**EARTHTONGUES,
GRAINY CLUBS,
MUSHROOM PIMPLES, etc.**

Plate 1

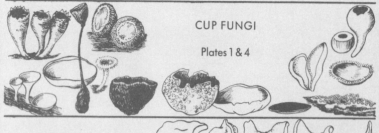

CUP FUNGI

Plates 1 & 4

**FALSE MORELS
AND LORCHELS**

Plates 2 & 3

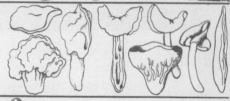

**MORELS
(SPONGE MUSHROOMS)**

Plate 2

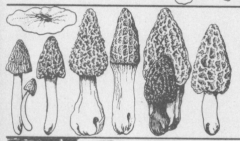

**JELLY FUNGI AND
OTHER CLUB FUNGI**

Plate 5

**CORAL FUNGI
AND
CHANTERELLES**

Plates 6 & 7

HYDNUMS
(TOOTH FUNGI)

Plates 8–10

BOLETES
(FLESHY PORE FUNGI)

Plates 10–13

WOODCRUSTS, GROUNDWARTS, AND POLYPORES

Plates 6 & 14

GILL MUSHROOOMS

Plates 15–42

STINKHORNS, FALSE TRUFFLES, AND BIRDS' NESTS

Plates 43 & 48

PUFFBALLS, EARTHBALLS, AND EARTHSTARS

Plates 43–48

THE PETERSON FIELD GUIDE SERIES®
Edited by Roger Tory Peterson

THE PETERSON FIELD GUIDE SERIES®

A Field Guide to
Mushrooms
North America

Kent H. McKnight
and
Vera B. McKnight

Illustrations by
Vera B. McKnight

*Sponsored by the National Audubon Society
and the National Wildlife Federation*

HOUGHTON MIFFLIN COMPANY BOSTON NEW YORK

WARNING: Do not eat any wild mushroom without first obtaining an expert opinion on identification of the mushroom. This book is intended to be a field guide to mushrooms, and as such, it focuses on identification, not on mushroom toxicology. For details on that subject, we refer you to one of the excellent treatises now available (see Selected References, p. 407).

For information about this and other Houghton Mifflin trade and reference books and multimedia products, visit The Bookstore at Houghton Mifflin on the World Wide Web at http://www.hmco.com/trade/.

Library of Congress Cataloging-in-Publication Data

McKnight, Kent H.
A field guide to mushrooms of North America.

(The Peterson field guide series; 34)
"Sponsored by the National Audubon Society and the National Wildlife Federation."
Bibliography: p. 407
Includes index.
1. Mushrooms—North America—Identification.
2. Mushrooms—North America—Pictorial works.
I. McKnight, Vera B. II. National Audubon Society.
III. National Wildlife Federation. IV. Title.
V. Series.
QK617.M424   1987   589.2'097   86-27799
ISBN 0-395-42101-2
ISBN 0-395-910900 (pbk.)

Printed in the United States of America

VB 18 17 16 15 14 13 12 11 10

Editor's Note

Nearly all nature-oriented people profess a love affair with the flowers, but only a limited number admit to a similar passion for mushrooms, other than as a table delicacy. Some people would dismiss them as "toadstools," to be ranked with spiders, snakes, bats, and other things that have become symbolic of the dark side of life.

By contrast, many country folk on the continent of Europe adore the various edible fungi. They are mushroom lovers—"mycophiles," if you will. But other cultures who live in the lands bordering the North Sea, notably the English, might be called "mycophobes"—toadstool haters.

Why this dichotomy? The answer probably lies in tradition, inherited from the lost legends and superstitions of antiquity. Or, the prejudice against mushrooms may have developed because a small minority of species, notably the Amanitas and a few others, are dangerous if eaten. They are toxic; sometimes deadly, or at least hallucinogenic.

North America has inherited the English tradition and therefore might be expected to have an anti-mushroom bias, regardless of the fact that the greater bulk of our population originally emigrated from continental Europe where the prejudice did not exist.

The average person on our side of the Atlantic can probably not put a name to a single mushroom other than the familiar meadow mushroom that is grown commercially. This new *Field Guide* by the McKnights aims to correct this, to make us more aware and knowledgeable about this important botanical galaxy.

The fungi, numbering some 100,000 species, range in size from minute unicellular yeasts to gross growths such as the giant puffballs and bracket fungi. Those with caps and stems we call mushrooms; some are edible, even delicious. Some of the lesser forms of fungi have medicinal properties. Penicillin and some of the other antibiotics so valuable in modern medicine were derived from molds, which are primitive fungi.

The identification of fungi is more akin to the identification of flowers than it is to the field recognition of birds; they may be examined in the hand. Their recognition is a visual process nevertheless, but more comparable to the bird-in-hand techniques of early ornithology. The approach to serious mushroom study is somewhat technical, and a fairly complex terminology is often unavoidable. Instead of the binocular, the hand lens becomes the most useful optical instrument.

A great many of the lesser-known mushrooms have never been assigned common names in English. They have their scientific names, of course, bestowed upon them by taxonomists, some dating as far back as Linnaeus. To take the edge off nomenclatural formality, so forbidding to many amateurs, the McKnights have coined appropriate common names for some of the species which lacked them. But it is best to try to memorize the scientific names as well.

If your principal interest in mushrooms is gastronomic, read the sections on **edibility** with care. Aside from the few notoriously lethal kinds you just might have a severe allergic reaction to a mushroom that could be eaten with pleasure by someone else.

No one is better qualified to write and illustrate *A Field Guide to the Mushrooms of North America* than Kent and Vera McKnight. These attractive fungi have been their lifelong obsession. If the gestation period of this book from original concept to the printed page has seemed a long one, it is because of the complexity of the subject and the authors' desire for perfection. Drawings in themselves take time and the exquisite color plates by Vera McKnight are a perfect counterpoint to the informative text.

All mycophiles will treasure this book in their library, and if you are a newcomer to the game, take this field guide with you on your rural rambles. It will help you to put names to most of the mushrooms that decorate the woodlands and wet meadows when conditions are just right.

ROGER TORY PETERSON

Preface

With a continual bombardment of mass media "hype," late twentieth century Americans are avocationally preoccupied with violent sports and electronic gadgetry to a degree unbelievable in other times and other cultures. By contrast, and by tradition, Eastern Europeans are likely to take to the woods the way we take to the football mayhem on the TV screen on a free weekend. In explaining this, a distinguished Czech mycologist wrote, "There are 13 million people living in Czechoslovakia, and 13 million of them are mushroom lovers."

Immigrants from Europe and their American-born offspring have preserved these traditions and have always been represented in disproportionately high numbers among the relatively few mushroom hunters in America. Most often they prize mushrooms for food, and they brought with them from the homeland a knowledge of a few familiar species of mushrooms. Very few people were interested in mushrooms and related fungi for reasons other than edibility and possible poisoning. The immigrants who learned something about mushrooms in the "old country" are vulnerable to certain realities of life in America, such as (1) the diversity and richness of our land, which offers more types of ecological niches than Europe. Many more species of plants and fungi have evolved in North America than in Europe; the ecology of our continent is more complex. (2) The American species are not as well known as the European species. (3) Favored edible European species may have poisonous "look-alikes" among the American species. This occasionally leads to fatal mistakes.

With the increased affluence of post-war Americans, however, we are experiencing rising interest in the natural environment, its importance to people, and details of its structure and function. As a part of this, the serious study of wild mushrooms and related fungi as an avocational interest now has a large cadre of participants. In the words of a world-renowned taxonomist, "mushroom study is starting to become respectable." However, prejudice and misinformation still enshroud mushroom mycology to such an extent that a large segment of the American population sees no value in their study.

Many mushroom enthusiasts are organized in local clubs or societies that sponsor monthly meetings and numerous activities and projects, including lectures, study groups, hunting excursions, forays, walks, displays, cooking and photography sessions. These groups often publish newsletters, cookbooks, recipes, etc. Many of the local groups are chapters of a national organization. For information on local clubs and societies, contact The North American Mycological Association, 4245 Redinger Road, Portsmouth, Ohio 45662.

Although "pothunters" still predominate, other, often more academic interests are common. Many seek knowledge of the diverse roles of mushrooms in the earthly ecosystems, and almost with religious devotion they enthusiastically protect it. Far too few people realize how essential mushrooms are to the welfare of mankind. Tragically, this is too little appreciated by executives, managers, and other power brokers and decision makers, some of whom are responsible for resource management in federal, state, or local government or private agencies. Sometimes even people who work in research agencies do not appreciate the role of fungi; sometimes they are scientists trained in other subject areas.

Many of our forests, especially those made up of pine trees and their relatives, would not exist without the mushrooms which grow among their roots. This association of a fungus and a tree such as a pine is called symbiosis. It is a relationship beneficial to both organisms, and is the basis for one of the great benefits of mushrooms to mankind. Fungus partners in the relationship are called mycorrhizae. In the mycorrhizal association, the mushroom invader of the tree roots helps the host tree in mineral nutrition, resistance to disease, and water stress under drought conditions. Without these fungi, the forest giants would be dwarfed, scrawny and spindly, or unable to grow at all in some now-forested locations. These trees would obviously be incapable of providing the cover, soil stabilization, wood, fiber, and other products which we take for granted.

Equally important is the role of mushrooms and related fungi in nutrient recycling, whereby they make food available for many organisms. By decaying wood, forest trash, and diverse kinds of plant and animal wastes, fungi release minerals and nutrients for use by a great variety of other organisms. Some mushrooms are a primary food source for animals of diverse kinds and others are a preferred food of many animals, including man. Like their wild counterparts, cattle pastured in the vast forests of our western mountains aggressively seek certain wild mushrooms after summer rainstorms.

For many people, the fascination with mushrooms lies simply in the traditional aura of folklore and mysticism which has long engulfed them. But whatever their interests, this book was written for novice mushroom hunters—for those whose fascination with the sport is just beginning.

Mushrooming has been a lifelong pursuit for us and for our

family. It provides a common outlet for our two professional interests, mycology and art. The watercolor paintings reproduced here are mostly copies from originals in various media painted in the course of many pleasant seasons collecting and studying in the wilds. A few were painted from our own color slides and three species were painted from transparencies kindly loaned by Harry Knighton and Harry Thiers. Species descriptions and comments on biology and ecology of the species are based mostly on the author's own research.

By contrast, the comments on edibility of the species are based almost entirely on the cumulative experience of others, almost none on our own experience. We have received many first-hand reports, both oral and written, and we have drawn heavily on the literature, including some unpublished written accounts. Although we have checked the information on edibility very carefully to make sure that it is accurate and up-to-date, neither we nor the publisher assume any responsibility for others' experiences, whether based on recommendations published herein or otherwise.

Many people have contributed in numerous ways to the production of this book. Countless specimens have come from near and far. Most important was the faithful support, patience, tolerance, understanding, encouragement and free labor given by our four children: Jeffry, Karl, Larry, and Kathleen. When other families went on vacations, we went mushroom hunting.

A special acknowledgement is due to Anne Dow, who wrote the chapter on mushroom cooking (and patiently read the entire manuscript), to Karl B McKnight, who wrote the chapter on mushroom poisoning, and to Joan Boyce McKnight for the Glossary. Richard Baird also edited the entire manuscript, as did Todd Williams. We deeply appreciate Peter Katsaros' help in correcting citations for the 4th edition. We received much valuable help from the following scientists, each of whom critically reviewed parts of the manuscript in their special fields: Lekh Batra, Howard Bigelow, William Cibula, Martina Gilliam-Davies, Linnea Gilman, Kenneth Harrison, Richard Homola, David Jenkins, Josiah Lowe, Walter Sundberg, Nancy Smith Weber, and Carl B. Wolfe. Whereas we gratefully acknowledge both the quality and quantity of their help, we retain for ourselves the responsibility for any errors, factual or conceptual, which may be contained in the finished book.

KENT AND VERA MCKNIGHT

Contents

ILLUSTRATIONS

Color and black-and-white plates
Plates 1–48, grouped after p. 208

Line drawings
Figures 1–32, scattered throughout the text

A Field Guide to
Mushrooms
of North America

1

How to Use This Book

This Field Guide is designed to make your mushroom collecting outings as safe and enjoyable as possible. Although no pocket-sized book can cover all the North American fungi, we have attempted to include most of the common edible and poisonous species you are likely to encounter, along with many others that are of interest. The information is presented in a way that is aimed at satisfying the needs of both the beginner and the experienced collector, with an emphasis on distinguishing characteristics — field marks — that can be readily observed in mushrooms that are growing in their natural habitat. As in other Peterson Field Guides, these key features are pinpointed with arrows on the illustrations and highlighted with italics in the text. The most important field marks are noted on the page facing each plate.

Experts and serious amateurs frequently confirm identifications of mushrooms by examining them under a microscope (see p. 9), but as a Field Guide, this book focuses primarily on identifying characteristics that can be observed in the hand. Although this approach limits the number of species that can be identified as well as the accuracy of the identifications, if you follow the recommended procedures carefully, with practice, you should be able to identify many species of mushrooms with reasonable accuracy by comparing the specimen in hand with the illustrations and detailed descriptions in this guide. We suggest the following steps:

1. Pick a mushroom. Be sure to get the *whole* mushroom, not just part of one. Missing parts (such as the base of the stalk) may include the most important characteristics that are essential for correct identification. *Dig,* do not pull, the mushroom out of the soil or wood where it is growing. Use a garden trowel or fairly sharp, sturdy knife.

2. Wrap each mushroom in waxed paper or aluminum foil. *Do not use plastic* bags or plastic wrap. Plastic does not allow any moisture to escape and clings too tightly to the mushroom. Waxed paper will trap the right amount of moisture to keep the mushroom fresh, without making it too slimy. Place the mushroom on a piece of wax paper and roll the paper into a cylinder, twisting the ends to seal the packet. *Do not mix* different types of mushrooms in the same packet, especially if you are not sure of their

identity. Wrap each one separately, to avoid contamination.

3. Carry mushrooms in a shallow basket. Try to keep them standing up (cap up).

4. Be sure that you have collected a mushroom—not a lichen, insect gall, bone, seedpod, piece of manure or rotten wood, or an Indian Pipe—a non-green flowering plant that feeds on decaying material in soil. Some people have even brought us a bit of plastic trash or a burned pancake, both suspected of being mushrooms.

5. Take notes on the size, shape, color, odor, and surface texture of each mushroom at the time you collect it. Many wild mushrooms look very different once they have started to dry out, and others, such as the inky caps (*Coprinus,* p. 276), soon turn into a slimy mess if you keep them too long.

6. *Make a spore print* (see Fig. 1). Spore color is an essential clue to the identity of many species of mushrooms, and should be used to confirm your identifications. Individual spores are much too small to be visible without a microscope, but you can collect them in a mass by cutting off the cap or head of a mature, fresh mushroom and placing it, with the gills or other spore-bearing surface (hymenium) facing downward, on a sheet of white paper. Be sure to use *white* paper—any other color will distort the color of white or pale-colored spores when they are deposited on the paper. Pure white spore prints may be difficult to see on white paper, but can usually be detected by slanting the paper. This disadvantage is more than offset by the fact that differences among pale-colored and white spore prints (which may indicate a poisonous species such as an *Amanita,* p. 215) can not be detected at all on colored paper. It takes a while—sometimes several hours—for some species (such as chanterelles, p. 81) to deposit their spores, so be patient.

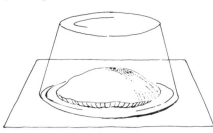

Fig. 1. How to make a spore print from a mushroom cap.

7. Study the shapes and descriptions of mushroom fruiting bodies on pp. 18–23 of Chapter 2, where the major groups (families and genera) of mushrooms are introduced. Try to match your unknown mushroom specimen with one of the illustrations. For easy access, illustrations of the most common and important groups of mushrooms are repeated on the inside front cover, with cross-references that will direct you to the correct plates at the center of this book.

8. Once you have found a group of mushrooms on a plate that seem to resemble your specimen closely, use the arrows on the plate and the brief descriptions of key features on the legend page facing the plate to narrow down your choices.

9. Turn to the more detailed descriptions in the text to confirm your identification. Be sure to check the information under **Similar species,** where confusing look-alikes are contrasted.

10. Check the **Edibility** section to see whether your species is considered edible or not. Keep in mind that individual people vary widely in their sensitivity to mushroom toxins, and be sure to read the cautions on p. 10 before tasting or eating any wild mushroom. *Never eat a wild mushroom raw.*

Illustrations and Legend Pages. More than 500 mushrooms are illustrated in this guide, on 48 color and black-and-white plates that are grouped at the center of the book for convenient use in the field. Within the space limitations of this pocket-sized guide, we have attempted to show as many variations in color, size, and developmental stages as possible, including some color changes that occur when the mushroom's flesh is cut or bruised. However, some variations in color could not be shown, especially for species that gradually change color over time, depending on their age and moisture content. Although the illustrations and legend pages highlight the most important and typical characteristics of the species, neither the art nor the brief legend can take the place of the more detailed description in the text. Supplemental illustrations in black-and-white are scattered throughout the text. Many of these show important structural features, including some that are difficult or impossible to show clearly on the plates.

About 450 species are illustrated in color in this guide. The terms used to describe the color of the cap and stalk in the legends (pages facing the plates) and the text are expressed in common English terms, following the Universal Color Language of Kelly and Judd (see p. 407) which allows a range of colors to be given with considerable precision. This is important, as mushrooms rarely, if ever, exhibit a single color and their colors may change with age or under different light and moisture conditions (see p. 6). The system for naming basic hues and intermediate colors is illustrated in the chart below. By combining these and using the appropriate modifiers (pale, moderate, strong), up to 267 three-dimensional blocks of color can be named.

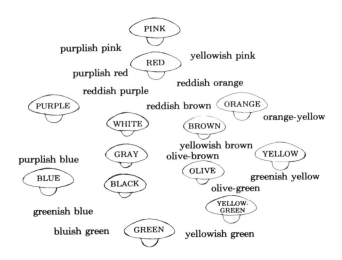

Fig. 2. Basic hues and intermediate colors
(Kelly and Judd, 1976).

General Organization. For convenience, the mushrooms in this guide are grouped into three different parts of the book, depending on whether or not they produce spores by means of gills on the underside of the cap. Part I covers the non-gilled fungi, a group which includes many mushrooms that are important as edible species, such as morels (p. 36), chanterelles (p. 81), and boletes (p. 100). Although the mushrooms in this first part of the book do not have gills, they have other structural modifications for producing spores that are important for identification. (See Chapter 2 and individual species accounts in the running text for details.)

Part II covers the gilled fungi, which have a series of gills or spore-producing plates on the underside of the cap, as do the commercially cultivated mushrooms available in the supermarket.

Part III covers the puffballs and related mushrooms that have yet another type of structural design for producing and releasing spores — usually a round spore case that completely

encloses the spore mass until it matures. All three of these
groups include both edible and poisonous species.

Within each of the three major groups in the text, mushrooms are divided into large groups (families) and smaller sub-
groups (genera) on the basis of structural characteristics. (For
more details about the structure and classification of mushrooms, turn to Chapter 2.) The order of the families and genera
in the text roughly follows the order in which the mushrooms
are illustrated on the plates: non-gilled fungi first, then gilled
fungi, and finally the puffballs and their relatives (Gastromycetes). A list of mushrooms in order by family appears in the
Contents (p. xi).

Species Descriptions. Each description starts with a brief
statement summarizing the distinctive characteristics of the
mushroom, with the most important field marks for that species highlighted in italics. This capsule description is essen-
tially the same as the brief legend on the page facing the plate
where the mushroom is illustrated; both pinpoint the most
conspicuous features that will help you distinguish one mushroom species from another. It is very important to consult the
more detailed description that follows in the text, however, in
order to confirm your identification. Although with experience,
you can train yourself to size up several characteristics at a
glance, and to zero in on the ones that distinguish a particular
species; for safety's sake, particularly if you are new to mushroom identification, it is essential for you to *compare each feature* of the mushroom you have collected with the diagnostic
features described for the most likely candidate or candidates
in the text. You may find, for example, that you have collected
a closely related species that seems to match a description and
illustration in all but one or two respects. Those differences
may be very important, especially if one species is edible but
the other one is not. *Do not assume* that an unknown mushroom is edible just because it seems to be very similar or is
closely related to one in the text that is known to be edible.
The italics in the descriptions and the **Similar species** entries
will help you sort out these differences between species. To
further facilitate comparisons between species, the structural
details of the mushroom are described in roughly the same
order from one species account to the next: first the cap (shape,
surface texture, margin, undersurface, and flesh); then the
stalk, if one is present (shape, thickness, attachment to cap,
color and texture—exterior and interior); followed by the
spore print color and a brief summary—under **Technical
notes**—of microscopic characters that aid identification.

Unlike the mushrooms that are cultivated commercially and
sealed in packages at the supermarket, wild mushrooms are
subject to changes in weather; nibbling or bruising by wild
animals, small and large; and other factors that may affect

their appearance. You must obtain specimens *in good condition* in order to be able to identify the mushroom accurately — in some cases, a single fresh mushroom in good condition will yield more clues that are useful for identification than a number of specimens in poor condition. Excessive drying, moisture, or handling may destroy or obscure important characters you will need to recognize the species. As emphasized above, it is also important to have the *entire* mushroom, or better yet, several intact specimens that represent different stages of maturation. To obtain an accurate estimate of the color of the gills, for example, be sure to examine the undersurface of immature caps, before they have fully expanded. Of course, a single specimen or even two cannot show the full range of variation possible within a species, so it is best to gather several good specimens of the mushroom, if possible.

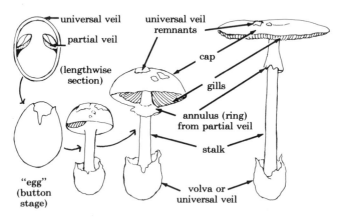

Fig. 3. Growth stages of a gill mushroom, such as an *Amanita*.

As noted above, make written notes on the mushroom's characteristics when you first collect it, before its color and shape are altered by excessive moisture or drying. Record the overall size; the shape, color, and texture of the cap, both at the center and at the margin (outer edge); and note any color changes that occur when you press your finger against the cap or stalk or scratch the surface. Notice whether the cap surface is dry or sticky, scaly, or warty, and whether there are any fibrillose streaks or zones on the cap. Pay particular attention to the type of spore-producing structures (gills, pores, or spines) on the underside of the cap. Gills, pores, and spines provide information valuable for identification by their spacing, and attachment to the stalk (see illustrations on inside front cover), their size (both in thickness and breadth), shape, and color—both before and after the spores mature.

Notice how the stalk (if any) is attached to the cap. Study the size, shape, and texture of the stalk and the shape of its base. Be sure to note whether a ring is present on the stalk, whether any patches or scales are present on the cap or stalk, and whether any remnants (wispy shreds) of a veil hang from the cap margin or coat the stalk. Cut the cap and stalk in half lengthwise and record any color changes that occur in the flesh. Note the thickness of the cap and whether it varies from the center to the limb and margin (outer edge). Notice whether the stalk is hollow, solid, or partially stuffed with cottony filaments. Any one of these details or (usually) a combination of them may be critical for an accurate identification of the mushroom. Since you cannot always anticipate which features will be most important for identification purposes, it is better to record too much detail than too little. These features and others that are important for mushroom identification are illustrated below and on the inside front cover.

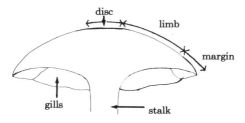

Fig. 4. Cap of a gill mushroom (lengthwise section).

In the species descriptions, the overall size of the cap and stalk is given first, in a range, as follows: small = less than 5 cm across; medium = 5–10 cm across; large = 10 cm or more. The size range refers to the size of the mushroom at maturity, when the spores have developed. The actual dimensions recorded for the cap and stalk of each species are listed under **Technical notes** in the species accounts.

Both the overall shape of the cap and the shape and texture of the cap margin may undergo significant changes as the mushroom grows and matures. Although individual mushrooms are too variable to match these categories exactly, typical variations in cap shape are illustrated below and on the inside front cover.

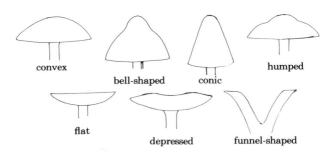

Fig. 5. Gill mushrooms: variations in cap shapes.

Pay special attention to the cap margin, as seen both from above (Fig. 6) and in lengthwise section (Fig. 7).

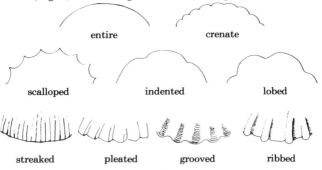

Fig. 6. Cap margins: variations in outline and surface texture.

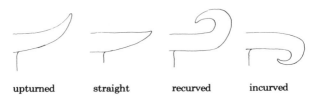

Fig. 7. Cap margins (lengthwise section).

Technical terms. As in other Field Guides, technical terms have been kept to a minimum, so that descriptions can be clearly understood by non-specialists. Our goal is to introduce everyone to the enjoyment of mushroom hunting, whether you are primarily interested in collecting for the pot or are curious in a wider sense about mushrooms. However, unless you simply want to admire the different forms and colors fungi take, without attempting to identify mushroom species, you will need to learn a few technical terms that are routinely used to describe the parts of a mushroom and their arrangement or variations. You cannot safely tell whether you have picked an edible field mushroom (*Agaricus*) or a poisonous *Amanita,* for example, without knowing what a **volva** is and where it is located (see Fig. 14, p. 20). You will find that you will quickly pick up these terms as you use this guide, since they are usually explained in context as well as defined in the Glossary (p. 399). The most important terms for structural features are also illustrated in figures throughout the text and on the inside front cover.

Experienced mushroom hunters (serious amateurs as well as professional mycologists) will already be familiar with these terms and with the best places to hunt for mushrooms. Although we have designed this book to make it as easy as possible for you to identify mushrooms safely and reliably on your own, we encourage you, particularly if you are a beginner, to contact a local club or mycological association to see if you can accompany some of the members on their forays. In addition to gaining practical field experience, you can also learn how to use a microscope to confirm your identifications (see below). The comparison of microscopic features, such as spore shape, size, and ornamentation, is a technique that is gaining popularity among serious amateurs.

The internal structure of the mushroom cap has features that are critical for identification but which can be studied in detail only by use of the high magnification of a microscope. Some of the important microscopic differences are mentioned in the **Technical notes** section of each species account. Although structural details can not be seen with a hand lens or with the naked eye, the major tissue areas and some special attributes imparted to them by the microscopic structure characteristic of the species can be recognized with no special tools or equipment. Color, thickness, and texture of tissue zones should be noted (see Fig. 8).

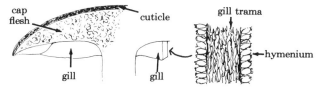

Fig. 8. Mushroom cap (lengthwise section): major tissue areas.

Odor and taste. The odor or taste of a mushroom may be restricted to one of the tissue zones, such as the cuticle, flesh, or gills. Odors may be fragrant or unpleasant or fairly innocuous. (Some mushrooms, for example, smell like raw potatoes.) Odors are often very faint, but may be detected by crushing the flesh between your fingers, or they may be concentrated by wrapping the specimens in waxed paper or aluminum foil (never plastic wrap) for a few hours.

Information on taste is included in some of the species descriptions, and refers to the taste of the raw flesh of the cap. Many mushroom hunters use taste as a supplemental characteristic to diagnose mushroom species; indeed, some mushrooms (such as the *Russulas* or brittlegills, p. 317) are very difficult to identify accurately without taking a tiny bite of the cap and chewing it for a second or two to pick up the distinctive taste of the species. Some taste reactions are delayed. **Do not** hold the piece of raw mushroom in your mouth until the taste develops — **always spit it out immediately. Do not swallow it.** This identification technique is **NOT RECOMMENDED** for beginners, however. You must first be acquainted with the species well enough to be sure that you are not about to taste a poisonous one by mistake. **Our recommendation is simple: Do not taste any wild mushroom without first obtaining an expert opinion on identification of the mushroom.** (Keep in mind that even an expert can make a mistake on this, particularly if the mushroom has appeared unusually early or late in the season.) If you do decide to check the taste of a wild mushroom, take only a tiny bite of the flesh or gills, chew it for a second or two, and then *spit it out immediately.* Do not eat an entire wild mushroom raw, and **never** taste a mushroom that could be an *Amanita* (see Pls. 25–28) or some other potentially poisonous species — even one bite could be fatal. If you think that you may have tasted a poisonous species by mistake, contact the nearest hospital or Poison Control Center at once. For more information on poisonous mushrooms, see Chapter 3 and the **Edibility** section of each species account in the text. Read that section first, *before* you decide to taste anything, and check the **Similar species** section to see whether your mushroom could be confused with a poisonous species.

Edibility often depends as much on the person as on the mushroom (see Chapter 3, p. 24). Even when properly cooked, some mushrooms that can be eaten safely by many people can nonetheless trigger a toxic reaction in a sensitive individual. Reports from many sources have been summarized in a capsule statement for each species. We have purposely taken a very conservative view on edibility, for the benefit of the inexperienced mushroom hunter. We do not wish to see anyone suffer the agony of even mild mushroom poisoning needlessly. We emphasize, however, that this book is intended to be a field guide to mushrooms — as such, it focuses on identification, not on mushroom toxicology. For details on that subject we refer you to one of the excellent treatises now available (see p. 407).

For those of you who enjoy collecting wild mushrooms for the pot, a number of recipes have been included at the back of this book. We hope that you will try them and enjoy them. Keep in mind, however, that proper collecting, preparing, and cooking techniques are as essential as identifying the mushroom species accurately: some cases of suspected mushroom poisoning are simple food poisoning. **Neither the authors nor the publishers assume any responsibility for the consequences of readers eating wild mushrooms. To repeat: do not eat any wild mushroom without first obtaining an expert opinion on identification of the mushroom.** The old saying is a wise one: if in doubt, throw it out!

Fruiting. Information on fruiting that is important for identification is given in each species account: the number of fruiting bodies produced by a species at one time, and their spatial relationships (whether the mushroom appears singly or in clusters or clumps); the type of soil or substrate where the species grows, and any other trees or plants that are characteristically associated with it; and the months (season) when it is known to appear. The type of soil or substrate and plants growing nearby (including hardwood or coniferous trees) may be an important identifying feature for certain mushrooms (see boletes, for example, pp. 100–124). Make a note of the type of habitat where you found the mushroom when you pick it — perhaps on the back of a spore print paper.

Area Covered. This guide includes 510 species found in the continental U.S. and Canada. Some species from Alaska are included. Some mushrooms are distributed widely throughout temperate N. America; others are restricted to the Pacific Northwest, the Southeast, or other regions. Although this Field Guide covers more North American species than most other pocket-sized guides currently available, out of necessity, we have included only a representative sampling. In the family Tricholomataceae alone, for example, there are more than 500 species in North America. To date no comprehensive inventory of North American fungi has been undertaken, so mycologists (scientists who study mushrooms) do not even know how many mushroom species occur within our borders. However, this guide will enable you to identify all the most common and important North American mushrooms, along with many others you will come across. For identification problems that go beyond the limits of this guide, see the references listed in the bibliography (p. 407), and check with the nearest college, university, museum, or appropriate government agency to see if a professional mycologist can help you.

Common and scientific names. Two kinds of names are used for mushrooms in this guide: (1) scientific or latinized names, and (2) common or folk names. The scientific name of each species is italicized and consists of two words. The first word, which is capitalized, is the name of the genus (plural, genera) or group to which the species belongs. The second part of the name, which is not capitalized, is the species name, and the combination is unique for each mushroom. Several closely related species may share the same genus name, such as *Boletus,* but each one will have been assigned its own specific name, such as *edulis* or *rubropunctus.* For example, there are many boletes (species of *Boletus,* or other genera within the family Boletaceae), but only one *Boletus rubropunctus* (see p. 108). The common name for this bolete is Red-dot, based on the same characteristic that was the basis for the scientific name.

In scientific literature and technical reports, the official name for this bolete would be listed as *Boletus rubropunctus* Peck. Peck is the name of the species author — the person who first formally described this mushroom species. We feel that author names are unnecessary in a field guide.

Mycologists (scientists who study fungi) unanimously prefer to use scientific (latinized) names for fungi, because they mean the same thing to people worldwide who know a particular mushroom. Common names can lead to confusion because the same mushroom species may carry several common or folk names in different languages. Scientific names have been assigned according to internationally accepted rules and are therefore less likely to change than common names, which may vary according to local custom or the preferences of an author who is proposing a common name for a species. In some parts of the U.S. the species *Morchella semilibera* (p. 40), an edible morel, is known as the Half-free Morel, or simply "Morel"; in others it is known as "Cow's Head" or *Mergel.* If you learn it as *Morchella semilibera,* there is no room for confusion. Although common names are emphasized in field guides, we encourage you to learn and use the scientific name for each mushroom.

As you become more familiar with scientific names, you will also increase your awareness of the relationships between species. Once you know the genus name for a certain group of mushrooms, you can see at a glance which species in this book or other mushroom guides are closely related and are likely to share characteristics that are useful for identification purposes. Closely related species are grouped in one or more genera; related genera are grouped in the same family, and so on, up through a hierarchy of related groups. For details on the structural basis of these classifications, see Chapter 2.

Since this guide, like other Field Guides, is intended primarily for non-specialists, each mushroom illustrated is listed under both a common and scientific name. Some of the mushrooms in this guide are well known and already carry traditional common or folk names; others do not have a widely accepted common name, particularly in this country, which does not have a strong folk tradition regarding mushrooms. Possibly because of the traditional aversion to the use of wild mushrooms for food among the British, who have tended to scorn all mushrooms as poisonous "toadstools," there are comparatively few common names in the vernacular in English. In cases where a widely accepted common name for a mushroom does exist in English, we have used it in this guide. *Amanita muscaria* (p. 227), for example, is commonly known as Fly Agaric or the equivalent in several languages. In other cases, however, we have coined new English names for this guide, after researching many sources for a precedent or sound scientific and etymological basis for each common name proposed here.

To come up with an appropriate common name in English, we have often gone to the European common names as a resource, since many are steeped in local folklore or tradition and are based on a characteristic of the group or species that is important for identification purposes. For example, the German name "Rötlinge" for *Entoloma* species (p. 310) can be translated into "Pinkgill" in English. Translations of German names often permit the grouping of several related species under the same folk or common name, much as mycologists do with scientific names for genera.

Many of the common names in this guide are based upon a translation of the scientific (latinized) name or its root, particularly if the translation helps call attention to an important field mark that will help you identify the mushroom and recognize its relationship to other species in the same genus or family. Thus, species of *Lentinellus* and *Lentinus* are called "sawgills," because of the serrated (sawtoothed) edges on their gills, and species of *Laccaria* are called "tallowgills," because of the waxy texture of their gills.

Other common names used in this guide represent a compromise between common names used elsewhere: *Rozites caperata* (p. 302) is widely known as "Gypsy" or the equivalent, but has been called by the Finnish common name — which translates as "Granny's Nightcap" — in a beautifully illustrated field guide to *Mushrooms of Northern Europe* (Nilsson and Persson, 1978) that is now available in English. We propose the common name "Gypsy Nitecap" for this species, which merges the common name used outside of Finland with a name that highlights a characteristic of the mushroom useful for identification. The young button stage of this species *(R. caperata)* has a wrinkled (sometimes ragged) veil peeking out from the billowing, lobed margin of the cap above that does indeed look like an old-fashioned nightcap. The "Nightcap" part of the common name not only helps one remember this characteristic but also encourages a search for the young button, the best stage of development to confirm identification of the species.

Because most of the common names used in this guide are merely recommendations, without an established precedent of accepted usage, references in the text are supplemented by scientific (latinized) names. We hope that this Field Guide will help promote a constructive dialogue among mycologists about common names that will eventually result in a widely accepted checklist of common and scientific names for North American mushrooms.

Edibility Symbols. ▰ = Edible for most people; see pp. 10–11 and 24–26. ◉ = **Not recommended;** see species descriptions for details. ☠ = **Poisonous.**

2

Mushrooms are Fungi

Mushrooms are fungi — members of a kingdom of living organisms that grow and fruit much the way plants do, but which lack roots, stems, leaves, flowers, and seeds. The simple-bodied organisms in this kingdom also lack a special green pigment, chlorophyll, which enables plants possessing it to manufacture a basic food — simple sugar — from water and carbon dioxide, using the energy of sunlight. Among these simple-bodied organisms that lack chlorophyll, the larger and more complex ones are known as fungi.

Fungi include crusts and molds (such as the one from which penicillin is derived) as well as larger fruiting bodies with a cap and stalk. Since ancient times, the larger edible fungi have been called mushrooms. The word "toadstool" is often applied to mushrooms that are poisonous to people. However, human sensitivity to mushrooms is known to be highly variable (see next chapter); consequently, the term mushroom as used here includes not only non-poisonous, edible fungi, but also those that are known to be poisonous, and the great majority of the related species, of which the edibility or toxicity is not known.

Lacking chlorophyll, mushrooms must obtain their food by absorption from the surrounding medium (usually soil or decaying wood) in which they grow. The body of a mushroom is made up of slender filaments, collectively known as mycelium. Many of these filaments are adapted for absorbing nutrients. The individual filaments, or hyphae (singular, hypha), penetrate the substrate, which may be soil, wood, bodies of other plants, or wastes such as dung, fallen leaves, twigs, and so on. Compact masses of hyphae remain vegetative under ground, like roots, until the fruiting season for the species, which may last only a few weeks, or may extend from early spring until late fall. The hyphae of mushrooms that grow in fairy rings may expand outward each year to reach new nutrients, so that the ring becomes larger each year. When a mushroom is actively growing during its fruiting season, the hyphae form organs that will produce and eventually disperse spores — the familiar mushroom fruiting body, which may be in the form of a cup, a club, a cap and stalk, a bracket, a coral-like head, or a puffball. This fruiting body is not the entire mushroom, but merely a reproductive part, in a way roughly comparable to the flowers or cones of more familiar plants.

Mushrooms reproduce by special microscopic cells known as spores. Spores serve three functions performed by seeds in higher plants: (1) they are reproductive bodies capable of initiating a new organism; (2) they are agents of dispersal which allow the plant (mushroom, in this case) to spread from one locality to another; and (3) they are structures of dormancy which enable the mushroom to withstand adverse environmental conditions, such as winter, drought, and so on.

Each mushroom spore is a single cell. The structure, production, and method of dispersal of these cells, along with the structures and tissues which produce them, are important in identification of mushrooms. Many structural details of mushroom fruiting bodies that are useful in identification (such as spore shape) can be seen only in a microscope. (Some of these details are mentioned in the **Technical notes** section of the species descriptions.) However, even if you do not have a microscope, you can learn to recognize the different kinds of spore-producing organs (such as gills or pores) and can predict how each will function after making field and "laboratory" observations of mushrooms, without actually seeing the details under a microscope.

Under favorable circumstances, a mushroom spore germinates and begins to grow by sprouting a single filament (hypha), which soon branches into a mass of filaments (hyphae or mycelium) that penetrates and expands throughout the growth substrate or medium. A hypha from one spore mates with that from another spore, beginning a reproductive process that eventually produces more spores by a special spore-producing cell. The cells of a mushroom which produce spores by this sexual process are of two types: (1) the sac-like ascus (*plural,* asci), which produces spores called ascospores internally, and (2) the club-shaped basidium (*plural,* basidia),

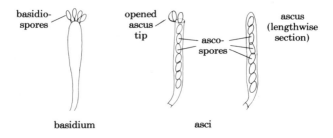

Fig. 9. Spore-producing cells: asci (at right)
and basidium (at left).

which produces basidiospores externally (see Fig. 9). These two methods of spore production characterize the two major groups of mushrooms — the Ascomycetes (sac fungi) and the Basidiomycetes (club fungi).

ASCOMYCETES (SAC FUNGI)

Many kinds of spores are produced by Ascomycetes (sac fungi). A few sac fungi produce ascospores from tip cells of the filamentous hyphae growing directly on the mycelial body, but most sac fungi develop special spore-bearing structures called ascocarps, which partially or wholly envelop the asci as they develop. The three types of ascocarps produced by sac fungi are illustrated in Fig. 10.

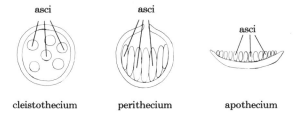

asci	asci	asci
cleistothecium	perithecium	apothecium

Fig. 10. Three types of ascocarps (spore-bearing structures).

The first type — the cleistothecium, characteristic of molds such as *Penicillium* that are not included in this guide — is a spherical ascocarp that completely encloses the developing asci. The perithecium — characteristic of the parasitic mushroom pimples, *Hypomyces*, p. 29 — is a globose or flask-shaped ascocarp with an opening at the top and sometimes a neck. The apothecium — found in **cup fungi** such as *Peziza,* p. 56 — is flat to saucer-shaped or cup-shaped or sometimes everted (turned inside out). Many of the sac fungi (Ascomycetes) produce apothecia that may be highly modified, as in the **morels** (p. 36) and other groups illustrated on p. 18.

The fruiting bodies shown in Fig. 11 are all modified apothecia. Most of the fungi which develop fruiting bodies that take these forms are sac fungi (Ascomycetes). Some are edible, some are not — see individual descriptions of species in Chapter 4 for details.

In sac fungi, the spore-producing cells (asci) form a layer called the *hymenium,* which is usually on the upper or outer surface of the club, cup, or cap (head). When these cells are mature, the ascus tip opens (see Fig. 9) and ascospores are shot into the air. A cloud of spores can often be released by jarring a mature ascocarp or blowing on its hymenium; in the wild, wind or rain can do this. The hymenium may be distinguished from other parts of the ascocarp by its position on the upper or outer surface and by its different color or texture. In the morels, for example, the spore-bearing hymenium is a wrinkled, convoluted, or pitted layer that is usually some shade of brown (see Pl. 2).

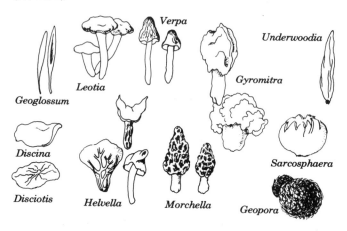

Fig. 11. Fruiting bodies of sac fungi (Ascomycetes).

BASIDIOMYCETES (CLUB FUNGI)

Basidiomycete mushrooms are far more numerous than Ascomycete mushrooms and their fruiting bodies are more diverse in form. The club fungi are divided into two major groups on the basis of their reproductive structures: the Hymenomycetes, which produce basidia (spore-producing cells) and spores in the open, or at least on surfaces that are exposed to the air; and the Gastromycetes (puffballs and related fungi), which have basidia enclosed within the fruiting body—usually a round spore case—at maturity. The basidiospores of Hymenomycetes are discharged forcibly from the fruiting body, usually from the gills on the underside of the cap; the spores of Gastromycetes are discharged passively, when the spore case collapses. Most of the common mushrooms are Hymenomycetes, but some, such as puffballs and earthstars (see Pls. 43–48) are Gastromycetes.

The most familiar fungi among the Hymenomycetes are the **gill fungi,** which are covered in Part II of this guide. They have a fruiting body made up of stalk and cap, with sheet-like gills hanging from the undersurface of the cap. The hymenium (spore-bearing layer) consists of club-shaped basidia (cells) that are produced on the gill surfaces. Some species have a thin membrane called the *partial veil* extending from the stalk to the cap margin in young (button-stage) fruiting bodies (see Fig. 12). As the cap expands, this veil breaks, leaving a complete or partial *ring* (*annulus*) on the stalk and often leaving *scale-like remnants* on the cap margin or outer surface. The presence of a veil, ring, or scaly remnants of the veil tissue on the cap or stalk may be important for identification purposes, since they are found in poisonous species such as Amanitas (p. 215).

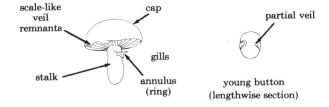

scale-like veil remnants — cap — partial veil

gills

stalk — annulus (ring)

young button (lengthwise section)

Fig. 12. Gill mushroom with partial veil.

Some gill mushrooms, such as cavaliers (*Tricholoma,* p. 185) lack a partial veil or ring, while others, such as webcaps (*Cortinarius,* p. 287) have a cobwebby or filamentous veil (see Fig. 13).

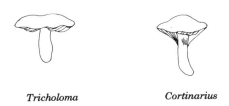

Tricholoma   *Cortinarius*

Fig. 13.

In *Amanita,* a genus that contains many deadly poisonous species, a second veil, called the *volva* or *universal veil,* is also produced (see Fig. 14 and Pls. 25–28).

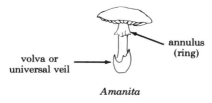

volva or universal veil

annulus (ring)

Amanita

Fig. 14.

In Hymenomycetes, each basidium produces four (rarely two) basidiospores, each on a conical sterigma (see Fig. 15). When the spores are mature, they separate from the sterigma with sufficient force that the spore is projected into the narrow space between two layers of hymenium and falls free of the hymenial surfaces. Air currents carry it away from the parent mushroom. Although there are many kinds of fruiting bodies in Hymenomycete club fungi, the form of the fruiting body always takes advantage of this method of spore dispersal, having the hymenium (spore-bearing tissue) on the lower or outer surface, so the spores can fall free. In contrast, the sac fungi (Ascomycetes) usually shoot their spores farther into the air than Hymenomycetes do. In morels and other Ascomycetes, the hymenium (spore-bearing tissue) is on the upper surface. Gastromycetes (puffballs and relatives) lack a method of actively propelling their spores away from the fruiting body, although the spores can be carried away by air currents once the spore case collapses.

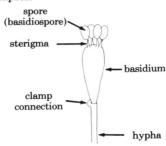

spore (basidiospore)

sterigma

basidium

clamp connection

hypha

Fig. 15. Mature basidium and spores.

A simple kind of Basidiomycete mushroom fruiting body is a flat crust or thin, cottony layer, often found on the underside of a log or other piece of wood. These **crust fungi** may be so thin and smooth that they appear to be painted on the wood (see Fig. 16). Some crust fungi have a wrinkled or folded hymenial surface; others grow outward from the wood, forming a shelflike or fanlike bracket (fruiting body) — see Pl. 6. In these brackets the spore-bearing layer (hymenium) is still on the undersurface, as in other Hymenomycetes.

crust fungus   *Cantharellus*

Fig. 16.   **Fig. 17.**

Most Hymenomycete **club fungi** have a stalk and cap or branches, but not all of them have gills. For example, the chanterelles (*Cantharellus*, p. 81, Pl. 7) have a wrinkled or folded spore-bearing surface on the underside of a funnel-like or top-shaped cap. These wrinkles or folds sometimes form prominent ridges that are developed well enough so that they resemble gills.

Pore fungi have a layer of tubes on the undersurface that look like tiny pores or holes when seen from below. In these fungi the spores are produced on the inner surfaces of the pores or tubes. Pore fungi with woody to tough or leathery fruiting bodies, such as Sulphur Shelf (*Laetiporus*, p. 127), are called **polypores.** Some polypores have a stalk and centrally attached cap, as gill mushrooms do, but most are brackets or shelves that are laterally attached to the substrate (usually wood) where they grow. Some are shaped like an oyster shell or a horse's hoof. Some polypores (p. 125) are crusts, often with upturned lobes or margins similar to those of the crust fungi mentioned above. They grow most frequently on wood and may cause disease or death of valuable trees. However, they are also important as "scavengers" that help break down and recycle woody debris into nutrient-rich soil in the forest.

Fig. 18. *Laetiporus*

Boletes (p. 100) are pore fungi with soft, fleshy fruiting bodies. A pore or tube layer is attached to the underside of the cap by a gelatinous layer which permits the tube layer to be peeled readily off the cap flesh, as in *Boletus,* p. 103, Pl. 13. Many good edible fungi are boletes, although a few are poisonous (see p. 117).

Fig. 19.   *Boletus*

The **tooth fungi,** or hydnums, produce basidia (spore-producing cells) and spores on teeth or spines on the underside of the cap (see *Hydnum,* Pls. 8 and 10). Like the polypores, some tooth fungi are fleshy and edible; others are tough and unpalatable. Some form crusts or brackets, as in the crust fungi and polypores.

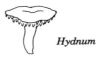

Hydnum

Fig. 20. Tooth fungus.

Coral mushrooms (p. 70, Pl. 6) produce basidiospores on a hymenial layer which coats the outer surface of the fruiting body. The fruiting body may take the form of a simple club, as in *Clavariadelphus* (p. 72, Pl. 6) or an intricately branched, coral-like head or mass, as in *Ramaria* (p. 74, Pl. 6).

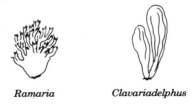

Ramaria   *Clavariadelphus*

Fig. 21. Coral fungi.

Puffballs are among the most common Gastromycetes. They produce spores inside a spore case which may be smooth or distinctively ornamented on the surface (see *Lycoperdon,* p. 354, Pl. 46). Some puffballs are stalked (see *Tulostoma,* p. 364, Pl. 48). Many puffballs are edible when young and white inside, but be sure to cut them in half to make sure that there are no developing gills.

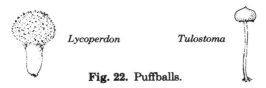

Lycoperdon   Tulostoma

Fig. 22. Puffballs.

Some Gastromycetes, called false truffles, grow under ground (see *Truncocolumella,* p. 349, Pl. 43). Many are the favored food of rodents and larger animals such as deer. Their presence may be revealed by humps or cracks in the soil.

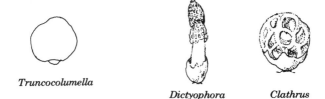

Truncocolumella

Dictyophora   Clathrus

Fig. 23. False truffle.   **Fig. 24. Stinkhorns.**

Unlike false truffles, stinkhorns and related fungi (*Dictyophora* and *Clathrus,* both on Pl. 43) are among the most conspicuous and colorful fungi known. Not only do they come in bizarre shapes, but they also usually have strong, offensive odors, which can make their presence known before they are seen.

The plates at the center of this book show a wide variety of mushroom fruiting bodies, but keep in mind that other species with different shapes, colors and textures could not be included in this pocket-sized guide.

3

Poisonous and Edible Mushrooms

Karl B McKnight

Even the most expert opinion about the edibility of a particular sample of mushrooms must be tempered with the time-proven qualifier, "for most of the people, most of the time." Cases abound of well-meant advice to "eat and enjoy" — given by amateurs and professionals alike — resulting in discomfort, or even death. Conversely, dire warnings of severe toxicity to those who might eat even the smallest portion of certain wild mushrooms have been contradicted by pleased palates and satisfied stomachs. Given such inconsistencies, how can anyone enjoy eating mushrooms? In order to do so safely, you must not only correctly identify the mushrooms under consideration but also know how your own body usually reacts to those particular mushrooms. It is possible for an individual to have an allergic reaction to certain mushrooms, even if they are commonly eaten and enjoyed by other people. Other mushrooms, of course, have long been established as deadly poisonous to humans.

Mushroom toxins (poisons) are usually categorized by the part of the body they affect and how quickly those effects are manifested. The toxins causing the most serious problems are those that act as cellular poisons. Deadly cyclopeptides and monomethylhydrazines act by rupturing cell membranes in the liver, inhibiting RNA synthesis in the liver, kidneys, intestinal mucosa, and central nervous system, or by disintegrating the red blood cells. Symptoms may include abdominal pain, vomiting, diarrhea, dehydration, jaundice, hypotension (low blood pressure), tachycardia (excessively fast heartbeat), and subnormal temperature. Poisoning can be quite severe or even fatal if certain species of *Amanita* (p. 215), *Galerina* (p. 296), *Gyromitra* (p. 48), or *Lepiota* (p. 241) are ingested. Unfortunately, many of the symptoms of cellular poisoning by mushrooms do not appear until after a long period of latency, which may vary from 6 to 48 hours, has passed.

Another category of very serious toxins is found in those species of *Amanita* (p. 215), *Clitocybe* (p. 138), *Inocybe* (p. 301), *Panaeolus* (p. 286), and *Psilocybe* (p. 274) that contain nerve poisons. The poisons found in these mushrooms include musca-rine, ibotenic acid-muscimol, muscazone, and psilocybin-psilo-cin. Symptoms of nerve poisoning usually appear much more quickly than symptoms of cellular poisoning, sometimes within minutes but rarely after more than 2 hours. In addition to abdominal pain, vomiting, diarrhea, and dehydration, symp-toms of nerve poisoning are manifested as either cholinergic effects on the peripheral nervous system — disrupting trans-mission of nerve impulses and causing a drop in blood pres-sure — or anticholinergic effects on the central and peripheral nervous systems, causing an increase in glandular secretions, slowing the heartbeat, and causing muscle spasms, convulsions, paralysis, and coma. The effects of the nerve toxins can be quite severe, even fatal. Nevertheless, many people foolishly persist in experimenting with mushrooms containing nerve poi-sons, in search of hallucinogenic or intoxicating effects.

A third group of mushroom toxins are those that cause gas-trointestinal irritations. The majority of toxins found in poi-sonous mushrooms are in this group. Admittedly, this group is just a "catch-all" collection of unidentified toxins that can cause severe distress (very unpleasant, but rarely fatal) in some people, but not necessarily bothering other people who have eaten the same mushrooms from the same pot. Species in more than 25 genera have often caused gastrointestinal irrita-tions. Some of the groups involved include well-known edible species as well as poisonous species: see *Agaricus* (p. 254), *Bo-letus* (p. 103), *Lactarius* (p. 326), *Morchella* (p. 37), and *Rus-sula* (p. 317). Onset of symptoms is usually within 2 hours.

A final category of mushroom toxins includes those that cause problems only when consumed with alcohol. Several spe-cies of *Coprinus* (p. 276), for example, if ingested without alco-hol, are perfectly safe. However, when alcohol is consumed be-fore, during, or even some time after a meal that includes these mushrooms, painful symptoms may begin almost immediately. The toxins in these mushrooms arrest metabolism of the eth-anol (alcohol) at the acetaldehyde stage, resulting in vasomo-tor reactions (dilation or contraction of blood vessels), nausea, and vomiting. The effect is very similar to the Antabuse reac-tion for alcoholics. Toxicologists are finding that some of the morels and other species of mushrooms in different genera (such as *Clitocybe*) have a similar effect when consumed with alcohol.

How can you tell whether a mushroom you have in hand is a poisonous species? Techniques based on myth and folklore, such as blackening silver spoons, peeling off skin, or boiling in water, are useless. Just as you readily recognize your best friends at a distance because you know so well their size, shape, posture, and stride, you can learn to recognize poison-ous mushrooms at a glance, once you have been around mushrooms long enough to have assimilated the characteristics of different species. You must invest some time first, studying their features and learning to recognize their size, shape, color, texture, habitat, smell, and so on, but with practice you can quickly narrow down the possibilities. With the many well-written books on mushrooms, clubs for amateur mushroom hunters, and professional mycologists available throughout North America, it is possible for anyone to learn to recognize several edible and poisonous species, whether they are collecting for the table or just for sheer enjoyment. We hope this book will help along the way.

Identification of edible species is only part of the process leading to safe and pleasurable mycophagy: correctly harvesting mushrooms in the field, transporting them home, storing them properly until they are used, preparing them for eating, and selecting the appropriate food and drink to accompany them are all important parts of the process. A mushroom is perishable like any other vegetable. Many cases of suspected mushroom poisoning have proven to be nothing more than common food poisoning, with no inherent blame for the mushroom involved. Also, just as some people are allergic to milk, chocolate, or oranges, individuals may react differently to mushrooms that are commonly eaten by other people. Remember the adage mentioned above, "for most of the people, most of the time." Some people can consume a small portion of a mushroom safely, but will have problems if they eat more at the same meal or over a period of several days. The toxins in certain species of *Verpa,* for example, often seem to have a cumulative effect (see p. 41).

What about all the mushrooms for which edibility is generally unknown? When we come across this problem while conducting mushroom walks with interested amateurs, we sometimes smile and say, "There is only one way to find out." The person posing the question usually laughs and quite sensibly responds, "Well, I'm not going to be the one to try it." Mushroom lovers often experiment with small portions of mushrooms to see whether they can eat them safely or not. This is part of the never-ending process that expands our knowledge about edible species. Nonetheless, we strongly discourage any experiments with mushrooms that might be suspected of being poisonous, or with mushrooms that have been known to cause problems for some people, even if others have eaten them safely. The entries in the **Edibility** section of the species descriptions that follow reflect this conservative approach.

See explanation of edibility symbols on p. 14.

PART I

Non-gilled Mushrooms

4

SAC FUNGI: ASCOMYCETES

Miscellaneous Sac and Cup Fungi

Family Clavicipitaceae

Grainy Clubs: Genus *Cordyceps*

Frequently parasitic on underground hosts such as truffles and insect pupae (see Pl. 1). At maturity, grainy clubs have pimple-like, *spore-bearing perithecia* on upper part of club (best seen in sections cut through the club).

SOLDIER GRAINY CLUB *Cordyceps militaris*　　　**Pl. 1**
Small to medium, *orange club;* upper part *pimpled at maturity* with spore-bearing perithecia that are darker than stalk in between. **Stalk:** Whitish at base, rising *singly or in clumps* of 2–5 *from insect pupae* buried in wood or in the ground. **Technical notes:** Club 2.5–4.5 cm high, to 0.5 cm across.
Fruiting: Widely distributed in N. America. Midsummer to late fall.
Edibility: Said to be unpalatable.
Similar species: A number of fungi have small, orange to yellow club-like fruiting stages that are commonly mistaken for this species, including: (1) Little Earthtongue (*Microglossum rufum,* not shown), (2) Irregular Earthtongue (*Spragueola irregularis,* not shown), and (3) coral fungi (species of *Clavaria,* p. 70). *Cordyceps* (grainy clubs) have the orange, pimple-like perithecia when mature. These may be seen best in sections cut through the club. (see Fig. 25, p. 31).

Family Hypocreaceae

Mushroom Pimples: Genus *Hypomyces*

Parasitic on fleshy fungi, especially gill fungi such as *Russula* or *Lactarius* — see Pl. 1. Mushroom pimples *distort cap and stalk of host* mushroom into white to brightly colored tissue with tiny, *pimple-like perithecia* embedded in flesh or gills of host (use a hand lens to look for them).

ORANGE MUSHROOM PIMPLE　　　　　　　　**Pl. 1**
Hypomyces lactifluorum
Parasite that grows on several *large, white* brittlegills (species

of *Russula,* p. 317) and milkcaps (*Lactarius,* p. 326). The host mushroom retains its general shape, but all parts (including gills) are distorted by parasite. This species is white at first, becoming orange as it matures. It produces *reddish orange pimple-like* perithecia on *gills or surfaces* of host where gills normally would be.

Fruiting: Hardwood forests throughout range of host mushroom. Summer and fall.

Edibility: Reportedly edible, but some people experience intestinal upset a few hours later. It is probably best to avoid eating this fungus, since the host fungus cannot be identified accurately and some may be mildly poisonous.

Remarks: Stubby Brittlegill (*Russula brevipes,* p. 318), Pepper Milkcap (*Lactarius piperatus,* p. 333), Cottonroll Milkcap (*L. deceptivus,* p. 329), and Fleecy Milkcap (*L. vellereus,* p. 339) are known to be hosts for this species (*H. lactifluorum*). No doubt other host species are involved. Deformity caused by this parasitic fungus usually makes identification of the host mushroom impossible.

GREEN MUSHROOM PIMPLE   **Pl. 1**
Hypomyces luteovirens
Parasitic on *brittlegills* (*Russula,* p. 317). White at first, but eventually becomes light olive-green as spores mature. *Olive-green* perithecia are embedded in soft tissue but project as small pimples on distorted gill surface of host.

Fruiting: On various species of *Russula* throughout temperate N. America. Common in wet weather wherever host species are found.

Edibility: Unknown, but **not recommended** because host can not be identified.

Remarks: There are several host species, including an orange-red *Russula* that has yellowish spores and is common in conifer and aspen forests of Rocky Mts. In eastern U.S. Green Mushroom Pimple frequently parasitizes a purple *Russula.*

Family Xylariaceae

Genus *Xylaria*

DEAD-MAN'S FINGERS *Xylaria polymorpha*   **Pl. 1**
Small to medium, *dark brown or black club;* occasionally an *irregular mass* of tissue (stroma). **Fruiting body:** Usually club-shaped (fingerlike), but often flattened, fanlike. Surface white to grayish and fleshy at first, becoming dark brown to black with a white interior (see Pl. 1). Tough at maturity and more or less woody in age. Surface powdery in young specimens but soon roughened by projecting tips of perithecia, which are easily seen when club is sectioned (see Pl. 1 and Fig. 25).

Fruiting: Single or clumped; rising from decaying stumps, logs, or buried wood. Throughout N. America. Summer to late fall.

Edibility: Unpalatable.

Similar species: (1) A similar species, *Xylaria hypoxylon* (not shown), is more slender (not more than 3 mm in diameter), with pointed tips. (2) Black earthtongues (*Geoglossum* and *Trichoglossum*, p. 32) are very similar, but lack embedded perithecia that typically give mature fruiting bodies of *Xylaria* a rough or pimpled surface. Perithecia are best seen in sections, however (see Fig. 25). (3) *Cordyceps ophioglossoides* (not shown) is often mistaken for *Xylaria* (Dead-man's Fingers), but *Cordyceps* (grainy clubs) are most commonly parasitic on subterranean hosts such as insect pupae and truffles.

Cordyceps   *Xylaria*   *Geoglossum*

Fig. 25. Cross-sections of some black club fungi (Ascomycetes).

Family Sclerotiniaceae

Genus *Sclerotinia*

BROWN CUP *Sclerotinia tuberosa*   **Pl. 1**

Small, dark brown cup rises from an *underground tuber* (*sclerotium*). **Cup:** Deeply concave; both inner and outer surfaces smooth. **Stalk:** Gradually expands into cup, sometimes expanded at base also. Surface smooth, dark brown. Sclerotium globular to irregularly nodular; black on surface, white inside.

Technical notes: Stalk 3–10 cm long, 1–2 mm thick. Sclerotium 5–8 mm in diameter, 1.0–1.5 cm long. Spores hyaline (transparent), smooth, ellipsoid (narrowed at each end); 12–17 $\times$ 9 μm.

Fruiting: Solitary or in small clusters. Widely distributed in N. American forests. Spring and early summer.

Edibility: Unknown.

Similar species: Little, brown, fleshy cups of many species in several genera resemble Brown Cup (*S. tuberosa*). Most are small and inconspicuous. They are distinguished on microscopic characters.

Remarks: A related species causes brown rot of fruits in eastern N. America. The fungus blights caused by *Sclerotinia* result in considerable economic loss.

Family Geoglossaceae

Because of their unusual appearance, members of this family are quite unlike other cup fungi (see Pl. 4). Species of *Leotia* (below), in particular, are often considered to be jelly fungi because of their texture and colors.

Earthtongues: Genus *Geoglossum*

Stalked, *club-shaped head;* round to flattened in cross-section (see Fig. 25, p. 31).

G. nigritum

BLACK EARTHTONGUE *Geoglossum nigritum*   **Pl. 1**
Small to medium, *dark brown* to *black club;* spore-bearing apothecium (see p. 17) *smooth;* upper portion (receptacle) typically compressed. **Stalk** (lower half or third of fruiting body): Cylindric, slender, smooth; surface minutely hairy, sometimes sticky; moderate brown to black. **Technical notes:** Stalk 1–6 cm long; 2–5 mm wide, 0.5–2.0 mm thick. Spores dark brown, clavate (club-shaped), 7-septate, straight or somewhat curved; 30–90 × 4.5–6.5 μm.
Fruiting: Forested areas throughout N. America. Scattered or in small groups on moss beds (including peat moss), on soil in well-drained areas, on wet soil by streams, in bogs, or occasionally on decaying logs. Summer to fall.
Edibility: Unknown.
Similar species: There are more than 20 species of black earthtongues in 2 genera (*Geoglossum* and *Trichoglossum*) in N. America; they are distinguished primarily on microscopic characters. Species of *Trichoglossum* have sharply pointed, thick-walled, brown spines projecting from the hymenium (spore-bearing layer) that are lacking in *Geoglossum*. (1) *Trichoglossum hirsutum* (not shown) is common from coast to coast. Several species, including (2) *G. glabrum,* (3) *G. simile,* and (4) *T. farlowii* (not shown), are more common in eastern N. America. All may be confused with (5) *Xylaria* (Dead-man's Fingers, p. 30), which is thicker, and with the dark brown to black species of (6) *Cordyceps* (grainy clubs, p. 29), which usually have more distinct stalks.

Genus *Leotia*

Leotia lubrica

Because of their gelatinous texture, these mushrooms are often considered to be jelly fungi (see p. 64). The stalked fruiting bodies might be thought of as cups turned inside out and fused with the stalk on the outer surface. In *Leotia* the undersurface of the cap does not produce spores.

SLIPPERY CAP *Leotia lubrica*   **Pl. 1**
Small to medium, *yellowish, gelatinous cap. Stalk same color.*
Cap: Irregularly hemispherical; often flattened, with margin
bent back. Surface smooth or wrinkled, frequently slippery,
sometimes with wart-like bumps. Buff to dingy yellow or yellowish to olive-green, often glistening. Odor faint or lacking,
not distinctive when present. Taste mild, not distinctive.
Stalk: Hollow, cylindrical or tapered upward, sometimes flattened; often fused toward base. Surface scurfy. **Technical
notes:** Cap 1–4 cm across. Stalk 5–10 mm × 2–6 cm. Spores
hyaline (transparent), smooth, fusiform (spindle-shaped);
18–28 × 5–6 μm; at maturity 5- to 7-septate.
Fruiting: Occasionally solitary, but usually in clusters and often in large clumps of 50 or more. On bare soil or in open
places in woods; sometimes on well-rotted wood. Widely distributed in N. America, but particularly common east of the
Mississippi R. Summer and fall.
Edibility: Edible, but little known. McIlvaine (see p. 407)
rated it good.
Similar species: (1) Green Slippery Cap (*L. atrovirens,* not
shown) and **Winter Slippery Cap** (*L. viscosa,* Pl. 1) both
have dark green caps; Green Slippery Cap is typically dark
green all over. These two species can be mistaken for green
forms of Slippery Cap (*L. lubrica*). Green Slippery Cap, which
is usually smaller, is reported from Florida to Canada and only
as far west as the Great Lakes; Winter Slippery Cap is known
from the West Coast as well. In Maryland and Virginia *L.
viscosa* often fruits in the winter, even after heavy frosts,
hence the name Winter Slippery Cap. Its edibility is unknown.

Family Sarcoscyphaceae

Elf Cups: Genus *Sarcoscypha*

Small to medium, pink to bright red cups with pale pink to
white exterior, on short to long stalks. Elf cups grow from decaying wood. Spores thin-walled, smooth, non-amyloid (do not
turn blue in iodine).

SCARLET ELF CUP *Sarcoscypha coccinea*   **Pl. 1**
Medium to large cups, *shallow* or *deeply concave.* **Cup:** Margin
incurved. *Interior scarlet,* fading as it dries; exterior nearly
white; cottony, with matted hairs. **Stalk:** Short or occasionally lacking; stout, whitish when present. **Technical notes:**
Cup 2–5 cm across. Stalk 4–5 mm thick and up to 2–3 cm long.
Spores hyaline (transparent), smooth, elliptic; 25–40 × 10–12
μm.

Fruiting: Solitary or in groups; on buried or partially buried sticks. Widespread in the East and Midwest and in California. Winter to early spring.

Edibility: Not recommended.

Similar species: (1) Western Scarlet Cup (*S. occidentalis* below) is similar but smaller; it is common in midwestern and eastern N. America during midsummer. It is not likely to be mistaken for Scarlet Elf Cup, considering their different fruiting times. (2) **Pink Hairy Goblet** (*Microstoma floccosa,* **Pl. 1**) is sometimes placed in the same genus (*Sarcoscypha*), but its goblet-shaped cups are much smaller, with more conspicuous, stiff white hairs, and it fruits later in the spring. Microscopic differences also distinguish the *Sarcoscypha* and *Microstoma* genera.

Remarks: The medium to large, bright scarlet, stalked cups arising from wood in early spring make this one of the easy species for the beginner to recognize. Reports claim Scarlet Elf Cup as a favored medicinal plant of the Oneida (and probably other) Indians, who may have used it as an antibiotic.

WESTERN SCARLET CUP *Sarcoscypha occidentalis*   **Pl. 1**
Small, shallow, pink cups on *long, slender stalks.* Texture cartilaginous. *Cup: Interior bright red,* fading to watermelon pink; *exterior lighter* and smooth or wrinkled at base. *Stalk:* Pink above, whitish at base. **Technical notes:** Cup 1–2 cm across. Stalk 1–4 mm $\times$ 0.5–2.0 cm. Spores hyaline (transparent), smooth, elliptic; 20–22 $\times$ 10–12 μm.

Fruiting: Solitary or clustered on buried sticks in deciduous forests. Midwest and East. Spring and early summer.

Edibility: Unknown.

Similar species: The smaller size, more purplish red color, and later fruiting distinguish it readily from Scarlet Elf Cup (above), to which it is obviously related.

Family Sarcosomataceae

These stalked cups are mostly inconspicuous because of their dark colors, resulting from the presence of melanin pigments, particularly in the outer tissues. A few have carotenoids (yellow to red pigments) in tissues of the upper surface (hymenium), but most do not. Some species have gelatinous internal tissues in the cup and most are tough or leathery. Spores are sometimes surrounded by gelatinous sheaths. As in the Sarcoscyphaceae (previous family), asci are cylindrical to club-shaped, thick-walled, suboperculate, and do not stain blue in iodine.

Most species are found in spring or early summer, and are distinguished from the Sarcoscyphaceae by their dark (often blackish) colors, contrasted with the bright colors of most species of Sarcoscyphaceae found in temperate N. America.

Genus *Galiella*

RUFOUS RUBBER CUP *Galiella rufa*   **Pl. 1**
Small to medium, *thick, brown,* more or less *top-shaped* to
shallowly cup-shaped. **Cup:** Margin incurved, thin, *irregularly
toothed;* teeth lighter than exterior. Upper surface *smooth,
pale reddish to reddish brown* or fading to yellowish brown.
Outer surface blackish brown; velvety below to sparsely scaly
toward margin. Interior gray; firm and *gelatinous* but not
fluid, giving flesh a *rubbery* feel. **Stalk:** *Short* and thick when
present; occasionally lacking. **Technical notes:** Cup up to 3
cm across. Stalk 0.5–1.5 cm (up to 2.5 cm) long, when present.
Spores warty, elliptic; 20 × 10 μm. Flesh stains (turns blue) in
cotton blue dye.
Fruiting: Solitary to clustered on buried wood. Hardwood forests, Midwest and eastern N. America. Spring to summer.
Edibility: Unknown.
Similar species: (1) Charred-pancake Cup (*Sarcosoma*, below) is larger and black, with a more liquid interior. When seen
under a microscope, the spores of Rufous Rubber Cup distinguish it even more clearly from *Sarcosoma* and from (2) Black
Felt Cup (*Plectania nannfeldtii,* not shown). Both of the latter
resemble Rufous Rubber Cup in having a gelatinous texture.

Genus *Sarcosoma*

CHARRED-PANCAKE CUP *Sarcosoma globosum*   **Pl. 1**
Medium to large, *thick-fleshed, black cup. Nearly globose
(round)* at first, then *top-shaped. No distinct stalk.* **Cup:** Upper surface concave to disk-shaped; black. *Interior gelatinous*
but *watery.* Outer surface brownish black; hairless but often
wrinkled. **Technical notes:** 3–8 (up to 10) cm across and
3.5–7.0 cm high.
Fruiting: Solitary or in groups, partially buried in soil; in conifer forests. Northern U.S. and Canada. Early spring.
Edibility: Unknown.
Similar species: (1) Rufous Rubber Cup (*Galiella rufa,*
above) has the same general shape and gelatinous texture, but
Charred-pancake Cup (*Sarcosoma*) is larger, with a black upper surface and liquid interior. (The upper surface of Rufous
Rubber Cup is light reddish brown.) The thick, watery flesh of
Charred-pancake Cup distinguishes it readily from the few
black species with a thin stalk, such as (2) Black Felt Cup
(*Plectania nannfeldtii,* not shown), or others that have thin
cups and no stalk. (3) *Sarcosoma latahensis* (not shown), a
western species, can be distinguished from Charred-pancake
Cup only on microscopic characters.

Genus *Urnula*

DEVIL'S URN *Urnula craterium*   **Pl. 1**
Medium-sized, *brownish black* to *gray, goblet-shaped cup* with
a *thin margin*. Grows on *rotting wood*. **Cup:** Shaped more or
less like an elongate egg at first, later *opening by a star-shaped
slit* that leaves the margin *notched* as the cup expands. Inner
surface *smooth, brownish black;* when moist, exterior darker
brownish black than inner surface, but as it dries out it becomes dingy grayish from a dense outer layer of soft, suede-like
hairs. **Stalk:** Solid, sometimes flattened or ribbed near base;
gradually expanding upward into cup. Black or brownish
black. *Attached* to substrate (wood) *by dense mat of black filaments*. **Technical notes:** Cup 2–5 cm across when fully expanded; up to 6 cm deep. Stalk up to 5 cm long and 1 cm thick.
Spores smooth, broadly ellipsoid; 25–35 × 12–14 μm.
Fruiting: Solitary or clustered, on *buried wood* (usually oak)
in hardwood forests. Midwest to Southeast. *Early spring.*
Edibility: Inedible.
Similar species: (1) Devil's Cigar (*U. geaster,* not shown) is
larger and more southerly in distribution. Upon opening its
splits about halfway down or farther into 3–6 broad rays that
resemble the rays on earthstars (Pl. 47). (2) Winter Urn (*U.
hiemalis,* not shown), reported from Alaska, has cups that are
most often smaller and proportionally broader than in Devil's
Urn. Winter Urn is often found on soil with no apparent attachment to decaying wood. It may be found under melting
snow.
Remarks: One of the first fleshy fungi to fruit each spring in
the eastern deciduous forests. The black cups emerging
through the fallen leaves from March to May are true harbin-
gers of spring.

Sponge Mushrooms: Morels

Morels: Family Morchellaceae

Large, mostly stalked, with sponge-like or bell-shaped caps
(caps are disk-like and lack a stalk in *Disciotis*). Color cream to
brown, sometimes with pink or olive tints. Stalk hollow, with a
single channel, or stuffed with cottony filaments. Asci operculate; do not stain blue in iodine. Ascospores thin-walled, hyaline (nearly colorless and transparent) or with some yellowish
content, and with apical clusters of external guttules (oil droplets).

All species are considered edible after cooking by some people, but bell morels (*Verpa*) do cause poisoning (see **caution**

under that genus). Also, the morels in genus *Morchella* occasionally are responsible for some poisoning, particularly when eaten with alcoholic beverages.

Genus *Disciotis*

Disciotis venosa

CUP MOREL *Disciotis venosa* **Pl. 2**
Large, brown, shallow cup or *disk.* Usually no stalk. **Cup:** Upper surface reddish brown, *smooth or* typically *wrinkled* or *veined,* often with a *network of ridges.* Exterior of cup whitish. **Stalk:** Very short if present; ribbed. **Technical notes:** Cup 6–20 cm across. Spores hyaline, smooth, elliptic; 14–16 × 8–10 μm. Thin-walled, with external apical guttules (oil droplets). **Fruiting:** Solitary to clustered; on soil in forested areas. Widespread. Spring.
 Edibility: Edible.
Similar species: Cup or Ear Morel (*Disciotis*) is virtually indistinguishable on field characters from (1) species of *Discina* such as Thick Cup (p. 47). *Disciotis* may also be confused with some of the larger species of (2) *Peziza* (p. 56) but these cup fungi have thinner flesh and the ascus layer turns dark blue if a drop of iodine solution is placed on it. *Disciotis* and *Discina* do not. Microscopic characters link *Disciotis* with other morels, including *Verpa* (bell morels), although the disk-like shape looks very different.

Morels: Genus *Morchella*

Morchella

Medium to large, *deeply pitted,* oval to conical cap on *hollow,* smooth to scurfy stalk. Ribs or ridges around pits are blackish in some species, such as the Black Morel (p. 38). Spore print yellowish. Spores have apical clusters of guttules (oil droplets). See **caution** on p. 38 about serving morels with alcohol.

NARROWHEAD MOREL *Morchella angusticeps* **Pl. 2**
Medium to large, *dark, narrow, cone-shaped* cap. **Cap:** Conic, *pointed at* apex; about half as broad at base as height; *narrow* in proportion to stalk. Cap and stalk fused from base of cap upward. Surface moderate to dark brown, often purplish or reddish brown, typically darkening to blackish in age. *Lengthwise furrows* with *few* or *indistinct crossribs. Ribs darker* (at least in age) than pits. **Stalk:** Hollow, fragile, cylindric but usually expanded toward cap; shallowly and indistinctly furrowed; usually slit at base. Surface white to pink or brownish. **Technical notes:** Cap 5–9 × 3–5 cm. Stalk 5–15 cm long, 2–5 cm wide. Spores hyaline, smooth, elliptic; 24–28 × 12–14 μm.

Thin-walled, with apical guttules (oil droplets).

Fruiting: Singly to scattered on ground in hardwood forests from Rocky Mts. eastward. In Rocky Mts. grows in conifer forests containing Douglas fir; sometimes found growing in mouths of rodent tunnels. Early spring.

Edibility: Edible; good, but see **caution** under Black Morel (below).

Similar species: Very similar to (1) *M. canaliculata* (not shown), which grows in the same area; the 2 species can be distinguished only by using microscopic characters. Narrowhead Morel is often confused with (2) Black Morel (*M. conica,* below) and seems to intergrade with other black morels, but the lower edge of its cap comes outward or upward from stalk and does not form a *downward-hanging lobe,* as in Black Morel (see Pl. 2) and *M. canaliculata.* Narrowhead Morel seems to fruit earlier than Black Morel (*M. conica*).

Remarks: It is clear from study of Peck's original collection (1897) and his original description of the species that the name *M. angusticeps* must go with the morel having the characteristics listed above for the Narrowhead Morel.

BLACK MOREL *Morchella conica*   **Pl. 2**
Medium to large, *dark cap, distinctly wider than stalk;* ribs dark, mostly vertical. *Cap* (head): Conic, often with a narrow, pointed tip; surface olive-gray to grayish tan or moderate brown, becoming blackish in age. Cap typically has a small rounded lobe on lower margin, as seen in lengthwise section (Pl. 2). Cap and stalk *fused* from *lower margin* of cap *upward.* *Stalk:* Narrow, hollow, cylindric; usually enlarged and *slit at base.* Surface soft, granular, white. **Technical notes:** Cap 4–7 cm high, 2.5–4.0 cm wide. Stalk 2.5–4.0 cm long, 1.5–2.5 cm wide. Spores hyaline, elliptic; 20–25 $\times$ 12–14 μm. Thin-walled, smooth, with clusters of apical guttules (oil droplets).

Fruiting: Scattered on ground in forested areas in spring. A large form is prevalent in hardwood forests across U.S. and under Douglas fir in Rocky Mts. Often found in disturbed soil and burned areas; especially abundant the first year after a burn. Time of fruiting depends on local conditions; overall, later than (1) Half-free Morel (*M. semilibera,* p. 40) and earlier than (2) Common Morel (*M. esculenta,* p. 39), although its season overlaps both. A common fungus of northern coniferous forests; at high elevations it may be found even in July or August.

Edibility: Edible; good, but use **caution:** We have received a number of reports that "the black ones are poisonous," and since very dark-colored ones are often old and overmature, this may be a wise precaution to apply to individual specimens. Some people feel that Black Morels are among our best edible mushrooms; however, reports persist of gastrointestinal upset, especially when these mushrooms are taken with alcohol.

Similar species: (1) See under Narrowhead Morel (above). (2)

Morchella crassistipa (not shown) can be distinguished from Black Morel (*M. conica*) only by microscopic characters; it grows in western conifer forests. See also **Remarks.**
Remarks: The name Black Morel applies to a variety of forms that represent more than 1 species; the species described here represents a common form, but there is much variation in size, shape, and color. It is also known as Conic Morel. *Morchella elata* (not shown) is widely recognized in Europe as a distinct species. It has tall but more rounded caps with less pointed apex and major ribs which are more vertically oriented and are connected by more distinctly horizontal short ribs, making rectangular pits. Long ribs can often be traced from one margin over the top and down to the margin on the opposite side; the marginal pits are typically open on the stalk and a distinct lip overhanging the stalk is not so evident as in *M. conica.* Our N. American black morels seem to intergrade more in these characters, making distinct species of "Black Morels" difficult to recognize.
THICK-FOOTED MOREL *Morchella crassipes*   **Pl. 2**
Cap: Large, conical; pits very wide, shallow, and *irregular; surface yellow,* with *thin, light-colored ribs.* **Stalk:** Hollow, *enlarged,* and *usually slit at base;* tends to be conspicuously large, so entire fruiting body may be as much as 45 cm (18 in.) high. Surface grayish yellow to pale yellow or orange-yellow, irregularly and shallowly ridged. **Technical notes:** Cap usually 8 cm or more long. Spores hyaline, elliptic; 20–22 × 12–14 µm. Thin-walled, smooth, with apical clusters of external guttules (oil droplets).
Fruiting: Scattered on ground in woods; common across northern U.S. and at least as far south as Virginia. Late spring.
Edibility: Edible; reportedly very good.
Remarks: Has appearance of a large, overgrown Common Morel (*M. esculenta,* below), and some specialists think that is what it is. Fruiting seasons coincide and habitats are similar. However, these 2 morels are recognizable as distinct forms or species and both are frequently found. Common Morel may be white at first, whereas Thick-footed Morel is distinctly yellow and more readily stains darker orange-yellow to brownish when cut or handled.
COMMON MOREL *Morchella esculenta*   **Pl. 2**
Medium to large, *conical to round, irregularly pitted cap.* **Cap:** Surface *nearly white* to *yellowish gray, yellow,* or *light yellowish brown,* usually becoming lighter as it matures. Ridges white to yellow or light yellowish brown (never black) and typically lighter than depressions (pits). Cap *fused* with stalk *from base of cap upward.* **Stalk:** Hollow, brittle; cylindrical, or expanded at base. Surface often shallowly and irregularly furrowed; white to yellowish. **Technical notes:** Cap 6–10 cm high, 4–5 cm wide. Stalk 3–5 cm high, 1.0–2.5 cm wide. Spores hyaline, elliptic; 20–25 × 12–14 µm. Thin-walled, smooth, with

clustered, external, apical guttules (oil droplets).

Fruiting: Scattered in small clusters or occasionally in rings on ground in forests, grassy places, or old orchards. Throughout temperate N. America. Late spring. Often particularly abundant in disturbed or burned-over soil. We have seen especially prolific fruiting where a bulldozer cleared a roadway in river bottomland. Because it consistently fruits in May, *M. esculenta* is also known as the May Mushroom, but fruiting varies locally, at least, from February to July. This is usually the latest morel to fruit in localities where more than 1 species are found. Although fruiting seasons overlap, this species normally comes later than the black morels (Narrowhead Morel and Black Morel, p. 38).

Edibility: Edible and generally considered one of the best. Stalks edible, but morel caps frequently are cut from stalks when gathered, to keep the heads free of soil and other debris. This practice is permissible when collecting morels, because they are so easy to recognize, but other fungi should **never** be collected without the entire stalk attached, since important identification characters may be on base of stalk.

Similar species: Some mycologists consider (1) Thick-footed Morel (*M. crassipes*, above) to be a giant form of this species (*M. esculenta*); others recognize several other species, including (2) *M. deliciosa* (see also **Remarks**). (3) Burnsite Morel (*M. atromentosa,* below), a closely related species found at burn sites the first year after a forest fire, is *almost black at first,* becoming lighter as it matures. As it grows, the edges of its ribs *crack* (see Pl. 2), giving it a distinctive mottled appearance (Common Morel also does this to some extent, but the cracking is less obvious.)

Remarks: Common Morel (*M. esculenta*) is one of the easiest mushrooms to recognize. Its mild, pleasant flavor and common occurrence throughout the U.S. add to its popularity. Attempts to cultivate this morel in laboratories or on "farms" have been only partially successful. The species is so variable that it is not known how many species pass under this name; there is little agreement on the subject among either professional or amateur collectors.

BURNSITE MOREL *Morchella atrotomentosa.*   **Pl. 2**
Cap: Dark brownish gray (almost black) at first, becoming *lighter with age.* Ribs eventually develop *cracks* along edges, giving the cap a distinctive mottled appearance.

Fruiting: First year after forest fires, on charred, carbon-rich soil.

Edibility: Edible, but see **caution** under Black Morel (p. 38).

Similar species: (1) See Common Morel (*M. esculenta,* above). (2) See Black Morel (*M. conica,* p. 38).

HALF-FREE MOREL *Morchella semilibera*   **Pl. 2**
Medium-sized, *bell-shaped cap. Cap: Small* in proportion to

stalk. Surface of cap has lengthwise ribs (often branched) and shallow depressions. Light to dark yellowish brown, darkening on ribs as it dries. *Cap and stalk fused from* about *middle of cap upward* (see Pl. 2 and Fig. 26). **Stalk:** *Hollow with basal slots;* cylindrical and typically expanded at base. White to yellowish; surface granular and usually faintly and shallowly grooved. **Technical notes:** Cap 2–4 cm long (width slightly less). Stalk 7–15 cm long. Spores hyaline, smooth, elliptic, with apical clusters of guttules (oil droplets); 22–26 × 12–14 μm. **Fruiting:** Common in hardwood forests. Fruits in early spring, usually March and April. Although the Early Morel (*Verpa bohemica*, p. 42) and this species may be found in the same locality, Half-free Morel usually grows on soil with better drainage. Also, Half-free Morel generally fruits later than the Verpas (bell morels) and is often collected along with black morels (p. 38) early in the "morel season."

Edibility: Edible and good, although reportedly of poorer quality than other morels. **Caution:** Be sure to distinguish this species from *Verpa bohemica* (Early Morel, p. 42). Persons known to be sensitive to the Early Morel and those who may be unaware of this sensitivity should rely on microscopic examination to confirm identification (see below).
Similar species: Easily confused with (1) Early Morel (*V. bohemica*, p. 42). Most reliable field characters are *attachment of cap and stalk,* ecology (soil type), and *time of fruiting.* Structural differences in stalk also help to distinguish them. Poisonous species of *Verpa* typically have *cottony filaments* "stuffed" in stalk interior and *lack slots* near base of stalk. Species of *Morchella* have *hollow* stalks, usually with *holes or slots* around the base (see Fig. 26). Accurate identification is most important for anyone who may be sensitive to *Verpa* poisons. Most dependable differences are microscopic: *V. bohemica* (Early Morel) has larger spores—only 2 spores in an ascus (rarely 3 or 4)—whereas Half-free Morel has 8. (2) A variety of *Verpa digitaliformis* (not shown) has reddish orange scales on stalk and 8 spores in an ascus.
Remarks: Half-free Morel (*M. semilibera*) is also known as "Cow's Head."

Bell Morels: Genus *Verpa*

Small to medium, bell-shaped cap with smooth to netted or wrinkled (but *not deeply* pitted) surface. Cap (head) attached at center to tip of long, slender, fragile, *cotton-stuffed* stalk (see Fig. 26 and Pl. 2). **Caution:** Some Verpas are poisonous, particularly when eaten over a period of several days— see Early Morel (*V. bohemica,* p. 42).

Verpa bohemica

Early Morel
(V. bohemica)

Half-free Morel
(M. semilibera)

Black Morel
(M. conica)

Common Morel
(M. esculenta)

Fig. 26. Morels *(Morchella)* and bell morels *(Verpa)*. Compare cap and stalk attachments and stalk interiors.

EARLY MOREL *Verpa bohemica* **Pl. 2**
Medium-sized, *brown, bell-shaped cap, attached* like a parasol — *only at tip of stalk. Cap:* Surface *strongly ridged or wrinkled,* with *lengthwise folds* and *shallow, irregular furrows.* Outer surface grayish yellow to moderate brown; undersurface white. Margin slightly flaring or incurved, wavy. *Stalk:* Cylindric, but somewhat narrowed toward top; brittle. Surface grainy to slightly scaly, whitish to yellowish or light yellowish gray. Stalk interior *stuffed with cottony threads* (Fig. 26). **Technical notes:** Cap 2.0–3.5 cm high and almost as wide. Stalk 6–9 cm long. Spores hyaline, elliptic; 60–80 × 15–20 µm. Thin-walled; smooth; with external, apically clustered guttules (oil droplets).
Fruiting: Singly or scattered on rich soil in moist places, as in riverbottom and similar lowland communities. Also in coniferaspen forests of the Rockies; widespread. Fruits in *early spring,* usually ahead of the other morels, hence the name Early Morel.

 Edibility: Not recommended, although edible, at least for some people, when well cooked. There are reports of mild to severe poisoning, particularly after eating large quantities or repeated meals of *Verpa* over several days. **Use great caution** in testing your own tolerance to this species — do not rely wholly on the experiences of others. If tempted to eat this species, test a small quantity (cook it first) and remember that sensitivity to its toxins seems to be cumulative.
Similar species: This species is easily confused with (1) Half-free Morel, but the two can be distinguished easily (when cut in half lengthwise) by the different *attachment of cap and stalk* (see Fig. 26 and Pl. 2). *Cottony filaments* stuffing the interior of *Verpa* stalks are usually evident even in old specimens. The enormous spores — 2–3 per ascus — are distinctive for Early Morel (*V. bohemica*). (2) A variety of *Verpa digitaliformis* (not shown), known only from southern California, has soft, reddish orange scales on stalk.

Remarks: Formerly known as *V. bispora.* The very soft, white scales on the stalk tend to be in rings. A large form common in the West is often twice as big but otherwise looks the same.

BELL MOREL *Verpa conica*   **Pl. 2**
Small to medium, *thin, bell-shaped cap.* **Cap:** Sometimes almost as wide as it is high; margin sometimes flaring. *Outer surface* (hymenium) *dark brown* and *smooth* or with *very fine, net-like ridges;* inner surface white. **Stalk:** Cylindric; white to pale dingy yellow. Surface smooth, or with bracelet-like rows of soft, cottony, white scales. **Technical notes:** Cap 1–3 cm high. Stalk 5–10 cm long. Spores 8 to an ascus; hyaline, smooth, elliptic; 22–26 × 12–16 μm. Thin-walled, with external apical guttules (oil droplets).
Fruiting: Scattered; on soil in woods. Early spring.
Edibility: Edible, but seldom found in sufficient quantity for a meal. **Caution:** May be confused with Early Morel (*V. bohemica,* above), which is poisonous to some people.
Similar species: See (1) Early Morel (above) and (2) Half-free Morel (p. 40). (3) *V. digitaliformis* (not shown) has a more distinct network of ridges on the cap, and reddish orange scales on the stalk. It is known from southern California.

False Morels and Lorchels

Family Helvellaceae

Large, usually with a distinct cap and stalk. Form of cap varies from a disk to a cup or a saddle-shaped to convoluted "head." Color mostly white to yellow, brown, or black. Ascus tip does not stain blue in iodine. Spores smooth to warty. This family contains both edible and poisonous species.

Lorchels: Genus *Helvella*

Medium to large, shallow to deep cup on a smooth to wrinkled, ribbed or fluted stalk. Cap (head) *often saddle-shaped or everted* (turned inside out) or somewhat convoluted (wrinkled or folded). Cap white to gray or grayish brown (mostly *dull-colored*).

Helvella

VINEGAR CUP *Helvella acetabulum*   **Pl. 2**
Medium to large, *brown, stalked cup.* **Cup:** Typically compressed at first, then expanded, and often irregular at maturity. Inside of cup (hymenium) light yellowish brown to dark brown (sometimes with a tinge of violet). Outside of cup light grayish brown to brown, sometimes whitish near the margin; pale brownish to cream-colored at base. Outer surface of cup minutely velvety to scurfy (under a hand lens). *Prominent,*

whitish to *cream-colored, angular* to *sharp-edged ribs extend* from stalk *almost to margin* of cup. Ribs are typically forked. Cup margin sometimes incurved at first, becoming straight and sometimes flaring outward; typically split at maturity. **Stalk:** Usually well developed, but not clearly distinct from cup. Cream-colored to brownish; strongly ribbed, sometimes with more or less angular ribs that are continuous with those of cup. Stalk interior chambered. **Technical notes:** Cup 1.5–8.0 cm across and up to 4 cm deep. Stalk 1–6 cm high × 1–3 cm thick. Spores thin-walled, smooth, uniguttulate, elliptic; 18–22 × 12–14 μm.

Fruiting: Solitary, or more often scattered to clustered; on soil in woods. Spring and summer.

Edibility: Sometimes reported as edible **with caution.**

Similar species: Several N. American species of *Helvella* are cup-shaped and have strongly ribbed stalks: Like Vinegar Cup, (1) *H. griseoalba* (not shown) has ribs that extend at least halfway up the sides of the cup, but the cups are gray and the ribs are white to grayish. (2) In *H. queletii* (not shown) the ribs extend from the stalk only to the *lower* part of the cup. (3) Cup Morel (*Disciotis venosa*, p. 37) and (4) species of *Discina* (p. 47) may be confused with Vinegar Cup, but the stalk is rarely well developed in *Disciotis* or *Discina* and the flesh is thicker in *Discina.* Also, the ribs are different. Vinegar Cup and other lorchels (species of *Helvella*) are dull-colored compared with those of *Disciotis* and *Discina.*

Remarks: The very large, light to dark brown cups with a whitish base are quite distinctive when they fruit in spring and early summer.

WAVY LORCHEL (SADDLE BACK) *Helvella crispa* **Pl. 2** Cap stalked, *saddle-shaped* to *lobed; pale cream color, both inside and outside.* **Cap:** Sometimes irregularly lobed or split; margin rolled inward when young. **Stalk:** Tapers upward; interior has longitudinal chambers. *Surface strongly ribbed, cream-colored,* hairless to powdery; *ribs branched, rounded.* **Technical notes:** Cap 1–5 cm across. Stalk 2–10 cm × 1.0–3.5 cm thick. Spores hyaline, thin-walled, smooth, uniguttulate, elliptic; 18–20 × 10–13 μm.

Fruiting: Solitary to scattered or clustered in small groups. On soil or rotting woody debris; conifer and hardwood forests of U.S. and Canada. Summer and fall.

Edibility: Reported as edible, but easily mistaken for Elfin Saddle (*H. lacunosa*) and related species that are not recommended. See **cautions** on edibility under *H. lacunosa* (p. 46) before experimenting with *H. crispa.* Mature specimens of *H. crispa* are said to be leathery and indigestible.

Similar species: The combination of white to cream or pale yellow color on all parts, the irregularly saddle-shaped cap, and the strongly ribbed stalk is distinctive. Still, this morel is likely to be confused frequently with white or pallid forms of several gray or brown species, particularly Elfin Saddle (below). Tinges of gray or brown on any part of the mushroom suggest a species other than Wavy Lorchel (*H. crispa*).

Remarks: The Latin species name *crispa* means irregularly wavy or curled and refers to the cap, especially its margin. In young caps the margin curves backward (or outward) at first and later typically curves inward as the cap matures. Although it is the source of the species name here, the characteristic is neither distinctive nor unique for *H. crispa* (Wavy Lorchel), as most lorchels and false morels do this to some degree.

FLEXIBLE LORCHEL *Helvella elastica*   **Pl. 2**
Cap: Convex; basically *saddle-shaped,* but often irregularly so. *Lobes often curl upward* and *sometimes overlap.* Cap *margin incurved at first,* but later flaring or curved toward stalk. Hymenium dull *yellow brown* to *olive-brown* or *grayish brown; outside of cap white* to *dingy yellowish,* smooth, occasionally ingrown with stalk at maturity. *Stalk:* Roughly *cylindrical,* sometimes tapering toward tip, flattened, wrinkled, or creased. *Cream to pale brownish;* surface smooth, or with fine powdery texture. **Technical notes:** Cap 1–5 cm across. Stalk 2–10 cm long $\times$ 3–8 mm thick. Spores hyaline, thin-walled, smooth, uniguttulate, elliptic; 19–22 $\times$ 11–13 μm.
Fruiting: Solitary or in small groups. On moist soil or rotting wood, in both hardwood and coniferous forests, throughout U.S. and Canada. Midsummer to fall.

Edibility: Reported as edible, but lacking in substance and seldom found in sufficient quantity to be significant.
Similar species: There are several lorchels with a dull brown, saddle-shaped cap on a slender, smooth, white or pale stalk. The species can be separated only with difficulty. In (1) *H. stevensii* and (2) *H. albella* (not shown), the outer surface of the young cap is mealy compared with the smooth outer margins of Flexible Lorchel (*H. elastica*). Although their fruiting seasons overlap, *H. stevensii* appears earlier than *H. elastica* (Flexible Lorchel), and *H. albella* typically comes later. (3) *Helvella atra* (not shown) and related species that are very similar to *H. elastica* in general appearance have jet black to grayish hymenial surfaces, in contrast to the tan to dull brown hymenium in Flexible Lorchel.

ELFIN SADDLE *Helvella lacunosa*   **Pl. 2**
Cap: Convex, with sides pressed against the stalk, to *irregularly saddle-shaped,* often with *conical, upward-projecting lobes.* Hymenium *pale neutral gray* (occasionally whitish) to *moderate gray* or *black;* coarsely wrinkled. Outer surface gray to black, smooth (hairless), with ribs that extend from stalk apex toward margin; ribs are often branched. *Stalk:* Cylindrical or *tapering upward,* often bent or contorted, sometimes with irregularly disposed pits; vertical ribs, often branched.

Dingy white to gray or black, often lighter at base than apex.
Technical notes: Cap 2–4 cm across, 1–5 cm high. Stalk 5–12 × 1–3 cm. Spores hyaline, thin-walled, smooth, uniguttulate, elliptic; 17–20 × 11–12 μm.
Fruiting: Solitary to clustered or scattered. On moist soil in both conifer and mixed conifer-hardwood forests, often in grassy places. Widely distributed throughout N. America.
Edibility: Although reported as edible after cooking by many authors we agree with Smith (1975), who says, **"not recommended."**
Similar species: Occasionally, nearly pure white forms of Elfin Saddle are found. These paler forms are easily mistaken for Wavy Lorchel (*H. crispa*, p. 44), but Wavy Lorchel has shorter ribs on the underside of the cap, and its cap (head) is characteristically white to yellowish, instead of whitish to grayish as in Elfin Saddle. (2) There are several large gray to blackish lorchels (species of *Helvella*) in N. America that have strongly ribbed stalks and more or less convoluted, convex to saddle-shaped caps. Specialists do not agree upon how many of the variants should be recognized as separate species. The name *Helvella sulcata* is given to those gray to blackish lorchels with more distinctly saddle-shaped to trilobed caps that lack ribs on the underside. Watch for *H. sulcata* on better-drained soil. (Elfin Saddle often shows a preference for boggy soil.) (3) Small specimens with a comparatively thin, solid stalk may be *Helvella palustris* (not shown).
Remarks: Because the species in this section (subgroup within genus *Helvella*) are not easily defined, and some are not well known, it may be dangerous to experiment with them for food. Elfin Saddle is often found in quantities great enough to be tempting, but there are so many doubtful factors involved that we must agree that these species are **not to be recommended** as food.

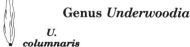

Genus *Underwoodia*

U. columnaris

IVORY CANDLE *Underwoodia columnaris*   **Pl. 2**
Cap (fruiting body): Columnar to *spindle-shaped;* or *club-shaped; straight* or *curved,* tapering gradually to a rounded tip. *Straw-colored* to *pale brownish,* with *lengthwise wrinkles* or *grooves.* **Stalk:** *Very short* or *lacking;* if present, stalk portion is spongy in cross-section, with many channels (see Pl. 2).
Technical notes: Cap up to 10 cm tall × 2–3 cm in diameter. Spores hyaline, coarsely warty, elliptic; 25–27 × 12–14 μm; uniguttulate.
Fruiting: Solitary or in groups; on soil in hardwood forests. Rare. Iowa eastward and north to Canada.

Edibility: Unknown.
Remarks: A most interesting and distinctive-looking fungus; microscopic characters show that it is related to the lorchels (species of *Helvella*).

Genus *Discina*

Discina perlata

Several species of *Discina* are found in the U.S. They are difficult to distinguish without examining the spores under a microscope.

THICK CUP *Discina perlata*   **Pl. 3**
Medium to large, *shallow, thick-fleshed, brown cup* or *disk,* attached to soil at a *central point, usually without a stalk.* (A few have a very short, solid, strongly ribbed stalk.) *Cap:* Upper surface *yellowish brown* to *moderate brown,* darkening somewhat in age; smooth or wrinkled. *Undersurface* hygrophanous — at first *light brownish gray when moist,* but *white* or nearly so *as it dries out.* Surface of cap smooth near margin and usually strongly wrinkled or ribbed toward base. **Technical notes:** Cap 7-18 cm across. Spores minutely warty; pointed, with a short, pointed spine at each end; typically with 1 large central guttule (oil droplet) and 2 small apical ones; elliptic to broadly fusoid, flattened in side view; 25-35 × 8-16 μm.
Fruiting: Solitary or clustered; on soil, often under or around snowbanks. Found in both coniferous and hardwood forests. *Early spring,* before or with the morels.
Edibility: Edible.
Similar species: Forms of Thick Cup that lack a stalk are almost indistinguishable in the field from (1) Cup Morel (*Disciotis,* p. 37). (2) Some cup fungi in genus *Peziza* (p. 56) resemble Thick Cup, but their flesh is *usually thinner,* and the ascus (spore-bearing) layer *turns blue* in iodine solution. (3) Other species of *Discina* (not shown) are very similar; they are best distinguished on microscopic characters. *Discina olympiana,* known only from the Northwest, has small fruiting bodies (cups), less than 2.5 cm (1 in.) across. One form of *D. leucoxantha* has a bright yellow hymenium (upper surface is brown in other species of *Discina*). *Discina warnei* grows on rotting wood in eastern states. *Discina macrospora,* widespread in northern forests, and *D. apiculatula,* common in the Sierra and Rocky Mts., are distinguished from Thick Cup (*D. perlata*) in the field only by very subtle color differences, but microscopic characters of their spores separate these 3 species readily. (4) False morels (*Gyromitra,* next group) have a *hollow* or *multichanneled stalk.* (If present, stalk of Thick Cup is short and solid.)
Remarks: These large, thick, brown cups are found *only in early spring,* in *both coniferous and hardwood forests.* The

spores of Thick Cup mature very slowly, sometimes requiring a
month or more to develop after cup expansion is virtually complete.

False Morels: Genus *Gyromitra*

G. *infula*
G. *gigas*

Medium to large, brown to reddish brown or purplish brown cap, on a thick, *hollow or multichanneled stalk.* Cap *saddle-shaped* to *wrinkled or
folded,* sometimes with brainlike convolutions.
Caution: Some people have died after eating certain false morels. The Hooded False Morels —
Gyromitra infula, p. 53, and *G. ambigua,* not
shown — are especially dangerous, although False
Morel (*G. esculenta,* p. 51) has also been impli-
cated in some fatal poisonings. The specific poisons
involved were found to be hydrazines, after it was
discovered that the symptoms of false morel poisoning were the same as those caused by rocket
fuels. These volatile compounds are not necessarily
boiled off during cooking.

BROWN FALSE MOREL *Gyromitra brunnea*   **Pl. 3**
One or more *large, brown, fused caps,* on a *single* or *compound
stalk.* **Cap:** *everted* (turned inside out), roughly *saddle-shaped,*
often *intricately lobed* and *folded.* Lobes *may overlap* but are
not fused at their margins and seldom with stalk. *Hymenium
strong brown* to *moderate reddish brown* or with more reddish
overtones; *wrinkled* or veined. External surface nearly white to
yellowish gray or tan. **Stalk:** *White, sometimes branched,* with
branches visible below the lowest lobes of cap. Stalk expanded
at base. Interior hollow or stuffed; often has *several branching
channels* (cut stalk in half lengthwise). **Technical notes:** Cap
5–12 cm across. Stalk 3–6 × 11–15 mm. Flesh turns yellowish
or brown (*not pink*) in weak potash (KOH) solution.
Fruiting: Solitary or scattered; on soil and well-decayed wood
in hardwood forests. East of the Rocky Mts.; found in southern Canada and eastern U.S. to mid-South.
Edibility: Questionable. Reports on the edibility of Brown
False Morel (*G. brunnea*) vary, but we do **not recommend**
eating it, as there are definite reports by reliable authors that
it is poisonous. Brown False Morel is also commonly confused
with 2 other false morels that are definitely **poisonous** — False
Morel (*G. esculenta*) and Hooded False Morel (*G. infula*). It
can also be mistaken for Carolina False Morel (*G. caroliniana*),
which is edible, at least for some people.
Similar species: (1) In Carolina False Morel (*G. caroliniana,*
p. 50) the lobes of the cap are usually *fused* at the edges, forming *seam-like ribs.* (2) The flesh of False Morel (*G. esculenta,*

p. 51) and Hooded False Morel (*G. infula,* p. 53) *turns pink* in a weak (2%) solution of potash (KOH). See details in **Similar species** entry under California False Morel (below).

Remarks: Although it is not really common, this beautiful fungus is frequently seen, as it fruits during the morel season. Its distinctive field characteristics are complex and must be studied carefully. Look for the *combination* of field marks described above; other false morels may share individual characters with this species. There is confusion in the Latin names applied to some of the false morels. Brown False Morel (*G. brunnea*) may be the same species (or a variety) known in some recent European books (and a recent edition of Smith's *Mushroom Hunter's Field Guide*) as *Gyromitra fastigiata.* We use the name *G. brunnea* here to avoid ambiguity, as this is clearly the species to which Underwood (1889) gave that name.

CALIFORNIA FALSE MOREL   **Pl. 3**
Gyromitra californica
A western false morel with a *thin, yellow-brown* to *olive-brown, wrinkled* cap. **Cap:** *Large,* typically a little taller than it is broad; *nearly round* to *broadly convex.* Hymenium usually *irregularly lobed* and *convoluted* or *furrowed,* sometimes nearly smooth; color varies from *yellowish brown* to *grayish brown* or *olive-brown.* Outer surface white, finely woolly, strongly ribbed. Margin of cap recurved. **Stalk:** *Deeply fluted,* with *conspicuous ribs* that extend outward onto underside of the cap, like ribs of an umbrella. *White* to pale grayish to yellowish in age; usually *pink* to *purplish at the base.* **Technical notes:** Cap 5–12 cm across. Stalk 2–10 × 2–5 cm. Spores hyaline (clear), smooth, uniguttulate, elliptic; 16–18 × 7–9 μm.
Fruiting: Solitary to scattered. On soil, often near decaying conifer logs, or along streams, dirt roads or trails. Sometimes very abundant along logging skid trails. U.S. and Canada, in coniferous forests from the Rocky Mts. to the Pacific Coast. Early spring to late summer.
Edibility: Uncertain; apparently some people have eaten it with no ill effects. Both McKenney and Stuntz (1971) and Smith and Weber (1980) advise **caution** in using it for food, even when identification is certain. We do **not recommend** it, because there is danger in confusing California False Morel (*G. californica*) with poisonous species such as False Morel (*G. esculenta*) and Hooded False Morel (*G. infula*) — see below.
Similar species: (1) Apart from the base of its stalk (which often lacks the pinkish tint), *Gyromitra sphaerospora* (not shown) is almost identical to California False Morel in the field, but is found only in eastern and midwestern N. America; their ranges apparently do not overlap. *G. sphaerospora* can be distinguished immediately on the basis of ecology and microscopic characters: it has spherical spores, as its species name suggests; California False Morel (*G. californica*) has el-

liptic spores. Both look enough like (2) False Morel (*G. esculenta*, p. 51) and (3) Hooded False Morel (*G. infula*, p. 53) — both **poisonous** — that great care must be used in identifying these species. California False Morel and *G. sphaerospora* both have *strongly ribbed stalks,* unlike False Morel and Hooded False Morel. To confirm the identification, crush a small piece of cap flesh in a drop of weak (2%) potash solution — the flesh of *G. esculenta* and *G. infula* will *turn pink.* This reaction is readily seen under low magnification of a microscope, but is also visible when tissue is prepared on thin glass over white paper or on a white ceramic or enamel spot plate. (4) See also California False Morel (*G. californica,* below).

CAROLINA FALSE MOREL *Gyromitra caroliniana*   **Pl. 3**
A large, *reddish brown* false morel with *seam-like fusion lines* along ridges on cap (head). *Cap:* Large, roughly *globose* (nearly round) to ellipsoid in overall shape. Surface strongly and *irregularly convoluted* to *pitted,* or with a combination of more or less lengthwise (vertical) pits and ribs. Hymenium moderate *reddish brown* to *moderate brown* or *darker;* reverse surface white or nearly so. Margin of cap pressed against stalk. *Stalk:* Club-shaped or abruptly expanded at base; *branched near apex,* but *branches hidden* by lobes of cap. *Interior multichanneled.* Surface white; strongly ribbed, with rounded ribs that branch and diverge on upper stalk. **Technical notes:** Cap 5–12 cm across; flesh 1–2 mm thick. Stalk 3–15 cm long, 2.5–7.5 cm thick. Spores hyaline (clear), thick-walled, uniguttulate to triguttulate; reticulate, with a network of thick, widely spaced ribs and isolated or fused spines or ribs; elliptic; 22–35 × 11–16 μm. Cap flesh does *not* turn pink in KOH.
Fruiting: Solitary or in groups; on soil in hardwood forests. Midwest to eastern and southern U.S. Early spring.
Edibility: Edible; sometimes mistaken for morels (*Morchella,* p. 37). **Use great caution** in identifying this species, since it can be confused with 2 **poisonous** false morels (False Morel, p. 51, and Hooded False Morel, p. 53) very easily, with painful results. See below, and details in **Similar species** entry under California False Morel, above.
Similar species: In addition to the 2 false morels mentioned above — (1) False Morel (*G. esculenta,* below) and (2) Hooded False Morel (*G. infula,* p. 53), (3) Brown False Morel (*G. brunnea,* p. 48), (4) *G. fastigiata* (Fig. 27, p. 53), and (5) Snow or Giant False Morel (*G. gigas,* p. 53) are often confused with Carolina False Morel, but they *lack* the *seams* or *fusion lines* along some of the convoluted ridges of the cap. Cap tissue of Carolina False Morel does not turn pink in potash (3% KOH) solution, as in *G. esculenta* and *G. infula.* The massive, multichanneled stalk is like that of *G. gigas* and *G. brunnea,* but in *G. caroliniana* it is more often expanded into a bulbous base. (6) The California False Morel (*G. californica,* p. 49) should be

readily distinguished from the Carolina False Morel on geographic and ecological considerations. Inasmuch as live specimens are never seen together, they could be confused from the descriptions. California False Morel has distinctly thinner cap flesh, a more grayish brown or yellowish brown to olive-brown cap (hymenium), sharper-edged ribs, and splotches of pink often low down on stalk. However, in this comparison there is danger in too much reliance on the pink to purplish colors usually seen on lower stalk of California False Morel, as young specimens are frequently suffused with pink overall and some show no pink.

Remarks: Carolina False Morel (*G. caroliniana*) seems to be a rare fungus and one not well understood. It is quite possible that most of the collections called *G. caroliniana* are actually other species that have been erroneously identified. The seamlike lines that are usually present on some ribs or ridges of the cap show where the lobes of the cap are fused, indicating that this false morel has a compound receptacle (cap).

FALSE MOREL *Gyromitra esculenta*   **Pl. 3**
A *reddish brown, wrinkled* false morel that fruits in *early spring.* **Cap:** Medium to large, *irregularly rounded,* often more or less flattened; sometimes almost smooth, but more often *strongly wrinkled* or *folded* and *irregularly lobed,* but *not distinctly pitted* as in a "true" morel (*Morchella,* p. 37). Surface occasionally yellowish to yellow-brown, but more often *light to dark reddish brown;* whitish on reverse side. Flesh *thin,* fragile. **Stalk:** Hollow, typically with a *single channel,* or *stuffed with soft, white, cottony filaments.* Usually *round* in cross-section, occasionally *flattened;* cylindric, but frequently tapering upward and often *expanded at base* to form a short, irregular bulb. Stalk and cap sometimes fused where stalk meets inner surface of cap. Surface of stalk white to brownish, often flushed with pink or purplish tones; smooth to scurfy, sometimes irregularly wrinkled or grooved. **Technical notes:** Cap 3–10 cm across. Spores hyaline (clear), thin-walled, smooth, biguttulate, elliptic; 18–22 × 9–12 μm. Flesh turns *pink or reddish* in KOH.
Fruiting: Solitary or in groups; on soil, in both coniferous and hardwood forests throughout N. America, but more abundant in the North. Common under pine and aspen. *Early spring,* from soon after the snow melts until about the time morels appear.
Edibility: Poisonous, at least to some people. Definitely **not recommended.** Although many people have eaten this mushroom with no apparent ill effects, others have died from false morel poisoning.
Similar species: Two Hooded False Morels — *G. infula* (p. 53) and *G. ambigua* (not shown) — are the two species most likely to be confused with *G. esculenta,* but their later fruiting and

generally less wrinkled caps help to distinguish them in the field. Accurate identification of these 3 species is possible only by use of a microscope, however. Hooded False Morel (*G. infula*) is definitely poisonous, and most likely *G. ambigua* also. (2) Brown False Morel (*G. brunnea*, p. 48) is a coarse mushroom with a more saddle-shaped cap; several caps are usually partially fused on a robust, sometimes branched stalk. Its flesh does not turn pink in KOH. (3) Two Giant False Morels — *G. gigas* (below), which is also known as Snow Morel, and *G. fastigiata* (Fig. 27) — fruit at about the same time as *G. esculenta* but, like Brown False Morel (*G. brunnea*) and Carolina False Morel (*G. caroliniana,* p. 50), they do not turn pink in weak potash (KOH). Reports on edibility of *G. brunnea* vary, but neither it nor *G. caroliniana* can be recommended for food without reservation. See also **caution** below.

SNOW MOREL (GIANT FALSE MOREL)   **Pl. 3**
Gyromitra gigas
A *yellow-brown, wrinkled or convoluted cap* on a *massive, multichanneled stalk.* **Cap:** Medium to large, *globose* (round) to *elliptic,* sometimes indistinctly saddle-shaped. Margin often irregularly lobed, bent backward and sometimes fused with stalk. Hymenium *light* to *dark yellowish brown;* lower surface nearly white. *Flesh thick.* **Stalk:** *Thick and fleshy,* irregularly ridged or wrinkled. Surface white or nearly white; interior *multichanneled.* **Technical notes:** Cap 5–18 cm across. Stalk 2–14 × 3–15.5 cm. Spores hyaline, minutely warty, uniguttulate or triguttulate; elliptic, flattened slightly in profile; 24–35 × 10.5–15.3 μm. Cap flesh (hymenium) slowly turns *yellow* in KOH.

Fruiting: Solitary or in groups; on soil, often originating around or under melting snowbanks. Common in coniferous forests of western and northern mountains; Rocky Mts. westward. Early spring.

Edibility: Widely eaten and highly prized by many people, but **use caution:** this species and *G. fastigiata* have been reported to contain hydrazines (see p. 24). **Avoid consuming large amounts.**

Similar species: Two Giant False Morels which occur in N. America — *G. gigas* and *G. fastigiata* (Fig. 27) — are indistinguishable in the field, but microscopic characters of their spores can be used to separate them. There is confusion regarding the correct Latin names, but this is of little importance to the amateur mushroom hunter, as long as only small amounts are eaten. *Gyromitra gigas* (Snow Morel, p. 27) is found from the Rocky Mts. westward. It has oval, almost smooth spores (Fig. 27), whereas (1) *Gyromitra fastigiata* has broadly fusiform (spindle-shaped) spores, with a knob-like apiculus at each end. *Gyromitra fastigiata* is found in the Northwest and east of the Rocky Mts. Both of these Giant False Morels are fre-

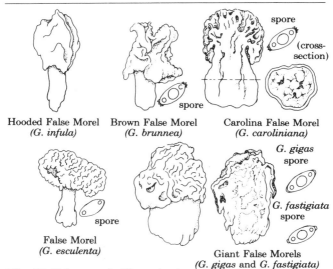

Hooded False Morel Brown False Morel
(G. infula)   *(G. brunnea)*

spore
(cross-
section)

Carolina False Morel
(G. caroliniana)

G. gigas
spore

G. fastigiata
spore

False Morel
(G. esculenta)

spore

Giant False Morels
(G. gigas and *G. fastigiata)*

Fig. 27. False morels *(Gyromitra)*.

quently confused with 2 false morels that are definitely **poisonous:** (2) False Morel *(G. esculenta,* p. 51) and (3) Hooded
False Morel *(G. infula,* p. 53). Flesh of these 2 species develops
pinkish tints in weak solutions of KOH (potash), whereas in *G.
gigas* (Snow Morel) the dark brown hymenium slowly changes
to *yellow* in KOH. (4) Brown False Morel *(G. brunnea,* p. 48),
which has also been reported as poisonous, and (5) Carolina
False Morel *(G. caroliniana,* p. 50) have *more reddish brown*
caps with a slightly different shape, but again, microscopic
characters of the spores are most reliable.
Remarks: The combination of the *massive, multichanneled*
stalk; the *thicker flesh* of the cap (receptacle); and the *more
yellow-brown* (rarely pinkish brown) colors on fresh specimens
is a set of characters by which Snow Morel *(G. gigas)* can be
recognized in the field.
HOODED FALSE MOREL *Gyromitra infula*   **Pl. 3**
Cap: Medium to large; *typically saddle-shaped,* but often indistinctly so, and *irregularly lobed.* Hymenial surface smooth
to wrinkled, dull *yellowish brown* to *dark reddish brown;* undersurface light brown to nearly white. *Stalk:* Hollow with a
single channel, or stuffed with cottony filaments. *Surface
smooth* to *irregularly depressed* or "*folded,*" but *never strongly
fluted. Dingy brownish* to *nearly white,* often with *purplish* or
red-purple tints. Sometimes expanded downward (toward
base). **Technical notes:** Cap 3–10 cm across. Stalk 1–6 ×
0.7–1.5 cm. Tissue fades to pink in potash (KOH). Spores hya-

line (clear), thin-walled, smooth or faintly roughened, biguttu-late, narrowly elliptic; 19–23 × 7–8 μm.

Fruiting: Solitary or in groups; on soil or decaying wood, in hardwood and coniferous forests throughout temperate N. America. Sometimes found in late spring, but more common in summer and fall.

Edibility: Poisonous.

Similar species: (1) Another Hooded False Morel, *G. ambigua* (not shown), cannot be satisfactorily distinguished from *G. infula* by using field characters alone. Although *G. ambigua* has larger, more purplish caps and fruits later in the year, a more reliable distinguishing character is spore shape (spores are longer and more pointed in *G. ambigua*). In field characters both species intergrade with (2) False Morel (*G. esculenta,* p. 51). All 3 of these false morels are **poisonous,** although some people can apparently tolerate *G. esculenta* after it is cooked. *Gyromitra infula* and *G. ambigua* are especially dangerous. False Morel (*G. esculenta*) fruits earlier than the 2 Hooded False Morels (*G. infula* and *G. ambigua*). Its cap is typically *more wrinkled or convoluted* and less saddle-shaped than in the latter 2 species. All 3 species resemble (3) Brown False Morel (*G. brunnea,* p. 48), and to a lesser degree, (4) Snow or Giant False Morel (*G. gigas,* p. 52). Possible confusion of these species may be responsible for the fact that *G. gigas* and *G. brunnea* are often said to be poisonous. Tissue of the 3 false morels that are definitely poisonous — *G. ambigua, G. esculenta,* and *G. infula* — fades to *pink* in KOH, whereas tissue of *G. brunnea* and *G. gigas* turns *yellow.*

Genus *Rhizina*

DOUGHNUT FUNGUS *Rhizina undulata*   **Pl. 3**
Medium-sized, *flat disk,* attached to soil by *several string-like strands.* Often grows in clusters, with disks fused together. *Surface brown, smooth* or *wrinkled* and sometimes marked with concentric zones. Margin thick, sterile; underside yellow-ish. No stalk. **Technical notes:** Cap 2–5 cm across. Spores hyaline, thin-walled, smooth, apiculate, with long, conical appendages; elliptic-fusiform; 20–35 × 8–11 μm.

Fruiting: In groups; on soil under coniferous trees, particularly in burned areas. Summer.

Edibility: Unknown, but likely to be tough and unpalatable.

Remarks: Bears a superficial resemblance to (1) species of *Discina* (p. 47), (2) *Disciotis* (Cup Morel, p. 37), and (3) *Peziza* (cup fungi, p. 56), but may usually be recognized by the numerous string-like projections on its underside, unless these are poorly developed or broken off. Spores are different from those of *Peziza* and *Disciotis* and similar to those of *Discina perlata* (Thick Cup, p. 47), but much larger.

Cup Fungi

Cup Fungi: Family Pezizaceae

Small to large cups or disks, usually centrally attached, without a distinct stalk. Color typically some shade of brown or violet. Ascus tip stains blue in iodine. Common on soil, decaying wood, manure piles, etc., where they are important decomposers that make nutrients available for reuse by other organisms. Some cup fungi form under the soil surface and break through at maturity. Few are of interest for food.

Genus *Geopora*

Geopora cooperi

Pine truffles (species of *Geopora*) originate under ground but may push up to the surface as they expand. They reveal their presence by a *hump or mound of soil* that is sometimes *split open* by the expanding fungi. See also false truffles (*Truncocolumella,* p. 349), which are more closely related to puffballs. The classic "gourmet" truffles (order Tuberales) are very uncommon in N. America; they may be found in Oregon and northern California, but are rare elsewhere.

PINE TRUFFLE *Geopora cooperi*   **Pl. 4**
Small to medium, *round,* or nearly so, with a small, inconspicuous opening. *Surface irregularly furrowed; fuzzy* from *long, soft, brown hairs.* Honey-colored to dark brown; interior white or nearly white, deeply convoluted. **Technical notes:** Apothecium 2–7 cm across. Spores hyaline, uniguttulate, thin-walled, smooth, broadly elliptic; 20–27 × 13–17 μm.
Fruiting: Solitary or in groups. Under conifers and *Eucalyptus;* often pushing up a mound of soil. Western N. America, from Calif. to Alaska and Rocky Mts. Spring and summer.
Edibility: Unknown.
Similar species: The fuzzy, brown external surface and white, coarse internal convolutions help to separate specimens of *Geopora* (Pine Truffle) from various common Gastromycetes (puffballs and related species) they resemble, such as species of (2) *Truncocolumella* (False Truffle, p. 349) and (3) *Gautieria* (not shown). Pine Truffle also is likely to be confused also with species of (4) true truffles (Tuberales), which are rare outside of Oregon and northern California. They are distinguished largely on microscopic characters.
Remarks: Young specimens exude milky juice when cut.

Genus *Pachyella*

BLACK DISK *Pachyella clypeata*   **Pl. 4**
Small to medium, *black cup,* shaped like a flattened ball at
first, but soon *expanding to a flat disk* that is *attached very
broadly to rotting wood* with only a very narrow portion free.
Cup: Irregular in outline and sometimes cleft. *Upper surface
smooth* to *wrinkled,* glistening; *dark reddish brown* at first,
developing olive tints and eventually becoming greenish black.
Underside whitish. **Technical notes:** Cup 1–4 cm across; tip
of ascus stains blue in iodine. Spores hyaline, smooth, thin-
walled, elliptic; 25–30 × 12–14 μm.
Fruiting: Single, scattered, or more often in small groups or
clusters; on decaying logs or wood. Reported from eastern N.
America and Oregon. Summer to fall.
Edibility: Unknown.
Similar species: (1) Fireplace Cup (*P. leiocarpa,* p. 57) and
(2) Pig-ear Cup (*P. phyllogena,* below) are similar in color,
but they lack the very broadly attached, flat cup or disk. Fireplace Cup and Pig-ear Cup also fruit earlier in the year, in
spring. Fireplace Cup appears on burned soil or charred wood;
Pig-ear Cup in hardwood forests, usually on soil but occasionally on well-decayed logs.

Cup Fungi: Genus *Peziza*

*Peziza
vesiculosa*

Medium to large, *thin-fleshed cups* that may become flat or recurved in age. Inner surface some
shade of yellow or brown. To confirm identifications of species and separate them conclusively
from other genera of cup fungi, the flesh (alternating layers of globose and filamentous cells in that
tissue) must be examined under a microscope.

PIG-EAR CUP *Peziza phyllogena*   **Pl. 4**
Medium to large *thin, fragile,* hemispherical cup; sides *frequently compressed* or *lobed.* Cup attached to soil or wood
without a distinct stalk, at a narrow, central point. Inner surface *dark purplish brown* to *dark reddish gray* or *moderate
brown.* Outer surface colored similarly or with more purplish
gray before it dries, particularly toward the base; scurfy. Margin thin, sharp-edged; turns black as it dries. **Technical
notes:** Cup 3–8 cm across. Asci stain blue in iodine. Spores
hyaline (transparent) to pale cream in mass, warty and usually
with apical thickening, elliptic; 17–23 × 8–13 μm.
Fruiting: Singly or in dense clusters; on soil or well-decayed
logs in hardwood forests. Eastern N. America. Early spring.
Edibility: Unknown.

Similar species: This species can be distinguished fairly readily from similarly colored species by its large, *thin* cups which
do not become completely flattened. Even young cups are thinner and have sharper rims (margins) than those of Fireplace
Cup (*P. leiocarpa,* below), which fruits at about the same time.
In addition, Fireplace Cup is usually associated with *burned
soil or wood.* Pig-ear Cup is most readily recognized by the
surface pattern on its spores, as seen highly magnified by a
microscope.

FIREPLACE CUP *Peziza leiocarpa*   **Pl. 4**
Medium to large, *fragile, shallow cup* or *disk,* often irregularly
shaped; margin sometimes incurved. Cup *broadly attached* to
burned soil or charred wood. *Inner surface of cup smooth; light*
to *dark grayish purple* at first, *becoming grayish brown* to
brownish black at maturity. Outer surface smooth or with
small, soft scales; purplish gray. **Technical notes:** Cup 4–15
cm across. Asci stain blue in iodine. Spores hyaline or faintly
brownish in mass, smooth, multiguttulate, globose; 8–9 μm in
diameter.
Fruiting: Solitary to scattered or occasionally in dense clusters. On burned soil or charred wood, especially in outdoor fireplaces. Western U.S. and Canada. Early spring.
Edibility: Unknown.
Similar species: (1) *Peziza trachycarpa* (not shown) is very
similar in appearance and is more common in eastern N. America. It often appears in greenhouses on sterilized soil. The two
are readily distinguished by microscopic examination of their
spores, which are smooth in *P. leiocarpa* and finely to coarsely
warty in *P. trachycarpa.* These species are included in a separate genus by some writers.
Remarks: The purple to brown disks or cups on burned soil or
old fireplaces are distinctive. Great masses are sometimes seen
in *burned areas* around melting snow.

WOODLAND CUP *Peziza sylvestris*   **Pl. 4**
Medium to large, *deep cup;* hemispherical at first, but soon
expanding to a *deep cup* and *sometimes spreading* to an *almost
flat disk.* Cup thin, fragile, attached by a central point. Inner
surface smooth, *yellow-brown* to moderate *dark brown.* Margin
incurved at first, thin, sharp-edged. Outer surface light brown,
becoming whitish as it dries. **Technical notes:** Cup 3–8 cm
across. Ascus tips stain blue in iodine. Spores hyaline, thin-
walled, smooth, elliptic; 15–20 × 9–10 μm.
Fruiting: Single to densely clustered; on soil in woods. U.S.
and Canada. Late spring and summer.
Edibility: Unknown.
Similar species: There are many large brown species of
Peziza which cannot be separated without examining their
spores and tissues of the flesh under a microscope. (1) Barnyard Cup (*P. vesiculosa,* p. 58) and (2) *P. pustulata* (not

shown) look very similar to *P. sylvestris* (Woodland Cup) but have coarse, wart-like pustules on the white to yellowish outer surface. They differ also in their habitats. (3) Several other species, such as *P. emileia* (not shown), may be distinguished for certain only on microscopic characters.

BARNYARD CUP *Peziza vesiculosa*   **Pl. 4**
Large, deep, yellowish brown cup. Round at first, soon expanding and becoming a *hemispherical* or *deep cup.* **Cup:** Often compressed or irregular in outline and sometimes lobed or crimped. Inside of cup smooth, *dark yellowish brown* to *strong yellowish brown; outer surface scurfy,* typically *mottled* and *strong brown at first,* fading to light yellowish brown and eventually becoming dingy white as it dries out. Cup attached at center to manure or soil by a very short stalk; stalk sometimes lacking. **Technical notes:** Cup 6–12 cm across. Spores hyaline, thin-walled, 20–23 × 10–11 μm. Ascus tips stain blue in iodine. **Fruiting:** Single or in groups, often in dense clumps; on *manure piles* or *heavily fertilized soil,* also reported from soil in greenhouses. Throughout N. America. Spring and summer. **Edibility:** Unknown.
Similar species: *Peziza pustulata* (not shown) also has a scurfy outer surface like that of *P. vesiculosa* (Barnyard Cup) but differs in that it is usually found on charcoal or burned soil and has warty spores.
Remarks: This is one of the largest and most prolific Pezizas and therefore, one of the most conspicuous.

 Genus *Sarcosphaera*

S. crassa

VIOLET STAR CUP *Sarcosphaera crassa*   **Pl. 4**
Large, pale-colored cup, usually *half-buried* in soil. **Cup:** Round or flattened underground sphere at first; soon *splits irregularly* at top, into rays that *bend backward* at the tips. *Inner surface smooth; white at first,* but soon becoming *lilac to lilac-brown.* Outer surface of cup *white, felty.* **Stalk:** Very short, if present; often lacking. Stalk tissue includes compacted soil particles. **Technical notes:** Cup 2–12 cm across. Ascus tips stain blue in iodine. Spores hyaline, thin-walled, smooth, biguttulate, broadly elliptic; 13–15 × 7–8 μm.
Fruiting: Solitary or in small clusters; on soil in coniferous forests. Northern U.S. and Canada. Spring and summer.
Edibility: Dangerous. Some report poisoning from it.
Similar species: *Sarcosphaera ammophila* (not shown) has a long stalk; it grows in sandy soil and has been reported from Florida.
Remarks: The delicate colors of the hymenium (inner surface) of fresh cups in good condition are most attractive. When the

cups are fully mature, a breath of air incites discharge of a huge cloud of spores.

Cup Fungi: Family Pyronemataceae

Mostly small to medium cups or disks, usually without stalks. These cup fungi sometimes fruit in great numbers. Colors vary widely — often bright yellow, orange, or red. Ascus tip does not stain blue in iodine. Common on soil and plant and animal debris.

Genus *Aleuria*

ORANGE FAIRY CUP (ORANGE PEEL)   **Pl. 4**
Aleuria aurantia
Medium to large, *bright orange to brilliant yellow, thin, brittle cup.* Varies greatly in size. *Cup: Deep* at first, with an incurved margin; expanding to a *shallow, irregular cup* or rarely becoming nearly flat. *Outer surface* has *whitish hairs* (visible under hand lens) that become more conspicuous as cups age and dry out. Cup attached to soil at a central point. *Stalk:* Lacking or very poorly developed. **Technical notes:** Cup 1–10 cm across. Spores hyaline (transparent), coarsely reticulate, elliptic; 18–24 × 8–11 μm. Asci do not stain blue in iodine.
Fruiting: Scattered, in groups, or densely clustered. Common across the continent from Tennessee and California north to southern Canada. Particularly abundant along logging roads and skid trails. Spring to fall or early winter. On the West Coast it fruits both in spring and fall, but is most abundant in the fall. One of the most common and widespread species among the more conspicuous cup fungi. In some seasons it is very abundant, especially in the Northwest.
Edibility: Edible and said to have good flavor.
Similar species: Thin, fragile cups of (1) Dazzling Cup (*Caloscypha fulgens,* below) are more yellow, typically flushed with green or blue-green on the exterior surface. It fruits in early spring and summer, whereas Orange Fairy Cup fruits most abundantly in the fall. Although Orange Fairy Cup is more orange, there is a certain resemblance. Both are very handsome fungi.

Genus *Caloscypha*

DAZZLING CUP *Caloscypha fulgens*   **Pl. 4**
Small to medium, *irregularly shaped* cup; varies from a *deep cup* to a *flat* or *recurved disk.* *Cup:* Often lopsided or split; fragile, thin. *Bright orange-yellow inside;* orange-yellow to green outside, with sparse hairs on external surface (use hand

lens). Margin of cup incurved at first, but soon expanded. **Technical notes:** Cup 1–3 cm across. Spores hyaline, thin-walled, smooth, elliptic; 10–12 × 6–8 μm.

Fruiting: Solitary, in groups, or in clusters; on moist soil, often around melting snowbanks. Northern conifer forests across the continent, typically under Douglas fir. Early spring and summer.

Edibility: Unknown, but probably not worth the effort.

Similar species: See Orange Fairy Cup (*Aleuria aurantia,* above).

Remarks: The small to medium-sized, fragile, bright yellow to orange cups, often green on the outside, are distinctive among the fungi which *appear following the melting snowbanks at high elevations.* A most attractive species.

Genus *Geopyxis*

DWARF ACORN CUP *Geopyxis carbonaria*   **Pl. 4**
Tiny, short-stalked, goblet-shaped cup. **Cup:** *Dull yellow inside; outside* usually *smooth* (sometimes blistered) and lighter in color. Margin *thin;* strongly incurved at first, but soon bending outward. Margin eventually splits and develops a characteristic ragged appearance. **Stalk:** Short, slender; expands abruptly into cup. **Technical notes:** Cup 3–10 mm across, depth about the same as diameter. Stalk about 2–3 × 1 mm. Spores hyaline (transparent), thin-walled, smooth, eguttulate; elliptic with pointed ends, and flattened on one side; 13–16 × 6–8 μm.

Fruiting: In groups, typically in very large clusters. *On soil in burned places,* or attached to charred wood. Throughout N. America. Spring and summer.

Edibility: Too small to be worth trying.

Similar species: (1) *Geopyxis vulcanalis* (not shown) fruits less abundantly, but is common in certain seasons in coniferous forests of the North and West, particularly where Douglas fir is present. It has a broader, less goblet-shaped cup with a lighter margin. (2) *Tarzetta cupularis* (not shown) is larger and has a smoother margin. Its spores contain oil drops.

Remarks: These tiny goblets remind one of miniature acorn cups. They are often conspicuous by their great numbers on burned soil the first season after a burn.

Genus *Jafnea*

DEEP CUP *Jafnea semitosta*   **Pl. 1**
Medium to large, *deep, flat-bottomed cup.* **Cup:** Inside *yellowish white;* exterior *brown,* with *soft, brown hairs.* Sides of cup fairly straight; margin broadly incurved, shallowly lobed. Cup

is constricted gradually at base, which is not clearly distinct from stalk. Interior darkens to brown as it ages. Flesh of cup thick, colored like interior surface. **Stalk:** *Short, thick,* and *fluted,* with deep, irregular, vertical ribs or pitted, with same color and texture as cup exterior. Stalk often partially buried in soil. **Technical notes:** Cup 2–6 × 2–3 cm. Stalk 1–2 cm, sometimes wider than it is long. Spores broadly fusoid, warty, biguttulate, 25–35 × 10–12 μm. Excipular trichomes 18–20 μm in diameter, with brown, tuberculate walls.
Fruiting: In groups or clumps on soil or (rarely) on well-decayed wood. Midwestern and eastern U.S., southward to North Carolina. Summer.
Edibility: Unknown.
Similar species: *Jafnea fusicarpa* (not shown), which fruits at about the same time and throughout the same area, is smaller and has less conspicuous ribs (if any) on stalk. The spores are longer, more slender, and sometimes slightly curved.
Remarks: On the basis of field characters, these 2 species (*J. semitosta* and *J. fusicarpa*) will usually be placed in the genus *Peziza* (see Pl. 4), in family Pezizaceae. However, microscopic characters, show their relationship with the other cup fungi in family Pyronemataceae.

Genus *Melastiza*

FALSE EYELASH CUP *Melastiza chateri*　　　　**Pl. 4**
Small, shallow cup or disk. No stalk. **Cup:** Upper surface *bright orange-red,* smooth. *Margin thick, sometimes wavy* or irregularly convoluted in age; *streaked* with *clusters of soft, dark brown hairs. Outer surface of cup sparsely hairy.* **Technical notes:** Cup 1.0–1.5 cm across. Spores hyaline, biguttulate, coarsely reticulate, ellipsoid; 17–20 × 10–13 μm.
Fruiting: Scattered to crowded; on bare or mossy soil. Northern U.S. and Canada. Spring and early summer.
Edibility: Unknown, but surely not worth the effort.
Similar species: These handsome little, shallow cups or disks are easily confused with (1) Eyelash Cup (*Scutellinia scutellata,* p. 63), but differences in the hairy margins may be seen with a hand lens. Eyelash Cup (*Scutellinia*) has *stiff,* brown, *bristle-like* hairs, whereas the soft, shorter, brown hairs of False Eyelash Cup (*Melastiza*) are *matted together,* giving the cup margin a streaked but not spiny appearance.

Genus *Otidia*

YELLOW EAR *Otidea leporina*　　　　**Pl. 4**
Small to medium, *elongated cup, attached near one side* with *opposite side extended upward;* often cleft on side nearest attachment. **Cup:** Margin rolled inward. Inner surface smooth;

bright yellow to *light yellowish brown*. Outer surface colored similarly, becoming dull in age. ***Stalk:*** Short or lacking. **Technical notes:** Cups 1–5 cm across. Spores hyaline, biguttulate, thin-walled, smooth, elliptic; 12–14 × 7–8 μm.

Fruiting: Single or in groups, or more often, in dense clusters; on soil and mosses in woods. Throughout N. America. Summer and early autumn.

Edibility: Sometimes reported as edible, but rarely found in sufficient quantity to be of interest.

Similar species: Yellow Ear is unlikely to be confused with any except (1) other species of *Otidea* (not shown), all of which are more or less ear-shaped, and possibly (2) Brown Ear Fungus (*Auricularia auricula*, p. 64), which is always found *on decaying wood.* Species of *Otidea* are distinguished mostly on microscopic characters. *Auricularia* is a jelly fungus. Its *rubbery* consistency and *dark brown* color, inside and out, contrast with the lighter colors and thin, comparatively fragile texture of Yellow Ear (*Otidea leporina*).

Remarks: The curious, off-center attachment of these narrow, medium-sized cups gives them a special appeal.

Genus *Pseudocollema*

CARTILAGE CUPS *Pseudocollema cartilagineum*   **Pl. 4**
Crowded masses of *tiny,* bright *orange cups* or *disks* on a *white, cartilage-like* mass of tissue *covering piles of mouse dung.* ***Cup:*** Smooth, more or less waxy, bright orange both inside and out. No hairs or spines on the margin. No stalk. **Technical notes:** Apothecia (cups) 1–2 mm in diameter.

Fruiting: Around melting snowbanks at high elevation in western mountains. Early spring. Very abundant in certain years, when the bright orange clusters are conspicuous dots of color on the lush green meadows and clearings of the alpine and subalpine life zones.

Edibility: Probably inedible, but not likely to be tried.

Similar species: Minute cups of *Pseudocollema* are individually almost indistinguishable in the field from those of many other species, including (1) *Octospora leucoloma* (not shown), but their habit of growing on a tough, white, cartilage-like mass of tissue which in turn caps a pile of rodent dung is distinctive. The orange cups of *Octospora* are directly on soil or vegetable debris, singly or in expansive masses. (2) Numerous other cup fungi produce minute, similarly colored cups or disks that are difficult to distinguish without microscopic characters. Some, like Eyelash Cup (*Scutellinia,* below), (3) *Cheilymenia* (not shown), and (4) *Dasyschphus* (not shown), have cups with hairy margins that are readily seen with a hand lens. The cups of *Pseudocollema* and *Octospora* lack hairs on margin.

Genus *Scutellinia*

Small cups with *spiny hairs on margin.* Specialists recognize more than a dozen species of *Scutellinia,* which can be identified only with the aid of a microscope. Eyelash Cup (*S. scutellata,* below) is the most common and widespread species. Some forms tend to be quite orange and resemble species of *Cheilymenia* (not shown). The latter also have brown, spine-like hairs and are distinguished on microscopic characters.

EYELASH CUP *Scutellinia scutellata*   **Pl. 4**
Small, flat, broadly attached cup. **Cup:** Upper surface bright *red* to *reddish orange;* outer surface colored similarly, but sparsely adorned with *stiff, brown, spinelike hairs* (easily seen under a hand lens). Young cup globose at first, with an incurved margin. **Technical notes:** Mature cup 0.5–2.0 cm across. Spores hyaline, minutely warty, broadly elliptic; 18–19 × 10–12 μm.
Fruiting: Solitary, in groups or dense clusters; on a wide range of substrates including wood, moist soil, and various kinds of plant debris. Throughout N. America. Spring and summer.
Edibility: Too small to be of interest.
Remarks: This is a most attractive little fungus, especially when magnified enough that the fringe of stiff hairs can be seen on the margin and outer surface. Although small, the bright red disks are readily seen in contrast with the substrate.

CLUB FUNGI: BASIDIOMYCETES
Jelly Fungi
Family Auriculariaceae
Genus *Auricularia*

BROWN EAR FUNGUS *Auricularia auricula*   **Pl. 5**
Small to medium, tough, *gelatinous* or *rubbery fruiting body,*
shaped like a *shallow cup* or an *ear lobe. Brown* inside and
out; outer surface usually has a hoary cast. **Technical notes:**
2–10 (up to 15) cm across. Spores curved-cylindrical; 12–14 ×
4–6 μm.
Fruiting: Solitary or clustered; on *decaying wood.* Throughout temperate N. America. Spring to fall.
Edibility: Edible. A related species is widely used in the Ori-
ent.
Similar species: Species of cup fungi of similar shape are less
rubbery and grow on soil: see (1) Yellow Ear (*Otidea leporina,*
p. 61) and (2) Cup or Ear Morel (*Disciotis venosa,* p. 37). (3) In
southeastern U.S. *Auricularia polytricha* (not shown) is more
common and is difficult to distinguish in the field; it has lilac
to purplish hues and longer hairs on the outer surface. Its flesh
has a zoned structure in cross-section when seen with a microscope.
Remarks: *Auricularia* is said to fruit in late summer and fall
in western U.S., however, in the Rocky Mts. we commonly find
it around melting snowbanks in the spring.

Family Dacrymycetaceae
Genus *Calocera*

CORAL JELLY FUNGUS *Calocera viscosa*   **Pl. 5**
Vivid yellow to *orange-yellow, repeatedly branched* stalks; *ge-*
latinous but *tough.* Branches are *sometimes flattened* and *usu-*
ally forked at tips; deep-rooted. ***Spore print:*** Orange-yellow.
Technical notes: Stalks 3–6 (up to 10) cm high × 1–3 mm
diameter. Basidia forked. Spores yellowish, 3.5–4.5 μm; eventually 1-septate.
Fruiting: On soil and decaying wood. Northern U.S. and Canada. Summer to fall.
Edibility: Unknown.
Similar species: Large specimens are easily confused with
branched coral fungi (*Ramaria*—see Pl. 6), but the *more ge-*

latinous texture throughout identifies Coral Jelly Fungus. Positive identification is possible only by studying microscopic characters (see **Technical notes**). (1) Gelatinous Coral (*R. gelatinosa,* not shown), from western N. America, also has a gelatinous texture, but it is much *larger* and more extensively branched than Coral Jelly Fungus. Small specimens on decaying wood may be mistaken readily for (2) *Calocera cornea* (not shown), which rarely exceeds 1.5 cm.

Genus *Guepiniopsis*

JELLY CUP *Guepiniopsis alpina*   **Pl. 5**
Small, light to *deep orange-yellow* jelly fungus; shaped like a *top,* a *thick disk,* or a *shallow cup.* Grows *on decaying wood.* Concave or flat; surface smooth, *shiny.* Outer surface dull, smooth to ribbed or minutely pimpled (under a hand lens).
Technical notes: Basidia (spore-producing cells) on concave or flat surface; forked. Fruiting body 0.5–2.0 cm across. Spores curved, 15–18 $\times$ 5–6 µm; eventually 3–4-septate.
Fruiting: Solitary or in groups; on decaying wood. Common on coniferous wood in early spring, often fruiting under snowbanks. Western U.S. and Canada.
Edibility: Unknown.
Similar species: (1) In Hairy Jelly Cup (*Femsjonia radiculata,* not shown) the outer surface of the cup is hairy (velvety, with very short white hairs), not dull as in Jelly Cup. Hairy Jelly Cup grows on dead wood of birches and other deciduous trees in eastern to midwestern U.S. and Canada. The gelatinous texture, thicker flesh, and shiny upper or inner surface distinguish Jelly Cup readily from (2) numerous species of true cup fungi (*Peziza,* p. 56).

Jelly Fungi: Family Tremellaceae

The gelatinous to rubbery texture distinguishes members of this family from most others, but positive identification of the Tremellaceae can be confirmed only by microscopic examination of the basidium, which is 4-celled (see Fig. 28), in contrast with the 1-celled basidium of most other Basidiomycetes. Many jelly fungi may be recognized by their distinctive shapes, although others are rather shapeless crusts, blobs, or globules that readily dry to nothing more than a spot on the substrate. Of the genera which have distinctive, recognizable forms, some jelly fungi will be confused with members of other families, such as corals, hydnums, and cup fungi, which they resemble in some details. Likewise, some fungi of closely related families with gelatinous fruiting bodies are often included in this family (Tremellaceae) and gelatinous to rubbery forms are sometimes found in distantly unrelated families.

A few species are edible; none is known to be poisonous.

Genus *Exidia*

WARTY JELLY FUNGUS *Exidia glandulosa*   **Pl. 5**
Wrinkled, sheet-like to *brain-like mass* of soft to fairly *tough, gelatinous tissue* (older specimens sometimes become watery in wet weather). Shrinks to a flat membrane when dry. *Brownish black* to *grayish yellowish brown.* Surface sparsely to thickly dotted with *tiny warts,* visible with a hand lens. **Technical notes:** Size varies — may be up to 20 cm (8 in.) across. Spores curved; 10–16 × 4–6 μm.
Fruiting: On a dead wood of deciduous trees. Temperate N. America, east of Rocky Mts.
Edibility: Unknown.
Similar species: A closely related species, *Exidia recisa* (not shown), lacks the warty surface; it has lighter colors (yellowish brown to dark brown) and is more erect, having a very short, stemlike base.

Genus *Phlogiotis*

APRICOT JELLY *Phlogiotis helvelloides*   **Pl. 5**
Small to medium, *fan-shaped* to *spatula-shaped cap;* margin *often curls over* at rear, like a little Calla Lily or split funnel. Cap *tapers* to a *short, thick stalk.* **Cap:** *Pale pink* to *apricot or deep rose.* Flesh *gelatinous* but *firm; translucent.* Upper and lower (spore-bearing) surfaces alike, or lower surface lighter and slightly wrinkled. **Technical notes:** 5–10 cm tall, 2.5–6.0 cm across. Spores smooth, hyaline, elliptic; 10–12 × 4–6 μm.
Fruiting: Solitary to clustered; on soil or much-decayed coniferous wood. Throughout temperate N. America. Fruits in spring in some areas, but more commonly in summer to fall.
Edibility: Edible. Usually pickled or candied. Old specimens are tough and indigestible, but young ones are sometimes eaten raw in salads.
Similar species: The *rubbery, gelatinous texture* and *smooth* undersurface distinguish Apricot Jelly from some chanterelles, such as Red Chanterelle (*Cantharellus cinnabarinus,* Pl. 7 and p. 82).
Remarks: This is one of the few wild mushrooms that can be eaten raw. Be sure to clean it carefully and make sure that you have a young specimen of Apricot Jelly, not a chanterelle or one of its poisonous look-alikes (see p. 82).

Genus *Pseudohydnum*

TOOTHJELLY *Pseudohydnum gelatinosum*   **Pl. 5**
Small to medium, *white to grayish, tongue-like* caps; attached to wood *at one side* or *off-center.* **Cap:** *White at first,* becoming

brownish. Gelatinous but tough; translucent. *Lower surface* of cap *toothed.* **Stalk:** *Short* and *thick* or *lacking.* **Spore print:** White. **Technical notes:** Caps 3–6 cm across. Spines 2–4 mm long. Spores subglobose; 5–7 μm diameter; basidia cruciate (cross-shaped).

Fruiting: Solitary to clustered; on well-decayed wood, often on moss-covered logs or branches. Throughout temperate N. America. Early spring to fall.

Edibility. Edible, but said to be tasteless.

Similar species: Because of its toothed spore-bearing surface, more often than not Toothjelly will be sought among the tooth fungi (Hydnaceae, Pls. 8–10) by novice mushroom hunters. However, the *translucent, gelatinous* texture of *Pseudohydnum* (Toothjelly) is unlike any of the true hydnums. As in true hydnums or hedgehog mushrooms, the teeth on the undersurface of this jelly fungus are spore-bearing surfaces, but the cells which produce spores (basidia) look different when seen under a high-power microscope. (Fig. 28).

Fig. 28. Basidium of Tremellaceae.

Jelly Fungi: Genus *Tremella*

Gelatinous. Fruiting body varies in shape, from an irregular, often folded mass, to a coralloid head or a cup. Often dries to a shapeless crust and revives after rain.

LEAF JELLY *Tremella foliacea*   **Pl. 5**
Dense clusters of medium to large, *brown, thin, leaf-like lobes. Reddish brown* to *purplish* or *blackish brown; gelatinous* but *firm.* Grows on decaying wood, especially of *oaks.* **Technical notes:** 3–12 cm across. Spores globose to ovate; 8–9 × 7–9 μm.
Fruiting: Solitary to scattered; on wood of dead trees, especially stumps of oaks. Widely distributed throughout temperate N. America. Summer and fall.

Edibility: Edible.

Remarks: The large size and thin, dark-colored lobes are quite distinctive.

WITCHES' BUTTER *Tremella mesenterica*   **Pl. 5**
Small to medium, *irregularly lobed* or *convoluted mass; gelatinous* but *firm. Orange-yellow* to *orange;* lighter in age. Grows *on wood.* **Technical notes:** Up to 10 cm long and 3–4 cm thick. Entire exposed surface fertile (bears spores). Basidio-

spores ovate (egg-shaped) to globose; 7–10 × 6–10 μm.

Fruiting: On wood. Spring to fall throughout N. America.

Edibility: Edible, according to McIlvaine (see p. 407).

Similar species: Not likely to be confused with anything except other species of *Tremella* and *Dacrymyces* (jelly fungi). (1) *Dacrymyces* (sometimes also called Witches' Butter or Fairy Butter) is usually smaller, but otherwise almost indistinguishable in the field. It grows only on wood of coniferous trees. The 2 genera can be distinguished readily with the aid of a microscope by examining the basidia (spore-bearing cells), which are 2-pronged in *Dacrymyces* and 4-pronged in *Tremella*. (2) Sulphur Butter (*Tremella lutescens*, not shown) is usually smaller and lighter in color (sulphur yellow to pale yellow), with hollow lobes. (3) Yellow Leaf Jelly (*T. frondosa*, not shown) is larger, lighter (straw-colored), and has more leaflike lobes.

WHITE CORAL JELLY *Tremella reticulata*   **Pl. 5**
Small to medium *clumps* of *repeatedly branched and fused stalks. White* to *dingy pale yellow.* Branches *hollow; flattened* at first, *tips blunt, rounded* at maturity. *Spore print:* White.
Technical notes: 3–8 cm high, width about the same. Spores ovoid, depressed on one side; 9–11 × 5–6 μm.
Fruiting: Solitary to scattered; on soil or well-rotted stumps. Northern U.S. and southern Canada, east of Rocky Mts. Summer to fall.
Edibility: Unknown.
Similar species: False corals (species of *Tremellodendron*, next group) growing in the same area have more flattened branches and a tougher, less gelatinous texture.

False Corals: Genus *Tremellodendron*

False corals (*Tremellodendron*) strongly resemble branched coral fungi (*Ramaria*, p. 74), but generally have a *tougher texture* and *more flattened* branches. Their basidia (spore-producing cells) look different under a microscope.

FALSE CORAL *Tremellodendron schweinitzii*   **Pl. 5**
Large rosettes of *coral-like, upright stalks* that are sometimes fused together. *Buff* to *dingy yellowish; texture fleshy, tough;* waxy when moist. Branches sparse; flattened in cross-section.
Spore print: White. **Technical notes:** Clumps up to 15 cm across and 10 cm tall. Basidia (spore-producing cells) restricted to lower branches and mid-portion of stalk. Spores subglobose (nearly round) to allantoid (slightly curved, with rounded ends); 7.5–10.0 × 4–6 μm.
Fruiting: Solitary to scattered; on ground in woods. Midwestern and eastern U.S. and Canada. Summer and fall.
Edibility: Unknown.
Similar species: The five American species of False Coral

(*Tremellodendron*) are commonly mistaken for branched coral fungi (*Ramaria*, p. 74). Although the texture of false corals and the shape of the branches (in cross-section) are somewhat distinctive, microscopic examination of basidia and spores is necessary to confirm indentification.

Rust and Smut Fungi

Family Pucciniaceae

Genus *Gymnosporangium*

CEDAR-APPLE RUST   **Pl. 5**
Gymnosporangium juniperi-virginiana
Small to medium, *rounded galls on* stems of *juniper* develop *orange, gelatinous, horn-like* outgrowths *after summer rainstorms.* Dormant galls appear as tough, woody growths on juniper stems. After rains, the galls swell and produce a cylindrical, usually pointed mass of orange, gelatinous horns (spore-bearing tissue). **Technical notes:** Galls 0.5–3.0 cm across; horns 1–2 cm high when fully expanded. Teliospores 2-celled, rhombic-oval to elliptic; thick-walled, moderate brown, on very long, gelatinous stalks.
Fruiting: Scattered or in groups; on young branches of juniper. (See alternate host and form under **Remarks.**) Maine to North Dakota, southward to Florida and Mexico. Summer and early autumn; after rains.
Edibility: Unknown. The galls are too woody to be edible.
Similar species: *Gymnosporangium juniperinum* (not shown) produces large, orange blobs like soft Jell-O® on branches of common juniper in the Rocky Mts., from Alberta south through Utah.
Remarks: This one of the larger, more conspicuous plant rusts. Some cause great economic loss as parasites of crop plants, lumber trees, etc. Rust fungi may parasitize 2 different host plants, producing different kinds of spores on each. The "alternate host" for the Cedar-Apple Rust is the apple tree and its relatives. Here it infects the leaves, forming small, dense clusters of minute, cylindrical, yellow spore cases.

Family Ustilaginaceae

Genus *Ustilago*

CORNSMUT *Ustilago maydis*   **Pl. 5**
Small to large, *irregularly shaped galls* that may form on any

part of *corn plants. Silvery galls* replace kernels and eventually become *filled with black spore powder.* Young galls appear first as swollen plant tissue having normal color, but soon form soft, irregular, tumor-like growths of indefinite shape and become silvery white. As spores mature, the interior (spore mass) blackens beneath a very thin, fragile outer layer.

Fruiting: Solitary to clustered and sometimes fused together on corn plants; most commonly forming giant, distorted growths that replace normal corn kernels. Widespread wherever corn is grown. Summer and fall.

Edibility: Young Cornsmut galls, harvested before they begin to turn black, are eaten in Mexico. Some reports indicate that they are highly regarded.

Coral Fungi

Coral Fungi: Family Clavariaceae

The coral fungi produce small to large, soft, fleshy fruiting bodies that vary from clublike to branched (coral-shaped), often lacking a distinct stalk. Colors range from white to yellow, orange, pink, and purple. Spores are produced on surfaces of clubs or branches. Many species are eaten, but some poisoning is reported from their use.

Some coral fungi have distinctive forms which are readily recognized, but both microscopic and chemical characters may be necessary for accurate identification. Details of branch tips (see Fig. 29, below) are sometimes useful in distinguishing genera. Because of their similar shapes and colors, many other fungi in such widely separated taxonomic groups as Ascomycetes and jelly fungi closely resemble the true corals, Clavariaceae. Microscopic characters distinguish them readily and subtle differences of surface structure and texture may be sufficient.

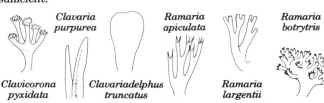

Fig. 29. Branch tips of coral fungi.

Coral Mushrooms: Genus *Clavaria*

Small to (rarely) large, fleshy fungi; coral-like or club-shaped. On soil or algae-covered rotting wood. Spore print white. Spores are not minutely spiny in branched forms.

PURPLE CORAL *Clavaria purpurea* **Pl. 6**
Clusters of pale purple, spindle-shaped clubs. No distinct stalk
or branches. Grows on *wet soil.* **Cap:** An irregularly cylindrical
club, tapered at each end, sometimes abruptly pointed at tip.
Surface smooth to shallowly wavy or grooved, sometimes
somewhat flattened, occasionally lumpy. Light purple to grayish reddish brown when fresh, changing to light yellowish
brown or light yellowish pink as it dries. Flesh white, brittle.
Odor and taste slight, not distinctive. **Stalk:** Very short,
white; distinct from spore-bearing part of club by color. **Spore**
print: White. **Technical notes:** Club 4–10 cm tall, 2–6 mm
thick. Spores smooth, ellipsoid; 6–9 × 3–5 μm. Cystidia cylindric to clavate (club-shaped); 50–125 × 5–10 μm.
Fruiting: In groups or clumps, or dense clusters; on soil in
coniferous forests across Canada and southward in mountains.
Common in Rocky Mts. and westward. Summer and fall.
Edibility: Edible.
Similar species: Old and faded specimens of Purple Coral (*C.*
purpurea) which have lost the characteristic purple colors may
be confused with (1) *Clavaria rubicundula* (not shown) or possibly with (2) *Clavaria fumosa* (not shown).

WHITE WORM CORAL *Clavaria vermicularis* **Pl. 6**
Clusters of small to medium, thin, white, brittle clubs with *no*
branches. Grows *on moist soil.* **Cap (club):** Very long and slender, cylindrical or stringy, with a pointed or rounded tip and
narrowed base; often curved or wavy, sometimes flattened.
Very fragile. White at first, but yellowing or brown-tipped
from withering in age. Flesh white. Odor iodine-like; taste not
distinctive. **Stalk:** Not clearly distinct, but fairly evident as a
short, translucent zone at base of club. **Technical notes:** Club
3–10 cm tall, 1–5 mm diameter. Spores ellipsoid in face view;
4–7 × 3–5 μm.
Fruiting: In groups or clusters or dense clumps; on moist soil.
Widespread in N. America, but more common east of Rocky
Mts. Summer and fall.
Edibility: Edible.
Similar species: (1) *Clavaria atkinsoniana* (not shown),
which has larger spores, can not be recognized as different in
the field. It is more common in the Southeast. (2) *Clavaria*
mucida (not shown) is smaller and grows on wet wood covered
with a slime layer of green algae.

MAGENTA CORAL *Clavaria zollingeri* **Pl. 6**
Medium-sized, *thick branches* with *rounded tips. Reddish pur-*
ple overall. Branches coral-like but not crowded; smooth, brittle. *Fruiting body (club):* Unbranched at base, with an indistinct stalk; uniformly reddish purple to moderate purple. No
odor; taste disagreeable, radish-like.* *Spore print:* White.

* See p. 10 for cautions about using taste as an identifying characteristic.

Technical notes: Club 2–8 × 1–3 cm. Basidia clavate (club-shaped), 4-spored with straight sterigmata. Spores subglobose to broadly elliptic; 4–7 × 3–5 μm. Hyphae strongly inflated.
Fruiting: Solitary, in groups, or clumps; on mossy soil. Great Lakes area eastward and southward. Summer and early autumn.
Edibility: Unknown.
Similar species: Very frequently misidentified as (1) *Clavaria amethystina* (not shown), which is less brittle and has more crowded branches. Although these 2 coral fungi are difficult to distinguish in the field, microscopic characters separate them readily: Magenta Coral (*C. zollingeri*) has spores that are significantly smaller than those of *C. amethystina*. On the basis of microscopic characters, contemporary mycologists usually include *C. amethystina* in a different family (Clavulinaceae) and genus (*Clavulina*).

Genus *Clavariadelphus*

FLAT-TOP CORAL *Clavariadelphus truncatus*   **Pl. 6**
Small to medium (rarely large), *flat-topped, yellow* to *brownish club; white at base. Sweet taste. Club:* Nearly cylindric at first, or enlarged at either end; tip rounded at first, but soon flattened and sometimes depressed in age, with a rounded, uplifted margin. Surface dry; smooth at first, developing irregular vertical wrinkles or grooves. Light orange-yellow to orange or yellowish brown. *Stalk* portion (lower part of club): *White* or yellowish; smooth, sometimes enlarged at base. *Spore print:* Pale yellowish. **Technical notes:** Club (including stalk) 6–12 cm tall, 2.5–8.0 cm wide. Spores ellipsoid; 9–12 × 5.5–7.0 μm.
Fruiting: Scattered or in groups or clusters; on soil. Widespread in coniferous forests. Late summer and fall.
Edibility: One of the best edible mushrooms. It has a sweet flavor that is especially appealing to some people.
Similar species: Two species of *Clavariadelphus* which give *white* spore prints are more common in the West: (1) *Clavariadelphus borealis* (not shown) is colored like Flat-top Coral (*C. truncatus*) and is indistinguishable in the field; it has differently colored, slightly smaller spores. (2) *Clavariadelphus lovejoyae* (not shown), found in northern Rocky Mts., has red to reddish orange overtones and larger spores. (3) *C. unicolor* (not shown) is pink to lilac at first; it grows in hardwood forests in southeastern U.S. Young specimens of Flat-top Coral are easily confused with a number of species which never develop the smooth to wrinkled or depressed flat top characteristic of *C. truncatus:* (4) *Clavariadelphus mucronatus* (not shown) has a

flattened top with a sharp point at center. (5) *Clavariadelphus pistillaris* (not shown) is smaller, with a round top; it stains brown or reddish brown when handled. (6) *Clavariadelphus ligula* (not shown), which has yellowish spores, and (7) *C. sacchalinensis* (not shown), which produces a white spore print, are both more slender than Flat-top Coral; their clubs have rounded to blunt tips. (8) *Clavariadelphus cokeri* (not shown) is found in New England under hemlocks in autumn. It grows in clusters of tall (up to 20 cm), pink brownish clubs with pointed to blunt, flattened, or antler-like branched tips.

Remarks: As far as we know, all species of *Clavariadelphus* are edible.

Genus *Clavicorona*

CROWN CORAL *Clavicorona pyxidata*   **Pl. 6**
Medium to large, *dingy yellowish, coral-like mass* with *many branches. Tips* of branches *depressed (indented)* and *ringed with pointed branchlets.* *Cap (club):* Extensively branched; surfaces smooth, moist. Yellowish white to pale yellow at first, darkening as it matures, with older branches often becoming yellowish brown to grayish brown. Flesh nearly white. May have a slight odor of raw potatoes; taste peppery.* *Stalk:* Very short; colored like lower branches. *Spore print:* White. **Technical notes:** 6–10 cm tall × 2–7 cm across. Spores smooth, amyloid, ellipsoid; 3.5–5.5 × 2–3 μm. Hyphae clamped; chrysocystidia present.

Fruiting: Solitary or in groups or clumps; on decaying stumps and logs of deciduous trees. Common, especially on aspen, willow, and cottonwood; widespread in N. America. Late spring through summer or early fall.

Edibility: Edible.

Similar species: Crown Coral is often confused with many other species of large, pale-colored, branched coral fungi, but the *crown-like branch tips* on species of *Clavicorona* are distinctive. *Clavicorona avellanea* (not shown) develops brown colors earlier and has a stronger, peppery taste.* It grows on wood of conifers in the Northwest.

Remarks: The enchanting Crown Coral is one of the most commonly collected coral mushrooms throughout the region. With a long fruiting season and its habit of growing on a variety of soft, woody substrates in deciduous and mixed forests, it often fruits when the ground is dry and few other mushrooms can be found.

* See p. 10 for cautions about using taste as an identifying characteristic.

Coral Mushrooms: Genus *Ramaria*

Ramaria

Medium to large, much-branched, coralloid mass. Fruiting body has short, often fused stalk. Spore print (rarely) white to yellow or dull orange-yellow; spores not amyloid (do not stain blue in iodine).

GREEN-TIPPED CORAL *Ramaria apiculata*   **Pl. 6**

Medium to large, *compact clumps* of *slender, coral-like branches*. *Cap (head): Light brown,* with *whitish* to *pink* or *green tips*. Branches arise directly from a white, string-like strand in substrate (wood or coniferous debris), or from a short, indistinct stalk. Two or more branches per node. Each branch forks 3–6 times, ending in sharply pointed, crested tips. Branches nearly parallel; slightly flattened, with rounded angles between branches. Actively growing tips are light to moderate yellowish green; may be moderate yellowish pink to light yellowish brown (color of older branches in age). All parts stain brown when cut or bruised. Texture waxy. Flesh tough; yellowish white, quickly darkening when cut. Odor may be fragrant; taste bitter. *Stalk:* Short and cylindric, colored like branches except for white, hairy base; attached to white, string-like strand penetrating and extending throughout the substrate. *Spore print:* Pale grayish yellow. **Technical notes:** Fruiting body 4–10 cm high, 2–10 cm across. Spores minutely roughened, with cyanophilous warts; ellipsoid, with a squared-off tip; $7–10 \times 3.5–5.0$ μm. Some hyphae thick-walled, clamped. **Fruiting:** In sparse to dense clusters, on wood or coniferous debris (cones, twigs, and needles); sometimes on buried, moss- or grass-covered wood. Southern Canada to northern and eastern U.S. Summer and fall.
Edibility: Unknown.
Similar species: A slender, more open-branched variety of this species may be confused with older specimens that no longer have the green color of actively growing tips. (1) *Ramaria tsugina* and (2) *R. ochraceovirens* (not shown) are very similar and are best distinguished by microscopic characters. Both species usually have green on their branches, but the green is concentrated less at the tips of the branches and more on the lower parts and at point of branching; in Green-tipped Coral (*R. apiculata*) green color is usually most conspicuous *on actively growing tips* of young branches. *Ramaria tsugina,* like *R. apiculata,* grows on rotting wood; *Ramaria ochraceovirens* grows on soil and develops green color with maturity or when bruised or injured. (3) The closely related *Ramaria stricta* (not shown) is a dull yellow species that develops brownish colors with age or injury, but is never green.

CAULIFLOWER CORAL *Ramaria botrytis* **Pl. 6**
Large, whitish head, with *many compact, red-* to *orange-tipped, coralloid branches.Cap (head):* Often nearly as wide as tall; branching 5–7 times above stalk. Branches short, *densely clustered,* sometimes flattened or rounded to angular, with rounded, knobby, or pointed tips (see Fig. 29). Stains yellow to brownish when bruised. Flesh fibrous to firm; white. Odor sweet, faint; taste not distinctive. *Stalk:* Single, *thick* or massive, unbranched; cylindric (with a blunt basal tip) or conic. *Spore print:* Pale yellow. **Technical notes:** Head 7–15 × 5–12 cm. Spores striate (streaked), cyanophilous, subcylindric; 11–17 × 4–6 μm. Stalk flesh weakly amyloid (turns faint blue in iodine).
Fruiting: Solitary, scattered, or in groups; sometimes in arcs under conifers and in mixed forests. Widely distributed in N. America. Summer and fall.
Edibility: Questionable. Reports that it is inedible may result from confusion with other species having red or pink branches, such as *R. formosa* (not shown), which is **poisonous.**
Similar species: (1) *Ramaria botrytoides* (not shown) found from the Great Lakes eastward, has slightly acidic taste* and more violet-pink at branch tips, but is best distinguished by microscopic examination of its spores, which lack streaks. Several of the closely related species in the *"botrytis* complex," distinguished by a combination of microscopic and field characters, have often been identified as *Ramaria botrytis.* In (2) *R. rubrievanescens* (not shown) the pink color of branch tips fades soon after collecting or as it matures; whereas in (3) *R. rubripermanens* (not shown) the dull pink to red color of branch tips persists and the branches do not stain reddish to violet-brown, as in *R. rubribrunnescens, R. maculatipes,* and *R. rubiginosa* (not shown). (4) *Ramaria strasseri* (not shown) has yellow to orange branch tips and a spicy odor. Spore dimensions also help to distinguish them. (5) *Ramaria caulifloriformis* (not shown), found in the Great Lakes region, has branch tips that darken as they age; its reddish brown tints sometimes become grayish red. (6) *Ramaria formosa* (not shown) has yellow tips on its branches; the branches are usually more pinkish than in *R. botrytis* (Cauliflower Coral).
GOLDEN CORAL *Ramaria largentii* **Pl. 6**
Large clumps of *slender, orange-yellow, coral-like branches* on *short, thick stalk. Does not change color* when wounded. *Fruiting body (head):* May be wider than tall. Branches rise from a single or fused stalk. Each branch forks up to 9 times before tips; tips rounded (see Fig. 29, p. 70). Bushy head; lower branches nearly parallel and widely spaced. Moderate to light

---

* See p. 10 for cautions about using taste as an identifying characteristic.

orange-yellow or pale orange-yellow, upper part sometimes lighter. Flesh white; fleshy-fibrous, brittle. Odor may be slightly sweet; taste not distinctive. **Stalk:** Cylindrical to broadly conical, often with small, abortive branches among main branches. *White to yellow,* with white, cottony hairs at base. **Spore print:** Pale orange-yellow. **Technical notes:** Fruiting body (head) 12–15 × 7–15 cm. Spores warty, streaked in spirals, subcylindrical, 11–15 × 3.5–5.0 μm. Clamps present. **Fruiting:** Scattered or in groups; under conifers. Rocky Mts. westward. Summer and fall.

Edibility: Not recommended. The probability of confusion with species that are definitely poisonous is too great.

Similar species: Golden Coral is frequently called (1) *R. aurea,* but its spores are too large and too strongly ornamented to be *R. aurea*; its branches are also darker orange than in *R. aurea* (not shown). Microscopic characters are needed to distinguish them with certainty. (2) *Ramaria longispora* (not shown) is difficult to distinguish on field characters, but is more slender than Golden Coral, and has a compound stalk. Its spores are slightly shorter and less distinctly ornamented; there are no clamp connections on hyphae. (3) *R. formosa* (not shown) is **poisonous;** it has *more pinkish* branches with *yellow tips.* (4) *R. gelatiniaurantia* (not shown) has *marbled flesh* in stalk: translucent grayish white, alternating with waxy, opaque white areas. It is also poisonous.

RUFFLES *Sparassis crispa*   **Pl. 5**
Large, rounded clumps of flat, wavy branches. White to pale yellow. Stalk poorly developed, arising from a cordlike strand at base.

Edibility: Edible. Some rate it highly, especially when it is young.
Fruiting: Solitary to scattered. Common on sandy soil under Virginia pine. Fall.
Similar species: The western species, *Sparassis radicata* (not shown), sometimes called Cauliflower Mushroom, has thinner branches and a thick, rooting stalk.

Groundwarts and Woodcrusts

Family Thelephoraceae

Fruiting body soft or fleshy to leathery, papery, or tough and fibrous. Grows as crust, bracket, branching coral, or fan-shaped to spatula-shaped cap, often on wood, frequently on underside of decaying logs. Fertile surface (which faces downward) is smooth to irregularly warty, streaked, wrinkled, or folded. Spore print white to brown. Spores smooth to warty or spiny, without germ pore.

Genus *Polyozellus*

Until recently, the species in this genus were grouped in with the chanterelles, in family Cantharellaceae (p. 81), but microscopic characters show that they are more closely related to the groundwarts (genus *Thelephora,* next group).

BLUE CHANTERELLE *Polyozellus multiplex*   **Pl. 7**
Large clumps of *thick, spoon-shaped* to *fan-shaped caps; dark bluish* to *purplish gray. Fused stalks. Undersurface* of cap *wrinkled* to *veined* or *nearly poroid.* Individual caps small to medium-sized. Upper surface smooth; margin wrinkled and lobed, often crenate (scalloped). Uniformly colored at first, but fading, with gill surface lighter. Flesh soft; colored like surface, blackening in age. Odor aromatic; taste not distinctive. ***Stalk:*** Thick, brittle, short; solid or occasionally hollow. ***Spore print:*** *White.* **Technical notes:** Cap 3–10 × 2–5 cm. Stalk 3–5 × 0.6–2.0 cm, in clumps up to 30 cm across. Spores warty, subglobose-angular; 5.5–6.5 × 4.5–5.5 μm across. Basidia turn olivaceous in KOH.
Fruiting: Clustered, on soil under conifers. Northern U.S. and southern Canada, coast to coast. Late summer and fall.
Edibility: Edible.
Similar species: (1) Pig's Ears (*Gomphus clavatus,* p. 86) has thicker, lighter purplish colors fading to brown. Its yellowish spore print and larger, long-ellipsoid spores separate it readily from Blue Chanterelle. (2) *Craterellus caeruleofuscus* (not shown) rarely forms compound clusters, usually has a centrally attached stalk and larger spores, and is not restricted to coniferous forests.
Remarks: This species looks like a chanterelle (*Cantharellus,* p. 81), but microscopic characters show that it is more closely related to species of *Thelephora* (groundwarts).

Groundwarts: Genus *Thelephora*

Thelephora terrestris

Shape of rosettes varies, from crust-like or bracketlike to coralloid or fan-shaped. Flesh flexible to leathery and tough. Fertile (spore-bearing) surface of fruiting body — on underside of each lobe of rosette — is smooth to roughened. Spore print light to dark brown. Spores warty to spiny, non-amyloid (spores do not stain blue in iodine).

CARNATION GROUNDWART   **Pl. 6**
Thelephora caryophyllea
Small to medium, *blackish purple, thin rosettes* of *variable shape; undersurface smooth or streaked.* ***Cap:*** Simple (un-

fused) and shallowly vase-shaped, with a flattened outer limb and margin, or compound, with several overlapping concentric disks or spatula-shaped lobes. Upper surface smooth, or with radiating fibrils (streaks), or irregularly roughened. Purplish brown to blackish brown or *blackish purple,* fading quickly as it dries and then becoming lighter and somewhat zoned. Margin irregularly torn or lobed. Flesh thin; deep brown. Odor and taste not distinctive. **Stalk:** *Short* to almost lacking; central or eccentric (off center); colored like cap surface. **Technical notes:** Cap 1–5 cm across. Spores angular-ellipsoid or lobed, with long spines, 6.5–8.5 × 5–7 µm. Clamps present on hyphae. **Fruiting:** Solitary or in groups; on soil, in coniferous woods. Widespread in N. America. Summer and fall.
Edibility: Inedible.
Similar species: The many variant forms of this fungus are often called by different names, but once the range of variation is understood, Carnation Groundwart (*T. caryophyllea*) is not likely to be confused with other species growing in the same locality. Similarly shaped forms of Groundwart (*Thelephora terrestris,* below) are thicker and more coarse.

GROUNDWART *Thelephora terrestris*   **Pl. 6**
Small to medium, *deep brown, irregular* or *shallowly funnel-shaped* cap; surface *coarsely hairy* to *scaly.* Undersurface has *warts* but *no gills, pores,* or *teeth.* **Cap:** Shape varies, from a thick, flat crust upturned near margin to a partial or complete funnel shape; often forms overlapping resettes. Dark brown to brownish black, with a whitish margin during active growth phase. Margin thin; smooth at first, then lobed or irregularly notched. Flesh colored like surface of cap. Odor and taste not distinctive. Undersurface smooth or with radiating wrinkles at first, becoming *finely and unevenly warty* (see detail on Pl. 6). **Stalk:** Short or lacking; colored like cap. **Spore print:** Purplish brown. **Technical notes:** Cap 2–6 cm across. Spores sparsely spiny, angularly ellipsoid or lobed; 8–12 × 6–9 µm. Clamps present on hyphae.
Fruiting: Solitary or in groups or clumps and sometimes fused; on soil, common in coniferous forests. Widespread in N. America. Summer and fall or early winter.
Edibility: Inedible.
Similar species: (1) *Thelephora americana* (not shown) has a smoother undersurface, with fewer warts; its spores are smaller than those of Groundwart. (2) *Thelephora griseozonata* (not shown) has *gray zones* on its cap. (3) *Thelephora intybacea* (not shown) is lighter in color when young; it has softer fibrils and scales on cap surface. (4) *Thelephora vialis* (not shown) is dingy whitish to yellowish grayish brown or grayish purple; it often forms a fused mass of *thick,* vase-like or spatula-shaped to fan-shaped lobes. These species of *Thelephora* are all inedible.

Family Corticiaceae

Woodcrusts: Genus *Merulius*

Crust-like fungi that grow on wood; brackets or caps are attached at one side. Underside strongly wrinkled. Hyphae hyaline (transparent), monomitic, mostly clamped. Spores hyaline.
non-amyloid (do not stain blue in iodine).

CORAL WOODCRUST *Merulius incarnatus*   **Pl. 6**
Medium-sized, *pink, overlapping crusts* or *brackets; undersurface* has *radiating ribs, folds,* or *elongated pores.* **Cap
(bracket):** Crust-like to shelf-like, often semicircular and irregularly lobed. No stalk. Upper surface wavy, minutely hairy.
Yellowish pink (fades rapidly in sunlight). Flesh *soft* and
spongy or *leathery,* thick; yellowish white. Margin thick, usually darker than limb. Undersurface pale yellowish pink to
pinkish yellow. **Spore print:** White. **Technical notes:** Cap
2–7 cm across. Spores smooth, ellipsoid; 4.0–4.5 $\times$ 2.0–2.5 μm.
Fruiting: Solitary to clumped; on decaying wood in hardwood
forests. Midwest to eastern and southeastern U.S.
Edibility: Unknown.
Remarks: The name Coral Woodcrust is derived from the
pinkish color of this fungus, not its shape.
GELATINOUS WOODCRUST *Merulius tremellosa*   **Pl. 6**
Medium to large, *dingy, variously colored sheet* of *fused, gelatinous crusts* with *radiating wrinkles.* Grows *on decaying wood.*
Crust: Stalkless, adhering to wood for entire width or with a
margin that curves outward to form a very narrow shelf or
bracket with a woolly, white upper surface. Lower surface
wrinkled, ribbed, or indistinctly angular-poroid (or a combination of these forms); dingy white to gray or tinged with yellow,
pink or orange. Flesh thin; fleshy to waxy or gelatinous, drying
hard. **Spore print:** White. **Technical notes:** Each crust up to
10 or 15 cm across; merged with other crusts. Spores smooth,
curved; 3–4 $\times$ 0.5–1.0 μm.
Fruiting: Summer to late fall, on hardwood logs and debris.
Widespread in N. America.
Edibility: Unknown.

Splitgills: Family Schizophyllaceae

split gills   **Genus** *Schizophyllum*

SPLITGILL *Schizophyllum commune*   **Pl. 6**
Small, stalkless, fan-shaped, light gray cap or bracket; upper
or outer surface *conspicuously hairy. Gill folds* on undersurface
develop *split edges* when spores mature. Grows *on decaying
wood.* **Cap:** Variable, ranging from a laterally attached cap or
bracket that is fan- or shell-shaped, to a centrally attached cap
or cup that is saucer-shaped or deeper. Outer or upper surface
dry, with white hairs over a white to gray background; often
split. Margin incurved or inrolled; lobed and often split. Flesh
thin, leathery; flexible but *tough.* Odorless. Undersurface of
cap has widely spaced, radiating ribs or folds which *split* when
mature. **Spore print:** White. **Technical notes:** Cap 1–3 cm
across. Spores smooth, cylindrical; 1.0–1.5 μm.
Edibility: Inedible but non-poisonous in the ordinary sense.
However, mycophagists are strongly urged to keep away from
this one, as it is clearly capable of eating humans! There are
several well-documented accounts of *Schizophyllum* (Splitgill)
being isolated from abnormal growths in the mouth or throat
of people who have eaten it, both in the U.S. and Europe.
Fruiting: Solitary or in groups or clusters; on decaying wood,
both hardwood and conifer forests. Widespread in N. America.
Fruits throughout the year, including warm spells in winter in
colder climates. Old fruiting bodies are persistent; thus the
fruiting season may seem longer than it actually is.
Similar species: *Plicaturopsis* (formerly *Trogia*) *crispa* (not
shown) is found on hardwoods in northern U.S. and southern
Canada, from the Great Plains eastward. It has wavy or
crimped "gill" folds, but they are not consistently split at maturity as in *S. commune* (Splitgill).

Family Stereaceae

Genus *Stereum*

FALSE TURKEYTAIL *Stereum ostrea*   **Pl. 6**
Small to medium, *very thin, gray brackets* with *multicolored
zones* on upperside; *smooth underneath.* Brackets *often overlap* each other; attached *at one side to wood.* **Cap (bracket):**
Broadly spatula-shaped to fan-shaped or semicircular in outline; narrowed to base or stalkless. Upper surface minutely
hairy, with narrow, concentric, grayish yellow to reddish orange or brown *zones between* broader *bands of gray.* Texture
tough and leathery to woody. Undersurface usually *smooth,*
sometimes indistinctly warty or radially roughened; pale grayish yellow to dingy orange-yellow or light brown. **Spore print:**
White. **Technical notes:** Cap 1–6 cm across, approx. 0.5 mm
thick. Spores smooth, cylindrical with one side flattened;
5.5–7.5 × 2–3 μm.

Fruiting: Common on decaying logs and stumps in hardwood forests of Midwest and eastern N. America. Early summer to late fall or early winter.

Similar species: This species is very commonly mistaken for Turkeytail (*Coriolus versicolor,* p. 125, Pl. 14). The 2 species are very much alike in the field and the thin, multicolored caps or brackets are hard to distinguish unless one studies the undersurface of the bracket carefully. Often a hand lens will be necessary, as the pores of very young specimens of Turkeytail (*C. versicolor*) can not be seen without magnification.

Remarks: Formerly known as *Stereum lobatum* or *S. fasciatum.*

Chanterelles

Family Cantharellaceae

Fruiting body soft and fleshy, upright, flared outward from a short, thick stalk or forming a flattened or depressed cap. Spore-bearing (under) surface smooth to wrinkled or with branching ribs, sometimes as shallow, thick gills. Cap margin often lobed or wrinkled. This group contains many edible species, but **great caution** is advised, as their similarity to poisonous look-alikes is one of the most common causes of mushroom poisoning!

Chanterelles: Genus *Cantharellus*

Small to large, more or less *trumpet-shaped,* fleshy fungi; mostly yellow to reddish. Hymenium (spore-bearing surface) *smooth* to *wrinkled* or *ribbed,* sometimes with *ridges* or *folds* that resemble gills.

C. cibarius

CHANTERELLE *Cantharellus cibarius*   **Pl. 7**
Medium to large, *egg-yolk yellow overall. Gills blunt, thick, branched, widely spaced;* gills *extend down stalk.* **Cap:** Shallowly convex at first, soon becoming flat, then shallowly to deeply depressed at center; may be funnel-shaped in older specimens. Margin of cap or "funnel" often wavy and indented. Vivid yellow to orange-yellow, darkening when bruised; sometimes bleaching to whitish in sunlight. Flesh firm, thick; yellow. Odor faintly reminiscent of dried apricots or lacking; taste not distinctive. **Stalk:** Solid; tapers downward from cap. Surface smooth; colored like cap or lighter. **Spore print:** Pale yellow. **Technical notes:** Cap 3–10 cm across. Stalk 3–8 × 0.5–2.0 cm. Spores thin-walled, smooth, ellipsoid; 8–11 × 4.5–5.5 μm.

Fruiting: Scattered to clustered; on *soil,* in both coniferous and hardwood forests. Widely distributed in N. America. Summer and fall.

Edibility: Edible. Usually considered one of the best. (See recipes, p. 386).

Similar species: Often confused with various other chanterelles (see Pl. 7). Most are edible, but (1) Scaly Chanterelle (*Gomphus floccosus,* p. 86) and related species are **poisonous** to some people. In these chanterelles, the flesh of the cap (center) and stalk breaks into *coarse scales* and a deep hollow forms at center of cap. (2) False Chanterelle (*Hygrophoropsis aurantiacus,* p. 154, Pl. 16) is deep orange overall; it has thin, narrow gills that are often repeatedly forked (see detail on Pl. 16). It is **not recommended,** especially because of its similarity to 2 other poisonous species that are often mistaken for chanterelles: (3) Jack-O-Lantern (*Omphalotus illudens,* p. 178, Pl. 17) and (4) Showy Flamecap or Big Laughing Mushroom (*Gymnopilus spectabilis,* p. 298, Pl. 37). Both of these poisonous look-alikes grow on *wood* (sometimes on tree roots), *not soil,* and they are usually *larger* and *darker* overall than edible chanterelles, but study the *gills* carefully to avoid confusion (see color plates). In Showy Flamecap (*G. spectabilis*), the gills are *thin* and *close together,* with *sharp edges;* in Jack-O-Lantern they are somewhat broader but still close and *sharp-edged, not bluntly rounded* as in an edible chanterelle such as *C. cibarius.* To confirm your identification, make a spore print: The spores of *C. cibarius* are pale yellow, not yellowish white as in Jack-O-Lantern, or bright brownish orange, as in Showy Flamecap.

RED CHANTERELLE *Cantharellus cinnabarinus*   **Pl. 7**
Small to medium, *reddish orange* to red or *pink cap, stalk, and gills. Gills forked. Cap:* Flat or *shallowly funnel-shaped;* circular in outline or irregularly lobed, margin incurved at first. Surface smooth, wavy near margin. Colors fade rapidly in sunlight and may become nearly white. Flesh thin, white. Odor not distinctive; taste slowly becomes hot, peppery. Gills decurrent (extending down stalk); thick, narrow with blunt edges, distant, interveined. *Stalk:* Cylindric, tapering downwards from cap, sometimes white or yellowish at base; does not stain (change color) when cut. *Spore print:* Pinkish. **Technical notes:** Cap 1–5 cm across. Stalk 2–5 cm × 4–8 mm. Spores thin-walled, smooth, ellipsoid; 7–10 × 4.5–5.5 μm.

Fruiting: Solitary or in groups; on soil under hardwoods. Eastern U.S. and southern Canada. Summer and early fall.

Edibility: Edible, but regarded by some as lower in quality than some other chanterelles.

Similar species: The relatively small size, more or less uniform color of all parts, pinkish spore print, and combination of blunt-edged, narrow, widely spaced, forked, decurrent gills dis-

tinguish Red Chanterelle from some waxycaps (species of *Hygrophorus*, p. 202, Pl. 22), which resemble it superficially.
Remarks: For whatever this species lacks in size and quality, it may compensate in quantity and ease of recognition. It is sometimes found in great numbers in the Chesapeake Bay area and southern U.S.

SMOOTH CHANTERELLE *Cantharellus lateritius*   **Pl. 7**
Medium to large, *thin, irregularly lobed, orange cap. Fragrant. Undersurface* of cap *smooth* to *wrinkled* or *shallow-gilled.* **Spore print:** *Pinkish.* **Cap:** Slightly humped or flat at first, soon becoming depressed or shallowly funnel-shaped. Outline often deeply lobed, folded, or wrinkled. Surface smooth. Light orange to vivid orange; margin often distinctly lighter. Cap fading to light or moderate orange-yellow, sometimes whitish. Flesh white to orange-yellow. Odor sweetish, somewhat reminiscent of pumpkin; taste not distinct or slightly bitter.* Gills often absent but may vary from narrow veins to extensively branched and wrinkled, slightly raised ribs. **Stalk:** Tapers gradually to base. Interior solid. Surface smooth; colored like cap or lighter. **Technical notes:** Cap 3–9 cm across. Stalk 2–6 × 0.5–2.0 cm. Spores smooth, ellipsoid; 6–10 × 4–6 μm.
Fruiting: Solitary to clustered; on soil in hardwood forests. America, but more common in mid-Atlantic states and South. Summer.
Edibility: Edible and choice. (See recipes, p. 386.)
Similar species: Often confused with (1) Chanterelle (*C. cibarius*, p. 81), but both species are edible and delicious. Chanterelle (*C. cibarius*) has slightly more yellowish (less pink) coloration, *thicker flesh,* and usually *better-developed gills.* The spore print of *C. lateritius* (Smooth Chanterelle) is distinctly *pinkish,* not pale yellow as in *C. cibarius.* (2) *Cantharellus odoratus* (not shown) is also fragrant, but it has a *hollow stalk.* It, too, is edible.

YELLOWISH CHANTERELLE *C. lutescens*   **Pl. 7**
Small to medium, *slender, thin, yellowish brown cap. Undersurface smooth* to *wrinkled or veined; orange-yellow.* Stalk *hollow.* **Cap:** Flat to convex with incurved margin at first, soon narrowly funnel-shaped, with a scalloped, wrinkled, or folded margin. Upper surface fibrillose or with sparse, soft scales; dull orange to yellow when young, soon becoming brown. Flesh very thin; pale orange-yellow. Odor faint, fragrant. **Stalk:** Slender, tapering downwards; often creased, flattened and bent. **Spore print:** Yellowish pink. **Technical notes:** Cap 2–5 cm across. Stalk 3–8 × 0.3–1.0 cm. Spores smooth, ellipsoid; 9–13 × 6.5–8.0 μm.
Fruiting: In groups or scattered, on damp mossy soil or moss-

* See p. 10 for cautions about using taste as an identifying characteristic.

covered wood; often around bogs or springs. Great Lakes area east to Newfoundland and south to Carolinas. Summer and fall.

Edibility: Edible and much sought after. (See recipes.)

Similar species: Young specimens, not yet brown on top, may be mistaken for (1) Smooth Chanterelle (*C. lateritius*, p. 83), which is also edible and delicious. It has a *solid* stalk. (2) In the Southeast, *C. odoratus* (not shown) may also be confused with young (yellow) specimens of Yellowish Chanterelle, especially since both have a hollow stalk; it, too, is edible. (3) Horn of Plenty (*Craterellus cornucopioides,* p. 85) and other species of *Craterellus* with a smooth to wrinkled undersurface have a similar cap upper surface when faded, but the *undersurface* is *never orange-yellow.* (4) Several closely related species of *Cantharellus,* such as Funnel Chanterelle (*C. tubaeformis,* below), have more distinctly *gill-like ridges or folds* on the undersurface. Funnel Chanterelle is **not recommended.**

SMALL CHANTERELLE *Cantharellus minor*   **Pl. 7**
Small to medium, *slender cap; depressed* at *center* or *shallowly funnel-shaped. Egg-yolk yellow overall. Cap:* Flat to convex, with an incurved margin at first; soon becoming irregularly lobed, indented, and wavy. Surface smooth to slightly scaly; hygrophanous (water-soaked) when fresh. Brilliant yellow to light orange-yellow. Flesh soft, fragile; yellow. Odor faint, fragrant; taste not distinctive. Gills orange-yellow, decurrent (extending down stalk), distant; forked near margin, becoming intervenose (developing minute crossribs) in age. Gills narrow (from stalk apex to cap margin) and thin, with blunt edges. *Stalk:* Central or eccentric (off center); interior hollow. Cylindric to flattened or grooved. Surface smooth; orange-yellow. *Spore print: Pale orange-yellow* or more pinkish. **Technical notes:** Cap 1–3 cm across. Stalk 3–6 × 0.4–1.0 cm. Spores smooth, thin-walled, ellipsoid; 7–11 × 4–6 μm.

Fruiting: Scattered or in groups or clumps; on soil in hardwood forests east of Great Plains.

Edibility: Presumably edible.

Similar species: (1) *Cantharellus ignicolor* (not shown) is common in the same area. It is described as "basically apricot orange" with gills that are *gray* or *tinged with violet* when mature (after spores have developed). It is slightly larger and less fragile and has larger spores. (2) Faded, small specimens of several other small to medium species may be confused easily with Small Chanterelle (*C. minor*). Small, yellow waxycaps (species of *Hygrophorus,* p. 202, Pl. 22) and navelcaps (species of *Omphalina,* p. 177, Pl. 17) that are often thought to be chanterelles have *sharp-edged, non-forked gills.*

FUNNEL CHANTERELLE *Cantharellus tubaeformis*   **Pl. 7**
Small to medium, *thin, often funnel-shaped, brown cap and stalk. Gills yellowish gray* to *pale grayish brown; narrow, forked near cap margin. Cap:* Convex to flat, with a broad,

shallowly depressed disc (center) and incurved margin at first; margin soon spreads and turns upward, forming a funnel; outline lobed or wavy; disc (center of cap) often open to hollow of stalk. Surface yellowish brown; smooth to slightly scaly. Flesh thin and membranous, fragile. Odor not distinctive. **Stalk:** Cylindric or tapered downwards; often flattened, bent, or creased. Colored like cap or lighter, whitish at base. Interior hollow. **Spore print:** White. **Technical notes:** Cap 1.0–3.5 cm across. Stalk 3–6 × 3–7 cm. Spores ellipsoid; 9–11 × 6–8 μm. **Fruiting:** In groups or scattered or clustered; on mosses or moss-covered wood in bogs or wet, springy areas. East of Great Plains.

Edibility: Edible **with caution. Not recommended**—some mild but uncomfortable poisonings are reported from species in this group.

Similar species: Several small, thin chanterelles with hollow stalks and caps that are some shade of brown are easily and frequently confused. A good spore print is essential to distinguish them. Spore prints are not always obtained readily from chanterelles (Cantharellaceae). Mature caps may require a full day to deposit enough spores for a satisfactory spore print.

Genus *Craterellus*

Similar to other chanterelles, but caps are usually *thinner* and *more funnel-shaped*. In *Gomphus* species (p. 86) the caps are thicker and more solid. As in other families of mushrooms, the genera are ultimately distinguished on the basis of microscopic characters.

HORN OF PLENTY *Craterellus cornucopioides*   **Pl. 7**
Size varies—small to medium or occasionally large. *Very thin, funnel-shaped cap;* no gills. Cap and stalk *dark grayish brown* to *blackish.* **Cap:** Surface smooth to wrinkled; dark at first, but drying quickly to light bluish gray with reddish brown on margin. Flesh very thin, brownish, brittle. Undersurface smooth to wrinkled, particularly near margin; appears more or less waxy, bluish gray to blackish. **Stalk:** Hollow; continuous with funnel-shaped cap, but lacks "waxy" sheen. **Spore print:** *Yellowish white.* **Technical notes:** Cap 2–7 cm across. Spores smooth, ellipsoid; 8–11 × 5–6 μm.
Fruiting: In groups or clusters, on soil in hardwood and conifer forests. East of Great Plains and West Coast. Summer and fall.
Edibility: Edible. Not so popular in N. America as in Europe. We know of no reports of poisoning.
Similar species: *Craterellus fallax* (not shown) has very slightly larger spores and a pinkish spore print which may tinge outer (spore-bearing) surface of cap. *Craterellus foetidus* (not shown) has lighter colors and a sweetish, sickening odor.

Genus *Gomphus*

Caps are *thicker* and *more solid* than in other chanterelles. These species can also be distinguished on the basis of microscopic characters.

PIG'S EARS *Gomphus clavatus*   **Pl. 7**
Medium to large, *firm, thick, purplish cap;* flat or depressed. *Usually in clumps; stalks often fused.* **Cap:** Clublike when young, with flattened tips; expanding to an irregularly lobed, often eccentric cap, sometimes overlapping other caps. Surface smooth to scaly; purplish gray, fading to light yellowish brown. Flesh firm, white. Odor and taste not distinctive. Gill surface colored like cap, but fading more slowly; wrinkled or veined, but lacks distinct gills. **Stalk:** Short, *thick,* often branched. **Spore print:** Dingy yellowish. **Technical notes:** Cap 3–10 cm across. Stalk 2–8 × 1–3 cm. Spores wrinkled, long-ellipsoid; 10–13 × 4–6 μm.
Fruiting: Clustered or in groups; on soil in northern coniferous forests. Coast to coast, southern Canada and northern U.S. Late summer and fall.
Edibility: Edible.
Similar species: *Gomphus pseudoclavatus* (not shown) has slightly smaller, smooth spores and grows in hardwood forests.

SCALY CHANTERELLE *Gomphus floccosus*   **Pl. 7**
Large, funnel-shaped, yellow to *orange* or *reddish orange, scaly cap. Undersurface wrinkled* or more or less *poroid.* Fruiting body (cap and stalk) nearly cylindric and rounded or flat on top at first. Center of cap becomes depressed and finally *funnel-shaped* as stalk becomes hollow. Surface cottony at first, soon developing *coarse, downturned scales* near center. Flesh thick, whitish. Odor and taste not distinctive. Spore-bearing surface shallowly wrinkled, ridged, or elongate-poroid. **Stalk:** Not distinct from cap; hollow, cylindric, tapered to base. **Spore print:** Pale orange-yellow. **Technical notes:** Cap 5–15 cm across. Stalk 8–15 × 1–3 cm. Spores faintly warty, ellipsoid; 12–15 × 6.0–7.5 μm.
Fruiting: Solitary or in groups; on soil, in coniferous and mixed hardwood-conifer forests. Coast to coast, but less common in the West; sometimes found in rhododendron thickets in the Southeast. Summer and fall.
Edibility: Not recommended. Apparently edible for some people but definitely not for others. There are numerous reports of people being made ill by it.
Similar species: Two related species found in the Northwest are *Cantharellus bonari* and *C. kauffmanii* (not shown). Both are more yellowish to brownish, not reddish and orange as in

Scaly Chanterelle (*C. floccosus*). In addition, *C. bonari* typically fruits in clumps, and *C. kauffmanii* has coarser scales. There are small differences in spore measurements.

Tooth Fungi (Hydnums)

Spine Fungi: Family Hydnaceae

Mostly medium to large, fleshy, leathery or woody. Stalk usually central, but off center or lateral or lacking in some species. Spores develop on thick spines, which hang down like icicles on undersurface of cap. Spore print white or brown.

Many spine fungi are edible. Others are important as decomposers of dead plant material. Some cause diseases in valuable trees.

Members of this family which do not have a distinct cap and stalk are not included here. These form crusts on the underside of logs and other forest debris.

Hydnums: Genus *Auriscalpium*

PINECONE MUSHROOM *Auriscalpium vulgare*   **Pl. 9**
Small to medium, *brown cap,* attached *at one side* or *off center. Long, slender stalk rises from decaying pine cones. Cap:* Flat to rounded; late fall specimens are often pleated, folded, or otherwise misshapen. Upper surface brown to dark purplish brown, covered with dark brown fibrils. Undersurface spiny. Flesh thin, flexible, tough. Spines light to dark brown. *Stalk:* Brown, hairy, rigid. *Spore print:* White. **Technical notes:** Cap 1–4 cm across. Stalk 2–7 cm × 2–3 mm. Spines about 2–3 mm or less in length. Spores hyaline, minutely roughened, amyloid, subglobose; 4–5 × 5–6 μm.
Fruiting: Solitary or in clumps; on partially buried, decaying pine cones or on litter under pines. Throughout U.S. and Canada. Summer to late fall. Reported from Nova Scotia after frosts in November.
Edibility: Inedible.
Remarks: This very distinctive and attractive little fungus is not likely to be mistaken for any other. As a scavenger on pine cones and other debris (it has also been found on corncobs!), it illustrates the important role of many mushrooms in forest ecology.

Hydnums: Genus *Bankera*

Fleshy tooth fungi that grow on soil. Cap (head) central on stalk. Cap and stalk more or less fleshy and brittle; flesh *not zoned* or *two-layered* as in *Hydnellum* (p. 92). Spore print white. Spores subglobose (nearly round); roughened.

FLESHY HYDNUM *Bankera carnosa*   **Pl. 10**
Medium-sized, *brown cap; often lobed* or *split and wavy*. *Cap:* Convex to flat; margin incurved, whitish to pale fawn. Surface *smooth* and *unpolished at first,* becoming *scaly.* Flesh pallid to light brown. Odor *fragrant,* becoming stronger as it dries; taste mild. Spines *white* to pinkish buff or pale gray. *Stalk:* Central or off-center; colored like cap but darker; darker brown at base than above. *Flesh* (interior) has a distinct *core. Spore print: White.* **Technical notes:** Cap 3–10 cm across. Stalk to 5 cm long and 2 cm thick. Flesh of dried cap turns pale olive in KOH. Spores minutely roughened, subglobose; diameter 4.0–5.5 μm. Clamps lacking.

Fruiting: Solitary to clumped; on soil in coniferous and mixed conifer-hardwood forests. U.S. and Canada. Midsummer to fall.

Edibility: Unpalatable.

Similar species: (1) Grayish White Hydnum (*B. fulgineoalba,* below) is usually larger; it is not grayish brown and is fleshy to fibrous, not scaly. (2) Species of *Sarcodon* (p. 95) and (3) *Hydnellum* (p. 92) produce spore prints that are *brown,* not white as in *Bankera.* (4) In the cork hydnums (*Phellodon,* p. 97) the cap is tough and fibrous.

Remarks: This species has been reported from widespread localities in N. America. In Canada it is said to be common in Nova Scotia, where a nearly white color variant occurs. Fleshy Hydnum has also been reported from New Brunswick, Quebec, and British Columbia. In the U.S. it is found in the Great Lakes region, Oregon, and New Mexico. Could be expected in many other localities when the species is better known.

GRAYISH WHITE HYDNUM *Bankera fuligineoalba* **Pl. 10**
Medium to large, *fleshy* to *fibrous cap; dark yellowish brown at center* to *yellowish pink* or *pinkish brown on margin.* Becomes much *darker* and quickly water-soaked in *wet weather. Cap:* Convex at first, becoming flat or depressed at center. Margin thin, incurved when young; lobed and wavy later. Pine needles and other forest litter *adhere to densely matted surface* fibrils. Flesh soft and *brittle* to fleshy-fibrous. Odor none or mild when fresh, faint but disagreeable as it dries; taste not distinctive. Spines extend *from upper stalk to cap margin;* close together, *nearly white. Stalk: Central, short; fleshy, without a hard central core.* Surface smooth, colored like cap surface and lighter above than below. *Spore print: White.* **Technical notes:** Cap 6–15 cm across. Stalk 2–4 × 1.3–2.5 cm. KOH and iodine negative on dried material. Spores globose to subglobose. Clamps lacking.

Fruiting: Solitary or scattered; on soil in coniferous forests, usually under pine. U.S. and southern Canada. Not common,

but often abundant when it does appear. Autumn, usually late.
Edibility: Unpalatable.
Similar species: Larger than (1) Fleshy Hydnum (*B. carnosa,*
p. 88) and more yellowish or pinkish brown rather than grayish
brown. Cap surface on Fleshy Hydnum tends to be scaly. The
readily water-soaked surface, with much intergrown forest debris, is characteristic of Grayish-white Hydnum. Compare also
with species of (2) *Sarcodon* (p. 95) and (3) *Hydnellum* (p. 92),
which are distinguished by their brown spore prints and (4)
Phellodon (p. 97), which have a thinner, more fibrous cap, usually of indeterminate growth. Lighter, softer colors (white to
pinkish), and smooth spores distinguish (5) hedgehog mushrooms (*Hydnum,* below).

Hedgehog Mushrooms: Genus *Hydnum*

Hydnum

Small to medium or (less often) large, fairly firm,
fleshy tooth fungi. *Stalk stout,* occasionally somewhat eccentric (off center). Spore print white.
Spores smooth. Until recently, the species in this
group were known as genus *Dentinum.*

WHITE HEDGEHOG *Hydnum albidum*   **Pl. 10**
Small to medium, *thick, white* to *pale grayish yellow cap* on a
thick, white stalk. Cap: Surface smooth; margin often lobed.
Flesh white, turning *dull yellow* to *orange* when cut or bruised.
Taste peppery; odor not distinctive. Spines white. **Technical
notes:** Cap 1–9 cm across. Spines to 0.5 cm long or longer.
Spores subglobose; 4.0–5.5 × 3.5–4.0 μm.
Fruiting: Solitary or scattered; in forests, under conifers or
hardwoods. Southeastern U.S. to southern Canada, west to
Great Lakes. Summer and early fall.
Edibility: Presumably edible. (See **Remarks.**)
Similar species: Often confused with (1) pallid or white
forms of Spreading Hedgehog (*H. repandum,* below, Pl. 8),
which has a mild (not peppery) taste and is more widely distributed. (2) Giant Hedgehog (*H. albomagnum,* not shown) is
larger and lacks peppery taste and color change when cut or
bruised; it is rarely found in southeastern U.S.
Remarks: Although no report of eating White Hedgehog has
come to our attention, neither has a case of poisoning by any
species in genus *Hydnum* (formerly *Dentinum*). This species
has no doubt been eaten by mushroom hunters seeking *H. repandum* (Spreading Hedgehog), an excellent edible mushroom
that sometimes comes in white forms.
SPREADING HEDGEHOG *Hydnum repandum*   **Pl. 8**
Medium to large, *fleshy* cap; pale *orange-yellow* (sometimes
whitish) to *pale reddish brown. Cap:* Thick, rounded or flat;

margin wavy and often indented or lobed. Flesh thick, soft, *brittle, white;* stains brownish orange where bruised. *Odor not distinctive;* taste mild to rather bitter when raw.* Spines *white* to *pinkish buff; small,* often *extending from lower cap down upper stalk.* **Stalk:** *Thick,* central or off center; colored like cap or lighter. **Technical notes:** Cap 2–15 cm across. Stalk to 7.5 cm long and 3.5 cm thick.

Fruiting: Solitary to clustered; on ground. Widely distributed in N. America. Common. Summer and fall.

Edibility: An excellent edible mushroom.

Similar species: (1) Depressed Hedgehog (*H. umbilicatum,* below) is usually darker, and more reddish, with a depressed disc (center of cap); it grows in *boggy lowland* habitats. Both Depressed Hedgehog and a white or nearly white variety of Spreading Hedgehog (often abundant late in season) frequently are confused with (2) White Hedgehog (*H. albidum,* p. 89). The similarity of Latin names is as confusing as their similar appearance. White Hedgehog has a peppery taste,* and so far is known only from Great Lakes region and southeastern U.S. in summer and early fall.

Remarks: The white variety of *H. repandum* (Spreading Hedgehog) occurs later in the season and is frequently confused with other hedgehogs (*Hydnum*). Mistaken identity among these species is of little consequence, however, as all are edible.

DEPRESSED HEDGEHOG *Hydnum umbilicatum*   **Pl. 10**
Small to medium, *irregular, rounded* to *flat* cap, with a *depressed center* and *wavy margin.* **Cap:** Pale *orange-buff* to moderate *reddish brown;* surface dull, slightly felty. Flesh brittle, thin; tasteless or mildly unpleasant when raw. Odor lacking. Long and short spines intermingled; colored like cap surface or more often lighter, color not extending down stalk. **Stalk:** Slender; paler than cap surface but darkening when bruised. **Spore print:** White. **Technical notes:** Cap 2.5–4.5 cm across. Spines to 7 mm in length. Stalk 2–6 × 0.5–1.0 cm. Spores ovoid; smooth, 7.5–9.0 × 6–7 μm.

Fruiting: On *boggy soil* under conifers. Great Lakes and eastern N. America.

Edibility: Edible.

Similar species: Frequently mistaken for (1) Spreading Hedgehog (*H. repandum,* above), which it closely resembles, and pallid forms may be mistaken for (2) White Hedgehog (*H. albidum,* p. 89). Smaller cap with thinner flesh and depression in center of cap distinguish *H. umbilicatum* (Depressed Hedgehog). Its association with "cedar," spruce, and balsam (fir) in low, swampy habitats also helps to separate it from

---

* See p. 10 for cautions about using taste as an identifying characteristic.

similar species. Slightly larger, more ovoid spores are distinctive.
Remarks: Since all species in this genus (*Hydnum*) are edible, no harm is likely in confusing them.

Hedgehogs: Genus *Hericium*

Medium to large, soft, white tooth fungi with thick, compact to loose branches; *long, sharply pointed (icicle-like) teeth* on underside. Hedgehogs (*Hericium*) grow on or inside decaying logs. Spore print white. Spores amyloid (stain blue in iodine).

CORAL HEDGEHOG *Hericium coralloides*   **Pl. 9**
Medium to large, *coral-like caps* with *many branches.* Coarse *spines hang downward in tufts,* especially *at ends* of branches. Branching is coarse, from a stout, main stalk. *Cap:* Laterally attached (at one side) to stalk. White to cream-colored. Odor and taste not distinctive. *Spore print:* White. **Technical notes:** Caps up to 30 cm or more across. Spines up to 18 mm. Spores 5–7 × 4.5–6.0 μm.
Fruiting: Solitary or clustered; on dead or living hardwood trees (especially beech, maple, and oak). N. America, east of Great Plains and north of Tennessee and Carolinas. Summer and fall.
Edibility: Edible.
Similar species: Although they look alike, (1) Western Coral Hedgehog (*H. abietis,* not shown) grows on conifers in West, and Coral Hedgehog grows on wood of broadleaf trees from Great Plains eastward. (2) Another hardwood species, Comb Hedgehog (*H. ramosum,* p. 92) is similar in appearance but has more slender branches, with shorter spines in continuous comblike rows along the lower surface of each branch. In Western Coral Hedgehog, the branches are coarser, with shorter teeth in tufts (not continuous rows along the underside), especially at ends of branches. Young stages of Western Coral Hedgehog are pale yellowish pink at first, becoming white. Coral Hedgehog and Comb Hedgehog are white but become yellowish in age. (3) See Bearded Hedgehog (below) and **Remarks.**
Remarks: A "tuberculate" form of Coral Hedgehog, with short branches that are reduced almost to knobs, occasionally occurs; it is sometimes confused with the Bearded Hedgehog (below), which is also edible.
BEARDED HEDGEHOG *Hericium erinaceus*   **Pl. 9**
Medium to large, *white, fleshy, rounded cap, covered with long, downward-projecting spines.* Surfaces discolor with age, becoming dingy yellow or brownish. *Stalk:* Very short if present; thick and lateral (attached at one side). *Spore print:* White.

Technical notes: Cap (including spines) up to 23 cm across; spines 1–4 cm long. Context and spores amyloid. Spores hyaline, finely roughened to smooth, subglobose; 5.5–6.5 × 4.5–5.5 μm.

Fruiting: Solitary. Grows from cracks or knot holes of living deciduous trees, most often oak, less often on logs or stumps. Widespread but never common in central and eastern U.S. and West Coast. Summer to fall in North, winter in Florida.

Edibility: Edible, good. (See recipes, p. 380).

Similar species: Compact, rounded form is quite distinctive among the large, white, fleshy tooth fungi (hydnums), although a short-branched, "tuberculate" form of Coral Hedgehog (*H. coralloides,* above) occasionally occurs. Since both are edible, no harm results from confusing them.

Remarks: This striking mushroom is the cause of a heart-rot disease in oaks. Occasionally the cap has a tendency to branch.

COMB HEDGEHOG *Hericium ramosum*   **Pl. 9**
Medium to large, *fleshy, white cap* with *slender branches.* Spines hang in *continuous, comblike rows along lower surfaces.* **Cap:** White, becoming cream or brownish in age. Odor and taste not distinctive. Spines typically short. **Spore print:** White. **Technical notes:** Cap up to 28 × 15 cm across. Spines 8 mm long or less. Spores subglobose; 3–5 × 3–4 μm.

Fruiting: On decaying logs of deciduous trees throughout N. America. Most common on maple, beech, and birch east of Rocky Mts. and on aspen and cottonwood in West.

Edibility: Edible, good.

Similar species: Frequently confused with (1) Coral Hedgehog (*H. coralloides,* p. 91) and (2) Western Coral Hedgehog (*H. abietis,* not shown), which is found only on wood of conifers. Coral Hedgehog has coarser branches and longer spines *in tufts,* not in *continuous rows* along lower surfaces.

Spine (Tooth) Fungi: Genus *Hydnellum*

Hydnellum *suaveolens*

(section)

Small to medium, tough, fibrous tooth fungi. Cap has *dense layer of short teeth* on underside. Cap *continuous* with short stalk. Flesh often *distinctly two-layered.* Spore print brown. Spores tuberculate, non-amyloid (do not stain blue in iodine).

ORANGE SPINE *Hydnellum aurantiacum*   **Pl. 8**
Medium to large, *orange, felty cap,* with *tough, fibrous, zoned flesh.* **Cap:** Convex to flat or depressed at center. Surface *smooth* to *rough* or with *bumps* or *vertical, finger-like lobes; felty,* becoming matted in age, sometimes zoned. Margin whitish to tan, or more often strong reddish orange; center darker, becoming moderate brown to reddish brown. *Flesh zoned with buff and rusty orange. Odor pungent, disagreeable. Spines* ex-

tend down stalk from lower surface of cap; dark *brown,* with *lighter* (buff or orange) *tips;* those at actively growing margin of cap are whitish. *Stalk:* Bulbous; one or more stalks grow from an orange mat. Interior woody, zoned orange-red. Surface orange to brown, velvety. *Spore print:* Brown. **Technical notes:** Cap to 18 cm across. Stalk 2-7 × 0.5-2.0 cm. KOH turns black on surface, dingy olive on flesh. Spores subglobose; 5.0-7.5 μm across.

Fruiting: Solitary to clustered or fused. On forest floor under conifers; throughout N. America. Summer and fall.

Edibility: Inedible.

Similar species: (1) Earl's Hydnum (*H. earlianum,* not shown) has a smoother cap; the spines hanging from its actively growing margin have *sulphur yellow tips* (not whitish tips, as in Orange Spine). (2) Funnel Hydnum (*H. conigenum,* p. 94) has thinner caps and (3) Northern Spine Fungus (*H. septentrionale,* not shown) is distinguished by paler colors. (4) In dried specimens of Rusty Spine (*H. ferrugipes,* not shown). The cap and stalk flesh has *bluish gray zones* (visible in lengthwise section). (5) Blue Spine (*H. caeruleum,* below) has *mauve to bluish zones* in flesh of fresh specimens.

BLUE SPINE *Hydnellum caeruleum* **Pl. 8**

Cap *light blue at first,* fading to *whitish* and eventually becoming *dark brown in age.* Surface *velvety or cottony,* later becoming *matted and pitted.* Flesh *dark brown; two-layered* — upper layer spongy; lower layer tough and fibrous, zoned with buff to mauve and brown. *Cap:* Medium to large; convex to flat or depressed. Stains rusty brown when bruised. Odor and taste not distinctive. Spines close, fine, short, extending down stalk; whitish with blue tinge when young, soon becoming dark brown with lighter tips. *Stalk:* Short and thick, often with a bulbous base made up of felty mycelium and decaying conifer needles. Buff-colored on surface; interior orange to rusty brown, with *zones of blue;* tough and fibrous. **Technical notes:** Cap 3-11 cm across. Stalk 2-4 × 1-2 cm. Spores subglobose; 4.5-6.0 μm across. Blue parts turn blue-green and reddish parts turn dark dull olive in KOH.

Fruiting: In groups or clusters; often fused. On forest duff in northern conifer forests. Late summer and fall.

Edibility: Inedible.

Similar species: (1) *Hydnellum cruentum* (not shown) has zones of blue in stalk interior and lilac to blue spines, but is readily differentiated from Blue Spine by its *strong odor of menthol* and the *drops of red juice* on its soft, actively growing margin. This species (*H. cruentum*), (2) Blue Foot (*H. cyanapodium,* not shown), and (3) Tough-stalk (*H. scleropodium,* not shown) all have the droplets of blood-red juice and a strong, medicinal odor, but Blue Spine does not. These 3 species all have blue on some parts, like Blue Spine, but they lack its orange to rusty brown stalk interior. They also differ in microscopic characters, having irregular, angular spores that resemble jacks. (Spores of Blue Spine are nearly round or spherical.) The bluish gray zones in the stalk interior separate (5) Rusty Spine (*H. ferrugipes,* not shown) and Blue Foot (*H. cyanapodium*). (6) Sweet Spine (*H. suaveolens,* p. 94) also has a stalk interior zoned with blue, but lacks blue tints elsewhere (see Pl. 8); it has a distinctive, strong, sickly sweet odor.

Remarks: Blue is often evident only on the actively growing parts of Blue Spine. It is brighter in cool weather.

FUNNEL HYDNUM *Hydnellum conigenum*   **Pl. 8**
Medium-sized, *thin, funnel-shaped caps;* may be *split* or *irregularly lobed; frequently fused,* forming medium to large *rosettes.* **Cap:** *Surface* radially ridged, *velvety* to *fibrillose* or *streaked;* bright orange at first, soon *zoned* with light yellowish brown to moderate yellow and moderate orange to moderate reddish brown (becoming darker and more brownish with age). Margin wavy and lobed. Flesh thin, tough; not zoned. Odor faint to lacking; taste mealy, strong.* Spines short, close, fine, extending down stalk; colored like cap surface, or brighter orange. **Stalk:** Single or fused, bulbous; orange-brown with a felty base. **Technical notes:** Cap 7 cm across. Stalk 3–6 × 0.5–2.0 cm. Spores subglobose to broadly ellipsoid, and angular; 4.0–5.5 × 3.5–4.0 μm.
Fruiting: Coniferous forests. New Mexico to British Columbia and Great Lakes region; also reported from Florida.
Edibility: Inedible.
Similar species: The thin, brightly colored, non-zoned flesh readily distinguishes this from other species with orange tones on surface or flesh of stalk or cap, such as (1) Orange Spine (*H. aurantiacum,* p. 92), (2) Earl's Hydnum (*H. earlianum*) and (3) Northern Spine Fungus (*H. septentrionale,* not shown).
Remarks: A very variable but distinctive species with especially bright colors when young, darkening in age and developing a very rough, radially ridged surface. Funnel Hydnum is very sensitive to weather, which can bring about striking color changes. It almost always forms fused masses and is notorious for incorporating into the fruiting body (cap and stalk) elements of the forest litter, such as twigs, cones, and needles.

SWEET SPINE *Hydnellum suaveolens*   **Pl. 8**
Medium to large, *soft, irregular cap.* **Cap:** Convex to flat. Surface *velvety at first; white,* becoming *dingy tan* to *brown* or with *olive to violet-gray tinges.* Margin sterile — has a broad band on underside that lacks spines. Flesh thick, fibrous, zoned. *Odor strong, fragrant; taste faint* or *lacking.** Spines crowded, short, light yellowish brown or more gray, with pale tips. **Stalk:** Short, woody; surface covered with bright violet

---

* See p. 10 for cautions about using taste as an identifying characteristic.

velvet, which darkens when rubbed; interior zoned with purplish-violet bands. **Technical notes:** Cap to 15 cm across, occasionally larger. Stalk 3–5 × 1.0–2.5 cm. Velvety layer on stalk stains blue-green in KOH. Spores warty, angular, broadly ellipsoid; 4.5–6.5 × 3–4 μm.

Fruiting: Solitary to grouped, sometimes fused together and often forming arcs. Grows from deep blue strands in the forest litter. On forest floor under conifers, across the continent. Mostly northern, but south to North Carolina in East and New Mexico in Rocky Mts. Late summer and fall.

Edibility: Inedible.

Similar species: Blue Spine (*H. caeruleum*, p. 93) could be confused with this species but lacks distinctive odor and has *blue tints* on young spines and actively growing cap; later, cap and spines are brown. Both have blue-zoned stalk interior (see lengthwise section on Pl. 8).

Remarks: Sweet Spine is typically thick and stout, but tends to be thin, rough, and tinged with blue (tones of flesh showing through) when developing under high-moisture conditions. Earliest developmental stages appear as a small pad of violet, cottony strands with a white tip, which enlarges to form stalk and cap.

Spine (Tooth) Fungi: Genus *Sarcodon*

Medium to large, fleshy tooth fungi. Cap often soft or brittle, with teeth (spines) on undersurface. Cap flesh *not distinctly layered* as in *Hydnellum* (p. 92). Stalk thick, fleshy; sometimes eccentric (off center) or lateral. Spore print brown. Spores angular, tuberculate. Until recently, the species in this group were known as genus *Hydnum*.

SCABER HYDNUM *Sarcodon scabrosus*   **Pl. 10**
Medium to large, *convex cap* with an *incurved, whitish margin*. **Cap:** Often has a broad, shallow depression and sometimes is open at center to hollow stalk. *Surface smooth* before emerging from soil, but *soon becoming* finely to coarsely *scaly; grayish yellow at first,* then *yellow-brown with* a *rusty tinge.* Sometimes has pinkish tints, darker scales, fading in age to light olive-gray. Margin incurved. Flesh soft, brittle; olive-buff, darkening on exposure to air and in age. Odor faint; *taste very bitter.*[*] Spines fine; colored like cap or lighter when young and becoming dark brown with paler tips. ***Stalk:*** Typically *long, with* a *pointed blackish green base.* ***Spore print:*** Brown. **Technical notes:** Cap to 20 cm across. Spines to 5 mm long. Spores warty, subglobose; 5.0–7.5 μm across.

Fruiting: Solitary to clustered. Widespread in coniferous or

---

[*] **See p. 10 for cautions about using taste as an identifying characteristic.**

deciduous woods in temperate N. America. Late summer and fall.

Edibility: Reported as inedible.

Similar species: (1) Scaly Hydnum (*S. imbricatus,* below, Pl. 8) lacks the olive to black stalk base and intensely bitter taste. (2) Finn Hydnum (*S. fennicum,* a European species) appears almost identical but its surface turns black, not green in KOH.

SCALY HYDNUM *Sarcodon imbricatus*   **Pl. 8**
Large, irregular, flat to *rounded, brown cap* with coarse, *often recurved, darker brown scales. Cap:* Often becomes depressed in the center as it matures, and in age usually develops a hole at center, connecting with the hollow stalk. *Surface light brown* with purplish tinge at first, dark brown all over in age. Margin *incurved at first.* Flesh thick; grayish buff to light brown; soft, fragile. *Odor and taste not distinctive.** Spines dull pale grayish brown with a lilac tinge at first, becoming darker as they mature. *Stalk:* Hollow, usually tapering at base; interior light brown. *Spore print: Brown.* **Technical notes:** Cap 6–25 cm across. Stalk 4–9 × 1.5–3.0 cm. Spores subglobose; 6–8 × 5–7 μm. Clamps present.

Fruiting: Solitary to clustered, often in fairy rings. On forest floor in both coniferous and hardwood forests. Widespread and common in temperate N. America.

Edibility: Edible, but some do not like the flavor. **Caution:** There are reports of persons being made ill by it; also it is easily confused with inedible species, such as Scaber Hydnum (above).

Similar species: Scaber Hydnum (*S. scabrosus,* above) is smooth at first and at maturity has less conspicuous scales than Scaly Hydnum (*S. imbricatus*). Also, Scaber Hydnum has a *bitter taste* compared with Scaly Hydnum, which has a mild taste when raw.*

CRACKED HYDNUM *Sarcodon rimosus*   **Pl. 10**
Medium to large, pinkish brown, *dry, cracked cap. Cap:* Convex to depressed at center. Surface *smooth at first,* then *scaly* and *typically cracking.* Flesh thick, soft, dry. Odor and taste not distinctive. Spines crowded, decurrent (extending down stalk); brownish pink. *Stalk:* Solid, fleshy; surface colored like spines, hoary. Interior grayish. *Spore print: Brown.* **Technical notes:** Cap to 12 cm across. Stalk 4–8 × 1–4 cm. Spores finely warty, subglobose; 5.0–6.5 × 4.5–5.0 μm. Clamp connections lacking on hyphae. Flesh *under cuticle* turns blue-green in KOH.

Fruiting: Scattered to clustered; on ground, under pines or in mixed conifer forest. Yellowstone National Park to Pacific Northwest. Late summer and fall.

Edibility: Unknown.

---

* See p. 10 for cautions about using taste as an identifying characteristic.

Similar species: Easily confused with (1) *S. fuligineo-violaceus* (not shown), which is found in similar habitats in Great Lakes region and southeastern U.S. Lack of odor and taste in Cracked Hydnum (*S. rimosus*) contrasts with acidic taste* and strong odor in *S. fuligineo-violaceus*. In both species, cap flesh turns blue-green in KOH (weak potash). This color reaction is restricted to the flesh just under the cuticle in Cracked Hydnum, but appears *throughout* the flesh in *S. fuligineo-violaceus*. In (2) Bluish Hydnum (*Hydnellum cyanellum*, not shown), reported only from northern California, the flesh turns blue-green throughout.

Cork Hydnums: Genus *Phellodon*

Small to medium, thin to fleshy tooth fungi. Cap soft to tough, with *two-layered flesh. Stalk tough;* often has conspicuous *mats of filaments* clumping soil particles together. Spore print white. Spores spiny. Odor *usually fragrant* and pleasant.

FUSED CORK HYDNUM *Phellodon confluens*   **Pl. 8**
Medium-sized, *velvety, pale yellowish to brown* caps on *short stalks; often fused* to form *large, irregular masses. Cap: Pale grayish yellowish gray,* becoming *dull brown* to *dark brown* where *velvety surface is worn away* on older parts. Margin *usually white,* becoming *gray to dark brown when bruised.* Flesh of cap *two-layered,* with a soft, cottony upper layer, colored like the surface, and a firm, dark, two-zoned lower layer. *Odor disagreeable;* taste mild to disagreeable.* Spines short, extending down upper stalk; nearly-white to buff at first, becoming buff to violet-gray and later brown. **Technical notes:** Cap 4–7 cm across, united in masses up to 13 cm (5 in.) across. Stalk to 2.5 cm long. Flesh turns darker in KOH when fresh; turns olivaceous in $FeSO_4$. No clamps. Spores minutely roughened, hyaline, subglobose; 4–5 × 3–4 μm.
Fruiting: Solitary or clustered; on soil in forested areas. Midwest to eastern N. America and Pacific Northwest.
Edibility: Unpalatable.
Similar species: Cap colors (usually darker with age) and shorter spines distinguish Fused Cork Hydnum from Dusky Cork Hydnum (*P. niger,* below), which often has fused caps but otherwise resembles *P. confluens* only slightly (see Pl. 10). Dusky Cork Hydnum has *black* flesh.
Remarks: Color of Fused Cork Hydnum varies greatly with moisture changes.
DUSKY CORK HYDNUM *Phellodon niger*   **Pl. 10**
Medium to large, *stalked caps; often fused together. Cap:* Rounded to *flat* or *depressed. Violet-black* to *dark brown,* or

---

* See p. 10 for cautions about using taste as an identifying characteristic.

pale gray to *grayish white* (2 forms — see **Remarks**); *darkest toward center.* Margin thick at first, but becoming thin with age; light-colored, but darkening and showing a fingerprint when pressed. Surface *velvety,* or with some coarse dark hairs. Flesh tough, fibrous, two-layered — upper layer soft and colored like surface; lower layer firm, black or dark brown. Odor slight or none when fresh; becomes sweetly fragrant as it dries. Taste mild to slightly acidic.* Spines light gray, darker when bruised. *Stalk:* Stout. Colored like cap or darker; covered at base with a thick, feltlike coating. *Spore print:* White. **Technical notes:** Cap 5–10 cm across. Stalk 2–6 × 0.5–3.0 cm. Spines 2.5–4.0 mm long. Spores spiny, globose or nearly so; 4–5 μm in diameter. Flesh of dried specimens turns blue-green in KOH.

Fruiting: Solitary to clustered; on soil under conifers and in mixed forests of conifers and hardwoods. Midwest to eastern N. America. Late summer and fall.

Edibility: Unpalatable.

Similar species: Dark-colored forms (var. *niger* — see **Remarks**) resemble a smaller species, (1) *Phellodon atratus* (not shown), which is more consistently bluish black, has a more slender stalk, and a less velvety cap surface. It is reported only from Pacific Northwest. Dusky Cork Hydnum (*P. niger*) is found in U.S. and Canada from Great Lakes east. (2) See Fused Cork Hydnum (p. 97) and (3) Zoned Cork Hydnum (below).

Remarks: Two distinct varieties of *P. niger* (Dusky Cork Hydnum) usually can be distinguished, mainly on size and coloration: *P. niger* var. *niger* (shown) and var. *alboniger.* The paler form, var. *alboniger,* grows larger than the dusky form, var. *niger* (Dusky Cork Hydnum); it is lighter when young, becoming darker brown when mature. Variety *alboniger* also has a more irregular surface than var. *niger* and a greater tendency to produce fused clumps that resemble Fused Cork Hydnum (*P. confluens,* p. 97) — see Pl. 8.

ZONED CORK HYDNUM *Phellodon tomentosus*   **Pl. 10**
Thin, small to medium, brown cap; flat or shallowly depressed. Surface *velvety, zoned.* Grows from buried, light brown, spongy, or feltlike pads.*Cap:* Velvety and pale dingy yellow on margin, *light* to *dark brown toward center.* Margin thick, wavy; often turned upward. Flesh thin, leathery; light brown. Odor faint, slightly fragrant; taste variable, sweet to bitter.* Spines crowded; white to buff, darkening somewhat when bruised. *Stalk:* Often flattened or irregular in shape, expanding upward into cap. Surface dull, fibrous; colored like cap. Interior zoned. *Spore print:* White. **Technical notes:** Cap flesh turns black in KOH and gray to black in FeSO₄. Cap 1–6

* See p. 10 for cautions about using taste as an identifying characteristic.

cm across. Stalk 2–5 cm long, less than 0.5 cm thick. Spores spherical or nearly so; 3–4 μm in diameter.

Fruiting: Single to clumped or in large, intergrown patches or masses; under conifers. Eastern N. America and Pacific Northwest. Fall.

Edibility: Inedible.

Similar species: Dusky Cork Hydnum (above) is more grayish to blackish; surface *not distinctly zoned.* It has a stouter stalk and *black flesh* (see lengthwise section on Pl. 10).

Hydnums: Genus *Steccherinum*

Medium to large, bracket or stalked cap is *tough to leathery* and *persistent.* Teeth (spines) somewhat flattened. Spore print white. Spores smooth, non-amyloid (do not stain blue in iodine).

SMOKY HYDNUM *Steccherinum adustum*   **Pl. 8**
A medium-sized tooth fungus; *shape and attachment vary — sometimes stalkless.* **Caps:** *Circular* to *fan-shaped* or *shell-like;* often *two-layered.* Surface uneven, often ridged, *hairy;* sometimes with faint concentric zones near margin. *Buff* to *pale* or *light brown,* often dark on margin; turns *smoky where rubbed.* Flesh white; odor and taste not distinctive. Spines often fused; white to dingy pink or purplish. **Stalk:** May be *attached to center* of cap, or *at one side* of cap; stalk sometimes lacking entirely. If present, stalk is stout, white, and velvety.
Technical notes: Cap to 8 cm across. Stalk to 2–3 cm long. Spines 1.5–3.5 mm long.
Fruiting: Solitary to scattered; on logs and dead branches of deciduous trees. Central and eastern N. America. Summer and fall.
Edibility: Unpalatable.

Genus *Climacodon*

STACKA HYDNUM *Climacodon septentrionalis*   **Pl. 9**
Large, shelf-like fruiting bodies; white to *dingy yellowish* and *eventually brownish.* Shelves (caps or brackets) numerous, tough, thick; each attached at one side to a common thick stalk. **Cap:** Surface velvety to coarsely roughened. Margin thick and rounded at first; later thin. Teeth fine, not tapering to a point; white at first, then yellow. Odor yeasty when young; taste not distinctive. **Technical notes:** Individual brackets up to 27 cm across. Spores 4.5–5.5 μm; cystidia numerous. Teeth 1–2 cm long.
Fruiting: On living hardwoods, especially hard maple (*Acer saccharum*). Northern U.S. and southern Canada. Late summer and fall.

Edibility: Inedible.
Remarks: Until recently, this species was placed in genus *Steccherinum* (above).

Fleshy Pore Fungi (Boletes)

Boletes: Family Boletaceae

Boletes are pore fungi with soft, fleshy fruiting bodies and a pore or tube layer attached to the cap by a gelatinous layer which permits the tube layer to be peeled readily off the cap flesh (as in *Boletus,* Pl. 11). Many good edible fungi are boletes; only a few are poisonous (see p. 117).

Boletus
edulis
round pores

Suillus
americanus
angular pores

Suillus
cavipes
elongate pores

Boletinellus
merulioides
gill-like folds

Fig. 30. Pore patterns in boletes.

Genus *Austroboletus*

BIRCH BOLETE *Austroboletus betula*   **Pl. 12**
Medium to large, *shiny, brightly colored, convex cap* with *yellow* to *brown tubes* on underside. Long, *slender, reticulated stalk.* **Cap:** Surface sticky, often pitted or reticulated; reddish orange to reddish brown or brilliant yellow, with yellow colors becoming more prominent in age; often lighter on margin. Flesh thin at margin to moderately thick on disc (center); yellow to greenish just above pores and colored more like surface near the cuticle. Tube layer thick, deeply depressed around stalk; yellow at first, but soon greenish and finally olive-brown. **Stalk:** Cylindric or tapered upwards, usually crooked or twisted. Surface rough, with a coarse network of ridges; yellow to red or reddish brown. Interior solid, brittle, reddish. **Spore print:** Olive-brown. **Technical notes:** Cap 3–7 cm across. Stalk 10–20 × 0.8–1.5 cm. Spores smooth, ellipsoid; 15–19 × 6.5–9.3 μm.
Fruiting: Scattered or in groups; on soil in hardwood and mixed hardwood-conifer forests. Northeastern U.S. south to Georgia. Summer and fall.
Edibility: Unknown.
Similar species: See Shagnet (*Boletellus russellii,* p. 101).

| *Boletus badius* smooth to minutely fibrillose | *Suillus granulatus* glandular dots | *Leccinum aurantiacum* glandular scales | *Boletus edulis* white net | *Tylopilus felleus* brown net | *Boletus russellii* shaggy net |

Fig. 31. Stalk surface patterns in boletes.

Genus *Boletellus*

Medium to large pore fungi with *soft, fleshy pore layer* on underside of cap. Cap surface mostly dull, non-sticky. Spores are long and narrow, with longitudinal streaks, grooves, or flanges.

SHAGNET *Boletellus russellii*   **Pl. 12**
Medium to large, *brown cap* with *dry, irregularly cracked surface. Olive tubes* on underside. *Stalk reddish,* with *coarse shaggy, net-like scales.* **Cap:** Convex; smooth at first, but soon cracking to form irregular scales. Yellowish brown to olive-gray or reddish orange. Flesh moderately thick; yellow and unchanging when cut or bruised. Tubes yellow to *olive;* pores (mouths) large and angular. **Stalk:** Slender, cylindric or tapered upwards. Surface scales small in wet weather. Grayish pink to reddish brown. Interior yellow. **Spore print:** Olive-brown. **Technical notes:** Cap 3–9 cm across. Stalk 8–20 × 1.0–2.5 cm. Spores longitudinally ridged, ellipsoid; 13–17 × 7–10 μm. Cuticle a trichodermium of inflated cells.
Fruiting: Solitary or in groups; on soil under hardwoods (usually containing oak). Northeast to Great Lakes and southward. Late summer and fall.
Edibility: Edible.
Similar species: The very slender reddish stalk with a net-like pattern of ridges reaches an extreme stage of development in Shagnet *(B. russellii*—see Fig. 31). (1) Birch Bolete *(Austroboletus betula,* p. 100) has a stalk most like it, but cap colors and surface textures distinguish them readily. Both Frost's Bolete *(Boletus frostii,* p. 106) and Goldstalk *(B. ornatipes,* p. 107) also have stalks with coarse, raised, net-like patterns, but they are more robust and are colored differently — see Pl. 13. Goldstalk is edible, but Frost's Bolete is **not recommended.**

Genus *Boletinellus*

SHALLOW-PORE *Boletinellus merulioides*   **Pl. 12**
Medium to large, *olive-brown* to *yellow-brown cap,* with *shallow, angular pores radiating from stalk* (see Fig. 30). Pores *stain blue-green,* then *reddish brown* when cut or bruised.

Cap: Irregularly shaped; slightly rounded to flat, with an in-rolled margin, becoming flat or depressed at center as it ex-pands, with a wavy, flaring outer limb and sterile margin. Sur-face smooth to fibrillose or velvety; grayish yellow to yellowish brown, sometimes with dark brown spots; stains darker brown when bruised. Flesh pale greenish yellow except pink just un-der cuticle; stains blue-green, then brown, when cut. Odor not distinctive; taste of raw potatoes or lacking.* Tubes strongly decurrent (extending down stalk); light yellow, often tinged with green; very shallow, distinctly veined with branched, ster-ile, radiating ridges. *Stalk:* Often flattened (in cross-section), tapered downwards; *eccentric* (off center) to lateral (attached to one side of cap). Solid, firm; surface colored like tubes or same color as cap in lower part, sometimes blackish at base. Stains reddish brown from injury or handling. *Spore print:* Yellowish to olive-brown. **Technical notes:** Cap 5–20 cm across. Stalk 2–5 × 1.0–2.5 cm. Spores thin-walled or slightly thickened, no apical pore; subglobose to broadly elliptic or in-equilateral; 7–10 × 6.0–7.5 μm. Pleurocystidia uncommon, no larger than basidia; narrowly fusoid-ventricose. Cheilocystidia similar, rare to lacking.

Fruiting: Scattered or in groups; on soil in hardwood forests, often around the edge of clearings and usually under ash trees. Widespread in eastern N. America. Summer and fall.

Edibility: Edible, but said to be of poor quality. **Not recom-mended.** Experienced collectors will find better species to eat, and for the novice, it is not worth risking the possibility of confusion with some blue-staining boletes that are **toxic.**

Similar species: A number of boletes, particularly (1) certain slipperycaps (species of *Suillus,* p. 113, Pl. 11) have large, angu-lar, radiating pores intervened with sterile ribs that do not produce spores (see Fig. 30). Some of these boletes also stain blue to green, but the other characters listed above will distin-guish Shallow-pore *(B. merulioides).* Focusing attention on a single character, in this case the blue staining, could cause some confusion with (2) Cornflower Bolete (*Gyroporus cyanes-cens,* p. 110) and poisonous species such as (3) *Boletus erythro-pus,* (4) *B. lurideus,* and (5) *B. calopus* (not shown).

Remarks: The thin, angular, blue- to green-staining pores separated by radiating veins and the eccentric (off-center) to lateral stalk supporting an irregularly shaped cap make this a distinctive, easily recognized species, especially if one notes the association with ash trees. The Latin name for this species — *merulioides* — refers to the resemblance of the underside of the cap in this bolete to the wrinkled spore-bearing surface of *Merulius* (see Pl. 6), a genus of crust-like or bracket fungi often

---

* **See p. 10 for cautions about using taste as an identifying char-acteristic.**

found on decaying wood. In addition to having similar wrinkles or veins, *Boletinellus merulioides* (Shallow-pore) also has shallow, angular tubes and thicker, soft flesh.

Boletes: Genus *Boletus*

**Boletus
edulis**

Small to medium or large pore fungi with a *soft, fleshy pore layer* that separates readily from cap flesh. Cap surface usually dry and smooth to fine-velvety. Spore print olive- to grayish brown or yellowish brown.

SPOTTED BOLETE *Boletus affinis* var. *maculosus*   **Pl. 13**
Medium to large, *dry, yellowish brown cap; often spotted,* as shown. *White flesh* and *tubes. White* or *yellowish pores.* **Cap:** Convex to nearly flat. Surface smooth to more or less roughened. Yellowish to olive-brown, or occasionally grayish reddish brown; sometimes with irregularly distributed pale yellowish spots (variety *maculosus,* shown). Tubes *white* to yellowish; adnate (broadly attached) or depressed near apex of stalk; pores round to angular. Flesh *white* in cap, pinkish in stalk. Odor and taste not distinctive. **Stalk:** Solid. Cylindric or tapered toward base. Surface colored like cap or lighter. **Spore print:** Light yellowish brown. **Technical notes:** Cap 5–12 cm across. Stalk 5–10 × 1.0–2.5 cm. Spores smooth, ellipsoid; 10–16 × 3–4 μm. Pleurocystidia fusoid-ventricose, 35–50 μm. Cap cuticle a trichodermium with clavate (club-shaped) end cells.
Fruiting: In groups or scattered; on soil under hardwoods. East of Great Plains. Summer and fall.
Edibility: Edible.
Similar species: The dry, brown cap with dull, pale yellowish spots characteristic of the spotted form (var. *maculosus*) is easy to recognize. The unspotted form or variety of this species may be confused with Question Bolete (*Tylopilus indecisus,* p. 123). Spore print color distinguishes them readily — Question Bolete produces a yellowish pink to grayish yellowish pink or pinkish brown spore print.

BAY BOLETE *Boletus badius*   **Pl. 13**
Medium to large, more or less *sticky, dark brown cap. Pores greenish yellow, staining bluish* when wounded. **Cap:** Convex at first, becoming nearly flat in age. Surface smooth to faintly felty or minutely velvety with a somewhat grainy appearance; sticky when young and moist. Reddish brown to dark or moderate brown. Flesh white with tints of yellow or pink, especially near tubes; unchanging or becoming light blue when cut or bruised. Odor and taste not distinctive. Tubes adnate (broadly attached), decurrent (extending down stalk), or depressed around apex of stalk; pale yellow at first, becoming

olive-yellow, then dull yellow. Tubes very broad on limb of cap (between center and margin). Pore mouths of medium size, often somewhat angular; staining *light blue-green* or occasionally grayish brown when bruised. *Stalk:* Cylindric or enlarged downwards and tapering to whitish base; solid. Surface fibrillose, may be netted in upper part (see Fig. 31, p. 101); reddish brown over yellow background. *Spore print:* Brown. **Technical notes:** Cap 3–10 cm across. Stalk 4–9 × 1.0–2.5 cm. Spores smooth, narrowly ellipsoid; 10–16 × 3.5–5.0 μm. Flesh turns bluish green in $FeSO_4$. Cap surface (cuticle) turns greenish in ammonia.

Fruiting: Solitary to scattered; on soil or well-rotted logs and stumps, in coniferous and mixed hardwood-conifer forests. U.S., east of Great Plains. Summer and early autumn.

Edibility: Edible.

Remarks: Notice color of pores *before* you touch them. Some boletes with *red pores that stain blue* are **poisonous.**

KING BOLETE (CEPE) *Boletus edulis*   **Pl. 13**
A *large, robust* mushroom with a *brown, thick-fleshed cap. Thick, whitish to brown stalk* (sometimes tinged with pink); *white net* over upper stalk (see Fig. 31, p. 101). Pore surface *white at first,* on young (unexpanded) caps; *pores minute. Cap:* Convex, becoming flat or nearly so. Surface smooth, moist to slippery or slightly sticky when wet, otherwise dry; yellowish brown to moderate brown, often lighter on margin. Flesh white, unchanging when cut or bruised. Odor and taste not distinctive. Tubes white at first, slowly becoming grayish yellow to olive-brown; pores (tube mouths) *very small,* round (see Fig. 30, p. 100). *Stalk:* Thick, stout; cylindric to club-shaped or bulbous. Interior solid. *Spore print:* Olive-brown. **Technical notes:** Cap 7–27 cm across. Stalk 10–20 × 2–5 cm (up to 10 cm long in bulbous forms—see **Remarks**). Spores thin-walled, ellipsoid; 12–20 × 4.0–6.5 μm. Pores (tube mouths) are covered by a soft layer of white hyphae when young.

Fruiting: Solitary to scattered; on forest soil. Widespread in N. America. Summer and fall.

Edibility: Edible and highly regarded. See recipes (pp. 376–379).

Similar species: Some forms are confused with a number of related species that have a white pore surface when young, minute pores, and a netted stalk surface: (1) *Boletus separans* (not shown), is found only in deciduous forests in central and eastern N. America. *B. separans* is variable also, but the typical form has *more purplish* tones in colors of cap and stalk. Its tubes do not develop olive tones; the tubes separate conspicuously from the stalk, often leaving connecting fibers. One form of *B. separans* has pores which develop a weak blue-green color when cut or injured. (2) *Boletus variipes* and (3) *B. aureus* (not shown) have blackish brown caps when young. (4) If you look only for the netted stalk surface and ignore the color of the pore surface on the underside of the cap, you could make the dangerous mistake of confusing King Bolete *(B. edulis)* with certain toxic boletes, such as Bitter Bolete (*Tylopilus felleus,* p. 122, Pl. 12). Bitter Bolete has a pink pore surface and a bitter taste.* (Spit it out immediately if you try it.) **Remarks:** Numerous varieties of King Bolete *(B. edulis)* have been described, varying in color of cap or stalk and in size and shape of stalk. The thick, club-shaped to bulbous-stalked form illustrated on Pl. 13 is common in the West. Eastern forms have a more cylindric stalk. In all forms the white network over the upper stalk surface; the white pore surface when young; the very tiny, round pore mouths; and the eventual development (with age) of olive colors on tubes are important identification features.

SUMMER REDCAP *Boletus fraternus*   **Pl. 13**
Small to medium, *red, velvety cap cracks in age, exposing yellow flesh. Stains blue* or *greenish* when cut or bruised. *Cap:* Usually medium-sized, but varies from small to occasionally large. Convex at first, becoming flat in age, sometimes with margin turned up. Surface dry; dark reddish orange to deep or moderate reddish brown, lighter on margin and fading quickly as it ages. Flesh thick; yellow but quickly staining *bluish when cut,* then fading back to yellow. Odor and taste not distinctive or taste slightly acidic.* Tubes adnate (broadly attached), with decurrent lines extending down stalk, or deeply depressed around apex of stalk. Pore surface uneven and mouths large, angular and irregular, larger near stalk; bright yellow at first, then darker greenish yellow and finally yellowish brown, turning temporarily dark blue-green when bruised. *Stalk:* Cylindric, often bent, solid, firm. Surface of upper stalk often ridged; yellow at apex and reddish below. Interior yellow, sometimes flushed with red below. *Spore print:* Olivaceous. **Technical notes:** Cap 4–7 cm across, sometimes larger. Stalk 4–6 × 0.6–1.0 cm. Spores smooth, ellipsoid (subfusiform in face view); 10–14 × 4–5 μm. Cuticle a trichodermium of short, inflated cells, 7–15 μm wide; end cells rounded or beaked.
Fruiting: In groups or clumps in lawns, roadsides, and open woods. Mid-Atlantic states and southward; common in Maryland and Virginia. Summer.
Edibility: Unknown, but **not recommended.** Some boletes with blue-staining flesh are **poisonous.**
Similar species: Species closely related to Summer Redcap are very difficult to identify. (1) *Boletus chrysenteron* (not shown) has a brown to olive-colored cap with red flesh showing in cracks; the flesh stains blue when cut or bruised. (2) *Boletus campestris* (not shown), a very rare species among the many red-capped boletes that resemble Summer Redcap *(B. frater-*

---

* See p. 10 for cautions about using taste as an identifying characteristic.

nus), is known from southern Michigan to West Virginia. It is distinguished by its smaller pores and microscopic characters. (3) A similar species sometimes known as *Boletus subfraternus* (not shown) has reddish pore mouths and flesh when mature. (Like all other boletes with red pore mouths, it should be avoided.) Unlike Summer Redcap, it has a stalk that is red *throughout,* and its cap does *not* crack to expose yellow flesh. (4) *Boletus parvulus* (not shown) is a *much* smaller species, otherwise similar in appearance.

FROST'S BOLETE *Boletus frostii*   **Pl. 13**
Medium to large, *shiny red cap. Red, strongly netted stalk. Red pore surface. All parts quickly stain blue* when cut. **Cap:** Convex at first, becoming flat in age. Surface sticky; minutely hoary at first, but soon becoming smooth. Deep red overall, or fading from red to yellow in some areas, particularly toward margin. Flesh yellowish. Odor not distinctive. Tubes greenish yellow; pores small, round, with *red mouths* that are beaded with yellow droplets. **Stalk:** Club-shaped, with a rounded base at first, becoming almost cylindrical at maturity. Surface sometimes yellow at base and usually conspicuously ribbed (see **Remarks**). **Technical notes:** Cap 5–12 cm across. Stalk 4–11 × 0.7–2.5 cm. Spores elliptic; 12–17 × 5.0–6.5 μm.
Fruiting: Scattered or in groups; common in oak woods. Eastern N. America. Summer.
Edibility: Sometimes reported as non-poisonous, but definitely **not recommended.** Some blue-staining boletes with red pore mouths are **poisonous.** We discourage experimenting with any having that combination for food.
Similar species: See Shagnet (*Boletellus russellii,* p. 101) and Goldstalk (*Boletus ornatipes,* p. 107).
Remarks: Forms of this species in southeastern U.S. sometimes have irregular ridges or a roughened texture on lower part of stalk, with the network pattern of ridges confined to the upper stalk. Yellowish forms of this species may be *Boletus floridanus.*

BRAGGER'S BOLETE *Boletus mirabilis*   **Pl. 13**
Cap and stalk dark reddish brown to *grayish brown. Cap surface woolly* to *grainy* or *slightly roughened. Surface of upper stalk coarsely netted. Pores yellow.* **Cap:** Convex; surface changes with age — young buttons more or less slippery but soon dry; then minutely velvety, sometimes cracking and becoming more or less scaly. Flesh firm; nearly white to yellowish, unchanging or reddish where bruised. Tubes deeply but very narrowly depressed around apex of stalk. Pores small and more or less angular. **Stalk:** Solid; club-shaped, with a rounded base; upper part has a *coarse network* on surface. **Spore print:** Grayish yellowish brown. **Technical notes:** Cap 5–16 cm across. Stalk 8–20 × 1–5 cm. Spores 15–24 × 7–9 μm.
Fruiting: Solitary to clustered; on or beside decaying logs or stumps of conifers, especially hemlock. Common in northwest-

ern U.S. and adjacent Canada; less common in Great Lakes area. Summer and fall.

Edibility: An excellent edible species.

Similar species: *Boletus projectellus* (not shown) is found on sandy soil under pines (not on decaying wood) in southeastern U.S. and less commonly in Great Lakes area. Its cap surface is less grainy or scaly and it has a sterile margin that projects slightly beyond the tube (spore-producing) layer. Spores of *B. projectellus* are larger than in *B. mirabilis* (Bragger's Bolete).

GOLDSTALK *Boletus ornatipes*   **Pl. 13**
Medium to large, *gray* to *yellowish brown cap,* with *bright yellow pores* on underside. *Slender, bright yellow stalk* with *netted or shaggy surface.* **Cap:** Convex to nearly flat. Surface dull and smooth to velvety. Olive-gray at first, but soon lighter and more brownish, sometimes with a slight yellow bloom. Flesh thick, bright yellow. Odor and taste not distinctive. Tubes adnate (broadly attached), rarely depressed around apex of stalk; bright yellow. Pores small; yellow, slowly becoming brownish when injured. **Stalk:** Cylindric, sometimes broader at base. Bright yellow throughout, surface strongly and coarsely netted. **Spore print:** Olive-brown. **Technical notes:** Cap 4–18 cm across. Stalk 8–15 × 1–3 cm. Spores smooth, long-elliptic; 9–13 × 3–4 μm.

Fruiting: Solitary to clumped; on soil, often in disturbed areas along trails, roads or in lumbered woods, hardwood forests. Eastern N. America, north to Great Lakes and south to Alabama.

Edibility: Edible.

Similar species: (1) *Boletus retipes* (not shown) is more robust and has a yellow to brown, often more or less powdery cap. See other boletes with a coarsely netted stalk: (2) Shagnet (*Boletellus russellii,* p. 101) and (3) Frost's Bolete (*Boletus frostii,* p. 106).

PARASITE BOLETE *Boletus parasiticus*   **Pl. 10**
The only bolete that is parasitic on a puffball. Small to medium, *dry, yellowish brown cap,* with *yellow pores* on underside. **Cap:** Convex. Surface dull; smooth to velvety, sometimes cracked. Margin sterile (no pores on outermost edge). Pale yellow flesh shows through cracks in cap surface. Tubes adnate (broadly attached) or decurrent (extending down stalk), but depressed around apex of stalk in age; moderate to dark yellow, orange-yellow to brownish. **Stalk:** Cylindric, solid; interior yellow. Surface fibrillose to scaly; grayish brown to yellowish brown. **Spore print:** Dark olive. **Technical notes:** Cap 2–7 cm across. Stalk 3–6 × 0.8–1.5 cm. Spores smooth, elliptic; 12–18 × 4–5 μm.

Fruiting: Solitary or clumped; attached to puffballs (*Scleroderma,* p. 359). Reported from Canada to Florida. Common in southeastern states. Summer and fall.

Edibility: Reportedly edible.

Remarks: Very distinctive if parasitic habit is observed.

PEPPER BOLETE *Boletus piperatus*   **Pl. 13**
Medium-sized, *reddish orange* to *brown cap and stalk.* *Pore mouths red. Taste strong,* and *sharply peppery.** (Spit it out immediately if you try it.) *Cap:* Hemispheric to convex, flattening in age. Surface mostly *dry* to tacky (not truly sticky); felty to minutely hairy near margin. Flesh thick on disc (center), tapering sharply on limb; soft pale yellow, flushed with pink near tube layer. Tubes adnate (broadly attached) or decurrent (extending down stalk); red to reddish brown, darkening when bruised. Tubes vary in size — larger and more angular near margin. *Stalk:* Cylindric or tapered at base and slightly enlarged toward cap. Surface almost smooth, with yellow, felty filaments at base. Interior *solid;* yellow, with reddish streaks. *Spore print:* Brown. **Technical notes:** Cap 2–8 cm across. Stalk 2–8 cm × 3–7 mm. Spores smooth, ellipsoid; 7–10 × 3–4 μm. Cheilo- and pleurocystidia similar; fusoid-ventricose, 40–60 × 8–13 μm.

Fruiting: Solitary or in groups; on soil, in both coniferous and hardwood forests. Southern Canada to mid-South; coast to coast. Summer and fall.

Edibility: Not recommended. Some people have experienced severe stomach pains from eating *B. piperatus* (Pepper Bolete).

Similar species: Other boletes with similar coloration *lack the red pore mouths.*

RED-DOT *Boletus rubropunctus*   **Pl. 13**
Small to medium, *rounded, shiny, orange* to *red* or *reddish brown cap. Slender, soft-scaled stalk.* Flesh and tubes *yellow,* usually *unchanging* when cut or bruised. *Cap:* Convex *(rounded).* Surface smooth to veined, *sticky* when wet. Flesh thick; soft but solid. Odor and taste not distinctive. Tubes adnate (broadly attached) or deeply depressed around apex of stalk; tube length about equal to thickness of cap flesh. Pores small, round; yellow, sometimes staining brownish when bruised. *Stalk:* Solid; gradually tapering upward toward cap. Upper stalk yellow (like tubes); lower part darker, sometimes reddish to brownish, blackening when bruised. Surface fibrillose, with soft, red, tuft-like scales or streaks. Base more or less sheathed with pale yellow mycelium. *Spore print:* Olivebrown. **Technical notes:** Cap 4–8 cm across. Stalk 5–15 cm long × 8–12 mm. Spores fusiform (spindle-shaped) to elliptic; 12–15 × 4.5–6.0 μm.

Fruiting: Solitary to scattered or clustered; on soil in deciduous, coniferous, or mixed forests, often in moist, mossy places. Southeastern U.S. Summer and fall.

Edibility: Unknown.

Similar species: The lighter and particularly more yellowish

---

* See p. 10 for cautions about using taste as an identifying characteristic.

forms of Red-dot *(B. rubropunctus)* may be confused easily
with *Boletus longicurvipes* (not shown). They can be distinguished with confidence only by microscopic characters. The
sticky, bright-colored caps distinguish these two boletes from
related species having similar fruiting habits.

Genus *Fuscoboletinus*

ROSY BOLETE *Fuscoboletinus ochraceoroseus*   **Pl. 12**
Large, dry, fibrillose, rose-tinted cap with *large, yellow, angular pores.* Grows *under larch trees in Northwest.* **Cap:** Broadly
convex to nearly flat, sometimes more or less humped. Surface
fibrils sometimes form soft scales. Color varies—whitish to
pink or yellow, fading readily in bright sun, or whitish at first,
then pink and darkening in age. Flesh thick; bright yellow
with a pink zone just under surface fibrils; unchanging or turning slightly greenish blue when cut. Odor faint and acidic;
taste slightly peppery or bitter.* Tubes shallow, adnate
(broadly attached) or decurrent (extending down stalk); dull
yellow at first, darkening and more greenish to brown in age.
Pores large, elongated to angular, tending to form radial rows
(see **Remarks**), sometimes with distinct branching ribs. **Stalk:**
Short, sometimes enlarged at base; dry, yellow with white
base. Thin white veil breaks from stalk at an early stage and
may leave scattered, thin flecks on cap margin. **Spore print:**
Reddish brown. **Technical notes:** Cap 8–20 cm across. Stalk
3–8 × 1–2 cm. Spores cylindric; 7.0–9.5 × 2.5–3.5 μm.
Fruiting: Scattered or in groups; on soil *under larch.* Northwestern U.S. and Canada. Late spring to fall.
Edibility: Edible, but **not recommended,** as some report
that a bitter flavor develops when cooked.
Similar species: Frequently confused with (1) Lake's Slipperycap *(S. lakei,* p. 116) which grows under Douglas fir in the
same region. It has darker, more orange to brownish colors. (2)
In eastern N. America Painted Slipperycap *(S. pictus,* p. 118) is
a similar species found under eastern white pine, but with
darker red colors and more olive-brown spore print.
Remarks: The large size, angular-elongate shape, and radial
arrangement of pores in this species is sometimes called "bole-
tinioid." In its extreme form, its pore layer resembles that of
Shallow-pore *(Boletinellus merulioides*—see Fig. 30, p. 100).

Genus *Gyroporus*

Small to large, dry, thick-fleshed cap on hollow stalk. Tubes on
underside of cap are yellowish white before spores develop.
Spore print yellow.

---

* See p. 10 for cautions about using taste as an identifying characteristic.

CHESTNUT BOLETE *Gyroporus castaneus*   **Pl. 11**
Small to medium, *dry, yellowish* to *reddish brown* cap with
whitish tubes on underside. *Slender, brown, hollow stalk.* **Cap:**
Convex to flat or shallowly depressed, sometimes with a flaring
margin at maturity and often split. Surface color varies — usually some shade of brown, but sometimes yellowish pink to
orange-yellow. Flesh thick, white, unchanging when cut or
bruised. Odor and taste not distinctive. Tubes shallow; free
(unattached) to adnexed (notched) and deeply depressed
around apex of stalk; *white,* staining yellow. **Stalk:** Very fragile; cylindric, often irregularly flattened or depressed. Surface
dry, colored like cap. **Spore print:** *Yellow.* **Technical notes:**
Cap 3–8 cm across. Stalk 3–7 × 0.6–1.5 cm. Spores smooth,
elliptic; 7.5–12.0 × 4.5–6 μm.
Fruiting: Solitary or in groups; on soil in hardwood forests,
from midwestern N. America to East and South. Common
from late spring to fall.
Edibility: Edible. Some rate it excellent, but not often found
in sufficient quantity for food.
Similar species: *Gyroporus purpurinus* (not shown) has a
more grayish red cap. Check spore color with a spore print.
CORNFLOWER BOLETE *Gyroporus cyanescens*   **Pl. 11**
Medium to large, *dry, yellowish cap* with *white* to *yellow tubes*
on underside. Yellow stalk. *All parts immediately stain blue
when cut or bruised.* Eastern N. America. **Cap:** Convex to
nearly flat or shallowly depressed. Surface uneven to wrinkled
or pitted, cottony; nearly white to grayish yellow. Flesh brittle; white, but instantly turning *blue* when cut or damaged.
Odor and taste not distinctive.* Tubes deeply depressed
around apex of stalk; white at first, becoming yellow in age,
changing to *blue* whenever tube layer is cut or bruised. Pores
small, round. **Stalk:** Irregular in shape, cylindric to club-
shaped; hollow and more or less brittle; straw yellow like cap
or lighter. **Spore print:** Light yellow. **Technical notes:** Cap
4–11 cm across. Stalk 5–9 × 1.5–3.5 cm. Spores smooth, elliptic
(sometimes curved); 8–10 × 5–6 μm.
Fruiting: Solitary to clustered on soil in hardwood forests,
often along roads, trails, or in waste places. Eastern N. America. Summer and early fall.
Edibility: This species has been listed as **poisonous** in older
books, but recent reports indicate that it is edible **with caution.** (Be sure to distinguish it from blue-staining boletes that
are definitely poisonous, such as *Boletus calopus, B. erythro-
pus,* and *B. lurideus,* not shown). Cornflower Bolete is easily
recognized by its straw yellow cap and *instant blue stain* when
cut or bruised.

---

* See p. 10 for cautions about using taste as an identifying characteristic.

Similar species: Woollycap (*Suillus tomentosus*, p. 119) has *brown pores* from the first and stains blue-green more slowly.

Scaberstalks: Genus *Leccinum*

Medium to large, thick-fleshed cap with a thick pore layer that separates readily from stalk. Stalk cylindric to club-shaped; surface scaly — roughened or dotted with *dark scabers* (*tufts of scales*).

Leccinum scabrum

Spores smooth.

ASPEN SCABERSTALK *Leccinum aurantiacum*   **Pl. 12**
Large, dry, reddish orange, fleshy cap. Solid, whitish stalk roughened with *dark scales. Flesh turns pink, then black* when cut or bruised. **Cap:** Convex; margin clasps stalk at first, becoming flat and breaking into segments as cap expands. Margin is sterile (extends beyond tubes). Surface of cap uneven; rough to felty. Dull to bright *reddish orange.* Flesh *thick,* white, slowly turning *pink,* then gray or *black* when cut; sometimes slowly staining blue in interior of stalk base. Odor and taste not distinctive. Tubes nearly free from apex of stalk; light yellowish brown. Pores minute, ochraceous (dull orange-yellow). **Stalk:** Solid; cylindric, sometimes with a slightly swollen middle portion. Surface rough from scales (Fig. 31), which are white at first but eventually become black-tipped. **Spore print:** Yellowish brown. **Technical notes:** Cap 5–15 cm (or more) across. Stalk 10–15 × 1.5–3.5 cm. Spores narrowly elliptic to pyriform (pear-shaped); 13–18 × 3.5–5.0 μm. **Fruiting:** Scattered on soil under aspen and pine. Northern U.S. and Canada. Early summer to fall.
Edibility: Excellent. See recipes (pp. 376 and 378).
Similar species: (1) Another species known as **Aspen Scaberstalk** (*L. insigne*) is common under quaking aspen in central U.S. and Rocky Mts. in late spring and summer. The cap is more orange and has more distinctly dull *yellow* pores with no olive tints before spores mature. Flesh of cap and stalk stains purplish gray to gray when cut, but without first staining red or pink (see Pl. 2). It, too, is an excellent edible mushroom. (2) *Leccinum atrostipitatum* (not shown) has dark-colored scales, even in the young button stage.
Remarks: A number of species with reddish orange or similarly colored caps can now be recognized in the field by paying careful attention to details such as those above, but some can be identified only on microscopic examination. As far as we know, all *Leccinums* (scaberstalks) are edible and generally well liked.
BIRCH SCABERSTALK *Leccinum scabrum*   **Pl. 12**
Medium to large, *grayish brown* to *yellowish brown, fleshy cap.*

Solid, whitish stalk, with *dark brown* to *black, rough-edged scales.* **Cap:** Convex or depressed (flat); sometimes flushed with olive in age. Surface moist to sticky or dry, smooth but often depressed in age. Flesh *thick;* white and unchanging, or slowly turning brownish when cut. Odor and taste not distinctive. Tubes deeply depressed around stalk; nearly white at first, but soon becoming grayish yellowish brown as spores mature. Pores small; pore surface white to brownish and unchanging, or staining yellowish to brownish when bruised. **Stalk:** Thick and even or enlarged downwards. Interior *solid;* white and unchanging or slowly turning pale pinkish near edge, sometimes developing patches of blue or red stains in localized areas. **Spore print:** Brown. **Technical notes:** Cap 4–10 cm across. Stalk 5–15 cm × 8–15 mm. Depression between tubes and stalk 1.0–1.5 cm deep. Spores smooth, fusiform to flattened, with distinct suprahilar depression; 15–19 × 5–7 μm. **Fruiting:** Scattered or in groups; on soil under birch. Widely distributed in N. America. Common in summer and fall. **Edibility:** Good.

Similar species: *Leccinum holopus* (not shown) is a small, similarly colored species found in moist birch forests and bogs from the Great Lakes eastward. *Leccinum holopus* is readily distinguished from Birch Scaberstalk *(L. scabrum)* by its small size and consistently red or bright brownish-staining flesh near apex of stalk.

Genus *Strobilomyces*

OLD-MAN-OF-THE-WOODS   **Pl. 10**
Strobilomyces floccopus
Medium to large, *pale gray* to *nearly black* cap, with *coarse, dry, dark gray* to *blackish scales. Whitish* to *nearly black tubes* on underside *stain red* when cut or bruised. *Slender, tough stalk;* surface *fibrillose* to *shaggy.* **Cap:** Convex at first, becoming flat on disc (at center) or occasionally broadly depressed at maturity. Surface breaks into dark, angular to pyramidal or (more commonly) shaggy scales at a very early stage, exposing lighter, dingy flesh between scales. Margin of cap often has cottony scales (remnants from veil). Flesh soft; stains orange-red, then black, when cut or bruised — occasionally stains black directly. Odor and taste not distinctive. Tube layer wide; broadly adnate (attached) or depressed around apex of stalk. Pores large, angular; those near stalk often elongated. **Stalk:** Cylindric or enlarged downward, solid. Surface unpolished and streaked or netted with extensions of tube walls at apex; *fibrillose to scaly* or ringed with veil remnants in midportion, and minutely velvety at base. Color varies from gray to color of cap. **Spore print:** Black. **Technical notes:** Cap 4–15 cm across. Stalk 5–12 × 1.0–2.5 cm. Spores reticulate, with broad ridges and prominent apiculus; subglobose;

10–15 × 9–12 μm. Pleurocystidia numerous; fusoid-ventricose to clavate (club-shaped) and mucronate (with a short, abrupt tip). Caulocystidia clavate.
Fruiting: Solitary to scattered or in groups, but rarely in great numbers; on soil in hardwood and mixed hardwood-coniferous forests. Midwest to Atlantic Coast, from southern Canada southward. Summer and fall.
Edibility: Apparently not poisonous, but no one seems very enthusiastic about eating it. **Not recommended.**
Similar species: *Strobilomyces confusus* (not shown) is another shaggy bolete that cannot be distinguished from *S. floccopus* without examining the spores microscopically. (In *S. confusus,* the spores have warts or ridges that do not form a complete network.) Both species are called Old-Man-of-the-Woods and are very easily distinguished from all other boletes.

Slipperycaps: Genus *Suillus*

Suillus brevipes

Medium to large, soft, thick-fleshed cap with a *soft pore layer* on underside; pores often angular (see Fig. 30, p. 100) and in rows that radiate from stalk. Upper surface of cap *often sticky.* Stalk sometimes dotted at apex and may have remains of fibrillose-gelatinous veil. Spore print olive-brown to moderate or dingy yellowish brown.

AMERICAN SLIPPERYCAP *Suillus americanus*   **Pl. 12**
Small to medium, *slimy, bright yellow cap,* with *red to reddish brown scales embedded in slime. Thin, yellow stalk,* dotted with *dark reddish glands. Tubes dingy yellow; pores angular.*
Cap: Obtuse to convex at first, sometimes becoming flat in age. Margin has soft, cottony, yellowish veil material which leaves brownish patches as it dries. Flesh thin; yellow, staining brown when bruised. Odor not distinctive; taste acidic. **Stalk:** Cylindric, tough, slender; often bent. Yellow, *dotted* with brown and becoming reddish brown (especially in lower part) when handled. Base attached to substrate (mossy soil) by coarse, white to brownish, string-like strands. **Spore print:** Light brown to brownish orange. **Technical notes:** Cap 3–10 cm across. Stalk 3–8 × 0.5–1.0 cm. Spores smooth, narrowly subfusiform (nearly spindle-shaped), flattened in one view; 8–12 × 3–5 μm.
Fruiting: Solitary to clustered; on soil under white pine. Often comes up through dense beds or masses of lichens or moss. Eastern U.S. and Canada; common. Late summer and fall.
Edibility: Edible, but considered not worthwhile by some because of thin flesh.
Similar species: *Suillus sibiricus* (not shown) is occasionally found in western N. America. It has lighter, less red but more greenish colors and a thicker stalk that is often ringed.

STUBBY-STALK *Suillus brevipes*   **Pl. 11**
Medium-sized, *slimy, grayish brown cap* with a *thick, yellow tube layer* on underside. *Stubby, white* to *yellowish stalk* with *no ring;* seldom has *glandular dots.* **Cap:** Hemispherical at first, later broadly convex to nearly flat; sometimes slightly lobed. Margin in button stage extends beyond tubes and is naked to slightly hairy, but not with a distinct white, cottony roll—see **Similar species** below. Surface smooth, sticky, sometimes streaked under thick slime layer. Grayish brown to reddish brown when young, becoming lighter and more yellow to orange brown in age. Flesh soft, thick; white at first, but soon becoming yellowish above tubes and stalk; unchanging when cut or bruised. Odor and taste not distinctive. Tubes yellow, darkening and becoming more olive-colored as spores mature. Pores minute, round. **Stalk:** *Short,* cylindric, sometimes tapering at base; interior solid, white at first, becoming yellow, at least at apex. Surface smooth; white at first, later becoming yellow at apex or eventually yellowish overall or brownish from handling. Glandular dots *usually lacking,* or at maturity poorly and irregularly formed. **Spore print:** Light brown. **Technical notes:** Cap 4–9 cm across. Stalk 2–5 × 1–2 cm. Spores narrowly elliptic to oblong, indistinctly and variously inequilateral in profile; 6–9 × 3–4 μm. **Fruiting:** Scattered to clustered; on soil under 2- and 3-needle pine or spruce; common at times. Widely distributed throughout N. America. Late summer and fall.
Edibility: Edible and often found in sufficient quantity for food. Some dislike the texture.
Similar species: Although it is one of the most common and widespread species of our western coniferous forests, *S. brevipes* (Stubby-stalk) is easily confused with several less common species such as (1) *S. borealis* (not shown), (2) Pale Slipperycap (*S. neoalbidipes,* p. 117), and (3) Pine Slipperycap (*S. pseudobrevipes,* p. 119), all of which have a *cottony roll* on the margin of young caps and often have recognizable *veil remnants,* either on stalk or cap margin (or both), when mature. (4) Granulated Bolete (*S. granulatus,* p. 115) has more distinct glandular spots on stalk and usually a more mottled cap surface. (5) Lake's Slipperycap (*S. lakei,* p. 116) grows under Douglas fir in the western mountains and has a scaly cap and a ringed stalk.
Remarks: Inasmuch as all of these species are edible, no harm results from their confusion.
HOLLOW STALK *Suillus cavipes*   **Pl. 10**
Medium to large, *rounded* to *flat, brown cap;* surface *fibrillose* to *scaly. Cap yellow* on underside, with *large, angular pores. Stalk soon becomes hollow.* **Cap:** Rounded to triangular, sometimes with an indistinct knob at first, soon becoming broadly rounded to nearly flat. Margin thin, whitish; incurved on

young (unexpanded) caps. Surface moist but not sticky. Brownish orange; lighter between scales, which are sometimes tipped with dingy yellow. Flesh thick, soft; yellow to nearly white. Odor and taste not distinctive. Tube layer adnate (broadly attached) or decurrent (extending down stalk); pores (tube mouths) *angular* and radially elongated at maturity (see Fig. 30), becoming tinged with olive as spores mature. *Stalk:* Cylindric or tapering upwards from a slightly enlarged, rounded base, colored like cap or lighter; has indistinct ring from thin, fibrillose veil which may leave whitish wisps on cap margin; interior solid above but *soon hollow* at base. *Spore print:* Dark olive-brown when moist. **Technical notes:** Cap 3–10 cm across. Stalk 4–10 × 1.0–1.5 cm. Spores 7–10 × 3.5–4.0 μm.

Fruiting: Solitary or scattered to clustered; *always under larch.* Sometimes common in both eastern and western N. America. Fruits in fall.

Edibility: Edible.

Similar species: Hollow stalk (especially at base) on young specimens is usually sufficiently distinctive, but careful attention to colors, thickness and texture of veil tissue, and associated trees will distinguish it easily from (1) the reddish Painted Slipperycap (*S. pictus,* p. 118, Pl. 11), which is always associated with eastern white pine, and (2) the more reddish brown-scaled Lake's Slipperycap (*S. lakei,* p. 116, Pl. 11), which is always associated with Douglas fir.

GRANULATED BOLETE *Suillus granulatus*   **Pl. 11**
Medium to large, *brown* to *yellowish* or *pallid, sticky cap. Grayish yellow tubes* on underside have *small round pores.* Tubes and pores *do not change color* when cut. *Stalk slender;* upper part strongly *dotted* with *brown or pink glands.* **Cap:** Convex, with a very thin, membranous margin. Surface smooth, but often more or less mottled, streaked, or spotted with pinkish brown on pale pinkish yellow background, darkening as it matures to pinkish brown overall. Flesh soft; pallid at first, becoming pale yellow with a watery, greenish yellow line above tubes. Odor lacking to slightly fragrant; taste none or slime layer faintly acidic. Tubes pallid to yellowish when young, later becoming grayish yellow as spores mature, not staining when bruised. Pores (tube mouths) at first often beaded with droplets of cloudy liquid, in age becoming brownish-spotted and darkening slightly when bruised. *Stalk:* Cylindrical or tapered downward, solid. Surface smooth; pallid to yellow and conspicuously dotted with *pink* or *brown* overall (Fig. 31, p. 101). Interior white at first, but soon bright yellow at apex and brown at base. *Spore print:* Light reddish brown to light brown. **Technical notes:** Cap 5–12 cm across. Stalk 4–9 × 1.0–2.5 cm. Spores oblong or tapered slightly at apex, inequilateral in side view; 7–10 × 2.0–3.5 μm.

Fruiting: Scattered to clustered; on soil in coniferous forests, particularly pine woods. Widespread in N. America. Summer and fall, often common and abundant during September in northern forests.

Edibility: Edible and commonly harvested for food, due partly to its common and often abundant occurrence. The relatively thin slime layer compared with other common species of *Suillus* enhances its appeal for some mushroom lovers.

Similar species: The conspicuous glandular dots on its stalk and the lack of any white cottony veil tissue distinguish Granulated Bolete readily from related look-alikes. (1) Pale Slipperycap (*S. neoalbidipes*, p. 117) has a *white, cottony roll* on margin of young caps and Stubby-stalk (*S. brevipes*, p. 114) has few (if any) glandular dots on stalk surface.

LAKE'S SLIPPERYCAP *Suillus lakei*   **Pl. 11**
Medium to large, *dingy pinkish* to *yellowish cap;* surface *fibrillose* to *scaly, often sticky. Yellow tubes* and *large, angular pores* on underside. *Short, thick, ringed stalk.* **Cap:** Convex to flat, with an inrolled margin at first; margin may be upturned at maturity. Surface of young caps covered with a superficial layer of reddish to pink or brownish scales (easily removed); surface may be almost smooth later; more or less streaked under scales. Flesh thick, yellowish. Odor and taste not distinctive. Tubes shallow, dingy brownish yellow. Pores stain brown when bruised. **Stalk:** *Short, thick;* cylindric or tapered downwards. Bright to moderate yellow, staining brown when handled and darkening at base in age. Interior pale yellow at first, except sometimes staining green in lower part and brown at base in age. **Spore print:** Light brown to brownish orange. **Technical notes:** Cap 5–20 cm across. Stalk 6–10 × 1–4 cm. Spores ellipsoid to subcylindric or ventricose; 8–10 × 3–4 μm.

Fruiting: Scattered or in groups; on soil under conifers, usually Douglas fir. Rocky Mts. to West Coast. Summer and fall.

Edibility: Reported as edible.

Similar species: Lake's Slipperycap *(S. lakei)* can be distinguished from a number of look-alikes by their associations with certain trees: (1) Painted Slipperycap (*S. pictus*, p. 118) is an eastern species, always found *under eastern white pine.* (2) Hollow Stalk (*S. cavipes*, p. 114, Pl. 10) and (3) Rosy Bolete (*Fuscoboletinus ochraceoroseus*, p. 109, Pl. 12) are associated with *larch.* (4) *Suillus ponderosus* (not shown) has a gelatinous veil. It grows in mixed coniferous forests.

SLIPPERY JACK *Suillus luteus*   **Pl. 11**
Slimy, brown cap. Short to *stubby stalk* has *brown glandular dots* and a *well-developed ring. Undersurface of ring* has a *sticky* or *slimy layer,* tinged with *reddish purple* to *reddish brown.* **Cap:** Rounded to nearly flat. Surface smooth and shiny, but often streaked under slime layer. Moderate to dark reddish brown, fading to yellow tinged with brown. Flesh soft;

white to yellowish above tubes and stalk, unchanging when cut or bruised. Odor and taste not distinctive.* Tubes thick; some shade of dingy yellow, darkening with age. Pores minute; yellow dotted with brown, unchanging when bruised. **Stalk:** Cylindric or tapered downwards; solid. Yellow and glandular-dotted above ring; whitish below, especially at base. Purplish to pinkish gray, gelatinous veil material sheaths stalk below ring, usually extending to base in young specimens. **Spore print:** Light brown. **Technical notes:** Cap 4–12 cm across. Stalk 3–6 × 1–3 cm. Spores oblong to narrowly inequilateral; 6–9 × 3–4 μm. Pleurocystidia and cheilocystidia more or less clavate (club-shaped), with acute to rounded tips; encrusted. **Fruiting:** Scattered or in groups; on soil in coniferous forests. Southern Canada and U.S. Summer and fall.
Edibility: Although this species is edible for some people and is often rated as choice, recent reports confirm that it is **toxic** to other people. Remove slime layer and tubes before cooking.
Similar species: Numerous species of *Suillus* with a slimy cap and ringed stalk are frequently misidentified as Slippery Jack. (1) *Suillus acidus,* (2) *S. subluteus,* and (3) *S. cothurnatus* (not shown) all have narrower stalks. Another species which grows under larch trees can be distinguished from Slippery Jack by its greenish colors: (4) *Suillus grevillei* (not shown) has brighter, more olivaceous colors and a yellowish rather than a purplish or grayish purple outer layer on stalk ring. (5) Pine Slipperycap (*S. pseudobrevipes,* p. 119) has a cottony veil and lacks glandular dots on stalk. (6) A Florida species, *Suillus pseudogranulatus* (not shown) is very closely related to Slippery Jack, but usually lacks glandular dots on stalk. A few rare specimens of Slippery Jack have a ring that separates from stalk and leaves soft, cottony patches (veil remnants) on margin of cap. These could easily be mistaken for (7) dark specimens of Pale Slipperycap (*S. neoalbidipes,* below).

PALE SLIPPERYCAP *Suillus neoalbidipes*   **Pl. 11**
Medium to large, *rounded, pale-colored, smooth cap,* with *pale yellowish tubes* on underside. *White* to *yellowish* or *reddish brown stalk.* **Cap:** Surface sticky when wet; dingy yellowish pink when young to pinkish yellow or light grayish yellow in age, and then often spotted or more or less mottled by the drying slime. *Margin* of cap (when young) has *cottony, white* to *pinkish remains* of *partial veil.* Flesh white, slowly becoming yellow. Odor and taste not distinctive. Tubes pale dingy yellow. Pores round, minute; yellow, not staining or only slightly staining when bruised. **Stalk:** Cylindric to bulbous or tapered at base; solid. Surface white and not glandular-dotted at first, but later darkening and developing minute glandular

---

* See p. 10 for cautions about using taste as an identifying characteristic.

dots on lower portion in age; then becoming yellow above to reddish brown at base. Interior colored similarly. *Spore print:* Dull reddish brown. **Technical notes:** Cap 4–10 cm across. Stalk 3–6 × 1.0–1.5 cm. Spores oblong, flattened in one view; 6.5–9.0 × 2.5–3.0. μm.

Fruiting: Scattered or in groups *under pine,* especially white pine; often common in plantations. Late summer and fall. **Edibility:** Recently reported as **toxic.**

Similar species: Stubby-stalk (*S. brevipes,* p. 114) has a darker cap and lacks the white cottony veil tissue on cap margin characteristic of Pale Slipperycap *(S. neoalbidipes).*

PAINTED SLIPPERYCAP *Suillus pictus*   **Pl. 11**
Medium to large, *dry, pink* to *red, scaly cap* with *small, yellow, angular pores* on underside. *Thin, ringed stalk;* usually *soft-hairy* to *scaly.* **Cap:** Conic to rounded, with an incurved margin, expanding to broadly conic or nearly flat, sometimes with an upturned margin at maturity; occasionally shallowly depressed towards center. Surface *dry*—never truly sticky but may be slightly tacky when wet, at least on young caps. Dark red to brownish red at first, becoming lighter as it expands and ages. Scales on cap often recurved. Patches of reddish veil remnants typically hang from margin of cap. Flesh soft; yellow, but changing to pinkish gray or reddish upon exposure to air. Tubes adnate (broadly attached) or decurrent (extending down stalk); tube layer not readily separable from cap. Tubes yellow at first, but becoming brown as spores mature. Pores (mouths) large near margin to small near stalk; yellow, but discoloring with brownish or reddish tints when injured. Odor and taste not distinctive. **Stalk:** Cylindrical or enlarged downward; solid or rarely hollow. Surface yellow at apex and typically netted from decurrent tubes; base colored like cap and fibrillose or scaly up to ring. *Spore print:* Grayish brown to olive-brown. **Technical notes:** Cap 3–12 cm across. Stalk 4–9 × 0.8–2.5 cm. Spores narrowly oblong, inequilateral; 8–12 × 3.5–5.0 μm.

Fruiting: Scattered or in groups; on soil *under eastern white pine,* throughout the range of host tree. Common in late summer and fall. **Edibility:** Edible and often highly rated. (See recipes, p. 376.) **Similar species:** (1) Hollow Stalk (*S. cavipes,* p. 114, Pl. 10) is more brownish and typically has a hollow stalk; it grows under larch trees. (2) Lake's Slipperycap (*S. lakei,* p. 116) grows only in association with Douglas fir. The consistent association of Painted Slipperycap *(S. pictus)* only with eastern white pine separates it readily from both of these "look-alikes."

PINE SLIPPERYCAP   **Pl. 11**
Suillus pseudobrevipes
Cap *more distinctly streaked* than in Stubby-stalk (*S. brevipes,*

---

* See p. 10 for cautions about using taste as an identifying characteristic.

p. 114); some cottony *veil remnants* remain on stalk as an *incomplete ring*. Compare also Pale Slipperycap (*S. neoalbidipes*), which has a cottony veil when young that remains on margin of expanded caps.
Edibility: Unknown, but presumably edible, as it was long considered the same as Stubby-stalk (*S. brevipes*, p. 114).
Fruiting: Single to scattered or small groups, under lodgepole pine in northern Rocky Mts. Summer.
WOOLLYCAP *Suillus tomentosus*   **Pl. 11**
Medium to large, *yellow, woolly cap* and *stalk. Brown tubes* on underside of cap. *All parts stain blue* when cut or bruised.
Cap: Convex, with an incurved margin at first; margin sterile (extends beyond tubes). Surface *velvety* to *soft-scaly*, with yellow to yellow-orange, red, or grayish fibrils on young (unexpanded) and developing caps; gradually becoming almost smooth. Cap surface yellow and sticky below fibrils. Flesh thick, soft to firm; yellow but *staining blue* or *greenish blue* when cut or bruised. Odor and taste not distinctive or taste acidic.* Tubes adnate (broadly attached) or decurrent (extending down stalk), or rarely depressed around apex of stalk; dingy yellow to olive-yellow, *staining dingy greenish blue* when cut or bruised. Pores (mouths) small, brown, *staining blue* when cut or bruised. *Stalk:* Cylindrical or enlarged toward base; solid. Surface yellow like cap or more orange, with dark reddish brown glandular dots overall. No ring. Often has yellow to orange filaments attached to soil at base. Interior yellow, *staining blue* when cut or bruised. *Spore print:* Brown to olive-brown. **Technical notes:** Cap 5–15 cm across. Stalk 5–11 × 1–2 cm. Spores oblong, inequilateral and more or less fusoid, with a slight suprahilar depression in side view; 7–10 × 3–4 μm.
Fruiting: Scattered or in groups; on soil under 2-needle pines. Pacific Coast and Rocky Mountains to Great Lakes region and, rarely, Cape Breton Isle (Nova Scotia). Summer and fall (see Remarks).
Edibility: Edible, but not highly rated; often has a disagreeable acidic taste. **Caution:** Be sure to distinguish this species from other blue-staining boletes that are poisonous.
Similar species: (1) American Slipperycap (*S. americanus*, p. 113), (2) *S. hirtellus* (not shown), and (3) *S. subaureus* (not shown) all *lack blue-staining reaction* when injured or cut. These 3 yellow species do not occur in pine forests of Rocky Mts. where Woollycap is one of the most common boletes, but they may be confused in the Midwest and East.
Remarks: Woollycap *(S. tomentosus)* is highly variable in important field characters such as color of young tubes or pores; color of fibrils on cap and stalk; and intensity, color, and speed

---

* See p. 10 for cautions about using taste as an identifying characteristic.

of wound reaction. Some differences are geographic and suggest that races or varieties of the species could be recognized,
but in areas where the species fruits both commonly and abundantly the wide range of variation argues against that. It is
one of the most common summer mushrooms under pine in the
Rocky Mts. It fruits in fall along the Pacific Coast.

MOUNTAIN SLIPPERYCAP *Suillus umbonatus*   **Pl. 11**
Small to medium, *thin, greenish yellow cap,* with a *sticky,
brown-streaked surface. Large, angular pores* on underside of
cap. *Slender, ringed stalk.* Grows *under pine.* **Cap:** Convex to
broadly conic or nearly flat, with a low, rounded, central
hump. Surface smooth to uneven; sometimes with brownish
streaks or mottling from drying gluten (slime), variegated with
yellow to greenish or brown clumps of fibrils under slime. Flesh
pale dingy yellow; very slowly and faintly staining blue-green
and eventually dingy pinkish brown when cut. Odor and taste
not distinctive. Tubes adnate (broadly attached) to subdecurrent (extending slightly down stalk); greenish yellow, staining
dingy pinkish brown when bruised. Pores (mouths) large, angular; irregularly or more or less radially disposed. **Stalk:** Cylindrical, often twisted or bent; solid. Interior and surface pale
yellow at apex, lighter downwards, becoming whitish near
base; stains dingy brownish from handling. *Ring* gelatinous,
pinkish brown. **Spore print:** Dull brown. **Technical notes:**
Cap 3–8 cm across. Stalk 3–6 × 0.4–0.8 cm. Spores narrowly
elliptic to oblong, inequilateral; 7.0–9.5 × 4.0–4.5 μm.

Fruiting: Solitary or in groups or clusters; in low, mossy or
grassy soil under pines; frequent where there is also peat moss
and *Vaccinium* (blueberries). Rocky Mts. from Utah north-
ward and Pacific Northwest. Late summer and fall.

Edibility: We know of no reports, but presumably edible.

Similar species: (1) *Suillus sibiricus* (not shown) is similar in
color and stature, but has a *cottony veil* which adheres to the
cap margin rather than the pinkish, gelatinous veil and ring on
stalk characteristic of Mountain Slipperycap *(S. umbonatus).*
Both grow under pines and their geographic ranges overlap,
but Mountain Slipperycap is always associated with 2-needle
pines, whereas *S. sibiricus* is found under western white pine.
(2) The eastern bolete *Suillus americanus* (American Slipperycap, p. 113) is associated with eastern white pine. It has
red scales on a more *orange-yellow* rather than greenish yellow
background.

Remarks: This handsome little mushroom is often very abundant. Because of its affinity for moist habitats, it may be the
only species found in dry seasons.

Boletes: Genus *Tylopilus*

Medium to large, thick-fleshed cap with a thick, white tube
layer that becomes pinkish as spores mature. Stalk solid, often

tough; surface sometimes netted (Fig. 31, p. 101). Spore print pink to pinkish brown or dark reddish to purplish brown.

BITTERSWEET BOLETE *Tylopilus ballouii*   **Pl. 12**
Medium to large, *thick, smooth, reddish orange cap,* with *pale yellowish tubes* that *stain brown* when bruised. *Thick, yellowish stalk.* **Cap:** Convex (rounded) to flat, with a narrow, membranous margin when young (before cap expands); may have a flaring margin in age. Margin sterile (extends beyond tubes). Cap often irregular in outline. Surface sometimes pitted or depressed at center; slightly sticky when moist. Color varies, but usually some shade of reddish to pinkish orange when young and fresh, becoming brown as it dries out or is damaged. Flesh thick, firm; yellowish white, staining pale purplish pink, then pinkish brown, when cut. Odor and taste not distinctive, or taste slightly acidic or bitter.* Pores small. **Stalk:** Short, *thick;* flaring at apex and tapered at base. Interior solid; firm to spongy. Surface smooth or wrinkled to lined at apex; yellowish white at first, becoming *pale yellow* flushed with cap color (reddish or pinkish orange); stains brown with aging, drying, or wounding. **Spore print:** Light brown. **Technical notes:** Cap 5–15 cm across. Stalk 3–10 × 1–3 cm. Spores thick-walled, elliptic, flattened in profile; 7–10 × 3–5 μm.
Fruiting: On soil under hardwoods (oak and beech); frequent in clearings or roadsides, sometimes abundant. Southern New England to Pennsylvania, south to Alabama and eastern Texas. Early summer to September.
Edibility: Not recommended.
Similar species: (1) Yellow Foot (*Tylopilus chromapes,* below) has a more purplish pink, not bittersweet orange cap, and a distinctive *chrome yellow stalk base* that is not found in Bittersweet Bolete *(T. ballouii).* The following boletes are more slender, with a shiny, *more sticky* cap: (2) Red-dot (*Boletus rubropunctus,* p. 108, Pl. 13), (3) *Boletus longicurvipes* (not shown), and (4) Birch Bolete (*Austroboletus betula,* p. 100).
Remarks: Bittersweet Bolete is easily recognized by its colors and color changes, its small pores, and its association with oak and beech trees in eastern and southern U.S. We have never found the stalk or pore surface truly white, as it is sometimes described; in our collections it is always pale to moderate creamy yellow, quickly staining warm brown.

YELLOW FOOT *Tylopilus chromapes*   **Pl. 12**
Medium to large, *pink* to *red cap;* surface *dry. Tubes yellowish white* to *pinkish,* with *small mouths (pores). Slender stalk; bright yellow at base.* **Cap:** Convex to hemispheric *(round-topped),* becoming broadly convex to flat, sometimes with a flaring margin in age. Light to moderate pink or grayish to moderate red at first, but fading to pinkish gray with age. Sur-

---

* **See p. 10 for cautions about using taste as an identifying characteristic.**

face smooth to uneven or somewhat pitted, more or less felty or fibrous; *dry* or at times somewhat tacky. Flesh thick, soft; white to pinkish, unchanging or occasionally slowly becoming yellowish with age. Odor and taste not distinctive or taste of cuticle slightly acidic. Tubes depressed around apex of stalk or nearly free (unattached); white to yellowish, then grayish pink and eventually brownish pink with age; unchanging or occasionally staining pink when injured. Pores *small,* round to angular; white when young. **Stalk:** Cylindric to narrowly fusoid or tapered at one end; solid, firm. Surface dry; pink to dingy whitish with pink glandular dots on upper part; bright yellow, unpolished, and uneven at base. Interior whitish above, *strong yellow* at base. **Spore print:** Light reddish brown. **Technical notes:** Cap 5–10 cm across. Stalk 4–15 × 1.0–2.5 cm. Spores smooth, oblong in face view, inequilateral with suprahilar depression in profile; 11–16 × 4–6 μm. Pleurocystidia subcylindric to fusoid with blunt to rounded tips; cheilocystidia fusoid-ventricose; caulocystidia variable, clavate (club-shaped) to ventricose.

Fruiting: Solitary to scattered; on soil under pine, hemlock, or aspen. Southeastern Canada to Great Lakes, south to Georgia. Late spring to late summer.

Edibility: Said to be edible.

Remarks: This bolete is easily recognized in the field by its pink cap and lighter stalk, which is dotted at apex and *bright chrome yellow* at base. It is as handsome as it is distinctive.

BITTER BOLETE   **Pl. 12**
Tylopilus felleus

Medium to large, *rounded* to *flat, light brown cap;* surface *smooth. White* to *pinkish tubes* on underside. *Solid, firm stalk* with a *distinctly netted surface pattern at apex* (see Fig. 31, p. 101). **Cap:** Hemispheric to convex, with a sterile, membranous margin when young, becoming rounded to flat at maturity; occasionally depressed in age. Surface minutely felty at first, becoming *smooth* in age; dry, sometimes slightly sticky when wet and occasionally splitting or becoming pitted near margin as it matures. Moderate yellowish brown to grayish red or light brown, often paler on margin. Flesh thick, firm; white, unchanging when cut or slowly staining pinkish brown, especially around holes left by tunneling larvae. Odor not distinctive; *taste very bitter.** Tubes adnate (broadly attached) or subcurrent (extending slightly down stalk) when young, becoming deeply depressed around apex of stalk in age. Tubes white to pale yellowish brown when young, soon becoming pinkish to light reddish brown in age; staining light brown to dark orange-yellow when cut or bruised. **Stalk:** Rarely cylindric, but more often tapering upward from an enlarged base or

---

* See p. 10 for cautions about using taste as an identifying characteristic.

tapering in both directions and thicker in the middle. Interior solid, firm. Surface dry; whitish at apex to pale brown or darker below, often staining olivaceous with handling; strongly netted, occasionally smooth toward base. No veil. *Spore print:* Brownish pink. **Technical notes:** Cap 4–16 cm across. Stalk 4–16 cm long × 0.5–3.0 cm at apex, often thicker below. Spores thin-walled, nearly fusoid in face view; inequilateral, with a shallow suprahilar depression in profile; 11–16 × 3–5 μm. Cheilo- and pleurocystidia fusoid-ventricose; caulocystidia similar or clavate (club-shaped).

Fruiting: Solitary or in groups; or clusters; on soil or decaying forest debris, including well-decayed wood, in both coniferous and hardwood forests. Southern Canada southward in eastern and midwestern N. America. Common in summer and fall.

Edibility: Unpalatable. (Bitter taste remains after cooking.)

Similar species: (1) *Tylopilus rubrobrunneus* (not shown) has the same very bitter taste, but little or no netted pattern on stalk surface. (2) Question Bolete (*T. indecisus,* p. 123) lacks the bitter taste of *T. felleus* (Bitter Bolete), but its edibility is unknown. (3) King Bolete (*Boletus edulis,* p. 104, Pl. 13), one of the choice edible species, looks enough like Bitter Bolete *(T. felleus)* that the two are sometimes confused; however, *B. edulis* lacks the bitter taste of *T. felleus* and its pores do not develop the pink to pinkish brown colors typical of *T. felleus* (Bitter Bolete).

Remarks: The strong network on stalk surface, brown cap, pink tubes, and very bitter taste* make this common and handsome species quite distinctive. It is appreciated more for its appearance than culinary qualities, however, as the bitter taste apparently does not leave even after cooking.

QUESTION BOLETE *Tylopilus indecisus*   **Pl. 12**
Medium to large, *rounded to flat, brown cap* with *white* to *pink* or *pinkish brown tubes. Lacks* bitter taste.* *Stalk* may be *netted near top,* but *always smooth below.* **Cap:** Convex to rounded at first, expanding to flat or nearly so; sometimes irregular in outline. Surface minutely velvety or soft-scaly and slightly sticky when wet, or dry and unpolished. Light brown to yellowish brown. Flesh white, slowly staining yellowish to brownish pink when cut. Odor and *taste not distinctive.* Tubes adnate (broadly attached) at first, then somewhat depressed; white to yellowish pink or darker, staining brown when cut or injured. Pores minute, angular; colored like sides of tubes, becoming brown in age. **Stalk:** Cylindrical to club-shaped; solid. Surface smooth to scurfy, or occasionally faintly and incompletely netted at apex. Pallid to brownish, darkening with age and slowly staining brown from handling. No ring. *Spore print:* Yellowish pink to grayish yellowish pink or pinkish

* See p. 10 for cautions about using taste as an identifying characteristic.

brown. **Technical notes:** Cap 5-15 cm or more across. Stalk
4-10 × 1-3 cm. Spores narrowly inequilateral to narrowly fusiform (spindle-shaped); 10-13 × 3-4 μm.
Fruiting: In groups or scattered on soil; in hardwood forests.
New England to Great Lakes states and southward. Summer
and fall.
Edibility: Unknown.
Similar species: The lack of a strong bitter taste distinguishes Question Bolete *(T. indecisus)* from (1) Bitter Bolete
(T. felleus, p. 122) and (2) *T. rubrobrunneus* (not shown). Bitter Bolete is further distinguished by its more consistently and
distinctly netted stalk. (3) See unspotted form of Spotted Bolete *(Boletus affinis)*, discussed on p. 103.

GRAY-VIOLET BOLETE   **Pl. 12**
Tylopilus plumbeoviolaceous
Medium to large, *grayish purple* to *brown cap* with *small,
round, brownish pink pores* on underside. *Thick, club-shaped,
purplish stalk.* **Cap:** Convex, with an inrolled margin at first,
expanding to flat; often irregular in outline and more or less
wavy, with a flaring outer limb at maturity. Surface dry and
unpolished; sometimes cracking in age. Grayish purple to dark
purplish gray when young, fading to yellowish brown at maturity. Flesh firm, white, unchanging. Odor not distinctive;
taste very bitter.* **Stalk:** Cylindric or enlarged downwards,
occasionally lobed in cross-section; firm. Interior white, unchanging when cut. Surface smooth, sometimes with a faint
net pattern, only on upper part. Dark violet-gray, sometimes
more or less mottled at first, with gray fading and color becoming more violet-purple as it matures. Base white, sometimes
stained olive on surface or interior. **Spore print:** Dull yellowish pink to reddish brown. **Technical notes:** Cap 4-15 cm
across. Stalk 8-12 × 1-2 cm at apex. Spores nearly fusoid to
inequilateral, with shallow suprahilar depression; 11-14 × 2-5
μm. Pleurocystidia abundant; fusoid-ventricose with a long,
slender neck. Flesh turns pink in FeSO$_4$.
Fruiting: Single to scattered or clumped; on soil in deciduous
woods, often on sandy soil in open woods. Great Lakes area
eastward and southward. Late summer and fall.
Edibility: The persistent bitter taste makes it unpalatable.
Similar species: (1) *Tylopilus eximius* (not shown) is more
brownish; it has white tubes that stain blackish when injured.
(Bruises or wounds do not stain black on Gray-violet Bolete.)
(2) See Bitter Bolete *(T. felleus,* p. 122).
Remarks: Apart from its strongly bitter taste, Gray-violet
Bolete *(T. plumbeoviolaceous)* is an attractive and distinctive
species, with its violet to gray or brown cap, violet-tinged stalk
with a white base, and pleasant odor.

---

* See p. **10 for cautions about using taste as an identifying characteristic.**

Pore Fungi (Polypores)
Pore and Shelf Fungi: Family Polyporaceae

Fruiting bodies are mostly large and tough to woody in texture and produce spores in a layer of tubes on the under surface. Some species have a distinct cap and stalk; others form crusts, brackets, or shelves, usually on logs, stumps, or decaying wood. Many cause serious diseases in living trees and those which decompose dead wood and woody debris are important in recycling nutrients in forests and other wild lands. A few polypores are edible when young and tender; some cause mild poisoning.

Genus *Coriolus*

TURKEYTAIL *Coriolus versicolor*   **Pl. 14**
Small to medium, *thin, leathery caps* or *brackets,* attached *at one side* to wood. Brackets *often overlap* each other. *Cap (bracket):* Upper surface *multicolored; zoned,* with bluish brown to light yellowish brown between narrow concentric stripes that are whitish to yellow, reddish orange, bluish, or greenish to grayish brown and less velvety than broader zones. Brackets may be flat or wavy, semicircular or irregularly lobed in outline, sometimes narrowed to a short, stalk-like attachment. Undersurface nearly white, with minute pores (see detail on Pl. 14). Flesh thin, white. **Technical notes:** Cap 2–7 cm across, 3–5 pores per mm of undersurface. Flesh less than 1 mm thick. Spores smooth, hyaline (clear), cylindric or curved; 4–6 × 1.5–2.0 μm.
Fruiting: Densely clustered on dead wood or wounded parts of deciduous trees. Alaska to Newfoundland, south to Mexico. Summer and fall.
Edibility: Inedible.
Similar species: The combination of thin flesh; conspicuous, multicolored concentric zones lacking pink or violet; and very fine, velvety hairs on upper surface make this species distinctive among the polypores, but it is frequently confused with (1) False Turkeytail (*Stereum ostrea,* p. 80, Pl. 6), which has a similarly zoned upper surface. Young specimens are distinguished with great difficulty, but in *Stereum ostrea* the lower surface remains smooth to slightly wrinkled but never develops pores as in *C. versicolor* (Turkeytail). (2) Rufescent Polypore (*Hirschioporus pergamenus,* not shown) and related species have violaceous tinge on margin and pore surfaces.

Mazegills: Genus *Daedalea*

OAK MAZE-GILL *Daedalea quercina*   **Pl. 14**
Medium to large, *tough, yellowish gray* to *brownish brackets.*

Pore walls thick, maze-like. Grows *on stumps* and *rotting logs.*
Brackets: Convex to flat, with a thick, more or less wavy margin. Flesh thick, leathery to woody. Brackets are attached at one side, lacking a stalk. Pores very wide, elongated and connected to form a *maze-like pattern* on undersurface; walls *thick;* white to gray. **Spore print:** White. **Technical notes:** Bracket 4–20 × 3–8 cm across, 1.5–5 cm thick. Tubes 1–3 cm long × 1–3 mm wide. Spores smooth, cylindric; 5–7 × 2.0–3.5 μm.
Fruiting: Solitary or in groups; sometimes in 2–3 layers. Common on oak and other hardwood *stumps and logs* (rarely from wounds in live trees). U.S. east of Mississippi River. Seen throughout the year. Perennial.
Edibility: Inedible.
Similar species: (1) Birch Maze-gill (*Lenzites betulina,* p. 128) and (2) lamellate forms of Currycomb Bracket (*Daedaliopsis confragosa,* not shown) with a gill-like undersurface have similar, maze-like patterns of elongated pores, but caps are thinner and upper surfaces more distinctly zoned and multicolored. Pore surface of Currycomb Bracket *(D. confragosa)* becomes flushed with pink in age or with handling, inspiring one of its common names, Blushing Bracket.

Genus *Fomitopsis*

*Fomitopsis
pinicola*

REDBELT *Fomitopsis pinicola*   **Pl. 14**
Large, thick, woody bracket; attached *at one side* to wood. Upper surface *mostly brown* to *gray; white* to *red-banded near margin when fresh. Pores yellowish.* **Cap:** Irregularly convex to hoof-shaped; margin thick, rounded. Surface at first covered with a shiny, resinous, red to brown or blackish crust; later becoming gray to black and finally grooved. Flesh corky to woody; yellow to light brownish, turning pinkish where wounded. Pore surface white to yellow or light brown. No stalk. **Spore print:** White. **Technical notes:** Cap 5–35 cm across × 2–20 cm thick. KOH on context (woody flesh) turns deep red to deep reddish brown. Spores hyaline (transparent), ovoid; 5–7 × 4–5 μm.
Fruiting: Solitary or in groups of several; on both coniferous and deciduous dead trees, stumps or logs; occasionally on living trees, and commonly so in Alaska and the Yukon. Canada and Alaska to Mexico, but more common in North. Perennial.
Edibility: Inedible.
Remarks: Fresh specimens are readily recognized by the red band near the margin. They lack a white or brown layer between successive years' growth.

Genus *Ganoderma*

ARTIST'S FUNGUS *Ganoderma applanatum*   **Pl. 14**
Large, flat, woody, grayish brown bracket. Pore surface white, but quickly stains brown on injury. ***Cap (bracket):*** Semicircular to fan-shaped; attached at one side to wood. (No stalk.) Upper surface of cap a dull crust, with more or less concentric zones or grooves. Flesh soft and corky to punky (spongy and fibrous); brown. Pores minute. ***Spore print:*** Brown. **Technical notes:** Cap 5–50 cm across × 1.5–10.0 cm thick. Spores minutely spiny, brownish, ovoid; 6–9 × 4.5–6.0 µm.
Fruiting: Solitary or in groups; on deciduous trees, logs, or stumps. Mostly on dead wood, but frequently growing from wounds of living trees. British Columbia to Newfoundland, south to Mexico.
Edibility: Inedible.
Remarks: The instant and permanent color change to brown of the fresh pore surface upon injury invites "artists" to record messages or drawings, hence the common name, Artist's Fungus. Techniques for etching on *Fomes* are described by Hodge (1985) as follows: A large needle or a sharp engraving tool will be adequate to do most of the etching. If the fungus is etched lightly, a light brown color will appear and if it is scratched heavily, a dark brown color will result. To get special effects, a knife or a scalpel blade can be used. Soft shading (for subjects such as clouds) can be made by lightly pressing the surface of the fungus with fingers or a Q-tip. The etching must be made shortly after the fungus is cut from the tree—preferably the same day, although a day or two later might be satisfactory, depending on the humidity and temperature. The fungus starts drying after being cut off and within a week or two becomes quite hard. In time, it can be handled without danger of further discoloration. After it has thoroughly dried, white spaces and highlights can be scratched into the surface. Sometimes white retouch paint is applied sparingly for highlights and brown watercolor for the very dark areas.

Genus *Laetiporus*

SULPHUR SHELF *Laetiporus sulphureus*   **Pl. 14**
Large, soft, stalkless brackets in *overlapping rosettes. Yellow to orange,* weathering to nearly white. Grows on *living trees* and dead wood. ***Bracket:*** Fleshy and moist to firm, drying rigid and brittle. Upper surface smooth to wrinkled; margin thick, often lobed or wavy. Flesh white to yellowish pink or yellow. Pore surface yellow. ***Spore print:*** White. **Technical notes:** Cap 5–30 cm across × 0.5–2.5 cm thick. Spores smooth, ovoid; 5–7 × 3.5–4.5 µm.

Fruiting: Solitary or in groups; on both living and dead hardwoods and conifers. Alaska to Ontario and south to Mexico. Summer and fall.

Edibility: Edible, **with caution.** Young specimens are highly prized. However, some people have experienced digestive upset and other mild poisoning symptoms from eating Sulphur Shelf.

Genus *Lenzites*

BIRCH MAZE-GILL *Lenzites betulina*   **Pl. 14**
Medium to large, *thin, leathery* to *woody brackets* on *dead wood. Upper surface zoned; lower surface whitish, gill-like. Cap (bracket):* Irregularly semicircular in outline; attached at one side to wood (no stalk). Sometimes forms a crust-like layer over substrate (wood) below attached edge. Flexible when fresh, but drying rigid. Upper surface gray to brown, often with thin, *multicolored zones;* hairy and often suffused with green from algae growing on surface. Lower surface *whitish;* occasionally elongate-pored, but more often *gill-like,* with gills that are thick and branched near margin of cap. Pore layer does not change color with age or wounding. Flesh white. *Spore print:* White. **Technical notes:** Cap 2–12 cm across, 0.3–1.5 cm thick. Spores short-cylindric; 4–7 × 1.5–3.0 μm.
Fruiting: Solitary or in groups; common on decaying wood of many deciduous species, occasionally on conifers. Nova Scotia to Florida and Pacific Northwest.
Edibility: Inedible.
Similar species: This is one of numerous zoned polypores. (1) Currycomb Bracket (*Daedaleopsis confragosa,* not shown) has a similar, distinctly zoned upper surface, but its different undersurface distinguishes it readily. (2) False Turkeytail (*Stereum ostrea,* p. 80, Pl. 6) never forms gilled to poroid lower surface. Even at maturity it is smooth to wrinkled. (3) Oak Maze-gill (*Daedalea quercina,* p. 125) has a much thicker cap or bracket.

Genus *Grifolia*

HEN-OF-THE-WOODS *Grifolia frondosus*   **Pl. 14**
Large clumps of small to medium, *soft, grayish brown, fan-shaped caps, overlapping* and *fused to stalk. Cap:* Upper surface smooth to hairy; indistinctly streaked or zoned. Caps are attached at one side to a *massive, fleshy* stalk. Pores on undersurface of cap white, becoming yellowish in age; pores do not quickly turn brown from handling. *Spore print:* White. **Technical notes:** Cap 2–8 cm across × 2–7 mm thick, in clumps up to 60 cm across. Spores smooth, ovoid; 5–7 × 3.5–5.0 μm.
Fruiting: Clumps single or in groups, around stumps and either living or dead, standing trees; mostly on hardwoods but

occasionally on conifers. Southern Canada and U.S. to Louisiana and Idaho. Fall.

 Edibility: Edible and highly prized, but tends to be tough in age. See recipes (p. 388).

Similar species: (1) *Polyporus umbellatus* (not shown) also forms giant clumps and has similar caps, but they are mostly attached at the center instead of at one side as in *G. frondosus* (Hen-of-the-Woods). (2) *Meripilus giganteus* (not shown) has larger, more brownish caps; it stains brown readily upon bruising.

Genus *Polyporus*

DRYAD SADDLE *Polyporus squamosus*   **Pl. 14**
Large, thick, brown caps on *eccentric* (off-center) *stalks* growing out of *old stumps or logs.* Upper surface *scaly; Pore surface white* to *yellowish. Pores large, angular,* and *decurrent* (extending onto stalk). *Cap:* Fan-shaped and flat or broadly depressed over stalk and then sometimes more or less funnel-shaped. Pale grayish yellow between brown to blackish scales at first, later brown overall. Texture fleshy-firm and watery at first, drying tough and rigid. Flesh white. *Stalk: Eccentric* (off center) to lateral (attached at one side); often rudimentary. Upper part white to yellowish like pores; brownish black at base. *Spore print:* White. **Technical notes:** Cap 5–30 cm across × 0.5–4 cm thick. Spores cylindric; 10–15 × 4–6 μm. **Fruiting:** Solitary to clumped; on wounds of living deciduous trees or less commonly on logs or stumps. Southern Canada to Tennessee and westward to Rocky Mts. Spring and summer.

Edibility: Edible, but *use only young caps.* Anything older will be too tough to be palatable.

Similar species: The large, black-tipped, brown scales; and shallow, wide, more or less angular pores; together with its size and habitat, make this species easy to recognize, even by novice mushroom hunters.

Family Fistulinaceae

Genus *Fistulina*

BEEFSTEAK *Fistulina hepatica*   **Pl. 14**
Large, flat, red to *reddish brown,* soft and *fleshy cap* (bracket). *Attached at one side* to wood, sometimes by a short stalk. *Cap (bracket):* Upper surface streaked; moist to sticky when young and fresh. *Undersurface buff* to *cream-colored; poroid* from mouths of innumerable individual cylinders with walls that are distinct from each other. Tubes stain pink when damaged. Flesh streaked like meat, oozing red juice when cut. *Stalk:*

Short, thick; sometimes lacking. ***Spore print:*** Pale brownish.
Technical notes: Cap 8–30 cm across, 1–6 cm thick. Stalk up
to 6 cm long and 1–3 cm thick. Pores about 1 mm diameter, up
to 12 mm long. Spores ovate; 4–6 × 3–4 μm.
Fruiting: Solitary or in clumps; on dead trees, logs, or stumps,
or living trees, especially oak; hardwood forests, east of Rocky
Mountains. Summer and fall.
Edibility: Edible. Reports vary on its quality — perhaps the
less enthusiastic ones are based on older specimens. Some people recommend serving it raw in salad mixed with greens.

PART II

Gilled Mushrooms

6

MORE CLUB FUNGI: BASIDIOMYCETES (continued)

Gill Fungi (Agarics)

White and Pale-spored Mushrooms: Family Tricholomataceae

This family is very large and difficult to define on field characters. Spore prints vary from white to pale yellowish or grayish violet to grayish pink in color; veils are present or absent on small and delicate to very robust, solid fruiting bodies; and the cap and stalk are not readily separable. Many edible and some poisonous species are included.

Bracelet Mushrooms: Genus *Armillaria*

Armillaria straminea

Medium to large, white-spored gill fungi; usually white or with yellow to grayish brown colors. Gills adnate (broadly attached to stalk), tending to extend down it in some species. Stalk and cap do not separate readily. Spores smooth, non-amyloid (do not stain blue in iodine). Spore print white.

SCALY BRACELET *Armillaria albolonaripes*　　**Pl. 15**
Medium to large, *rounded* to *flat, yellow cap; sometimes sticky* and *tinged with gray,* may appear *scaly. Gills yellow,* with *sawtoothed edges. Stalk scaly.* **Cap:** Convex or humped at first, becoming nearly flat; sometimes retaining a hump and having an upturned outer limb and margin. Surface smooth and shiny to somewhat sticky at first, usually with *streaks* or *flat scales under slime layer,* but soon becoming dry and sometimes more distinctly scaly towards margin in age. Flesh thick, firm, white or with yellow zone under cuticle. Odor and taste not distinctive. Gills broad, close to subdistant (see inside front cover), notched near stalk; white when young, but soon tinged with yellow, may become orange-yellow in age, edges becoming minutely and irregularly toothed. **Stalk:** Solid, firm, cylindrical. Surface white to yellow or eventually brownish; smooth on upper half of stalk. Stalk has membranous ring and is sheathed below ring with ragged, fibrillose *(shaggy) or scaly* veil remnants, often in concentric zones. **Spore print:** White. **Technical notes:** Cap 4–12 cm across. Stalk 2–8 × 0.8–2.5 cm. Spores smooth, weakly amyloid, ellipsoid; 6–8 × 4.0–4.5 μm.

Fruiting: Scattered or in groups; on soil under conifers. Rocky Mts. to Pacific Northwest. Frequently seen, but usually not in great abundance. Summer and early fall.
Edibility: Edible.
Similar species: Two closely related species, recently segregated from *A. albolonaripes* (Scaly Bracelet) are distinguished with some difficulty in the field. *Armillaria albolonaripes* has brighter yellow colors, particularly on the cap margin, compared to the grayish yellow to more grayish brown colors of (1) *Armillaria pitkinensis* (not shown). Still more gray colors are seen in (2) *Armillaria fusca* (not shown), in which yellow is completely lacking. All 3 species are found from Colorado westward through Utah and north to Yellowstone Park, frequently fruiting together. Microscopic differences help to distinguish them. In the same region (3) Yellow Bracelet (*A. straminea*, p. 135) is found under aspen and in aspen-conifer forests. It has bright yellow colors that fade quickly in bright sun and conspicuous, dry, yellow scales on the cap—if they haven't been washed off by the summer rainstorms, which are often torrential. Both Yellow Bracelet and Scaly Bracelet are known to be edible and presumably the other 2 species are edible also, as they have long been confused and frequently regarded as a single species.
Remarks: The shaggy stalk and yellow to brown, more or less scaly cap with yellow, "sawtooth-edged" gills are good field characters for Scaly Bracelet *(A. albolonaripes)*. Some researchers place it in genus *Floccularia,* along with *A. straminea* (Yellow Bracelet), *A. pitkinensis,* and *A. fusca.*
MISTY BRACELET *Armillaria caligata*   **Pl. 15**
Medium to large with streaks of *dark brown fibrils* (hairs) and *flattened scales* over *whitish cap surface* and *lower stalk. Gills white. Ring white, membranous; flares upward. Cap:* Convex to broadly conic at first, becoming flat, usually with a persistent, low hump and thin, dry, minutely fibrillose margin which may flare upward at maturity. Flesh firm, white. Odor and taste not distinctive, or with a pungent to fragrant odor. Gills close, broad, adnate (broadly attached); white, may stain brown when cut. *Stalk:* Cylindric or slightly enlarged downward; solid, firm. Nearly white and smooth above ring and sheathed with coarse brown fibrils or scales below. Ring soft and *membranous* to fibrillose; white on upper surface, brown below. Ring sometimes leaves scales on cap margin. *Spore print:* White. **Technical notes:** Cap 6–12 cm across. Stalk 4–9 × 1–2 cm. Spores smooth, non-amyloid, elliptic; 6–8 × 4.5–5.5 μm.
Fruiting: Single to scattered or in groups; on soil under hardwoods or in mixed conifer-hardwood forests from Great Lakes eastward; may be found under conifers in Pacific Northwest. Late summer and fall.

Edibility: Edible.

Similar species: Often confused with (1) *Armillaria matsutake* (Oriental Matsutake, not shown) in northern U.S. and Canada. (2) *Armillaria ponderosa* ("White Matsutake," not shown) is larger and white overall, staining brown when cut or bruised. (3) The brown, scaly *Lentinus edodes* (Shiitake), which grows on wood, is now widely cultivated in N. America and may be expected to naturalize (grow wild).

Remarks: Cap of *A. caligata* (Misty Bracelet) may be flushed with bluish gray on margin or may stain that color when injured. In Maryland and Virginia we find bluish gray fibrils matted with soil and coating the stalk base. The wide variety of odors and tastes reported for this species suggests either great variability in the species or frequent misidentification, or both.

YELLOW BRACELET   **Pl. 15**
Armillaria straminea var. *americana*
Medium to large, *bright yellow cap* with *light yellow gills.* White stalk. Cap and *stalk* have *yellow, recurved scales.* *Cap:* Rounded to humped, expanding to nearly flat with a downturned margin; Surface smooth or fibrillose on disc (center) at first, scaly on limb and margin; soon becoming scaly overall, but more distinctly so toward margin. Margin strongly incurved at first and scaly from veil remnants; remaining thin as it expands, often with scattered scales at maturity. Cap *brilliant yellow* at first, but fades quickly in sunlight. Flesh white, firm to soft; thick on disc. Odor and taste not distinctive. Gills close, broad, adnate (broadly attached) or notched around apex of stalk; edges irregularly torn at maturity. *Stalk:* Cylindrical or tapered and curved to a short, thick, pointed base. Surface smooth at apex; scaly (like cap) below ring. *Spore print:* White. **Technical notes:** Cap 5–20 cm across. Stalk 5–12 × 1.5–2.5 cm. Spores smooth, weakly amyloid, ellipsoid to oblong; 6–8 × 4–5 μm. Clamp connections present on hyphae.

Fruiting: Scattered or in groups; often in distinct fairy rings; on grassy soil in aspen woods. Rocky Mts. Summer.

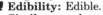

Edibility: Edible.

Similar species: Often confused with (1) forms of *A. albolonaripes* (Scaly Bracelet, p. 133), which has a similar scaly stalk but *flat,* not recurved *scales* on cap. The association with quaking aspen will sometimes distinguish them. Both species occur in aspen-conifer forests, but Yellow Bracelet *(A. straminea)* is not found in conifer stands that lack aspen. (2) The eroded gill edges cause many people to look for this mushroom among species of *Lentinus* (sawgills, p. 159) and the very well-developed ring with bracelets of recurved to shaggy scales on the lower stalk may even suggest (3) a species of *Amanita* (p. 215).

Remarks: This handsome species fruits abundantly after summer rains. The fairy rings are often recognized at a distance by the darker green grass stimulated to more vigorous growth by the mushroom. This is evident even when the mushroom is not fruiting.

HONEY MUSHROOM *Armillaria mellea*   **Pl. 15**
Clumps of small to medium or occasionally large, *thin, flat* to *humped caps;* surface *fibrillose* or *scaly. Color varies* from *grayish pink* to *yellow* or *brown.* Stalk *ringed. Spores white.*
Cap: Rounded at first, expanding to broadly convex or flat with a persistent low, rounded hump. Margin sometimes indented or wavy, with a flaring outer limb or margin, usually splitting in age. Surface sticky to dry, *streaked* inward from margin; *scales* usually darker than background (cuticle). Flesh firm; nearly white at first, sometimes brownish in age. Odor and taste not distinctive or taste disagreeable.* Gills close, broad, adnate (broadly attached) or subdecurrent (extending slightly down stalk); white to yellowish at first, flushed or spotted with brown in age and powdered by the white spores at maturity. **Stalk:** Cylindrical to club-shaped; often fused at base. Interior hollow or stuffed with cottony fibrils. Surface colored like cap or darker at base. Attached to wood by coarse white or blackish strands. **Spore print:** White. **Technical notes:** Cap 3–15 cm across. Stalk 5–15 × 0.5–3.0 cm. Spores smooth, not amyloid, ellipsoid; 7–10 × 5.0–6.5 μm. Cheilocystidia abundant, clavate (club-shaped) to fusoid-ventricose with rounded tips, occasionally nearly cylindric or contorted. No pleurocystidia.
Fruiting: Densely clustered or in groups; around bases of living or dead trees or stumps of either coniferous or hardwood species. Widely distributed in N. America. Midsummer to late fall.
Edibility: An excellent edible species when well cooked, for those who can tolerate it. **Not recommended** — some people eat it with impunity, but others experience mild poisoning. **It should never be eaten raw.** We advise **caution** in collecting either Honey Mushroom *(A. mellea)* or Friendship Mushroom *(A. tabescens* — see p. 137) for food, as both are very variable species and there are a number of closely related species and subspecies whose culinary qualities are unknown. They also resemble other unrelated species that are **poisonous** (see below).
Similar species: (1) Except for its *more decurrent gills* (which extend farther down stalk) and the *lack of a ring* on its stalk, Friendship Mushroom (*A. tabescens,* p. 137) is almost identical to Honey Mushroom *(A. mellea).* Both occur on the same woody hosts, fruit at the same time, and exhibit a similar

---

* See p. 10 for cautions about using taste as an identifying characteristic.

range of variation in color, size, and texture (see Pl. 15). Friendship Mushroom (*A. tabescens*) is more common in southern U.S. than in northern states and Canada, and is not found west of the Great Plains. Although there is little or no harm in confusing these two species with each other if you can tolerate Honey Mushroom *(A. mellea),* serious problems could result from confusing Honey Mushroom with a number of un-related, brown-spored species that also grow on wood and are **poisonous** or undesirable. See (2) Autumn Skullcap (*Galerina autumnalis,* p. 294, Pl. 37), (3) Sulphur Tuft (*Naematoloma fasciculare,* p. 267, Pl. 33), and (4) Showy Flamecap or Big Laughing Mushroom (*Gymnopilus spectabilis,* p. 296, Pl. 37). Spore prints will distinguish them readily. (5) The poisonous Jack-O-Lantern (*Omphalotus illudens,* p. 178) is a white-spored species that *lacks a ring* on the stalk and has *more greenish to bright orange* colors, of a hue never seen on even the brightest yellow forms of Honey Mushroom *(A. mellea)* and Friendship Mushroom *(A. tabescens).*

Remarks: Both *A. mellea* (Honey Mushroom) and *A. tabescens* (Friendship Mushroom) are sometimes placed in the ge-nus *Armillariella.* Unfortunately, these fungi cause a root-rot disease which kills both coniferous and hardwood trees, includ-ing some fruit trees such as apple trees. Recent research sug-gests that *A. mellea* is less common in N. America than previ-ously supposed. Much of what passed under that name in the past may be a closely related species, *A. bulbosa.*

FRIENDSHIP MUSHROOM *Armillariella tabescens*   **Pl. 15**
No ring on stalk. Gills usually more strongly decurrent than in Honey Mushroom (*A. mellea*). See discussion under **Edibility** and **Similar species** sections for Honey Mushroom.

Genus *Catathelasma*

C. imperiale

COMMANDER *Catathelasma imperiale*   **Pl. 15**
Very large, dingy brown, rounded to *flat cap. Gills close, decur-rent* (extending down stalk). ***Cap:** Thick;* convex to obtuse, expanding to flat or humped. Margin incurved at first. Surface sticky when young and fresh, later dry and often cracking. Yel-lowish brown to olive-brown at first, darkening and becoming more grayish brown with age. Flesh thick and tapering gradu-ally toward margin; hard, white. Odor and taste "mealy"; taste somewhat peppery also. Gills narrow at first, often forked; dingy yellowish to pale olive-gray. ***Stalk:** Thick, pointed.* Short; sheathed with dingy yellowish brown veil which forms a *double ring.* Upper ring membranous and

streaked on upper surface; lower ring gelatinous. ***Spore print:***
White. **Technical notes:** Cap 15–40 cm across. Stalk 12–18 ×
5–8 cm. Spores smooth, amyloid; subfusoid to subcylindric,
with suprahilar depression; 11–15 × 4.0–5.5 μm. No cystidia.
Fruiting: Solitary to scattered on soil: in coniferous forests,
sometimes in river bottom woods. Rocky Mts. to West Coast.
Late summer and fall.

Edibility: Edible.
Similar species: The sheathing, *double-edged ring* distinguishes Commander (*C. imperiale*) from (1) large species of *Armillaria* of similar stature. (2) *Catathelasma ventricosum* (not
shown) is smaller, has a dry cap at all stages, is nearly white
when young, and has a disagreeable taste.

Funnelcaps: Genus *Clitocybe*

Clitocybe
clavipes

Small to large, fleshy fungi, with thin, broadly adnate (attached) or decurrent gills. Cap does not
separate easily from stalk. Stalk lacks ring. Spore
print white to grayish yellowish, grayish pinkish,
or grayish violet. Some funnelcaps are poisonous.

WHITE STRINGS *Clitocybe albirhiza*   **Pl. 16**
Small to medium (or rarely large), *thin, white* to *pinkish yellow
cap. Thin, white stalk, attached to conifer needles* by a *dense
mat* of *white, threadlike strands.* Grows *under* or *near melting
snowbanks.* **Cap:** Convex at first, expanding to flat, sometimes
with a low, rounded hump on disc (center) or shallowly depressed. Cap sometimes eccentric (off center) on stalk. Margin
occasionally lobed or indented. Hygrophanous (water-soaked)
at first, but drying very quickly. Surface smooth, dingy pale
orange-yellow when moist, drying to yellowish white or light
yellowish brown; at times indistinctly zoned, with a hoary
cast. Flesh thin. Odor and taste not distinctive, or odor occasionally faintly sweet. Gills close, narrow, adnate (broadly attached) or short-decurrent (extending slightly down stalk),
forked or intervened at times; white or colored like cap.
Stalk: Cylindric or tapering slightly; sometimes compressed or
fluted. Interior stuffed at first, but soon hollow; exterior colored like cap. ***Spore print:*** White. **Technical notes:** Cap
2.5–6.0 cm (rarely larger) across. Stalk 3–8 × 0.5–2.0 cm.
Spores smooth, non-amyloid, ellipsoid; 4.5–6.0 × 2.5–3.5 μm.
Cystidia lacking.
Fruiting: Scattered or in groups or clusters; on soil in coniferous forests. Rocky Mts. to Pacific Coast. Early spring.
Edibility: Unknown.
Similar species: The combination of decurrent gills when old,
pale pinkish yellow caps when young and moist, and abundant
white strands at base of stalk distinguishes White Strings from

(1) Snow Funnel (*Lyophyllum montanum,* p. 164), which fruits simultaneously in the same area. When mature and dried somewhat, the two are often impossible to distinguish in the field. Young specimens of *L. montanum* are distinctly *gray* in the moist condition, contrasted with the *white to pinkish yellow* color of *C. albirhiza* (White Strings) at the same age. As they mature and colors fade they look more alike. (2) Other white species of *Clitocybe* which have numerous white strands from stalk base (as in *C. albirhiza*) are smaller and less robust.
Remarks: This is one of the most common and at times one of the most abundant species in our western snowbank fungus flora. These mushroom species produce young, but often sizable fruiting bodies under the snowbanks during winter or early spring months. They do not develop spores until after the snow melts. When formed under the snow, they frequently have a characteristically curved lower stalk (see Pl. 16).
CLUBFOOT FUNNELCAP *Clitocybe clavipes*   **Pl. 16**
Small to medium, *gray-brown, flat* or *depressed cap* with *strongly decurrent gills* extending down *bulbous stalk. Cap:* Flat, often with an incurved margin and a slight, narrow, pointed hump at first, developing a broadly depressed to funnel-shaped disc (center) and inner limb as it expands. Surface moist, smooth to felty; sometimes wavy and uneven to coarsely ribbed near margin in age. Grayish brown to olive-brown. Flesh thick on disc (at center) to thin at margin; white to watery gray and limp in wet weather, brittle in dry conditions. Odor and taste not distinctive* or odor fruity. Gills narrow to moderately broad, close to subdistant, often forked and interveined; white at first, becoming grayish yellow with broadly wavy edges in age. *Stalk:* Sometimes eccentric (off-center); colored like cap. Surface vertically streaked with fibrils; base covered with abundant white, cottony fibrils. Interior white. *Spore print:* White. **Technical notes:** Cap 2–9 cm across. Stalk 3–6 cm long $\times$ 0.5–1.0 cm thick at apex, 1.0–3.5 cm thick at base. Spores smooth, non-amyloid, ovoid (egg-shaped); 6–9 $\times$ 3.5–5.0 μm.
Fruiting: Solitary or scattered or in groups or clusters, often in fairy rings; on soil or needle beds (sometimes moss-covered), under conifers or hardwoods. Widely distributed from Canada to Mexico. Late summer to fall.
Edibility: Edible with caution — **not recommended.** Although some people report that this mushroom has good flavor, when **alcohol is consumed with or following *C. clavipes,*** some people develop **mild poisoning symptoms,** such as headaches, and a flush or rash on the upper body.
Similar species: Except for (1) *Clitocybe subclavipes* (not shown), a very closely related species, Clubfoot Funnelcap (*C.*

---

* See p. 10 for cautions about using taste as an identifying characteristic.

clavipes) is easily recognized in the field. *Clitocybe subclavipes* and *C. clavipes* are almost indistinguishable in the field, but can be readily separated on microscopic characters (spores and hyphae). *Clitocybe subclavipes* has a less bulbous stalk, a paler cap, and is found under *hardwoods,* rarely under conifers, which seems to be the preferred habitat of *C. clavipes.* (2) Cloudy Funnelcap (*C. nebularis,* p. 142) has similar coloration (see Pl. 16) but the gills are more crowded and produce a yellowish spore print.

SWEAT MUSHROOM   **Pl. 16**
Clitocybe dealbata subspecies *sudorifica*
Small, white, rounded to *flat, dry cap* with *decurrent, white gills* extending down *slender, white stalk. Common in grassy areas.* **Cap:** Convex with an incurved margin at first, soon becoming flat or broadly and shallowly depressed or with a flaring limb and margin at maturity. Surface smooth and somewhat slippery at first, soon becoming dry and often cracked in age; dull white or discolored to yellowish gray. Flesh thin, dingy white. Odor not distinctive (subspecies *sudorifica*); taste absent or disagreeable.* Gills close, narrow, adnate (broadly attached) at first, soon decurrent (extending down stalk); dingy white. **Stalk:** Cylindric or tapering slightly downward, often curved, thin. Surface smooth or downy; white to dingy at base. **Spore print:** White. **Technical notes:** Cap 1.0–3.5 cm across. Stalk 1–5 × 0.3–0.8 cm. Spores thin-walled, smooth, non-amyloid, ellipsoid; 4–5 × 2.5–3.5 μm. Cystidia lacking.
Fruiting: Single or in groups or clusters on grassy soil; frequent in lawns, parks, old fields. Widely distributed. Summer and fall.
Edibility: Poisonous. Sometimes included by mistake in collections of white edible species.
Similar species: Easily confused with numerous small, white to brownish species of *Clitocybe,* although the habitat and persistently white color of this mushroom help to eliminate many look-alikes. (1) Another poisonous whitish mushroom, which has a mealy odor and taste (see **Remarks**), is *C. augeana* (not shown). It grows on grassy soil, manure, commercial mushroom beds, and in greenhouses. (2) *Clitocybe morbifera* (not shown) resembles Sweat Mushroom and is often regarded as a discolored form of it, but *C. morbifera* in good condition has grayish brown colors that are lacking in *C. dealbata. Clitocybe morbifera* is known from Tennessee to Washington, D.C., but is probably distributed more widely; it has often been misidentified and reported as a brownish form of *C. dealbata.*
Remarks: Two distinct species are called *C. dealbata* in Europe. One of these European species has a mealy odor, but the subspecies described here *(sudorifica)* does not have an odor.

---

* See p. 10 for cautions about using taste as an identifying characteristic.

FOREST FUNNELCAP   **Pl. 16**
Clitocybe gibba
Medium to large, *funnel-shaped, light pinkish brown cap* with
narrow, *crowded, decurrent gills* that extend down stalk. ***Cap:***
Flat or shallowly depressed, with an inrolled margin at first;
sometimes streaked, becoming deeply funnel-shaped. Surface
smooth, or occasionally tending to scaliness around disc (center); pinkish to yellowish brown. Flesh thin, white, fragile.
Odor and taste not distinctive. Gills white to pale dingy yellow; sometimes forked. ***Stalk:*** Usually *short;* cylindric or with
an expanded base. Surface smooth to minutely fibrillose, cottony at base. White to dingy pale orange-yellow. **Technical
notes:** Cap 3–8 cm across (5–25 in *C. gibba* var. *maxima*).
Stalk 3–7 × 0.5–1.2 cm. Spores smooth, non-amyloid, elliptic;
6–10 × 4–6 μm.
Fruiting: Solitary or in groups; on soil, in both coniferous and
deciduous forests. Widely distributed. Summer and fall.
Edibility: Unknown.
Similar species: (1) Overmature specimens of *Melanoleuca*
(p. 169) may be confused with *C. gibba* (Forest Funnelcap). (2)
The *repeated forking* in gills (see detail on Pl. 16) and generally *brighter orange* colors distinguish False Chanterelle (*Hygrophoropsis aurantiacus,* p. 154). (3) *Clitocybe inversa* (not
shown) is difficult to distinguish from *C. gibba* in the field, but
the more persistently *downturned* outer limb and cap margin
are important characters of *C. inversa*. (4) In *C. squamulosa*
(not shown) the cap and stalk are both the same color (cap is
darker than stalk in *C. gibba*).
Remarks: Although Forest Funnelcap is widespread in N.
America, the type form of the species (subspecies *gibba*) is
more common in hardwood forests east of the Rocky Mts. A
much larger variety of the species, var. *maxima,* found in the
Northwest, is sometimes regarded as a separate species.
BLUSHING BOWLCAP *Clitocybe irina*   **Pl. 16**
Medium to large, *dry, white* to *dull pinkish cap; flat* or *depressed* at center. *Gills crowded; adnate* (broadly attached to
stalk) or *short-decurrent* (extending down it slightly). Pleasant
odor. Stalk *cylindric* or *club-shaped*, with *no ring*. ***Cap:*** Obtuse, with a cottony, inrolled margin at first, expanding to a
flat cap with a shallowly depressed disc (center) or retaining a
low, rounded hump; outline sometimes lobed or indented. Surface smooth; slightly sticky at first, but soon becoming dry or
occasionally pitted or with watery spots. White at first, but
soon becoming yellowish pink to brownish pink; in age water-
soaked caps may be yellowish brown. Flesh thick, soft; white
to pinkish. Odor faint; fragrant to pungent; taste not distinctive.* Gills narrow to moderately broad; white at first, soon

---

* See p. 10 for cautions about using taste as an identifying characteristic.

becoming dingy yellowish pink. **Stalk:** Solid; surface fibrillose to slightly roughened or with lengthwise (vertical) streaks. Whitish at first, becoming dingy pale pinkish brown in age. Base usually coated with white fibrils binding surrounding humus. **Spore print:** Pale grayish pink. **Technical notes:** Cap 3–13 cm across. Stalk 4–8 × 1.0–2.5 cm. Spores ellipsoid, non-amyloid, smooth to faintly warty or roughened. Pleurocystidia lacking or scattered; filamentous, flexuous (zigzag).

Fruiting: In groups or clusters; on soil and woody debris. Widespread in N. America. Late summer and fall.

Edibility: Poisonous to some people. Recent reports confirm gastrointestinal irritants.

Similar species: Easily confused with faded specimens of a number of colored species such as (1) Blewit *(Clitocybe nuda).* Be sure to examine fresh young specimens. (2) *Clitocybe pseudoirina* (not shown) has smooth spores.

CLOUDY FUNNELCAP *Clitocybe nebularis*   **Pl. 16**
Medium to large, *thick, brownish gray cap;* surface *smooth. Disagreeable odor. Dingy gills. Thick stalk. Pale grayish yellow spore print.* **Cap:** Convex, with an incurved margin at first, expanding to flat or shallowly depressed, sometimes with a low, rounded hump. Margin often remains downturned, sometimes shallowly grooved or incised. Surface moist but not hygrophanous (water-soaked). Light to moderate grayish brown; slightly sticky in moist weather, at times with radiating streaks. Flesh thick, firm; white. Odor and taste disagreeable.* Gills adnate (broadly attached to stalk) at first, becoming short-decurrent (extending slightly down it); close, broad in midportion but narrowed toward stalk and cap margin, sometimes forked. Gill edges even at first, soon becoming uneven or incised; gills white to yellowish white. **Stalk:** Cylindric or enlarged at base, solid, firm; often curved or flattened, occasionally eccentric (off center). Surface fibrillose, with pale grayish brown fibrils over a whitish background; becomes dingy overall from handling. **Technical notes:** Cap 6–15 cm across. Stalk 7–10 × 1.5–4.0 cm. Spores smooth, non-amyloid, ellipsoid; 5.5–9.0 × 3.5–4.5 μm. Clamps present on hyphae.

Fruiting: Solitary or in groups or small clumps, sometimes in fairy rings; on soil, in coniferous and mixed forests. British Columbia to Mexico and eastward to Great Lakes; common in Pacific Northwest, less so in Midwest. Late summer through autumn.

Edibility: Some have reported gastrointestinal irritation.

Similar species: Faded specimens of Cloudy Funnelcap *(C. nebularis)* may be confused with numerous other pale gray or dingy white mushrooms, but the combination of grayish yellow

---

* See p. 10 for cautions about using taste as an identifying characteristic.

spore print; the disagreeable, often skunk-like odor; and the more or less distinctive, "cloudy" cap surface help to identify *C. nebularis.*

BLEWIT *Clitocybe nuda* **Pl. 16**

Medium to large, *violet cap* (color varies as it ages and dries); surface *water-soaked* to *dry, smooth. Violet gills* and *stalk. Spore print dull yellowish pink.* **Cap:** Convex with an inrolled margin at first, becoming flat; sometimes indented or wavy with a flaring outer limb and margin, and occasionally with a low, rounded hump at maturity. Surface slippery to slightly sticky, at least when young (before cap expands); often cracking in dry weather. Violet to grayish violet, flushed with yellow or light brown, becoming more yellow to brown as it ages; sometimes faintly streaked near margin. Flesh thick, soft and flexible, watery at first; dull lilac to yellowish lilac or dingy white. Odor pleasant, faintly fragrant or absent; taste not distinctive. Gills adnate (broadly attached to stalk) or subdecurrent (extending down it slightly) or notched; close, narrow. Gill edges smooth or uneven; gills violet at first, grayish yellow to brownish in age. **Stalk:** Short and cylindric to club-shaped or bulbous at base; interior solid. Surface fibrillose, streaked with white fibrils over violet ground color similar to that of young gills, in age often brownish at base. **Technical notes:** Cap 4–12 cm across. Stalk 3–6 × 1.0–2.5 cm. Spores non-amyloid, warty to smooth, ellipsoid; 5.5–8.0 × 3.5–5.0 μm. Clamps present on hyphae.

Fruiting: Solitary, in groups, or dense clumps; on soil, in coniferous or hardwood forests, meadows, lawns, orchards, or on compost heaps or trash piles. Common and widely distributed from Canada to Mexico. Late spring to fall.

Edibility: Edible, highly rated, and frequently collected for food. See recipes (pp. 390–391).

Similar species: (1) *Clitocybe saeva* (not shown) lacks the pleasant odor and violaceous tints in gills and intensive violet young cap of Blewit *(C. nuda),* but may have faint tinges of violet on stalk and similar field characters otherwise. (2) *Clitocybe glaucocana* (not shown) is faintly tinged with violet when fresh, not more intensely violet as in *C. nuda,* but faded specimens of the two are practically indistinguishable in the field. These three species are all edible and have been frequently misidentified. They are so closely related that they may indeed be regarded as varieties of a single species. Both (3) *Clitocybe graveolens* and (4) *Clitocybe bartelliae* (not shown) can be distinguished from *C. nuda* by their different, less pleasant odors and tastes. (5) Some forms of Dingy Bowlcap (*C. tarda,* p. 145) have coloration similar to Blewit, but *C. tarda* is noticeably more slender. (6) Violet-colored webcaps (species of *Cortinarius,* p. 287, Pl. 36) have a rusty brown spore print; young specimens have a *cobwebby veil.*

Remarks: Blewit is extremely variable, particularly in color. This popular species will fruit in culture. In mulch piles and thick accumulations of decaying leaf litter in hardwood forests it sometimes fruits in clumps and often has a very thick, rimmed bulb on stalk base (not shown). A British common name for this mushroom is Blewits, which may be translated roughly as Blue Caps.

ANISE FUNNELCAP *Clitocybe odora*   **Pl. 16**
Small to medium; cap tinted *bluish green. Odor* of *anise. Gills decurrent* (extend slightly down stalk). *Spore print yellowish pink* to *pale orange-yellow.* **Cap:** Convex at first, with an in-curved margin; expanding to flat or shallowly depressed, some-times with an upturned and wavy margin. Surface felty or with radiating streaks of fibrils (use hand lens). Color varies, but usually tinted with some pale blue-green; cap whitish to pale yellow or brown in some specimens. Flesh thin or moder-ately thick, firm; white to pale grayish yellow. Odor and taste of anise. Gills close to crowded, adnate (broadly attached) at first, finally decurrent (extending down stalk); grayish to pink-ish yellow or blue-green in var. *pacifica* (not shown). **Stalk:** Cylindrical or enlarged at either top or base; sometimes curved or bent. Interior solid at first, becoming hollow in age. Surface fibrillose, sometimes streaked. Pale dingy yellow, often darker at base when water-soaked. Base often covered with white, cottony threads. **Technical notes:** Cap 2–9 cm across. Stalk 2–6 × 0.4–1.0 cm. Spores smooth, non-amyloid, ellipsoid to ovoid; 6–8 × 3.5–5.0 μm. Clamps present on hyphae.
Fruiting: Solitary or in groups; on soil, in both coniferous and hardwood forests. Widespread from Alaska south. Midsummer to fall.
Edibility: Not recommended. Small amounts of muscarine.
Similar species: White spore print and lack of anise odor distinguish (1) *Clitocybe aeruginosa* and (2) *C. glaucoalba* (not shown) from *Clitocybe odora* (Anise Funnelcap). (3) Verdigris Mushroom (*Stropharia aeruginosa,* p. 262, Pl. 32) has a shiny blue-green cap, a *ringed stalk,* and produces a purple-brown spore print.

CLUSTERED FUNNELCAP *Clitocybe subconnexa*   **Pl. 16**
Clumps of medium to large, *smooth, white caps* with *dingy whitish stalks.* Grows in *hardwood forests. Odor pleasant or lacking, rarely disagreeable.* **Cap:** Convex, with an inrolled margin at first, expanding to flat or shallowly depressed; mar-gin bent down or flaring in age. Surface shining white and sat-iny at first, discoloring slowly; occasionally water-spotted on disc (center). Margin sometimes wavy or slightly ridged. Flesh white or faintly pinkish; thin, brittle. Taste faintly bitter or lacking, disagreeable in old specimens.* Gills crowded, adnate

---

* See p. 10 for cautions about using taste as an identifying char-acteristic.

(broadly attached) or short-decurrent (extending down stalk slightly), occasionally forked; white, soon becoming pale yellow to pale yellowish pink. *Stalk:* Cylindrical or tapered upward. Surface minutely fibrillose except for base, which is cottony, with adhering debris. Interior stuffed with cottony filaments at first, becoming hollow in age. *Spore print:* Pale grayish pink. **Technical notes:** Cap 3-9 cm across. Stalk 3-8 × 0.5-1.0 cm. Spores non-amyloid, minutely warty, ellipsoid; 4-6 × 2.5-3.5 μm. Clamps present on hyphae.

Fruiting: In small to large clumps on forest floor. Southern Canada to Tennessee, west to Pacific Coast. Late summer and fall.

Edibility: Edible when young and fresh, but **not recommended** because of the difficulty of identifying this species reliably on the basis of field marks—need to use microscopic characters to confirm identification. Avoid old, dried specimens.

Similar species: (1) *Clitocybe fasciculata* (not shown) is practically indistinguishable from Clustered Funnelcap *(C. subconnexa)* in the field. Young specimens of *C. fasciculata* have a disagreeable odor (unlike young specimens of *C. subconnexa,* which have a pleasant odor), but old specimens of both species may develop an unpleasant odor. *Clitocybe fasciculata* may be a species confined to disturbed soils, as it is found along road banks. (2) *Clitocybe densifolia* (not shown) is almost identical to *C. subconnexa* (Clustered Funnelcap); the two can be distinguished only by microscopic characters.

DINGY BOWLCAP *Clitocybe tarda*   **Pl. 16**
Small to medium, *hygrophanous* cap—*brownish pink* or *tinged with violet* (changes gradually with age and drying). *Odor lacking or alkaline. Gills close, decurrent* (extending down stalk) *at maturity. Cap:* Obtuse to convex at first, with an inrolled margin, becoming flat or developing a shallowly depressed disc (center); outer limb and margin often uplifted and sometimes wavy or lobed. Surface smooth or fibrillose, sometimes faintly streaked at margin. Flesh thin, firm, brittle; colored like moist cap surface at first, but soon fading to whitish with a violet or pinkish cast. Odor and taste not distinctive; or (in variety *alcalina*) odor strong, alkaline or disagreeable, and taste slightly acidic to bitter, persistent.* Gills adnate (broadly attached) or notched around apex of stalk at first, finally becoming decurrent (extending down stalk); narrow, at times forked; tinged with violet, dingy pinkish to yellowish when young (before spores develop), becoming light pinkish gray. *Stalk:* Slender; cylindric or tapering downward. Solid; sometimes flattened or curved. Surface smooth, or with whitish fibrils over a background color similar to that of cap.

---

* See p. 10 for cautions about using taste as an identifying characteristic.

Base often has soft, white to violet-tinged tufts of filaments. *Spore print:* Pinkish gray. **Technical notes:** Cap 1–7 cm across. Stalk 1.5–6.0 × 0.3–1.0 cm. Spores non-amyloid, warty or smooth, ellipsoid; 4.5–7.5 × 3–5 μm.

Fruiting: In groups or clusters, often in fairy rings; on lawns, cultivated or waste areas, compost piles, manure, or occasionally on sawdust heaps; sometimes on soil in woods or in greenhouses. Summer and fall. Widely distributed.

Edibility: Unknown, but **not recommended.** However, it may have been eaten by mistake, by someone who assumed it was *C. nuda* (Blewit).

Similar species: Forms of Dingy Bowlcap *(C. tarda)* with violet-tinged colors may be mistaken for the more robust Blewit *(C. nuda)*, which is a choice edible species (see p. 143).

Remarks: The description given here is broad enough to include variety *alcalina,* which can be distinguished by its smaller spores and alkaline odor. This variety has been found from the Chesapeake Bay south to Tennessee. However, there is considerable variation within the species. In addition to color differences with aging, there is a confusing variety of color forms within the species, some of which have been named separately. There is much intergradation in color, but at the extremes there are predominantly violet and predominantly brownish forms.

Coincaps: Genus *Clitocybula*

STREAKED COINCAP *Clitocybula abundans*   **Pl. 17**
Large, dense clusters of small to medium, *thin, light yellowish brown* to *grayish yellow caps,* with *gray* or *blackish streaks. Thin, white, hollow stalks.* **Cap:** Convex to hemispheric, sometimes with a slight knob when young; expanding to flat, with a narrow, low, central depression as it matures. Margin strongly inrolled at first, limb and margin later arched; frequently split at maturity. Surface has minute, radiating streaks of fibrils (denser at center); may be dry or moist. Flesh thin. Odor and taste not distinctive. Gills adnate (broadly attached) to short-decurrent (extending slightly down stalk); close, narrow, thin, white. **Stalk:** Cylindric, often curved; *hollow* and splitting readily. Surface smooth; lighter than cap color, sometimes white. *Spore print:* White. **Technical notes:** Cap 1.0–3.5 cm across. Stalk 3–12 cm × 2–5 mm. Spores smooth, amyloid, subglobose to ovate (egg-shaped); 4.5–6.5 × 3.5–5.5 μm. Cheilocystidia clavate (club-shaped) to saccate (sac-shaped). No pleurocystidia. Clamps present on hyphae.

Fruiting: Densely clumped on logs and decaying wood, in hardwood and mixed forests. Northern U.S. and southern Canada. Summer and fall. Infrequent.

Edibility: Unknown.

Similar species: (1) *Clitocybula familia* and (2) *Clitocybula lacerata* (not shown) are usually larger, characteristically with longer stalks. *Clitocybula familia* lacks the gray or blackish fibrils on cap and *C. lacerata* has a typically ragged cap margin.

Coincaps: Genus *Collybia*

Small to medium, *thin-fleshed* gill fungi with a *thin, cartilaginous,* often hairy stalk. Cap margin incurved to inrolled at first. Spore print usually white, rarely yellowish to pinkish.

Collybia acervata

CLUSTER COINCAP *Collybia acervata*   **Pl. 17**
Dense clusters of small to medium, *reddish brown caps* (color fades quickly with age). *Thin cap* and *stalk. White* to *pinkish gills.* Grows *on decaying wood.* **Cap:** Obtuse to convex, with an incurved margin at first, expanding to broadly convex or flat. Surface smooth, indistinctly streaked on outer limb and margin when wet. *Hygrophanous* — dark reddish brown when young and fresh, fading quickly to light reddish brown, sometimes becoming as light as pinkish white. Flesh thin, flexible; pinkish white. Taste bitter.* Gills close, narrow, notched around apex of stalk; white at first, sometimes tinged with pink with maturity. **Stalk:** Cylindrical. Surface dry, smooth; colored like cap or darker, white-cottony at base. **Spore print:** White. **Technical notes:** Cap 2–5 cm across. Stalk 4–10 cm × 3–5 mm. Spores smooth, elliptic; 5–7 × 2–3 μm.
Fruiting: On decaying stumps, logs, sticks, or buried wood of coniferous trees. Canada and northern U.S. Summer to fall or winter.
Edibility: Poisonous to some people.
Similar species: This is a very distinctive species when seen fresh and in good condition. Badly faded specimens may be confused with *Clitocybula familia* (not shown) and perhaps with some of the pinwheel mushrooms (species of *Marasmius,* p. 165, Pl. 19).
BUTTER COINCAP *Collybia butyracea*   **Pl. 17**
Medium-sized, *reddish brown cap* and *stalk. Flesh thin. Gills ragged-edged, close. Cap surface smooth—feels like butter.*
Cap: Broadly convex, with a low, rounded hump at first; expanding to flat, with a downturned outer limb and margin, sometimes with a shallow depression at center. Surface moderate reddish brown, fading to light brown or pale orange-yellow. Flesh watery when fresh, soft; moderately thick over disc (center) and tapering abruptly to thin limb and margin. Odor and taste not distinctive.* Gills adnate (broadly attached) or nar-

---

* See p. 10 for cautions about using taste as an identifying characteristic.

rowly notched around stalk apex; white to pale grayish pink. *Stalk:* Cylindric or flattened above a swollen base; *sometimes twisted.* Interior hollow in age. Surface smooth to streaked; white-cottony at base. Color of cap or lighter. No veil. *Spore print:* White to yellowish white. **Technical notes:** Cap 3–7 cm across. Stalk 3–10 × 0.4–1.0 cm. Spores smooth, short-elliptic; 5–7 × 3.0–3.5 μm.

Fruiting: Scattered or in groups; on soil and decaying needles. Common in pine plantations. S. Canada and northern U.S.

Edibility: Edible, but may be confused with several related species, including one that is **poisonous** (see below).

Similar species: Easily confused with other coincaps (species of *Collybia*), but the combination of reddish brown colors; smooth, buttery texture of cap surface; ragged gill edges; twisted stalk with swollen, cottony base; and habitat on pine needles help to distinguish it. Forest Friend (*Collybia dryophila,* p. 149) often fruits simultaneously in the same habitat, in a great range of variable forms. It usually is more yellowish brown, and has a thinner, not twisted stalk, and an inrolled cap margin that persists longer than in Butter Coincap. Forest Friend *(C. dryophila)* is **poisonous.**

TUFTED COINCAP *Collybia confluens* **Pl. 17**
Small to medium, *paper-thin, dry, brown, flat caps* on *slender, hairy stalks.* Grows in *groups* or *dense clusters, on decaying leaves of deciduous trees.* **Cap:** Convex with a strongly in-curved margin at first, soon becoming nearly flat, with a low, flattened hump or shallow depression on disc (center) and a wavy margin. Surface smooth, faintly streaked before fading; somewhat uneven at maturity. Dull reddish brown to moderate brown, fading to pale orange-yellow or yellowish white. Flesh very thin, tough. Odor and taste not distinctive. Gills free from stalk or notched around stalk apex; crowded, narrow; nearly white. *Stalk:* Cylindric or slightly enlarged at base, often compressed; tough, sometimes grooved. Surface light reddish brown beneath dense soft, white hairs which form a mat among decaying leaves. *Spore print:* White. **Technical notes:** Cap 2–5 cm across. Stalk 5–10 cm × 2–5 mm. Spores smooth, thin-walled, elliptic to narrowly obovate (shaped like an upside-down egg); 6–8 μm long.

Fruiting: *In groups* to *dense clusters;* on decaying leaves, in hardwood and mixed conifer-hardwood forests. Southern Canada to mid-South and Colorado to Northwest. Summer and fall.

Edibility: Nonpoisonous.

Similar species: The fairly tough, dry texture suggests (1) a pinwheel mushroom (species of *Marasmius,* p. 165), the group where it is classified by some authors. (2) *Collybia polyphylla* (not shown) has odor and taste of garlic when crushed and (3) *C. peronata* (not shown) has a strong, peppery taste.* (4)

Collybia subnuda (not shown) and (5) *Marasmius cohaerans* (not shown) have more widely spaced gills.

FOREST FRIEND *Collybia dryophila*   **Pl. 17**
Small to medium, *brown cap; margin lighter, incurved* at first. Gills *crowded, white. Stalk lighter-colored* than cap. Grows *on forest litter. Cap:* Convex at first, later becoming flat, often with elevated outer limb and margin. Surface smooth; *hygrophanous*—deep brown to light brown when young, fading as it ages and dries to orange-yellow or yellowish white. Flesh thin, watery at first, flexible; white. Odor variable or absent; taste not distinctive.* Gills adnate (broadly attached) or notched around apex of stalk; narrow. *Stalk:* Cylindrical or nearly so; not twisted. Surface smooth, dull; lighter color than cap. No veil. *Spore print:* White. **Technical notes:** Cap 2–6 cm across. Stalk 3–8 cm × 2–7 mm. Spores smooth, non-amyloid, elliptic; 5–7 × 3.0–3.5 μm. No hymenial cystidia.
Fruiting: Scattered to clustered; on soil or decaying wood, in a variety of forest types. Common and widespread in N. America. Spring to fall.
Edibility: Reports vary. **Not recommended**—edible for some, but others are made ill by it.
Similar species: Easily confused with the slightly larger and more reddish brown Butter Coincap (*Collybia butyracea,* p. 147), although colors vary widely in both species with age and weather conditions. The stalk is characteristically *twisted* in *C. butyracea* (see Pl. 17) and not in *C. dryophila.*
Remarks: Numerous varieties of *C. dryophila* (Forest Friend) are known, including one with yellow gills, and a Rocky Mountain form with a garlicky odor.

PURPLE COINCAP *Collybia iocephala*   **Pl. 17**
Small, rounded cap with a *central depression* and *streaked margin. Reddish purple gills. Whitish stalk. Cap: Light purple,* fading to light purplish gray. Convex to broadly convex; thin. Surface smooth, except sometimes faintly ribbed on outer limb and margin. Flesh thin to almost membranous. Odor and taste unpleasant. Gills adnate (broadly attached) to subdecurrent (extending slightly down stalk); narrow, distant; edges pale and ragged. *Stalk:* Cylindric or narrowed at base; hollow. Surface minutely velvety above, coarsely hairy in lower part. Nearly white at apex, sometimes flushed with dingy brown below. *Spore print:* White. **Technical notes:** Cap 1.5–3.5 cm across. Stalk 3–5 cm × 2–4 mm. Spores smooth, non-amyloid, short-ellipsoid; 6–7 × 3.0–3.5 μm. No pleurocystidia. Cheilocystidia few, slender, clavate (club-shaped).
Fruiting: Solitary or in groups; on decaying litter on forest floor. Southeastern U.S. Late summer.

* See p. 10 for cautions about using taste as an identifying characteristic.

Edibility: Unknown, but unattractive from a culinary point of view.

Similar species: Not likely to be confused with any other small, white-spored mushroom growing in our southeastern hardwood and mixed forests. Some small species of *Cortinarius* (webcaps, p. 287) and *Inocybe* (p. 301) approach it in color (see Pls. 36 and 37), but brown spore prints readily distinguish them. Some color variants of Lilac Fairy Helmet (*Mycena pura*, p. 175) are similar in color (see Pl. 19), but they are always water-soaked and smell like raw potatoes. The odor of Purple Coincap *(C. iocephala)* is different—Hesler describes it as "unpleasant, suggesting old cabbage."

SPOTTED COINCAP *Collybia maculata*   **Pl. 17**
Medium to large, *pale yellow, dry, convex* or *humped cap. All parts* develop *scattered reddish brown spots.* Grows *on decaying conifer wood.* **Cap:** Rounded, but may become flat, sometimes retaining a broad, low hump at maturity. Surface smooth, occasionally with depressed spots; nearly white to light dull yellow, sometimes light brownish in age. Flesh white; firm. Odor absent; taste bitter. Gills adnate (broadly attached to stalk); crowded, narrow; white to pale yellowish pink. **Stalk:** Cylindric or tapering downwards to a partially rooting base; firm, but hollow in age. Surface smooth and colored like cap above level of substrate; lower part intergrown with needles and wood fragments with white, cottony filaments. Upper part sometimes has vertical streaks or is twisted. **Spore print:** Nearly white to dull, pale yellowish pink. **Technical notes:** Cap 4–10 cm across. Stalk 5–15 × 0.6–1.8 cm. Spores smooth, dextrinoid (stain reddish purple in iodine), subglobose; 4.5–6.0 × 3.5–5.0 μm.

Fruiting: Solitary or in small clusters; on forest humus, or more commonly on decaying logs; often on buried wood in coniferous forests. Common throughout southern Canada and northern U.S. Summer and fall.

Edibility: Edible, but ratings vary from not very good to unpalatable. We have yet to hear anyone praise its culinary qualities.

Remarks: Spotted Coincap *(Collybia maculata)* is a fairly distinct species, marked by the pallid, rounded cap with crowded gills and a stalk that is deeply buried in well-rotted conifer wood. All parts develop characteristic *reddish brown spots* as the mushroom matures. This is an unusually large species for the genus and has numerous forms, varieties, or subspecies. In the central Rockies, the large, robust, and distinctly yellow variety *scorzonerea* may be locally much more common than the type variety *(maculata).* A group of species with faintly colored spore prints, including *C. maculata* and *C. butyracea* (Butter Coincap, p. 147) are sometimes placed in a different genus, *Rhodocollybia.*

APPLESEED COINCAP *Collybia tuberosa*　　**Pl. 17**
Tiny, dull white mushroom; surface *dry.* Look for *brown, hard, appleseed-like sclerotium rooted in* black remains of a larger *decaying mushroom.* ***Cap:*** Convex, with an incurved margin at first, expanding to flat, sometimes with a narrow, pointed central knob. Surface smooth but unpolished; white to dingy yellowish to pinkish white. Gills adnate (broadly attached to apex of stalk); close, white. ***Stalk:*** Slender, cylindrical, often curved; dull white. Attached to hard, brown, shiny sclerotium buried in host tissue — usually several sclerotia connected by fragile strands. ***Spore print:*** White. **Technical notes:** Cap less than 1 cm across. Stalk 1–3 cm long and approx. 1 mm thick. Spores smooth, elliptic; 4.5–5.5 × 2–3 µm.
Fruiting: Solitary or in small clusters; on mushroom remains. Widespread. Summer and fall.
Edibility: Unknown. (Who would try?)
Similar species: (1) Magnolia Coincap (*Strobilurus conigenoides,* p. 184) is smaller and grows on "cones" of magnolias. It may be found in eastern and southern U.S. where magnolia is a native tree. (2) Two other species of *Collybia* which grow on decaying mushrooms have a distribution similar to *C. tuberosa. Collybia cookei* (not shown) has nearly round, lighter brown to yellowish sclerotia. *Collybia cirrhata* (not shown) looks like *C. tuberosa* and *C. cookei* but does not produce sclerotia.

Coincaps: Genus *Cyptotrama*

GOLDEN COINCAP *Cyptotrama chrysopepla*　　**Pl. 15**
Very small, bright golden yellow, dry cap and *stalk. Gills white* to *yellow.* Grows *on wood.* ***Cap:*** Convex to flat, often lined or furrowed near margin. Surface dull to powdery or scaly. Gills adnate (broadly attached) or decurrent (extending down stalk); thick, broad, subdistant. Odor and taste not distinctive. ***Stalk:*** Cylindric; firm. Surface dry; color and texture like cap or lighter. No veil. ***Spore print:*** White. **Technical notes:** Cap 0.5–2.0 cm. Stalk 1–4 cm long × 2–3 mm thick. Spores smooth, non-amyloid, ellipsoid; 8–12 × 6.0–7.5 µm. Pleurocystidia and cheilocystidia fusoid to fusoid-ventricose. Cap cuticle a filamentous palisade.
Fruiting: Few to many; on logs, sticks, and buried wood of deciduous trees. Common and widespread, but never in great numbers. Spring to fall.
Edibility: Unknown.
Similar species: Golden Coincap is quite distinctive in size, texture, and color. Some very small species of *Pholiota* (scalecaps, p. 270, Pl. 33) have a similar dry appearance, but these are brownish and usually have a ring on stalk. They produce a brown spore print.

Grainy Caps: Genus *Cystoderma*

SAFFRON PARASOL *Cystoderma amianthinum*   **Pl. 15**
Small, fragile, light brown to *yellowish,* more or less *grainy cap*
on a *slender stalk* with a *faint ring.* **Cap:** Broadly convex to
humped. Surface dry, sometimes powdery or scaly or just powdery to grainy. Margin toothed or ragged from veil fragments;
sometimes lighter than disc (center). Flesh thin; white. Odor
and taste not distinctive. *Gills* close to crowded, narrowly attached to stalk, sometimes by a tooth; broad, *white* to *pale
yellowish.* **Stalk:** Thin, fragile, hollow; equal in diameter or
somewhat enlarged towards base. Surface colored like cap; ornamented with soft, granular scales below *poorly developed
ring.* Base clothed with cottony white filaments. **Spore print:**
White. **Technical notes:** Cap 2–4 cm across. Stalk 3–6 ×
0.3–0.7 cm. Spores ellipsoid; 5.5–6.5 × 3.0–3.5 μm.
Fruiting: Scattered to clustered; on mosses or needle beds under conifers. Summer to fall. Widespread, often common from
Virginia north to western N. America.
Edibility: Probably edible, but too small to be important as
food.
Similar species: Several other grainy caps (species of *Cystoderma*) are easily confused with Saffron Parasol *(C. amianthinum)*: (1) Deceptive Grainy Cap *(Cystoderma fallax,* not
shown) and (2) *Cystoderma granosum* (not shown) both have a
persistent ring. *C. granosum,* which is similarly covered with
grainy or powdery scales, is found on decaying hardwood logs
in central and eastern U.S. (3) Cinnabar Grainy Cap *(Cystoderma cinnabarinum,* not shown) is distinctly larger and
flushed with pinkish to pinkish brown. The species are more
readily distinguished on microscopic characters.

Genus *Flammulina*

VELVET SHANK *Flammulina velutipes*   **Pl. 17**
Clumps of small to medium, *shiny, orange-yellow caps* with
yellowish white gills. Stalk flexible; lower part dark brown and
velvety, often fused with other stalks *at base.* Grows *on wood.*
Cap: Convex, with an inrolled margin at first; becoming nearly
flat or with a low, indistinct hump, sometimes developing a
flaring outer limb and margin in age. Surface smooth, shiny;
sticky when wet. Yellow to orange or brownish orange; darker
on disc (center) and light at margin. Flesh thick on disc, thin
outward; white to yellowish. Odor and taste not distinctive.
Gills notched, subdistant, broad; yellowish white. **Stalk:**
Cylindric, or lower part tapers downward. Yellowish white at
apex, becoming darker to dark brown at base at maturity; surface minutely hairy. Interior becomes hollow in age. No ring.

Spore print: White. **Technical notes:** Cap 1.5–6.5 cm across. Stalk 2–7 × 0.3–1.0 cm. Spores smooth, ellipsoid; 6.5–9.0 × 2.5–4.0 µm. Pleurocystidia and cheilocystidia fusoid-ventricose with an obtuse apex. Pileocystidia project through slimy cuticle.

Fruiting: Widespread on hardwoods; fruits all year long. Common on aspen and willow in western states and on elm in the Midwest and East.

Edibility: Edible and easily grown in culture. Enotake, a very slender form with a poorly developed cap, is sold in Oriental food specialty stores.

Remarks: The dark brown to blackish, velvety stalk base; sticky yellow to orange or brown cap; and habit of growing in clusters on wood make this a distinctive species among N. American white-spored species that lack a ring on the stalk. It is one of the few species that fruits in winter, even in cold climates.

H. petaloides

Genus *Hohenbuehelia*

LEAF OYSTER *Hohenbuehelia petaloides*   **Pl. 20**
Small to medium, *fan-shaped, thin, brown cap* with *crowded gills. Grows singly* or *clustered* on *decaying, often moss-covered wood.* **Cap:** Wedge-shaped to *fan-shaped* or spatula-like; tapers to a stemlike base from the beginning but has *no true stalk.* Margin incurved at first, may be streaked in age. Surface moist to gelatinous, but not sticky; hygrophanous (fades as it dries). Moderate brown to moderate or grayish yellowish brown at base and center of cap, lighter toward margin. Flesh thick, pale brownish gray. Odor and taste not distinctive. Gills decurrent (extending down stalk); narrow, pale dingy yellowish gray. Gills may have fringed edges. ***Spore print:*** White. **Technical notes:** Cap 2–5 × 4–10 cm. Spores smooth, non-amyloid, elliptic; 7–9 × 4–5 µm. Pleurocystidia abundant; fusoid, thickwalled. Cheilocystidia similar but smaller. Flesh of cap has gelatinous layer (see **Remarks**).

Fruiting: Scattered or in groups; *on decaying wood* of both coniferous and deciduous trees. Sometimes grows from *moss-covered* stumps or logs. Quebec to North Carolina and West. Summer and fall.

Edibility: Edible.

Similar species: (1) *Hohenbuehelia mastrucatus* (not shown) has unpleasant odor. *Hohenbuehelia angustatus* (not shown) has a lighter, more pinkish-colored cap and globose spores.

Remarks: Species of *Hohenbuehelia* were formerly included in the genus *Pleurotus,* with the other oyster mushrooms that are shaped somewhat like an oyster shell (see Pl. 20). A combination of mostly microscopic characters distinguish them, although a lengthwise section of a fresh cap may show the *gelatinous layer* of the cap flesh as a somewhat watery line near the cap surface.

**H.
aurantiacus**

Genus *Hygrophoropsis*

FALSE CHANTERELLE   **Pl. 16**
Hygrophoropsis aurantiacus
Small to medium, *orange, flat* to *funnel-shaped cap* with *crowded, repeatedly forked, strongly decurrent gills. No ring* on stalk. *Cap:* Convex to flat at first, with a downturned outer limb and margin; soon becoming funnel-shaped, often lobed. Surface minutely hairy; orange-yellow to brownish orange. sometimes tinged with brownish gray over disc (center). Flesh thin, soft; nearly white or tinged with orange. Taste not distinctive.* Gills narrow; orange to orange-yellow. *Stalk:* Sometimes eccentric (off center), bent or twisted; tapers upward from enlarged base. Surface dry, minutely velvety to unpolished; orange-yellow to brownish orange. *Spore print: White* to *yellowish white.* **Technical notes:** Cap 2–6 cm across. Stalk 2.5–7.0 × 0.3–1.2 cm. Spores smooth, dextrinoid, elliptic; 5–8 × 3.0–4.5 μm.
Fruiting: Single to scattered or clustered; on soil or decaying wood, including charred wood. Hardwood and coniferous forests; widely distributed in northern U.S. and Canada. Late summer and fall.
Edibility: Questionable. Frequently reported as poisonous, but some people apparently eat it without ill effects. Its reputation for poisoning may be due to confusion with the toxic *Omphalotus illudens* (Jack-O-Lantern), just as its reputation as a non-toxic edible species may result from confusion with the highly prized *Cantharellus cibarius* (Chanterelle).
Similar species: False Chanterelle *(Hygrophoropsis aurantiacus)* is frequently misidentified, as mentioned above under **Edibility.** The colors and very narrow, repeatedly branched gills suggest (1) a chanterelle (*Cantharellus,* p. 81, Pl. 7) to some, but the gills or ridges of chanterelles are always *thick,* with *rounded edges,* and are *widely spaced* or reduced to little more than *faint ribs* or *lines.* (2) Gills of *Omphalotus* (Jack-O-Lantern, p. 178, Pl. 17) are broader than in *Hygrophoropsis* and are *not repeatedly* branched (see detail on Pl. 16). (3) Orange to

* See p. 10 for cautions about using taste as an identifying characteristic.

yellow species of *Gymnopilus*—such as Showy Flamecap or Big Laughing Mushroom (p. 298, Pl. 37)—which are sometimes confused with *Hygrophoropsis* produce brownish spore prints and usually have a *conspicuous ring* on stalk. Both Jack-O-Lantern and Showy Flamecap are **poisonous.**

Tallowgills: Genus *Laccaria*

Small to medium, rarely large, hygrophanous mushrooms (colors fade with age). Cap not readily separated from stalk. Stalk slender to thick, sometimes fibrous; ringless. *Gills somewhat waxy;* flesh- to violet-colored. Spore print white or flushed with violet. Spores smooth to ornamented; non-amyloid (do not stain blue in iodine).

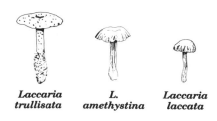

Laccaria   *L.*   *Laccaria*
trullisata   *amethystina*   *laccata*

AMETHYST TALLOWGILL *Laccaria amethystina*   **Pl. 18**
Small to medium, *slender mushroom. Purple all over.* Surface of cap *watery;* fades as it dries. Widely spaced gills extend down fragile stalk. ***Cap:*** Convex, soon becoming depressed at center and sometimes becoming shallowly funnel-shaped in age. Surface smooth at first, later becoming roughened as it breaks to form soft, somewhat powdery scales. Color varies, but some shade of *purple all over.* Hygrophanous—moderate violet to moderate purple when young and moist, fading to light reddish purple or lighter; flushed with reddish brown as purples fade and finally drying purplish gray. Cap may be streaked near margin when moist. Odor and taste not distinctive. Gills adnate (broadly attached) or decurrent (extending down stalk); subdistant. Gills broad; colored like cap surface or lighter, but violet persists longer than on cap. ***Stalk:*** Cylindric, zigzag, hollow at maturity. Surface fibrillose, colored like cap or lighter; base white-cottony. ***Spore print:*** *White* or flushed with *pale violet.* **Technical notes:** Cap 1–5 cm across. Stalk 3–8 × 0.4–1.0 cm. Spores echinate (spiny), non-amyloid, globose; 7–9 μm. Clamps present on hyphae.
Fruiting: Solitary or in groups or small clumps; in wet places, often in deep leaf litter. Hardwood forests east of Great Plains. Summer and early autumn.

Edibility: Reportedly edible, but few people get excited about eating purple food.

Similar species: Formerly considered a color variant of *Laccaria laccata* (Deceiver, below), but darker, more violet colors and tendency to develop a more funnel-shaped cap distinguish it. This is strictly a species of moist, shady hardwood forests, in comparison with (1) other tallowgills (species of *Laccaria*) that may be found in more open forests, grassy places or lawns (see *L. ochropurpurea,* p. 157), or sandy soils and dunes (see *L. trullisata,* p. 157). (2) Violet Webcap *(Cortinarius violaceus,* p. 294, Pl. 36) is larger. (3) *Inocybe lilacina* (not shown) is smaller than Amethyst Tallowgill *(L. amethystina).* Both *C. violaceus* and *I. lilacina* produce brownish spore prints.

DECEIVER *Laccaria laccata*   **Pl. 18**
Small, *pink* to *brownish cap* (fades quickly as it dries); *rounded* to *flat,* often *shallowly depressed* at center. *Gills waxy; pale purplish pink. Slender stalk.* **Cap:** Convex at first, later becoming broadly convex to flat, often flaring on outer limb and margin. Surface smooth at first, but usually breaking at a very early stage to form minute, very soft, upturned scales that give the cap a scruffy texture; sometimes with indistinct radiating streaks. *Hygrophanous* — yellowish pink to reddish orange or brownish orange when young, fading in sunlight. Flesh thin, soft; colored like surface; watery texture. Odor and taste not distinctive. Gills adnate (broadly attached) or short-decurrent (extending slightly down stalk); distant, broad, and thick; nearly white to yellowish pink or grayish pink. **Stalk:** Cylindrical, straight or bent; firm. Surface smooth to roughened, with minute lengthwise (vertical) scales or fibrils in age (use hand lens); colored like cap. No ring. **Spore print:** White. **Technical notes:** Cap 1–4 cm across. Stalk 2–6 cm × 3–7 mm. Spores echinulate (spiny), non-amyloid, subglobose to broadly ellipsoid; 7.5–10 × 7.0–8.5 μm.

Fruiting: Solitary to scattered or in groups; on damp soil, moss beds, and muck, often in open places or streamsides in a great variety of plant communities. Very widespread in N. America. Late spring to fall.

Edibility: Edible, but not highly rated.

Similar species: This nearly ubiquitous little mushroom appears in such an exasperating array of variant forms that, although it is one of our more common species, it is also one of the more difficult ones for inexperienced mushroom hunters to recognize in the field. Most often it simply causes bewilderment rather than confusion with any other species in particular. The waxy gills often suggest (1) a waxycap (species of *Hygrophorus,* p. 202), particularly when their color has faded. In general appearance Deceiver *(L. laccata)* resembles (2) a coincap (species of *Collybia,* p. 147), or a funnelcap (species of *Clitocybe,* p. 138), but it may be recognized in the field by its pinkish, waxy gills, visible in favorable condition. (3) Other tallowgills (species of *Laccaria*) are distinguished by their fairly distinctive size, color, odor, habitat, and so on.

PURPLE-OCHRE TALLOWGILL **Pl. 18**
Laccaria ochropurpurea
Medium to large mushroom; *often stout* or *coarse.* **Cap:** *Rounded* to *flat;* surface *smooth* or *roughened. Purple, fading* to *brownish* or *nearly white.* Convex, with an incurved margin at first; soon becoming shallowly depressed on disc (center), eventually flat or with an irregularly flaring limb and margin. Surface smooth and hygrophanous (water-soaked) at first, fading quickly to unpolished, sometimes with small soft scales. Flesh firm; watery when fresh. Odor not distinctive; taste unpleasant. Gills adnate (broadly attached) or subdecurrent (extending slightly down stalk); distant. Gills waxy, thick, broad; light purple at first, soon fading to purplish white. **Stalk:** Cylindric or enlarged in middle or base; solid, firm. Surface watery and streaked at first, soon becoming dry, smooth. Colored like cap or lighter and more brownish. No ring. **Spore print:** White to purplish white. **Technical notes:** Cap 4–15 cm. Stalk 4–15 × 1–3 cm. Spores echinulate (spiny), globose; 6–9 μm in diameter. Spines 1–2 μm long. Cheilocystidia irregular.
Fruiting: Solitary or in groups; on soil in hardwood forests, often in grassy open places, or in lawns, parks, etc. East of Rocky Mts. Summer and fall.
Edibility: Unenthusiastic reports claim it is edible.
Similar species: This tallowgill is fairly common, but its great variability and lack of truly distinctive characters make it difficult to recognize. A combination of rapidly fading, purplish colors; size; habitat; and the somewhat waxy, thick gills helps to distinguish it from (1) other tallowgills (species of *Laccaria*) and numerous species in other genera. *Laccaria ochropurpurea* is often confused with (2) violet-colored webcaps (species of *Cortinarius*), which produce rusty brown spore prints (see p. 294, Pl. 36).

SANDY TALLOWGILL *Laccaria trullisata* **Pl. 18**
Small to medium, *reddish brown cap,* with *purplish, waxy gills. Robust stalk.* Grows *in sand.* **Cap:** Convex but somewhat flattened at first, expanding to a flat cap with a broad, shallow depression and often a flaring limb and margin. Surface moist, streaked, or spotted, soon developing minute, soft, upturned scales. Reddish brown, fading quickly to light grayish pink. Flesh firm; brownish. Odor and taste not distinctive. Gills adnate (broadly attached) or with a decurrent tooth extending down stalk; subdistant. Gills thick, broad; purplish pink to purple. **Stalk:** Cylindrical to club-shaped, with the base rooted fairly deeply in sand and coated with cottony, purplish white filaments that are intergrown with sand. Surface fibrillose

above sand level and colored like cap. **Spore print:** White.
Technical notes: Cap 2.5–8.0 cm across. Stalk 3–10 × 0.8–2 cm. Spores long-ellipsoid; *smooth,* 16–20 × 6–8 μm.
Fruiting: Solitary or in groups, often in arcs or rows; on *very sandy soil, sand dunes,* or sand breaks above ocean or lake beaches or streamsides. Great Lakes eastward. Summer and fall.
Edibility: Unknown.
Remarks: Purplish to brown colors, waxy gills, and sandy habitat distinguish this species quite well. It is sometimes so deeply rooted in the sand that only the cap shows above it and all surfaces, but most particularly stalk and gills, are plastered with sand. The smooth pores are unusual in *Laccaria.*

Sawgills: Genus *Lentinellus*

Lentinellus ursinus

Medium-sized, tough, more or less fan-shaped caps (brackets) that grow on wood. Stalk may be absent; if present, it may be off center or attached at one side. *Gills have sawtoothed edges.* Spore print white. Spores minutely spiny, amyloid (turn blue in iodine solution).

NAVEL SAWGILL *Lentinellus omphalodes*   **Pl. 17**
Small to medium, *often lobed, smooth, brown, moist cap* with *depressed disc* (center). *Gill edges ragged. Short, ridged stalk.*
Cap: Convex, with an incurved margin, expanding to broadly convex or nearly flat but retaining depressed disc. Light to moderate grayish or yellowish brown, fading with age and becoming pale, dingy orange-yellow when dried. Flesh soft; white. Odor lacking; taste bitter to peppery.* Gills adnate (broadly attached), subdistant; broad, with irregularly torn or toothed edges: grayish yellowish pink. **Stalk:** Central or eccentric (off center); cylindric. Surface smooth to ridged or furrowed; reddish brown. **Spore print:** Pale grayish yellow.
Technical notes: Cap 1–5 cm across. Stalk 0.5–4.5 cm × 1–5 mm. Spores minutely spiny, amyloid, short-ellipsoid; 5–6.5 × 3.5–4.5 μm.
Fruiting: Solitary or in small groups; on soil and forest debris in both coniferous and hardwood forests. Widely distributed. Summer and fall.
Edibility: Unknown.
Similar species: Often confused with (1) *Lentinellus cochleatus* (not shown), which has fused stalks, a more slender vase-like shape, and a cap more eccentric on stalk. It is found in hardwood forests east of the Rocky Mts. (2) *Lentinellus vul-*

* **See p. 10 for cautions about using taste as an identifying characteristic.**

pinus (not shown) is more robust and has a hairy cap surface. In (3) *Lentinus ursinus* (Hairy Sawgill, below) and (4) *Lentinellus montanus* (not shown), both found near melting snowbanks at high elevations, the cap is laterally attached, sometimes with a rudimentary stalk or none at all. *Lentinellus montanus* is edible.

HAIRY SAWGILL *Lentinellus ursinus*   **Pl. 17**
Small to medium, *dry, brown cap; bracket-like.* Gills *close, ragged-edged. Clusters of brackets sometimes overlap.* Grows *on decaying wood.* **Cap:** Convex to flat. Surface smooth or minutely hairy near margin (use hand lens); sparsely to densely hairy toward center, with dark, fairly stiff hairs. Dark brown to dark orange-yellow. Flesh firm; nearly white. Odor sweet, aromatic; taste bitter or peppery.* ***Spore print:*** White. **Technical notes:** Cap 2–10 cm across. ***Stalk:*** Lacking or rudimentary. Spores echinulate (spiny), amyloid, subglobose; 3.0–4.5 × 2.0–3.5 µm.

Fruiting: Few to many; sometimes in overlapping clusters, on decaying wood of both coniferous and deciduous trees. Widely distributed in N. America. Summer and fall.

Edibility: Unknown, but *Lentinellus montanus* from high elevations in western mountains is edible and has long been confused with *L. ursinus.*

Similar species: (1) *Lentinellus montanus* (not shown) is always found *near or under melting snow;* otherwise best distinguished from *L. ursinus* by microscopic characters. (2) *Lentinellus vulpinus* (not shown) has *well-developed, fused stalks* and white to yellowish hairs on cap. It sometimes grows from wounds of living trees. (3) Species of several genera, including *Panus, Panellus* (p. 179), *Pleurotus* (p. 181), and *Hohenbuehelia* (p. 153) have a similar bracket-like growth form, but they all have *smooth-edged* gills and differ in microscopic characters.

Sawgills: Genus *Lentinus*

Small to large, firm to tough cap, with *sawtooth-edged gills.* Cap firmly attached to central to eccentric (off-center) stalk. Grows on wood. Spore print white to yellowish. Spores non-amyloid (do not turn blue in iodine solution).

*Lentinus
lepideus
(section)*

SCALY SAWGILL *Lentinus lepideus*   **Pl. 15**
Medium to large, *round cap,* with *brown scales. Gills white* to *yellowish,* with *sawtoothed edges. Tough, scaly stalk* with *high ring.* Grows from *conifer wood.* **Cap:** Convex at first, becoming

---

* **See p. 10 for cautions about using taste as an identifying characteristic.**

nearly flat, sometimes with an indistinct, rounded hump. Margin incurved at first and sometimes beaded with moisture. Surface fairly sticky when young, soon becoming dry and often cracking; yellowish white between brown scales. Flesh tough; white. Odor variable; taste faint, somewhat disagreeable. Gills notched around apex of stalk or subdecurrent, subdistant (see inside front cover); white at first, but soon tinged with yellow as they dry and cap expands. *Stalk:* Cylindric above, tapered below to a pointed base; solid, tough. Surface white and fibrillose above ring; white between scales below ring. Scales are white to reddish brown and recurved. Base of stalk stains reddish brown with handling or in age; upper part becomes dingy yellowish. *Spore print:* White. **Technical notes:** Cap 5–15 cm across. Stalk 3–10 × 1–2 cm. Spores smooth, non-amyloid, long-ellipsoid; 8–15 × 4–6 µm. Pleurocystidia fusoid-ventricose to nearly cylindric. Cheilocystidia filamentous, crooked.

Fruiting: Solitary to scattered, on *coniferous stumps and logs;* also on fenceposts, railroad ties, and construction timbers. Widespread in N. America. Fruits in warm weather throughout growing season.

Edibility: Edible. Young caps are highly rated by some, but may require long cooking time.

Similar species: (1) The stalk of Giant Sawgill (*Lentinus ponderosus,* not shown) develops patchy to recurved scales but *never produces a distinct ring* as in *L. lepideus* (Scaly Sawgill). *Lentinus ponderosus* is found in the Northwest on coniferous wood. (2) *Lentinus spretus* (not shown) is found in the East. It is usually more slender, with a thinner cap, smaller spores, and more decurrent gills that stain bright yellow when cut or bruised.

TIGER SAWGILL *Lentinus tigrinus*					**Pl. 15**
Small to medium, *dry cap* with *dark brown* to *blackish scales. Scaly white stalk.* Grows *on wood,* often *in clusters. Cap:* Round at first, sometimes with a low, indistinct knob; later flat or shallowly funnel-shaped as it matures. Surface fibrillose to scaly; yellowish white between dark scales. Flesh tough, white; thin over outer disc and limb. Odor weak or lacking; taste not distinctive. Gills close, short-decurrent (extending slightly down stalk); white to yellowish white, with ragged edges. *Stalk:* Central or eccentric (off center); cylindric above, tapered downward; often bent. Surface fibrillose to scaly, with a thin ring which may disappear with age. Upper stalk nearly white; brown at base. *Spore print:* White. **Technical notes:** Cap 1.5–6.0 cm across. Stalk 2–6 × 0.5–1.0 cm. Spores narrow, smooth, non-amyloid, ellipsoid; 6–10 × 2.5–3.5 µm. Cheilocystidia filamentous, contorted. No pleurocystidia.

Fruiting: Occasionally single, more often in groups or clusters; on hardwood logs or water-soaked wood. Widespread in deciduous forests, east of the Rocky Mts. Spring to early fall.

Edibility: Unknown, but presumably non-poisonous.

Similar species: Small size and hardwood substrate distinguish Tiger Sawgill (*L. tigrinus*) from most scaly species of *Lentinus* growing in this area, including (1) Scaly Sawgill (*L. lepideus,* above). (2) *Lentinus sulcatus* (not shown) is somewhat scaly; it is orange to brown and has a pale-colored spore print. Smith and Weber (1979) report it growing from avalanche debris (felled aspens) in the Rocky Mts.

Remarks: In variety *squamosum* of *L. tigrinus* — an unusual form that was at one time considered a separate species — the cap does not fully expand and the gills remain covered by the veil, even after the spores have developed. This variety was formerly regarded as an abortive or puffball form of a different fungus *(Lentodium squamulosum)* but is now known to belong to the species *Lentinus tigrinus.*

False Funnelcaps: Genus *Leucopaxillus*

Medium to large, dry caps, with solid, thick flesh. Gills narrow, adnate (broadly attached) or decurrent (extending down stalk); often crowded. Firm, fleshy stalk often has *masses of white strands radiating into substrate* (usually duff); no veils. Spore print white. Spores have amyloid ornamentation (turns blue in iodine).

L. gentianeus

FALSE FUNNELCAP *Leucopaxillus albissimus*   **Pl. 18**
Medium to large, *dry, white* to *pale yellow cap; brownish over disc* (center). *Gills close. Stalk chalky white; base* surrounded by a *mat* of *abundant white threads* and *conifer needles.* **Cap:** Broadly convex, with a strongly incurved margin at first; expanding to flat or remaining broadly convex to indistinctly humped, sometimes with an irregular, flaring outer limb and margin. Surface smooth and unpolished to scurfy; often ribbed on margin. Flesh thick, firm; white, dry. Odor pungent and unpleasant; taste bitter.* **Stalk:** Often eccentric (off center); cylindric or club-shaped, with a tapered base; tough. **Spore print:** White. **Technical notes:** Cap 5–15 cm across. Stalk 3–8 × 0.8–3.0 cm. Spores amyloid, minutely warty, ellipsoid; 5–8 × 3.5–5.0 μm. Cheilocystidia scattered, filamentous.

Fruiting: Solitary to clustered; on humus and well-decayed wood (usually of conifers). Widespread in N. America. Summer and fall.

Edibility: Inedible.

Similar species: Easily confused with large, white or light-colored funnelcaps (species of *Clitocybe,* p. 138), many of which have *faintly colored spore prints*. Be sure to check spore print

---

* See p. 10 for cautions about using taste as an identifying characteristic.

color carefully (use white paper). (1) *Clitocybe robusta* (not shown) has a *yellowish* spore print, compared with the white spore print of *Leucopaxillus albissimus* (False Funnelcap). The *mat of conifer needles,* held together by *white filaments* around the stalk base and surrounding soil, helps distinguish *Leucopaxillus* species from some species of *Clitocybe.* (2) See Early False Funnelcap (*L. laterarius,* p. 163).

Remarks: Contrary to advice given in some mushroom books, spore prints should always be made *on white paper,* never on black or other colored paper which could make pale-colored spore prints appear white.

BITTER FALSE FUNNELCAP   **Pl. 18**
Leucopaxillus gentianeus
Medium to large, *dry, reddish brown cap; rounded* to *flat. Gills white* or *yellowish, close* to *crowded. White filaments mat conifer needles* around *stalk base.* **Cap:** Convex at first, expanding to flat or nearly so, with a persistently downturned margin; sometimes shallowly funnel-shaped, with a flaring limb. Surface smooth, unpolished; often cracking in age. Reddish orange to reddish brown on center, lighter outwards, becoming pale orange-yellow or yellowish white at margin. Flesh firm, thick, dry, white; tapering gradually from disc (center) to narrow, thin margin. Odor faint but pungent when present; taste *bitter,* strong.* Gills adnate (broadly attached to stalk) or subdecurrent (extending down it slightly), rounded at stalk; narrow, and separable from cap. Gills are sometimes spotted or streaked with reddish brown in age. **Stalk:** Cylindric or club-shaped. Surface smooth or minutely powdered; white or stained brownish, especially from bruising or handling. **Spore print:** White (be sure to use white paper). **Technical notes:** Cap 4–15 cm across. Stalk 4–8 × 1–3 cm. Spores amyloid, warty, subglobose (nearly round); 4–6 × 3.5–5.5 μm. Cheilocystidia present. Clamps present on hyphae.

Fruiting: Solitary or in groups, often forming fairy rings on decaying humus under conifers. Common from Rocky Mts. westward. Summer and fall.

Edibility: Unknown.

Similar species: The combination of color, bitter taste, and round spores is distinctive among the false funnelcaps (species of *Leucopaxillus*). The white spore print, reddish brown color, dry cap, and mat of conifer duff clinging to lower stalk by white filaments helps to separate this species from similar large species of *Clitocybe.*

Remarks: This species is sometimes "squatty," having a stalk which is deeply buried in the duff and appears to be too short for the massive cap. It is often remarkably prolific and the clean, dry caps are most attractive.

* See p. 10 for cautions about using taste as an identifying characteristic.

EARLY FALSE FUNNELCAP   Pl. 18
Leucopaxillus laterarius

Medium to large cap; *round* to *flat* or *flaring*. Cap *dull white* or *flushed with yellowish pink*. Gills crowded. Stalk *white;* often *enlarged at base*. Grows in *hardwood forests*. **Cap:** Obtuse to broadly convex, with a low, rounded hump and an incurved margin at first; soon expanded to flat, often with a broad, low depression and a flaring limb and margin; outline sometimes lobed or indented. Surface smooth, dry and unpolished or minutely scurfy; often grooved near margin. Odor unpleasant; taste *very bitter*.* Gills narrow, adnate (broadly attached) or subdecurrent — sometimes continued down stalk by a line; white to dingy yellowish white. **Stalk:** Cylindric or *club-shaped;* solid. Surface dry, smooth to minutely downy; cottony at base. **Spore print:** White. **Technical notes:** Cap 5–15 cm across. Stalk 4–10 × 1–2 cm. Spores amyloid, warty, subglobose (nearly round); 3.5–5.5 × 3.5–4.5 μm. Cheilocystidia filamentous. Clamps present on hyphae.

Fruiting: Solitary to scattered or in groups; on soil and forest litter in hardwood forests. Great Lakes eastward. Early summer and fall.

 Edibility: Non-poisonous, but unpalatable (bitter-tasting).

Similar species: Lighter color; smaller, round spores; and fruiting in hardwood forests (not among conifers) distinguish Early False Funnelcap from (1) False Funnelcap (*L. albissimus,* p. 161). White spore print and bitter taste contrast with (2) large, white species of *Clitocybe* (funnelcaps, p. 138).

False Funnelcaps: Genus *Lyophyllum*

Cap medium to large, white to grayish brown or brownish black; often stains dark gray to black when cut or bruised. Cap central to eccentric (off center), on a ringless stalk. Cap and stalk do not *L.* separate readily. Spore print white or pale grayish *montanum* yellow.

FRIED CHICKEN MUSHROOM   Pl. 18
Lyophyllum decastes

Medium to large, *moist, grayish brown caps; rounded* to *flat,* often *irregularly shaped*. *White stalks stain brownish* when cut or bruised. Grows *in clumps on ground*. **Cap:** Convex or humped, with an incurved margin; outline often lobed or indented. Soon flat or nearly so, often with arching limb and margin. Surface smooth; moist to slippery. Hygrophanous — light grayish brown, sometimes yellowish brown on disc (center) and somewhat translucent. Flesh thin, firm; white. Odor

---

* See p. 10 for cautions about using taste as an identifying characteristic.

and taste slightly pungent. Gills adnate (broadly attached) subdistant, narrow, uneven; *dingy* — yellowish white, becoming brownish in age. **Stalk:** Cylindric or tapered at apex; usually bent or contorted. Fused at base. Surface smooth or minutely fibrillose; white or staining brownish. No ring. **Spore print:** White. **Technical notes:** Cap 3–12 cm across. Stalk 3–8 × 1.0–2.5 cm. Spores smooth, non-amyloid; subglobose to broadly ellipsoid; 4–6 × 4–5 μm.

Fruiting: Large clusters on soil, grassy areas, roadsides, waste places, around old sawdust piles. Widely distributed in N. America. Summer to late autumn.

Edibility: Edible and reportedly good.

Remarks: Although widespread and fairly common, this species is not always easily recognized.

SNOW FUNNEL *Lyophyllum montanum* **Pl. 18**
Small to medium, *thin, dingy grayish brown cap; rounded to flat. Slender, curved stalk with white, cottony base.* Grows *in or near melting snowbanks.* **Cap:** Broadly convex to obtuse, often with an irregular outline and downturned margin at first. Soon flat and often broadly and shallowly depressed on disc (center), frequently developing a flaring limb and margin in age, occasionally with a low, broad hump at center. Surface smooth, moist (partially water-soaked); dark grayish brown, fading to light grayish yellowish brown or grayish yellow with a hoary cast in all stages when fresh, becoming dingy pale yellow as it dries. The thin cap margin appears scorched in old specimens. Flesh thin; watery gray at first, fading to dingy yellowish white. Odor and taste not distinctive. Gills broadly notched around apex of stalk, close, thin; *dingy* — gray to yellowish white. **Stalk:** Cylindric or slightly enlarged at base; lower part typically curved in a wide arc. Surface smooth to minutely fibrillose; color dingy (similar to gills). Base of stalk clothed in *white, cottony filaments* which bind conifer needles and forest litter into a compact mat. No ring. **Spore print:** White. **Technical notes:** Cap 2–7 cm across. Stalk 3–8 × 0.5–1.5 cm. Spores non-amyloid, smooth, ellipsoid; 6.5–8.0 × 3.5–4.0 μm. Clamps present.

Fruiting: Solitary or in groups or small clumps; often in fairy rings or rows, frequently projecting from a *melting snowbank.* Rocky Mts. Spring and early summer.

Edibility: Unknown.

Similar species: Aged specimens are almost indistinguishable in the field from another snowbank mushroom growing in the same area, White Strings (*Clitocybe albirhiza,* p. 138). Both of these mushrooms originate under snowbanks and often attain a considerable size while held flat against the ground by the weight of the snow above them. As the temperature rises, the snow melts faster around the mushroom, which is often seen projecting from a hole in the snowbank. The filaments around stalk base in Snow Funnel *(L. montanum)* form a very smooth-surfaced, almost shiny mat, lacking the distinct stringlike strands characteristic of White Strings *(Clitocybe albirhiza).*

Pinwheel Mushrooms: Genus *Marasmius*

Small to medium cap, usually centrally attached and not readily separated from stalk. Stalk thin but tough, white to blackish. Dried specimens often revive when moistened. Spore print white to pale yellowish. Cap cuticle a layer of nearly parallel hyphal tips with end cells that are variously branched or ornamented but not threadlike.

Marasmius   **Marasmius**   **M. andro-**   **Marasmius**
oreades   **rotula**   **saceus**   **siccus**

HORSEHAIR MUSHROOM   Pl. 19
Marasmius androsaceus
Very small,. round to *flat, paper-thin cap; pinkish white* to *yellowish pink.* Stalk very thin, *hairlike; shiny, nearly black.* Grows *on conifer needles.* **Cap:** Broadly conic to convex at first, expanding to flat or broadly depressed, with a flaring, wavy margin. Surface dry, smooth at first then minutely roughened; faint wrinkles or streaks radiate from margin inward. Flesh very thin, somewhat membranous; yellowish white to light yellowish brown. Odor and taste not distinctive; taste rarely slightly bitter. Gills broad, adnate (broadly attached) or notched around apex of stalk, subdistant to distant, sometimes forked; yellowish white at first, soon becoming light grayish or yellowish brown or flushed with grayish pink. **Stalk:** Cylindric or thickening toward top; straight or curved and often flattened (in cross-section). Interior hollow. Surface shiny, smooth. Stalk slender but tough; brownish pink at apex, brownish black at base, often with black stringy filaments matting substrate (needles and duff). No ring. **Spore print:** White. **Technical notes:** Cap 2–12 mm across. Stalk 2–6 cm long × 0.5–1.5 mm thick. Spores smooth, elliptic; 6–9 × 3–4 μm.
Fruiting: In groups, often in large numbers on conifer needles and debris. Widely distributed. Spring to fall, following rainy periods.
Edibility: Unknown.
Similar species: (1) *Marasmius pallidocephalus* (not shown) has light yellowish brown to pale orange-yellow caps and dif-

fers in microscopic anatomical features. (2) *Marasmius thujinus* (not shown) has smaller caps with an incurved margin (sometimes not fully expanding) and the stalk is thicker and lighter in color. *Marasmius thujinus* is a common and widespread little species that has a garlic odor when crushed, both from fresh specimens and dried ones that have been remoistened.

FAIRY RING MUSHROOM *Marasmius oreades*   **Pl. 19**
Groups of small to medium, *bell-shaped* to *flat, brown* to *yellowish caps* on *slender, rigid stalks*. Grows *in fairy rings* on *grassy soil or fields*. *Cap:* Bluntly conic to bell-shaped, with a strongly incurved margin at first, soon becoming convex to humped or (in age) nearly flat, with an uplifted limb and margin. Hygrophanous (water-soaked) but drying out quickly; surface smooth and shiny when young and moist, sometimes with translucent streaks near margin, soon dull and opaque; may be finely felted upon drying. Young caps are deep brown, then light yellowish brown or more grayish brown, fading to yellowish white, sometimes tinged with yellowish pink or light yellow. Flesh thick on disc (center) and tapering abruptly over outer limb to a thin margin; white or pale yellowish white. Odor faintly fragrant; taste not distinctive. *Stalk:* Cylindric or enlarged at base; often rooting in soil. May be compressed and sometimes twisted in age. Firm and rigid; interior solid or stuffed with cottony filaments. Surface dry, dull, smooth to felty, opaque; yellowish white to moderate orange-yellow or light yellowish to reddish brown. Base covered with white fibrils, often matting dead grass leaves. *Spore print:* White. **Technical notes:** Cap 1–5 cm across. Stalk 2–7 cm long × 2–6 mm thick. Spores smooth, thin-walled, subglobose to ovate (egg-shaped); 7–10 × 3–6 μm.
Fruiting: Scattered, in groups or clusters (fairy rings) on grassy soil in lawns, parks, meadows, or shrubland; rarely under spruce trees. Widely distributed. Fruits throughout the season.
Edibility: Edible and choice, but make sure that you identify each mushroom you collect from the ring carefully. See below.
Similar species: Check the white spore print carefully to avoid confusion with numerous "little brown mushrooms" with brown spore prints, such as (1) *Galerina* (p. 296), (2) *Cortinarius* (p. 287), and (3) *Inocybe* (p. 301), some of which are **poisonous.** (4) The habitat distinguishes Fairy Ring Mushroom *(M. oreades)* from most other species of *Marasmius*. (5) In southern California a dingy gray species, *Marasmius albogriseus* (not shown), looks very much like *M. oreades* except for the color.

MAGENTA VELVET *Marasmius plicatulus*   **Pl. 19**
Small to medium, *bell-shaped* to *rounded, thin, reddish brown cap* with *velvety sheen*. *Long, wiry, brittle, deep brown stalk* with *white tuft at base*. *Cap:* Broadly conic to bell-shaped,

with a straight or slightly incurved margin at first, expanding to broadly convex with a broad, somewhat flaring limb. Long streaks extend inward from thin margin, which is flexible. Surface dry and minutely velvety; moderate to dark purplish red at first, becoming reddish brown overall. Flesh thin. Odor and taste not distinctive.* Gills very broad, rounded-adnate (broadly attached to stalk), subdistant; pale purplish pink to dingy, pale orange-yellow. *Stalk:* Cylindric, often bent or wavy; very long and slender. Surface polished when mature; purplish pink at first, soon darkening, first at base to dark reddish brown and eventually to blackish red overall. *Spore print:* White. **Technical notes:** Cap 1.0–4.5 cm across. Stalk 6–12 × 1.5–3.5 mm. Spores 11–15 × 5.0–6.5 μm.

Fruiting: In groups or clusters; on wood, leaf mold, or forest litter. Common under sitka spruce in fall in the Northwest; under live oak during winter rainy season in California.

Edibility: Caps are edible.

Similar species: Quite a distinctive species. Look for the relatively large caps for a *Marasmius*, the reddish brown colors, velvety sheen on cap, and dark, shiny stalk. Brown Roof (*Pluteus lutescens,* p. 251, Pl. 30) may have a cap of similar color, with a suggestion of velvety sheen, but it has a *yellow, fleshy stalk.*

PINWHEEL MUSHROOM *Marasmius rotula*   **Pl. 19**
Clumps of *small, thin, whitish, umbrella-shaped caps* with *widely spaced white gills* that are attached to a *collar* around the *wiry black stalk.* **Cap:** Hemispheric to broadly rounded, often with a slight central knob at first, soon expanding to flattened-convex with a narrow to broad, central depression and long, shallow to deep grooves radiating inward ⅓ to ¾ of cap radius from margin. Surface dry, dull, smooth; yellowish white overall or brownish, at least on depressed center; darker when young. Flesh thin, flexible. Odor not distinctive; taste mild, sometimes with a bitter aftertaste.* Gills adnate (broadly attached) or notched at broad or narrow collar which may be free or attached to stalk; thin but broad, distant; white. *Stalk:* Cylindric or slightly bulbous; straight or curved. Surface dry, smooth; dull or shiny, translucent at apex. Interior hollow. Pale light yellow at first, soon darkening at base to nearly black and becoming progressively lighter upward. *Spore print:* White or sometimes yellowish. **Technical notes:** Cap 1–2 cm across. Stalk 1.5–8.0 cm long × 0.5–1.0 mm diameter. Spores smooth, thin-walled, obovate to narrowly elliptic; 6.5–9.5 × 3.0–4.3 μm. Cystidia lacking.

Fruiting: Clustered on decaying wood of deciduous trees, less frequently on coniferous wood. Midwest to eastern North America. Spring to fall.

* See p. 10 for cautions about using taste as an identifying characteristic.

Edibility: Unknown.

Similar species: *Marasmius capillaris* (not shown) is smaller, darker colored, and grows on oak leaves.

ORANGE PINWHEEL   **Pl. 19**

Marasmius siccus

Small, rounded, dull orange to brown, very thin cap, with radiating folds or grooves. Stalk long and wiry, tough; yellowish to brown, shiny in age. **Cap:** Convex at first, soon becoming broadly convex to broadly bell-shaped, with a low, shallow central depression or low, rounded, narrow hump. Margin may be scalloped or lobed. Surface dry, dull, opaque; smooth at first, but soon roughened or minutely velvety. Flesh very thin, fragile to flexible; white. Odor not distinctive; taste usually mild, sometimes bitter or lacking. Gills notched around apex of stalk or free, thin, distant, fragile or flexible; narrow and straight at first (before cap expands), becoming moderately broad and bowed outward (toward cap margin) in age. Gill edges smooth. Gills white to yellowish white, rarely with a brownish orange edge. **Stalk:** Centrally attached; cylindrical or tapered slightly toward apex or occasionally distinctly swollen at apex or base. May be straight or curved. Surface dry; dull at first but becoming *polished* in age and on drying. Hollow; cartilaginous to horny. Yellowish white to pale yellow or rarely dark red at apex, becoming yellowish brown to deep brown overall; darker below than above and with a disk-like patch of yellowish white hairs at base. **Spore print:** White. **Technical notes:** Cap 0.25–3.0 cm across. Stalk 2–6 cm $\times$ 0.2–1.0 mm. Spores narrowly clavate (club-shaped), sometimes curved or irregular; 16–21 $\times$ 3.0–4.5 μm. Broom cells of gill edge and cap cuticle have yellowish to brown, fimbriate (fringe-like) projections.

Fruiting: Scattered or in small to large groups or troops; on leaf mold or forest litter of both hardwood and coniferous forests. East of Rocky Mts. from southern Canada to Carolinas and Tennessee. Summer and fall.

Edibility: Unknown.

Similar species: Frequently confused with several other species of *Marasmius,* including (1) *M. borealis* in northeastern U.S., which lacks the radial folds or grooves on cap. (2) *Marasmius bellipes* and (3) *M. pulcherripes* (not shown) have pink or purplish tints on cap, gills, or stalk apex that are lacking in *M. siccus.* (4) *Marasmius fulvoferrugineus* (not shown) is the common species of the southeastern U.S.; it is often mistakenly called *M. siccus.* The two are best distinguished on microscopic characters. *Marasmius fulvoferrugineus* is usually larger, has more brown, rather than orange colors. Although it has been reported as far north as New Jersey, it is found more commonly in the Great Smoky Mountains and southward, whereas *M. siccus* is more common north of the Great Smokies. They look very much alike in the field.

Cavaliers: Genus *Melanoleuca*

Medium to large, thin-fleshed cap; usually hygrophanous (fades with age or drying). Very slender, sometimes fragile stalk. Gills adnate (broadly attached) or notched around apex of stalk; often crowded. Spore print white to grayish yellow. Spores with amyloid ornamentation and plage (a non-ornamented zone near apicular end). Cystidia on gill edge often encrusted and with long, pointed apex.

YELLOWISH CAVALIER *Melanoleuca alboflavida*   **Pl. 18**
Small to medium, *thin, flat cap; yellow* to *brownish* or *whitish. Broad, white gills. Slender stalk; no ring.* **Cap:** Obtuse to broadly rounded at first, soon becoming flat with a shallow depression, sometimes with a low, rounded central knob. Margin incurved at first; finally upturned, sometimes with a flaring outer limb. Surface smooth; tacky when moist. Strong brownish yellow to pale yellow or yellowish white. Flesh whitish. Odor and taste not distinctive. Gills notched around apex of stalk, thin, crowded; white at first, later dingy yellowish white. **Stalk:** Cylindric above a slightly enlarged base; fragile. Dingy white with lengthwise streaks. **Spore print:** White. **Technical notes:** Cap 3–10 cm across. Stalk 3–9 × 0.5–1.0 cm. Spores ellipsoid, with amyloid warts; 7–9 × 4.0–5.5 μm. Pleuro- and cheilocystidia fusoid-ventricose with rounded tips.
Fruiting: Solitary or in groups; on soil in open, deciduous or mixed woods, along roads, or in fields; at low elevations east of Rocky Mts. Summer to early fall.
Edibility: Edible.
Similar species: *Melanoleuca evenosa* (not shown) is larger and more robust; it has more orange-yellow colors, sometimes with no trace of brown or with disc (center) flushed with brown. Cap shows a tendency to crack in age. Found at high elevations in Rocky Mts. and in northern boreal forests. *Melanoleuca evenosa* and *M. alboflavida* (Yellowish Cavalier) have similar microscopic characteristics, but their lighter, more yellow to orange-yellow colors set them apart from the numerous, grayish to gray-brown species that are common in the West.
COMMON CAVALIER *Melanoleuca melaleuca*   **Pl. 18**
Small to medium, *thin, flat, brown cap* with *wide, dingy white gills. Fragile, skinny, brownish stalk; no ring.* **Cap:** Convex at first, soon becoming flat, usually with a shallow central depression, sometimes with a low, rounded central hump. Surface smooth, hygrophanous; moist to slightly sticky, later dry. Brownish gray to grayish brown, yellowish brown, or olive-brown, center sometimes darker. Flesh thin, firm; white except brown or gray just under cuticle. Odor and taste not distinc-

tive or taste weak but unpleasant. Gills notched around apex of stalk, close, broad in center; white at first, but becoming dingy yellowish white in age. *Stalk:* Cylindric or with narrow basal bulb, fragile, white at apex to gray or brown below, lighter than cap color, fibrillose-streaked. *Spore print:* White. **Technical notes:** Cap 2–8 cm across. Stalk 3–10 cm × 3–10 mm. Spores amyloid, warty, ellipsoid; 6–9 × 4.0–5.5 μm. Cheilo- and pleurocystidia fusoid-ventricose, with sharply pointed tips; sometimes encrusted.

Fruiting: Solitary or in groups; on soil in pastures, meadows, or open woods in coniferous and hardwood forests. Widespread in N. America. Summer and fall (spring and fall in West).

Edibility: Edible in Europe, but no reliable reports in this country.

Similar species: Easily and commonly confused with several gray to brown species, particularly in the West. They can be distinguished only upon microscopic study. Yellowish Cavalier *(M. alboflavida)* is larger, with a nearly white to light yellowish brown cap and larger spores. It may be found from the Midwest to the East.

Genus *Micromphale*

STINKING PINWHEEL *Micromphale foetidum*   **Pl. 19**
Small, brown, round to *flat cap* with *depressed center; streaks* or folds extend *outward* to *ragged margin. Velvety brown stalk. Strong, unpleasant odor. Cap:* Convex at first, expanding to flat with a shallowly depressed disc (center); limb and margin tend to flare upward. Surface dry; light reddish brown, fading to light yellowish brown. Margin thin, incurved at first; later straight and irregularly indented or torn. Flesh thin. Gills adnate (broadly attached, to a collar around apex of stalk), distant, broad; moderate yellowish pink. *Stalk:* Cylindric, hollow; central or occasionally slightly eccentric (off center). Base cottony. *Spore print:* White. **Technical notes:** Cap 1–3 cm across. Stalk 2–3 cm × 1–2 mm. Spores smooth, elliptic; 8.5–10.0 × 3.5–4.0 μm.

Fruiting: In groups or clusters; on dead twigs, branches, and fallen wood. Great Lakes to Atlantic Coast and southern Canada to mid-South. Summer to early autumn.

Edibility: Unknown.

Remarks: Easily recognized by the foul odor, small size, color, and textures.

Fairy Helmets: Genus *Mycena*

Small to medium, often fragile, mostly *bell-shaped* to *conic caps.* In young specimens cap margin is *usually pressed against stalk,* which is very thin and fragile. Spore print white.

Mycena   M. haema-   Mycena   Mycena
epipterygia   topus   lilacifolia   overholtsii

STUMP FAIRY HELMET *Mycena alcalina*   **Pl. 19**
Thin, gray, bell-shaped caps. Alkaline (bleach-like) odor. Long,
thin, brittle stalks. Grows *singly* or *in clumps, on decaying*
wood or *forest litter.* **Cap:** Broadly conic to bell-shaped at first,
expanding and sometimes developing an upturned limb and
margin as it matures. Surface at first covered with a bluish
gray bloom, soon polished and slippery, partially water-
soaked; streaked. Gray to grayish brown, grayish yellowish
brown or black, sometimes nearly white on margin. Flesh thin;
white or grayish. Taste acidic. Gills adnate (broadly attached),
close to subdistant; white to grayish, sometimes with lighter-
colored edges. **Stalk:** Cylindric; tough but brittle, hollow. Surface colors and texture like cap, sometimes somewhat flattened. Sparse white mycelium (filaments) at base. **Spore**
print: White. **Technical notes:** Cap 1–3 cm across. Stalk 3–10
cm × 1–4 mm. Spores smooth, amyloid, elliptic; 8–11 ×
4.5–6.5 μm. Pleurocystidia and cheilocystidia abundant; fusoid-
ventricose with pointed to rounded, occasionally branched tips.
Fruiting: Solitary or in groups or clumps; on decaying conifer
wood, stumps, and rotting debris under conifers. Canada and
U.S., common and widespread in northern coniferous forests.
Spring and fall.
Edibility: Unknown.
Similar species: This is the most common and widespread of
a number of species that are indistinguishable in the field without the use of a microscope. It is also one of the most variable
in numerous characters, compounding the difficulty of distinguishing it from other ordinary-looking, gray species such as
Mycena leptocephala (not shown), which typically has a
weaker alkaline odor and more fragile stalk. Although the alkaline odor is usually strong in Stump Fairy Helmet *(M. alca-*
lina), it is sometimes so weak that it can be detected only by
crushing the flesh of a fresh specimen. Numerous Mycenas
that grow on wood lack an odor or have a different odor. In
most cases microscopic characters must be observed to identify
them accurately.

YELLOWSTALK FAIRY HELMET   Pl. 19
Mycena epipterygia

Small, *conic, dark yellow* to *light olive-brown, sticky cap,* on a *yellow, slimy stalk.* Grows *singly* or *in groups under conifers.* **Cap:** Broadly conic or ovoid with a prominent hump at first, becoming radially streaked; limb sometimes flared outward in later stages and margin may be irregularly torn. Surface smooth, *sticky;* lighter yellow toward margin, in age fading to yellowish white and sometimes flushed with pink or gray. Flesh thin, flexible; yellowish. Odor faintly fragrant or lacking; taste not distinctive. Gills adnate (broadly attached), subdistant, fairly broad; nearly white to yellow. **Stalk:** Cylindric, tubular; flexible. Surface *slimy* or sticky. Strong *yellow* at first, fading quickly in bright sunlight to yellowish white. **Spore print:** White. **Technical notes:** Cap 0.8–2.0 cm across. Stalk 5–8 cm × 1–2 mm. Spores amyloid, smooth, ovoid (egg-shaped); 8–11 × 5–6 μm. Cheilocystidia clavate (club-shaped), with irregular, sometimes branched, somewhat filamentous projections; gelatinizing. No pleurocystidia.

Fruiting: Scattered or in groups under conifers. Canada to Tennessee across the continent. Late summer to late fall.

Edibility: Unknown.

Similar species: The highly variable field characters of *Mycena epipterygia* (Yellowstalk Fairy Helmet) result in frequent confusion with related species which can be distinguished with certainty only on microscopic characters. A variety of the species that grows on wood and has more greenish to olivaceous colors may be distinguished by its *tendency to fade to white,* compared with (1) *Mycena epipterygioides* and (2) *M. griseoviridis* (not shown), which have olive-gray to olive-brown or darker colors that do not fade to white. (3) *Mycena viscosa* (not shown) has a strong, disagreeable odor and taste.

ROSY-GILL FAIRY HELMET *Mycena galericulata*   **Pl. 19**
Small to medium, *bell-shaped, grayish brown cap,* with *streaks radiating from center. Stalk brittle,* usually *smooth.* Grows *singly* or *in clusters,* on *decaying logs* of *deciduous trees.* **Cap:** Broadly conic with an incurved margin at first, expanded to bell-shaped with a low, obtuse hump and spreading limb and margin; margin frequently splitting with age. Surface covered with a hoary bloom at first, soon shining and polished, with radiating wrinkles or streaks; somewhat slippery but not sticky when wet. Dark gray to brownish gray when young, fading to light yellowish brown or sometimes yellowish gray. Flesh white or pale gray; tough and cartilaginous. Odor and taste not distinctive.* Gills adnate (broadly attached) or notched around apex of stalk, close to subdistant, strongly interveined. Gills white to pale gray or grayish pink, sometimes

---

* See p. 10 for cautions about using taste as an identifying characteristic.

spotted with dingy reddish brown. *Stalk:* Cylindric or slightly enlarged at base; hollow, tough and cartilaginous. Surface smooth or twisted; blackish to dingy gray or grayish brown, nearly white above. *Spore print:* White. **Technical notes:** Cap 3.5–6.5 cm across. Stalk 5–10 cm × 4–8 mm. Spores smooth, amyloid, elliptic; 8–10 × 5–6 μm. No pleurocystidia. Cheilocystidia clavate to subcapitate (club-shaped or nearly so), with numerous wavy, filamentous projections.

Fruiting: Scattered to clustered on decaying hardwood logs (occasionally on wood of coniferous trees). Pacific Northwest and Great Lakes states and southern Canada eastward. Spring and fall.

Edibility: Unknown, but **not recommended.**

Similar species: The very numerous gray species of *Mycena* (Fairy Helmet) growing on wood have been frequently misidentified, even when microscopic characters were used. Many are indistinguishable in the field, but with little reported harm to the mushroom pothunter, as their small size and delicate consistency render them unattractive for food. Among the common species, (1) the somewhat smaller *Mycena inclinata* (not shown) appears to be restricted to *hardwood* forests and has *whitish, fibrillose flecks* on the stalk, which tends to become brownish orange to yellowish at base. (2) *Mycena maculata* (not shown) is almost indistinguishable from *M. galericulata* (Rosy-gill Fairy Helmet) in the field, except for the *more pronounced reddish stains* on gills. (3) The *thinner, more fragile* consistency helps to distinguish *Mycena parabolica*.

BLEEDING FAIRY HELMET Pl. 19
Mycena haematopus
Blood-red juice oozes from cap and stalk when cut. Small, *reddish gray* to *reddish brown, bell-shaped caps,* on *slender, brittle stalks. Cap margin clasps stalk at first;* becomes torn or scalloped in old caps. Grows *in clumps on decaying wood.* **Cap:** Egg-shaped at first, expanding to bell-shaped or broadly conic, occasionally convex; in age, cap becomes flat with a low hump and often an upturned outer limb and margin. Margin sterile (extends beyond gills). Surface of cap dry and scurfy at first, soon becoming polished and moist; streaked or occasionally ribbed at maturity. Dark reddish brown on disc (center), lighter outward. Flesh thin, fragile; grayish pink or lighter; *"bleeds" when cut.* Odor and taste not distinctive or taste slightly bitter. Gills narrowly adnate (broadly attached) or notched around apex of stalk; narrow; dingy white to pinkish gray, (lighter along edge), soon becoming stained dingy reddish brown. *Stalk:* Cylindric, hollow; colored like cap except at base which is coated with thick, white hairs. *Spore print:* white. **Technical notes:** Cap 1–3 cm across. Stalk 4–8 cm × 1–2 mm. Spores smooth, amyloid, long-elliptic; 8–10 × 5–6 μm. Pleurocystidia infrequent; ventricose with tapered necks and sharp tips. Cheilocystidia similar.

Fruiting: In groups or clusters; on decaying wood of deciduous trees. Widespread and common throughout the continent. Spring and fall.

Edibility: Edible, but said to be tasteless and little used.

Similar species: The color, growth form, and habitat on decaying hardwood logs, and especially the presence of *thin, red latex,* make this a distinctive species. Other grayish brown species of *Mycena* and related genera that might be confused with it *lack the red latex.*

Remarks: *Mycena haematopus* (Bleeding Fairy Helmet) is one of the easiest members of the genus to recognize. In some specimens the latex is sparse and hard to see when flesh is cut, but the *cap margin* offers important identification clues at all ages. In young specimens the *sterile margin forms a clasping cylinder* around the slender stalk and in old age it usually *forms small teeth* or tiny lobes or scallops.

GOLDEN FAIRY HELMET *Mycena leaiana*   **Pl. 19**
Small, bright orange caps and *orange gills* with *red edges. Stalk color similar.* Grows *in clumps,* on *decaying logs* and *stumps* of *deciduous trees.* **Cap:** Bell-shaped, with an incurved margin at first, expanding to convex or sometimes nearly flat, with a shallow, central depression. Surface smooth, shiny, sticky when moist; reddish orange at first, fading to vivid orange, then paler and more yellowish, or eventually almost white at times. Flesh thick; watery yellowish white line beneath orange cuticle. Odor and taste faint and not distinctive or lacking. Gills adnate (broadly attached) or notched around apex of stalk; close to crowded. **Stalk:** Cylindric or flaring slightly at apex, often curved or somewhat wavy. Interior hollow. Tough, cartilaginous. Base has stiff, orange hairs; surface smooth otherwise except apex scurfy at first; sticky to slimy when wet. **Spore print:** White. **Technical notes:** Cap 1–4 cm across. Stalk 3–6 cm × 2–4 mm. Spores smooth, amyloid, elliptic; 7–9 × 5–6 μm. Pleuro- and cheilocystidia clavate to fusoid-ventricose, with one to several protruberances at apex and orange protoplasmic content.

Fruiting: Clumped on wood of various deciduous trees. Southern Canada to Missouri and eastward; common. Spring to fall.

Edibility: Unknown.

Similar species: May be confused with (1) species of *Hygrophorus* (waxycaps, p. 202). (2) Old specimens, in particular, may be confused with *Mycena texensis* (not shown), which is found in the Gulf states. It has predominantly grayish colors, flushed with orange on cap surface, and smaller spores.

LILAC-GILL FAIRY HELMET *Mycena lilacifolia*   **Pl. 19**
Small, sticky, yellow, umbrella-shaped cap with *lilac-tinted gills. Slimy yellow stalk.* Grows on *decaying logs* and *stumps* of *conifers.* **Cap:** Convex, with a flattened apex and straight margin; center sometimes depressed at maturity. Streaks radiate inward from margin. Surface smooth; light yellow (sometimes

flushed with pale purple at first). Odor and taste not distinctive. Gills narrow, decurrent, subdistant (see inside front cover); pale purple, fading to yellowish white but long *retaining purplish tinge.* *Stalk:* Cylindric, tubular, often curved. Surface smooth, slimy to sticky; purplish above and yellow below, sometimes with purplish tinges that fade completely to white except for a cottony tuft at base that retains lilac tinge. *Spore print:* White. **Technical notes:** Cap 0.5–2.0 cm across. Stalk 1–3 cm × 1–2 mm. Spores smooth, non-amyloid, short-elliptic; 6–7 × 3.0–3.5 μm. No cystidia on gills. Cap trama and cuticle stain reddish brown in iodine.

Fruiting: Scattered, in groups, or small clumps; on decaying stumps and logs of coniferous trees. Common but never very numerous; widespread. Spring to fall.
Edibility: Unknown.
Similar species: The colors, surface texture, decurrent gills, and habitat make this a distinctive species. The gills, which are somewhat waxy, may suggest a small species of *Laccaria* (tallowgill, p. 155) or *Hygrophorus* (waxycap, p. 202), but few of these grow on decaying wood.

SNOWBANK FAIRY HELMET *Mycena overholtsii*   **Pl. 19**
Small to medium, *gray, broadly humped caps,* on *gray* to *brownish stalks* with *white cottony filaments* over *lower part.* Usually grows *in clumps* on *decaying conifer wood.* *Cap:* Broadly bell-shaped to convex at first; becoming flat with a broad, rounded, central hump, or humped on disc (center) with an upturned outer limb and margin. Streaks extend from margin inward. Surface smooth, somewhat greasy, hygrophanous (water-soaked); dark to pale watery gray or bluish gray, sometimes with a yellowish tinge. Gills adnate (broadly attached) or subdecurrent (extending down stalk), broad, subdistant; gills stain gray when bruised. *Stalk:* Cylindric or enlarged at base, sometimes flattened; often penetrating deeply in well-decayed wood (logs or stumps). Surface smooth. Yellowish white to gray above; gray, then slowly brownish below. *Spore print:* White. **Technical notes:** Cap 2–5 cm across. Stalk 6–12 cm × 2–5 mm. Spores smooth, amyloid, elliptic; 6–8 × 3–4 μm.
Fruiting: Single, or more commonly in small clumps; on well-decayed logs or stumps of conifers (often on Douglas fir). Common around snowbanks—sometimes originates under the snow at high elevations in Rocky Mts. and Northwest. Spring.
Edibility: Unknown.
LILAC FAIRY HELMET *Mycena pura*   **Pl. 19**
Small, rounded to *flat, smooth, purple* to *pink cap,* with *lighter-colored gills. Fragile stalk. Odor and taste of radishes* (may be **poisonous**—do not try it intentionally).* *Cap:* Obtuse to convex, with straight or slightly incurved margin, ex-

---

* See p. 10 for cautions about using taste as an identifying characteristic.

panding to a nearly flat cap. Surface hygrophanous (water-soaked), often faintly streaked from margin inward; color variable, ranging from some shade of light purple to purplish pink or light purplish blue, rarely purplish white. Flesh thick over disc (center), tapering sharply on limb to a thin margin; fading to nearly white. Gills adnate (broadly attached) or notched around apex of stalk, subdistant, broad. Gills are ventricose (broader at middle) and sometimes interveined (use hand lens). Color of gills varies, but is similar to that of cap or lighter; edges are often nearly white. **Stalk:** Cylindric or enlarged toward base, sometimes flattened; hollow, fragile. Surface smooth or roughened, sometimes with twisted streaks. Colored like cap or nearly white with a tuft of white, cottony fibrils at base. **Spore print:** White. **Technical notes:** Cap 2–5 cm across. Stalk 3–8 cm × 2–6 mm. Spores smooth, amyloid, ellipsoid; 6–8 × 3–4 μm. Cheilo- and pleurocystidia similar; ventricose to fusoid-ventricose.
Fruiting: Single to scattered or in groups; on soil in both coniferous and deciduous forests. Often abundant in cool, moist seasons; widespread in N. America. Summer and fall.
Edibility: Poisonous.
Similar species: Frequently misidentified because of great variability and common occurrence. May be mistaken for a species of *Laccaria* (tallowgill, p. 155).

SCARLET FAIRY HELMET   **Pl. 19**
Mycena strobilinoides
Small, *round* or *bell-shaped, red cap; fades to yellow. Orange to yellow gills* have *darker edges. Skinny, orange stalk.* Grows *under conifers.* **Cap:** Conic at first, with margin incurved against stalk; expanding to bell-shaped or convex, with margin often flaring upward and minutely scalloped. Surface smooth, moist, somewhat slippery; translucent-streaked near margin and sometimes shallowly grooved. Vivid reddish orange, fading to strong orange or strong orange-yellow. Flesh thin; yellowish. Odor and taste not distinctive. Gills adnate (broadly attached) with a slightly decurrent tooth extending down stalk; subdistant, narrow. Gills yellow to orange, with *reddish orange edges.* **Stalk:** Cylindric; solid or nearly so. Fragile. Surface smooth except scurfy at apex. **Spore print:** White. **Technical notes:** Cap 1–2 cm across. Stalk 2–5 cm × 1–2 mm thick. Spores smooth, amyloid, elliptic; 7–9 × 4.0–5.5 μm. Cheilo- and pleurocystidia abundant, similar; clavate (club-shaped) or nearly fusoid; contents orange to hyaline; rod-like projections over upper surface.
Fruiting: Scattered or in dense groups; on needle beds and mossy forest litter. Common in Northwest and at high elevations in Rocky Mts.; less common in Great Lakes states and southern Canada eastward. Late summer and fall.
Edibility: Unknown, but too small to be of interest.

Similar species: (1) *Mycena rosella* (not shown) is another small *Mycena* (Fairy Helmet) with pink-edged gills. It has a lighter-colored, more pinkish to grayish pink cap. (2) *Mycena monticola* (not shown) has a red to pink cap and a pink stalk that becomes brown or darker. Its gills lack the red edges found on *Mycena rosella* and *M. strobilinoides* (Scarlet Fairy Helmet).

Navelcaps: Genus *Omphalina*

**O. chryso-
phylla**

Small to medium, brightly colored cap on a *slender stalk*. Yellowish orange to white gills extend down stalk. Cap margin incurved at first; cap has a *narrow depression* at center. Spore print white to pale yellowish. Spores non-amyloid (do not stain blue in iodine).

GOLDGILL NAVELCAP *Omphalina chrysophylla*   **Pl. 17**
Small to medium, *brown, funnel-shaped cap* with *orange-yellow, decurrent gills. Slender stalk*. Grows on *decaying conifer wood*. *Cap:* Thin, flat, with a low, convex knob or shallowly depressed disc (center) and inrolled margin at first; disc becomes more deeply depressed as it ages. Surface minutely fibrillose or scaly (use hand lens); yellowish brown. Flesh thin, flexible; orange. Odor and taste not distinctive. Gills subdistant, narrow and thin; light orange-yellow to light orange. *Stalk:* Cylindrical; often curved or flattened. Surface sooty or with scattered hairs; moist. Orange-yellow, sometimes flushed with brown; white-cottony at base. No veil. *Spore print:* Pale grayish yellow. **Technical notes:** Cap 0.5–4.0 cm across. Stalk 2–4 × 0.5–3.0 mm. Spores smooth, non-amyloid, elliptic; 8.5–15.5 × 4.5–6.0 μm.
Fruiting: Scattered to clustered on decaying conifer wood, often coming up through mosses. Widely distributed throughout N. America. Spring to fall.
Edibility: Unknown.
Remarks: Among the small species found on rotting conifer wood, these brown, *centrally depressed,* more or less scaly caps with *orange gills* are quite distinctive. They are often found in considerable numbers and in all stages of maturity at one time.

TINY NAVELCAP *Omphalina postii*   **Pl. 17**
Tiny, orange to *whitish cap* with *depressed disc* (center). *White gills extend down fragile, yellowish stalk*. Grows in *very wet, often moss-covered soil. Cap:* Convex to flat; very thin. Surface smooth, more or less translucent and streaked on limb and margin from gills when moist. Flesh soft; dull orange or yellow. Gills decurrent (extending down stalk), narrow, often interveined, distant (widely spaced); white to yellow or yellowish pink. *Stalk:* Hollow; cylindric or enlarged at base. Surface

smooth or at first powdered with scattered, minute wisps. Orange-yellow to yellow. No veil. *Spore print:* White. **Technical notes:** Cap 0.5–2.5 cm across. Stalk 2–6 cm × 1–3 mm. Spores smooth, non-amyloid, elliptic; 6.5–11.0 × 4.5–6.5 μm. **Fruiting:** Scattered or in groups; on wet soil around springs, seepage areas, or brooks. Northern U.S. and probably southern Canada. Spring to fall.
Edibility: Unknown, but of little concern as it would be hard to find enough for a mouthful.
Similar species: May be confused with some fairy helmets (species of *Mycena,* p. 170).

Jack-O-Lantern: Genus *Omphalotus*

JACK-O-LANTERN *Omphalotus illudens*   **Pl. 17**
Medium to large, *orange caps* with *broad, strongly decurrent gills.* Grows in *clumps* on *stumps, roots,* or *buried wood.* **Cap:** Convex to flat, often with a low, central, pointed knob and an incurved margin; soon becoming depressed on disc (center) and inner limb. Surface smooth to fibrillose (streaked); bright orange to orange-yellow (not olivaceous). Flesh firm, thin, yellow. Odor weak but disagreeable to some people; taste not distinctive.* Gills narrow to moderately broad, close; orange-yellow. **Stalk:** Cylindric or tapered to base; ringless. Surface dry; smooth to minutely downy or somewhat scaly in age. Interior solid; light orange-yellow. **Spore print:** Yellowish white. **Technical notes:** Cap 5–15 cm across. Stalk 5–20 × 1–3 cm. Spores smooth, subglobose; 3–5 μm.
Fruiting: Large, dense clusters on trunks, stumps, or coming from roots of dead or living hardwood trees, especially oaks. Common where trees have been removed for construction. East of Great Plains. Late summer and fall.
Edibility: Poisonous! This is **not** a chanterelle (see Pl. 7).
Similar species: This species is very commonly mistaken for (1) a chanterelle (*Cantharellus,* p. 81) by ill-advised but wishful-thinking mushroom pothunters in the eastern states. We have never seen chanterelles with *close, sharp-edged gills* growing *in large clumps on a woody* substrate decaying tree roots (stump or log), as is the case with *Omphalotus illudens,* but this mushroom is all too often brought into the laboratory all trimmed and ready for cooking by someone seeking confirmation of their misidentification. The ringless stalk, smooth cap, and white to yellowish spore print distinguish it from (2) species of *Gymnopilus* (flamecaps, p. 297, Pl. 37), which also vaguely resemble Jack-O-Lantern *(O. illudens)* and which also grow on recently cut or decaying wood, and often fruit at the same time. (2) A greenish-tinged species, *Omphalotus oliva-*

---

* See p. 10 for cautions about using taste as an identifying characteristic.

scens, is found in northern California. It has larger spores than
O. illudens and the European species, *Omphalotus olearus,*
which may also be tinged with green. *Omphalotus olearus* and
Omphalotus illudens are sometimes regarded as a single species, in which case the correct species name is *olearus.*

Remarks: Two interesting characteristics of *Omphalotus illudens* (Jack-O-Lantern) are its pathogenicity and its eerie luminescence. This mushroom eventually kills its host tree — by the
time its large clumps are found at the base of an otherwise
healthy-looking tree, nothing can be done to halt the disease.
The luminescence can be seen by observing moist, fresh mushrooms in the darkness for a time long enough for the observer's
eyes to become dark-adapted. This characteristic probably
suggested the widely accepted common name for the species.

Genus *Oudemansiella*

DEEP ROOT *Oudemansiella radicata*   **Pl. 20**
Medium to large, *flat, brown, streaked cap;* surface *sticky.*
Wide, white gills. Spindly, rigid, brittle, deep-rooted stalk.
Cap: Bell-shaped, with an incurved margin at first; soon becoming flat or nearly so, with a low, central hump or knob.
Surface smooth or sometimes wrinkled on disc (center) and
inner limb; slimy to sticky when moist. Color variable but usually some shade of grayish to yellowish brown, varying from
dark brown to yellowish white flushed with brown. Flesh thin,
white. Odor and taste not distinctive. Gills widely notched
around apex of stalk, subdistant (see inside front cover). Gills
thickish, white. **Stalk:** Spindle-shaped, tapering both upward
and downward from ground level. Surface dry, smooth or
scurfy at apex, often twisted-streaked and sometimes scaly or
zoned below; no veils. Nearly white above to brown (like cap)
below. *Deeply rooted* — portion below ground tapers to a narrow point deep in the soil. **Spore print:** White. **Technical
notes:** Cap 3–12 cm across. Stalk (above ground) 5–25 ×
0.5–1.5 cm. Spores non-amyloid, smooth, broadly elliptic;
14–17 × 9–11 μm. Clamps present. Cheilo- and pleurocystidia
large, variable.
Fruiting: Solitary or scattered; on soil under deciduous trees,
possibly from dead roots. Widespread. Late spring to early fall.
Edibility: Edible.
Similar species: This is a very variable species, frequently
confused in the Rocky Mts. with *Oudemansiella longipes* (not
shown), which has a moist to dry cap with a velvety sheen in
dry weather.

Oyster Mushrooms: Genus *Panellus*

Fan-shaped caps, mostly small. *Stalk often lacking;* if present, it is short and eccentric (off center) to lateral (attached at

one side). Gill edges smooth to torn, but *not toothed* as in saw-gills (*Lentinus,* p. 159, or *Lentinellus,* p. 158). Spore print white. Spores amyloid (stain blue in iodine).

LATE OYSTER *Panellus serotinus*   **Pl. 20**
Small to medium, *fan-shaped cap;* color varies—*green to yellow* or *violet. Yellow gills. Stalk short* if present. Grows *on wood in late fall.* **Cap:** Convex, with an incurved margin that is often deeply lobed or indented; expanding to nearly flat. Surface smooth, *sticky.* Color variable and often mixed—predominantly green to yellow; often flushed with violet at first, eventually yellowish olive. Flesh thick, firm, white. Odor and taste not distinctive. Gills adnate (broadly attached), close, narrow; bright orange-yellow or lighter at first, sometimes with violet edges, fading to pale yellow. **Stalk:** Very short or lacking; surface white, hairy. **Spore print:** Pale yellow. **Technical notes:** Cap 3–10 cm across. Spores smooth, amyloid, curved; 4–6 × 1–2 μm. Cheilocystidia cylindric, thin-walled.
Fruiting: Scattered to clustered, often overlapping; on wood of both coniferous and deciduous trees, widely distributed. *Late fall,* often fruiting after first frost.
Edibility: Edible, but not highly rated. May require long cooking.

BITTER OYSTER *Panellus stipticus*   **Pl. 20**
Clusters of small, *fan-shaped* to *kidney-shaped, dry, hairy caps. Caps orange-yellow* to *brownish; gills same color. Stalk stubby,* attached at one side. Fruits on decaying wood. **Cap:** Convex, with a depressed disc (center); margin flaring at maturity. Surface scurfy to woolly (use hand lens). Flesh tough, firm; light yellowish pink. Odor not distinctive; taste unpleasant, described as acidic to astringent or very bitter.* Gills adnate (broadly attached) or decurrent (extending down stalk), close, narrow; orange-yellow. **Stalk:** Cylindric or flattened; attached to cap off center or *at one side.* Dull yellowish white; base matted with hairs. **Spore print:** White. **Technical notes:** Cap 0.3–3.0 cm across. Stalk 5–10 × 3–8 mm. Spores smooth, amyloid, oblong; 3.0–4.5 × 1.5–2.5 μm.
Fruiting: In groups or dense clusters, often overlapping; on logs and stumps of deciduous trees. Widely distributed. Fruits in fall, but occasionally in spring and summer also.
Edibility: Not edible.
Similar species: Colors distinguish this from other common species of *Panus* (not shown) and *Panellus.* Species of *Crepidotus* (p. 295) having a similar shape can be distinguished by their brown spore print, compared with the white spore print of *Panellus stipticus* (Bitter Oyster).
Remarks: After several minutes in a completely dark room,

---

* See p. 10 for cautions about using taste as an identifying characteristic.

one can see the gills of *P. stipticus* glow with a faint, eerie, greenish light. This quality of luminescence is shared by a number of common mushrooms such as Jack-O-Lantern, (*Omphalotus,* p. 178), Oyster (*Pleurotus,* below), and Golden Trumpets (*Xeromphalina,* p. 195). These are all wood-rotting fungi. Microscopic filaments of the vegetative fungus penetrating the wood will make the moist wood appear to glow if it is not allowed to dry out.

Genus *Phyllotopsis*

NESTCAP *Phyllotopsis nidulans*   **Pl. 19**
Small to medium, *fan-shaped, dry, orange caps* with a *disagreeable odor.* Grows *in clusters* on *dead wood* of *both coniferous and deciduous trees.* **Cap:** Attached at one side, usually without a stalk. Convex at first, becoming semicircular in outline then elongating and eventually becoming fan-shaped, sometimes irregularly lobed. Margin remains incurved in older specimens. Surface densely clothed in coarse to soft, whitish hairs. Orange-yellow, becoming paler as it fades. Flesh thin; light orange-yellow, two-layered, with a marked color change when cut or bruised. Odor and taste usually strong, disagreeable.* Gills adnate (broadly attached), close, narrow; colored like cap or lighter. **Stalk:** Lacking or very short. No veils. *Spore print:* Yellowish pink. **Technical notes:** Cap 3–7 cm across. Spores smooth, short-elliptic; 4–5 × 2–3 μm.
Fruiting: In groups or clusters; on decaying logs, stumps, or standing snags (dead trees). Widespread in N. America but more common from Great Lakes eastward. Late summer to fall, winter in warmer climates.
Edibility: We know of no reports of poisoning, but we know of no one who has tried eating it, because of the persistent bad odor and taste.
Similar species: In eastern U.S., Nestcap is very frequently confused with *Phyllotopsis subnidulans* (not shown), which has more orange color; thinner, more widely spaced gills; and curved or sausage-shaped spores.

Oyster Mushrooms: Genus *Pleurotus*

Medium to large, bracket- to fan-shaped caps on eccentric (off-center) to lateral stalks. Gills decurrent (extending down stalk). **Spore print:** white to dingy yellowish or violet-gray. Spores thin-walled, hyaline (transparent), non-amyloid (do not stain blue in iodine).

OYSTER *Pleurotus ostreatus*   **Pl. 20**
Clumps of *white* to *light gray* or *grayish yellow, fan-shaped* to *shallowly funnel-shaped cap.* Stalk *very short* if present; *lat-*

| **Pleurotus ostreatus** | **Pleurotus porrigens** | **Panellus serotinus** | **Panellus stipticus** |

eral (attached at one side) or *eccentric* (off center). **Cap:** Convex with an incurved margin at first, expanding to fan-shaped, with a flat or shallowly depressed disc (center) and inner limb; sometimes shallowly funnel-shaped with a shallow, often off-center depression. Margin often lobed and sometimes arched toward center. Surface smooth, hygrophanous — brownish gray to grayish brown or yellowish brown at first, lighter as it dries out. Flesh firm, thick; nearly white. Odor and taste mild. Gills decurrent, branching on stalk; subdistant, broad; edges not toothed. Gills dry quickly and stain brown at times. **Stalk:** Eccentric (off center), lateral, or lacking; usually curved when present. Tough; surface white, velvety at base. **Spore print:** White. **Technical notes:** Cap 5–25 cm across. Stalk 0.5–1.5 × 0.5–1.0 cm. Spores smooth, non-amyloid, elliptic; 8–12 × 3.5–4.5 μm.

Fruiting: Single to densely clustered, often overlapping. Grows in clumps on *logs, stumps, and rotting wood* of various trees, including cottonwood and tulip poplar. Widespread. Spring and late fall.

Edibility: Edible and highly rated.

Similar species: Often confused with (1) *Pleurotus sapidus* (not shown), which has a lilac-gray spore print. (2) *Pleurotus cystidiosus* (not shown) grows on conifer wood and is distinguished on microscopic characters. (3) Angel Wings (*Pleurotus porrigens,* p. 182) also has a white spore print; it grows on wood of coniferous trees. It has smaller, thinner caps (see Pl. 20).

Remarks: This popular and widespread edible mushroom is named for its shape rather than its taste. It is sometimes found in great quantity and may be dried and stored for later use, with excellent results. It is easily cultivated and is grown commercially in Europe. Specimens collected for the table should be inspected carefully for shiny, black beetles, which lay their eggs on the gills, and beetle larvae, which tunnel into the mushroom flesh.

ANGEL WINGS *Pleurotus porrigens*   **Pl. 20**
Small to medium, *thin, white, fan-shaped caps; laterally attached* (at one side). Gills close or crowded. Grows *in overlapping clusters* on *coniferous wood.* **Cap:** Rounded or semicircular in outline; sometimes spatula-shaped or fan-shaped, with a

strongly incurved margin when young; margin may be lobed or indented at maturity. Surface smooth and shiny except for white hairs at point of attachment; not streaked. Flesh very thin, white, pliant. Odor and taste not distinctive. Gills decurrent (extending down stalk); yellowish in age. *Stalk:* Very short if present; always lateral. Surface hairy; no veils. *Spore print:* White. **Technical notes:** Cap 2–5 × 4–8 cm. Spores smooth, non-amyloid, subglobose; 5–7 × 4.5–6.5 μm. No hymenial cystidia. No gelatinous layer in flesh. Clamps abundant on hyphae.

Fruiting: In dense groups or clusters on decaying logs and stumps, especially hemlock. Widespread in northern conifer forests. Summer and fall.

Edibility: Edible.

Similar species: Thin, pure white cap with narrow, close gills, always growing on coniferous wood, separate Angel Wings *(P. porrigens)* from (1) larger, white to gray or brownish oyster mushrooms, such as *Pleurotus ostreatus* (p. 181), *P. sapidus,* and *P. cystidiosus* (not shown). (2) Faded specimens of Nestcap *(Phyllotopsis nidulans,* p. 181), which also have yellowish gills, can be distinguished readily by their strong odor and light-colored spore print. (3) Large white specimens of *Crepidotus,* such as Soft Stumpfoot (p. 295, Pl. 37), have brown spore prints.

Remarks: The white, wood-rotting oyster mushrooms with nearly round, non-amyloid spores are sometimes put in a separate genus, *Pleurocybella.*

Genus *Rhodotus*

ROSY VEINCAP *Rhodotus palmatus*   **Pl. 19**
Small to medium, *rounded, red* to *pink caps;* surface has *network of ribs.* Gills and stalk *pink.* Grows *singly* or *in clusters on wood.* **Cap:** Convex with an incurved margin, expanding somewhat as it matures to broadly convex. Surface smooth between ridges, dry; color fades with age. Flesh firm, somewhat rubbery; pink. Gills adnate (broadly attached), close, broad, interveined. **Stalk:** Often eccentric (off center); cylindric but typically bent, tough. Surface dry, fibrillose; light pink. No ring. *Spore print:* Yellowish pink. **Technical notes:** Cap 2–7 cm across. Stalk 1.5–5.0 cm × 2–6 mm. Spores tuberculate, globose to subglobose; 5–8 × 4.5–6.5 μm. Clamps present on hyphae.

Fruiting: Solitary to clustered; on logs in deciduous forests. Eastern Canada to Great Lakes and south to Virginia. Not common. Summer and early fall.

Edibility: Unknown.

Remarks: The strongly ribbed, red caps, fading to orange-yellow; off-center stalk; and pale-colored spore print make this a very distinctive mushroom.

Coincaps: Genus *Strobilurus*

Small to medium, whitish to olive or grayish brown cap, firmly attached to stalk. Flesh thin but fairly tough. Stalk firm, slender; sometimes rooting. Spore print: White. Spores non-amyloid (do not stain blue in iodine).

MAGNOLIA COINCAP *Strobilurus conigenoides*   **Pl. 17**
Very small, rounded to flat, whitish caps on *thin, white stalks. Grows in clusters* from *dead "cones" of magnolias.* **Cap:** Convex to broadly conic, with an incurved margin at first; expanding to a flat cap with a narrow central depression. Surface downy or hairy; *dry.* Pale yellowish gray on disc (center), nearly white outwards. Odor and taste not distinctive. Gills white to yellowish white. **Stalk:** Cylindric, white at apex, tinged yellowish gray below, white cottony at base. **Spore print:** white. **Technical notes:** Cap up to 1 cm across. Stalk 1.5–3.5 cm long, less than 1 mm in diameter.
Fruiting: Scattered to clustered; on fallen magnolia "cones" throughout the range of this tree. Late summer and fall.
Edibility: Unknown.
Similar species: Not likely to be confused with any other white mushroom this small, especially since it grows on decaying magnolia "cones." However, there are numerous small white species in several genera that grow on cones of other trees: (1) *Strobilurus trullisatus* (not shown) is common on cones of Douglas fir in the Northwest and (2) *Baeospora myosura* (not shown) is a slightly larger species that grows on cones of eastern white pine, spruce, and other conifers in northern forests from coast to coast. It was formerly placed in genus *Collybia* (p. 147).
WESTERN COINCAP *Strobilurus occidentalis*   **Pl. 17**
Small, rounded to flat, grayish brown, rubbery cap on a *rooting stalk* growing from *buried cones* of *spruce trees.* **Cap:** Convex at first; later broadly conic and finally almost flat, often with a low, shallow central depression. Surface smooth or slightly wrinkled, sometimes streaked or ribbed near margin. Dark grayish brown to light brown or yellowish gray. Flesh thin; white. Odor none or slightly of radishes; taste absent. **Stalk:** Cylindric, often curved or bent; interior hollow. Surface smooth above ground; white at apex, becoming brown on lower portion and hairy below ground level. **Spore print:** White.
Technical notes: Cap 0.5–3.0 cm across. Stalk 1–2 cm in diameter; 1.0–3.5 cm long above ground, up to 6 cm long below ground. Spores smooth, non-amyloid, elliptic; $4–7 \times 2–3$ μm.
Fruiting: Solitary or in groups. Early spring.
Edibility: Unknown.
Similar species: This coincap is almost indistinguishable in the field from (1) *Strobilurus wyomingensis* and (2) *S. lignitilis*

(not shown). (3) *Strobilurus albipilata* (not shown) is smaller and grows from pine cones. Numerous species of *Mycena* (fairy helmets, p. 171, Pl. 19) closely resemble these species of *Strobilurus*.

Cavaliers: Genus *Tricholoma*

Tricholoma Medium to large, fleshy cap; gills notched around apex of stalk. Solid, fleshy to fibrous stalk; centrally attached to cap. Stalk may have slight fibrillose, non-membranous ring but *no volva* (compare with *Cortinarius*, p. 287). Spore print *white to pale yellowish*. See **caution** on p. 189 about eating white or grayish *Tricholomas* — some are poisonous.

BROWNSTAIN CAVALIER   **Pl. 21**
Tricholoma flavobrunneum
Medium-sized, *brown,* slightly sticky, *streaked cap.* Gills pale yellow, *spotted with brown.* Stalk *same color as cap; no veil.* **Cap:** Convex at first, becoming humped and eventually flat; margin sometimes flared and irregular in outline. Surface smooth or nearly so; *moist to slightly sticky* when wet. Dull reddish brown to moderate brown. Flesh white, tinged with reddish brown in age; thick on disc (center) but tapering sharply to a thin margin. Odor and taste of fresh meal.* Gills notched around apex of stalk, close, moderately broad; *staining brownish* when bruised. **Stalk:** Cylindric, solid. Surface dry, smooth or minutely fibrillose; same color as gills at first, lower part staining to brown of cap. **Spore print:** White. **Technical notes:** Cap 3–10 cm across. Stalk 4–8 × 0.6–2.0 cm. Spores non-amyloid, subglobose to short-elliptic; 5.0–6.5 × 3–4 μm.
Fruiting: Scattered or in groups or clumps; on soil under pines and other conifers. Southern Canada and northern U.S.; rare in Rocky Mts. Late summer and fall.
Edibility: Not recommended — sometimes reported as poisonous.
Similar species: Commonly confused with (1) *Tricholoma populinum* (not shown), which grows under cottonwood trees, and with (2) *Tricholoma albobrunneum* (not shown), which grows under hardwood trees east of the Great Plains.
GOLDEN CAVALIER *Tricholoma aurantium*   **Pl. 21**
Medium to large, *rounded* to *flat cap;* cap and stalk *orange, often flushed* with *green;* surface *sticky when wet.* Stalk *firm,* has a faint ring (veil line) but *no fibrils. Yellowish gills* become *spotted* with *brown in age.* **Cap:** Convex with an inrolled mar-

* **See p. 10 for cautions about using taste as an identifying characteristic.**

gin at first, often with a low, obtuse hump; may be lobed or irregular in outline; expanding to nearly flat, sometimes with an arched limb and margin. Surface at first smooth, *sticky when wet* over embedded dark fibrils, breaking into small, flattened scales. Vivid reddish orange to brownish orange, usually streaked or splashed with dark green, often with orange droplets on margin. Flesh white to yellowish; firm. Odor and taste disagreeable. Gills close, narrowly adnate (attached) or slightly notched around stalk apex or short-decurrent (extending down stalk slightly); yellowish white, soon spotted or stained with reddish brown, often with droplets on edges. *Stalk:* Cylindric or enlarged downward and tapered to a thick tip at base. Solid and *firm* at first, becoming hollow and often splitting as it matures. Surface pale yellow and smooth to fibrillose above veil ring, which is set high on stalk; stalk *colored like cap* below ring. Ring a band or separate droplets of thin slime, drying quickly and breaking into patches of scales. Ring sometimes an indistinct veil line or zone; *not fibrillose* or membranous. *Spore print:* White. **Technical notes:** Cap 4–12 cm across. Stalk 3–8 × 1.0–2.5 cm. Spores smooth, non-amyloid, subglobose to short-elliptic; 4–6 × 3–5 μm.

Fruiting: Solitary or in groups or clumps; sometimes in rows, arcs, or fairy rings on soil in mixed or coniferous woods. Widespread and sometimes abundant in southern Canada and northern U.S. Summer and fall.

Edibility: Not recommended. Unpalatable, but supposedly not toxic.

Similar species: Frequently confused with Zeller's Bracelet (*Tricholoma* or *Armillaria zelleri*, p. 193), which often fruits at the same time in the West. The two are readily distinguished by the *veil*, which leaves a *fibrillose or membranous ring* high on the stalk of *T. zelleri* and a shiny to dull or slimy sheath or zone *without fibrils* on *T. aurantium* (Golden Cavalier). In wet weather they can be very difficult to distinguish.

CAVALIER (MAN-ON-HORSEBACK)   **Pl. 21**
Tricholoma flavovirens
Medium to large cap; *vivid yellow, brown* at *center; no black streaks* or *fibrils. Gills yellow. Stalk thick, yellow; no ring.*
Cap: Convex to broadly conic, with an inrolled margin at first; expanding to broadly convex or flat, often with a broad, low, central hump. Surface has thin sticky outer layer at first, soon drying and in age sometimes forming small, scurfy scales on disc (center). Pale yellow at first, then greenish yellow to vivid yellow and usually remaining yellow on margin but gradually becoming brown to reddish brown from disc (center) outward. Flesh thick, firm; white or tinged with yellow under cuticle. Odor and taste mealy when raw. Gills notched around apex of stalk, close, broad; edges become ragged with age. Gills bright yellow, not staining when bruised. *Stalk:* Cylindric or enlarged

at base; solid or hollowed in age. Surface smooth to fibrillose; pale to light yellow. *Spore print:* White. **Technical notes:** Cap 4-12 cm across. Stalk 3-9 × 1.0-2.5 cm. Spores elliptic; 6.0-7.5 × 4-5 μm. Pleurocystidia as embedded chrysocystidia or lacking. No cheilocystidia.

Fruiting: Single or in groups or clusters; in coniferous and hardwood forests. Widespread in N. America; common under pine and aspen in western states. Fall to early winter.

Edibility: A popular edible mushroom. Be sure to distinguish it from Sulphur Cavalier *(T. sulphureum)* and from *T. sejunctum* (see below), both of which are **poisonous.**

Similar species: (1) *Tricholoma intermedia* (not shown) has a white stalk and gills but its cap is similar in color to *T. flavovirens* (Cavalier). (2) *Tricholoma sejunctum* (not shown) is poisonous. It is more slender than *T. flavovirens,* with a more conic cap when young; the cap is more greenish yellow and has black to grayish brown fibrils under the slime layer on its surface. (3) As its name suggests, Sulphur Cavalier (*Tricholoma sulphureum,* p. 191) is more sulphur yellow in color and has a *strong, unpleasant odor.* It has a bitter or nauseating taste and has been reported as poisonous. It also has dry cap and stalk surfaces. (4) *Tricholoma leucophyllum* (not shown) has white gills. It is more grayish brown on the disc and duller yellow on the limb and margin of the cap. The edibility of this species, which grows in the West, is unknown.

SHINGLE HEAD *Tricholoma imbricatum*   **Pl. 21**
Medium to large, *rounded, brown cap;* surface *dry, smooth to scaly. Stout, dull brownish stalk. Gills pale, sometimes spotted.*
Cap: Convex to broadly conic, with a downy, inrolled margin at first, becoming broadly convex or humped in age. Surface minutely fibrillose to fibrillose-scaly (use hand lens); sometimes ribbed at first along margin or developing radiating streaks or cracks as it matures. Moderate brown to moderate yellowish brown or grayish brown. Flesh firm; nearly white but slowly flushed with reddish brown when cut or bruised. Odor and taste mild or absent. Gills notched around apex of stalk, close, broad; yellowish white to pinkish white at first, sometimes spotted with reddish brown in age. *Stalk:* Cylindrical or enlarged at base; solid. Yellowish white, but soon becoming brown to pinkish brown at base; lighter above. Surface smooth and unpolished. **Technical notes:** Cap 5-10 cm across. Stalk 4-8 × 1-3 cm. Spores smooth, with a large central oil drop, ellipsoid; 5-7 × 4-5 μm. No cystidia on gills. No clamps on hyphae.

Fruiting: Scattered or in groups; or occasionally in small clusters; on soil under coniferous trees. Widespread in northern forests. Fall to early winter.

Edibility: Edible. Be sure to distinguish it from Fuzztop (see below), which may be **poisonous.**

Similar species: Sometimes confused with (1) Fuzztop (*Tricholoma vaccinum*, p. 191), but Shingle Head *(T. imbricatum)* is more robust, has a less fibrillose cap surface (use hand lens), and is usually duller brown in color. (2) White gills and tinges of yellow on limb and margin of cap distinguish *Tricholoma leucophyllum* (not shown), a western species.

IRKSOME CAVALIER *Tricholoma inamoenum*   **Pl. 21**
Small to medium, *dull pale yellow cap; flat* to *rounded* or *humped. Slender stalk.* Odor and taste *strong, disagreeable (tar-like).* **Cap:** Convex or slightly depressed, but with a low, narrow, rounded hump on disc (center). Surface smooth; pale grayish yellow, unchanging with age or drying. Flesh white; moderately thick on disc, tapering abruptly to a thin margin. Gills broad, adnate (broadly attached to stalk), subdistant; *whitish,* unstaining or sometimes tinged with gray. **Stalk:** Solid, cylindric or enlarged slightly toward base. Surface smooth, dry; colored like cap or lighter. **Spore print:** White. **Technical notes:** Cap 2–4 cm across. Stalk 4–8 cm × 3–7 mm. Spores ellipsoid; 5–10 × 4.0–5.5 μm.
Fruiting: Solitary or in groups; on soil in coniferous forests from Rocky Mts. westward. Summer and fall.
☠ **Edibility: Poisonous.**
Similar species: The pale colors, smooth, "clean" appearance, and strong, unpleasant odor and taste make this quite distinctive. *Tricholoma platyphyllum* (not shown) may be just a large-spored variety of this species *(T. inamoenum)* that is often tinged with brown on disc.

TIGERTOP *Tricholoma pardinum*   **Pl. 21**
Medium to large, *gray, rounded* to *flat cap; dry surface* forms *small scales. Whitish gills. Dingy white stalk;* surface *smooth* to *fibrillose* (use hand lens). **Cap:** Convex, with an incurved margin at first; soon becoming flat, with a downturned margin or with a shallowly depressed limb and a low, rounded hump on disc (center). Surface fibrillose at first, soon breaking into small, brownish gray, hairy scales. Cap darker in center, nearly white at margin; unchanging when cut or bruised. Flesh firm; white, unchanging when cut or bruised. Odor and taste of "fresh meal" (**poisonous**—do not try it intentionally).* Gills narrowly to broadly notched around apex of stalk, close, broad; yellowish white or rarely flushed with pale pink; edges become ragged in age. **Stalk:** Cylindric or widened somewhat toward base. White to grayish, sometimes staining pinkish brown at base. **Spore print:** White. **Technical notes:** Cap 4–15 cm across. Stalk 6–15 × 1–2 cm. Spores smooth, elliptic; 6–10 × 5.0–6.5 μm.
Fruiting: Solitary to scattered or in groups; on soil in cool, coniferous or mixed forests, northern U.S. and Canada. Fall.

---

* See p. 10 for cautions about using taste as an identifying characteristic.

Edibility: Poisonous. It is dangerous to eat any of the white to gray or grayish brown species of *Tricholoma,* as the poisonous and edible ones are usually most difficult to distinguish in the field.

Similar species: Very easily and frequently confused with several other whitish to gray Tricholomas, including (1) **Waxygill Cavalier** (*T. myomyces,* Pl. 21), which is smaller and has remnants of a fibrillose veil when young and more widely spaced, thick, somewhat waxy, torn-edged gills. (2) Silver Streaks (*T. virgatum,* p. 192) has a less scaly cap with a shinier, more extensively streaked surface and a narrower knob or hump. It usually has a pinkish flush at base of stalk. (3) *Tricholoma atroviolaceum* (not shown) has a darker, more violaceous cap and brownish to grayish gills. It fruits under conifers in Pacific Northwest.

SOOTY HEAD *Tricholoma portentosum*   **Pl. 21**
Medium to large, *broadly conic, gray cap; surface sticky, streaked* with darker gray. Gills and stalk *flushed with greenish yellow.* *Cap:* Bell-shaped to conic, with an incurved margin and sometimes with a pointed knob at first; expanding to a broadly convex or flat cap with a flaring margin at maturity. Sometimes lobed or irregular in outline. Surface covered with a thin *sticky* layer, streaked with radiating dark fibrils. Cap dark gray to purplish gray or lighter and tinged with yellow. Flesh whitish, slowly staining yellowish when cut. Odor and taste somewhat "mealy."* Gills notched around apex of stalk, subdistant, broad; yellowish white with gray to greenish yellow tinge; edges ragged. *Stalk:* Cylindric or sharply tapered at base; solid, stout. Surface minutely fibrillose-streaked; colored like gills. *Spore print:* White. **Technical notes:** Cap 4–12 cm across. Stalk 5–10 × 1–2 cm. Spores smooth, ellipsoid; 5.5–7.0 × 3.5–5.0 μm.

Fruiting: Scattered or in groups; on soil (more common on sandy soil) under pines and in mixed woods. Widespread in N. America. Fall to winter.

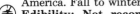

Edibility: Not recommended, although it is edible and highly rated by some people. **Use great caution**—it is easily confused with other gray Tricholomas, including some that are poisonous (see below).

Similar species: *Tricholoma sejunctum* (not shown) lacks purplish tints and has a more yellowish cap with blackish to grayish brown fibrils beneath a thin, sticky layer. It has a bitter to nauseating taste and has been reported as **poisonous.**

SHINY CAVALIER *Tricholoma resplendens*   **Pl. 21**
Medium-sized, *rounded* to *flat, sticky cap,* on a *stout stalk. All parts white. Gills not waxy. No veils* on stalk. *Cap:* Convex, with an incurved margin at first, sometimes irregular in outline

---

* See p. 10 for cautions about using taste as an identifying characteristic.

or lobed; expanding to a flat cap, typically with an uplifted outer limb and margin. Surface smooth, shiny, *sticky* when wet; white and remaining so, or occasionally light brown-spotted in age. Flesh white; firm, neither fragile nor brittle. Odor and taste not distinctive.* Gills adnate (broadly attached) or narrowly notched around apex of stalk, close, moderately broad; white or occasionally faintly flushed with pink. *Stalk:* Cylindric or slightly enlarged downward; solid. Surface smooth, dry; white. *Spore print:* White. **Technical notes:** Cap 4–10 cm across. Stalk 3–7 $\times$ 0.5–2.0 cm. Spores smooth, ellipsoid; 6.0–7.5 $\times$ 3.5–4.5 μm.

Fruiting: Solitary to scattered or in groups; on soil in hardwood or mixed coniferous-hardwood forests east of Great Plains. Late summer and fall.

Edibility: Edible, but **use great caution.** Some white and pale-colored species are poisonous (see below).

Similar species: Easily and frequently confused with many white, veil-less species in several genera, such as (1) *Tricholoma venenata* (not shown), which is poisonous; (2) Whitish Brittlegill (*Russula albidula,* p. 317, Pl. 39); and (3) several species of *Hygrophorus* (waxycaps, p. 202, Pls. 22–24), including *H. ponderosus* (not shown). **Caution:** *Tricholoma resplendens* (Shiny Cavalier) grows along with some poisonous species of *Amanita* (p. 215, Pls. 25–28). Great care must be exercised in collecting not to miss the sometimes fragile veils which identify the *Amanita* species.

SOAPY CAVALIER *Tricholoma saponaceum*   **Pl. 21**
Medium to large cap; *rounded* to *flattened, often humped.* Cap usually *tinged with olive;* may be *brownish* on *disc* (center). *Gills close. Stalk thick; stains reddish when injured. Odor "soapy"* or *lacking. Cap:* Convex, with an incurved margin and often with a low, broad, rounded hump; expanding to flat or nearly so, often with a persistent low hump and frequently also with a flaring outer limb and margin. Outline typically has irregular lobes or folds and splits. Cap occasionally is off center on stalk. Surface of cap dry to moist; smooth at first, but soon streaked and tearing into small scales. Color varies — olive-gray to light greenish yellow, yellowish white, brownish orange, or moderate to grayish brown; darkest on disc or in folds, with a lighter-colored margin and outer limb. Flesh thick, tapering sharply near margin; white, except showing cap color just under cuticle. Odor usually unpleasant ("soapy") if present — sometimes faintly "mealy"; taste strong, unpleasant.* Flesh and gills slowly stain faintly brownish pink when cut or wounded. Gills adnate (broadly attached) or notched around apex of stalk, close, sometimes with wavy or irregularly ragged edges; yellowish white with a greenish tinge. *Stalk:* Cylindri-

---

* See p. 10 for cautions about using taste as an identifying characteristic.

cal or slightly thicker below, sometimes tapered at base; often bent. Surface smooth to fibrillose or minutely scaly (use hand lens); white or weakly flushed with cap colors, brownish pink at base or staining that color around insect holes or when cut or injured. *Spore print:* White. **Technical notes:** Cap 4–12 cm across. Stalk 4–8 × 1.5–3.0 cm. Spores smooth, short-ellipsoid; 5–7 × 3.5–5.0 μm. No cystidia.

Fruiting: Solitary or in groups; on soil in deciduous and coniferous forests. Widely distributed in N. America; common in northern forests. Summer and fall.

Edibility: Questionable. Reports vary. **Not recommended. Remarks:** This is an extremely variable species. The peculiar odor and pink-staining flesh and gills are good characters when well developed, but they are often weak or lacking. People who eat Tricholomas should be alert for "non-typical" forms which may be this species.

SULPHUR CAVALIER *Tricholoma sulphureum*   **Pl. 21**
Small to medium, *rounded cap,* on a *slender stalk. All parts yellow. Odor strong, unpleasant. Cap:* Convex with a low, broad hump; margin incurved at first. Surface smooth; moist to dry. Light greenish yellow tinged with brown at center. Flesh yellow; thick on disc, tapering sharply to a thin outer limb and margin. Odor of coal tar or "sulphur"; taste disagreeable.* Gills adnate (broadly attached) or notched around apex of stalk, subdistant, broad (from apex to cap margin) and thick; yellow at first. *Stalk:* Cylindric, sometimes curved or flattened; interior solid or stuffed with cottony filaments. Surface smooth to minutely fibrillose; lacks ring or veil fibrils. Interior yellow. *Spore print:* White. **Technical notes:** Cap 2–8 cm across. Stalk 4–8 × 0.5–1.0 cm. Spores smooth, ellipsoid; 8–10 × 5–6 μm.

Fruiting: Solitary or in groups; on soil in deciduous woods. Widely distributed. Summer to fall.

Edibility: Reported as **poisonous.** Odor and taste make it an unlikely candidate for table use.

Similar species: Faded forms of *T. sulphureum* (Sulphur Cavalier) are likely to be confused with *Tricholoma inamoenum* (Irksome Cavalier, p. 188) and (2) *Tricholoma* (not *Tricholomopsis*) *platyphyllum*. (3) If odor and taste are ignored, *T. sulphureum* could be mistaken for small specimens of the highly sought edible, *Tricholoma flavovirens* (Cavalier or Man-on-Horseback, p. 186).

FUZZTOP *Tricholoma vaccinum*   **Pl. 21**
Medium-sized, *rounded, reddish brown cap;* surface *dry, fibrillose* to *scaly; cottony at margin. Stalk similar to cap.* Often grows *in clumps. Cap:* Broadly conic to bell-shaped, with an incurved margin at first, soon expanding to a broadly rounded

* See p. 10 for cautions about using taste as an identifying characteristic.

cap with a flat or humped disc (center); often irregular in outline. Surface densely fibrillose, splitting to form fibrillose scales
on outer disc and limb; less so on margin. Light brown to
brownish orange or dark reddish brown; usually lighter on
disc. Flesh white at first, but slowly staining reddish brown in
age or where bruised or cut; thick on disc, tapering sharply to
a thin margin. Odor and taste weak, somewhat disagreeable.*
Gills adnate (broadly attached to stalk) at first, soon becoming
notched around stalk apex, close, broad; nearly white when
young (before spores develop), slowly becoming tinged with
pinkish brown in age. *Stalk:* Cylindric, usually with a tapered
base. Surface fibrillose to minutely scaly (use hand lens); colored like cap except nearly white at apex and often white-
cottony at base. Interior soft to hollow. No veils. *Spore print:*
White. **Technical notes:** Cap 4–7 cm across. Stalk 5–8 ×
0.8–1.5 cm. Spores non-amyloid, subglobose; 4–5 μm in diameter.
Fruiting: In groups or clumps, on soil under coniferous trees.
Widely distributed in northern U.S. and Canada. Late summer
and fall.
Edibility: May be poisonous; **not recommended.**
Similar species: Shingle Head (*Tricholoma imbricatum*, p.
187) is more robust, with a solid, firm stalk and less hairy,
duller brown colors.

SILVER STREAKS   **Pl. 21**
Tricholoma virgatum
Medium to large, *conic* to *flattened, gray cap;* often with *radiating streaks. White gills. Thick, whitish stalk, usually flushed
with pink at base. Cap:* Conic, with an incurved outer limb
and margin, to bell-shaped at first; expanding to a nearly flat
cap with a low, narrow, broadly conic to rounded knob or
hump; often irregularly indented or lobed in outline or split.
Surface dry and fibrillose (typically streaked); may split to
form minute scales. Cap grayish brown to brownish gray or
dark reddish gray; usually lightest on margin and darker
toward center, but tip of hump sometimes yellowish gray.
Flesh thin; white. Odor faint and earthy or lacking. Gills
widely and deeply notched around apex of stalk, close; nearly
white to gray or spotted with gray. Gill edges may be uneven
or ragged. *Stalk:* Cylindric or tapered slightly upward. Surface
unpolished or minutely fibrillose. White, except usually flushed
with pale pink to pale purplish pink at base. Interior white;
solid. No veils. *Spore print:* White. **Technical notes:** Cap
4–9 cm across. Stalk 6–12 × 1–2 cm. Spores smooth, non-
amyloid, short-ellipsoid; 6.0–7.5 × 4.5–6.0 μm.
Fruiting: Solitary to scattered in coniferous and mixed forests. Widespread in N. America. Late summer and fall.
Edibility: Said to be edible, but **not recommended.**
Similar species: Very easily confused with other gray species,

including the poisonous *T. pardinum* (Tigertop, p. 188), which usually has more pronounced scales on cap and a less pointed and less distinct knob or hump on center of cap. (2) Waxygill Cavalier (*Tricholoma myomyces,* Pl. 21) is smaller, with a less robust stalk; it often has remnants of a fibrillose veil when young. (3) *Tricholoma terreum* and *Tricholoma atroviolaceum* (not shown) have darker, more violet or bluish colors, particularly on disc (center of cap). None of these has a stalk base that is flushed with pink, as is often the case with Silver Streaks.

ZELLER'S BRACELET *Tricholoma zelleri*   **Pl. 21**
Medium to large, *rounded, orange* to *brown* or *greenish cap; surface sticky, streaked* or with *flat scales. Thick, pointed, stalk* with a *high, fibrillose ring.* **Cap:** Broadly conic to convex or humped, with a strongly inrolled margin at first; expanding to a nearly flat cap, sometimes with a persistent low, rounded hump. Surface *sticky* at first, with fibrils (streaks) under the glutinous layer; may be dry and frequently cracked in age. Colors are usually mixed and quite variable. Flesh firm, thick on disc, tapering abruptly to a thin margin; white, slowly staining brownish orange when cut or wounded. Odor and taste weak to strongly "mealy."* Gills close, narrow, adnate (broadly attached) or notched around apex of stalk; pale grayish yellow at first, but soon becoming spotted or flushed with brown. **Stalk:** Cylindrical or tapered downward, narrowed to a pointed base; solid. Surface smooth and yellowish white above ragged ring; colored like cap below ring and fibrillose to scaly. **Spore print:** White. **Technical notes:** Cap 5–15 cm across. Stalk 4–12 × 1–3 cm. Spores smooth, non-amyloid, ellipsoid; 4–5 × 3–4 μm. Cystidia lacking.
Fruiting: In groups or scattered on soil under pines. Northern U.S. and Canada; often abundant in Rocky Mts. and Pacific Northwest. Late summer and fall.
Edibility: Edible **with caution. Not recommended.**
Similar species: An unpalatable species, Golden Cavalier (*Tricholoma aurantium,* p. 185), is almost identical in appearance with Zeller's Bracelet *(T. zelleri)* but has a fragile veil which quickly disappears and leaves no distinct ring of veil tissue on stalk, although there is usually a distinct color difference and often a ring of droplets marking the zone of contact between cap margin and stalk in the button stage. Both species fruit in the same area and season, but *T. aurantium* (Golden Cavalier) is commonly associated with other conifers, such as spruce, whereas *T. zelleri* appears to grow only in association with pine trees. Both species have been placed in the genus *Armillaria* (p. 133) by many mycologists.

* See p. 10 for cautions about using taste as an identifying characteristic.

Genus *Tricholomopsis*

T. rutilans

Medium to large, firm cap on a slender, solid, ringless stalk. Gills adnate (broadly attached) or notched around apex of stalk. Spore print white. Spores thin-walled, pseudoamyloid (stain purple to reddish brown in iodine). Hyphae clamped. Grows on decaying wood.

BROADGILL *Tricholomopsis platyphylla*   **Pl. 20**
Medium to large, *flat, gray cap,* with *wide, white gills. Slender, white stalk; no veils.* Grows *on decaying wood* in *springtime.*
Cap: Convex, with an inrolled margin at first, soon becoming broadly convex or flat, occasionally with a low, broad central hump; margin often upturned and disc (center) shallowly and broadly depressed. Surface smooth; moist and often with faint, narrow streaks when wet. Pale dingy pinkish white to yellowish white, yellowish gray, or brownish gray; often darkest on disc and lighter toward margin. Flesh thin, flexible; white to watery grayish. Odor and taste not distinctive. Gills adnate (broadly attached) at first, but soon notched around apex of stalk, subdistant. Each gill is thin but very wide (from stalk apex to cap margin); edge smooth to ragged. Gills white to grayish. *Stalk:* Cylindric or slightly enlarged downward; may be hollow or stuffed. Surface smooth; white or tinged with gray. Base usually attached to substrate by white strands. *Spore print:* White. **Technical notes:** Cap 5–18 cm across. Stalk 6–14 × 1–3 cm. Spores smooth, ellipsoid; 7–10 × 4–6 μm. Cheilocystidia abundant, variable. Clamps present on hyphae.
Fruiting: Solitary to scattered or in groups; on well-decayed stumps, logs, or woody debris. Common on hardwoods. Widespread in N. America. Spring and early summer; less common in fall. Often one of the first large gill fungi to appear in spring.

Edibility: Edible, but not highly rated. Older caps may have strong, disagreeable flavor and are frequently riddled with insect larvae.
Similar species: Broadgill *(Tricholomopsis platyphylla)* is likely to be mistaken for (1) a species of *Tricholoma* (previous group). (2) *Tricholomopsis fallax* (not shown), known only from the northern Rocky Mts., has a yellowish stalk and gills and smaller, broader spores. (2) Species of *Pluteus* (roof mushrooms, p. 248, Pl. 30) fruiting at the same time and in the same habitat and (3) species of *Entoloma* (pinkgills, p. 310) have *pink* spore prints and pink gills when mature.
RED RIDER *Tricholomopsis rutilans*   **Pl. 20**
Medium to large, *scaly red cap* with *yellow background between scales. Yellow gills. Scaly yellow and red stalk.* Grows on

decaying wood. **Cap:** Broadly convex, with a low, flat hump and an incurved margin at first; expanding to broadly rounded or nearly flat. Surface fibrillose to almost velvety on disc (center), soon fibrillose-scaly on limb and margin. Reddish brown to dark red or purplish red scale color dominates vivid yellow to orange-yellow ground color of flesh showing between scales, or yellow colors predominate near margin. Cap sometimes stains yellow when bruised or injured. Flesh thick, firm. Odor and taste absent or taste faint and radish-like. Gills adnate (broadly attached), becoming notched around apex of stalk, narrow, close to crowded; yellow. Gill edges irregularly torn. **Stalk:** Central or sometimes slightly eccentric (off center); cylindric or enlarged at base. Firm; interior stuffed with cottony filaments, becoming hollow in age. Surface dry to moist; color and texture like that of cap. No veil. *Spore print:* White. **Technical notes:** Cap 3–14 cm across. Stalk 4–10 × 0.5–2.0 cm. Spores smooth, non-amyloid, elliptic; 5–7 × 3.0–4.5 μm. Pleurocystidia clavate (club-shaped). Cheilocystidia abundant; variable. Clamps present on hyphae.

Fruiting: Solitary or in small clumps; on decaying conifer wood. Widely distributed; common in northern forests. Summer and fall.

Edibility: Edible, but with gummy consistency and strong, unattractive flavor, according to some reports.

Similar species: Often confused with (1) Yellow Rider (*Tricholomopsis decora,* below, Pl. 20), which is a predominantly yellow fungus with less conspicuous brown to blackish scales. In *T. rutilans* (Red Rider) the red color of the scales predominates. Pale or faded old specimens of Red Rider may resemble (2) *T. sulphureoides* (not shown), which is entirely yellow, with a fibrillose veil at first. It may develop brownish tinges on the cap and stalk scales in age.

YELLOW RIDER *Tricholomopsis decora*   **Pl. 20**
Very similar to Red Rider (above), but cap is *predominantly yellow,* with less conspicuous *brown* to *blackish scales.*
Fruiting: Common but not in quantity; on conifer logs. Northern U.S. and Canada. Late summer and fall.
Edibility: Unknown.

Genus *Xeromphalina*

Small, thin, umbrella-shaped caps on thin stalks. Stalk has *brownish orange matted hairs* at base. Grows on decaying wood.

GOLDEN TRUMPETS *Xeromphalina campanella*   **Pl. 20**
Small, brown to *yellow, thin, umbrella-shaped cap,* with *brownish streaks. Thin, brown stalk* with *yellow hairs at base.* Grows *in clumps* on *conifer wood.* **Cap:** Convex, with an inrolled margin at first, becoming broadly convex or nearly flat;

soon with a narrow, shallow central depression. Surface smooth or shallowly ribbed; moist. Strong brown to brownish orange on disc (center) to orange-yellow on margin. Flesh thin and flexible; yellow. Odor and taste not distinctive.* Gills broadly adnate (attached) at first, soon becoming decurrent (extending down stalk), distant to subdistant (see inside front cover), often interveined; narrow and tapering toward margin of cap. **Stalk:** Cylindric or appearing to be thickened at base, from *mat of brownish orange hairs;* usually curved. Tough but flexible. Surface yellow and smooth at first underneath yellow scurf, which quickly disappears (flakes off), becoming yellow at apex and grading to dark reddish brown at base. **Spore print:** White. **Technical notes:** Cap 0.5–2.5 cm across. Stalk 1–4 cm long × 1–2 mm thick. Spores hyaline (clear), smooth, amyloid, narrowly ellipsoid to subcylindric; 5–8 × 3–4 μm. Pleurocystidia scattered; ventricose to subcylindric. Cheilocystidia similar; abundant.
Fruiting: In clumps or very dense clusters, often numerous; on decaying, often moss-covered logs, stumps, and woody debris of coniferous trees. Widespread in conifer areas of N. America. Common throughout the growing season.
Edibility: We know of no reports of poisoning, but this is not likely to be a popular edible species because of its size and texture.
Similar species: Golden Trumpets *(Xeromphalina campanella)* has been confused with a number of species of *Xeromphalina* that grow on decaying wood: (1) *Xeromphalina kaufmannii* (not shown) is common on decaying oak in central and eastern hardwood forests. (2) *Xeromphalina crickiana* (not shown) is more reddish brown and is restricted to redwoods on the West Coast.

Waxycaps: Family Hygrophoraceae

Dry to sticky or greasy cap, centrally attached on stalk. Cap has waxy-appearing, thickish gills. Spore print white. Most species have no veil. Microscopic characters are necessary to confirm family and genus identification. A few species are known to be edible, but experimentation with others is not advised.

Arched-gill Waxycaps: Genus *Camarophyllus*

Medium to large, white-spored gill fungi with *waxy, mostly arched gills* that extend down stalk. Dry cap. Gill trama tangled.

---

* See p. 10 for cautions about using taste as an identifying characteristic.

SNOWY WAXYCAP *Camarophyllus niveus* **Pl. 24**
Small, white, thin, somewhat *greasy cap. Widely spaced, white, waxy gills extend down slender, white stalk.* **Cap:** Convex, sometimes with a shallowly depressed center, then flat or nearly so. Surface smooth, with translucent streaks from margin to disc; *greasy* to slightly sticky when moist and fresh, soon becoming dry. Flesh very *thin,* flexible; white. Odor and taste not distinctive.* Gills *decurrent* (extending down stalk), *distant,* narrow, somewhat interveined, thin; white. **Stalk:** Cylindric, sometimes tapered downward; interior stuffed with cottony filaments. Surface smooth or slightly fibrillose (streaked), dry. **Spore print:** White. **Technical notes:** Cap 1–4 cm across. Stalk 1.5–6.0 cm × 2–5 mm. Spores smooth, ellipsoid; 7–10 × 4–6 µm. No cystidia. Clamps present on hyphae. Gill trama interwoven.
Fruiting: Scattered or in groups; on soil in coniferous and deciduous woods. Widespread. Late summer to winter.
 Edibility: Unknown, but **not recommended.** Some species of *Clitocybe* (p. 138, Pl. 16) of similar appearance are **poisonous** (see below).
Similar species: Very hard to distinguish from (1) *Camarophyllus borealis* (not shown), if indeed they are different species, and from (2) *Camarophyllus virgineus* (not shown). Snowy Waxycap (*C. niveus*) has a thinner, more distinctly translucent-streaked cap with a thicker slime layer. Caps of *Camarophyllus virgineus* and (3) pallid forms of Butter Meadowcap (*C. pratensis,* below, Pl. 22) are not slimy or sticky. (4) Small species of *Clitocybe* (p. 138) have non-waxy, thinner gills and usually a dry cap. Some are poisonous.
BUTTER MEADOWCAP *Camarophyllus pratensis* **Pl. 22**
Small to medium, *orange cap fades quickly to orange-yellow. Gills lighter orange than cap. Stalk usually whitish.* **Cap:** Convex or obtuse, expanding to nearly flat or top-shaped; sometimes shallowly depressed. Surface smooth and unpolished; moist at first, but soon becoming dry and sometimes cracking around disc (center). Reddish orange to moderate or strong orange, fading to light or moderate orange-yellow. Flesh thick, brittle; whitish or pale orange-yellow. Odor and taste not distinctive. Gills thick but narrow, subdistant, often interveined, decurrent (extending down stalk). **Stalk:** Stout, cylindric or tapered downward. Surface smooth, dry and unpolished; *whitish* or tinged with cap color. Interior stuffed with cottony filaments. **Spore print:** White. **Technical notes:** Cap 2–7 cm across. Stalk 3–8 × 0.5–2.0 cm. Spores smooth, short-ellipsoid to subglobose; 5.5–8.0 × 3.5–5.0 µm. Clamps present on hyphae. No cystidia.
Fruiting: Solitary or in groups or clumps; in open woods or grassy places. Widespread in N. America. Late spring to fall.
Edibility: Reported as edible in Europe.

Similar species: Faded orange caps of (1) *Hygrocybe margi-nata* and (2) *H. turunda* (not shown) are more scaly and are easily distinguished from Butter Meadowcap (*Camarophyllus pratensis*) on microscopic characters.

Waxycaps: Genus *Hygrocybe*

Small to medium cap of various shapes and colors (see Pl. 22). *Gills waxy,* broadly attached to apex of stalk or decurrent (extending down stalk). Stalk slender, often brittle. Spore print white. Distinguished from *Hygrophorus* (p. 202) and *Camaro-phyllus* (previous genus) accurately only with a microscope. Gill trama bilateral.

Hygrocybe conica

SCARLET HOOD *Hygrocybe coccinea*   **Pl. 22**
Small to medium, *waxy cap; conic, spreading in age.* Cap and upper stalk *scarlet. Gills red* to *yellowish orange; close. Stalk fragile. Cap:* Obtusely *conic* to broadly bell-shaped when young, with an incurved margin; *expanding* to flat or humped, sometimes with a flaring margin at maturity. Surface smooth and remaining so as it dries out; moist to slightly slippery. Strong to *vivid red;* margin somewhat streaked when moist. Flesh thin, fragile; red to reddish orange. Odor and taste not distinctive. Gills adnate (broadly attached) or notched around apex of stalk, sometimes subdecurrent (extending down stalk slightly), thick, interveined; *red to yellowish orange,* drying pale yellow. *Stalk:* Nearly cylindric; typically bent irregularly, flattened, or grooved. Interior hollow. *Upper stalk colored like cap;* lower part yellow. Base of stalk sometimes coated with white, cottony mycelium. **Technical notes:** Cap 2–5 cm across. Stalk 3–7 × 0.4–0.8 cm. Spores smooth, ellipsoid; 7–10 × 4–5 μm. Clamps present on hyphae. No cystidia.
Fruiting: Scattered or in groups; on soil in both coniferous and hardwood forests. East of Great Plains and in the Pacific Northwest. Summer and fall.
Edibility: Edible, according to some reports.
Similar species: Easily confused with numerous other red to orange species, particularly when dealing with faded specimens. (1) *Hygrophorus puniceus* (not shown), which has a slightly sticky cap, may belong to the same species. (2) *Hygrocybe cantharellus* (not shown) and (3) Vermilion Waxycap (*H. miniata,* p. 201) are usually smaller. Their caps appear minutely scaly under a hand lens.
CONIC WAXYCAP *Hygrocybe conica*   **Pl. 22**
Small to medium, *brilliant red* to *orange* or *yellow, translucent, conic cap. All parts stain black* when injured. *Cap:* Narrowly *conic* when young, with a slightly incurved margin at first; soon becoming obtusely conic (or rarely convex) with a

conic hump on disc (center). Surface smooth; slightly sticky
when moist, soon drying and streaked or fibrillose or minutely
scaly at times (use hand lens). *Red* on disc and *red to orange
or yellow* outward, sometimes flushed with green. Flesh thin,
fragile; colored like surface of cap. Odor and taste not distinctive.* Gills close, broad, free from stalk or nearly so; yellowish
white at first, darkening to yellow or yellowish orange, sometimes flushed with green; edges wavy to irregularly torn.
Stalk: Cylindric; fragile and sometimes splitting. Interior hollow. Surface smooth to fibrillose; often develops vertical
streaks, in a spiral pattern. Stalk colored like cap or lighter,
with a white mycelium at base. *Spore print:* White. **Technical notes:** Cap 2–6 cm across. Stalk 4–10 × 0.5–1.0 cm. Spores
smooth, ellipsoid; 9–12 × 5.0–6.5 μm. Clamps present on hyphae. Lateciferous hyphae in gill trama. No cystidia.
Fruiting: Single or in groups. Widespread in N. America.
Throughout the season.
Edibility: Not recommended, as reports vary; apparently
poisonous, at least for some people.
Similar species: A number of cone-shaped waxycaps *do not
blacken* when bruised, including (1) the red *Hygrocybe cuspi-
data* and (2) the orange to yellow *H. acutoconica* (not shown).
H. acutoconica turns bright orange-red as it dries. (3) *Hygrocybe erinaceus,* (4) *H. nitratus,* (5) *H. tahquamenonensis,* and
(6) *H. nigrescens* (not shown) all blacken when bruised, but
they are not red. *Hygrocybe erinaceus* is *gray* to *yellow* and is
found in Mexico and the Caribbean Islands. The broader, usually convex to flat caps of *H. nitratus* are *brown* at first.
YELLOW WAXYCAP *Hygrocybe flavescens*   **Pl. 22**
Bright yellow to *orange overall; does not blacken* when bruised
(see Conic Waxycap, above). **Cap:** *Slimy* to *sticky; waxy,
translucent.* Small to medium, broadly convex cap has an incurved margin when young. Surface smooth and faintly
streaked when moist, soon dry and shiny; later becoming flat
or slightly depressed on disc (center), with margin remaining
somewhat downturned. Vivid orange to brilliant yellow or
lighter. Flesh thin, waxy; yellowish. Odor and taste not distinctive. Gills close, notched near stalk, broad; yellow with
lighter edges. *Stalk:* Fragile, hollow, splits readily; cylindric,
sometimes narrowed at base; often flattened or grooved. Surface smooth to faintly fibrillose; moist to slick or dry, but not
slimy or sticky. Upper part colored like gills, lower part darker
and sometimes orange down to whitish base. *Spore print:*
White. **Technical notes:** Cap 2–6 cm across. Stalk 4–6 ×
0.8–1.2 cm. Spores smooth, ellipsoid; 7–9 × 4–5 μm. No cystidia. Clamps present on hyphae.
Fruiting: In groups; on soil in coniferous and deciduous for-

ests. Widespread in N. America. Throughout the season.
Edibility: Edible, according to some.
Similar species: Easily confused with numerous yellow waxycaps that have a rounded to flat cap. (1) Both cap and stalk surfaces are sticky to slimy in *Hygrocybe chlorophana* (not shown). (2) *Hygrocybe marchii* (not shown) has yellow caps when dried out, but when fresh and moist the caps have red colors not found in Yellow Waxycap (*H. flavescens*).

PINKGILL WAXYCAP *Hygrocybe laeta* **Pl. 22**
Small, slimy to *sticky cap* and *stalk. Color* of cap and gills *variable,* but both become *pink* when they fade. *Cap:* Convex to flat, may be depressed at center; sometimes upturned on outer limb and margin. Surface smooth, with weak translucent streaks; *highly variable in color,* ranging from violet gray to pink, orange-yellow, or pale yellowish brown, sometimes flushed with olive. Flesh thin, tough; colored like surface or paler. Odor none to fishy; taste not distinctive. Gills adnate (broadly attached) or decurrent (extending down stalk), sub-distant, narrow; variously colored at first, but *fading to pink* — sometimes darker toward edges. *Stalk:* Slender, cylindric; interior hollow. Surface smooth; color similar to that of cap.
Spore print: White. **Technical notes:** Cap 1–3 cm across. Stalk 3–7 × 0.2–0.4 cm. Spores smooth, ellipsoid; 5–7 × 3–4 μm. Cheilocystidia filamentous, sometimes branched. Clamps present on hyphae.
Fruiting: Scattered or in groups; on damp soil, often in mossy places. Widespread in N. America. Summer and fall.
Edibility: Reported as edible by some authors. Few published accounts deal with its edibility, possibly because of the small size and slimy texture.
Similar species: *Hygrophorus hondurensis* (not shown) is closely related and has a similar appearance but it shows *yellow,* not pink, as it dries out. It has a more southerly distribution.
Remarks: The highly variable colors may be responsible for this small waxycap having been called by several names in N. America: *H. peckii, H. davisii, H. roseiceps,* and possibly *H. houghtonii.*

ORANGE-GILL WAXYCAP *Hygrocybe marginata* **Pl. 22**
Cap and stalk *bright orange* to *yellow,* with a *waxy texture overall.* Cap *conic. Gills remain orange-yellow* after *other parts fade. Cap:* Small to medium, obtusely *conic* to bell-shaped, with a downturned margin; expands to convex or nearly flat, with a low, obtuse hump. Surface smooth at first, moist to somewhat slippery, may become minutely scaly or cracked at maturity. Hygrophanous — strong orange to strong orange-yellow, sometimes tinged with olive when moist, fading to pale yellow or yellowish white. Margin at times faintly translucent, streaked. Flesh thin, waxy, fragile; colored like cap

surface. Odor and taste not distinctive. Gills subdistant, broad, notched near stalk, interveined; gills same color as cap or brighter — *vivid orange color persists,* at least on edges. *Stalk:* Cylindric, sometimes enlarged downward; often curved or wavy. Fragile; interior hollow. Surface smooth, dry, not sticky or slippery; pale orange-yellow. *Spore print:* White. **Technical notes:** Cap 1–5 cm across. Stalk 4–8 × 0.3–0.6 cm. Spores smooth, ellipsoid; 7–10 × 4–6 μm. No cystidia or clamps. Lateciferous hyphae rare.

Fruiting: Single or in groups; on soil in mixed coniferous and deciduous woods. Widespread. Late spring to fall.

 Edibility: Reported as edible. Do not confuse this waxycap with *H. conica* (see below).

Similar species: May be confused with other small, orange to yellow species, such as Yellow Waxycap (*H. flavescens,* p. 199), but the *persistent orange color of gills* when other parts fade or dry is distinctive. Orangish forms of Conic Waxycap (*H. conica,* p. 198) turn *black* when touched or bruised. Yellow Waxycap is edible, according to some people, but Conic Waxycap is **poisonous.**

VERMILION WAXYCAP *Hygrocybe miniata*   **Pl. 22**
Small, shiny, scarlet cap; fades quickly to *orange* or *yellow. Matching gills* and *stalk. Cap:* Convex, with an incurved margin; often shallowly depressed on disc (center), may be nearly flat when fully mature. Surface smooth and strong orange-red when moist, sometimes with translucent streaks near margin; soon drying to orange or yellow, with minute fibrillose scales (use hand lens). Margin eventually splits somewhat as it dries. Flesh thin, brittle, waxy; colored like surface or lighter, odor and taste not distinctive. Gills *waxy,* subdistant, broad, ventricose (wider at middle), broadly adnate (attached) to notched; red, fading to orange or yellow. *Stalk: Thin,* cylindric, sometimes flattened or grooved; interior stuffed with cottony filaments. Surface smooth; colored like cap, but fades to orange or yellow more slowly than cap. *Spore print:* White. **Technical notes:** Cap 1.5–4.5 cm across. Stalk 3–5 × 0.2–0.4 cm. Spores smooth, ellipsoid; 6–9 × 4–5 μm. No cystidia. Clamps present. Gill trama nearly parallel.

Fruiting: In groups or scattered; on soil, forest litter, or well-decayed wood in coniferous and deciduous forests. Widespread. Midsummer to late fall.

 Edibility: Said to be edible, but not worth the effort.

Similar species: Very commonly confused with (1) *Hygrocybe cantharellus* (not shown), which is usually slightly smaller and more slender, with decidedly *decurrent,* more orange to yellow, *widely spaced gills.* (2) Note cap shape carefully to avoid confusion with several similarly colored waxycaps (species of *Hygrocybe* and *Hygrophorus*) that have conic caps. (3) Faded specimens of Vermilion Waxycap (*H. miniata*) may also be confused with small chanterelles (*Cantharellus,* p. 81, Pl. 7) that have *more widely spaced, thick gills or gill-like ribs* on the spore-bearing surface which are *forked* or often *interveined.*

PARROT WAXYCAP *Hygrocybe psittacina*   **Pl. 22**
Small to medium, *sticky cap* and *stalk. Yellowish green all over,* or with *reddish orange* or *yellow* on *stalk and gills. Cap:* Conic to bell-shaped, expanding to convex or nearly flat, often with an obtuse hump. Surface sticky or slimy, shiny and remaining so when dry; translucent-streaked when moist, drying opaque. Moderate yellowish green to dark yellowish green, sometimes partly reddish to brownish orange to yellowish pink, yellow, or olive-green; greens fade first. Flesh thin, colored like surface; fragile, but sometimes held together by thick lime layer on cap surface. Odor and taste not distinctive. Gills subdistant, narrow, adnate (broadly attached); greenish gray at first, *soon becoming reddish orange* to *vivid yellow. Stalk:* Cylindric, sometimes tapering upward; interior sometimes hollow. Surface smooth, slimy or sticky; dark green above to yellow or orange at base when young and fresh, *soon losing green color* and eventually fading to pinkish like cap. *Spore print:* White. **Technical notes:** Cap 1–3 cm across. Stalk 3–6 cm × 2–5 mm. Spores smooth, ellipsoid; 6–9 × 4–6 μm. No cystidia. Few clamps. Gill trama nearly parallel.
Fruiting: Scattered or in groups; on soil, in various habitats. Widespread, but seldom abundant. Spring to fall.

Edibility: Edible.
Similar species: Faded specimens are commonly confused with various yellow to orange, slimy species, especially (1) *H. laeta* (Pinkgill Waxycap).
Remarks: The green colors (at first bluish in some California collections) of *H. psittacina* are distinctive, but fade quickly to orange, yellow, or pink. We emphasize again that *young, fresh specimens* which have *not faded* are essential for accurate identification, as there may be no trace of green on any but the youngest caps.

Waxycaps: Genus *Hygrophorus*

Small to medium, rarely large cap with *waxy gills.* Cap and gills continuous with stalk. Spore print white. Distinguished from other waxycaps (*Hygrocybe* and *Camarophyllus*) only with a microscope: Gill trama bilateral, as in *Hygrocybe* (p. 198), but spores smooth and thin-walled.

H. erubescens

ALMOND WAXYCAP *Hygrophorus agathosmus*   **Pl. 23**
Medium to large, *smooth, gray cap;* surface *sticky. White* to *grayish gills* and *stalk. Odor strong, fragrant, almond-like. Cap:* Convex to obtuse, with an incurved, thin, faintly hairy

margin; expanding to flat or becoming broadly depressed over
inner limb and disc (center). Surface glutinous to *sticky* when
moist; dark to light grayish yellowish brown, sometimes indistinctly zoned; color changes little as cap loses moisture. Flesh
soft; grayish above to white below. Gills subdistant, adnate
(broadly attached) or short-decurrent (extending slightly down
stalk), thin and narrow; *white to grayish.* **Stalk:** Cylindric,
sometimes narrowed slightly at base; solid. Surface smooth or
nearly so; white at first, but soon flushed with cap color; may
be dry or moist but not gelatinous or sticky. **Spore print:**
White. **Technical notes:** Cap 4–10 cm across. Stalk 4–8 ×
5.0–1.5 cm. Spores 7.5–10.5 × 4.5–5.5 μm. Clamps on divergent
gill trama. No cystidia.
Fruiting: Scattered or in groups; in coniferous and mixed
woods. Northern U.S. and Canada. Midsummer to winter.
Edibility: Edible.
Similar species: No other gray waxycap has the combination
of almond-like odor; dingy white to gray colors; sticky to
slimy, non-scaly cap; and dry, nearly smooth stalk. (1) *Hygrophorus bakerensis* (not shown) has *brown* to *pale orange-yellow* colors. (2) *Hygrophorus fuligineus* (not shown) has a
thicker, slimy stalk and *lacks the almond-like odor.* It is more
commonly reported from the Midwest to eastern N. America,
but has been found in Idaho and Wyoming.

GOAT WAXYCAP *Hygrophorus camarophyllus*   **Pl. 23**
Medium to large, *brownish gray, streaked cap. Grayish* to
white gills. Gray stalk. Fruits in fall. **Cap:** Convex (*rounded*)
to top-shaped or *flat,* with an inconspicuous, low, broad hump.
Margin incurved at first, but soon merely downturned or (in
age) margin and limb sometimes flaring upward. Surface
smooth, slightly to moderately sticky, often streaked; margin
minutely hairy or grainy. Flesh thick but fragile; white. Odor
slight, unpleasant; taste not distinctive.* Gills adnate (broadly
attached) or short-decurrent (extending slightly down stalk) in
age; subdistant, thin but broad. **Stalk:** Cylindric or tapered
downward slightly. Surface dry; smooth or faintly scurfy
above. White at base; lower part same color as cap or lighter,
gradually becoming lighter upward, to an abrupt line at point
where gills are attached. Interior solid; pale gray. **Spore
print:** White. **Technical notes:** Cap 5–12 cm across. Stalk
3–10 × 1–2 cm. Spores hyaline (clear), smooth, non-amyloid,
ellipsoid; 7–9 × 4–5 μm. Gill trama divergent; clamps present
on hyphae.
Fruiting: Solitary or in groups, on soil under pine and spruce.
Southern Canada and northern U.S. Summer and fall to early
winter.

---

* See p. 10 for cautions about using taste as an identifying characteristic.

Edibility: Edible, **with caution. Not recommended,** because it is easily confused with species of unknown or questionable edibility (see below).

Similar species: (1) Gills flushed with pink, together with the evenly colored, more sticky cap surface distinguish the very closely related *H. calophyllus* (not shown). (2) Almond Waxycap (*H. agathosmus,* above) has an almond-like odor; it is edible. (3) March Mushroom (*H. marzuolus,* p. 207) fruits in early spring, around and under melting snowbanks. It is **not recommended.** Fibrillose, streaked to mottled stalk surface distinguishes (4) *Hygrophorus inocybiformis* (not shown) and (5) Olive-gray Waxycap (*H. olivaceoalbus,* p. 208).

GOLDEN-TOOTH WAXYCAP   Pl. 24
Hygrophorus chrysodon

Small to medium, *white cap;* surface *greasy to sticky when moist.* Soft, *golden yellow granules* on *cap margin,* and sometimes on *stalk apex* or *gill edges,* as shown. **Cap:** Convex, with a thin, soft, incurved margin at first; later broadly convex, obtuse, or indistinctly humped. Margin remains incurved or downturned, even in older specimens. Flesh soft, thick; white. Odor and taste not distinctive. Gills widely spaced but sometimes interveined; decurrent (extending down stalk). Gills are white or *powdered with yellow.* **Stalk:** Cylindric, sometimes tapered at base; interior stuffed with cottony filaments. Surface white or yellow at apex, with *soft granules* or a yellow zone or ring; slimy to sticky when moist. **Spore print:** White. **Technical notes:** Cap 2–8 cm across. Stalk 3–8 × 0.5–1.5 cm. Spores sometimes curved or with unequal sides, smooth, ellipsoid; 7–10 × 3.5–5.0 μm. No cystidia. Clamps present. Gill trama divergent.

Fruiting: Solitary or in groups or small clusters; on soil in coniferous or mixed woods. Widespread. Midsummer to winter.
Edibility: Edible, according to reports.
Similar species: Frequently confused with pure white waxycaps when telltale golden granules are overlooked, or not well developed. The combination of decurrent gills, lack of distinctive odor, and fairly greasy to sticky stalk when wet will help in recognition of Golden-tooth Waxycap (*H. chrysodon*).

CLAY WAXYCAP *Hygrophorus discoideus*   Pl. 24
Small, sticky, thin cap; reddish brown at center, buff at margin. Gills pinkish tan. Stalk thin, whitish. **Cap:** Convex, sometimes with a slight hump, expanding to a nearly flat cap with a downturned margin. Surface smooth, sticky; strong reddish brown to moderate brown on disc (center), yellowish pink to pale orange-yellow near margin. Flesh thin; white, or tinged with dingy reddish orange to reddish brown. Odor and taste not distinctive. Gills short-decurrent (extending slightly down stalk), close, narrow; white or flushed with *yellowish pink.* **Stalk:** Cylindric; solid at first but soon hollow. Surface

smooth or with white fibrils on upper part; sticky below, sometimes brownish at base. *Spore print:* White. **Technical
notes:** Cap 2-5 cm across. Stalk 4-8 × 0.3-0.5 cm. Clamps
present on cuticle. Lateciferous hyphae in flesh. No cystidia.
Fruiting: Scattered or in groups; in coniferous forests. Southern Canada and northern U.S.; Midwest to West Coast. Fall
and early winter.

Edibility: Reported to be edible in Europe.

Similar species: *Hygrophorus leucophaeus* (not shown)
grows in *hardwood* forests. The margin of its cap is *white,* not
buff, and the surface of its stalk is *dry,* not sticky.

IVORY WAXYCAP *Hygrophorus eburneus*   **Pl. 24**
Small to medium (occasionally large), *white, slimy cap* and
stalk. Slender stalk. **Cap:** Convex to humped, with an incurved margin at first; becoming flat, sometimes with a depressed center. Margin hairy at first; margin and outer limb
flare upward in older specimens. Surface smooth, *slimy;* remains white or becomes yellowish when it dries out. Flesh
white; thick on disc (center), thin on limb and margin. Odor
and taste not distinctive. Gills *distant* (widely spaced); adnate
(broadly attached) and arched at first, soon decurrent (extending down stalk); broad at stalk and converging sharply toward
cap margin. *Gills white;* may become yellowish white in age or
on drying. **Stalk:** Cylindric or tapered downward, sometimes
sharply so at base; often curved or flattened. Surface *slimy;*
smooth, except fibrillose to scurfy at apex. *Pure white* or (in
age) dingy white. Interior stuffed with cottony filaments at
first, then hollow. *Spore print:* White. **Technical notes:** Cap
2-7 cm across. Stalk 4-15 × 0.2-1.0 cm. Spores smooth, ellipsoid; 6-9 × 4-5 μm.

Fruiting: In groups or scattered on soil. Common and often
abundant from Canada to North Carolina and Tennessee in
eastern N. America across the northern states to Rocky Mts.
and northwest to California. Late summer and fall to early
winter.

Edibility: Reportedly edible, but of poor quality. **Not recommended.**

Similar species: Easily confused with numerous white
waxycaps (species of Hygrophoraceae). (1) *Camarophyllus virgineus* (formerly *Hygrophorus virgineus,* not shown) *lacks
slime layers* on cap and stalk surfaces and often has streaked
margin and outer limb when moist. (2) Golden-tooth Waxycap
(*Hygrophorus chrysodon,* p. 204) has *yellow, granular scales*
on upper part of stalk and cap margin. Several white waxycaps
(species of *Hygrophorus*) develop pinkish to brownish colors in
age or upon drying. Among these, (3) *Hygrophorus chrysapsis*
(not shown) is white, fading to yellowish pink and has gills
which become *brownish* in age; (4) *Hygrophorus cossus* (not
shown) has a *strong, fragrant odor;* and (5) *H. glutinosus* (not

shown) has a scaly stalk under the slime and *develops yellow-ish brown stains or spots* on upper stalk as it matures.

PINK WAXYCAP *Hygrophorus erubescens*   **Pl. 23**
Medium to large, *thick, red to pink, sticky cap. Waxy gills extend down short, thick stalk* and are *farther apart* than in False Russula (p. 209). ***Cap:*** Convex when young, with an in-curved margin, becoming broadly humped or flat, sometimes with an upturned margin and outer limb at maturity. Surface moist to slimy or sticky, smooth or with spotty scales in age. Color variable — grayish red to grayish reddish brown or darker on disc (center); lighter outward, varying from deep pink to yellowish pink; often somewhat mottled, spotted, or streaked over a white or yellowish background. Flesh white, sometimes staining yellowish where bruised; soft, thick on disc (center), tapering to a thin margin. Odor and taste not distinc-tive. Gills *subdistant,* adnate (broadly attached to stalk apex) at first, but soon becoming *short-decurrent;* yellowish white or flushed with yellowish pink; darker pink stains or spots, espe-cially on the even or slightly ragged edges. ***Stalk:*** *Short* and cylindric or distinctly tapered toward base. Surface fibrillose or with rough scales. White at apex and sometimes beaded with drops of liquid; brownish pink below to whitish base. Interior solid or stuffed. ***Spore print:*** White. **Technical notes:** Cap 5–11 cm across. Stalk 4–8 × 0.5–1.5 cm. Spores smooth, ellip-soid; 7–11 × 5–6 μm. Clamps present.
Fruiting: Solitary or in groups or dense clusters; on soil under conifers, especially pine and spruce. Southern Canada from Great Lakes south to Tennessee and from Rocky Mts. to West Coast. Late summer to fall or early winter.
Edibility: Unknown.
Similar species: (1) False Russula (*Hygrophorus russula,* p. 209) has *close to crowded gills* and usually grows in hardwood forests. (2) Microscopic characters, especially the narrower spores, distinguish *H. russuliformis* (not shown), known only from Florida. (3) A western species, *H. amarus* (not shown), has yellowish gills, buff to yellow colors on cap, and a bitter taste. *H. amarus* and *H. erubescens* (Pink Waxycap) inter-grade and may be indistinguishable in the field. (4) Darker colors, more uniformly distributed over the cap, gills, and stalk, distinguish *H. capreolaris* (not shown). (5) *Hygrophorus purpurascens* (not shown) has a fibrillose veil that is evident on young specimens with unexpanded caps.

SLIMY WAXYCAP *Hygrophorus gliocyclus*   **Pl. 24**
A medium-sized waxycap. Cap and stalk *pale yellow,* from *yel-lowish slime* on surface. *Gills dull pale yellow.* ***Cap:*** Convex to obtuse, expanding to flat, sometimes with a low, humped disc or flaring margin and outer limb in age. Margin thin. Surface sticky to *slimy* or drying shiny and smooth. Light to moderate yellow; yellowish white on margin. Flesh *solid, white,* firm; thick on disc (center), tapering abruptly on outer limb. Odor

and taste not distinctive. Gills subdistant, decurrent (extending down stalk). *Stalk:* Abruptly tapered at base; upper stalk cylindric, mid-portion thicker. Interior solid. Surface sheathed by moderate yellow *slime* from obscure, slimy ring downward; white, with cottony hairs or fibrils above ring. *Spore print:* White. **Technical notes:** Cap 4–8 cm across. Stalk 3–6 × 1–2 cm. Spores smooth, ellipsoid; 8–10 × 4–6 μm. No cystidia. Clamps present on hyphae. Gill trama divergent.

Fruiting: In groups or clusters; on soil under conifers, particularly pine and spruce. Southeastern U.S. and western mountains. Fall and winter.

Edibility: Unknown.

Similar species: In young specimens of *Hygrophorus flavodiscus* (not shown), the gills are *pink* and the cap is white with a yellow to orange-yellow disc (center), drying yellowish pink. The spores of *H. flavodiscus* are smaller than those of *H. gliocyclus* (Slimy Waxycap) and *H. gliocyclus* is typically slightly larger and more robust.

WINTER HERALD *Hygrophorus hypothejus* **Pl. 23**
Small to medium, *slimy cap* and *stalk. Color variable — yellow* to *olive-brown,* or *reddish. Gills yellow* at maturity. *Cap:* Obtuse, with an incurved margin at first; then broadly convex to nearly flat, with a low, broad, obtuse hump; sometimes with a depressed disc (center) and slightly upturned margin at maturity. Surface smooth; brownish gray to grayish yellowish brown on disc to lighter yellowish brown, orange-yellow, or greenish yellow outward; brighter in age, sometimes becoming reddish orange or red. Flesh thin; yellow near cuticle, lighter below, becoming watery and whitish above gills. Odor and taste not distinctive. Gills subdistant, broad, decurrent (extending down stalk); white at first, but soon becoming *pale yellow. Stalk:* Cylindric, tapered toward base; solid. Upper part pale yellow, with silky fibrils; lower part *slimy* and variable in color, often matching cap. *Spore print:* White. **Technical notes:** Cap 2–7 cm across. Stalk 5–10 × 0.5–1.2 cm. Spores smooth, ellipsoid; 8–10 × 4–6 μm. No cystidia. Clamps present on hyphae. Gill trama divergent.

Fruiting: Scattered or in groups; on soil under conifers — common under 2-needle pines. Widespread. Spring to late fall or early winter.

Edibility: Edible.

Similar species: Commonly confused with (1) *Hygrophorus fuligineus* (not shown), which is *more grayish* — sometimes nearly black, but never yellow, orange, or red, as in Winter Herald. Faded caps of *H. fuligineus* may be streaked.

MARCH MUSHROOM *Hygrophorus marzuolus* **Pl. 23**
Large, robust, dingy whitish to *gray* or *black cap;* surface shiny. *Waxy gray gills. Thick, streaked stalk. Fruits under snowbanks. Cap:* Convex, with an incurved margin at first, expanding to broadly humped or flat, often with a flaring outer

limb and disc (center). Surface smooth, sticky; dingy white to olive-gray or olive-black, sometimes streaked. Flesh thick, firm; watery light yellowish gray, may be somewhat spotted. Odor and taste not distinctive.* Gills distant, broad and thick; gray to dingy white. **Stalk:** Thick, solid, firm. Surface moist, but not slimy or sticky; colored like cap or lighter. **Spore print:** White. **Technical notes:** Cap 4–10 cm across. Stalk 4–7 × 1–2 cm. Spores smooth, ellipsoid; 7–9 × 4–5 μm. No cystidia. Clamps present on hyphae. Gill trama divergent.

Fruiting: Solitary or in groups; on soil in coniferous forests at high elevations, *under and around snowbanks.* Early spring. **Edibility: Not recommended.** Widely eaten in Europe.

Similar species: Frequently confused with (1) Goat Waxycap (*Hygrophorus camarophyllus,* p. 203), which fruits from mid-summer to fall and has more closely spaced gills and warmer, grayish brown colors. (2) White to *yellowish or pinkish* gills distinguish *Hygrophorus calophyllus* (not shown). (3) Almond Waxycap (*Hygrophorus agathosmus,* p. 202) is distinguished by its *fragrant, almond-like odor.*

OLIVE-GRAY WAXYCAP   **Pl. 23**
Hygrophorus olivaceoalbus
Medium-sized, *slimy, black* to *smoky gray cap; surface streaked* and *lighter toward margin. Stalk* has *blackish bands.*
Cap: Convex at first, usually with a distinct, low, narrow to broad, pointed hump on disc (center); becoming nearly flat at maturity and often shallowly depressed over disc and inner limb. Surface smooth or wavy; slimy to sticky, conspicuously streaked or somewhat scaly below slime layer. Brownish black to dark olive-brown on disc and streaks; nearly white to pale gray on margin and limb between darker fibrils (streakes). Flesh thick on disc; soft, white. Odor and taste not distinctive. Gills white or tinged with pale grayish; close, moderately broad, adnate (broadly attached) or subdecurrent, (extending slightly down stalk). **Stalk:** Solid; interior white. Cylindric, sometimes tapered at base; often bent or wavy. Surface smooth from glutinous outer layer; banded with *blackish streaks or zones* from poorly developed ring downward; white and smooth or scurfy at apex **Spore print:** White. **Technical Notes:** Cap 3–8 cm across, Stalk 6–12 × 1–3 cm. Spores ellipsoid; 9–12 × 5–6 μm. No cystidia. Gill trama divergent. Clamps on cuticular hyphae.

Fruiting: Scattered or in clumps; on soil, in coniferous forests of West and North. Midsummer to late fall or winter.
Edibility: Widely eaten in Europe.
Similar species: Easily confused with numerous slimy, gray waxycaps (species of *Hygrophorus*). The habitat—on soil under conifers—and the dark-streaked, slimy cap and peculiar ragged, scaly zones on the stalk are key characters that identify the Olive-gray Waxycap.

Plates

Edibility symbols: = **Edible** for most people;
see pp. 10–11 and 24–26

 = **Not recommended;**
see text for details.

= **Poisonous.**

PLATE 1   ×½

MISCELLANEOUS SAC AND CUP FUNGI

1. **SOLDIER GRAINY CLUB** *Cordyceps militaris*   p. 29
   Bright orange clubs with spore-bearing pimples (perithecia). Single
   or in clusters of 2–5 from insect pupa.

Hypomyces (next 2 species): Parasites on several kinds of mushrooms.

2. **ORANGE MUSHROOM PIMPLE**   p. 29
   Hypomyces lactifluorum
   White at first, but at maturity produces bright reddish orange,
   pimple-like perithecia where gills of host normally would be.

3. **GREEN MUSHROOM PIMPLE**   p. 30
   Hypomyces luteovirens
   Green perithecia, embedded in soft tissue over badly deformed gills
   of host *(Russula),* may be evident only with hand lens.

4. **DEAD-MAN'S FINGERS** *Xylaria polymorpha*   p. 30
   Dark brown or black clubs on or around decaying stumps and logs.

5. **BROWN CUP** *Sclerotinia tuberosa*   p. 31
   Small, brown cup on long stalk rising from underground tuber.

6. **BLACK EARTHTONGUE** *Geoglossum nigritum*   p. 32
   Small to medium, dark brown to black, stalked, club-shaped head;
   round to flattened in cross-section.

7. **SLIPPERY CAP** *Leotia lubrica*   p. 33
   Yellowish, gelatinous cap; stalk same color. Cap irregularly hemispherical; often flattened, with margin bent back.

8. **WINTER SLIPPERY CAP** *Leotia viscosa*   p. 33
   Similar to Slippery Cap, but cap dark green.

9. **SCARLET ELF CUP** *Sarcoscypha coccinea*   p. 33
   Deeply concave cup with scarlet interior, exterior nearly white.
   Stalk short or lacking. Fruits in early spring.

10. **WESTERN SCARLET CUP** *Sarcoscypha occidentalis*   p. 34
    Shallow cup; interior bright red, fading to pink, exterior lighter.
    Slender stalk.

11. **PINK HAIRY GOBLET** *Microstoma floccosa*   p. 34
    Small, pink, goblet-shaped cup with coarsely hairy margin. Grows
    on buried sticks. Early spring.

12. **RUFOUS RUBBER CUP** *Galiella rufa*   p. 35
    Thick, brown, more or less top-shaped cup; margin toothed. Upper
    surface smooth; reddish brown, fading to light orange-yellow.

13. **DEEP CUP** *Jafnea semitosta*   p. 60
    Deep, flat-bottomed cup on short, thick, fluted stalk. Inside of cup
    yellowish white; outside brown, with soft, brown hairs.

14. **CHARRED-PANCAKE CUP** *Sarcosoma globosum*   p. 35
    Thick-fleshed, black cup; round at first, then top-shaped. No dis-
    tinct stalk. Cup interior gelatinous but watery.

15. **DEVIL'S URN** *Urnula craterium*   p. 36
    Brownish black, goblet-shaped cup; opens by star-shaped slit. In-
    ner surface smooth, brownish black. Stalk attached to rotting wood
    by dense mat of black filaments.

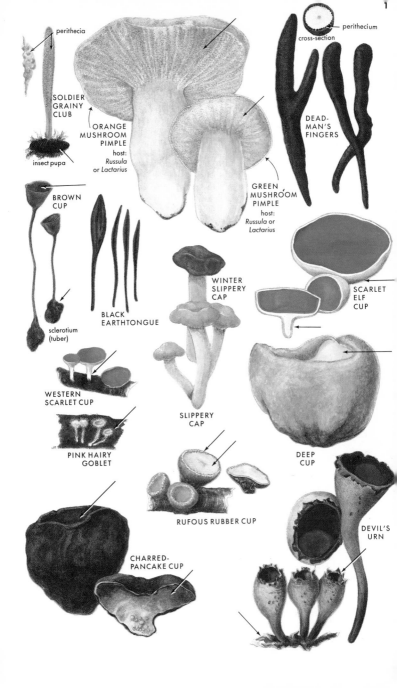

1

perithecia

SOLDIER GRAINY CLUB

insect pupa

ORANGE MUSHROOM PIMPLE
host: *Russula* or *Lactarius*

GREEN MUSHROOM PIMPLE
host: *Russula* or *Lactarius*

perithecium

cross-section

DEAD-MAN'S FINGERS

BROWN CUP

sclerotium (tuber)

BLACK EARTHTONGUE

WINTER SLIPPERY CAP

SCARLET ELF CUP

WESTERN SCARLET CUP

PINK HAIRY GOBLET

SLIPPERY CAP

DEEP CUP

RUFOUS RUBBER CUP

DEVIL'S URN

CHARRED-PANCAKE CUP

PLATE 2   **MORELS AND LORCHELS**   ×½

1. **CUP MOREL** *Disciotis venosa*   p. 36
   Shallow, brown cup or disk. Upper surface smooth or wrinkled to
   veined, often with network of ridges. Usually no stalk.

*Bell morels: Stalk usually stuffed with cottony filaments; often has
folds but no slots at base (Fig. 26, p. 42). Cap attached to stalk only at
tip. See cautions on edibility in text—many people have adverse reactions to Verpas, especially V. bohemica.*

2. **BELL MOREL** *Verpa conica*   p. 43
   Small to medium, bell-shaped, thin cap. Outer surface dark brown;
   smooth, or with very fine, net-like ridges.

3. **EARLY MOREL** *Verpa bohemica*   p. 42
   Medium-sized cap; strongly ridged or wrinkled, with lengthwise
   folds and shallow, irregular furrows.

*Morels (Morchella): Stalk hollow; often has slots at base. Cap sponge-
like, pitted. Edible, but see cautions in text (pp. 38, 41).*

4. **BLACK MOREL** *Morchella conica*   p. 38
   Dark cap, distinctly wider than stalk. Ribs mostly vertical.

5. **HALF-FREE MOREL (COW'S HEAD)**   p. 40
   Morchella semilibera
   Medium-sized, bell-shaped cap, small in proportion to stalk. Cap
   and stalk fused from about middle of cap upward.

6. **THICK-FOOTED MOREL** *Morchella crassipes*   p. 39
   Large, conical cap; yellow to tan with thin, light-colored ribs and
   wide, shallow, irregular pits. Stalk enlarged at base.

7. **COMMON MOREL** *Morchella esculenta*   p. 39
   Conical to globose, irregularly pitted cap (head). Surface whitish to
   yellowish gray, yellow, or light yellowish brown.

8. **BURNSITE MOREL** *Morchella atrotomentosa*   p. 40
   Fruits first year after forest fires. Cap dark brownish gray at first,
   lighter with age. Cracks on rib edges.

9. **NARROWHEAD MOREL** *Morchella angusticeps*   p. 37
   Narrow, pointed cap (head); surface brown, with darker lengthwise
   furrows and few or indistinct crossribs.

*Lorchels (Helvella): Cup-shaped to more or less saddle-shaped cap, on
a round or ribbed stalk. Stalk sometimes lacking.*

10. **ELFIN SADDLE** *Helvella lacunosa*   p. 45
    Gray to black cap. Ribbed stalk has small, round holes.

11. **WAVY LORCHEL (SADDLE BACK)** *Helvella crispa*   p. 44
    Cap saddle-shaped to lobed; pale cream overall. Stalk strongly
    ribbed; ribs branched, rib edges rounded.

12. **FLEXIBLE LORCHEL** *Helvella elastica*   p. 45
    Lobes of cap often curl up and overlap. Margin may curve inward
    at first. Cap dull brown; underside white to dingy yellow.

13. **VINEGAR CUP** *Helvella acetabulum*   p. 43
    Brown cup, with whitish to cream-colored, angular to sharp-edged
    ribs that run from stalk almost to margin.

14. **IVORY CANDLE** *Underwoodia columnaris*   p. 46
    White to brownish, columnar cap with shallow ribs or grooves;
    tapers gradually to round tip.

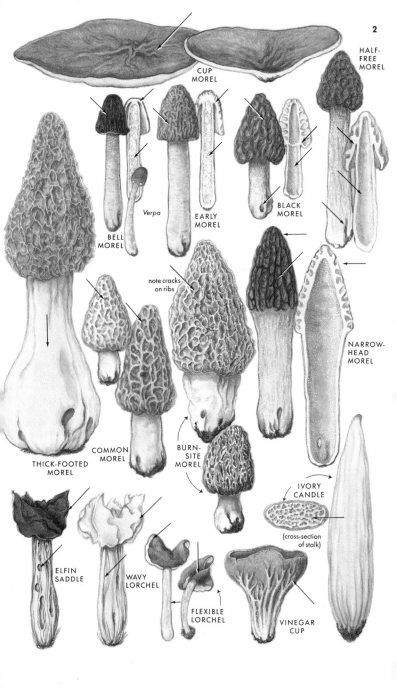

2

CUP MOREL

HALF-FREE MOREL

BELL MOREL

Verpa

EARLY MOREL

BLACK MOREL

note cracks on ribs

COMMON MOREL

THICK-FOOTED MOREL

BURN-SITE MOREL

NARROW-HEAD MOREL

IVORY CANDLE

(cross-section of stalk)

ELFIN SADDLE

WAVY LORCHEL

FLEXIBLE LORCHEL

VINEGAR CUP

PLATE 3   ×½

FALSE MORELS

1. **THICK CUP** *Discina perlata*   p. 47
   Shallow, thick-fleshed, brown cup or disk, attached at central point, usually without a stalk. Found only in early spring, in both coniferous and hardwood forests.

2. **DOUGHNUT FUNGUS** *Rhizina undulata*   p. 54
   Flat disk attached to soil by several string-like strands. Often in clusters and fused together. Surface brown, smooth or wrinkled.

False morels (Gyromitras): Brown, saddle-shaped to wrinkled or folded cap; sometimes convoluted. Thick stalk; hollow or multichanneled.

3. **BROWN FALSE MOREL** *Gyromitra brunnea*   p. 48
   One or more large, brown caps on a white stalk. Cap roughly saddle-shaped; surface wrinkled. Stalk single or compound, hollow; sometimes branched, with branching channels.

4. **CALIFORNIA FALSE MOREL** *Gyromitra californica*   p. 49
   Cap large, nearly globose or broadly convex; brown, irregularly lobed and convoluted or furrowed. Stalk deeply fluted, with conspicuous ribs; usually pink to purplish at base.

5. **FALSE MOREL** *Gyromitra esculenta*   p. 51
   Light to dark reddish brown cap, somewhat rounded; strongly wrinkled or folded and irregularly lobed. Stalk hollow, typically with a single channel; round in cross-section or flattened. Early spring. **Poisonous.**

6. **HOODED FALSE MOREL** *Gyromitra infula*   p. 53
   Cap typically saddle-shaped and irregularly lobed; yellowish brown to dark reddish brown. Stalk surface smooth or shallowly grooved, but never strongly fluted; dingy brownish to whitish, often tinted purplish. **Poisonous.**

7. **CAROLINA FALSE MOREL** *Gyromitra caroliniana*   p. 50
   Caps rounded, brown; irregularly convoluted to pitted. Cap usually shows seam-like fusion lines along some ribs. Stalk branched near tip, but branches are hidden by lobes of cap; interior multichanneled.

                                                                 p. 52
8. **SNOW MOREL (GIANT FALSE MOREL)** *G. gigas*
   Cap medium to large, rounded or flattened on top; light to dark yellowish brown. Stalk thick and fleshy; interior multichanneled. **Edible with caution — see text.** Avoid eating large amounts.

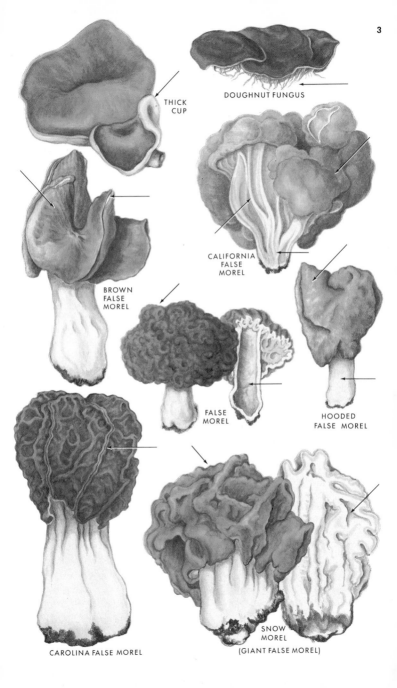

3

THICK CUP

DOUGHNUT FUNGUS

BROWN FALSE MOREL

CALIFORNIA FALSE MOREL

FALSE MOREL

HOODED FALSE MOREL

CAROLINA FALSE MOREL

SNOW MOREL (GIANT FALSE MOREL)

PLATE 4   × ½

CUP FUNGI

1. **BARNYARD CUP** *Peziza vesiculosa*   p. 58
   Large, deep, yellowish brown cup. Outer surface scurfy; somewhat mottled and strong brown at first. Grows on manure, fertilized soil.

2. **FIREPLACE CUP** *Peziza leiocarpa*   p. 57
   Fragile, shallow cup, broadly attached to burned soil. Inner surface smooth; grayish purple to grayish brown or brownish black.

3. **PIG-EAR CUP** *Peziza phyllogena*   p. 56
   Cup frequently compressed or lobed; fragile. Inner surface dark purplish brown to dark reddish gray or moderate brown.

4. **WOODLAND CUP** *Peziza sylvestris*   p. 57
   Medium to large, deep cup, sometimes spreading or almost flat. Inner surface yellow-brown to moderate dark brown. No stalk.

5. **DWARF ACORN CUP** *Geopyxis carbonaria*   p. 60
   Tiny, short-stalked, goblet-chaped cup. Dull yellow inside; outside smooth and lighter in color.

6. **BLACK DISK** *Pachyella clypeata*   p. 56
   Flat, black to dark reddish brown cup, attached very broadly to substrate (wood). Upper surface smooth to wrinkled.

7. **DAZZLING CUP** *Caloscypha fulgens*   p. 59
   Irregularly shaped; varies from a deep cup to a flat or recurved disk. Bright orange-yellow inside. Often grows near melting snow.

8. **ORANGE FAIRY CUP (ORANGE PEEL)**   p. 59
   Aleuria aurantia
   Bright orange to brilliant yellow cup; irregular, thin, brittle. Outer surface has whitish hairs (use a hand lens).

9. **FALSE EYELASH CUP** *Melastiza chateri*   p. 61
   Upper surface bright orange-red. Margin of cup thick, sometimes wavy; outer surface streaked with clusters of soft, dark brown hairs.

10. **PINE TRUFFLE** *Geopora cooperi*   p. 55
    Round, or nearly so. Surface irregularly furrowed; fuzzy from long, soft, brown hairs. Interior convoluted.

11. **YELLOW EAR** *Otidea leporina*   p. 61
    Elongated cup, attached near one side with opposite side extended upward. Surface bright yellow to light yellowish brown.

12. **EYELASH CUP** *Scutellinia scutellata*   p. 63
    Upper surface red to reddish orange. Outer surface sparsely adorned with stiff, brown, spinelike hairs.

13. **CARTILAGE CUPS** *Pseudocollema cartilagineum*   p. 62
    Crowded masses of tiny, orange, disk-like cups on a white, cartilage-like mass of tissue covering piles of mouse dung.

14. **VIOLET STAR CUP** *Sarcosphaera crassa*   p. 58
    Large cup, usually buried in soil; soon splits irregularly at top and rays bend backward. Inner surface white at first, but soon becomes lilac to lilac-brown. Outer surface white. **Poisonous?** (Reports vary).

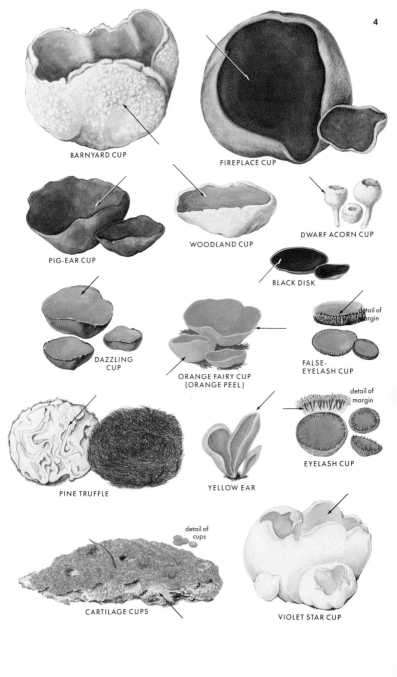

BARNYARD CUP

FIREPLACE CUP

PIG-EAR CUP

WOODLAND CUP

DWARF ACORN CUP

BLACK DISK

DAZZLING CUP

ORANGE FAIRY CUP
(ORANGE PEEL)

FALSE-
EYELASH CUP

detail of margin

PINE TRUFFLE

YELLOW EAR

detail of margin

EYELASH CUP

detail of cups

CARTILAGE CUPS

VIOLET STAR CUP

PLATE 5   ×½

JELLY FUNGI AND
MISCELLANEOUS CLUB FUNGI

1. **BROWN EAR FUNGUS** *Auricularia auricula*   p. 64
Brown, gelatinous or rubbery; shaped like a shallow cup or an ear-lobe. Outer surface usually has a hoary cast. Grows on decaying wood.

2. **JELLY CUP** *Guepiniopsis alpina*   p. 65
Small, gelatinous, orange-yellow; shaped like a top, a thick disk, or a shallow cup. Grows on decaying wood.

3. **TOOTHJELLY** *Pseudohydnum gelatinosum*   p. 66
White to grayish, tongue-like caps; attached at one side or off center. Gelatinous. Lower surface toothed.

4. **CORAL JELLY FUNGUS** *Calocera viscosa*   p. 64
Vivid yellow to orange-yellow, repeatedly branched stalks; gelatinous but tough. Branches sometimes flattened; usually forked at tips.

5. **FALSE CORAL** *Tremellodendron schweinitzii*   p. 68
Large rosettes of coral-like, upright stalks, with sparse, flattened branches. Dingy yellowish; fleshy, tough. Grows on soil.

6. **LEAF JELLY** *Tremella foliacea*   p. 67
Dense clusters of brown, thin, leaf-like lobes; gelatinous but firm. Grows on wood, especially dead oaks.

7. **WITCHES' BUTTER** *Tremella mesenterica*   p. 67
Irregularly lobed or convoluted, orange-yellow mass; gelatinous but firm. Grows on wood.

8. **APRICOT JELLY** *Phlogiotis helvelloides*   p. 66
Pink, fan-shaped to spatula-shaped cap; margin often curls over at rear. Cap tapers to short, thick stalk. Gelatinous but firm; translucent.

9. **CEDAR-APPLE RUST**   p. 69
Gymnosporangium juniperi-virginiana
Gelatinous, orange horns grow from tough, woody ball on branches of juniper. Appears seasonally, after rains.

10. **WARTY JELLY FUNGUS** *Exidisa glandulosa*   p. 66
Wrinkled, sheetlike to brainlike mass of tough, gelatinous tissue; black to yellowish brown. Tiny warts (use hand lens).

11. **WHITE CORAL JELLY** *Tremella reticulata*   p. 68
White to pale yellow stalks, repeatedly branched and fused; branches hollow, with blunt, rounded tips.

12. **RUFFLES** *Sparassis crispa*   p. 76
Large, rounded clumps of flat, wavy branches. White to pale yellow. Stalk poorly developed or lacking.

13. **CORNSMUT** *Ustilago maydis*   p. 69
Irregular silvery galls, replacing kernels in distorted ears of corn. Filled with black spore powder at maturity.

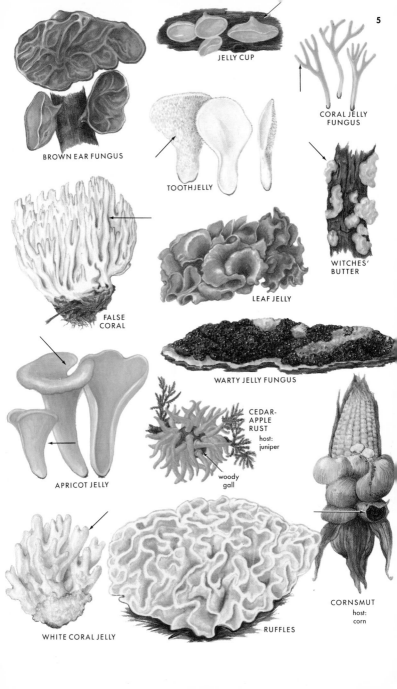

5

JELLY CUP

CORAL JELLY
FUNGUS

BROWN EAR FUNGUS

TOOTHJELLY

WITCHES'
BUTTER

FALSE
CORAL

LEAF JELLY

WARTY JELLY FUNGUS

APRICOT JELLY

CEDAR-
APPLE
RUST:
host:
juniper

woody
gall

CORNSMUT
host:
corn

WHITE CORAL JELLY

RUFFLES

PLATE 6 ×½

CORAL AND CRUST FUNGI

1. **MAGENTA CORAL** *Clavaria zollingeri* p. 71
   Thick branches with rounded tips. Reddish purple overall.

2. **PURPLE CORAL** *Clavaria purpurea* p. 71
   Clusters of pale purple, spindle-shaped clubs with no distinct stalk or branches. Grows on wet soil.

3. **WHITE WORM CORAL** *Clavaria vermicularis* p. 71
   Clusters of thin, white, brittle clubs with no branches. Grows on moist soil.

4. **FLAT-TOP CORAL** *Clavariadelphus truncatus* p. 72
   Flat-topped, yellow to brownish club; white at base. Sweet taste.*

5. **CROWN CORAL** *Clavicorona pyxidata* p. 73
   Dingy yellowish, coral-like mass with many branches; tips depressed (indented) and ringed with pointed branchlets.

6. **GREEN-TIPPED CORAL** *Ramaria apiculata* p. 74
   Compact, light brown clumps with green-tipped, coral-like branches. Grows on wood or woody debris.

7. **GOLDEN CORAL** *Ramaria largentii* p. 75
   Large clumps of orange-yellow, slender, coral-like branches on short, thick, white to yellow stalk. Does not stain when cut or bruised. **Not recommended.**

8. **CAULIFLOWER CORAL** *Ramaria botrytis* p. 75
   Large, dense, whitish head, with many compact, red- to orange-tipped, coral-like branches. Thick stalk. **Not recommended.**

9. **CORAL WOODCRUST** *Merulius incarnatus* p. 79
   Pink, soft to leathery, overlapping crusts or brackets. Undersurface has radiating ribs, folds, or elongated pores.

10. **GELATINOUS WOODCRUST** *Merulius tremellosa* p. 79
    Dingy, variously colored sheet of fused, gelatinous crusts, with radiating wrinkles. Grows on decaying wood.

11. **SPLITGILL** *Schizophyllum commune* p. 80
    Small, stalkless, fan-shaped, light gray cap; hairy, tough. Gill folds split-edged. Grows on decaying wood.

12. **FALSE TURKEYTAIL** *Stereum ostrea* p. 80
    Very thin, gray brackets, often overlapping; laterally attached to wood. Upperside has multicolored zones; underside smooth, with minute pores.

13. **CARNATION GROUNDWART** p. 77
    Thelephora caryophyllea
    Thin, blackish purple rosettes on short stalks. Shape varies. Undersurface smooth or streaked.

14. **GROUNDWART** *Thelephora terrestris* p. 78
    Deep brown, irregular or funnel-shaped cap. Upperside coarsely hairy to scaly. Underside may have warts, but no gills, pores, or teeth.

* See p. 10 for cautions about using taste as an identifying characteristic.

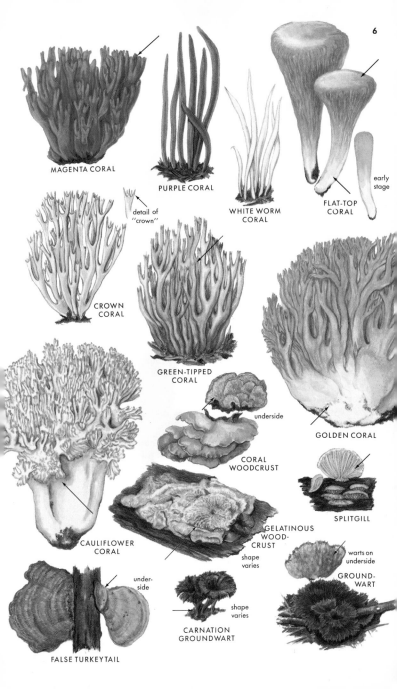

6

MAGENTA CORAL

PURPLE CORAL

detail of "crown"

WHITE WORM
CORAL

early
stage

FLAT-TOP
CORAL

CROWN
CORAL

GREEN-TIPPED
CORAL

GOLDEN CORAL

underside

CORAL
WOODCRUST

SPLITGILL

CAULIFLOWER
CORAL

GELATINOUS
WOOD-
CRUST

shape
varies

warts on
underside

GROUND-
WART

under-
side

FALSE TURKEYTAIL

shape
varies

CARNATION
GROUNDWART

PLATE 7   ×1/2

CHANTERELLES

Chanterelles (Cantharellaceae): All species soft and fleshy. Spore-producing surface smooth or with folds or wrinkles that are often called gills.

1. **PIG'S EARS** *Gomphus clavatus*   p. 86
    Firm, thick, purplish cap; flat or depressed. Thick stalk. Usually in clumps; stalks often fused. Spore print yellowish.

2. **SCALY CHANTERELLE** *Gomphus floccosus*   p. 86
    Large, funnel-shaped, yellow to orange or reddish orange cap; surface scaly. Underside wrinkled or somewhat poroid. Spore print pale orange-yellow. **Poisonous.**

3. **BLUE CHANTERELLE** *Polyozellus multiplex*   p. 77
    Large clumps of thick, spoon-shaped to fan-shaped caps; dark bluish to purplish gray. Fused stalks. Underside of cap wrinkled to veined or nearly poroid. Spore print white.

4. **HORN OF PLENTY** *Craterellus cornucopioides*   p. 85
    Very thin, funnel-shaped cap; no gills. Cap and stalk dark grayish brown to blackish. Spore print yellowish white.

5. **SMALL CHANTERELLE** *Cantharellus minor*   p. 84
    Slender cap; depressed at center or shallowly funnel-shaped. Egg-yolk yellow overall. Spore print pale orange-yellow.

6. **SMOOTH CHANTERELLE** *Cantharellus lateritius*   p. 83
    Thin, irregularly lobed, orange cap. Fragrant. Undersurface smooth to wrinkled or shallow-gilled. Spore print pinkish.

7. **FUNNEL CHANTERELLE** *Cantharellus tubaeformis*   p. 84
    Thin, often funnel-shaped, brown cap and stalk. Gills yellowish gray to pale grayish brown; narrow, forked near cap margin. Spore print white. **Not recommended.**

8. **RED CHANTERELLE** *Cantharellus cinnabarinus*   p. 82
    Reddish orange to red or pink cap, stalk, and gills. Cap flat or shallowly funnel-shaped. Gills forked. Spore print pinkish.

9. **YELLOWISH CHANTERELLE**   p. 83
    Cantharellus lutescens
    Slender, thin, yellowish brown cap; undersurface smooth to wrinkled or veined, orange-yellow. Stalk hollow. Spore print yellowish pink.

10. **CHANTERELLE** *Cantharellus cibarius*   p. 81
    Egg-yolk yellow overall. Gills blunt, thick, branched, widely spaced; gills extend down stalk. Spore print pale yellow. One of the best edible species, but be sure to distinguish it from poisonous look-alikes.

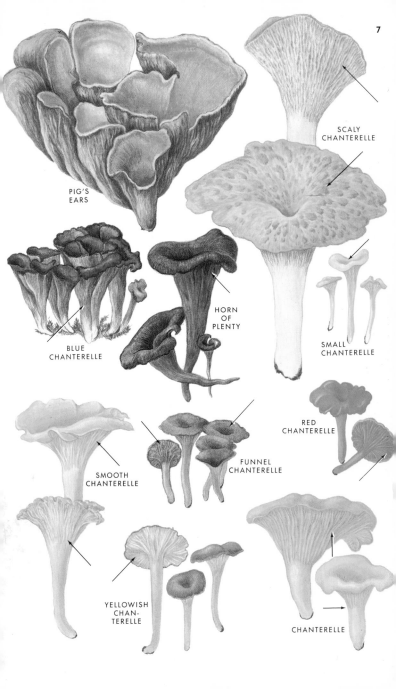

7

PIG'S
EARS

SCALY
CHANTERELLE

BLUE
CHANTERELLE

HORN
OF
PLENTY

SMALL
CHANTERELLE

SMOOTH
CHANTERELLE

FUNNEL
CHANTERELLE

RED
CHANTERELLE

YELLOWISH
CHAN-
TERELLE

CHANTERELLE

PLATE 8   ×¹/₂

TOOTH FUNGI (1)

Tooth fungi have spore-bearing spines on underside (lower surface) of cap. See also Pls. 9, 10.

1. **SPREADING HEDGEHOG** *Hydnum repandum*   p. 89
   Fleshy, orange-yellow to whitish cap on thick stalk. Spines white to pinkish yellow. No odor.

2. **SMOKY HYDNUM** *Steccherinum adustum*   p. 99
   Circular to fan-shaped or shell-shaped cap with central or lateral stalk. Cap often two-layered. Surface hairy, light brownish; turns smoky where rubbed.

3. **FUSED CORK HYDNUM** *Phellodon confluens*   p. 97
   Irregular masses of velvety, pale yellowish to brown caps that are often fused. Short stalks. Margin of cap usually white; stains gray to brown when bruised. Odor disagreeable.

4. **SCALY HYDNUM** *Sarcodon imbricatus*   p. 96
   Large, irregular, flat to rounded, brown cap with coarse, often re-curved, darker brown scales. Flesh thick, light brown, soft, fairly fragile. Spore print brown.

5. **ORANGE SPINE** *Hydnellum aurantiacum*
   Orange, felty cap with tough, fibrous, zoned flesh. Spines brown with buff or orange tips. Pungent odor.

6. **FUNNEL HYDNUM** *Hydnellum conigenum*
   Rosettes of thin, funnel-shaped caps; may be split, lobed, or Surface ridged, velvety, or streaked. Flesh zoned, with brown yellow or orange bands.

7. **BLUE SPINE** *Hydnellum caeruleum*   p. 93
   Surface velvety or matted and pitted. Cap light blue to w dark brown (in age). Flesh dark brown, two-layered.

8. **SWEET SPINE** *Hydnellum suaveolens*
   Soft, irregular, convex to flat cap; dingy white to brown. dark violet stalk. Flesh thin, fibrous, zoned (see lengthwise se Odor strong, fragrant—sickly sweet.

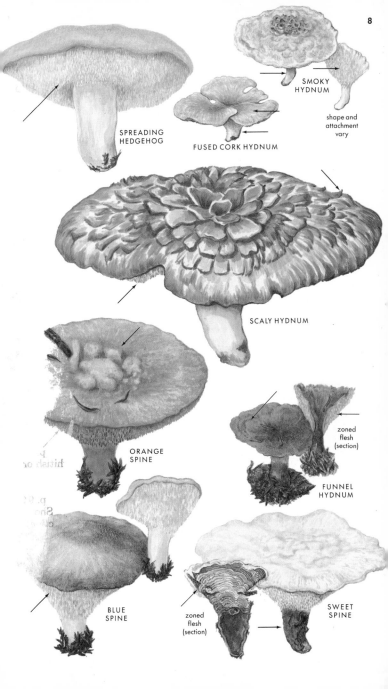

8

SPREADING
HEDGEHOG

SMOKY
HYDNUM

shape and
attachment
vary

FUSED CORK HYDNUM

SCALY HYDNUM

ORANGE
SPINE

FUNNEL
HYDNUM

zoned
flesh
(section)

BLUE
SPINE

zoned
flesh
(section)

SWEET
SPINE

PLATE 9   ×1/2

TOOTH FUNGI (2)

Toothlike spines on underside of cap produce spores. See also Pls. 8, 10.

1. **CORAL HEDGEHOG** *Hericium coralloides*   p. 91
    Coral-like caps with many branches. Coarse spines hang downward in tufts, especially at ends of branches.

2. **COMB HEDGEHOG** *Hericium ramosum*   p. 92
    Fleshy white cap with slender branches. Spines hang in continuous, comb-like rows along lower surfaces.

3. **BEARDED HEDGEHOG** *Hericium erinaceus*   p. 91
    White, fleshy, rounded cap, covered with long, downward-projecting spines.

4. **STACKA HYDNUM** *Climacodon septentrionalis*   p. 99
    Large, shelf-like fruiting bodies; white to dingy yellowish and eventually brownish.

5. **PINECONE MUSHROOM** *Auriscalpium vulgare*   p. 87
    Brown cap, attached at one side or off center. Long, slender stalk rises from decaying pine cones.

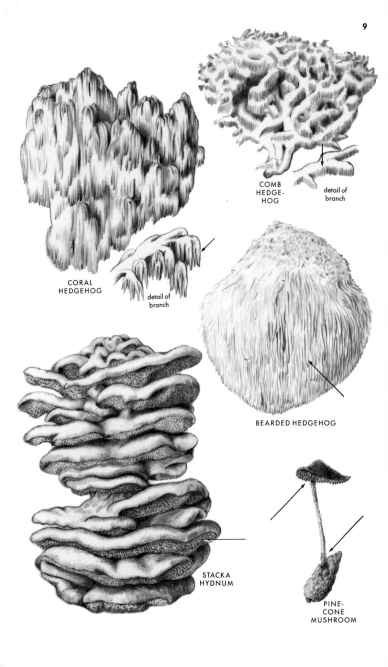

9

CORAL
HEDGEHOG

detail of
branch

COMB
HEDGE-
HOG

detail of
branch

BEARDED HEDGEHOG

STACKA
HYDNUM

PINE-
CONE
MUSHROOM

TOOTH FUNGI (3) AND BOLETES

First 8 species: Toothlike spines on underside of cap produce spores. See also Pls. 8, 9.

1. **GRAYISH WHITE HYDNUM** *Bankera fuligineoalba*   p. 88
   Cap dark yellowish brown (at center) to dingy yellowish pink (on margin); darker when wet. Brittle. Whitish spines. Forest debris adheres to cap surface. White spore print.

2. **FLESHY HYDNUM** *Bankera carnosa*   p. 88
   Brown cap, smooth at first, sometimes scaly in age; often lobed or split and wavy. Fragrant. Teeth whitish. Spore print white.

3. **CRACKED HYDNUM** *Sarcodon rimosus*   p. 96
   Cap convex to depressed at center. Surface dry; smooth at first, then scaly and typically cracking. Brown spore print.

4. **WHITE HEDGEHOG** *Hydnum albidum*   p. 89
   Thick, white to pale grayish yellow cap on a thick, white stalk. Flesh white, turning dull yellow to orange when cut or bruised; peppery taste when raw.* Often confused with white forms of the Spreading Hedgehog *(H. repandum),* Pl. 8.

5. **DEPRESSED HEDGEHOG** *Hydnum umbilicatum*   p. 90
   Irregular, rounded to flat cap, with depressed center and wavy margin; orange-buff to reddish brown. Grows on boggy soil under conifers.

6. **DUSKY CORK HYDNUM** *Phellodon niger*   p. 97
   Rounded to flat, stalked caps, often fused together. Surface velvety; black to brown, or gray; center darkest. **Not recommended.**

7. **ZONED CORK HYDNUM** *Phellodon tomentosus*   p. 98
   Thin, brown, cap; flat or shallowly depressed. Surface velvety, zoned; light to dark brown toward center.

8. **SCABER HYDNUM** *Sarcodon scabrosus*   p. 95
   Brown, convex, smooth (at first) to scaly cap, with an incurved, whitish margin. Pointed stalk is blackish green at base. Taste bitter.* **Not recommended.**

Next 3 species (boletes): Tubes or pores on underside of cap produce spores. See also Pls. 12, 13.

9. **OLD-MAN-OF-THE-WOODS** *Strobilomyces floccopus*   p. 112
   Coarse, dry, gray to blackish scales on cap; cap white to nearly black, with red-staining tubes on underside. Slender, tough stalk; surface fibrillose to shaggy. **Not recommended.**

10. **PARASITE BOLETE** *Boletus parasiticus*   p. 107
    Dry, yellowish brown cap with yellow pores on underside. The only bolete that is parasitic on a *Scleroderma* (puffball).

11. **HOLLOW STALK** *Suillus cavipes*   p. 114
    Rounded to flat, brown cap; surface fibrillose to scaly. Cap yellow on underside, with large, angular pores. Stalk soon becomes hollow. Always grows under larch.

* See p. 10 for cautions about using taste as an identifying characteristic.

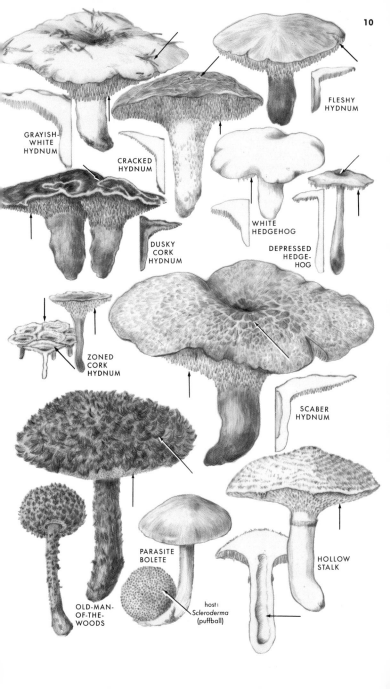

10

GRAYISH-WHITE HYDNUM

CRACKED HYDNUM

FLESHY HYDNUM

DUSKY CORK HYDNUM

WHITE HEDGEHOG

DEPRESSED HEDGE-HOG

ZONED CORK HYDNUM

SCABER HYDNUM

OLD-MAN-OF-THE-WOODS

PARASITE BOLETE

host: *Scleroderma* (puffball)

HOLLOW STALK

PLATE 11 ✕ 1/2

BOLETES (2)

Boletes (all 12 species): Note spore-bearing tube layer with round or angled pores on underside of cap. First 2 species (Gyroporus) have yellow spore print; other 10 species (Suillus) have brown spore print.

1. **CORNFLOWER BOLETE** *Gyroporus cyanescens*   p. 110
   Dry, yellowish cap with white to yellow tubes. Stalk yellow. All parts immediately stain blue when cut or bruised. **Not recommended.**

2. **CHESTNUT BOLETE** *Gyroporus castaneus*   p. 110
   Small to medium, dry, yellowish to reddish brown cap with whitish tubes. Stalk slender, brown, hollow.

3. **AMERICAN SLIPPERYCAP** *Suillus americanus*   p. 113
   Bright yellow cap, with red to reddish brown scales embedded in slime. Thin, yellow stalk, dotted with dark reddish glands. Tubes dingy yellow; pores angular. Grows under white pine.

4. **LAKE'S SLIPPERYCAP** *Suillus lakei*   p. 116
   Cap surface fibrillose to scaly, often sticky; dingy pinkish to yellowish, with yellow tubes and large, angular pores on underside. Short, thick, ringed stalk.

5. **PAINTED SLIPPERYCAP** *Suillus pictus*   p. 118
   Dry, pink to red, scaly cap, with small, yellow, angular pores. Stalk usually soft-hairy to scaly. Grows under eastern white pine.

6. **MOUNTAIN SLIPPERYCAP** *Suillus umbonatus*   p. 120
   Thin, greenish yellow cap with sticky, brown-streaked surface. Large, angular pores. Stalk slender, ring slimy. Grows under pine.

7. **SLIPPERY JACK** *Suillus luteus*   p. 116
   Slimy, brown cap. Short stalk has brown glandular dots and well-developed ring. Undersurface of ring has sticky or slimy layer, tinged reddish purple to reddish brown. Grows under conifers.

8. **GRANULATED BOLETE** *Suillus granulatus*   p. 115
   Cap brown to yellowish; sticky. Grayish yellow tubes have small, round pores; tubes and pores do not stain (change color) when cut. Stalk dotted with brown (or pink) glands near cap.

9. **WOOLLYCAP** *Suillus tomentosus*   p. 119
   Yellow, velvety to soft-scaly cap; brown tubes on underside. All parts stain blue when cut or bruised. Be sure to distinguish this bolete from other blue-staining species that may be **poisonous.**

10. **PALE SLIPPERYCAP** *Suillus neoalbidipes*   p. 117
    Rounded, pale-colored, smooth cap, with pale yellowish tubes. Margin of cap (when young) has cottony, white to pinkish remnants of partial veil. Stalk white to yellowish or reddish brown. Grows under pine. Recently reported as **toxic.**

11. **STUBBY-STALK** *Suillus brevipes*   p. 114
    Slimy, grayish to reddish brown cap with thick, yellow tube layer. Stubby, white to yellowish stalk lacks glandular dots; no ring.

12. **PINE SLIPPERYCAP** *Suillus pseudobrevipes*   p. 118
    Cap more distinctly streaked than in Stubby-stalk *(S. brevipes)*; Cottony veil remnants on margin of young cap, or on stalk, as an incomplete ring.

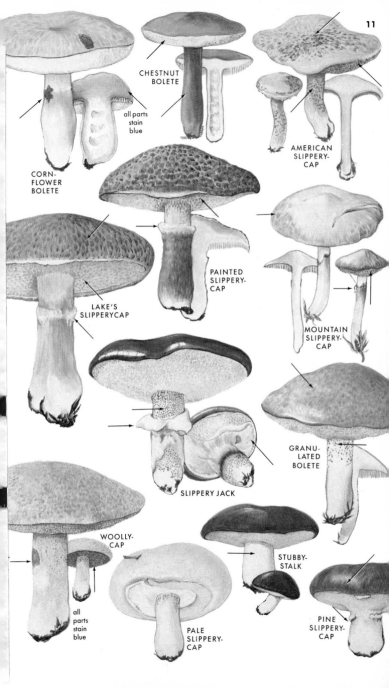

11

CHESTNUT BOLETE

all parts stain blue

CORN-FLOWER BOLETE

AMERICAN SLIPPERY-CAP

PAINTED SLIPPERY-CAP

LAKE'S SLIPPERYCAP

MOUNTAIN SLIPPERY-CAP

GRANU-LATED BOLETE

SLIPPERY JACK

WOOLLY-CAP

all parts stain blue

PALE SLIPPERY-CAP

STUBBY-STALK

PINE SLIPPERY-CAP

PLATE 12 × ½

BOLETES (3)

Boletes (next 12 species): Note tubes and pores on underside of cap. See also Pls. 10, 11, and 13. First 5 species (*Tylopilus*): Spore print pink to reddish brown.

1. **BITTER BOLETE** *Tylopilus felleus* p. 122
   Rounded to flat, smooth, brown cap with white to pinkish tubes. Stalk solid, firm; distinctly netted at top. Taste very bitter.*

2. **BITTERSWEET BOLETE** *Tylopilus ballouii* p. 121
   Thick, smooth, reddish orange cap, with pale yellowish tubes that stain brown when bruised. Stalk thick, yellowish. Taste slightly bitter or acidic.* **Not recommended.**

3. **QUESTION BOLETE** *Tylopilus indecisus* p. 123
   Rounded to flat, brown cap, with white to pink or pinkish brown tubes. Stalk may be netted near top, but always smooth below. Taste not distinctive.*

4. **GRAY-VIOLET BOLETE** *Tylopilus plumbeoviolaceous* p. 124
   Grayish purple to brown cap, with small, round, brownish pink pores. Thick, club-shaped, purplish stalk. **Not recommended.**

5. **YELLOW FOOT** *Tylopilus chromapes* p. 121
   Pink to red, rounded, dry cap, with small-mouthed, yellowish white to pinkish tubes. Slender stalk; bright yellow at base.

6. **SHAGNET** *Boletellus russellii* p. 101
   Brown cap with dry, irregularly cracked surface; olive tubes. Stalk reddish, with coarse, shaggy, net-like scales.

7. **BIRCH BOLETE** *Austroboletus betula* p. 100
   Shiny, bright-colored, convex cap; yellow to brown tubes. Slender stalk with coarse network of ridges.

8. **ROSY BOLETE** *Fuscoboletinus ochraceoroseus* p. 109
   Large, dry, fibrillose, rose-tinted cap; large, yellow, angular pores. Grows under larch in the Northwest. **Not recommended.**

9. **SHALLOW-PORE** *Boletinellus meruliodes* p. 101
   Irregularly shaped, olive- to yellow-brown cap, with shallow, angular pores that stain blue-green, then reddish brown. Pores radiate from stalk. **Not recommended.**

10. **BIRCH SCABERSTALK** *Leccinum scabrum* p. 111
    Grayish brown to yellowish brown, fleshy cap. Solid, whitish stalk has dark brown to black, rough-edged scales.

11. **ASPEN SCABERSTALK** *Leccinum aurantiacum* p. 111
    Large, dry, reddish orange, fleshy cap on a solid, whitish stalk roughened with dark scales. Flesh thick; turns pink, then black, when cut or bruised. See also *L. insigne.*

12. **ASPEN SCABERSTALK** *Leccinum insigne* p. 111
    Similar to *L. aurantiacum,* but cap more orange; tubes yellow. Flesh stains gray without turning red or pink first.

* See p. 10 for cautions about using taste as an identifying characteristic.

BITTER
BOLETE

12

QUESTION
BOLETE

BITTERSWEET
BOLETE

YELLOW
FOOT

BIRCH
BOLETE

SHAG-
NET

GRAY-VIOLET
BOLETE

BIRCH
SCABER-
STALK

ROSY
BOLETE

SHALLOW-
PORE

L. aurantiacum
ASPEN
SCABERSTALKS

L. insigne

PLATE 13 $\times 1/2$

BOLETES (4)

Boletes: *Soft tube layer with round pores on underside of cap. See also Pls. 10–12.*

1. **KING BOLETE (CEPE)** *Boletus edulis* p. 104
Brown, thick-fleshed cap. Pore surface of young cap white; pore mouths very small. Stalk thick; whitish to brown, sometimes tinged with pink. Whitish net over stalk surface.

2. **GOLDSTALK** *Boletus ornatipes* p. 107
Gray to yellowish brown cap with bright yellow pores. Slender, bright yellow stalk with netted or shaggy surface.

3. **RED-DOT** *Boletus rubropunctus* p. 108
Rounded, shiny, orange to red or reddish brown cap. Flesh and tubes yellow; no color change when cut or bruised. Slender stalk with soft scales.

4. **PEPPER BOLETE** *Boletus piperatus* p. 108
Reddish orange to brown, dry cap on a solid, similarly colored stalk. Pore mouths red. Taste strong, sharply peppery.* **Poisonous — do not try it intentionally.**

5. **SUMMER REDCAP** *Boletus fraternus* p. 105
Red, velvety cap; cracks in age, exposing yellow flesh. Stains blue or greenish when cut or bruised.

6. **BRAGGER'S BOLETE** *Boletus mirabilis* p. 106
Cap and stalk dark reddish brown to grayish brown. Cap surface woolly to grainy or slightly roughened. Pores yellow. Upper stalk coarsely netted.

7. **SPOTTED BOLETE** *Boletus affinus* var. *maculosus* p. 103
Dry, yellowish brown cap; often spotted, as shown. White flesh and tubes; white or yellowish pores.

8. **BAY BOLETE** *Boletus badius* p. 103
Dark brown cap; more or less sticky. Pores greenish yellow, sometimes staining bluish when wounded.

9. **FROST'S BOLETE** *Boletus frostii* p. 106
Shiny red cap on a red, strongly netted stalk. Pore surface red. All parts quickly stain blue when cut. **Not recommended.**

* **See p. 10 for cautions about using taste as an identifying characteristic.**

KING
BOLETE
(CEPE)

GOLDSTALK

RED-
DOT

PEPPER
BOLETE

BRAGGER'S
BOLETE

SUMMER
REDCAP

stains
blue or
greenish

all
parts
quickly
stain
blue

SPOTTED
BOLETE

BAY
BOLETE

sometimes
stains
bluish

FROST'S
BOLETE

PLATE 14   ×½

PORE AND SHELF FUNGI

Polypores (all except #5): Tough to woody at maturity.

1. **ARTIST'S FUNGUS** *Ganoderma applanatum*   p. 127
   Large, flat, woody, grayish brown bracket. Pore surface (underside)
   white, but quickly turns brown when cut or bruised.

2. **BIRCH MAZE-GILL** *Lenzites betulina*   p. 128
   Thin, leathery to woody brackets on dead wood. Upper surface
   zoned; lower surface whitish, gill-like.

3. **TURKEYTAIL** *Coriolus versicolor*   p. 125
   Thin, leathery caps (brackets), often overlapping; laterally attached to wood. Upper surface multicolored, zoned; lower surface
   has tiny pores (compare with False Turkeytail, Pl. 6).

4. **DRYAD SADDLE** *Polyporus squamosus*   p. 129
   Large, thick, brown, scaly caps on eccentric (off-center) stalks
   growing out of old stumps or logs. Pore surface white to yellowish;
   pores large, angular, decurrent (extending down stalk). Grows on
   old stumps or logs.

5. **BEEFSTEAK** *Fistulina hepatica*   p. 129
   Large, red, bracket-like cap; flesh streaked somewhat like meat.
   Undersurface yellow, with minute tubes.

6. **REDBELT** *Fomitopsis pinicola*   p. 126
   Large, thick, woody bracket; laterally attached to dead wood or
   living trees. Upper surface mostly brown to gray; white to red-
   banded near margin when fresh. Pores white.

7. **OAK MAZE-GILL** *Daedalea quercina*   p. 125
   Tough, yellowish gray to brownish brackets. Pore walls thick,
   maze-like. Grows on stumps and rotting logs.

8. **HEN-OF-THE-WOODS** *Grifolia frondosus*   p. 128
   Large clumps of soft, grayish brown, fan-shaped caps that overlap
   each other and are fused by massive fleshy stalk.

9. **SULPHUR SHELF** *Laetiporus sulphureus*   p. 127
   Large, soft, yellow to orange, stalkless brackets. Grows in overlapping rosettes in living trees and dead wood. Edible **with caution**
   (young specimens only)—some people have experienced mild poisoning symptoms.

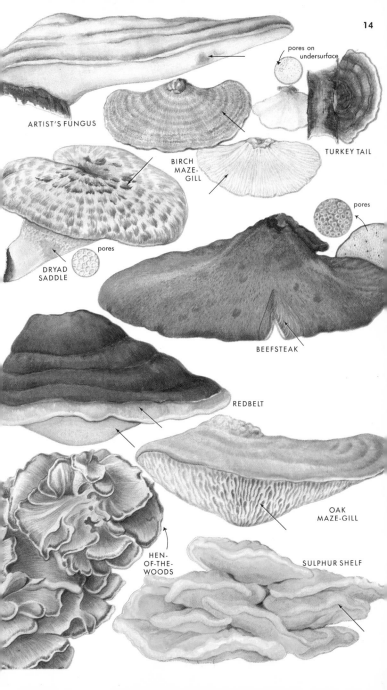

14

ARTIST'S FUNGUS

pores on undersurface

TURKEY TAIL

BIRCH MAZE-GILL

DRYAD SADDLE

pores

pores

BEEFSTEAK

REDBELT

OAK MAZE-GILL

HEN-OF-THE-WOODS

SULPHUR SHELF

PLATE 15   all ×½ (except #8)

WHITE- AND PALE-SPORED MUSHROOMS:
Tricholomataceae (1)

1. **MISTY BRACELET** *Armillaria caligata*   p. 134
   Streaks of dark brown fibrils (hairs) and flattened scales on whitish
   cap surface and lower stalk. Gills white. Ring white, membranous;
   flares upward.

2. **SCALY BRACELET** *Armillaria albolonaripes*   p. 133
   Rounded to flat, yellow cap; sometimes sticky and tinged with
   gray, may appear scaly. Gills yellow, with sawtoothed edges. Stalk
   scaly.

3. **FRIENDSHIP MUSHROOM** *Armillaria tabescens*   p. 137
   No ring on stalk. Gills usually extend farther down stalk than in
   Honey Mushroom. **Not recommended.**

4. **HONEY MUSHROOM** *Armillaria mellea*   p. 136
   Clumps of thin, flat to humped caps; surface fibrillose or scaly.
   Ringed stalk. Cap color varies from grayish pink to yellow or
   brown. Spores white. **Not recommended.**

5. **YELLOW BRACELET**   p. 135
   Armillaria straminea var. *americana*
   Bright yellow cap with light yellow gills and white stalk. Cap and
   stalk have yellow, recurved scales.

6. **SAFFRON PARASOL** *Cystoderma amianthimum*   p. 152
   Fragile, light brown to yellowish, grainy cap on a slender stalk with
   a faint ring. Gills white to pale yellowish.

7. **GOLDEN COINCAP** *Cyptotrama chrysopepla*   p. 151
   Very small, bright golden yellow, dry cap and stalk. Gills white to
   yellow. Grows on wood.

8. **COMMANDER** *Catathelasma imperiale* (×¼)   p. 137
   Very large, dingy brown, thick cap; rounded to flat. Thick, pointed
   stalk with a double ring. Gills close, decurrent (extending down
   stalk).

9. **TIGER SAWGILL** *Lentinus tigrinus*   p. 160
   Cap round at first, later shallowly funnel-shaped. Surface dry, with
   brown scales. Flesh tough. White gills with ragged edges extend
   down scaly white stalk. Grows on wood, often in clusters.

10. **SCALY SAWGILL** *Lentinus lepideus*   p. 159
    Round cap with brown scales, on a tough, scaly stalk. Gills white to
    yellowish, with sawtoothed edges. Grows from conifer wood
    (stumps and logs).

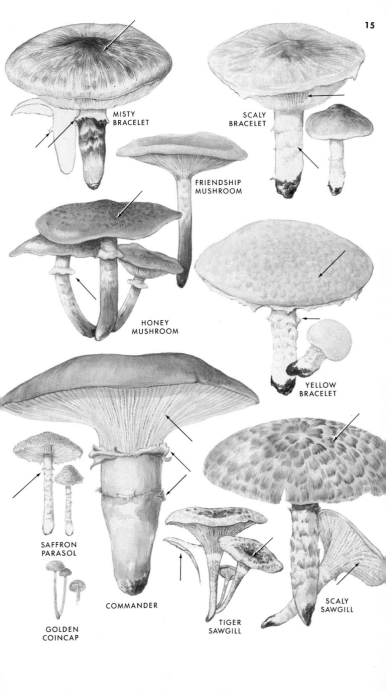

15

MISTY
BRACELET

SCALY
BRACELET

FRIENDSHIP
MUSHROOM

HONEY
MUSHROOM

YELLOW
BRACELET

SAFFRON
PARASOL

GOLDEN
COINCAP

COMMANDER

TIGER
SAWGILL

SCALY
SAWGILL

PLATE 16   ×½

WHITE- AND PALE-SPORED MUSHROOMS:
Tricholomataceae (2)

1. **BLUSHING BOWLCAP** *Clitocybe irina*   p. 141
   Dry, white to dull pinkish cap; flat or depressed at center. Gills crowded; attached to stalk or extending down it slightly. Stalk cylindrical or club-shaped, with no ring. Pleasant odor. **Not recommended—poisonous** to some people.

2. **CLUSTERED FUNNELCAP** *Clitocybe subconnexa*   p. 145
   Clumps of smooth, white caps with dingy whitish gills. White to dingy whitish stalks. Odor pleasant or lacking, rarely disagreeable. Grows in hardwood forests. **Not recommended.**

3. **CLUBFOOT FUNNELCAP** *Clitocybe clavipes*   p. 139
   Gray-brown cap; usually flat or depressed at center. Gills extend down stalk. Stalk bulbous. **Not recommended.**

4. **BLEWIT** *Clitocybe nuda*   p. 143
   Smooth violet cap; hygrophanous (color varies as it dries). Violet gills and stalk. Spore print dull yellowish pink.

5. **DINGY BOWLCAP** *Clitocybe tarda*   p. 145
   Cap brownish pink to violet-tinged; hygrophanous. Gills close; extend down slender stalk at maturity. **Not recommended.**

6. **WHITE STRINGS** *Clitocybe albirhiza*   p. 138
   Thin, white to pinkish yellow cap on thin, white stalk; attached to conifer needles by numerous white, threadlike strands. Grows under or near melting snowbanks.

7. **SWEAT MUSHROOM** *Clitocybe dealbata*   p. 140
   Small, white, dry cap; rounded to flat. Gills white, sometimes extending down slender white stalk. Common in grassy areas. **Poisonous.**

8. **ANISE FUNNELCAP** *Clitocybe odora*   p. 144
   Cap tinted bluish green. Gills extend slightly down stalk. Spore print yellowish pink to pale orange-yellow. Odor of anise.

9. **CLOUDY FUNNELCAP** *Clitocybe nebularis*   p. 142
   Thick, brownish gray, smooth cap. Dingy whitish gills extend down thick stalk. Disagreeable odor. **Poisonous.**

10. **FOREST FUNNELCAP** *Clitocybe gibba*   p. 141
    Light pinkish brown, funnel-shaped cap, with crowded gills that extend down stalk.

11. **FALSE CHANTERELLE** *Hygrophoropsis aurantiacus*   p. 154
    Orange, flat to funnel-shaped cap. Gills crowded, repeatedly forked; gills extend down stalk. No ring on stalk. Spore print white to yellowish white. **Not recommended.** Compare with true chanterelles (edible), Jack-O-Lantern (poisonous), and Showy Flamecap (poisonous).

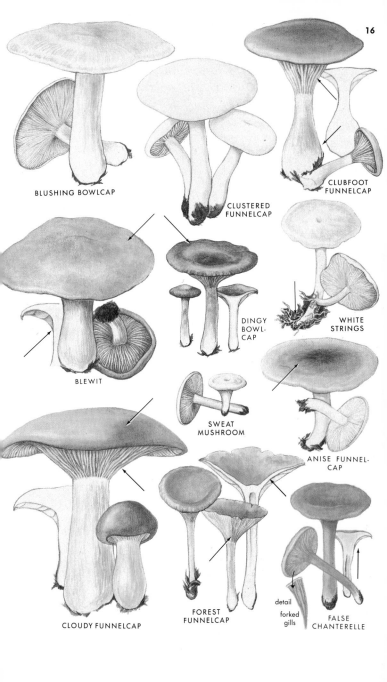

16

BLUSHING BOWLCAP

CLUSTERED FUNNELCAP

CLUBFOOT FUNNELCAP

BLEWIT

DINGY BOWL-CAP

WHITE STRINGS

SWEAT MUSHROOM

ANISE FUNNEL-CAP

CLOUDY FUNNELCAP

FOREST FUNNELCAP

detail forked gills

FALSE CHANTERELLE

PLATE 17   most ×½ (see plate)

WHITE- AND PALE-SPORED MUSHROOMS:
Tricholomataceae (3)

1. **STREAKED COINCAP** *Clitocybula abundans* p. 146
   Thin, light yellowish brown to grayish yellow cap, streaked with gray. Stalk thin, white, hollow. Grows in dense clusters.

2. **FOREST FRIEND** *Collybia dryophila* p. 149
   Cap brown, hygrophanous; margin lighter, incurved at first. Gills crowded, white. Stalk lighter than cap. **Poisonous.**

3. **SPOTTED COINCAP** *Collybia maculata* p. 150
   Pale yellow, convex or humped cap. All parts develop scattered reddish brown spots. Grows on decaying conifer wood.

4. **APPLESEED COINCAP** *Collybia tuberosa* p. 151
   Dull white, dry mushroom. Brown sclerotium (looks like apple seed) is rooted in black remains of decaying mushroom.

5. **TUFTED COINCAP** *Collybia confluens* p. 148
   Paper-thin, dry, brown, flat cap. Slender stalk is hairy at base. Grows in dense clusters on decaying leaves.

6. **PURPLE COINCAP** *Collybia iocephala* p. 149
   Small, rounded, light purple cap with a central depression and streaked margin. Reddish purple gills. Stalk whitish.

7. **CLUSTER COINCAP** *Collybia acervata* p. 147
   Reddish brown, thin, cap and stalk; hygrophanous. Gills white to pinkish. Grows in dense clusters on decaying wood. **Poisonous.**

8. **BUTTER COINCAP** *Collybia butyracea* p. 147
   Cap feels like butter. Gills ragged-edged. Stalk may be twisted.

9. **VELVET SHANK** *Flammulina velutipes* p. 152
   Shiny, orange-yellow cap; yellowish white gills. Lower part of stalk dark brown, velvety; stalks often fused at base.

10. **NAVEL SAWGILL** *Lentinellus omphalodes* p. 158
    Brown, moist cap has ragged gill edges. Stalk short, ridged.

11. **GOLDGILL NAVELCAP** *Omphalina chrysophylla* p. 177
    Brown, funnel-shaped cap. Orange-yellow gills extend down stalk.

12. **MAGNOLIA COINCAP** *Strobilurus conigenoides* p. 184
    Very small, rounded to flat, dry, dingy white cap on a thin, white stalk. Grows from dead "cones" of magnolia trees.

13. **HAIRY SAWGILL** *Lentinellus ursinus* p. 159
    Dry, brown cap with close, ragged-edged gills. Grows in bracket-like clusters (sometimes overlapping), on decaying wood.

14. **TINY NAVELCAP** *Omphalina postii* p. 177
    Orange to whitish cap; center depressed. White gills extend down fragile, yellowish stalk. Grows in very wet, mossy ground.

15. **WESTERN COINCAP** *Strobilurus occidentalis* p. 184
    Grayish brown, rubbery cap on a rooting stalk. Grows from buried cones of spruce trees.

16. **JACK-O-LANTERN** *Omphalotus illudens* p. 178
    Large, orange cap with broad gills that extend down stalk. Grows in clumps on stumps, roots, or buried wood. **Poisonous.**

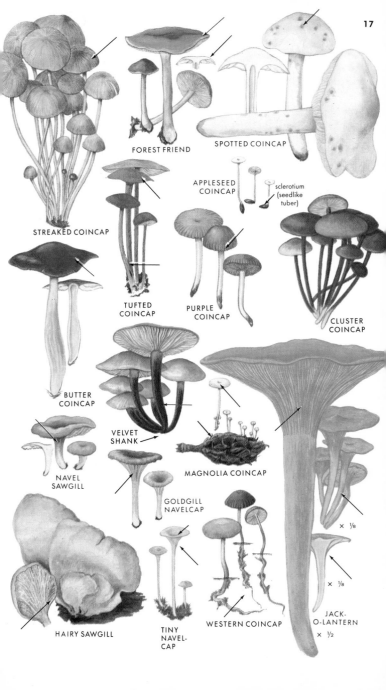

17

FOREST FRIEND

SPOTTED COINCAP

STREAKED COINCAP

APPLESEED
COINCAP

sclerotium
(seedlike
tuber)

TUFTED
COINCAP

PURPLE
COINCAP

CLUSTER
COINCAP

BUTTER
COINCAP

VELVET
SHANK

MAGNOLIA COINCAP

NAVEL
SAWGILL

GOLDGILL
NAVELCAP

× ⅛

HAIRY SAWGILL

TINY
NAVEL-
CAP

WESTERN COINCAP

× ⅛

JACK-
O-LANTERN

× ½

PLATE 18   × ½

WHITE- AND PALE-SPORED MUSHROOMS:
Tricholomataceae (4)

Tallowgills (Laccaria — first 4 species): Waxy-textured gills. Spore print white or flushed with violet.

1. **PURPLE-OCHRE TALLOWGILL**   p. 157
   Laccaria ochropurpurea
   Purple cap fades to brownish or whitish. Gills purple.

2. **DECEIVER** *Laccaria laccata*   p. 156
   Small, pink to brownish cap fades as it dries; center often shallowly depressed. Gills pale purplish pink. Stalk slender.

3. **AMETHYST TALLOWGILL** *Laccaria amethystina*   p. 155
   Slender, purple mushroom; hygrophanous (water-soaked). Widely spaced gills extend down fragile stalk.

4. **SANDY TALLOWGILL** *Laccaria trullisata*   p. 157
   Reddish brown cap and stalk. Purplish gills. Grows in sand, often on dunes.

5. **FALSE FUNNELCAP** *Leucopaxillus albissimus*   p. 161
   Dry, white to pale yellow cap; brownish at center. Gills close. Stalk chalky white; base surrounded by a mat of abundant white threads and conifer needles.

6. **EARLY FALSE FUNNELCAP**   p. 163
   Leucopaxillus laterarius
   Cap dull white or flushed with yellowish pink; round to flat or flaring. Gills crowded. Stalk white, enlarged at base. Grows in hardwood forests. Taste bitter.*

7. **BITTER FALSE FUNNELCAP**   p. 162
   Leucopaxillus gentianeus
   Dry, reddish brown cap; rounded to flat. Gills close to crowded; white or yellowish. Base of stalk surrounded by mat of white filaments and conifer needles. Taste bitter.*

8. **COMMON CAVALIER** *Melanoleuca melaleuca*   p. 169
   Thin, flat, brown cap with wide, dingy white gills. Fragile, skinny, brownish stalk.

9. **FRIED CHICKEN MUSHROOM** *Lyophyllum decastes*   p. 163
   Rounded to flat, moist, grayish brown caps; often irregular. White stalks stain brownish when cut or bruised. Grows in clumps on ground.

10. **SNOW FUNNEL** *Lyophyllum montanum*   p. 164
    Thin, dingy grayish brown cap; rounded to flat. Stalk slender, curved, with a white, cottony base. Gills dingy. Grows in or near melting snowbanks.

11. **YELLOWISH CAVALIER** *Melanoleuca alboflavida*   p. 169
    Thin, flat, yellow to brown or whitish cap, with broad, white gills. Slender stalk; no ring.

* See p. 10 for cautions about using taste as an identifying characteristic.

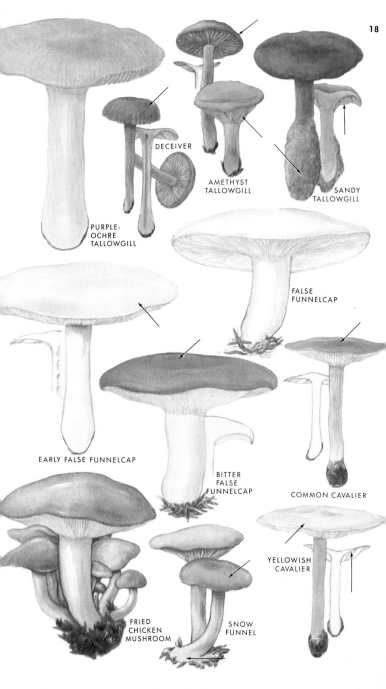

18

DECEIVER

AMETHYST
TALLOWGILL

SANDY
TALLOWGILL

PURPLE-
OCHRE
TALLOWGILL

FALSE
FUNNELCAP

EARLY FALSE FUNNELCAP

BITTER
FALSE
FUNNELCAP

COMMON CAVALIER

YELLOWISH
CAVALIER

FRIED
CHICKEN
MUSHROOM

SNOW
FUNNEL

PLATE 19   most ×½ (see below)

WHITE- AND PALE-SPORED MUSHROOMS:
Tricholomataceae (5)

1. **MAGENTA VELVET** *Marasmius plicatulus*   p. 166
   Thin, reddish brown cap with velvety sheen. Stalk brittle, with white tuft at base; stalk darkens to deep brown.

2. **ORANGE PINWHEEL** *Marasmius siccus*   p. 168
   Dull orange to brown, very thin cap; folds or grooves radiate from center. Stalk long and wiry, tough.

3. **HORSEHAIR MUSHROOM** *M. androsaceus* (×1)   p. 165
   Paper-thin cap. Blackish, hairlike stalk. On conifer needles.

4. **PINWHEEL MUSHROOM** *M. rotula* (detail ×1)   p. 167
   Clumps of small, thin, whitish, umbrella-shaped caps with widely spaced, white gills that are attached to a collar around stalk.

5. **FAIRY RING MUSHROOM** *Marasmius oreades*   p. 166
   Bell-shaped to flat, brown to yellowish caps, on slender, rigid stalks. Grows in groups (fairy rings) on grassy soil or fields.

6. **YELLOWSTALK FAIRY HELMET**   p. 172
   Mycena epipterygia
   Small, conic, dark yellow to light olive-brown, sticky cap, on a yellow, slimy stalk. Grows singly or in groups under conifers.

7. **STUMP FAIRY HELMET** *Mycena alcalina*   p. 171
   Thin, gray, bell-shaped cap. Brittle stalk. Odor alkaline (like bleach). Grows singly or in clumps on decaying wood or litter.

8. **LILAC-GILL FAIRY HELMET** *Mycena lilacifolia*   p. 174
   Sticky, yellow cap and stalk. Gills lilac-tinted. Grows on decaying logs and stumps of conifers.

9. **ROSY-GILL FAIRY HELMET** *Mycena galericulata*   p. 172
   Bell-shaped, grayish brown cap, with streaks radiating from center. Stalk brittle. Grows singly or in clusters, on decaying logs of deciduous trees.

10. **SCARLET FAIRY HELMET** *Mycena strobilinoides*   p. 176
    Red cap fades to yellow. Orange to yellow gills have darker edges. Stalk skinny, orange. Grows under conifers.

11. **BLEEDING FAIRY HELMET** *Mycena haematopus*   p. 173
    Bell-shaped cap; margin clasps stalk at first. Cap and stalk exude red juice when cut. Grows in clumps on decaying wood.

12. **SNOWBANK FAIRY HELMET** *Mycena overholtsii*   p. 175
    Gray, broadly humped cap. Stalk has white, cottony filaments over lower part. Grows in clumps on decaying conifer wood.

13. **GOLDEN FAIRY HELMET** *Mycena leaiana*   p. 174
    Bright orange cap and orange gills with red edges. Grows in dense clumps on decaying logs and stumps of deciduous trees.

14. **LILAC FAIRY HELMET** *Mycena pura*   p. 175
    Smooth, purple to pink cap; lighter-colored gills. Fragile stalk.

15. **ROSY VEINCAP** *Rhodotus palmatus*   p. 183
    Round, red to pink cap; surface has network of ribs. Gills and stalk pink. Grows singly or in clusters on wood.

16. **STINKING PINWHEEL** *Micromphale foetidum*   p. 170
    Cap has depressed center and dark streaks extending outward to ragged margin. Velvety brown stalk. Strong, unpleasant odor.

17. **NESTCAP** *Phyllotopsis nidulans*   see p. 181

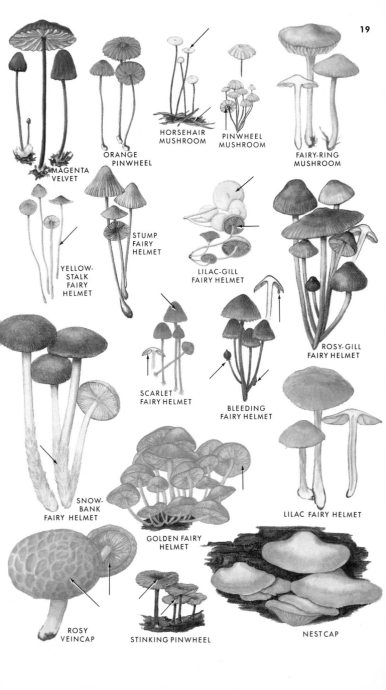

19

MAGENTA
VELVET

ORANGE
PINWHEEL

HORSEHAIR
MUSHROOM

PINWHEEL
MUSHROOM

FAIRY-RING
MUSHROOM

YELLOW-
STALK
FAIRY
HELMET

STUMP
FAIRY
HELMET

LILAC-GILL
FAIRY HELMET

ROSY-GILL
FAIRY HELMET

SCARLET
FAIRY HELMET

BLEEDING
FAIRY HELMET

SNOW-
BANK
FAIRY HELMET

LILAC FAIRY HELMET

GOLDEN FAIRY
HELMET

ROSY
VEINCAP

STINKING PINWHEEL

NEST CAP

PLATE 20 $\times\frac{1}{2}$ (except #6)

WHITE- AND PALE-SPORED MUSHROOMS:
Tricholomataceae (6)

1. **OYSTER** *Pleurotus ostreatus*   p. 181
   White to light gray or grayish yellow, fan-shaped to shallowly
   funnel-shaped cap. Stalk very short or lacking; attached at one
   side or off center if present. Grows in clumps, on stumps, logs, and
   rotting wood.

2. **ANGEL WINGS** *Pleurotus porrigens*   p. 182
   Thin, white, fan-shaped cap; close to crowded, narrow gills. Grows
   in overlapping clusters, laterally attached to conifer wood.

3. **BITTER OYSTER** *Panellus stipticus*   p. 180
   Small, fan-shaped to kidney-shaped, dry, hairy, orange-yellow to
   brownish caps; gills same color. Stalk stubby, laterally attached.
   Grows in clusters on decaying wood.

4. **LATE OYSTER** *Panellus serotinus*   p. 180
   Sticky, fan-shaped cap; green to yellow or violet. Gills yellow.
   Stalk short or lacking. Grows on wood in late fall.

5. **LEAF OYSTER** *Hohenbuehelia petaloides*   p. 153
   Thin, fan-shaped brown cap with crowded gills. No stalk. Grows
   singly or in clusters on decaying, often moss-covered wood.

6. **GOLDEN TRUMPETS** *Xeromphalina campanella* ($\times$1)   p. 195
   Small, brown to yellow, thin, umbrella-shaped cap, with brownish
   streaks. Thin, brown stalk with yellow hairs at base. Grows in
   clumps on conifer wood.

7. **BROADGILL** *Tricholomopsis platyphylla*   p. 194
   Flat, gray cap with wide, white gills. Stalk slender, white; no veils.

8. **YELLOW RIDER** *Tricholomopsis decora*   p. 195
   Yellow overall; blackish scales on cap.

9. **RED RIDER** *Tricholomopsis rutilans*   p. 194
   Yellow cap, densely covered with red scales. Scaly, yellow and red
   stalk. Yellow gills. Grows on decaying wood.

10. **DEEP ROOT** *Oudemansiella radicata*   p. 179
    Flat, brown, streaked cap; surface sticky. Wide, white gills. Stalk
    spindly, rigid, brittle; deeply rooted in soil.

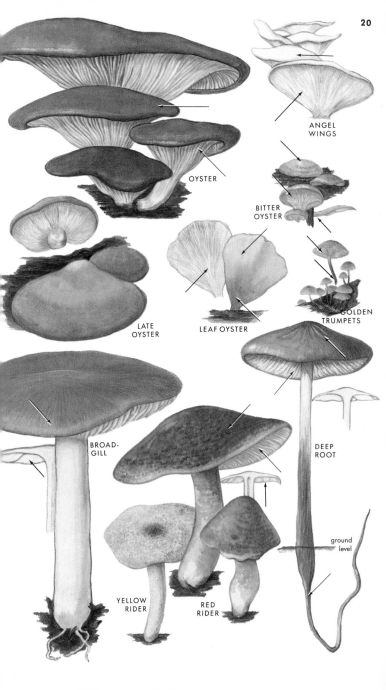

20

ANGEL
WINGS

OYSTER

BITTER
OYSTER

LATE
OYSTER

LEAF OYSTER

GOLDEN
TRUMPETS

BROAD-
GILL

DEEP
ROOT

YELLOW
RIDER

RED
RIDER

ground
level

PLATE 21   ×½

WHITE- AND PALE-SPORED MUSHROOMS:
Tricholomataceae (7)

1. **ZELLER'S BRACELET** *Tricholoma zelleri*   p. 193
Orange to brown or greenish cap; surface sticky, streaked, or with flat scales. Thick, pointed stalk; high, fibrillose ring. **Not recommended.**

2. **GOLDEN CAVALIER** *Tricholoma aurantium*   p. 185
Orange cap and stalk, often flushed with green. Cap sticky when wet. Stalk firm; has a veil line (faint ring), but no fibrils. Gills yellowish, spotted with brown in age. **Not recommended.**

3. **SHINGLE HEAD** *Tricholoma imbricatum*   p. 187
Dry, brown, rounded cap; surface smooth to scaly. Stout, dull brownish stalk. Gills pale, sometimes spotted.

4. **FUZZTOP** *Tricholoma vaccinum*   p. 191
Reddish brown cap; surface dry, hairy to scaly, cottony at margin. Stalk similar. Often grows in clumps. **Not recommended.**

5. **IRKSOME CAVALIER** *Tricholoma inamoenum*   p. 188
Dull pale yellow cap; flat to rounded or humped. Gills white. Stalk slender. Odor strong, disagreeable.

6. **SULPHUR CAVALIER** *Tricholoma sulphureum*   p. 191
All parts yellow. Odor strong, unpleasant. **Poisonous.**

7. **CAVALIER (MAN-ON-HORSEBACK)**   p. 186
Tricholoma flavovirens
Cap vivid yellow, brown at center; no black streaks or fibrils. Gills yellow. Stalk thick, yellow; no ring.

8. **TIGERTOP** *Tricholoma pardinum*   p. 188
Gray, rounded to flat cap; surface dry, forms small scales. Gills whitish. Firm, smooth to fibrillose, dingy white stalk. **Poisonous.**

9. **SILVER STREAKS** *Tricholoma virgatum*   p. 192
Conic to flattened, gray cap with white gills. Thick, whitish stalk, usually flushed with pink at base. **Not recommended.**

10. **BROWNSTAIN CAVALIER** *T. flavobrunneum*   p. 185
Brown cap; surface slightly sticky. Gills pale yellow, spotted with brown. Stalk colored like cap. **Not recommended.**

11. **SOAPY CAVALIER** *Tricholoma saponaceum*   p. 190
Cap olive-tinged; may be brownish at center. Gills close. Stalk thick; stains reddish when injured. Odor "soapy" or lacking. **Not recommended.**

12. **SHINY CAVALIER** *Tricholoma resplendens*   p. 189
Medium-sized, rounded to flat cap; surface sticky. All parts white. Gills not waxy as in white waxycaps *(Hygrophorus,* Pls. 23, 24). Stalk stout; no veil. **Not recommended.**

13. **WAXYGILL CAVALIER** *Tricholoma myomyces*   p. 193
Smaller than Tigertop. Has remnants of a fibrillose veil when young. Gills more widely spaced, thick, waxy; edges ragged.

14. **SOOTY HEAD** *Tricholoma portentosum*   p. 189
Broadly conic, gray cap; surface sticky, streaked with darker gray. Gills and stalk flushed with greenish yellow. **Not recommended.**

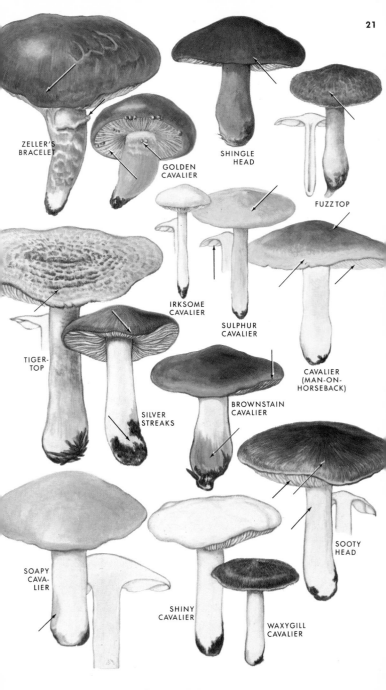

21

ZELLER'S BRACELET

GOLDEN CAVALIER

SHINGLE HEAD

FUZZ TOP

IRKSOME CAVALIER

SULPHUR CAVALIER

CAVALIER (MAN-ON-HORSEBACK)

TIGER-TOP

SILVER STREAKS

BROWNSTAIN CAVALIER

SOOTY HEAD

SOAPY CAVALIER

SHINY CAVALIER

WAXYGILL CAVALIER

PLATE 22   × 1/2

WAXYCAPS (1)

*Waxycaps (Hygrophoraceae): Gills have waxy texture. See also Pls.
23, 24.*

1. **VERMILION WAXYCAP** *Hygrocybe miniata*   p. 201
   Small, shiny, scarlet cap; fades quickly to orange or yellow. Matching gills and stalk. Thin stalk.

2. **LARCH WAXYCAP** *Hygrophorus speciosus*   p. 210
   Bright red, slimy cap; fades to orange. Gills white to yellowish. Slimy, white or orange-staining stalk. Grows under larch.

3. **PARROT WAXYCAP** *Hygrocybe psittacina*   p. 202
   Yellowish green, sticky cap and stalk. Stalk and gills fade quickly to reddish orange or yellow or pink.

4. **SCARLET HOOD** *Hygrocybe coccinea*   p. 198
   Scarlet cap and stalk. Cap waxy; conic at first, spreading in age. Stalk fragile. Gills red to yellowish orange; close.

5. **CONIC WAXYCAP** *Hygrocybe conica*   p. 198
   Brilliant red or orange or yellow, translucent, conic cap. All parts stain black when injured. **Poisonous.**

6. **ORANGE-GILL WAXYCAP** *Hygrocybe marginata*   p. 200
   Cap and stalk bright orange to yellow; both have waxy texture. Cap conic. Gills remain orange-yellow after other parts fade.

7. **BUTTER MEADOWCAP** *Camarophyllus pratensis*   p. 197
   Orange cap fades quickly. Gills lighter orange than cap. Stalk whitish.

8. **YELLOW WAXYCAP** *Hygrocybe flavescens*   p. 199
   Bright yellow to orange overall; does not turn black when bruised (see Conic Waxycap). Cap slimy to sticky, waxy, translucent.

9. **TENNESSEE WAXYCAP** *Hygrophorus tennesseensis*   p. 212
   Cap sticky; clay-colored to tawny or brownish at center, margin lighter. Odor of raw potatoes; taste bitter.* **Not recommended.**

10. **PINKGILL WAXYCAP** *Hygrocybe laeta*   p. 200
    Small, slimy to sticky cap and stalk. Color of cap and gills variable, but both become pink when they fade.

11. **BLUSHING WAXYCAP** *Hygrophorus pudorinus*   p. 209
    Orange-yellow to pinkish, rounded, sticky cap. Stalk solid; pale, with scurfy granules at apex; no ring. **Not recommended.**

* See p. 10 for cautions about using taste as an identifying characteristic.

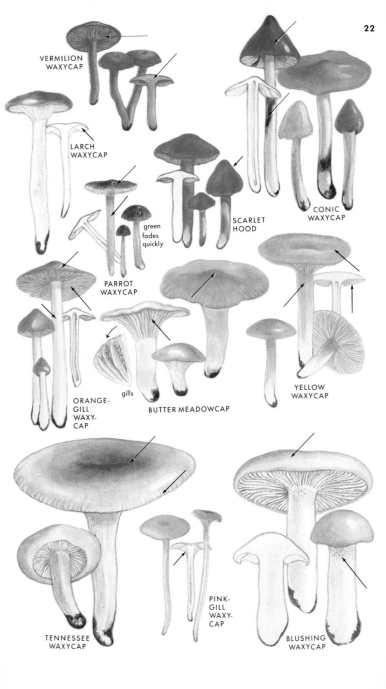

22

VERMILION WAXYCAP

LARCH WAXYCAP

PARROT WAXYCAP

green fades quickly

SCARLET HOOD

CONIC WAXYCAP

ORANGE-GILL WAXY-CAP

gills

BUTTER MEADOWCAP

YELLOW WAXYCAP

TENNESSEE WAXYCAP

PINK-GILL WAXY-CAP

BLUSHING WAXYCAP

PLATE 23   ×½

WAXYCAPS (2)

Waxycaps (Hygrophoraceae): Gills have waxy texture. See also Pls. 22, 24.

1. **FALSE RUSSULA** *Hygrophorus russula*   p. 209
   Medium to large, stout, sticky cap with close, narrow gills. Gills and cap purplish red, often streaked with pink. Compare with true Russulas (brittlegills—see Pls. 39 and 40).

2. **PINK WAXYCAP** *Hygrophorus erubescens*   p. 206
   Thick, red to pink cap; surface sticky. Gills extend down short, thick stalk and are farther apart than in False Russula.

3. **SPOTTED-STALK WAXYCAP**   p. 212
   Hygrophorus tephroleucus
   Small, thin, gray cap; surface sticky. Slender, white stalk; very small, fibrillose (hairy) scales become dark gray at maturity.

4. **OLIVE-GRAY WAXYCAP**   p. 208
   Hygrophorus olivaceoalbus
   Slimy overall when moist. Cap black to smoky gray in center; streaked and lighter toward margin. Stalk has blackish bands.

5. **GOAT WAXYCAP** *Hygrophorus camarophyllus*   p. 203
   Brownish gray, streaked cap; rounded or flat. Gills grayish to white. Gray stalk. Fruits in fall.

6. **ALMOND WAXYCAP** *Hygrophorus agathosmus*   p. 202
   Smooth, gray cap; surface sticky. Gills and stalk white to grayish. Almond-like odor.

7. **WINTER HERALD** *Hygrophorus hypothejus*   p. 207
   Slimy cap and stalk. Cap color varies—yellow to olive-brown, or reddish. Gills yellow at maturity. Fruits in late fall.

8. **MARCH MUSHROOM** *Hygrophorus marzuolus*   p. 207
   Large, robust, dingy whitish to gray or black cap; surface shiny. Gray gills. Thick, streaked stalk. Fruits under snowbanks in early spring.

23

PINK WAXY-CAP

FALSE RUSSULA

SPOTTED-STALK WAXY-CAP

OLIVE-GRAY WAXY-CAP

GOAT WAXYCAP

ALMOND WAXYCAP

WINTER HERALD

color varies

MARCH MUSHROOM

PLATE 24   ×½

WAXYCAPS (3) AND SLIME MUSHROOMS:
Hygrophoraceae and Amanitaceae

Waxycaps (first 7 species): Gills have waxy texture. See also Pls. 22, 23.

1. **SUBALPINE WAXYCAP** *Hygrophorus subalpinus*   p. 211
   Snowy white overall. Stubby, bulbous stalk has a thin, membranous ring. Fruits under or near snowbanks.

2. **IVORY WAXYCAP** *Hygrophorus eburneus*   p. 205
   White, slimy cap on a slender, white stalk. Gills white, distant (widely spaced). **Not recommended.**

3. **SNOWY WAXYCAP** *Camarophyllus niveus*   p. 197
   Small, white, thin cap; surface somewhat greasy. Widely spaced, white gills extend down slender, white stalk. **Not recommended.**

4. **HARDWOOD WAXYCAP** *Hygrophorus sordidus*   p. 210
   Medium to large, white cap; surface somewhat sticky. Gills white. Pointed white stalk. Grows in oak-hickory woods.

5. **SLIMY WAXYCAP** *Hygrophorus gliocyclus*   p. 206
   Cap and stalk pale yellowish, from yellowish slime on surface. Flesh solid, white. Gills yellowish.

6. **GOLDEN-TOOTH WAXYCAP**   p. 204
   Hygrophorus chrysodon
   Cap white, with soft, golden yellow granules on margin; gill edges and upper part of stalk may also have granules on surface, as shown. Sticky when moist; shiny. Grows on soil in coniferous or mixed woods.

7. **CLAY WAXYCAP** *Hygrophorus discoideus*   p. 204
   Small, sticky, thin cap; reddish brown at center, buff at margin. Gills pinkish tan. Stalk thin, whitish.

Next 2 species (Limacella): May be mistaken for waxycaps, but closely related to Amanitas (see Pls. 25–28). Edibility unknown; not recommended.

8. **WHITE SLIME MUSHROOM** *Limacella illinita*   p. 214
   Cap and stalk white, heavily coated with colorless slime. No ring on stalk except in very young specimens.

9. **SLIME MUSHROOM** *Limacella glischra*   p. 213
   Bright reddish brown slime coats cap and stalk; bits of slime (veil remnants) often dangle from margin of cap. Ring obscure.

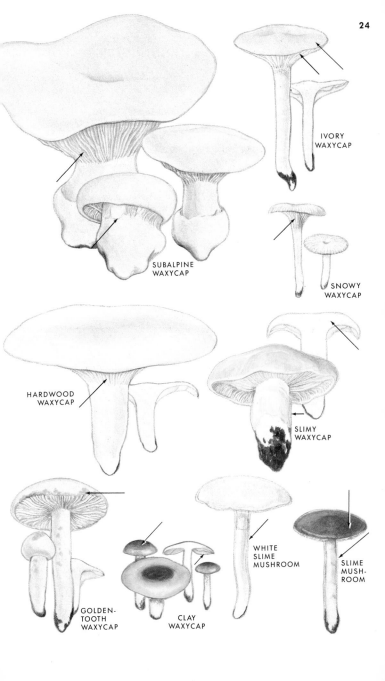

24

IVORY
WAXYCAP

SUBALPINE
WAXYCAP

SNOWY
WAXYCAP

HARDWOOD
WAXYCAP

SLIMY
WAXYCAP

GOLDEN-
TOOTH
WAXYCAP

CLAY
WAXYCAP

WHITE
SLIME
MUSHROOM

SLIME
MUSH-
ROOM

PLATE 25 ×½

AMANITAS (1): GRISETTES

Grisettes: Thin-fleshed cap with free gills (gills are not attached to apex of stalk). Membranous volva forms loose cup at base of stalk. Some species have a ring set high on stalk. Spore print white. Some species may be poisonous. See also Pls. 26–28.

1. **FLIMSY VEIL** *Amanita parcivolvata* p. 230
   Small to medium, red to orange cap, sometimes with loose yellow warts. Slender, powdery stalk; no ring. Cap has long streaks extending inward from margin. **Poisonous.**

2. **CAESAR'S MUSHROOM** *Amanita caesarea* p. 217
   Bright yellowish orange to red cap. Yellow gills, stalk, and ring. Deep, white, cuplike volva at base of stalk. **Not recommended.**

3. **TAWNY GRISETTE** *Amanita fulva* p. 238
   Similar to Grisette *(A. vaginata)*, but cap is light orange-yellow to brownish orange. Note *developing gills* in button stage (see lengthwise section).

4. **GILDED GRISETTE** *Amanita inaurata* p. 226
   Medium-sized, rounded, grayish brown to golden brown cap expands and flattens with age; small, gray to brown, wart-like scales (remnants of volva) adhere to surface. Stalk has no ring, but often has gray scales (remnants of volva tissue) scattered on surface.

5. **MEALY CAP** *Amanita farinosa* p. 223
   Small, fragile, gray cap on a thin, white to gray stalk. Cap and stalk have powdery to cottony remains of volva on surface. Stalk cylindrical; base slightly enlarged and rounded.

6. **GRISETTE** *Amanita vaginata* p. 237
   Medium-sized, rounded to flat, shiny gray cap; margin conspicuously ribbed. Slender, fragile stalk; no ring. Volva a white to grayish, loose sheath at base of stalk. Cap occasionally has an irregular white patch (remnants of veil) on surface, as shown. **Not recommended.**

7. **GLUE CAP** *Amanita peckiana* p. 230
   Medium to large; cap and stalk yellowish white, flushed with light pinkish brown. Surface of cap sticky, with slightly darker scales under slime. No ring on stalk; volva a loose, membranous sheath around lower stalk. Sometimes stains pink when cut or bruised.

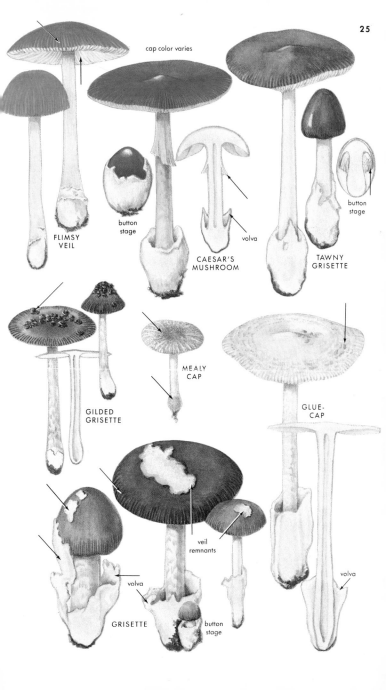

25

cap color varies

FLIMSY
VEIL

button
stage

CAESAR'S
MUSHROOM

volva

TAWNY
GRISETTE

button
stage

GILDED
GRISETTE

MEALY
CAP

GLUE-
CAP

veil
remnants

GRISETTE

volva

button
stage

volva

PLATE 26   ×½

AMANITAS (2): DEATHCAPS

Amanitas: Some species are **poisonous.** *See also Pls. 25, 27, and 28.*

1. **FLY AGARIC** *Amanita muscaria*   p. 227
Cap color varies — bright red to orange, yellow, or white, with soft, white to yellowish warts (volva tissue). White to yellowish volva tissue (universal veil) is intergrown with bulb of stalk in button stage; veil breaks and forms "bracelets" around stalk after cap expands. **Poisonous.**

2. **PANTHERCAP** *Amanita pantherina*   p. 229
Cap color varies — brown to dull yellow or buff. Stalk solid, with a rounded bulb topped by a collar or roll of volva tissue. **Poisonous.**

3. **YELLOW WART** *Amanita flavoconia*   p. 224
Fragile, slender, bulbous stalk. Cap bright orange to yellow, with yellow, felty or cottony warts on surface. East of Great Lakes. **Not recommended**—said to be **poisonous.**

4. **WARTY DEATHCAP** *Amanita francheti*   p. 216
Dark brown cap with soft, flat to pyramidal warts. Stalk has tinges of yellow on volva and ring. Pacific Northwest. **Poisonous.**

5. **JEWELED DEATHCAP** *Amanita gemmata*   p. 225
Medium-sized, yellow cap, flushed with pink. Ringed stalk has round bulb at base, topped with narrow ring or zone of volva tissue. Compare with pale forms of Panthercap *(A. pantherina).* **Poisonous.**

6. **BLUSHER** *Amanita rubescens*   p. 235
Medium to large, pinkish yellow to brownish red cap; streaked or splotched with grayish to pink volva remnants. Stalk bulbous, with a membranous ring below cap; ring thin but persistent — covers gills until comparatively late in expansion of cap. All parts stain pink when bruised or handled. **Not recommended.**

7. **YELLOW BLUSHER** *Amanita flavorubescens*   p. 225
Medium-sized, rounded to flat cap; surface sticky, yellow to orange (fades in sunlight). Yellow volva fragments on cap surface, lower stalk, and in soil around bulbous base. All parts stain pink when cut or bruised. **Poisonous.**

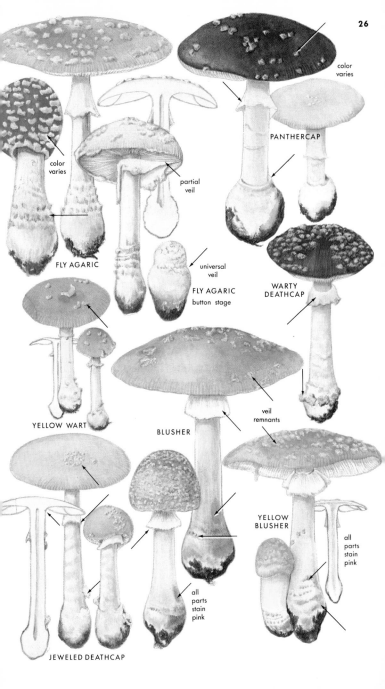

color
varies

color
varies

PANTHERCAP

partial
veil

FLY AGARIC

universal
veil

FLY AGARIC
button stage

WARTY
DEATHCAP

YELLOW WART

BLUSHER

veil
remnants

YELLOW
BLUSHER

all
parts
stain
pink

all
parts
stain
pink

JEWELED DEATHCAP

PLATE 27 ×½

AMANITAS (3): MORE DEATHCAPS

*Amanitas: Some species are **poisonous**. See also Pls. 25, 26, and 28.*

1. **DEATHCAP** *Amanita phalloides* p. 231
   Rounded to flat, greenish cap; often streaked with gray. Stalk ringed; rounded bulb at base is enclosed in a long, sac-like, membranous, white to green volva sheath, typically with an upward-projecting lobe on one side. **Poisonous.**

2. **FALSE DEATHCAP** *Amanita citrina* p. 221
   Shiny, lemon yellow cap. Slender white stalk with broad bulb at base. Volva leaves thin, cottony patches on cap that are white to gray with a pinkish cast. Odor of raw potatoes. **Poisonous.**

3. **PORPHYRY DEATHCAP** *Amanita porphyria* p. 233
   Flat or slightly humped, gray-brown cap. Stalk slender, ringed; broad, abrupt bulb (volva) with a short, thin, sharp limb. **Poisonous.**

4. **FOOL'S MUSHROOM** *Amanita verna* p. 238
   Pure white, sticky to shiny cap. Stalk slender, bulbous; sometimes tapers upward from rounded base. Ring membranous; hangs like a skirt from upper stalk. **Poisonous.** Compare early (button) stage with "eggs" of puffballs.

5. **CLEFT-FOOT DEATHCAP** *Amanita brunnescens* p. 216
   Cap usually brown, often with lighter streaks. Stalk has a large bulb with a distinct rim and one or more vertical clefts. A pale form (var. *pallida,* not shown) also exists. **Poisonous.**

6. **HOODED GRISETTE** *Amanita calyptrata* p. 218
   Stocky mushroom on a short, stout stalk. Cap shiny, yellow to orange, with a thick, white patch of volva tissue at center. Ring thin, set high on stalk; ring sometimes disappears at an early stage. **Not recommended.**

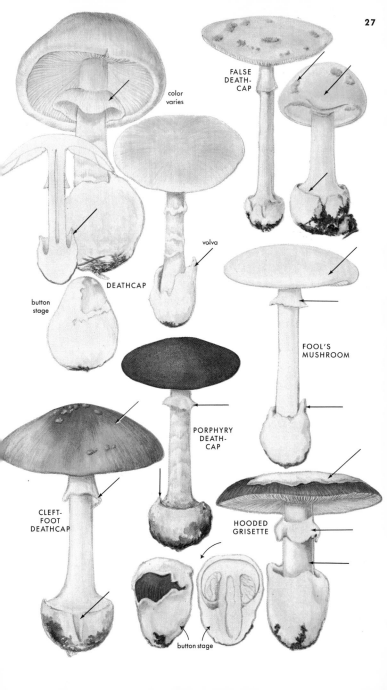

27

FALSE DEATH-CAP

color varies

DEATHCAP

volva

button stage

FOOL'S MUSHROOM

PORPHYRY DEATH-CAP

CLEFT-FOOT DEATHCAP

HOODED GRISETTE

button stage

PLATE 28   × 1/2

AMANITAS (4)

Amanitas (section Lepidella — next 11 species): Species in this sub-group are suspected of being poisonous. See also Pls. 25–27.

1. **CHLORINE LEPIDELLA** *Amanita chlorinosma*   p. 219
   White cap with a dry, powdery surface; occasionally has small, soft warts toward center. Flesh has strong, pungent, disagreeable odor (smells like lime or chlorine).

2. **GRAY LEPIDELLA** *Amanita tephrea*   p. 237
   Same size, shape, and odor as Chlorine Lepidella, but cap is a pale neutral gray. **Not recommended.**

3. **OLIVE LEPIDELLA** *Amanita pelioma*   p. 231
   Same size, shape, and odor as Chlorine Lepidella, but cap is grayish olive. **Not recommended.**

4. **CLUB FOOT** *Amanita rhopalopus*   p. 234
   Dingy white to yellowish, broadly convex cap; surface covered with white to pale yellow or brownish warts (volva remnants) that usually form cottony to felty patches near margin of cap. Stalk has cylindrical to rounded bulb under ground, at base. Odor heavy, unpleasant. **Not recommended.**

5. **SOLITARY LEPIDELLA** *Amanita cokeri*   p. 222
   White, shiny to sticky cap, with pyramidal warts at center. Bulb at base of stalk is covered with tough, pyramidal warts or recurved scales. Odor not distinctive.

6. **TURNIP-BULB LEPIDELLA** *Amanita daucipes*   p. 223
   White to yellowish pink cap, with patches of grayish pink veil, sometimes in the form of pointed scales that are fused at tips. Stalk has pointed bulb, often cleft.

7. **LOADED LEPIDELLA** *Amanita onusta*   p. 228
   Cap is crowded with gray to gray-brown, conical or irregularly shaped warts. Odor unpleasant. **Not recommended.**

8. **PINECONE LEPIDELLA** *Amanita ravenelii*   p. 234
   Stout, white to yellowish cap with conical to flattened, whitish to brown warts or scales (volva remnants). Ring thick, cottony to felty, fragile; bulb round, pointed. Odor strong. **Not recommended.**

9. **WOODLAND LEPIDELLA** *Amanita silvicola*   p. 236
   Medium-sized, white cap with felty patches of volva tissue on surface. Stalk white, bulbous; ring sparse, disappears at an early stage. California and Pacific Northwest. **Not recommended.**

10. **MANY WARTS** *Amanita polypyramis*   p. 232
    Thick, white cap, on a stout stalk. Soft, white, powdery to cottony patches or warts of volva tissue on cap surface. Odor weak to strong, disagreeable.

11. **GRAY DUST** *Amanita cinereoconia*   p. 220
    Dry, dingy whitish to gray cap, with soft, yellowish gray to brownish gray, powdery to cottony scales (volva remnants). Odor unpleasant. Stalk usually lacks ring. **Not recommended.**

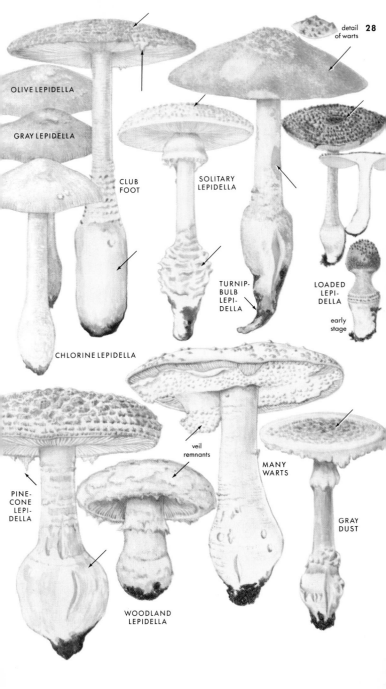

detail of warts **28**

OLIVE LEPIDELLA

GRAY LEPIDELLA

CLUB FOOT

SOLITARY LEPIDELLA

TURNIP-BULB LEPI-DELLA

LOADED LEPI-DELLA

early stage

CHLORINE LEPIDELLA

veil remnants

MANY WARTS

PINE-CONE LEPI-DELLA

WOODLAND LEPIDELLA

GRAY DUST

PLATE 29   ×1/2

PARASOL MUSHROOMS: LEPIOTAS AND OTHERS

Parasol mushrooms (Lepiotaceae): *All have gills that are free from stalk (not attached to apex). Stalk has a ring but no volva at base. Spore print usually white.*

1. **GREEN GILL** *Chlorophyllum molybdites*   p. 240
   Large, white cap; may have pinkish brown tinge on disc (center) and on tips of scales. Spores color gills light greenish gray when mature. Stalk slender. **Poisonous.**

2. **PARASOL MUSHROOM** *Leucocoprinus procera*   p. 245
   Large, white to brownish cap on a long, skinny, brown stalk. Gills and spore print white. Develops fibrillose scales on cap and stalk as it matures.

3. **SMOOTHCAP PARASOL** *Leucoagaricus naucina*   p. 243
   Smooth, white caps on graceful, ringed stalks. Cap nearly round to egg-shaped at first, soon spreading and becoming convex or nearly flat, with a low, broad, rounded hump; surface smooth (like kid leather). Grows in small clumps or "fairy rings" in grassy places. **Not recommended.**

4. **SHAGGY PARASOL** *Leucocoprinus rachodes*   p. 246
   Large, white cap with fibrillose scales that are often brown at tips. Spore print white. Flesh thick, white; stains slightly pink to intensely reddish orange when cut or bruised (see lengthwise section). **Not recommended.**

5. **SHIELD PARASOL** *Lepiota clypeolaria*   p. 242
   Small to medium, ragged brownish cap. Cap separates very readily from fragile, ragged stalk. **Not recommended.**

6. **SHARP-SCALED PARASOL** *Lepiota acutesquamosa*   p. 241
   Medium-sized, pallid to brown, round to humped cap with dark, tough, pointed scales that vary from sparse to crowded. **Not recommended.**

7. **ONION STEM** *Leucocoprinus cepaestipes*   p. 245
   Small to medium, fragile, white cap; surface mealy. Cap streaked or split at margin. Stalk slender, tapered. Usually grows in clumps.

8. **YELLOW PLEATED PARASOL**
   Leucocoprinus birnbaumii   p. 245
   Bright yellow overall; otherwise looks like Onion Stem. **Poisonous.**

9. **AMERICAN PARASOL** *Leucocoprinus americana*   p. 244
   Clumps of medium-sized but fragile-looking, bell-shaped caps. Cap white or pink-scaled; thick on disc (center), tapering to very thin on margin (see lengthwise section). Flesh white, staining yellow, then quickly grayish red or pink when cut.

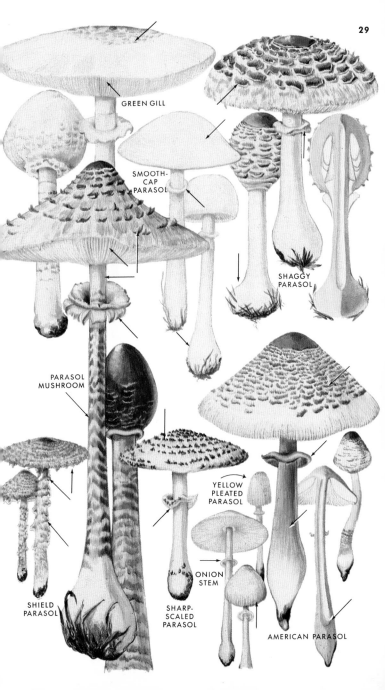

GREEN GILL

SMOOTH-CAP PARASOL

SHAGGY PARASOL

PARASOL MUSHROOM

YELLOW PLEATED PARASOL

ONION STEM

SHIELD PARASOL

SHARP-SCALED PARASOL

AMERICAN PARASOL

PLATE 30   ×½
ROOF AND SHEATH MUSHROOMS

1. **SILKY SHEATH** *Volvariella bombycina*   p. 252
   White, hairy cap on a shiny white stalk. Stalk ringless; broad,
   white, membranous sheath with gray patches. Grows on wood.
   Caution: Do not confuse this with an Amanita (see p. 253).

2. **BROWNISH YELLOW ROOF** *Pluteus flavofuligineus*   p. 250
   Thin, shiny, yellow caps on slender, twisted stalks. Grows on decaying wood.

3. **BIG SHEATH MUSHROOM** *Volvariella speciosa*   p. 253
   Whitish, sticky cap on a slender white stalk. Stalk has a white,
   membranous sheath but no ring. Gills *pink* from spores. **Caution:**
   Poisonous species of *Amanita* that resemble this species have *white*
   spores. Get a spore print!

4. **YELLOW ROOF** *Pluteus admirabilis*   p. 248
   Small, translucent, yellow caps on thin stalks arising from decaying
   wood. Stalk fragile, often split. Gills close, free from stalk (not
   attached to apex of stalk).

5. **DWARF ROOF** *Pluteus nanus*   p. 252
   Small, fragile, reddish brown cap on a yellow stalk. Gills yellow;
   spores pink. Grows on wood.

6. **SIENNA ROOF** *Pluteus chrysophaeus*   p. 250
   Small, brown, hygrophanous cap. Gills white at first, but soon become pink from maturing spores. Stalk slender, fragile; white or
   grayish. Grows on wood.

7. **DEER MUSHROOM** *Pluteus cervinus*   p. 248
   Bell-shaped, gray to grayish brown cap on a white to gray stalk.
   Cap separates readily from stalk. Grows on decaying wood or saw-
   dust.

8. **SAWDUST MUSHROOM** *Pluteus petasetus*   p. 252
   Cap white, streaked with brownish fibrils; disc (center) dingy yellowish, with minute scales. Stalk color and texture similar.

9. **BROWN ROOF** *Pluteus lutescens*   p. 251
   Small, fragile, olive to brown cap on a yellow stalk. Gills yellow
   when young (before spores develop). Grows singly or in small
   groups, on decaying wood.

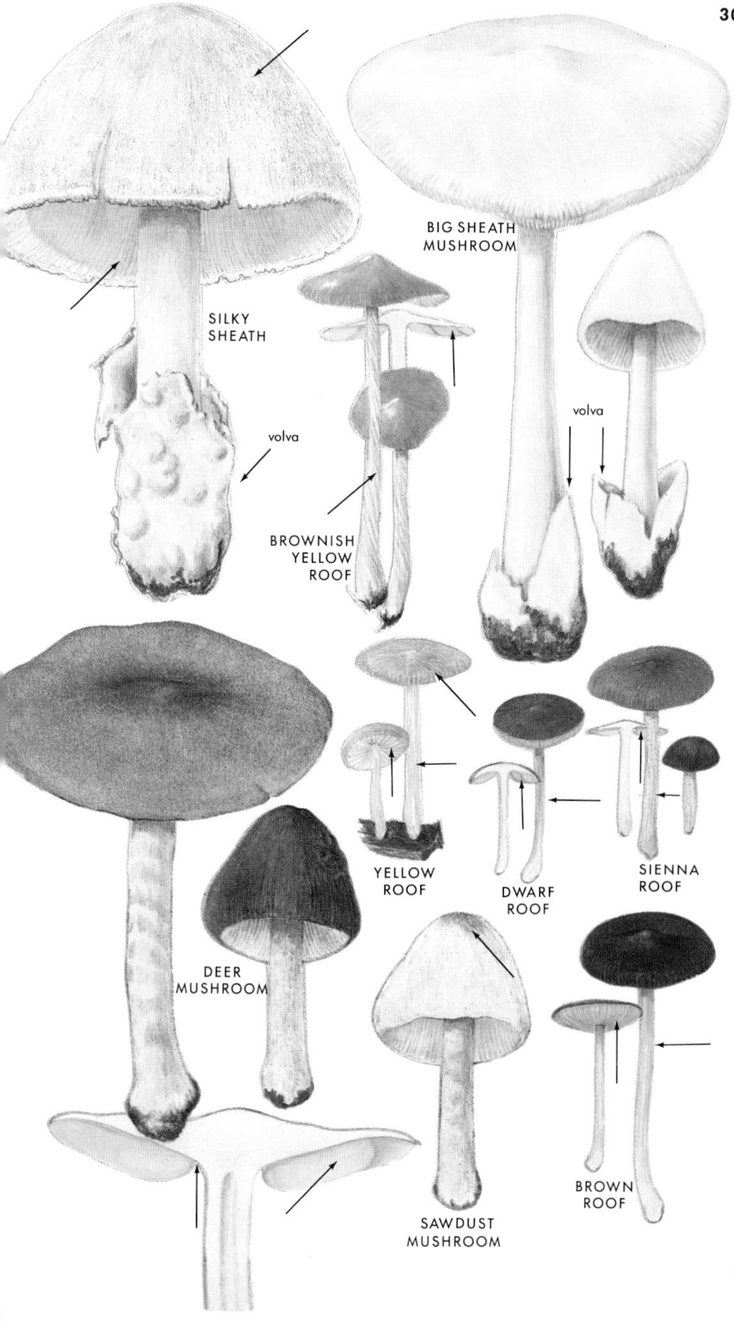

30

SILKY
SHEATH

BIG SHEATH
MUSHROOM

volva

volva

BROWNISH
YELLOW
ROOF

YELLOW
ROOF

DWARF
ROOF

SIENNA
ROOF

DEER
MUSHROOM

SAWDUST
MUSHROOM

BROWN
ROOF

PLATE 31 $\times \frac{1}{2}$ (except #10)

COMMON FIELD MUSHROOMS AND
RELATIVES: Agaricaceae (1)

Agaricus: All species have free gills (gills are not attached to apex of stalk). Spore print purple-brown. Stalk has a ring but no volva.

1. **CROCODILE MUSHROOM** *Agaricus crocodilinus*   p. 257
    Large, white cap on a short, stout stalk. Cap surface often cracks, forming angular scales. Flesh thick.

2. **MEADOW MUSHROOM** *Agaricus campestris*   p. 256
    Pure white to brownish cap on a short stalk with an indistinct ring; *no volva.* Gills crowded; pale pink when young, (before spores develop), becoming bright pink before ring breaks.

3. **SYLVAN MUSHROOM** *Agaricus sylvicola*   p. 262
    Smooth, white cap; slowly stains yellow when bruised. Flesh thin. Gills dingy white at first, then pink, finally becoming dark brown as spores mature. **Not recommended.**

4. **SHEATHED STALK** *Agaricus rodmani*   p. 259
    Medium-sized, squat, smooth, white cap on a short stalk with a double-flanged ring. Flesh thick (see lengthwise section).

5. **FLAT-BULB MUSHROOM** *Agaricus abruptibulbus*   p. 254
    Medium-sized, white cap on a slender stalk. Stalk has a wide, flat bulb at base. Flesh stains yellow when cut or bruised. Grows on soil under hardwoods.

6. **FOREST MUSHROOM** *Agaricus sylvaticus*   p. 260
    Small to medium, brown, scaly cap on a slender, white to brownish stalk. Flesh stains red. Grows under conifers.

7. **BLOODY AGARIC** *Agaricus haemorrhoidarius*   p. 258
    Medium to large, brown, scaly cap on a slender, white to brownish stalk. Flesh quickly stains red when cut or wounded (scratched). Grows under deciduous trees.

8. **HORSE MUSHROOM** *Agaricus arvensis*   p. 254
    Medium to large, white cap and stalk. Stalk has a membranous ring but no volva. Flesh stains yellow when bruised. Odor of anise.

9. **YELLOW CAP** *Agaricus comptuliformis*   p. 257
    Small, pale greenish yellow cap; vivid orange at first, fading to pale greenish yellow; scales darker. Odor of almonds. **Not recommended.**

10. **PRINCE** *Agaricus augustus* ($\times \frac{1}{6}$)   p. 255
    Robust, brown, scaly cap on a thick stalk. Stalk scaly below ring. All parts stain yellow.

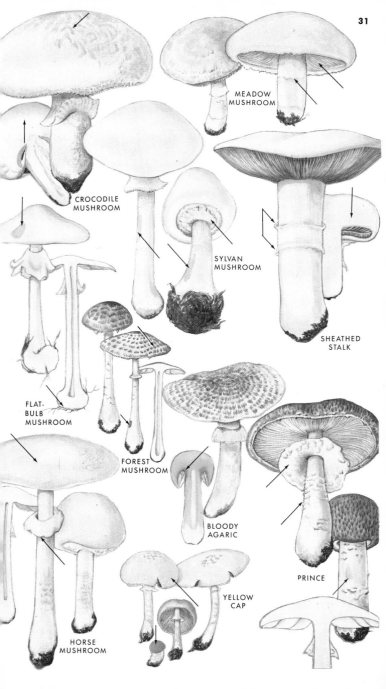

31

MEADOW
MUSHROOM

CROCODILE
MUSHROOM

SYLVAN
MUSHROOM

SHEATHED
STALK

FLAT-
BULB
MUSHROOM

FOREST
MUSHROOM

BLOODY
AGARIC

PRINCE

HORSE
MUSHROOM

YELLOW
CAP

PLATE 32   × ½

COMMON FIELD MUSHROOMS (2)
AND RINGSTALKS

1. **GRAYSCALE** *Agaricus meleagris*   p. 258
   Large cap, with a dark gray, fibrillose center and dark gray scales on a whitish background. Stalk thick, white. Flesh stains yellow, then dark purplish brown, when cut. **Not recommended.**

2. **FLAT-TOP** *Agaricus placomyces*   p. 258
   Medium-sized, thin cap, with a flattened, dark brown center. Stalk slender, bulbous; interior vivid yellow at base. Odor unpleasant (creosote-like), but mild. **Not recommended.**

3. **WOOLLYSTALK** *Agaricus subrutilescens*   p. 260
   Looks like Flat-top, but with reddish brown scales on cap. Flesh does not stain yellow. No odor. Stalk has woolly fibrils. **Not recommended.**

Ringstalks (Stropharia — next 8 species): Gills attached to stalk. Spore print purple-brown.

4. **MANURE ROUNDHEAD** *Stropharia semiglobata*   p. 266
   Small, shiny, yellow, hemispherical cap; gills adnate (broadly attached to apex of stalk). Stalk very long, skinny. Grows singly or in small groups, on horse or cow manure. **Not recommended.**

5. **SCALY RINGSTALK** *S. squamosa* var. *squamosa*   p. 267
   Shiny, reddish brown to orange or yellow cap with soft, white scales. Grows on decayed wood. **Not recommended.**

6. **PUMPKIN RINGSTALK** *S. squamosa* var. *thrausta*   p. 268
   Similar to Scaly Ringstalk, but more slender and more orange.

7. **CROWN TOADSTOOL** *Stropharia coronilla*   p. 264
   Small to medium, dingy light yellow cap; short, squat stalk. Gills attached to stalk. Grows in grassy places. **Poisonous.**

8. **FRINGED RINGSTALK** *Stropharia ambigua*   p. 263
   Pallid to yellow or brown-tinged cap; surface shiny or slimy. Ragged, white veil remnants hang from margin of cap.

9. **ROUGH-RING** *Stropharia rugosoannulata*   p. 265
   Large, purplish brown, streaked cap. Dingy stalk has thick, two-layered ring; lower layer has recurved, claw-like scales.

10. **VERDIGRIS MUSHROOM** *Stropharia aeruginosa*   p. 262
    Slimy, blue-green cap; margin often ragged. Stalk similar in color, with a whitish ring. **Not recommended.**

11. **LUXURIANT RINGSTALK** *Stropharia hornemannii*   p. 265
    Shiny, pale yellowish brown to dingy purplish or reddish brown cap. Stalk white, scaly; ring white. Grows on decaying conifer logs.

32

FLAT-
TOP

WOOLLYSTALK

GRAY-
SCALE

PUMPKIN
RINGSTALK

FRINGED
RING-
STALK

SCALY
RING-
STALK

MANURE
ROUNDHEAD

CROWN
TOADSTOOL

ROUGH-
RING

VERDIGRIS
M.

LUXURIANT
RINGSTALK

PLATE 33 **STROPHARIACEAE (2)** ×1/2

1. **ORANGE STUMP MUSHROOM** p. 268
   Naematoloma capnoides
   Rounded, orange to yellow-brown cap; surface moist but not
   sticky. Slender stalk; may have scattered buff fibrils. Grows in clusters on decaying conifer wood.

2. **SULPHUR TUFT** *Naematoloma fasciculare* p. 269
   Small to medium, greenish yellow to orange-yellow cap on a slender stalk. Grows in clusters on decaying logs or stumps. Bitter
   taste.* **Poisonous**—do not try it intentionally.

3. **BRICKCAP** *Naematoloma sublateritium* p. 270
   Small to medium cap; brick red at center, yellowish pink near margin. Margin of cap incurved or downturned. Thin, fibrillose veil
   leaves ring on stalk or patches on cap margin. Grows on hardwood
   logs or stumps.

4. **DUNG SMOOTHCAP** *Psilocybe coprophila* p. 274
   Small, dark reddish brown, rounded, smooth cap. Slender, fibrillose, pallid to brownish stalk. Grows singly or in clusters on manure.

5. **BLUESTAIN SMOOTHCAP** *Psilocybe cubensis* p. 275
   Small to medium, rounded to nearly flat, thin, yellowish cap. Cap
   separates readily from stalk. Stalk thin; stains blue at base when
   handled. **Poisonous.**

6. **FLAME SCALECAP** *Pholiota flammans* p. 272
   Small to medium, bright orange-yellow, shaggy cap, with bright
   yellow gills. Thin, shaggy, orange-yellow stalk. Grows on well-
   decayed conifer wood.

7. **CHARCOAL SCALECAP** *Pholiota carbonaria* p. 271
   Small to medium, brown, shiny cap. Reddish orange veil leaves
   scattered wisps on cap and thin zones on yellowish stalk. Grows on
   charcoal or burned soil.

8. **SPRING SCALECAP** *Pholiota vernalis* p. 274
   Clusters of shiny brown caps on thin, brown stalks. Gills narrow,
   crowded. Fruits in spring.

9. **SHARPSCALES** *Pholiota squarrosoides* p. 273
   Colored like Shaggy Scalecap, but lacks olive-greenish tones on
   gills. Surface of cap has gelatinous layer underneath scales.

10. **STRAW SCALECAP** *Pholiota veris* p. 273
    Thin, yellowish to light brown cap; smooth, hygrophanous. Slen-
    der, ringed stalk. Grows in clusters on decaying wood.

11. **TWO-TONED SCALECAP** *Pholiota mutabilis* p. 272
    Thin, brown, smooth cap; color fades from center outward. Brown
    gills. Stiff brown stalk. Grows in clusters.

12. **SHAGGY SCALECAP** *Pholiota squarrosa* p. 272
    Dry, scaly, yellowish brown cap. Gills tinged with olive-green when
    young. Grows in clumps on decaying wood.

13. **GOLDSKIN SCALECAP** *Pholiota aurivella* p. 270
    Orange-yellow, rounded cap; sticky, with scattered, flattened, red-
    dish orange scales. Stalk cottony above poorly developed ring;
    scales usually more prominent toward base.

* **See p. 10 for cautions about using taste as an identifying characteristic.**

33

ORANGE STUMP
MUSHROOM

SULPHUR
TUFT

BRICKCAP

DUNG
SMOOTHCAP

BLUESTAIN
SMOOTHCAP

FLAME SCALECAP

CHARCOAL SCALECAP

SPRING
SCALECAP

SHARP-
SCALES

STRAW
SCALE-
CAP

TWO-
TONED
SCALECAP

SHAGGY
SCALECAP

GOLDSKIN
SCALECAP

PLATE 34   ×½

INKY CAPS

Inky caps (Coprinus): Dissolve into a black, inky fluid at maturity. Most species (except #3 and #4) are edible when young—before self-digestion begins—but see precautions in text.

1. **INKY CAP** *Coprinus atramentarius*   p. 276
   Large, gray to brownish cap, with gray sheen; tinged with brownish, particularly toward pointed tip of cap.

2. **UMBRELLA INKY CAP** *Coprinus plicatilis*   p. 279
   Small, gray, wrinkled cap; very thin and fragile. Long, thin, fragile stalk. Gills attached to a collar around apex of stalk. Grows on grassy soil.

3. **DESERT INKY CAP** *Montagnites arenarius*   p. 281
   Dry, whitish cap, with fragile, narrow, gill-like plates. Slender, bulbous stalk. Grows on sandy soil or dunes.

4. **FELTSCALE INKY CAP** *Coprinus quadrifidus*   p. 280
   Medium-sized, bell-shaped, gray cap, with felt-like, patchy scales. Grows in clusters on hardwood logs. **Not recommended.**

5. **GRAY SHAG** *Coprinus cinereus*   p. 277
   Small to medium, gray cap; surface fibrillose to scaly or shaggy. Slender, gray stalk. Grows on dung or heavily manured soil.

6. **SNOWY INKY CAP** *Coprinus niveus*   p. 278
   Egg-shaped to bell-shaped cap; pure white before it dissolves. Surface of cap powdery, with a dense coating of granules (veil tissue).

7. **GLISTENING INKY CAP** *Coprinus micaceus*   p. 278
   Very thin, light brownish cap, with long streaks on surface; hygrophanous. Thin, whitish stalk. Cap is covered with a thin layer of glistening powder at first. Grows in dense clumps.

8. **SHAGGY MANE** *Coprinus comatus*   p. 277
   Medium to large, white cap; cylindrical, with a rounded tip. Surface of cap fibrillose to scaly. Stalk has a loose ring at first that often has disappeared in older specimens.

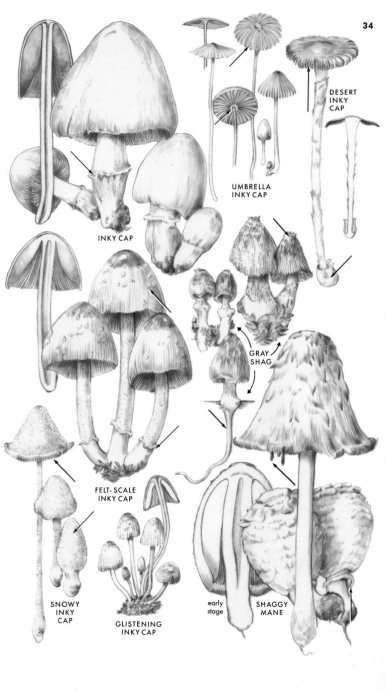

34

INKY CAP

UMBRELLA INKY CAP

DESERT INKY CAP

GRAY SHAG

FELT-SCALE INKY CAP

SNOWY INKY CAP

GLISTENING INKY CAP

early stage

SHAGGY MANE

PLATE 35   ×¹⁄₂

CRUMBLECAPS AND MOTTLEGILLS

1. **ASPEN CRUMBLECAP** *Psathyrella ulignicola*   p. 284
   Gray, brittle, streaked cap; cap separates readily from stalk. Stalk thick; white, sometimes flushed with pink at base. Grows under aspen.

2. **WEEPING WIDOW** *Psathyrella velutina*   p. 285
   Thin, fragile, brown cap; surface coarsely hairy. Deep brown, somewhat mottled gills. Thin, hairy stalk.

3. **FRINGED CRUMBLECAP** *Psathyrella candolleana*   p. 281
   Thin, yellowish, streaked cap; hygrophanous. Margin of cap thin, ragged, with shreds of white veil. Whitish, fragile stalk. **Not recommended.**

4. **ARTIST CRUMBLECAP** *Psathyrella delineata*   p. 282
   Thin, brown cap; more reddish brown at center, often wrinkled. Stalk whitish. Grows on decaying wood of deciduous trees.

5. **CLUSTER CRUMBLECAP** *Psathyrella hydrophila*   p. 283
   Smooth, brown, rounded cap; hygrophanous. Margin of cap incurved in young specimens, with wisps of white, fibrillose veil.

6. **HAYMAKER MUSHROOM** *Psathyrella foenesecii*   p. 282
   Smooth, brown, bell-shaped cap; hygrophanous. Brown gills. Very fragile, spindly, whitish stalk. Grows in lawns. **Not recommended.**

7. **THIMBLECAP** *Psathyrella gracilis*   p. 283
   Small, fragile cap; brown to yellowish or gray—sometimes whitish, with a pink tinge. Very thin, whitish stalk.

8. **TROOP CRUMBLECAP** *Pseudocoprinus disseminatus*   p. 285
   Small, fragile, brownish to gray, pleated caps on delicate, white stalks. Grows in large masses.

9. **STICKY MOTTLEGILL** *Panaeolus semiovatus*   p. 287
   Yellowish, bell-shaped cap; surface sticky. Black gills. Cap separates readily from long, hollow stalk. **Not recommended.**

10. **BELL MOTTLEGILL** *Panaeolus campanulatus*   p. 286
    Thin, gray, bell-shaped cap, on a brittle, skinny stalk. Gills become black from maturing spores. **Poisonous.**

35

ASPEN CRUMBLECAP

WEEPING WIDOW

ARTIST CRUMBLECAP

veil remnants

veil remnants

FRINGED CRUMBLECAP

CLUSTER CRUMBLE-CAP

cap color varies

THIMBLECAP

BELL MOTTLE-GILL

HAYMAKER MUSHROOM

cap color varies

STICKY MOTTLE-GILL

TROOP CRUMBLECAP

PLATE 36   × ½

WEBCAPS:
Cortinariaceae (1)

Webcaps (Cortinarius): Brown spore print. Cobweb-like veil.

1. **COPPER-RED WEBCAP** *Cortinarius orichalceus*   p. 293
    Large, firm, rounded or flat cap; reddish brown and yellow or greenish. Stalk greenish yellow, with a thick bulb that has a distinct rim.

2. **SORREL WEBCAP** *Cortinarius orellanus*   p. 292
    Thin, reddish orange to brownish orange cap. Cylindrical, yellow stalk. **Poisonous.**

3. **GOLDBAND WEBCAP** *Cortinarius gentilis*   p. 290
    Smooth, brown cap; rounded or depressed. Cylindrical brown stalk, zoned with golden yellow fibrils (veil remnants). **Poisonous.**

4. **BLUE-FOOT WEBCAP** *Cortinarius glaucopus*   p. 291
    Yellow to olive or brownish orange cap. Yellowish stalk, flushed with blue-green at apex. **Not recommended.**

5. **RED-GILL WEBCAP** *Cortinarius semisanguineus*   p. 294
    Orange-yellow to brown cap; nonhygrophanous. Red gills. Yellow stalk. Grows singly or in clusters. **Not recommended.**

6. **HOARY WEBCAP** *Cortinarius laniger*   p. 292
    Moderate reddish brown, rounded cap. Robust, club-shaped stalk. Grows under conifers. **Not recommended.**

7. **SMITH'S WEBCAP** *Cortinarius ahsii*   p. 288
    Brown cap, often flushed with yellow; hygrophanous. Brown gills. Stalk brownish, sometimes flushed with pink near top; veil remnants leave bright greenish yellow ring.

8. **SPLENDID WEBCAP** *Cortinarius splendidus*   p. 294
    Very similar to Greased Webcap, but veil tissue forms less distinct zones or rings on stalk. Great Lakes to Northwest.

9. **GREASED WEBCAP** *Cortinarius collinitus*   p. 289
    Shiny, yellow to brown cap; convex to humped. Stalk cylindrical; white to violet, zoned with slime. **Not recommended.**

10. **HELIOTROPE WEBCAP** *Cortinarius heliotropicus*   p. 291
    Slimy, heliotrope-violet cap and stalk. Violet to brown gills. Grows on soil.

11. **VIOLET WEBCAP** *Cortinarius violaceus*   p. 294
    Dark violet to dark purple cap and stalk. Spore print rusty brown. Grows on ground, in both coniferous and hardwood forests.

12. **BLUE-GILL WEBCAP** *Cortinarius delibutus*   p. 289
    Shiny, yellow cap. Stalk club-shaped, sticky; tinged with bluish lilac near top, banded with yellow on lower part, from sticky remnants of universal veil. **Not recommended.**

13. **CINNABAR BRACELET WEBCAP**   p. 288
    Cortinarius armillatus
    Rounded or humped, reddish brown cap. Thick, bulbous stalk, with cinnabar-red bands ("bracelets"). **Not recommended.**

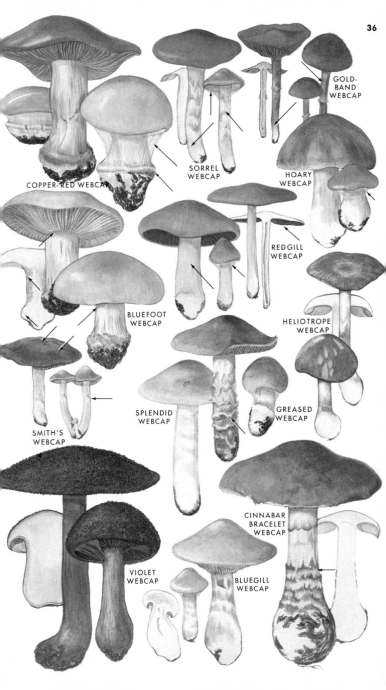

36

COPPER-RED WEBCAP

SORREL
WEBCAP

GOLD-
BAND
WEBCAP

HOARY
WEBCAP

REDGILL
WEBCAP

BLUEFOOT
WEBCAP

HELIOTROPE
WEBCAP

SMITH'S
WEBCAP

SPLENDID
WEBCAP

GREASED
WEBCAP

VIOLET
WEBCAP

CINNABAR
BRACELET
WEBCAP

BLUEGILL
WEBCAP

PLATE 37 $\times \frac{1}{2}$ (except #3)

FLAMECAPS AND OTHERS:
Cortinariaceae (2)

1. **SOFT STUMPFOOT** *Crepidotus mollis*   p. 295
    White to brownish, fan-shaped cap; smooth at first, soon develops
    yellowish to brown fibrils (hairs) and scales. Laterally attached to
    hardwood debris.

2. **AUTUMN SKULLCAP** *Galerina autumnalis*   p. 296
    Thin, brown, rounded to flat cap on a thin, brown stalk. Scattered
    to clustered on wood. **Poisonous.**

Flamecaps (Gymnopilus — next 4 species): Spore print bright brown-ish orange. The first species is sometimes mistaken for a chanterelle.

3. **SHOWY FLAMECAP (BIG LAUGHING MUSHROOM)** p. 298
    Gymnopilus spectabilis ($\times \frac{1}{6}$)
    Medium to large, orange-yellow cap on thick stalk. Gill usually
    lighter than cap; thin, sharp-edged, close. Grows in large clumps on
    decaying wood. **Poisonous.**

4. **ORANGE FLAMECAP** *Gymnopilus terrestris*   p. 299
    Orange cap, stalk, and gills; all hygrophanous, fading to yellow.
    Grows singly or in clusters on soil in western coniferous forests.

5. **FIR FLAMECAP** *Gymnopilus sapineus*   p. 297
    Dry, orange-yellow cap; stalk light-colored, becoming flushed with
    brown. Grows on conifer wood, especially on slashings in forests.

6. **BLUE-GREEN FLAMECAP** *Gymnopilus punctifolius*   p. 297
    Orange-brown cap, gills, and stalk, flushed with blue-green; all hy-
    grophanous. Grows on decaying wood. **Not recommended.**

7. **DARK DISK** *Hebeloma mesophaeum*   p. 300
    Shiny, brown cap. Stalk slender, more or less hairy, with a thin
    ring. Odor radish-like. **Poisonous.**

8. **POISON PIE** *Hebeloma crustuliniforme*   p. 300
    Rounded, cream to brownish cap; surface smooth. Gills beaded
    with water droplets along edges. Stalk robust. Odor radish-like.
    Poisonous.

9. **FLAKY SCALECAP** *Tubaria furfuracea*   p. 303
    Smooth, brown, fragile cap with wispy margin; hygrophanous.
    Stalk slender. Grows on soil or decaying wood.

10. **GYPSY NITECAP** *Rozites caperata*   p. 302
    Orange-yellow to brownish cap; frosted at center; wrinkled near
    margin. Stalk fleshy, whitish, with a white ring. Spores brown.

11. **EARTHBLADE FIBERHEAD** *Inocybe geophylla*   p. 301
    Thin, white, streaked cap; pointed knob. Slender white stalk. **Poi-
    sonous.**

12. **FLUFF FIBERHEAD** *Inocybe lanuginosa*   p. 302
    Dry, dark brown cap with fluffy scales. Stalk slender, scaly. Grows
    on well-rotted wood. **Poisonous.**

13. **CONIC FIBERHEAD** *Inocybe fastigiata*   p. 301
    Conic, brown, streaked or split cap, on a twisted stalk. **Poisonous.**

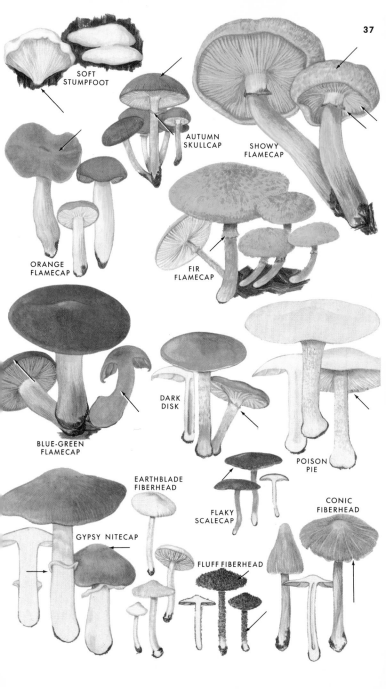

37

SOFT STUMPFOOT

AUTUMN SKULLCAP

SHOWY FLAMECAP

ORANGE FLAMECAP

FIR FLAMECAP

BLUE-GREEN FLAMECAP

DARK DISK

POISON PIE

EARTHBLADE FIBERHEAD

CONIC FIBERHEAD

GYPSY NITECAP

FLAKY SCALECAP

FLUFF FIBERHEAD

PLATE 38 $\times\frac{1}{2}$

MISCELLANEOUS BROWN- AND
PINK-SPORED GILL FUNGI

1. **MAPLE EARTHSCALE** *Agrocybe acericola* p. 304
   Obtuse to rounded or humped, yellowish brown cap; hygrophanous. Slender, white, ringed stalk. Grows singly or scattered, on decaying hardwood logs.

2. **ROUNDTOP EARTHSCALE** *Agrocybe pediades* p. 306
   Small, rounded cap on a very slender stalk. Cap strong brown to strong yellowish brown at first, fading quickly to light yellowish brown. Grows on grassy or disturbed soil.

3. **LEATHER EARTHSCALE** *Agrocybe erebia* p. 305
   Dark brown, wrinkled cap; hygrophanous. Stalk light brown, ringed.

4. **CRACKED EARTHSCALE** *Agrocybe dura* p. 305
   Round to flat, yellow cap; irregular cracks in surface reveal whitish flesh. Firm, whitish stalk with a high ring. Check spore print.

5. **GOLDGILLS** *Phylloporus rhodoxanthus* p. 314
   Rounded, red, velvety cap. Bright yellow gills extend down stalk.

6. **MILK BONNET** *Conocybe lactea* p. 308
   Delicate whitish, conic to bell-shaped cap on a spindly stalk. Common in lawns on summer mornings.

7. **RUSTY HOOD** *Conocybe tenera* p. 309
   Delicate reddish brown, bell-shaped cap on a fragile, ringless stalk.

8. **WRINKLE RING (FAIRY BONNET)** *C. arhenii* p. 307
   Small, fragile cap. Slender, two-toned stalk, with cuff-like ring. **Poisonous.**

9. **MANURE MUSHROOM** *Bolbitius vitellinus* p. 307
   Thin, sticky, watery, yellow cap on a thin, yellow stalk. Grows singly or in clumps, on manure or rich, moist soil.

Entolomas (next 5 species): Mature gills pink from spores. Gills attached to stalk.

10. **GRAY PINKGILL** *Entoloma lividum* p. 311
    Grayish cap on thick, white stalk. Grows in oak woods.

11. **SALMON PINKGILL** *Entoloma salmoneum* p. 311
    Orange, conic cap with nipple-like tip. Fragile, skinny stalk.

12. **UNICORN (YELLOW) PINKGILL** *Entoloma murraii* p. 311
    Looks like a bright yellow version of Salmon Pinkgill.

13. **STRAIGHT-STALK PINKGILL** *Entoloma strictior* p. 312
    Brown, conic cap on grayish stalk. Fruits in early spring. **Poisonous.**

14. **ABORTED PINKGILL** *Entoloma abortivum* p. 310
    Light brownish gray cap with grayish to pink gills. Pale stalk. Often has soft, whitish, irregular masses of tissue nearby.

15. **VELVET-FOOT BRIMCAP** *Paxillus atrotomentosus* p. 313
    Large, brown, velvety cap on a short, robust, velvety stalk. Laterally attached to decaying conifer wood.

16. **NAKED BRIMCAP** *Paxillus involutus* p. 313
    Dry, brown, fibrillose cap; margin strongly inrolled. Crowded gills extend down stalk. Stalk firm. Grows on ground. **Poisonous.**

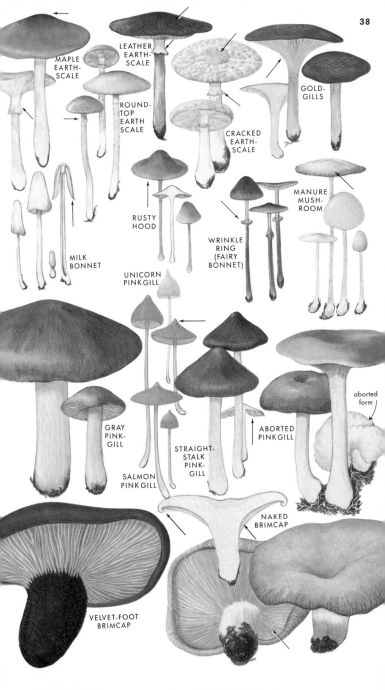

38

MAPLE EARTH-SCALE

LEATHER EARTH-SCALE

ROUND-TOP EARTH SCALE

CRACKED EARTH-SCALE

GOLD-GILLS

RUSTY HOOD

MILK BONNET

WRINKLE RING (FAIRY BONNET)

MANURE MUSH-ROOM

UNICORN PINKGILL

GRAY PINK-GILL

SALMON PINKGILL

STRAIGHT-STALK PINK-GILL

ABORTED PINKGILL

aborted form

NAKED BRIMCAP

VELVET-FOOT BRIMCAP

PLATE 39 ×½

BRITTLEGILLS (1) AND SLIMECAPS

Next 3 species (Gomphidiaceae): Gills extend down stalk. Spore print blackish.

1. **SLIMECAP** *Gomphidius glutinosus* p. 316
   Slimy, gray to brown, rounded cap; stains black when cut or bruised. White to smoky gills extend down white to yellow stalk.

2. **BROWN SLIMECAP** *Chroogomphus rutilus* p. 315
   Rounded to flat, reddish brown cap; surface sticky. Stalk firm; brownish orange.

3. **ORANGE WOOLLYCAP** *Chroogomphus tomentosus* p. 315
   Dry, woolly, orange cap. Widely spaced gills extend down orange stalk. Western N. America.

Brittlegills (Russula—next 7 species): Cap often white or brightly colored. Flesh brittle. Spore print white to yellow. See also Pl. 40.

4. **WHITISH BRITTLEGILL** *Russula albidula* p. 317
   Fragile, white cap on a thick, white, brittle stalk. Mature gills pale yellowish. Taste peppery.* Spore print pale yellow.

5. **COMPACT BRITTLEGILL** *Russula compacta* p. 318
   Stout, whitish cap; surface dry, unpolished. Gills close. All parts stain orange-brown. Spore print white.

6. **STUBBY BRITTLEGILL** *Russula brevipes* p. 318
   Large, dry, white cap; broadly funnel-shaped. Stalk stubby; attached to center of cap. Gills faintly flushed with green. Spore print pale yellowish.

7. **SCALLOP BRITTLEGILL** *Russula pectinatoides* p. 322
   Thin, fragile, light brownish cap, with radiating streaks and grooves; surface sticky. Fragile stalk. Spore print pale orange-yellow.

8. **SAND BRITTLEGILL** *Russula ventricosipes* p. 324
   Yellow to brown, firm, rounded to flat cap; center depressed, surface sticky. Short, hard stalk. Grows in sandy soil. Spore print pale orange-yellow.

9. **DENSE BRITTLEGILL** *Russula densifolia* p. 319
   Large, white to dingy brown cap on a thick stalk. Cap convex to depressed; surface dry to sticky. All parts stain red, then black when injured. Spore print white. **Not recommended.**

10. **STINKING BRITTLEGILL** *Russula fragrantissima* p. 321
    Large, yellow to yellow-brown, sticky cap. Yellowish gills stain brown when injured. Spore print pale orange-yellow. Firm, yellowish stalk. Odor strong, offensive.

* See p. 10 for cautions about using taste as an identifying characteristic.

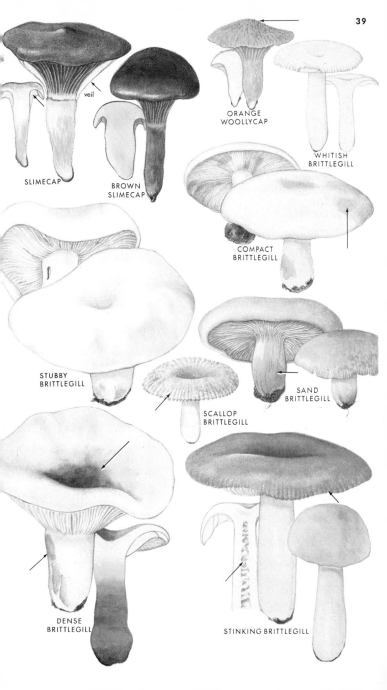

39

SLIMECAP

veil

BROWN
SLIMECAP

ORANGE
WOOLLYCAP

WHITISH
BRITTLEGILL

COMPACT
BRITTLEGILL

STUBBY
BRITTLEGILL

SCALLOP
BRITTLEGILL

SAND
BRITTLEGILL

DENSE
BRITTLEGILL

STINKING BRITTLEGILL

PLATE 40   × 1/2

BRITTLEGILLS (2) AND MILKCAPS (1)

Brittlegills (Russula—first 6 species): Cap often white or brightly colored. Flesh brittle. Spore print white to yellow. See also Pl. 39.

1. **FRAGILE BRITTLEGILL** *Russula fragilis*   p. 321
   Thin, fragile, multicolored cap on a brittle white stalk. Gills and spore print pale yellowish. Taste slightly peppery.*

2. **SHELLFISH BRITTLEGILL** *Russula xerampelina*   p. 325
   Cap color varies; flesh firm. All parts slowly stain dingy yellow-brown when injured. Fish odor (may develop slowly). Spore print yellowish.

3. **SICKENER** *Russula emetica*   p. 320
   Fragile, shiny, red cap with white gills. Thick, white stalk. Taste sharply peppery.* **Poisonous—do not try it intentionally.** Spore print white.

4. **GREEN BRITTLEGILL** *Russula virescens*   p. 325
   Dull green cap; surface breaks into crust-like patches. Does not change color when handled. No distinctive taste.* Spore print yellowish white.

5. **VARIEGATED BRITTLEGILL** *Russula variata*   p. 323
   Large, multicolored or predominantly green to pink, purplish, or gray cap. Gills repeatedly forked. Spore print white. Mild taste.*

6. **GOLDEN BRITTLEGILL** *Russula flavipes*   p. 320
   Yellow to orange, dry cap; rounded to flat. Short, firm, yellow stalk. Spore print yellowish.

Milkcaps (Lactarius—next 7 species): Latex (milky fluid) seeps from gills or flesh when cut. See also Pls. 41, 42.

7. **DARK-SPOTTED MILKCAP** *Lactarius atroviridis*   p. 327
   Large, dingy green cap and stalk; often spotted. Latex white; slowly stains gills greenish when cut.

8. **WRINKLED MILKCAP** *Lactarius corrugis*   p. 329
   Dry, brown cap with concentric wrinkles. Gills and flesh stain brown when injured, oozing abundant white latex.

9. **TAWNY MILKCAP** *Lactarius volemus*   p. 340
   Similar to Wrinkled Milkcap, but cap more orange; rarely wrinkled.

10. **SMOKY MILKCAP** *Lactarius fumosus*   p. 331
    Similar to Sooty Milkcap, but lighter and more grayish.

11. **SOOTY MILKCAP** *Lactarius lignyotus*   p. 332
    Thin, blackish brown cap; surface dull velvety. Slender stalk. Latex white; slowly stains cut surfaces pink. Gills close.

12. **SLIMY MILKCAP** *Lactarius mucidus*   p. 332
    Shiny, brown to gray cap; surface slimy to sticky. Latex white, drying as green to olive spots.

13. **WATERDROP MILKCAP** *Lactarius aquifluus*   p. 327
    Brown cap; sometimes indistinctly spotted or zoned. Latex transparent, watery. Odor of brown sugar. **Not recommended.**

* See p. 10 for cautions about using taste as an identifying characteristic.

40

color varies

FRAGILE BRITTLEGILL

SHELLFISH BRITTLEGILL

GREEN BRITTLEGILL

SICKENER

TAWNY MILKCAP

VARIEGATED BRITTLEGILL

GOLDEN BRITTLEGILL

WRINKLED MILKCAP

SMOKY MILKCAP

DARK-SPOTTED MILKCAP

SOOTY MILK-CAP

SLIMY MILKCAP

WATER-DROP MILK-CAP

PLATE 41 ×½

MILKCAPS (2)

Milkcaps (Lactarius): Latex (milky fluid) seeps from gills or flesh when cut. See also Pls. 40 and 42.

1. **FLEECY MILKCAP** *Lactarius vellereus* p. 339
   Large, hard, white cap; surface dry, minutely velvety at first. Cap convex, depressed at center. Gills widely spaced. Taste hot, peppery.* **Not recommended.**

2. **COTTONROLL MILKCAP** *Lactarius deceptivus* p. 329
   Dull white, dry cap; margin incurved in young specimens, with a large, cottony roll. Gills white to pale yellowish. Flesh stains brownish when cut or bruised. **Not recommended.**

3. **PEPPER MILKCAP** *Lactarius piperatus* p. 333
   Dry, white cap with thin, narrow, very crowded gills. White latex. Taste very peppery.* **Poisonous—do not try it.**

4. **POWDERPUFF MILKCAP** *Lactarius torminosus* p. 337
   Pink overall. Cap hairy, especially on margin. Latex white; does not stain cut surfaces. Taste hot, peppery.* **Poisonous.**

5. **SHAGGY BEAR** *Lactarius representaneus* p. 334
   Scaly, yellow cap with a hairy margin; surface sticky. Stalk spotted. Whitish latex quickly stains cut surfaces purple. Grows under conifers. **Poisonous.**

6. **SPOTSTALK** *Lactarius scrobiculatus* p. 335
   Straw yellow cap; young specimens have sticky surface and hairy margin. Latex white, but changes quickly to yellow when exposed to air (when gills are cut). Stalk spotted. **Poisonous.**

7. **INDIGO MILKCAP** *Lactarius indigo* p. 331
   Indigo blue overall, including the abundant latex. Cap surface sticky, with a silvery sheen. Cap slowly turns greenish with age. Taste may be peppery or bitter.*

8. **MARYLAND MILKCAP** *Lactarius subplinthogalus* p. 336
   Dry, pale orange-yellow cap; gills and stalk slightly darker. Latex stains cut surfaces strong yellowish pink. Gills very widely spaced. Spore print pale orange-yellow.

9. **ORANGE MILKCAP** *Lactarius hygrophoroides* p. 331
   Orange to reddish orange cap. Latex white; does not stain gills or flesh when cut. Spore print white.

10. **RED-WINE MILKCAP** *Lactarius subpurpureus* p. 336
    Purplish to yellowish pink overall, with darker spots or zones. Latex purplish red; slowly stains cut surfaces light green.

* See p. 10 for cautions about using taste as an identifying characteristic.

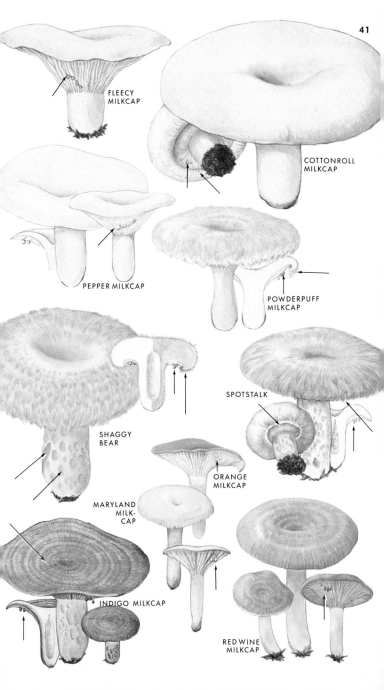

41

FLEECY
MILKCAP

COTTONROLL
MILKCAP

PEPPER MILKCAP

POWDERPUFF
MILKCAP

SHAGGY
BEAR

SPOTSTALK

ORANGE
MILKCAP

MARYLAND
MILK-
CAP

INDIGO MILKCAP

RED WINE
MILKCAP

PLATE 42   ×½

MILKCAPS (3)

Milkcaps (Lactarius): White to colored latex seeps from gills or flesh when cut. Spore print white to cream-colored. See also Pls. 40, 41.

1. **RED-HOT MILKCAP** *Lactarius rufus*   p. 335
   Reddish brown cap and stalk; surface moist to dry. Gills lighter brown. Latex white. Peppery taste develops slowly.* **Not recommended.**

2. **ORANGE-RING MILKCAP** *Lactarius thyinos*   p. 337
   Orange, slimy to sticky cap stalk; cap zoned. Latex orange; does not stain flesh or gills green when cut (see next species).

3. **RED-JUICE MILKCAP** *Lactarius rubrilacteus*   p. 334
   Orange cap with concentric rings. Latex scanty; dark red to orange-red. All parts slowly turn blue-green when injured.

4. **SAFFRON MILKCAP** *Lactarius deliciosus*   p. 330
   Orange overall; stains green from handling or bruising. Cap zoned. Latex orange at first; turns green when exposed to air.

5. **PECK'S MILKCAP** *Lactarius peckii*   p. 333
   Reddish orange overall; cap zoned with darker spots and streaks. Latex white; does not change color. Taste very peppery.* **Not recommended.**

6. **KINDRED MILKCAP** *Lactarius affinis*   p. 326
   Slimy, dull yellow or brownish cap. Latex white; unchanging, or sometimes drying as green spots on gills or flesh when cut.

7. **GRAY MILKCAP** *Lactarius caespitosus*   p. 328
   Firm, gray to grayish brown cap and stalk; surface slightly sticky. Latex white; unchanging. Taste develops slowly, but becomes extremely hot and persistent.* **Not recommended.**

8. **GOLD-DROP MILKCAP** *Lactarius chrysorrheus*   p. 328
   Yellowish, convex to flat, shiny cap. Latex abundant; changes quickly from white to bright yellow. Taste peppery.* **Not recommended.**

9. **ORDINARY MILKCAP** *Lactarius trivialis*   p. 338
   Cap and stalk gray, suffused with violet; both fade to brown. Cap surface sticky. Latex white. Grows under conifers in western N. America. **Not recommended.**

10. **DAMP MILKCAP** *Lactarius uvidus*   p. 339
    Sticky, gray to brown cap, flushed with purple. Latex white to yellowish; slowly stains cut surfaces purplish, then brown. Taste slow to develop, but bitter.* **Poisonous — do not try it.**

* See p. 10 for cautions about using taste as an identifying characteristic.

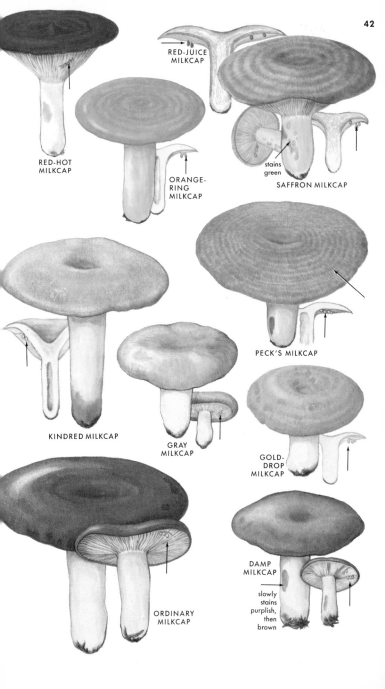

42

RED-JUICE
MILKCAP

RED-HOT
MILKCAP

ORANGE-
RING
MILKCAP

stains
green

SAFFRON MILKCAP

KINDRED MILKCAP

GRAY
MILKCAP

PECK'S MILKCAP

GOLD-
DROP
MILKCAP

ORDINARY
MILKCAP

DAMP
MILKCAP

slowly
stains
purplish,
then
brown

PLATE 43 $\times \frac{1}{2}$

STINKHORNS, PUFFBALLS (1),
AND RELATED FUNGI

1. **NET STINKHORN** *Dictyophora duplicata*   p. 347
   Spongy stalk with a net-like skirt that is attached underneath a
   thin, slime-covered cap. Dark olive spore slime has bad odor.
2. **EASTERN STINKHORN** *Phallus ravenelii*   p. 348
   Thin cap has olive, fetid spore mass. Stalk spongy, white.
3. **DOG STINKHORN** *Mutinus caninus*   p. 347
   No cap. Upper part of pointed stalk coated with spore slime.
4. **ASPIC PUFFBALL** *Calostoma cinnabarina*   p. 344
   Red spore case has orange, gelatinous outer layer. Stalk net-like.
5. **LATTICE PUFFBALL** *Calostoma lutescens*   p. 343
   Net-like, tough stalk has round, red-mouthed spore sac.
6. **CHAMBERED STINKHORN**   p. 346
   Simblum sphaerocephalum
   Round head has greenish spore mass on inner surfaces of lattice.
   Odor strong, repulsive.
7. **STINKY SQUID** *Pseudocolus fusiformis*   p. 345
   Small to medium, soft, pink, spongy columns, united at base; tips
   free or fused, but usually touching. Odor unpleasant.
8. **SAC STINKHORN** *Phallogaster saccatus*   p. 346
   White head and stalk, flushed with pink or lilac. Greenish spore
   slime inside slowly develops stinky odor.
9. **RIBBED LIZARD CLAW** *Lysurus mokusin*   p. 345
   Large, pink to reddish orange, hollow, deeply grooved stalk rises
   from whitish, membranous cup. Slimy, brown spore mass.
10. **LIZARD CLAW** *Anthurus gardneri*   p. 344
    Large, white, sponge-like stalk. Orange and brown head splits ver-
    tically. Unpleasant odor.
11. **LATTICE STINKHORN** *Clathrus ruber*   p. 345
    Reddish, round, lattice-like, hollow ball (spore case) emerges from
    white, cuplike outer membrane. Spore mass forms on inside of lat-
    tice.
12. **COLUMN STINKHORN** *Clathrus columnatus*   p. 345
    Pink, spongy receptacle (spore case), consisting of 2–5 thick col-
    umns that are united at tips. Odor unpleasant.
13. **CITRINE FALSE TRUFFLE** *Truncolumella citrina*   p. 349
    Greenish yellow; irregularly rounded or lobed. Matures under
    ground.
14. **FALSE BRITTLEGILL** *Macowanites americanus*
    Nearly round, lavender to yellowish outer spore case with white
    stalk and flesh. Compare with true brittlegills (*Russula,* p. 317).
15. **SLIMY POUCH** *Thaxtergaster pinguis*   p. 350
    Slimy, yellow, rounded cap. Does not open completely and does not
    give a spore print.
16. **BOLETE FALSE TRUFFLE** *Gastroboletus turbinatus*   p. 349
    Thick, dry, red to brown cap, with red to yellow tubes on under-
    side. Stubby stalk. Flesh stains blue when injured.

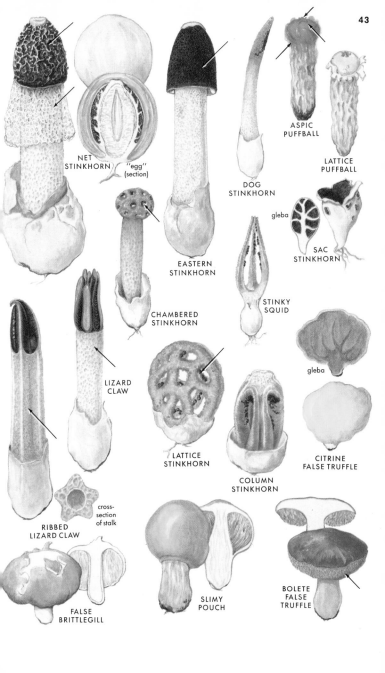

43

NET
STINKHORN

"egg"
(section)

ASPIC
PUFFBALL

LATTICE
PUFFBALL

DOG
STINKHORN

EASTERN
STINKHORN

CHAMBERED
STINKHORN

gleba

SAC
STINKHORN

STINKY
SQUID

LIZARD
CLAW

gleba

LATTICE
STINKHORN

COLUMN
STINKHORN

CITRINE
FALSE TRUFFLE

cross-
section
of stalk

RIBBED
LIZARD CLAW

FALSE
BRITTLEGILL

SLIMY
POUCH

BOLETE
FALSE
TRUFFLE

PLATE 44   ×½ (except #4)

GIANT PUFFBALLS

1. **VASE PUFFBALL** *Calvatia cyathiformis*   p. 352
   Large, round to pear-shaped, white to brownish spore case, with
   violet gleba (spore mass) at maturity.

2. **SMOKY PUFFBALL** *Calvatia fumosa*   p. 352
   Gray, thick-walled spore case has smooth to slightly wavy or very
   shallowly cracked surface. Grows in western mountains.

3. **SCULPTURED PUFFBALL** *Calvatia sculpta*   p. 353
   Pear-shaped to top-shaped spore case, with large warts that are
   usually united at tips. Grows at high elevations in western mountains.

4. **GIANT PUFFBALL** *Calvatia gigantea* (×⅛)   p. 353
   One of the largest puffballs. Round, white spore case has smooth
   outer layer that flakes away at maturity.

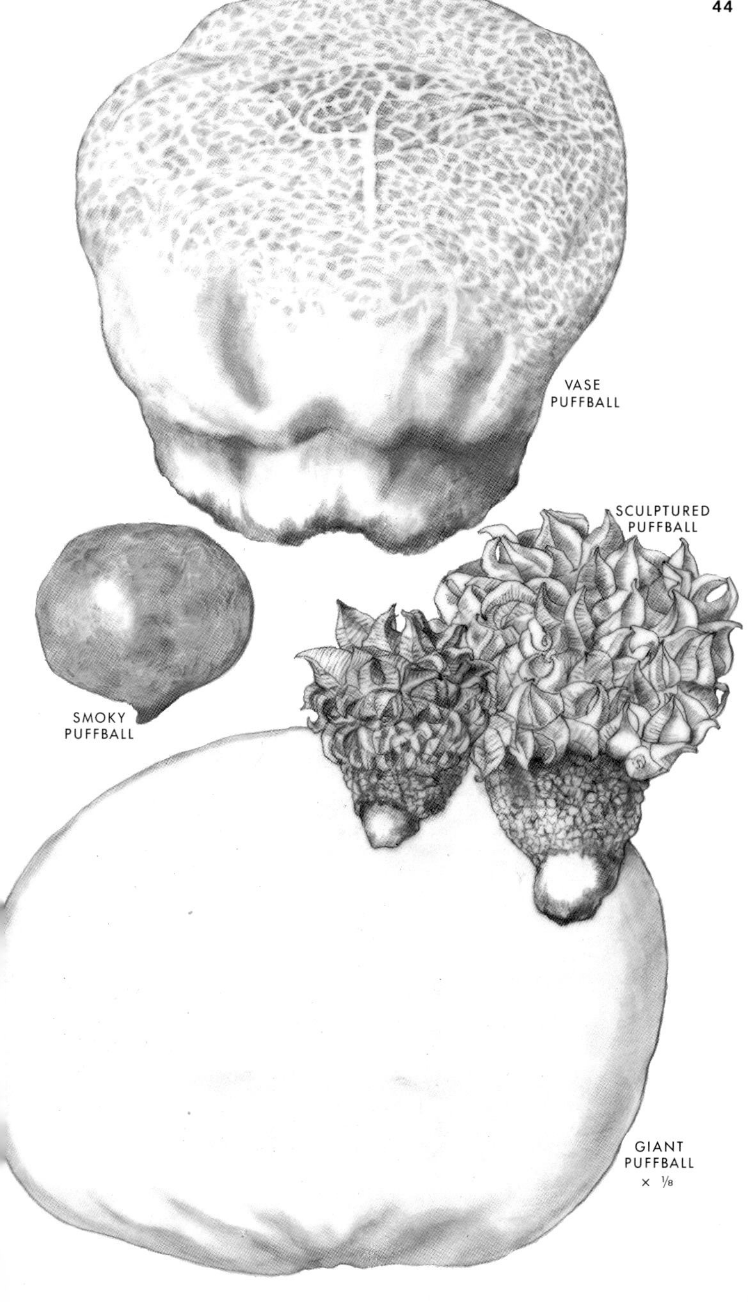

44

VASE
PUFFBALL

SCULPTURED
PUFFBALL

SMOKY
PUFFBALL

GIANT
PUFFBALL
× ⅛

PLATE 45   scale varies

GIANT PUFFBALLS (2)
AND TRUE PUFFBALLS

1. **GIANT PASTURE PUFFBALL**   p. 358

Mycenastrum corium ($\times 1/4$)
Flattened spore case has comparatively thin, felty outer wall that breaks into patches or is shed, exposing a thick, tough, persistent inner wall that breaks into irregular lobes.

2. **PASTURE PUFFBALL** *Vascellum depressum* ($\times 1/4$)   p. 357
Top-shaped puffball with olive-brown gleba (spore mass). Broad, chambered, sterile base is separated from gleba by a papery membrane (see lengthwise section).

3. **SANDCASE PUFFBALL** *Disciseda candida* ($\times 1$)   p. 354
Small, flattened, acorn-like spore case; opens by a single pore. Grows on exposed soil.

4. **PUFFBALL** *Bovista pila* ($\times 1$)   p. 351
Round, brown spore case with paper-thin wall; opens by an irregular pore or tear at apex. Grows on surface of ground.

5. **SCULPTURED GIANT PUFFBALL**   p. 357
Calbovista subsculpta ($\times 1/2$)
Rounded, white to brownish spore case; usually wider than it is tall. Outer wall breaks into thick, angular patches that separate from the very thin, shiny, inner spore case.

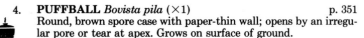
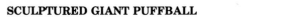

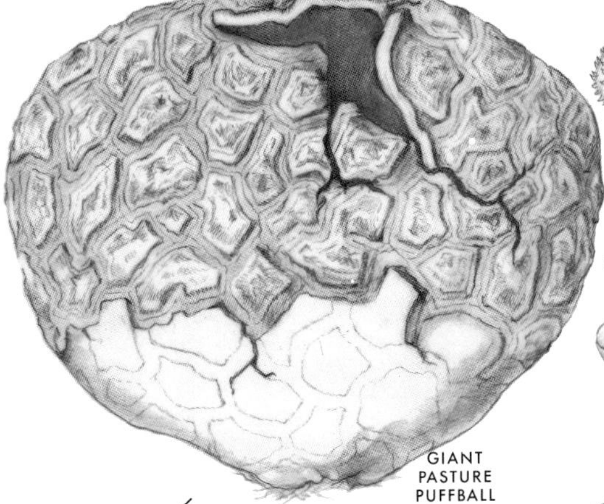

45

GIANT
PASTURE
PUFFBALL

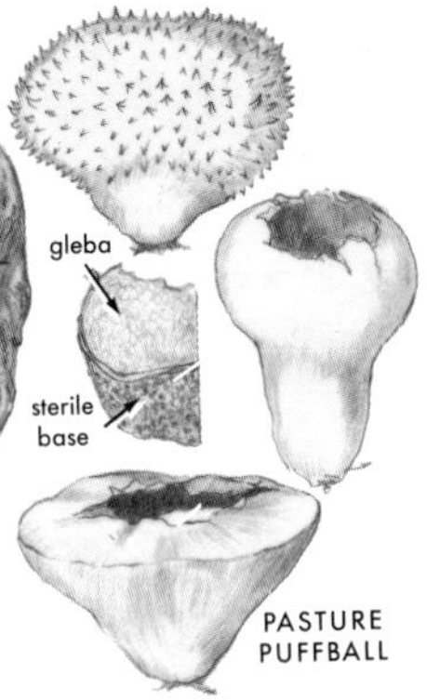

gleba

sterile
base

PASTURE
PUFFBALL

sand
case

inner
case

SANDCASE PUFFBALL

PUFFBALL

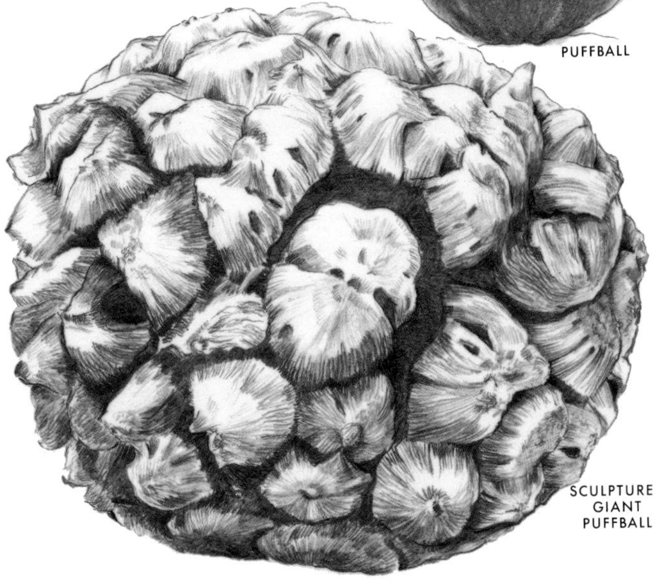

SCULPTURED
GIANT
PUFFBALL

PLATE 46   ×1

MORE PUFFBALLS

1. **NAKED PUFFBALL** *Lycoperdon marginatum*   p. 355
   Outer wall of spore case has thick, long spines that are shed in small sheets or scales, exposing brown, scurfy or pitted inner spore case.

2. **BEAUTIFUL PUFFBALL** *Lycoperdon pulcherrimum*   p. 356
   Similar to Naked Puffball, but lacks network of minute scurfy scales on inner spore case when outer scaly case is first shed.

3. **SPINY PUFFBALL** *Lycoperdon echinatum*   p. 354
   Rounded spore case, tapering to a stubby sterile base. When shed, long spines leave a netted pattern on surface of inner spore case.

4. **SMOOTH PUFFBALL** *Lycoperdon molle*   p. 355
   Brown spore case with small spines or granules on surface; case usually pear-shaped. Gleba (spore mass) dark brown.

5. **MINI PUFFBALL** *Lycoperdon pusillum*   p. 356
   Small, round spore case, attached to ground by one or more string-like strands; lacks sterile base. Outer wall of spore case smooth or nearly so; apical pore large, with lobed margin.

6. **GEM PUFFBALL** *Lycoperdon perlatum*   p. 355
   Pear-shaped or top-shaped, white to grayish spore case with cone-shaped scales that are easily shed. Gleba (spore mass) olive-brown. Grows on the ground.

7. **PEAR PUFFBALL** *Lycoperdon pyriforme*   p. 356
   Clusters of round to pear-shaped, smooth, white to brownish spore cases, attached by conspicuous, string-like strands to decaying wood.

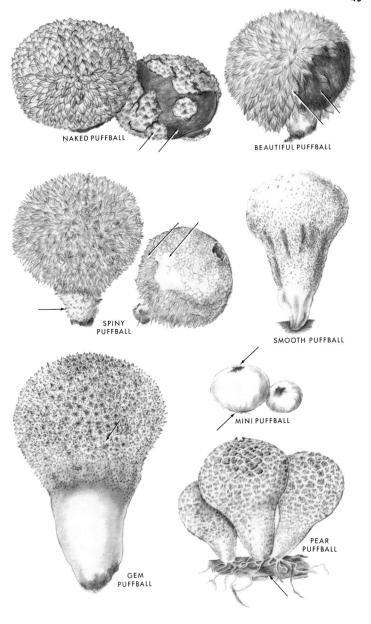

46

NAKED PUFFBALL

BEAUTIFUL PUFFBALL

SPINY PUFFBALL

SMOOTH PUFFBALL

MINI PUFFBALL

GEM PUFFBALL

PEAR PUFFBALL

PLATE 47   ×1 (except #1)

PUFFBALLS AND EARTHSTARS

1. **STAR EARTHBALL** *Scleroderma polyrhizum* (×1/2)   p. 363
   Large, whitish, thick-walled spore case with roughened surface;
   splits into wide, star-like rays. Forms under ground. **Not recommended.**

2. **WATER-MEASURE EARTHSTAR**   p. 358
   Astraeus hygrometricus
   Flattened spore case sits on 6 or more rays; no stalk. Rays expand
   or recurve when wet and fold inward when dry.

3. **REDDISH EARTHSTAR** *Geastrum rufescens*   p. 360
   Round, dull brownish spore case; tapers to a central point. When
   frehs, case often has pinkish tints after soil debris is brushed off.
   Mouth area fibrillose; opening not distinct.

4. **FLOWER EARTHSTAR** *Geastrum floriforme*   p. 359
   Small, round spore case with a small, indistinct apical pore
   (mouth). Outer wall has a ring of tough, pointed lobes that bend
   inward when dry and expand outward when moist.

5. **BOWL EARTHSTAR** *Geastrum saccatum*   p. 361
   Nearly round, light grayish brown spore case, recessed in a bowl of
   recurved rays. Spore case has a distinct conical mouth, surrounded
   by fibrils. Often grows under juniper.

6. **FRINGED EARTHSTAR** *Geastrum fimbriatum*   p. 359
   Small, round, smooth-walled spore case, recessed in a bowl of 5–8
   recurved rays. No stalk. Spore case has an indistinct, fibrillose
   mouth.

7. **COLLARED EARTHSTAR** *Geastrum triplex*   p. 361
   Nearly round spore case, with wide, pointed, recurved rays. Prominent "beak." No stalk. Cracked upper surface of rays forms a
   saucer-like base for inner spore case.

8. **GROOVED EARTHSTAR** *Geastrum pectinatum*   p. 360
   Small spore case with pointed, grooved mouth and grooved lower
   portion just above attachment to stalk. Outer rays remain recurved
   in older, fully mature specimens.

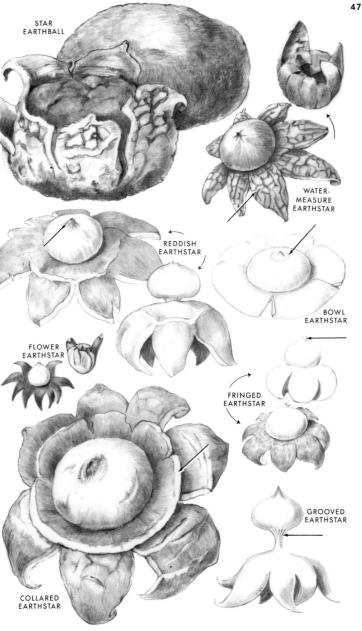

47

STAR EARTHBALL

WATER-MEASURE EARTHSTAR

REDDISH EARTHSTAR

BOWL EARTHSTAR

FLOWER EARTHSTAR

FRINGED EARTHSTAR

GROOVED EARTHSTAR

COLLARED EARTHSTAR

PLATE 48   scale varies

PUFFBALLS, BIRD'S NESTS, AND RELATED FUNGI

1. **STREAKED BIRD'S NEST** *Cyathus striatus* (×1)   p. 367
   Small, brownish, goblet-shaped cup with streaked and grooved inside wall. Contains dark spore cases, attached to inner surface of cup by a coiled cord.

2. **SPLASH-CUP BIRD'S NEST** *Cyathus stercoreus* (×1)   p. 367
   Small, goblet-shaped cup with smooth inner wall. Contains brown, flattened spore cases, attached to wall of cup by a thin, coiled cord. Grows on soil and manure.

3. **GEL BIRD'S NEST** *Nidula candida* (×1)   p. 368
   Small, brownish, nearly straight-sided cup. Contains tiny, dark-colored, flattened spore cases, embedded in gelatinous matrix at first. Grows on decaying wood or soil.

4. **BIRD'S NEST** *Crucibulum levis* (×1)   p. 366
   Small, brownish, thin-walled, dry cup with whitish spore cases, each attached to inner cup surface by a tiny cord. Grows on vegetable debris.

5. **SMOOTH EARTHBALL** *Scleroderma flavidum* (×1)   p. 362
   Small to medium, comparatively thin-walled, brownish spore case; smooth or sometimes split, forming shallow, angular scales. Spore case opens by recurved scales. **Not recommended.**

6. **EARTHBALL** *Scleroderma citrinum* (×1)   p. 362
   Medium to large, nearly round, yellowish to brownish spore case. Angular scales, usually with a smaller wart at center of each scale. **Poisonous.**

7. **FLATCAP STALKED PUFFBALL**   p. 363
   Battarraea stevensii (×½)
   Flattened to round spore case on a thick, coarse-scaled, woody stalk. Opens by a marginal tear. Grows on desert soil.

8. **STALKED PUFFBALL** *Tulostoma brumale* (× 1)   p. 364
   Nearly round, smooth, papery-thin spore case on a thin, woody, somewhat bulbous stalk. Case has a distinct tubular opening (mouth). Grows on sandy soil.

9. **PEA ROCK** *Pisolithus tinctorius* (×½)   p. 366
   Large, top-shaped to club-shaped, brown, thin-walled spore case. Contains pea-sized nodules of powdery spore mass, separated by fragile filaments. Grows on soil.

10. **GIANT STALKED PUFFBALL** *Podaxis longii* (×½)   p. 364
    Large, white, oval spore case with a thick but fragile wall. Contains dark reddish brown spore powder. Thick, scaly stalk.

11. **KHUMBI** *Podaxis pistillaris* (×½)   p. 365
    White to brownish, oval spore case wtih a papery-thin wall. Contains powdery, dark brown spores. Slender, bulbous stalk.

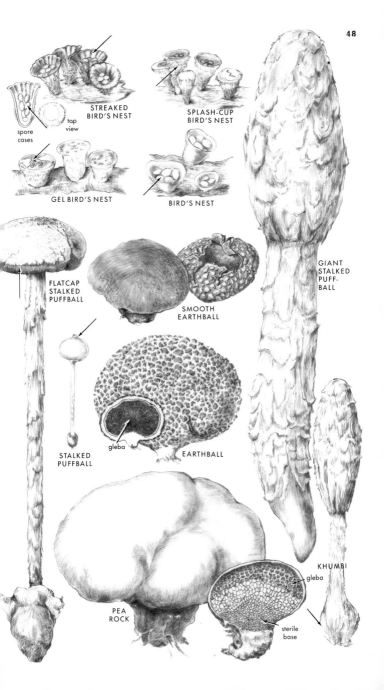

48

STREAKED
BIRD'S NEST

spore
cases

top
view

SPLASH-CUP
BIRD'S NEST

GEL BIRD'S NEST

BIRD'S NEST

GIANT
STALKED
PUFF-
BALL

FLATCAP
STALKED
PUFFBALL

SMOOTH
EARTHBALL

STALKED
PUFFBALL

gleba

EARTHBALL

KHUMBI

gleba

PEA
ROCK

sterile
base

Remarks: The stalk is sheathed by a *double-layered veil* from its base to the poorly developed ring. The outer layer of veil tissue is slimy; the inner layer consists of dark fibrils similar to those on cap and forms the ring and patchy scales.

BLUSHING WAXYCAP *Hygrophorus pudorinus*   **Pl. 22**
Medium to large, *orange-yellow* to *pinkish, rounded* cap; surface *sticky. Solid, pale stalk* with *scurfy granules at apex; no ring. Cap:* Convex to obtuse, with a strongly incurved, downy margin at first; expanding to a broadly bell-shaped or nearly flat cap with a broad, low hump. Surface smooth; pale orange-yellow to yellowish pink or light orange; margin lighter. Flesh thick, firm; colored like cap above to white in stalk. Odor faintly fragrant or absent; taste resembles that of turpentine or absent.* Gills subdistant, sometimes forked or interveined, narrow, short-decurrent (extending slightly down stalk); yellowish white to pinkish, but not red-staining or spotted. *Stalk:* Stout, *solid;* white above, sometimes tinged with cap color below. *Fluffy granules at apex* of stalk become reddish on drying or in KOH (weak potash). *Spore print:* White. **Technical notes:** Cap 5–12 cm across. Stalk 4–9 × 1–2 cm. Spores ellipsoid; 7–10 × 5–6 μm. Clamps present on hyphae. No cystidia. Gill trama divergent.

Fruiting: Scattered or in groups or fairy rings; on soil in coniferous forests. Western N. America and eastward along northern states and Canada. Late summer and fall.

Edibility: Not recommended. Extremely variable — difficult to identify.

Similar species: (1) Not clearly distinct from a European species, *Hygrophorus poetarum* (not shown). Pallid or white forms of *H. pudorinus* (Blushing Waxycap) may be recognized by the *scurfy granules* or glandular points at the stalk apex that turn *reddish* in KOH. (2) See False Russula (below).

FALSE RUSSULA *Hygrophorus russula*   **Pl. 23**
Medium to large, *stout cap;* surface *sticky. Gills* and *cap purplish red,* often *streaked with pink. Cap:* Convex, sometimes with a broad, low hump or flattened disc (center). Margin remains incurved in older specimens, sometimes becoming upturned (along with outer limb) at maturity; minutely cottony (use hand lens). Surface of cap smooth or wavy, *sticky* at first, but soon becoming dry and often breaking into small, scaly patches. *Purplish pink* to dark pink or yellowish pink, often *streaked;* may stain yellow when bruised. Margin is lighter than rest of cap. Flesh thick, firm; white or flushed with pink. Odor and taste not distinctive. *Gills close, narrow;* whitish at first, but soon becoming flushed with pink and eventually becoming *spotted or stained with purplish red* in age; adnate

---

* See p. 10 for cautions about using taste as an identifying characteristic.

(broadly attached), becoming decurrent (extending down stalk). **Stalk:** Stout, solid; short-cylindric, sometimes tapering slightly downward. Surface dry; pinkish white at apex, colored like cap below. **Spore print:** White. **Technical notes:** Cap 5–12 cm across. Stalk 3–8 × 1.5–3.5 cm. Spores smooth, ellipsoid; 6–8 × 3–5 μm. No cystidia. Clamps present on hyphae. Gill trama divergent.

Fruiting: Scattered or in groups or fairy rings; in oak forests. East of Great Plains and Washington state.

Edibility: Edible.

Similar species: Blushing Waxycap (*H. erubescens,* above) has more *widely spaced gills* that are *not* spotted or stained with purplish red. It grows in coniferous woods. (2) Brittlegills (species of *Russula,* p. 317, Pl. 40) have *brittle flesh.*

HARDWOOD WAXYCAP *Hygrophorus sordidus*   **Pl. 24**
Medium to large, *white cap;* surface *somewhat sticky. White gills. Pointed white stalk.* Grows in *oak-hickory woods.* **Cap:** Shallowly convex, with an inrolled margin at first; sometimes shallowly depressed on disc (center), expanding and becoming flat with age. Surface smooth; *sticky* when moist. *White* overall, or yellowish on disc. Flesh firm, thick. Odor and taste not distinctive.* Gills subdistant, broad, adnate (broadly attached) or subdecurrent (extending slightly down stalk); white at first, but later becoming flushed with yellowish. **Stalk:** Solid, firm; cylindric, or more commonly tapering downward to a *blunt point.* Surface smooth or very slightly cottony at apex, *white,* dry. **Spore print:** White. **Technical notes:** Cap 5–15 cm across. Stalk 5–10 × 0.5–3.0 cm. Spores smooth, non-amyloid, ellipsoid; 6–8 × 4.0–5.5 μm. Clamps present on cuticle.

Fruiting: Scattered or in groups; in open woods. Eastern and central U.S. and southern Canada. Sometimes abundant in late summer and fall.

Edibility: Although it has been reported as edible, we have no reports on its quality. **Not recommended** — easily confused with species of questionable edibility in several white-spored genera.

Similar species: The large size, habitat — under hardwoods, not conifers — and lack of slimy or sticky tissues coating stalk distinguish *H. sordidus* (Hardwood Waxycap) from other white species with which it might be confused readily. A robust southern species, *H. ponderatus* (not shown), has a *shorter,* more stocky growth form, with a *thin slime layer* on the stalk that is often difficult to detect.

LARCH WAXYCAP *Hygrophorus speciosus*   **Pl. 22**
Small to medium, *bright red, slimy cap; fades* to *orange. Gills white* to *yellowish. Slimy, white* or *orange-staining stalk.* Grows *under larch.* **Cap:** Shallowly convex or humped, with a

---

* See p. 10 for cautions about using taste as an identifying characteristic.

downturned or incurved margin; expanding to nearly flat, sometimes with a broad, shallow central depression. Surface smooth and very slimy; orange-red, *fading to orange* or orange-yellow, often remaining darker-colored on disc. Flesh soft; white to yellowish. Odor and taste not distinctive.* Gills subdistant, adnate (broadly attached) or subdecurrent (extending slightly down stalk), narrow; white to yellowish, with darker edges. *Stalk:* Cylindric or enlarged at base. Surface has white fibrils or more or less fibrillose scales under yellow- to orange-staining slime layer. *Spore print:* White. **Technical notes:** Cap 2–5 cm across. Stalk 5–10 × 0.4–0.8 cm. Spores smooth, ellipsoid; 8–10 × 4–6 μm. Clamps on cuticular hyphae. No pleurocystidia or cheilocystidia.

Fruiting: Scattered or in groups; in moist places *under larch* in Canada and U.S. Late summer and fall.

Edibility: Unknown.

SUBALPINE WAXYCAP *Hygrophorus subalpinus*   **Pl. 24**
Medium to large; *snowy white overall. Stubby, bulbous stalk has a thin, membranous ring. Fruits under or near snowbanks.* *Cap:* Broadly convex, expanding to obtuse or flat, sometimes with a low, broad hump remaining and an upturned margin in age. Patches of veil remnants may adhere to margin. Surface smooth, sticky or shiny; *pure white* or discoloring slightly when bruised. Flesh thick over disc and inner limb; white. Odor and taste not distinctive.* Gills decurrent (extending down stalk), close to subdistant (see inside front cover), narrow; white. *Stalk:* Short-cylindrical or enlarged downward, with a broadly rounded or pointed base. Surface white and silky smooth above ring; matted with fibrils below ring; not sticky. *Spore print:* White. **Technical notes:** Cap 5–15 cm across. Stalk 3–9 × 1–3 cm. Spores smooth, ellipsoid; 8–10 × 4–5 μm. No cystidia. Clamps present on hyphae. Gill trama divergent.

Fruiting: Scattered or in groups; on soil *in and around snowbanks.* Rocky Mts. to Pacific Northwest. Spring and summer.

Edibility: Edible, but said to be lacking in flavor.

Similar species: (1) A little-known, fall-fruiting species of southeastern forests, *Hygrophorus ponderatus* (not shown) is similar in stature (size and shape), but its slimy to sticky stalk surface, fibrillose (not membranous) veil, and narrower gills separate it from *H. subalpinus* (Subalpine Waxycap). (2) Small specimens of *Armillaria* (p. 133), particularly *A. arenicola* (not shown) are hard to distinguish from *H. subalpinus,* but this waxycap characteristically grows *near melting snowbanks* in high mountains. However, the thick, fleshy fruiting bodies of the Subalpine Waxycap often persist after the snow has completely melted.

---

* See p. 10 for cautions about using taste as an identifying characteristic.

TENNESSEE WAXYCAP   **Pl. 22**
Hygrophorus tennesseensis
Medium to large, *yellow* to *brown, sticky cap. Odor of raw
potatoes; taste bitter.** *Cap:* Broadly convex, with an incurved
margin at first; expanding to a flat cap, sometimes with a shallowly depressed disc (center). Surface smooth; slimy to *sticky.*
Brownish orange to reddish brown on disc, to light yellowish
brown or lighter on margin, which is cottony to fibrillose
(streaked). Flesh white; firm, thick on disc, tapering to a thin
margin. Gills adnate (broadly attached) or short-decurrent (extending slightly down stalk), subdistant; white. *Stalk:* Cylindric and tapered toward base; solid. Surface fibrillose to
streaked; dry. Dingy yellowish white. *Spore print:* White.
Technical notes: Cap 5–12 cm across. Stalk 5–10 × 0.8–2.0
cm. Spores smooth, ellipsoid; 6–9 × 4–6 μm. No cystidia.
Clamps present. Gill trama divergent.
Fruiting: In groups or scattered; on soil under conifers. Eastern U.S. and California.
Edibility: Unknown; **not recommended.**
Similar species: Odor and taste separate Tennessee Waxycap
(*H. tennesseensis*) and (1) *Hygrophorus bakerensis* (not
shown), which has an *almond-like odor* and no taste. (2)
Lighter colors, different odor and taste, and scurf on stalk that
turns reddish in KOH (weak potash) distinguish Blushing
Waxycap (*Hygrophorus pudorinus*, p. 209).

SPOTTED-STALK WAXYCAP   **Pl. 23**
Hygrophorus tephroleucus
Small, thin, gray cap; surface *sticky. Slender white stalk,* with
very small, *fibrillose scales* that become *dark gray* at maturity
(see **Remarks**). *Cap:* Convex, with a strongly incurved margin
at first; soon becoming flat except at margin, which long remains downturned; cap sometimes has a shallow central depression. Surface smooth, *sticky* and somewhat fibrillose
(streaked) under gluten; may be streaked on margin. Medium
gray on disc (center) to light brownish gray or light greenish
gray outward, fading with age. Flesh *thin,* soft; dingy whitish.
Odor and taste not distinctive. Gills adnate (broadly attached)
or short-decurrent (extending slightly down stalk), subdistant,
broad; white or dingy yellowish in age. *Stalk:* Cylindric; solid.
White overall at first, but soon *spotted with tufts of gray fibrils*
on upper part and midportion, often remaining white and fibrillose on lower part. *Spore print:* White. **Technical notes:**
Cap 1–3 cm across. Stalk 3–6 cm × 2–4 mm. Spores smooth,
ellipsoid; 7–10 × 4–5 μm. No cystidia. Clamps present on hyphae. Gill trama divergent.
Fruiting: Scattered or in groups; on soil under conifers and in
bogs. Widespread but not common — seldom abundant. Fall
and winter.
Edibility: Unknown.

Similar species: Very subtle differences separate this waxycap from (1) *Hygrophorus pustulatus* (not shown), which is slightly more robust, less distinctly fibrillose on cap, and has a smoother stalk surface, with dark dots that are not so scaly as in *H. tephroleucus* (Spotted-stalk Waxycap).

Remarks: In variety *aureofloccus* of *H. tephroleucus,* the dark scales on the upper stalk have golden yellow tips.

Deathcaps, Grisettes, and Slime Mushrooms: Family Amanitaceae

White (to yellowish) spore print, free gills, volva, and easy separation of stalk and cap (clean break) characterize the Amanitaceae. The volva may vary from a boot-like cup that is not attached to the stalk to one partially attached to the stalk or remaining as a thin ring, fibrils, slime layer, or powdery granules on the lower stalk and sometimes on the cap surface (see Fig. 32). The volva is the most important identification character, so *be sure you get it* when digging up the mushroom. The base of the stalk is often deep in soil. This family contains many poisonous species.

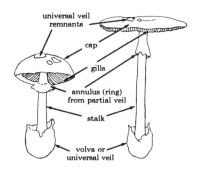

Fig. 32. Amanita. Note volva at base of stalk.

Slime Mushrooms: Genus *Limacella*

Medium-sized, *slimy* cap with free gills. Cap separates very easily from slender, slimy stalk. Spore print white.

SLIME MUSHROOM *Limacella glischra*   **Pl. 24**
Small to medium, *slimy, light brown cap* on a *slippery white*

stalk. ***Cap:*** Broadly rounded, sometimes with a low, broad hump. Pale to moderate *yellowish brown* or *reddish brown.* Margin incurved at first and often with *dangling bits of slime* as cap expands. Flesh soft; light reddish brown (just under cuticle) to white (below). Odor and taste not distinctive.* Gills free from stalk, close, thick; white to pale pinkish brown. ***Stalk:*** Separates easily from cap; solid, cylindric or slightly expanded downward. Surface white to pale brownish; *slimy* from thick *volva remains,* which coat *both cap and stalk* surface. *Ring obscure.* **Spore print:** White. **Technical notes:** Cap 2–5 cm across. Stalk 4.5–7.5 × 0.7–1.5 cm. Spores spherical or nearly so; 3.0–5.0 μm in diameter.

Fruiting: Solitary to scattered; on soil in woods. Seldom found in large numbers. Widespread.

Edibility: Unknown. **Not recommended.**

Similar species: The combination of the white spore print and the slimy cap and stalk surfaces may lead one erroneously to seek this species among (1) the waxycaps (*Hygrophorus,* p. 202, Pls. 22–24). Careful examination of young specimens, however, shows that the slimy coating on the stalk and cap comes from a *volva,* and a mixture of slime and filaments covers the young gills of unexpanded caps. The stature of this mushroom and its readily separable cap and stalk suggest relationships with (2) *Amanita* (next genus) and (3) *Lepiota* (p. 241). (4) Two other species of slime mushroom (*Limacella*) have a *membranous ring* on the stalk that distinguishes them readily from *L. glischra.* In addition, one of them—*L. glioderma* (not shown)—has a distinct, "mealy" odor; soft, reddish scales; and very scant slime on the stalk below the ephemeral ring. (5) Fischer's Slime Mushroom (*L. guttata,* not shown) has pale colors and fruits in fall in the north-central U.S. The European form of this species has yellowish to greenish drops on the stalk apex and lower ring surface. (6) White Slime Mushroom (*L. illinita,* below) is white to yellowish, with an *evanescent ring* on the stalk that is *not evident* on specimens with expanded caps.

WHITE SLIME MUSHROOM   Pl. 24
Limacella illinita

Small to medium, *white cap and stalk,* heavily *coated with colorless slime. No ring* evident on stalk. ***Cap:*** Obtuse to bell-shaped, with an incurved margin, expanding to broadly convex or nearly flat, with an indistinct, low, broad hump. Surface smooth; pure white to yellowish white or brownish. No odor or taste.* Gills close, broad, free from stalk but almost reaching it; white. ***Stalk:*** Cylindric, thin; often curved. White or nearly so. White fibrils comprising ring are not evident on expanded stalk. **Spore print:** White. **Technical notes:** Cap 2–7 cm

---

* **See p. 10 for cautions about using taste as an identifying characteristic.**

across. Stalk 5–9 cm × 3–8 mm. Spores smooth, subglobose; 4.5–6.5 μm.

Fruiting: Solitary or in groups; on soil in woods and fields. Widespread. Summer and fall.

Edibility: Unknown.

Similar species: Likely to be mistaken for (1) a white waxycap (*Hygrophorus,* p. 202) or (2) *Lepiota* (p. 241).

Remarks: Variety *argillacea* of *L. illinita* has a grayish brown disc (center of cap), evident when cap is fresh and moist. In variety *rubescens* base of stalk stains red.

Deathcaps and Others: Genus *Amanita*

A. phalloides

A. calyptrata

A. sylvicola

Small to medium or large gill fungi with *white spores*. Gills are not attached to stalk and are usually white—sometimes yellow to pinkish when young (before spores develop). Cap separates readily from stalk. Stalk has a *membranous ring* or a *volva boot,* or *both*. Volva varies, from a free, membranous boot at base of stalk to a ring or lip on the stalk (sometimes at the top of the bulb at the stalk base), to scales or powder on the lower stalk and sometimes on the cap surface (see Fig. 32, p. 213). As the young cap expands, the universal veil (volva tissue) ruptures, leaving a ring or boot on the stalk and scaly or powdery veil remnants on the cap and stalk.

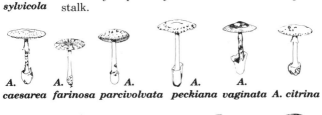

A. caesarea   **A. farinosa**   **A. parcivolvata**   **A. peckiana**   **A. vaginata**   **A. citrina**

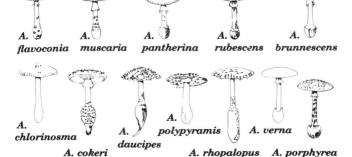

A. flavoconia   **A. muscaria**   **A. pantherina**   **A. rubescens**   **A. brunnescens**

A. chlorinosma   **A. cokeri**   **A. daucipes**   **A. polypyramis**   **A. rhopalopus**   **A. verna**   **A. porphyrea**

WARTY DEATHCAP *Amanita francheti*   **Pl. 26**
Medium-sized, *flat* or *slightly humped cap; dark brown,* with
many soft warts that are sometimes *tinged with yellow.* **Bulbous stalk.** *Cap:* Surface shiny; sticky between warts, which
are often in concentric rings. Very dark brown in center,
lighter and sometimes with a yellow cast toward margin. Flesh
white or yellowish below cuticle (surface), *unchanging* when
cut. No odor. Gills close together, almost touching stalk apex
or attached to it by a tooth; white at first, but developing a
yellow cast, especially near cap margin. *Stalk:* Gradually tapers upward from a narrow, round or egg-shaped *bulb,* which
may be pointed or flattened at base. Surface streaked and pale
to brownish yellow above ring; powdery or with scurfy, yellowish zones below ring. Interior slowly stains reddish brown in
bulb base when cut or bruised. *Ring pale yellow above; yellowish* to *grayish* and more or less *scaly below. Volva powdery to
cottony,* forming *flat to pyramidal scales* on cap surface and
around upper part of bulb. Scales are *easily removable. Spore
print:* White. **Technical notes:** Cap 4–8 cm across. Stalk 8–12
× 1.0–1.5 cm. Spores amyloid, broadly elliptic; 8–10 × 6–7 μm.
Volval scales made up of globose cells up to 60 μm in diameter.
Fruiting: Solitary or scattered on ground under conifers. California to Idaho and Maine to New Jersey; also in Minnesota.
Fairly common in fall.
Edibility: Unknown, but best regarded as **poisonous.** Experimentation is **not recommended.**
Similar species: Even for experienced collectors, the probability of confusing Warty Deathcap (*A. francheti*) with (1)
Panthercap (*A. pantherina,* p. 229) is great, because of the
overall similarity in color, size, and stature. Panthercap is definitely known to be **poisonous.** Differences in color and texture
of volva will usually distinguish most specimens—look for a
collar or roll of volva around upper surface of stalk bulb, which
is present in Panthercap. (2) Faded specimens of Warty Deathcap may resemble Blusher (*A. rubescens,* p. 235), but Blusher
slowly *stains pink* when handled.

CLEFT-FOOT DEATHCAP *Amanita brunnescens*   **Pl. 27**
Cap: Medium to large, *convex* to *nearly flat,* with a low, broad
central hump. Surface *sticky; brown,* often with *lighter
streaks;* usually sparsely decorated with small, cottony scales
of volva tissue. Flesh white; thin. Odor not distinctive, or like
that of raw potatoes. Gills close together, nearly touching stalk
apex but free from it, broad (from stalk apex to cap margin);
white, sometimes with scalloped edges. *Stalk:* Hollow; gradually enlarged downward to a *large, collared bulb* which typically has *one or more vertical clefts.* Surface white; slowly
stains reddish brown when bruised or handled. Ring white;
membranous or hanging in patches from the upper stalk. Volva
breaks into coarse scales or rarely forms an incomplete collar
around bulb margin or is pulled away from upper bulb com-

pletely. *Spore print:* White. **Technical notes:** Cap 3–13 cm across. Stalk 5–13 cm long × 1.0–1.5 cm thick at apex. Spores amyloid, globose; 7–10 μm.

Fruiting: Solitary or in small clumps (up to 5 or 6). Common on forest soil in mixed woods. Central and eastern N. America. Summer and fall.

Edibility: Poisonous.

Similar species: Potential danger lies in the similar appearance of this species and (1) Blusher (*A. rubescens,* p. 235), which is non-poisonous but easily confused with poisonous Amanitas. The differences in field characters are subtle and considerable experience with both species is needed for positive identification. The white varieties of these 2 species are particularly hard to distinguish. In age or when cut or bruised, Blusher (*A. rubescens*) stains *pale to light wine-red* and typically *lacks* the distinct rim (collar) and vertical clefts in the bulb characteristic of Cleft-foot Deathcap (*A. brunnescens*). The color change in Cleft-foot Deathcap is less conspicuous and *more dingy reddish brown.* (2) Panthercap (*A. pantherina,* p. 229), (3) Warty Deathcap (*A. francheti,* p. 216), (4) Deathcap (*A. phalloides,* p. 231), and (5) Porphyry Deathcap (*A. porphyria,* p. 233) do *not* turn reddish brown when bruised and typically have a more distinct volval lip or ring on the bulb margin. (6) See False Deathcap (*A. citrina,* p. 221).

Remarks: Variety *pallida* of *Amanita brunnescens* is pure white or nearly so. The cleft bulb and dingy reddish brown stains which usually develop on handling or bruising help to show its relationship to brown forms of the species. The odor of raw potatoes may be present in either the brown or white forms of the species. False Deathcap (*A. citrina,* p. 221) also has this odor and the 2 species are commonly confused. Blusher (*A. rubescens,* p. 235) consistently lacks this odor, but the character must be used with great caution, as it cannot always be detected in False Deathcap or in Cleft-foot Deathcap (*A. brunnescens*).

CAESAR'S MUSHROOM *Amanita caesarea*   **Pl. 25**
Medium to large, *bright yellowish orange* to *red cap.* **Cap:** Conical to convex at first, but becoming flat and lighter in color as it matures. Surface sticky, lacking scales; *smooth,* with *long streaks extending inward* from lighter-colored *margin.* Flesh yellow just below thin cuticle; white below. Odor not distinctive. Gills pale to moderate yellow; close, broad, free from stalk. **Stalk:** Typically slender, slightly tapering upward. Interior hollow. Surface dry; smooth to somewhat cottony. Pale to moderate yellow or light pinkish orange, with a *yellow, membranous ring* near apex. *Deep, membranous, cup-like, white universal veil sheaths base. Spore print:* White. **Technical notes:** Cap 5–18 cm across. Stalk 10–18 × 0.7–2.0 cm. Spores elliptic; 7–10 × 5–8 μm.

Fruiting: Solitary or in small clumps; often in fairy rings. On

soil in hardwood forests. Southern California to central and
eastern U.S. and adjacent Canada. More common in the
South; now known from 20 states. Summer and early autumn.
Edibility: Reported as edible, but **not recommended** because
of similarity to several poisonous species (see below).
Similar species: Colors are similar to those of (1) some forms
of the poisonous Fly Agaric (*Amanita muscaria,* p. 227), which
has small, soft universal veil warts on cap surface and rings of
universal veil warts on bulb instead of the sheathing membranous volva of Caesar's Mushroom (*A. caesarea*). (2) Yellow
Wart (*A. flavoconia,* p. 224), also similarly colored, is usually
smaller and has small, membranous universal veil scales on cap
surface. (3) Hooded Grisette (*A. calyptrata,* p. 218, Pl. 27)
which occurs on the West Coast, has more yellow to greenish
colors. (4) Flimsy Veil (*A. parcivolvata,* p. 229), has similar
colors, but its stalk lacks a ring and its universal veil breaks
into small scales, mostly remaining around lower stalk. It is
suspected of being poisonous and could be mistaken very easily
for Caesar's Mushroom by collectors who carelessly neglect the
bottom of the stalk.
Remarks: *Amanita caesaria* is regarded as a delicacy in Europe, particularly in Italy, where it has been eaten since the
time of the Caesars. Great caution should be used, however, as
there are several poisonous species of similar appearance in N.
America that are not found in Europe.
HOODED GRISETTE *Amanita calyptrata*   **Pl. 27**
Medium to large, *stocky* mushroom on a *short, stout stalk.*
Shiny yellow to *orange cap* has a *thick, white patch* of volva
tissue (*veil remnant*) at center. *Cap:* Rounded at first, then
flat, sometimes with an elevated margin at maturity and then
appearing depressed on disc (center). Surface sticky when
moist; smooth where it is exposed underneath the white, felty
volva remnants. Margin wavy. Flesh thick, soft; white beneath
the yellow to orange cuticle (cap surface), but often slowly
turning grayish yellow when cut. Gills narrowly adnexed
(notched at stalk apex), broad; white to yellowish, with cottony edges. *Stalk: Stout;* cylindric or tapering upward. Surface
fibrillose; white or tinged with pale yellow. Interior hollow.
Thin, white to yellowish ring, set high on stalk; ring often disappears at an early stage. Volva thick, firm; typically splits
around cap margin, leaving a single broad, *thick, felted patch*
that *covers most of cap,* but sometimes breaks up later into
several to many smaller white scales that cling to surface.
Basal part of veil persists as a thick, white, flaring cup (volva)
sheathing lower stalk or remaining in ground. **Technical
notes:** Cap 10–22 cm across. Stalk 10–15 (up to 20 cm) × 2–4
cm. Spores ellipsoid; 9–14 × 6–8 μm.
Fruiting: Single or clustered; on soil in conifer or mixed conifer-hardwood forests. California to British Columbia. Late fall
to early winter, also spring.

Edibility: Reported as edible, but **not recommended.** As with other Amanitas, the probability of confusion with poisonous species is too high and the penalty too great to justify the risk. We hear the report frequently that this mushroom is eaten, often by people of European descent, on the West Coast. But we hear also reports of mushroom poisoning among these people frequently enough to question the wisdom of recommending any Amanita for food. See discussion under Flimsy Veil (*A. parcivolvata*, p. 229).

Similar species: Hooded Grisette *(A. calyptrata)* is closely related to (1) Caesar's Mushroom (*A. caesaria*, p. 217), which in American forms is less robust and has caps with brighter colors, tending more to orange or red. Inasmuch as both are edible, there is little harm in their confusion, but faded forms could be confused with any of several poisonous species. A less stout form of this species, found in Oregon, has more yellow colors with greenish tints. It is sometimes known as *A. calyptroderma*. It is very dangerous to collect yellow Amanitas for food, particularly those *with greenish tints,* because of the likely confusion with the deadly Deathcap (*A. phalloides,* p. 231).

Remarks: Reports from the high Sierra Mts. describe late-season fruiting for this mushroom, even after frosts begin. As with some species of *Russula* (p. 315), these stout mushrooms often develop deep in the forest soil and never come above the surface. Collectors dig for them wherever they see a hump or crack in the ground.

CHLORINE LEPIDELLA *Amanita chlorinosma*   **Pl. 28**
Medium to large, *white cap;* surface *dry, powdery, occasionally* with *small, soft* to firm *warts* or patches *toward center.* **Cap:** Convex at first, becoming almost flat with a torn margin. Flesh white; has a *strong, pungent, disagreeable odor* (smells like *lime or chlorine*). Gills crowded, moderately broad, white with cottony edges. **Stalk:** Thick, solid; tapers upward from a pointed bulb. Surface white, with powdery granules. Ring often poorly developed, breaking up at an early stage or lacking at maturity; sometimes leaves tiny shreds on cap margin. Volva powdery. **Spore print:** White. **Technical notes:** Cap 5–16 cm across. Stalk 10–15 × 1.0–2.5 cm. Spores amyloid, elliptic to elongate; 8.5–10.5 × 5–6 μm. Volva remnants consist of more or less parallel, erect, irregular, easily broken chains of globose to clavate (club-shaped) or ellipsoid (sometimes elongate) cells *with very few hyphae. Clamps abundant* on tramal tissues.

Fruiting: Solitary or in small groups; on soil in hardwood and coniferous forests. Eastern U.S. Mid- to late summer.

Edibility: Suspected of being poisonous.

Similar species: Several large, dry, white or nearly white species in eastern N. America have been called "Chlorine Amanitas" erroneously because they have the same odor or a similar smell. The white, stout cap and stalk, the powdery volva, which forms few warts, and these typically only toward the center of the cap, are distinctive field characters. Two microscopic characters — presence of clamps and small spores — are necessary to verify the identification. (1) The white *Amanita longipes* (not shown) has smaller spores and *lacks clamps* on tramal tissues. (2) Gray Lepidella (*A. tephrea,* p. 237) and (3) Olive Lepidella (*A. pelioma,* p. 231) have the same stature and powdery veil remnants, but Gray Lepidella is pale neutral gray and Olive Lepidella is grayish olive (see Pl. 28). (4) Turnip-bulb Lepidella (*A. daucipes,* p. 223, Pl. 28) is confused with those 2 Amanitas, but it has tougher, *more distinct volval scales* that are tinged with orange-yellow to orange-brown or light reddish brown. Although their appearance may be quite different, several other species with a strong smell similar to that of Chlorine Lepidella *(A. chlorinosma)* are very often confused with it, when too much reliance is placed on the odor: Most common are (5) Many Warts (*A. polypyramis,* p. 232) and (6) *A. microlepis* (not shown), which are stouter, with more conspicuously *bulbous stalks* and *more cottony* universal veils, most often forming conical warts on the cap and bulb. (7) Club Foot (*A. rhopalopus,* p. 234) is pale to light *creamy yellow,* with distinctly *yellowish gills;* it often has a large bulb (volva) below ground. Both Club Foot (*A. rhopalopus*) and Many Warts (*A. polypyramis*) lack clamps. There are several species with clamps (visible under a microscope) that also have nearly white to gray or brownish volva remnants and a similar odor, including (8) Pinecone Lepidella (*A. ravenelii,* p. 234), (9) Loaded Lepidella (*A. onusta,* p. 228), and (10) *A. atkinsoniana* (not shown). (11) *Amanita smithiana* (not shown) found only on the West Coast, has a *more shaggy* appearance, from its more cottony veil remnant.

Remarks: Chlorine Lepidella (*A. chlorinosma*) is one of the most frequently misidentified species in the genus *Amanita.* Certainly one would be ill advised to eat any pure white *Amanita,* but especially one that is so frequently misidentified.

GRAY DUST *Amanita cinereoconia*   **Pl. 28**
Small to medium, convex to flat, *dingy whitish* to *gray cap;* surface *dry,* covered with *soft, yellowish gray* to *brownish gray, powdery* to *cottony volva scales* that form an easily removable layer on cap, particularly toward the center. Veil remnants also typically leave a fringe hanging from margin of cap. Flesh white. *Odor unpleasant* — smells like lime or "old ham." Gills close, free (unattached) or narrowly adnexed (separated from stalk by a narrow notch), rounded near margin of cap; white to pale cream, with cottony edges. *Stalk:* Cylindric or tapering upward above a rooting, bulbous base. Solid, white beneath sparse, thin, coating of powdery veil remnants which occasionally form an incomplete cottony rim at top of bulb; *ring usu-*

ally lacking. **Spore print:** White. **Technical notes:** Cap 3–7
cm (up to 10 cm) across. Stalk 5–10 × 0.5–1.0 cm. Spores hyaline, amyloid, elongate to cylindrical; 8.5–11.5 × 5.0–6.5 μm.
Clamps lacking. Volval remnants consist of comparatively
small, subglobose, ellipsoid, or pyriform, often brownish cells,
in loose rows on limb of cap and more compact, erect rows
mixed with thin hyphae at center of cap.

Fruiting: Solitary or scattered; on the ground in deciduous
forests. Southeastern U.S. Summer and fall.

Edibility: Not recommended.

Remarks: The species name — *cinereoconia* — refers to the
gray, dust- or powder-like remains of veil tissues on cap and
stalk. Because it is often mistakenly thought to refer to gray,
conical scales on the top, this species name is often applied
erroneously to Loaded Lepidella (*Amanita onusta,* p. 228) or
(2) *A. atkinsoniana* (not shown) — 2 eastern N. American species which have gray to brownish, conical scales. These 2 species also range farther north and west, in contrast to Gray
Dust, which may be restricted to the Southeast. (3) Another
gray species, Gray Lepidella (*A. tephrea,* p. 237), has a completely *powdery* cap, as in Chlorine Lepidella (*A. chlorinosma,*
p. 219). Thus, in forming soft, powdery to cottony scales, Gray
Dust is intermediate between Loaded Lepidella (*A. onusta*),
which forms *conical to warty scales,* and Gray Lepidella, which
has a *completely powdery* cap surface. (4) A larger species, *Amanita cinereopannosa* (not shown) has a *sticky* cap.

FALSE DEATHCAP *Amanita citrina*   **Pl. 27**
Small to medium, *shiny lemon yellow,* rounded to flat *cap.*
Slender white stalk with a *broad bulb* at base; *volva remnants*
are occasionally lacking *on mature caps* but are *usually present
as thin, cottony patches* of variable size over smooth cap surface. Volva remnants *white* to *gray* with a *pinkish cast.* Flesh
white except yellow just under skin. *Odor of raw potatoes*
(sometimes lacking or simply unpleasant in old caps). Gills free
from stalk, close; pale yellowish at first, but soon white with
fringed edges. *Stalk:* Hollow; gradually narrowed upwards,
above a *short, thick, rounded bulb,* which usually has a *sharp*
or *angular edge.* Ring membranous, but thin and soon collapsing against stalk; yellow to dingy white or flushed with brown.
Universal veil soft, cottony, pinkish gray, sometimes forming a
thin collar at top of bulb; soon breaking to form soft scales or
patches that cling tightly to the cap surface. *Spore print:*
White. **Technical notes:** Cap 3–10 cm across. Stalk 8–12 ×
0.5–1.5 cm. Spores hyaline (clear), amyloid, subglobose; 7–10
μm.

Fruiting: Solitary or clustered. Common and often abundant
in forests, central and eastern N. America. Late summer and
fall.

Edibility: Reports vary, but as it may be confused very easily with some of the most deadly species, such as *A. phalloides* (see below), it is foolish to experiment with any mushroom which looks like this as food.

Similar species: Color and general appearance of (1) Death-cap (*A. phalloides,* p. 231) and False Deathcap (*A. citrina*) are much alike. Deathcap (*A. phalloides*) is usually *more green,* but both species have white or light-colored forms which are difficult to distinguish from each other and from pure white species, including (2) Destroying Angel (*A. virosa,* not shown) and (3) Fool's Mushroom (*A. verna,* p. 238). The many soft, pinkish gray volval scales or patches are distinctive when present in *A. citrina* (False Deathcap), but they are frequently washed off by rain and the odor of raw potatoes characteristic of fresh specimens may be lacking. In old specimens the normally sharp edge of volva on the margin of the bulb (see Pl. 27) may not be evident. Although their different colors usually distinguish them readily, the general appearance of False Death-cap (*A. citrina*) and (4) Cleft-foot Deathcap (*A. brunnescens,* p. 216) is similar enough that they have sometimes been regarded as different varieties of the same species. There are nearly white forms of both species which are particularly confusing, but the "*raw potato*" *odor* characteristic of False Deathcap is not found consistently in Cleft-foot Deathcap (*A. brunnescens*). (5) See also Porphyry Deathcap (*A. porphyria,* p. 233), which is very similar except for its *more grayish brown* color.

SOLITARY LEPIDELLA *Amanita cokeri*   **Pl. 28**
Medium to large, *white cap; surface shiny (sticky when wet).* *Cap:* Convex, then flat, with large, *white* to *pale brownish pyramidal warts* over center. Warts are smaller and gradually become more cottony toward margin of cap. Flesh firm; white, unchanging when cut or bruised. *Odor not distinctive.* Gills crowded, free or narrowly attached to stalk, broad; white, sometimes with a pale yellowish or pinkish tinge and white, cottony edges. *Stalk:* Solid, tapering upward from a *large, scaly bulb at ground level.* Surface white; silky, with *tough, pyramidal warts* or *recurved scales* over *lower portion.* Ring membranous, hangs from upper stalk; ring appears two-layered, with upper surface minutely streaked and lower surface fibrillose-torn (use hand lens). Universal veil breaks up into rather large warts of soft, cottony tissue over cap and stalk; veil remnants quite inconspicuous on stalk. *Stains brownish* when handled. *Spore print:* White to pale cream. **Technical notes:** Cap 6–15 cm across. Stalk 1–2 cm thick at apex × 8–14 cm long. Bulb up to 3.5 cm thick. Spores amyloid, ellipsoid to elongate; 10.5–13.5 × 7–9 μm. Volval warts a mixture of globose to clavate (club-shaped) or nearly ellipsoid cells mixed with slender, branching hyphae; hyphae predominate at base of scale.

Fruiting: Solitary or in small groups; on soil in woods. Eastern U.S., from Chesapeake drainage southward. Summer.
Edibility: Suspected of being poisonous.
Similar species: Most often confused with (1) *Amanita solitaria* (not shown) and (2) Club Foot (*A. rhopalopus,* p. 234),
but with others as well. *Amanita solitaria* (formerly *Amanita
echinocephala*) is a European species that differs mostly on
microscopic characters. Club Foot (*A. rhopalopus*) is more distinctly colored, has smaller spores, and (most often) has a long,
rounded, underground bulb. In Solitary Lepidella (*A. cokeri*)
the spindle-shaped bulb is formed at ground level; it usually
tapers downwards and has conspicuous rings of coarse, tough,
sometimes recurved scales. Moreover, the scales are sometimes
in vertical rows. (3) Smith's Lepidella (*Amanita smithiana,* not
shown), a species of the Pacific Northwest, is sometimes called
A. cokeri. It has a poorly developed ring on the stalk, the stalk
has a more cottony to scaly surface, and the cap *lacks* the
distinct volval warts characteristic of Solitary Lepidella (*A. cokeri*).

TURNIP-BULB LEPIDELLA *Amanita daucipes*   **Pl. 29**
Medium to large, *white* to *yellowish pink* cap. **Cap:** Convex at
first, becoming flat, sometimes with a broad, low hump. Surface has patches of grayish pink veil, sometimes as *pointed
scales* that are fused at tips. **Stalk:** Colored like cap; has a
large, *pointed bulb,* often cleft, and a heavy ring that usually
drops off at an early stage.
Fruiting: Solitary or grouped; on soil in hardwood and mixed
coniferous-hardwood forests, often in disturbed areas (roadsides, trailsides, etc.). Pennsylvania and New Jersey to the
Carolinas and Tennessee. Common in summer and early fall.
Edibility: Unknown.
Similar species: May be confused with other large, bulbous
Lepidellas, but the *turnip-shaped bulb* and *yellowish pink* colors are quite distinctive. The *pointed volval scales,* united at
their tips as in some puffballs, are one of the best recognition
characters. Although they are often few in number, some scales
have been found on almost every cap we have studied.

MEALY CAP *Amanita farinosa*   **Pl. 25**
Small, fragile, gray to *grayish brown* cap on a *thin, white* to
gray stalk. **Cap:** Surface smooth on disc (center), beneath
powdery to *cottony remains of volva.* Cap flesh very thin
toward margin, with ridges (over gills) alternating with lighter-
colored depressions; in age cap is often depressed on disc and
has an upturned margin. Flesh white. Odor not distinctive.
Gills white or nearly so; close, free from stalk. **Stalk:** Cylindrical above a slightly enlarged and rounded base; surface white
to gray. Interior hollow or stuffed with cottony filaments. No
ring present, but gills of unexpanded caps are covered by a
cottony to *powdery veil.* Volva gray, sometimes tinged with yel-

low when dry; remnants powdery to cottony, lightly dusting cap and stalk. *Spore print:* White. **Technical notes:** Cap 2–5 cm across. Stalk 5–9 cm × 3–6 mm. Spores subglobose to broadly elliptic; 4.5–7 µm.

Fruiting: Solitary to clustered; on sandy soil in open, decidious woods or along trails or old roads, late spring to fall. Eastern U.S.; common in Southeast, Texas, California, and Oregon.

Edibility: Unknown.

Similar species: The combination of small size and gray to brownish, more or less powdered (but not scaly) surface distinguishes Mealy Cap (*A. farinosa*) from most species which fruit with it. (1) Some small, fragile species of *Russula,* including *R. pectinata* (not shown) look much like Mealy Cap, but these Russulas *have no trace of a veil at any age* and *do not have a pure white spore print.* (2) Unusually small specimens of other *Amanita* species, such as Gray Lepidella (*A. tephrea,* p. 237) may be mistaken for Mealy Cap; so may species such as (3) Loaded Lepidella (*A. onusta,* p. 228) that have lost their characteristic scales on the cap surface.

Remarks: Mealy Cap *(A. farinosa)* is one of the species which may not seem to belong in genus *Amanita* because of the apparent lack of either ring or volval tissues (veil remnants). However, if one looks very carefully at the stalk just above ground level, some remnant of a powdery to cottony universal veil can usually be seen. This is very easily destroyed by handling the specimen and powdery remains of volva tissue on cap surface are readily washed away by rain. Young specimens are best to show these characters, as well as the cottony layer over the gills.

YELLOW WART *Amanita flavoconia*   **Pl. 26**
Small to medium, *fragile species* with a *slender, bulbous stalk. Cottony* to *felty warts* scattered over *sticky cap surface* and *lower stalk. Margin* of cap *faintly streaked.* Flesh thin, soft and fragile; yellow just under surface, white below. Odor not distinctive. Gills free (not attached to stalk) but nearly reaching it, close; white, with delicately fringed edges (use hand lens). *Stalk:* Fragile; straight or curved below, cylindrical or tapered slightly above rounded bulb. White or tinged with yellow. Interior stuffed with cottony filaments at first but later hollow. Ring membranous; yellow all over or white with a yellow rim. Ring collapses against stalk in age, but persistent. Volva breaks into soft yellow patches of tissue on lower stalk and cap surface. *Spore print:* White. **Technical notes:** Cap 3–8 cm across. Stalk 5–10 × 0.5–1.0 cm. Spores amyloid, elliptic; 7.0–9.5 × 4.5–5.0 µm.

Fruiting: Common. Scattered to clustered; on soil, in both coniferous and deciduous forests east of Great Plains. Summer to early autumn.

Edibility: Said to be **poisonous.**

Similar species: The small size and orange to orange-yellow colors with dark yellow volva patches distinguish Yellow Wart *(A. flavoconia)* from most other species growing in this region. However, (1) Frost's Amanita *(A. frostiana,* not shown), which is common in the Southeast, is easily confused with Yellow Wart *(A. flavoconia).* The fact that the two are very hard to distinguish in the field is significant, because there are reports that Frost's Amanita is sometimes eaten, apparently with no ill effect. Pale yellow to white volva fragments are characteristic of Frost's Amanita, but the most reliable characters for separating them are microscopic: Frost's Amanita has nearly round or spherical spores which do not stain (turn blue) in iodine, whereas Yellow Wart has elliptic spores with gray spore walls in iodine (amyloid). (2) Fly Agaric *(A. muscaria,* p. 227) and (3) Yellow Blusher *(A. flavorubescens,* below) may be colored similarly to Yellow Wart, but both are typically larger. In addition, Fly Agaric has *broken rings* of lighter-colored, softer volva remnants around the top of the bulb that are not found in Yellow Wart. The pink-staining wound reaction of Yellow Blusher distinguishes it from Yellow Wart, but this is an elusive character, to be used with caution.

YELLOW BLUSHER *Amanita flavorubescens*   **Pl. 26**
Medium-sized, *convex* to *flat cap;* surface *sticky, yellow* to *dark orange-yellow,* with *numerous yellow warts.* Flesh white. Odor not distinctive. Gills close; white to cream-colored. **Stalk:** Tapers upward from a narrow to thick, often pointed bulb. Upper stalk sometimes yellow, grading to white at base. Ring membranous, breaking irregularly and sometimes leaving patches hanging from cap margin; ring yellow (often white on upper surface). *Volva breaks* into *soft* to *coarse yellow fragments,* more or less *in rings,* on *cap surface, lower stalk,* and *in soil around bulbous base. All parts slowly stain pink* when cut or bruised. **Technical notes:** Cap 6–12 cm across. Stalk 8–12 × 1–4 cm. Spores amyloid, elliptic to subglobose, 7.5–10.0 × 5.0–6.5 μm.
Fruiting: Solitary to clustered; on ground in forests or grassy clearings. East of Great Plains. Late spring to early fall.
Edibility: Poisonous.
Similar species: Except for its typical bright yellow to orange (but quickly fading) colors, Yellow Blusher *(A. flavorubescens)* strongly resembles (1) Blusher *(Amanita rubescens,* p. 235), even to the pinkish stains when handled or bruised. Collectors should be warned, however, that the yellow colors of Yellow Blusher fade readily in sunlight, making its identification difficult. (2) Yellow Wart *(A. flavoconia,* p. 224), and (3) Frost's Amanita *(A. frostiana,* not shown) are smaller, more slender species and lack the pink discoloration characteristic of Yellow Blusher.
JEWELED DEATHCAP *Amanita gemmata*   **Pl. 26**
Small to medium, *dull yellow, short, bell-shaped* to *rounded* or

flat cap; often flushed with pink. Slender, bulbous stalk. **Cap:** Surface shiny, sticky when moist, typically with many small, soft, *white to cream-colored patches of volva tissue;* volva remains sometimes not readily evident. Margin of cap thin, streaked. Flesh thin; buff-colored, except yellow just below cuticle. Odor not distinctive. Gills white; close, thin and narrow, free from stalk but approaching it closely or slightly attached to apex; short gills truncate (squared off). **Stalk:** Cylindric or tapered upward above rounded bulb. Surface buff to dingy white. *Ring thin, membranous; white or tinged with yellow; frequently lacking at maturity. Volva white to cream-colored,* forming *soft, cottony patches or scales* that are easily removed from cap, or a partial to complete, narrow-collared ring. Volva (veil) sometimes leaves wispy shreds on margin of cap. **Spore print:** White. **Technical notes:** Cap 3–10 cm across. Stalk 5–12 × 0.5–2.5 cm. Spores non-amyloid, elliptic to subglobose; 7.5–11.0 × 6–9 μm.

Fruiting: Solitary to clustered; on soil in coniferous and hardwood forests. Summer and fall. Apparently widespread in N. America.

Edibility: Poisonous.

Similar species: Field characters of Jeweled Deathcap *(A. gemmata)* intergrade with those of a number of other *Amanita* species in N. America, making it very difficult to distinguish them without a microscope. Worse yet, some of them may be hybridizing, producing intermediate or hybrid forms that may be encountered. The characteristic light dull yellow to pinkish yellow colors, medium size, and round, collared bulb are neither constant nor distinctive enough to exclude pallid forms of Panthercap *(A. pantherina,* p. 229) and several other species. **Remarks:** The volval collar around the top of the bulb should be sufficient warning that the mushroom likely belongs in a group of very dangerous poisonous species.

GILDED GRISETTE *Amanita inaurata*   **Pl. 25**
Medium-sized, *rounded cap; grayish brown* to *brownish black* or *golden brown.* **Cap:** *Rounded* when young, expanding to a flat cap, sometimes with a low, rounded hump; *margin ribbed or striated.* Surface sticky, with a number of small, gray to brown, wart-like scales of volva tissue adhering to surface; distinct *furrowed streaks* extend inward from margin. Gills free (not attached to stalk at its apex), close; white to pale cream, with more or less fringed edges (use hand lens). **Stalk:** Cylindric or tapering upward; hollow, fragile. White, with *no ring,* but often with *scattered gray scales* of volva tissue, especially at base. **Technical notes:** Cap 5–10 cm across. Stalk 3–8 × 1.0–1.5 cm. Spores non-amyloid, globose; 10–14 μm. Universal veil tissue contains sphaerocysts (globose cells).

Fruiting: Solitary to scattered. Widely distributed in forests or grassy places, in summer and fall.

Edibility: Reportedly non-poisonous, but we can **not recommend** it, as it is easily confused with numerous and varied poisonous species, such as Cleft-foot Deathcap (*A. brunnescens*, p. 216) and Panthercap (*A. pantherina*, p. 229).

Similar species: Species and varieties related to Gilded Grisette *(A. inaurata)* are not well understood in N. America, but the gold-toned, grayish brown cap and the way the gray volva breaks up into scales are important characters. (1) *Amanita umbrinolutea* (not shown) has similar colors, but its white volva is like that of Grisette (*A. vaginata*, p. 237); in both species the volva remains as a *membranous cup sheathing the lower stalk.* (2) Both Cleft-foot Deathcap (*A. brunnescens*, p. 216) and (3) Panthercap (*A. pantherina*, p. 229) have a *well-developed ring* on the stalk.

FLY AGARIC *Amanita muscaria* **Pl. 26**
Medium to large, *shiny cap*, with *soft, cottony warts; color varies,* from *red* to some shade of *orange, yellow, or whitish.* Stout, *bulbous stalk. Cap:* Rounded to flat, often with a low, shallow depression on disc when fully expanded. Surface *shiny* (sticky when moist); color darkest on disc and lighter toward margin, or, less frequently, uniformly colored. Margin wavy and streaked. Flesh thick; white. Odor not distinctive. Gills close, broad, free or barely touching stalk and appearing decurrent by a line extending down stalk. Gill edges even or with delicate fringes (use hand lens). *Stalk:* Typically robust, but separating readily from cap. Interior hollow at maturity. Stalk tapers upward from a round or pointed bulb. White to pale yellow. Ring membranous, persistent; white, smooth or streaked with "gill lines" above, undersurface cottony, with soft lumps. Universal veil *white* to *pale yellowish, intergrown with bulb* at base and sides *in button stage, but breaking* as cap expands, usually forming 2–3 *complete rings or rows of soft scales ("bracelets")* around *upper bulb* and producing numerous soft, cottony scales on cap surface. *Spore print:* White. **Technical notes:** Cap 7–15 cm across. Stalk 8–15 × 2.0–2.5 cm. Spores non-amyloid, ellipsoid; 8–11 × 6–9 μm.

Fruiting: Scattered or in groups; on soil in coniferous and hardwood forests. Common and widely distributed in N. America. Late spring to fall.

Edibility: Poisonous, though rarely fatal.

Similar species: (1) See Caesar's Mushroom (*A. caesaria*, p. 217, Pl. 25). (2) See Yellow Wart (*A. flavoconia*, p. 224). (3) See Flimsy Veil (*A. parcivolvata*, p. 229, Pl. 25) and other Amanitas. **Caution:** Young (button-stage) specimens of Fly Agaric (*A. muscaria*) are frequently misidentified as (1) puffballs (compare with puffball "eggs" on Pl. 43). People who eat puffballs should always cut them in half lengthwise and examine them carefully to make sure that there are *no developing gills.*

Remarks: *Amanita muscaria* (Fly Agaric) shows much vari-

ation in characters essential for accurate identification, making
it difficult to distinguish reliably from several similar species,
even for experienced collectors. Volva tissue is *intergrown with
the bulb* of the stalk and is recognizable only as *scales or
"bracelets" on bulb* and just above it, but in old specimens
these may have weathered away both here and on cap surface,
where they are superficial. As shown on Pl. 26, cap colors range
from scarlet to nearly white. Also, red pigments fade quickly in
bright sunlight, particularly at high elevations, leaving a
washed-out orange or yellow cap surface. On dingy yellow
specimens collected at 10,000 feet elevation in the Rocky
Mountains, I have removed volval warts, exposing a bright
scarlet cap (cuticle) beneath. *Amanita muscaria* is usually a
medium to large, robust species, but smaller, more slender
forms are common.

LOADED LEPIDELLA *Amanita onusta*   **Pl. 28**
Small to medium, *gray to whitish cap* on a *slender stalk.* Cap
is crowded with *gray to gray-brown, conical* or *irregularly
shaped warts.* **Cap:** Surface dry to somewhat sticky between
the dark warts. Warts vary in size and tend to be *larger at
center of cap,* becoming progressively smaller toward the margin. Flesh pale buff to gray. Odor unpleasant (smells like lime),
varies from weak to strong. Gills close to crowded, free or narrowly adnate (attached to stalk); each gill is wide at center but
tapers toward margin of cap and stalk. Gills dingy white to
cream with white, cottony edges. **Stalk:** Solid; bulbous, sometimes *tapering upward* from a slightly to sharply *thickened
base.* Bulb extends downward like a root into soil. Surface of
stalk dark gray to brownish gray at ground level; lighter
above, sometimes almost white at apex. Volva remnants are in
circles or scattered, *dark gray, wart-like* or recurved *scales.*
Ring usually lacking, but cottony to felty when present; gray
to dingy white, not well developed. **Spore print:** White. **Technical notes:** Cap 2.5–10.0 cm across. Stalk 3.5–15.0 × 0.5–1.5
cm; bulb fusiform (spindle-shaped); up to 4 cm thick, with tapering rooting portion up to 6 cm long. Spores hyaline (transparent), amyloid, broadly ellipsoid to elongate; 8–11 × 5–8 μm.
Clamps present on hyphae.
Fruiting: Solitary or scattered. On soil in deciduous forests,
eastern N. America. Late summer and fall.
Edibility: Unknown. Suspected of being **poisonous.**
Similar species: Several species of *Amanita* with gray to
brown volval warts grow in eastern N. America. A very small
species (not shown) with firm warts and large spores has been
called *A. nitida.* The more persistent ring, rooting stalk, and
thicker volva warts with more gray tones distinguish Loaded
Lepidella *(A. onusta)* from (2) *Amanita atkinsoniana* (not
shown), which grows in the same area. (3) Gray Lepidella *(A.
tephrea,* p. 237, Pl. 28) has a *completely powdery* volva and (4)

A. cinereopannosa (not shown) and (5) Gray Dust (*A. cinereoconia*, p. 220) have *softer, less conical warts* on the cap and *lack* the colored warts or recurved scales on the bulbous portion of the stalk. Under a microscope, *A. cinereoconia* and *A. cinereopannosa* also *lack clamps*.

Remarks: The Latin name *onustus* (meaning laden, burdened, or full) is appropriate in reference to the load of *sharp, gray* volval scales on cap surface and top of bulb. The scales are sometimes so crowded they seem almost to be spilling off.

PANTHERCAP   **Pl. 26**
Amanita pantherina

Medium to large, *brown* to *dull yellow* or *buff cap* on a *solid, bulbous stalk. Cap:* Surface sticky when moist, shiny as it dries; uniformly brown to yellowish buff, or with colors in streaks or patches beneath *cottony, white* to *buff, often pyramidal volval scales.* Margin thin, streaked. Flesh thick on disc (center) but tapers abruptly on limb to a thin margin; mostly white, except often yellow just under cuticle. Gills free, close to crowded; white, with finely scalloped edges. May have odor of radishes or turnips. *Stalk:* Tapers upward from a *rounded bulb,* which has a *collar* or *roll of volva* around its *upper surface.* Surface white, smooth above the ring but with soft hairs below it. Ring membranous, white; smooth, but sometimes with a toothed edge. Volva breaks into small, soft, white to cream-colored, flat to pyramidal scales, scattered mostly in concentric rings over cap surface and fused with bulb, except for very short, often recurved collars or rolls on upper bulb. *Spore print:* White. **Technical notes:** Cap 5–12 cm across. Stalk 6–12 × 1.0–2.5 cm. Spores not amyloid; broadly elliptic to subglobose; 9–12 × 6–8 μm.

Fruiting: Solitary or in small groups; on soil under conifers or in mixed hardwood-conifer forests. Northern U.S. and Canada. Spring and fall.

Edibility: Poisonous.

FLIMSY VEIL *Amanita parcivolvata*   **Pl. 25**

Small or occasionally medium-sized, *red* to *orange cap* on a *slender, ringless stalk. Cap:* Convex at first, expanding to flat. Surface shiny, smooth, sticky when wet; *streaked near margin.* Bright red on center, sometimes shading to orange on margin, beneath *scattered, loose, yellow warts.* Flesh thin; red under cuticle to yellow below it. Odor and taste not distinctive.* *Gills* close to crowded, broad, free from stalk; pale *yellow. Stalk:* Slender; tapers gradually upwards from a moderate bulb. *Surface yellow, powdery above; ring entirely lacking.* Universal veil fragile, breaking into small, yellow particles that are sparsely scattered on cap surface and bulbous part of stalk;

---

* See p. 10 for cautions about using taste as an identifying characteristic.

scales or warts sometimes in rings, easily lost or removed.
Technical notes: Cap 2.5–8.0 cm across. Stalk 7–15 × 0.5–1.8
cm. Spores white, short-elliptic to cylindric; 6.0–9.5 × 9.5–11.0
μm (up to 14 μm).
Fruiting: Solitary to clustered; on ground in deciduous woods,
lawns, or rarely in cultivated places. Spring to late summer.
Eastern N. America. Common at times.
Edibility: Reported as **poisonous.**
Similar species: May be mistaken for (1) Fly Agaric (*A. muscaria,* p. 227), (2) Yellow Wart (*A. flavoconia,* p. 224), or possibly (3) Yellow Blusher (*A. flavorubescens,* p. 225). The distinctly streaked cap margin distinguishes Flimsy Veil (*A.
parcivolvata)* from Yellow Blusher; also, the volval warts are
different. Yellow Wart *(A. flavoconia)* has sparse volval warts,
more like those of Flimsy Veil, but all of these Amanitas have
a *ring* on the stalk except Flimsy Veil, although the ring may
not be evident on some older specimens. No problems are likely
to arise from confusion of these Amanitas, however, if all are
treated as **poisonous.** Serious problems could arise in confusing Flimsy Veil (*A. parcivolvata)* with Caesar's Mushroom (*A.
caesaria,* p. 217), which has similar colors, although the ring
and volva are different. These 2 Amanitas have similar geographic ranges and their fruiting times coincide.
Remarks: The presence of a well-developed ring and persistent volva on the edible *Amanita caesaria* (Caesar's Mushroom) and the absence of these features on *A. parcivolvata*
(Flimsy Veil) would seem sufficient to distinguish the two, for
even the most incautious mushroom picker, but the possibility
of confusing the reportedly poisonous *Amanita parcivolvata*
with the edible *Amanita caesaria* is great for inexperienced
people or those who collect carelessly. I have frequently seen
just this kind of mistake made by inexperienced collectors —
both those whom I have accompanied in the field and those
who have brought their collections to our laboratory for identification. Because such errors are all too common, **we advise
against eating any *Amanita.***
GLUE CAP *Amanita peckiana*   **Pl. 25**
Small to medium, thin, convex to flat cap, on a slender, tapered stalk. *Cap: Yellowish white, flushed* with *light pinkish
brown. Surface sticky,* with fibrillose, *light pinkish brown
scales* in concentric *zones* as it matures. Flesh very thin; white.
Odor not distinctive. Gills free, close; pale cream, often with
pinkish edges. *Stalk:* Tapers gradually upwards and is sometimes expanded just below cap. Surface fibrillose, with inconspicuous fibrillose or cottony scales on upper part. *Colored like
cap; ring lacking. Volva* membranous, *loosely sheathing lower
stalk* and attached at its base. All parts very slowly stain pink
to pinkish brown when cut, handled, or bruised. *Spore print:*
White. **Technical notes:** Cap 4–8 cm across. Spores ellipsoid

to subcylindrical; 8–11 × 4–5 μm.
Fruiting: Solitary or grouped; on ground in hardwood forests. Eastern U.S. and Canada.
Edibility: Unknown, but **not recommended.**
Similar species: The light pinkish brown scales and tendency to stain pinkish when bruised or handled distinguish Glue Cap (*A. peckiana*) from similar whitish Amanitas, including forms of *A. fulva* (Tawny Grisette, Pl. 25) with a more evenly colored cap surface.
Remarks: Note particularly the *lack of a ring* on the stalk.

OLIVE LEPIDELLA *Amanita pelioma*   **Pl. 28**
Size, shape, and odor of Chlorine Lepidella (*A. chlorinosma*, p. 219), but grayish olive.
Edibility: Suspected of being **poisonous.**
Fruiting: Mid-Atlantic and southern hardwood forests. Summer.

DEATHCAP *Amanita phalloides*   **Pl. 27**
Medium to large, *rounded* to *flat, greenish cap;* often with *streaks* radiating from center. *Stalk ringed, bulbous.* **Cap:** Nearly round to convex at first, expanding to flat, often with a broad hump. Surface moderate olive to pale greenish yellow (sometimes white!); slightly sticky. No volva scales, warts, or patches. Flesh thin; white, except for a thin, green layer just under the cuticle (cap surface). No odor or faintly like that of honey. Taste said to be "mild, sweet, delicate" — **do not try it (one bite may kill!).*** Gills free (not attached to stalk), close; white to cream-colored. **Stalk:** Slender, from a broad bulb; solid. White or colored like the cap, shiny at first but soon with bands of delicate to coarse scales. Ring broad, membranous, persistent; grooved by gills on upper surface, white or colored like stalk, or lighter on either one or both surfaces. *Bulb rounded;* enclosed in a *long, sac-like, membranous, white* to *green volva sheath,* typically with an *upward-projecting lobe* on *one side.* **Spore print:** White. **Technical notes:** Cap 5–20 cm across. Stalk 5–18 × 1.0–2.5 cm; bulb to 3.5 cm across. Spores subglobose to short-elliptic; 8–10 × 7–9 μm.
Fruiting: Solitary or clustered; on soil in forests or clearings, sometimes in great numbers. Eastern N. America and Pacific Coast. Late summer and fall.
Edibility: Deadly poisonous.
Similar species: Pure white forms of *A. phalloides* (Deathcap) appear almost identical with pure white species such as (1) Destroying Angel (*A. virosa,* not shown) and (2) Fool's Mushroom (*A. verna,* p. 238). (3) False Deathcap (*A. citrina,* p. 221) is easily confused with Deathcap (*A. phalloides*) — the size, shape, and color variations of these 2 species overlap. The

---

* **See p. 10 for cautions about using taste as an identifying characteristic.**

odor (like raw potatoes) and numerous soft, *pinkish gray volval scales* characteristic of False Deathcap *(A. citrina)* are distinctive when present, but they are often lacking. Deathcap has a wider, free limb on the volva. (4) Cleft-foot Deathcap *(A. brunnescens,* p. 216) is most frequently confused with Deathcap where color variants intergrade, but it too lacks the long volval limb characteristic of Deathcap. The strongly margined bulb of Cleft-foot Deathcap has one or more *vertical clefts* that are not found in Deathcap. If the base of the stalk is not collected, Deathcap could also be mistaken for some edible green Russulas, such as Green Brittlegill *(Russula virescens,* p. 325, Pl. 40).

Remarks: This is one of the most dangerous poisonous mushrooms in temperate regions of the world. Its occurrence in N. America is subject to confused reports, probably because of its great variability. Although the early N. American mycologists reported *A. phalloides* from the eastern U.S., it was later thought that those early reports referred mistakenly to related species mentioned above. Recent collections have verified its occurrence on the West Coast and in the East from New York to Virginia. It may be uncommon, but it sometimes fruits consistently in great abundance year after year in localities where it has been found. Deathcap mushrooms collected at Belleplaine State Forest in New Jersey caused 3 deaths in 1969. Literally bushels of Deathcaps were produced in the same small woods in October 1972.

MANY WARTS *Amanita polypyramis*   **Pl. 28**
Medium to large, *thick, white cap* on a *stout stalk.* **Cap:** Rounded at first, but slowly spreading and becoming flat as it matures. Surface smooth beneath *soft, white, powdery* to *cottony patches* or *warts of volva tissue* (veil remnants). Flesh white. Odor weak to strong, *disagreeable* (smells like lime or alkali). Gills thick, close to crowded, free to narrowly adnexed (notched at stalk apex); white to cream-colored, with delicately cottony edges (use hand lens). **Stalk:** Solid, thick, tough (but readily separable from cap), tapering upward from a *large, rounded bulb.* Surface *white, completely powdery to warty* from universal veil at first, but in age only *fragments* of the veil remain, as powdery tissue or rings of scales on and just above the bulb. *Ring fragile, powdery* to *warty* on lower surface; present only before expansion is complete. Ring separates from stalk and sometimes leaves fragments hanging from cap margin. **Spore print:** White to cream-colored. **Technical notes:** Cap 6–15 cm (up to 21 cm) across. Stalk 8–18 cm (up to 20 cm) × 1.0–3.5 cm above bulb; bulb oval to elongate, with a rounded base. Spores thin-walled, hyaline, ellipsoid to elongate; 10–13 × 6–8 μm. Clamps lacking. Volval warts consist of subglobose to ellipsoid or elongate to subcylindrical cells on a basal tissue of branching, more or less erect, elongate elements and scattered slender hyphae.

Fruiting: Solitary or in small groups; on soil in coniferous and hardwood forests. Eastern and southeastern U.S. Late autumn — usually not before October 1.

☠ **Edibility: Poisonous.**

Similar species: (1) Solitary Lepidella (*A. cokeri*, p. 222) has larger, firmer volval warts on cap, a more persistent ring, coarser, (usually recurved) scales, on a rooting bulb and indistinct odor. (2) *Amanita microlepis* (not shown) has a whitish to pale-colored cap; it also has a more persistent ring, recurved scales on bulb, earlier fruiting time, and unpleasant odor. (3) Several other white species can be distinguished mostly by microscopic characters.

Remarks: This is one of several species frequently misidentified as Chlorine Lepidella (*Amanita chlorinosma*, p. 219) because of the strong, unpleasant odor. The two species are easily separated by microscopic characters. The best field characters are the *knob-like bulb* at the base of the stalk of Many Warts and the more powdery volva of Chlorine Lepidella.

PORPHYRY DEATHCAP *Amanita porphyria*   **Pl. 27**
Medium-sized, *flat* or *slightly humped, gray-brown cap* on a *slender, ringed stalk.* Stalk has a *broad, abrupt bulb* at base; bulb has a *short, thin, sharp-edged volval limb.* **Cap:** Brown, usually slightly tinged with purplish. Surface sticky beneath the soft, gray patches of volval tissue (few to many). Margin incurved at first. Flesh thin; white, unchanging when cut or bruised. Odor of raw potatoes. Gills close, free but almost touching apex of stalk; white or pale cream-colored. **Stalk:** Tapers slightly upward from the round to flattened, *distinctly collared bulb.* Surface white or gray above the thin, gray, membranous ring; zoned below ring with gray or purplish gray patches. **Spore print:** White. **Technical notes:** Cap 4–9 cm across. Stalk 6–10 × 0.7–2.5 cm, including bulb. Spores amyloid, globose; 7–9 μm in diameter.

Fruiting: Scattered on ground under conifers and less commonly in mixed conifer-hardwood forests. Widespread in northern U.S. and Canada. Late summer and fall.

☠ **Edibility: Poisonous.**

Similar species: The close similarity in all field characters except color of Porphyry Deathcap to (1) False Deathcap (*A. citrina*, p. 221) suggests the obvious close relationship of these 2 species. A gray form of *A. citrina* is indeed very similar to *A. porphyria*, but some *yellow tints* are always found on *A. citrina* and not on *A. porphyria*. (This is an unusual case where color is about the only field character that distinguishes the 2 species; in other cases characters besides color are usually available and often more reliable.) Forms of *A. porphyria* (Porphyry Deathcap) that lack the purplish tinge also resemble (2) Cleft-foot Deathcap (*A. brunnescens*, p. 216) in most respects, but the *cleft bulb*, the typically streaked cap surface (with fewer, firmer volval scales), and the usual lack of a potato-like odor in *A. brunnescens* will separate them. (3) *Amanita spreta* (not shown) is also gray, but it has a white, membranous volva and lacks the bulbous stalk base.

PINECONE LEPIDELLA *Amanita ravenelii*   **Pl. 28**
Large, rounded, *stout, white* to *yellowish cap,* with *conical to flattened, whitish* to *brown warts* or *scales. Tips of warts* are more or less *felted,* with *fibrils radiating* down the *sides.* In older specimens, each wart is *seated on a scale* formed by the splitting cap surface (cuticle). Flesh firm; white to pale cream-colored. Odor strong, unpleasant (smells like lime or chlorine). Gills crowded, wide, free; cream-colored, with pale edges. *Stalk:* Solid; stout, narrowed upwards from a thick, rounded bulb. White to cream-colored, with cream to grayish cottony zones or scales above bulb, often with thick scales on upper part of bulb. *Ring thick, cottony* to *felted; often breaks up soon after cap expands* and frequently is lacking at maturity. **Technical notes:** Cap 9–16 cm across. Stalk 10–25 × 1.0–2.5 cm above. Spores ovoid (egg-shaped), thin-walled, hyaline, amyloid; 8–11 × 5.5–7.0 μm. Clamps present. Volval warts consist of more or less parallel upright hyphae and clavate (club-shaped) cells at base, changing abruptly to a mixture of globose to elliptic cells in chains on irregularly disposed, branching hyphae. Warts are yellowish and refractive in KOH.
Fruiting: Solitary or scattered; on soil in deciduous forests, southeastern U.S. Late summer and fall.
Edibility: Not recommended.
Similar species: Among the "chlorine-smelling" Amanitas, Pinecone Lepidella is distinctive because of the large, often onion-like bulb at the base of its stalk and the coarse, felt-tipped volval warts or patches with fibrillose sides that are eventually seated on coarse, fibrillose scales formed by the splitting cap surface. Club Foot (*A. rhopalopus,* below) has a *longer bulb* and *more felted warts,* on a cap surface that is *not split* around the warts. The 2 species are easily and frequently confused. It may be necessary to examine the structure of the volval warts under a microscope to confirm identification, as *A. ravenelii* (Pinecone Lepidella) is a variable species.

CLUB FOOT *Amanita rhopalopus*   **Pl. 28**
Medium to large, *dingy white* to *yellowish cap;* surface nearly covered with *soft, white* to *pale yellow* or *brownish warts* (*volva remnants*) that usually form *cottony* to *felty patches near margin* of cap. *Cap:* Broadly convex, with an incurved margin when young. *Veil remnants* often *hang in shreds* at margin. Flesh white; firm. Odor heavy, unpleasant — smells like lime. Gills close, free or narrowly attached to apex of stalk; pale yellow. *Stalk:* Solid; cylindrical or tapering upward above a *large, cylindrical* to *rounded underground bulb.* Surface of stalk white, staining brownish when handled. Stalk sometimes has cottony remnants of ring near the top and usually has

cottony to felty warts or rings of volva tissue at top of bulb or just above it. *Spore print:* White to pale yellowish. **Technical notes:** Cap 6–18 cm across. Stalk 9–12 × 1–2 cm above bulb; bulb 5–10 × 2–4 cm. Spores ellipsoid to elongate; 8–11 × 5.5–7.0 μm. Clamps present. Volva remnants consist of branched hyphae and abundant globose to elongate cells (30–60 × 25–80 μm) in rows or at tips of hyphae.

Fruiting: On soil in woods. Eastern U.S. Summer and early autumn.

Edibility: Not recommended.

Similar species: On Club Foot *(A. rhopalopus)* the cap surface under the volva scales or patches *does not split* into more or less angular scales as in Pinecone Lepidella *(A. ravenelii,* p. 234). The weak but pungent odor, shaggy volva remnants on stalk and cap, and differently shaped stalk distinguish the West Coast species, Smith's Lepidella *(A. smithiana,* not shown), which is the closest American relative of Club Foot.

Remarks: The more or less distinctive long, thick bulb often comes as a surprise, as it is usually completely under ground and the slender stalk above gives no hint of what is below. This, along with the strong odor and wound reaction—the pale yellowish colors darkening to brownish upon handling—make Club Foot *(A. rhopalopus)* rather distinctive. However, very confusing varieties of this species and Pinecone Lepidella *(A. ravenelii)* have been described, in which the bulb shapes are just the opposite of those described here for the 2 species.

BLUSHER *Amanita rubescens*   **Pl. 26**

Medium to large, *pinkish buff* to *brown* or *brownish red cap* on a *stout, bulbous stalk.* All parts *slowly stain pink* when bruised or handled. *Cap:* Ovoid (egg-shaped) at first, then bell-shaped to convex or nearly flat when fully expanded. Surface sticky when moist; *colors variable* and sometimes *streaked or splotched* beneath *cottony patches* of *grayish to pink volval remnants. Margin streaked.* Flesh thin, soft, fragile; white, but stains dull reddish when cut or bruised. Odor and taste not distinctive. *Gills close,* moderately broad and narrowing toward stalk, free or attached to stalk apex by a narrow line; *white* or *soon stained or flushed with pink;* edges cottony. *Stalk:* Tapers only slightly above a narrow, rounded bulb. Surface minutely fibrillose to cottony (use hand lens); sometimes indistinctly zoned. Colored like cap surface or lighter. *Interior pale buff, staining reddish* when exposed to air; *stuffed* with cottony filaments. *Ring membranous; thin,* but *covering gills until comparatively late* in expansion of cap, then collapsing to a broad ring sheathing upper stalk. Ring white and finely striated on upper surface. *Volva forms many small,*

---

* See p. 10 for cautions about using taste as an identifying characteristic.

soft, gray scales on *bulb of stalk, surrounding soil,* and *cap surface.* **Spore print:** White. **Technical notes:** Cap 5–15 cm across. Stalk 8–20 × 1.0–2.5 cm. Spores amyloid, ellipsoid; 8–10 × 5–7 μm.

Fruiting: Single or grouped; on soil in hardwood forests; also in lawns or clearings. Summer to fall, less common in spring.

Edibility: Not recommended because the probability of confusing it with poisonous species is so great. (See below.)

Similar species: In addition to (1) Yellow Blusher (*A. flavorubescens,* p. 225), Blusher is readily confused with (2) Cleft-foot Deathcap (*A. brunnescens,* p. 216), which typically has a *sharper margin* on the stalk bulb and flesh that turns *brown* when bruised or wounded. Blusher often develops dull pink to red colors under similar conditions. A white form of Cleft-foot Deathcap also exists, making their identification even more confusing. Yellow Blusher is distinguished by its initial bright yellow colors. (3) Light or faded forms of Warty Deathcap (*A. francheti,* p. 216) are easily mistaken for Blusher.

Remarks: This medium to large, yet fragile species is so variable in color, size, and surface textures that it is not easy to recognize; this is particularly true for a white form, variety *alba,* often encountered in the Southeast. Also, we have seen brilliantly colored forms of this species — both in Florida and at high elevations in the Rocky Mts. — with colors so bright as to be almost unreal for the species. The pink to dull reddish stains which develop on all parts are the best recognition character. These appear upon handling, bruising, wounding, or sometimes evidently simply from drying or aging. **Caution:** American collectors are often misled by the generally positive endorsement of Blusher as an edible mushroom in European books, contrasted with the reserve of American authors. However, it is foolish to ignore the fact that European collectors do not have to contend with several poisonous or suspect species native to N. America which do not grow in Europe, such as Yellow Blusher *(A. flavorubescens)* and Cleft-foot Deathcap *(A. brunnescens).*

WOODLAND LEPIDELLA *Amanita silvicola*   **Pl. 28**
Medium-sized, *white, dry cap* on a *thick, bulbous stalk.* **Cap:** Broadly convex to flat. *Surface at first completely covered with fluffy, white volva remnants;* later with *large* to *small, cottony* to *felted, irregular volval patches* on smooth, slightly sticky ground tissue. Flesh white; soft. Odor and taste not distinctive.* Gills white; crowded, free or narrowly attached by thin lines to upper stalk; narrow, with cottony edges. **Stalk:** Stout, *bulbous; white. Solid,* with *cottony surface* and *cottony* to *felty volval remnants* on *outside of bulb,* sometimes forming a slight, fluffy rim. *Ring cottony; sparse* or *lacking* on *old specimens.*

---

* See p. 10 for cautions about using taste as an identifying characteristic.

Spore print: White. **Technical notes:** Cap 5–12 cm across. Stalk 6–10 (up to 12) × 1.5–2.5 cm. Spores amyloid, ellipsoid; 8–10 × 4.5–6 μm. Volva remnants a mixture of filamentous to spherical or clavate (club-shaped) cells. No clamps.

Fruiting: On the ground in conifer forests and clearings. Northwestern U.S. and western Canada, frequently along roadsides. Fall.

Edibility: Unknown, but as with other Amanitas, we advise against experimenting with it.

Similar species: These stout, medium-sized, bulbous-stalked mushrooms with cottony surface textures are distinctive among the white Amanitas which fruit in the Northwest. The sparse ring, often evident only as cottony scales or fibrils on the cap margin, or not at all evident on fully expanded mushrooms, is an important character. Collectors in California and the Northwest should get to know it well because it can be confused easily with common edible species such as (1) the young stages of white species of *Agaricus*—for example, Meadow Mushroom (*Agaricus campestris,* p. 256, Pl. 31) or (2) Smoothcap Parasol (*Leucoagaricus naucina,* p. 243). Woodland Lepidella (*Amanita silvicola*) is distinguished from (3) several white species of *Amanita* (lepidellas) found in midwestern and eastern N. America by the lack of a chlorine odor and by the *large, cottony volva patches* — not powdery to firm conical warts — on the cap. (4) A similar white species, which usually has a faint but pungent odor, is Smith's Lepidella (*Amanita smithiana,* not shown), found in the Pacific Northwest.

Remarks: The dark, silty soils of open, grassy "prairies" in the Puget Sound region appear to be especially favorable for Woodland Lepidella *(A. silvicola),* for it reportedly fruits abundantly there, often in dense clusters of 5 or 6 mushrooms. It may be colored gray by the fine, dark silt adhering to the fluffy cap surface.

GRAY LEPIDELLA *Amanita tephrea*   **Pl. 28**
Size, shape, and color of Chlorine Lepidella (*A. chlorinosma,* p. 219) but pale neutral gray.

Edibility: Suspected of being **poisonous.**

Fruiting: Hardwood forests in mid-Atlantic and southern states.

GRISETTE *Amanita vaginata*   **Pl. 25**
Medium-sized, *rounded* to *flat, shiny gray cap* with a *thin, conspicuously ribbed margin. Slender, fragile stalk. **Cap:*** Disc forms a low, rounded hump on mature specimens. Surface *occasionally* has an *irregular white patch* of *membranous tissue* (remnant of universal veil). Flesh white; thin, tapering gradually outward from stalk. Gills free from stalk, close; white or dingy cream-colored, sometimes with white, fringed edges. Odor not distinctive. ***Stalk:*** Slender, club-shaped; white. Surface covered with loose, cottony flecks, often in zones. No ring. Volva a loose white sheath at base of stalk. **Technical notes:**

Cap 5–10 cm across. Spores not amyloid, globose; 8–10 μm. Volva tissue mostly lacks sphaerocysts (globose cells).

Fruiting: Solitary or clustered. Widely distributed in forests and in clearings throughout Canada and the U.S. Common on lawns in eastern U.S. Summer and fall.

Edibility: Reportedly edible, but **we advise against eating any Amanita.** There is great danger in confusing the edible species with abnormal or atypical poisonous ones or with poisonous species that have been improperly collected or not critically studied.

Similar species: Easily confused with (1) Gilded Grisette (*A. inaurata,* p. 226), which has a *gray volva* that breaks into small fragments, leaving several to *many small scales* on the cap, in contrast to the white volva, occasionally present on the cap (if at all) as a single *large white patch* in Grisette (*A. vaginata*). (2) In midwestern to eastern U.S. there is a whole series of species or varieties related to *A. vaginata* (Grisette). These fungi range in color from white to yellow and various shades of gray and brown. They have the general appearance of Grisette (*A. vaginata*), but in addition to color, they vary in size, stature, volva texture, and in microscopic characters. One of the most common is **Tawny Grisette** (*A. fulva,* Pl. 25), which has a light reddish brown to light orange-brown cap with a stalk and volva that are sometimes nearly white but usually tinted with cap color. (3) *Amanita pachycolea* (not shown), a gray to blackish, western species, has lumpy volval fragments on cap surface, gray-edged gills, and stalk flushed with dull orange or light brown.

FOOL'S MUSHROOM *Amanita verna*   **Pl. 27**
Medium to large, *pure white cap* on a *slender, bulbous stalk.* *Cap:* Ovoid (egg-shaped) when young, but soon convex to bell-shaped. Surface *shiny* and *smooth* to *minutely fibrillose; sticky when wet.* Flesh white; thick. Odor pleasant to nauseating; **poisonous — do not taste it.*** Gills close to crowded, free but nearly touching stalk, tapering toward stalk. *Stalk:* Cylindric or *tapering upwards* from a *rounded bulb.* Surface *white,* sometimes becoming scaly as it matures. *Ring membranous, hanging like a skirt* from the *upper stalk. Volva membranous, cup-like,* with a *wide, often lobed limb* that is *free* from the stalk. No color change when cut or bruised. *Spore print:* White. **Technical notes:** Cap 4–10 cm across. Stalk 6–15 cm long; 0.8–2.0 cm thick at apex. Spores amyloid, short-ellipsoid; 9–11 × 7–9 μm. Cap color mostly unchanging in KOH. Gills pinkish purple in H_2SO_4.

Fruiting: Solitary or in groups or rings. Common in hardwood and coniferous forests. East and Midwest, rare on West Coast. Spring to summer and fall.

---

* See p. 10 for cautions about using taste as an identifying characteristic.

Edibility: Deadly poisonous.

Similar species: At least 3 other deadly poisonous species of pure white deathcaps (Amanitas) resembling Fool's Mushroom *(Amanita verna)* are found in N. America: (1) Destroying Angel (*A. virosa,* not shown), (2) Two-spored Death Angel (*A. bisporigera,* not shown), and (3) Slender Death Angel (*A. tenuifolia,* not shown). These Amanitas are practically impossible to distinguish accurately on field characters alone, but can be readily separated by using a combination of chemical and microscopic characters. (4) White or nearly white forms of *A. phalloides* (Deathcap, p. 231) look like *A. verna* (Fool's Mushroom) and may be confused with it easily. However, the white forms usually grow in association with the typical green forms of *A. phalloides.* (5) A white *Amanita* with comparatively sparse volva remnants and a broad, *vertically cleft bulb* at the base of the stalk may be the pallid variety of *Amanita brunnescens* (Cleft-foot Deathcap, p. 216). More dangerous is the possible confusion of the deadly white Amanitas and (6) the edible Smoothcap Parasol (*Leucoagaricus naucina,* p. 243, Pl. 29), or in the young button stage, (7) a white *Agaricus,* such as Flat-bulb Mushroom (*Agaricus abruptibulbus,* p. 254, Pl. 31). The parts above ground look alike, but these edible white mushrooms *lack the volva at the base of the stalk* characteristic of the deadly Fool's Mushroom and other white deathcaps (Amanitas). Before eating any mushroom, *always examine the base of the stalk* carefully. If it is perfectly clean, that is, if there are no soil particles or other debris adhering to the bottom one or two inches of the stalk, part of the stalk was probably left in the ground. And that part is absolutely essential for correct field identification, as it may include the tell-tale universal veil. (See Fig. 32, p. 213.)

Remarks: The several poisonous white Amanitas and related colored forms such as Deathcap *(A. phalloides)* are the most toxic mushrooms known. Their unfortunate use through mistaken identity is common enough to recommend the utmost caution. Their extreme toxicity and the usual one-way finality of its effects encourage one to use extreme measures in order to avoid eating any *Amanita* and any other mushroom which could possibly be confused with it.

Parasol Mushrooms: Family Lepiotaceae

Typically slender mushrooms. Cap and stalk separate readily by a clean break. Free gills; mostly white spore print (green in 1 species). Veil leaves a distinct ring on stalk; no volva. These fungi grow mostly on soil. The family contains both excellent edible and deadly poisonous species.

Genus *Chlorophyllum*

GREEN GILL *Chlorophyllum molybdites*   **Pl. 29**
Large, white cap; may have *pinkish brown tinge on disc* (center) and *tips of scales. Slender stalk.* Forms fairy rings in grassy places. Spores color *gills light greenish gray* when mature. *Cap:* Convex to bell-shaped, with thin, incurved margin, expanding to broadly convex. Surface at first covered by a thin layer of shiny, "pale pinkish buff" to "light pinkish cinnamon" volva tissue that soon cracks into superficial scales, exposing white, smooth to fibrillose cap surface. Scales become fibrillose and often curl back with age. Flesh soft, thick on disc (center) to very thin at margin; white, but sometimes quickly yellow to pink before turning brown. Odor faint and pungent or lacking; taste mild or lacking.* *Gills close, broad, free* and remote from stalk; *pale yellowish,* but becoming *distinctly green as spores mature,* finally grayish yellow to dingy brown. Gill edges dark, fringed. *Stalk:* Noticeably slender, enlarged toward base. Surface smooth or slightly powdered above ring; white, staining light grayish brown when cut or bruised. Interior white, but slowly turns reddish brown when cut. Ring thick, firm, two-layered; edges ragged. Ring white at first but becomes brown and scaly on underside at maturity. Ring is loosely attached to upper stalk or movable. *Spore print:* Pale yellowish green, light greenish gray when fresh. **Technical notes:** Cap 7–30 cm across. Stalk 10–25 cm long × 2.0–2.5 cm thick at apex; 4–6 cm thick at base. × 6.5–8.0 μm. Pleurocystidia lacking. Cheilocystidia clavate (club-shaped) to fusoid-ventricose, thin-walled. Cuticle consists of interwoven to more or less upright hyphae but not a distinct "turf," as in Shaggy Parasol (p. 246).
Fruiting: Singly or in groups, typically forming fairy rings; in grassy places such as meadows, lawns, pastures, or waste land. Late spring to early fall. Southern U.S. and north to mid-Atlantic states, Colorado, south Utah, and California.
Edibility: Poisonous. Some deaths have definitely been caused by Green Gill, but some people are affected less than others. Also, some varieties of this species appear to be less toxic.
Similar species: Although the spores readily distinguish Green Gill from other Lepiotas, without a spore print, Green Gill *(Chlorophyllum molybdites)* is almost indistinguishable in the field from (1) Shaggy Parasol *(Leucocoprinus rachodes,* p. 246) and (2) Browning Parasol *(L. brunnea,* not shown). Shaggy Parasol is edible (see **Remarks**), but Browning Parasol is **poisonous.** A reliable microscopic character to distinguish Green Gill from Shaggy Parasol is the microscopic structure of

***

* See p. 10 for cautions about using taste as an identifying characteristic.

the cap cuticle (see **Technical notes**). In addition, exposed cut surfaces of fresh specimens of Shaggy Parasol turn *pink to bright reddish orange,* whereas Green Gill and Browning Parasol both slowly turn *brown* when cut or bruised. Spores of Browning Parasol are white; that species appears most commonly at the base of deciduous trees and stumps. When fresh, the exposed cap between the gills near the stalk is sometimes flushed with light olive-green, but the gill faces and spore print of Browning Parasol are *never green,* as they are in Green Gill when spores mature.

Remarks: Although Shaggy Parasol (*L. rachodes*) is a good edible species, it should probably be avoided in regions where *Chlorophyllum molybdites* (Green Gill) grows because young stages of the two are so much alike that anyone could easily confuse them in the field. There seems to be a recent increase in poisoning by Green Gill, as drug users seek a mushroom "high." Apparently the green-tinged gills of *Chlorophyllum* (Green Gill) are mistaken for the blue-green oxidation reaction which occurs in some hallucinogenic mushrooms when tissues are damaged by cutting, breaking, or handling. We recommend against experimenting with Green Gill for food. More information is needed about the distribution of this species in N. America.

Parasol Mushroom (Lepiotas): Genus *Lepiota*

Small to large gill fungi with free (unattached) gills. Cap thin, often fragile. Cap separates readily from stalk. Stalk slender, with a fixed or movable ring. Spore print white to grayish yellow.

Lepiota clypeolaria

SHARP-SCALED PARASOL   Pl. 29
Lepiota acutesquamosa

Medium-sized *pallid* to *brown, round* to *humped cap* with *dark, sparse* to *crowded, tough, pointed scales.* **Cap:** Rounded at first, and covered with dense coating of pale round hairs, expanding to nearly flat or humped. Dingy brownish gray to yellowish brown between dense, dark brown, pointed scales that are often in concentric rows; sometimes dingy whitish near margin. Flesh white. Odor pungent or lacking; taste not distinctive.* Gills thin, narrow, crowded, free from stalk, sometimes forked; white with torn edges. **Stalk:** Nearly cylindric or distinctly tapered upwards from a bulbous base, which may be rounded or more or less pointed. Surface fibrillose; colored like cap cuticle or lighter. Ring fibrillose, often disappearing early; typically white, with a dark brown edge or surface fibrils.

---

* See p. 10 for cautions about using taste as an identifying characteristic.

Spore print: White to pale cream. **Technical notes:** Cap 4.5–8.5 cm across. Stalk 6–11 cm long, 8–12 mm thick at apex; bulb 15–22 mm across. Spores subcylindric; 6.5–9 × 2–3.5 μm. Pleurocystidia lacking. Cheilocystidia clavate (club-shaped); 20–25 × 7–10μm.

Fruiting: *Solitary* to *scattered* on *rich soil* in *coniferous* and *hardwood forests;* also in *grassy places,* sometimes in swamps. Summer and fall. Central and eastern U.S.

Edibility: Reported as edible, but **not recommended.**

Similar species: Sharp-scaled Parasol (*L. acutesquamosa*) is one of several species with dark, pointed scales on the cap. These Lepiotas are hard or impossible to distinguish without the use of microscopic characters. Several of these species, such as (1) Woolly Parasol (*L. eriophora,* not shown) are smaller than Sharp-scaled Parasol, but (2) Rough Parasol (*L. aspera,* not shown) is typically larger. Dark scales on the cap and lower stalk make these species easily confused with (3) certain species of *Amanita,* such as Loaded Lepidella (*A. onusta,* p. 228, Pl. 28). The surface scales of the Amanitas originate from volva tissue, but in Sharp-scaled Parasol the scales—both on cap and stalk—originate from the cap cuticle.

SHIELD PARASOL *Lepiota clypeolaria*   **Pl. 29**
Small to medium, *ragged, brownish cap.* Cap separates very readily from *fragile, ragged stalk.* **Cap:** Rounded to humped or broadly bell-shaped. Surface moderate brown to strong yellowish brown or lighter (sometimes yellow); cuticle splits on limb and margin, forming dry, ragged, colored scales exposing whitish flesh between. *Margin* thin but not streaked, incurved until late in development; *ragged,* from *shreds of colored cuticle* and *veil tissue.* Flesh thin, fragile. Gills close, thin, white, free from stalk but coming almost to it; Odor slightly pungent or lacking; taste not distinctive.* **Stalk:** Cylindric or nearly so; hollow, *fragile.* Surface scaly as on cap, sometimes zoned. Ring poorly developed; whitish, cottony at first, eventually remaining as *shreds* or disappearing. *Spore print:* White. **Technical notes:** Cap 2.5–7 cm across. Stalk 4–10 × 0.3–0.8 cm. Spores cylindric-fusoid; 12.5–18 × 4–6 μm. Cuticle of cap stains brown in KOH. End cells 100–250 μm long, in fascicles.

Fruiting: *Solitary* or *grouped;* on *soil* in *forests or clearings,* frequently under conifers. Summer and fall. Widely distributed in N. America; common in the Northwest and mountains. A small form is often seen under sagebrush in the shrub zone in the West.

Edibility: Not recommended. Several species in this group can not be distinguished without a microscope and at least one of similar appearance is known to be **poisonous.**

Similar species: The shaggy appearance, together with long,

* See p. 10 for cautions about using taste as an identifying characteristic.

spindle-shaped spores, characterizes a group of small to medium parasol mushrooms (*Lepiotas*) that is not well understood, even by specialists, at this time. There is a superficial resemblance to (1) species of *Cystoderma* (grainy parasols, p. 152). Shield Parasol (*L. clypeolaria*) has a more shaggy appearance, with a distinctly *scaly, not powdery,* cap surface and *more ragged,* shaggy scales on stalk. The smaller size, color differences, and softer scales on both cap and stalk readily distinguish Shield Parasol from (2) Shaggy Parasol (*Leucocoprinus rachodes,* p. 246). Also, the flesh of *L. rachodes* (Shaggy Parasol) *stains pink to reddish orange* when cut. *Lepiota clypeolaria* (Shield Parasol) does not.

Genus *Leucoagaricus*

SMOOTHCAP PARASOL *Leucoagaricus naucina*   **Pl. 29**
Medium to large, *smooth, white mushrooms* on *graceful, ringed stalks.* Grows in *small clumps or fairy rings in grassy places.* **Cap:** Nearly round to egg-shaped at first, soon spreading to convex or nearly flat, with a low, broad, rounded hump. *Surface smooth (texture "kid-like");* white or pale dingy buff at first, sometimes with a grayish tinge on hump at maturity. Flesh white and unchanging; thick, firm. Odor and taste not distinctive.* Gills free (not attached to apex) but close to stalk, close together, broad near cap margin and tapering toward stalk; white at first and usually becoming dingy grayish pink at maturity, drying light pinkish brown; edges delicately fringed (under a lens). **Stalk:** Cylindric or slightly enlarged at base; hollow at maturity. White throughout, sometimes discoloring slightly in age or when handled. Ring white, membranous, persistent, often collar-like (sheathing the stalk) and flaring above; rim cottony, with a double lip. No sign of a volva. **Spore print:** White. **Technical notes:** Cap 4–12 cm across. Stalk 6.5–14 cm long, 6–13 μm thick at apex. Spores ovoid (egg-shaped) with a small apical pore; spores stain rusty brown in iodine. Pleurocystidia lacking. Cheilocystidia abundant; spindle-shaped to saccate (sac-shaped).
Fruiting: Scattered or grouped, sometimes in fairy rings; on grassy soil, frequent on lawns and in parks and pastures. Late summer and fall. Widespread throughout temperate N. America.
Edibility: Edible, but **not recommended** because of the very close similarity to several white species of *Amanita* (p. 215) which cause fatal poisonings (see below).
Similar species: Several species of *Amanita* (deathcaps), are easily and frequently mistaken for Smoothcap Parasol (*L. naucina*). In the field they can be distinguished by careful exami-

---

* See p. 10 for cautions about using taste as an identifying characteristic.

nation of the stalk. In Smoothcap Parasol the basal part of the stalk is slightly enlarged, but completely *lacks any sign of a cup or volva.* By contrast, in the Amanitas, the base of the stalk is *sheathed with a membranous tissue,* which is the *"cup" or volva* (compare with *Amanita verna,* Fool's Mushroom, p. 238, Pl. 27). When Amanitas are pulled from the soil, the volva is often left behind. Because the essential structure for accurate identification is at the bottom of the stalk, it is important to *dig,* not *pull,* these mushrooms from the soil.

Remarks: The probability of misidentification is very high where this mushroom *(Leucoagaricus naucina)* is concerned and in this case it is **very dangerous,** because the species most likely to be mistaken for *L. naucina* (Smoothcap Parasol) are among the most poisonous mushrooms known. Worse yet, there are no immediate symptoms of poisoning—by the time the symptoms appear (see p. 24), it is usually too late.

Genus *Leucocoprinus*

AMERICAN PARASOL *Leucocoprinus americana*   **Pl. 29**
Clumps of *medium-sized* but *fragile-looking, thin, white* or *pink-scaled, bell-shaped caps stain pink* on *wounding* or *aging or drying.* **Cap:** Oval to bell-shaped at first, with an incurved margin, expanding to convex or nearly flat with a narrow hump. Surface covered with thin, grayish reddish brown cuticle which breaks into irregular rings, then large scales, exposing white ground tissue. *Flesh* thick on disc to very thin on margin; *white, staining yellow,* then *quickly grayish red when cut.* Odor and taste not distinctive.* Gills close, free from stalk; white, but reddening when bruised. **Stalk:** Solid at first, later hollow; enlarged near base and often tapering both up and down from there. Surface white but readily staining when handled. Ring large, membranous; sometimes disappearing early. *Entire mushroom turns grayish red on drying.* **Spore print:** White. **Technical notes:** Cap 5–15 cm across. Stalk 7–15 cm long; 0.5–1.5 cm thick at apex. Spores elliptic-ovate; 8–10 × 5–7 μm. Cheilocystidia clavate (club-shaped), with short to long, sometimes contorted necks.

Fruiting: Sometimes solitary, but more commonly in small to large clumps; on soil in grassy places or deciduous woods. Frequent on mulch piles. Summer. Central to eastern U.S.

Edibility: Edible, but **great caution** advised (see below). **Not recommended.**

Similar species: Young specimens of *Leucocoprinus americana* (American Parasol) look enough like *Chlorophyllum molybdites* (Green Gill, p. 240) that there is great danger of

---

* See p. 10 for cautions about using taste as an identifying characteristic.

fatal error. They fruit at the same time and grow in the same kinds of places. Great care must be taken not to confuse them. Even experienced collectors are frequently confused.

YELLOW PLEATED PARASOL Pl. 29
Leucocoprinus birnbaumii
Bright yellow overall; otherwise looks like Onion Stem (*L. cepaestipes,* below).
Edibility: Reported to be **poisonous.**
Fruiting: Widely distributed in southern U.S., fruiting in summer. Common in greenhouses and potted plants, especially woody plants; fruits during winter in the North.

ONION STEM *Leucocoprinus cepaestipes* Pl. 29
Small to medium, *fragile, white cap;* surface *mealy, streaked* or *split at margin. Slender, tapered stalk.* Usually grows *in clumps. Cap:* Long and bell-shaped, expanding to convex or humped, with a smooth disc and powdery to fibrillose-granular scales that often become grayish brown. Surface white to pale yellow under or between scales. Flesh thin, soft; white, but sometimes light dull yellow under cuticle (cap surface) when cut or bruised, or staining yellowish when handled. Gills thin, free from stalk, crowded; white, then dingy. Odor not distinctive; taste absent or bitter when raw. *Stalk:* Narrowly bulbous or swollen at base, *tapering* to a very narrow apex; hollow. Surface white, smooth under sparse, easily removed, mealy to filamentous fragments. Ring well developed but thin and easily detached. *Spore print:* White. **Technical notes:** Cap 2–8 cm across. Stalk 4–12 × 0.3–0.6 cm. Spores thick-walled, with an apical germ pore; broadly elliptic; 8–10 × 5–6 μm.
Fruiting: In *clusters* or *dense clumps;* on *rich soil, mulch piles,* or in greenhouses or potted plants. Widely distributed.
Edibility: Said to be edible.
Similar species: Several species that grow in similar habitats look very similar except for color. (1) Yellow Pleated Parasol (*Leucocoprinus birnbaumii,* above) is fairly common. Compare also with species of *Cystoderma* (grainy parasols), such as Saffron Parasol (p. 152, Pl. 15).
Remarks: The bulbous base of the stalk is the distinctive character which is the source of the popular common names of this graceful little mushroom. Its slender shape recalls that of a green onion. In some European (especially German) books these small Lepiotas are placed in a separate genus known by the folk name "Faltenschirmlinge," which means "pleated parasol."

PARASOL MUSHROOM *Leucocoprinus procera* Pl. 29
Large, scaly, white to *brownish cap* on *long, skinny, brown, scaly stalk. Gills* and *spore print white. Cap:* Egg-shaped when young, expanding to convex or flat, often with low hump at center. Surface at first covered with thin, brown, smooth volva tissue which early breaks into scattered, thin more or less flat

scales, exposing whitish to yellowish brown, cottony-fibrillose tissue. Cap *develops fibrillose scales* as it matures. Flesh soft; white or slightly reddish. Odor and taste not distinctive. Gills free and distant from stalk but close to each other, broad but tapered toward stalk; white to pinkish with fringed edges (use a lens). *Stalk:* Tapers upward from a small bulbous base; separates readily from cap. Surface colored like cap or lighter; smooth at first, but soon breaks into a *"snakeskin" pattern* of incomplete rings, exposing white flesh beneath. Interior hollow or stuffed with long fibrils. Bulb not sheathed or ringed with volva. Ring on upper stalk, soon loose from stalk and movable. *Spore print: White.* **Technical notes:** Cap 6–24 cm across. Stalk 15–40 cm long, 8–15 mm thick at apex. Spores smooth, broadly ellipsoid, with a minute apical pore; 12–16 × 8–11 μm. Spores stain purple-brown in iodine. Pleurocystidia lacking. Cheilocystidia clavate to nearly cylindric. Cuticle a turf of slightly inflated brown cells that are sometimes pointed at tips. **Fruiting:** *Single* or *scattered;* in *lawns, pastures,* or *weedy or grassy areas in open woods* (both coniferous and deciduous woods). Summer and fall. Central and eastern U.S. and adjacent Canada.

Edibility: Edible and widely recognized as one of the best. Be sure to distinguish it from Green Gill (*Chlorophyllum molybdites*) and other poisonous species (see below).

Similar species: Immature specimens of *L. procera* (Parasol Mushroom) are easily confused with poisonous species such as (1) Green Gill (*Chlorophyllum molybdites,* p. 240) and (2) Browning Parasol (*Leucoagaricus brunnea,* not shown). The "snakeskin" pattern of brown scales on the more slender stalk of *Leucocoprinus procera* (Parasol Mushroom) is a good field character but the stalks of other species sometimes break into irregular scales, particularly when they develop under humid conditions that dry abruptly. Both Green Gill *(C. molybdites)* and Browning Parasol *(L. brunnea) stain brown* when handled or bruised, adding to the possible confusion. Collectors in the areas where all 3 species have been reported should be especially alert.

SHAGGY PARASOL *Leucocoprinus rachodes*   **Pl. 29**
Large, white cap, with pinkish brown volval remnants (coarse scales); later develops *white, fibrillose scales,* often with *brown tips. Spore print: White.* Flesh thick; white, becoming *slightly pink* to *intensely reddish orange* when cut or bruised. *Cap:* Convex at first, expanding to broadly convex or nearly flat. Young buttons covered at first with grayish to pinkish brown or grayish red, thin, smooth volva tissue that soon breaks into coarse, recurved scales, more or less concentrically arranged. These scales (volva remnants) expose white, fibrillose tissue which later forms shaggy scales, particularly on cap margin. All parts may eventually turn brown from handling or weath-

ering. Odor and taste not distinctive.* Gills close, broad, free from stalk; white, staining yellowish and slowly brown when cut or bruised, or weathered. **Stalk:** Firm, slender, club-shaped; white, but soon staining grayish brown with age. Ring thick, double, fringed, scaly on underside; white at first, but soon dark brown. **Technical notes:** Cap 10–20 cm across. Stalk 10–20 × 1–2.5 cm thick at apex; bulb up to 5 cm thick. Spores ovoid to ellipsoid; 8–10.5 × 5–6.5 μm; pseudoamyloid. Pleurocystidia lacking. Cheilocystidia balloon-shaped to clavate (club-shaped). Cap cuticle a compact, turf-like palisade with terminal cells 18–36 × 3–14 μm. Cells turn pale brown in KOH.

Fruiting: *Solitary* to *grouped;* on *soil in grassy places* and *open woods* or *on mulch piles* (common in spruce woods in eastern Europe). Late summer to fall. Widespread, but range not well known.

Edibility: Edible, but **not recommended** because it is so easy to mistake for poisonous species (see below).

Similar species: Frequently confused with 2 **poisonous** species: (1) *Chlorophyllum molybdites* (Green Gill, p. 240) and (2) *Leucoagaricus brunnea* (Browning Parasol, not shown). Young specimens of the three are almost impossible to distinguish without a microscope, but see comparison of the three under Green Gill (*C. molybdites*). (3) American Parasol (*Leucocoprinus americana,* p. 244), which is edible, *stains pink* when cut, handled, or dried out. In the Chesapeake Bay region, at least, it has a series of highly variable color forms, including brown ones which could be mistaken for Shaggy Parasol.

Remarks: Careful studies will probably show significant ecological differences in N. American species of the parasol mushrooms and their relatives. Their frequent misidentification at present makes such conclusions impossible. Because of this and the exceptional range of variation in the American species, we advise **utmost caution** if parasol mushrooms are considered for food.

Roof and Sheath Mushrooms: Family Pluteaceae

This family is sometimes known as Volvariaceae. Pink spore print. Free gills (not attached to stalk). Clean, easy separation of cap and stalk. Volva may be present, but no ring. These fungi grow on soil, wood, or vegetable debris. Both edible and poisonous species, as well as many of unknown edibility.

* See p. 10 for cautions about using taste as an identifying characteristic.

Roof Mushrooms: Genus *Pluteus*

Pluteus cervinus

Thin-fleshed, often fragile cap; separates very easily from thin stalk. Gills free from stalk, pink when mature (after spores develop). Spore print some shade of pink.

YELLOW ROOF *Pluteus admirabilis*   **Pl. 30**
Small, translucent yellow caps on *thin stalks* rising from decaying wood. *Stalk fragile, often split. Cap:* Bell-shaped to rounded at first, becoming flat, sometimes with a very low, rounded hump. Surface often *wrinkled on disc* but smooth elsewhere. Bright yellow, occasionally flushed with olive on surface; hygrophanous, translucent, streaked near margin when moist. Flesh thin; dingy white. Odor and taste not distinctive.* *Gills close, free from stalk,* broad; yellow, but soon becoming flesh pink from maturing spores. *Stalk: slender, fragile.* Surface smooth; yellow above, white and cottony at base. Interior becomes hollow in age. *Spore print:* Pink. **Technical notes:** Cap 1.5–4 cm across. Stalk 2–6 × 0.2–0.4 cm. Spores subglobose; 5.0–6.5 μm in diameter. Cap cuticle consists of stalked, globose cells, 30–35 × 20–25 μm, with yellow content.
Fruiting: Single or in groups; in coniferous and mixed conifer-hardwood forests. Widespread. Spring to early autumn.
Edibility: Reported as nonpoisonous.
Similar species: The tendencies to develop a wrinkled disc and split stalk are good field characters for this small, fragile, bright yellow species. The pink spore print distinguishes Yellow Roof readily from (1) small yellow waxycaps (*Hygrophorus*, p. 202, Pl. 24) and from (2) Golden Coincap (*Cyptotrama chrysopepla*, p. 151, Pl. 15). A number of closely related species of *Pluteus* (roof mushrooms) are distinguished with difficulty from Yellow Roof (*P. admirabilis*); look for Yellow Roof's bright orange-yellow cap, yellow stalk, and yellow gills (before spores mature). These observations must be made on fresh specimens in good condition, as faded caps of Yellow Roof are yellowish brown, not bright yellow, and resemble (3) Sienna Roof (*P. chrysophaeus*, p. 250). (4) A form of *Pluteus lutescens* (Brown Roof, p. 251) having an odorless, yellowish brown cap and yellow gills and stalk is common in the Rocky Mts. (5) *Pluteus rugosidiscus* (not shown) is olive to yellowish green or greenish yellow. Under the microscope, cuticle cells of *P. admirabilis* (Yellow Roof) are white to yellowish in KOH (potash), whereas those of *P. rugosidiscus* are olive to brownish.
DEER MUSHROOM *Pluteus cervinus*   **Pl. 30**
Medium-sized, *gray* to *grayish brown, bell-shaped cap* on a

---

* See p. 10 for cautions about using taste as an identifying characteristic.

white to *gray,* medium-sized *stalk.* Cap *separates readily* from stalk. Grows on *decaying wood* or *sawdust.* **Cap:** Broadly convex at first, expanding to nearly flat, with a low, rounded hump at center. Surface smooth or occasionally wrinkled, sometimes with clumps of hairs over disc (use hand lens). Sometimes dingy white, but more often some shade of gray tinged with brown, often with a whitish margin. Flesh thick on disc, thin outwards; soft, white. Odor not distinctive; taste somewhat radish-like when raw (disappears when cooked). Gills free from stalk, close, broad; white to pallid at first, becoming flesh pink from maturing spores. **Stalk:** Firm, solid; tapering upward. Surface smooth or fibrillose; white or tinged with cap color, sometimes with sparse blackish fibrils. **Spore print:** Flesh pink. **Technical notes:** Cap 3–14 cm across. Stalk 5–12 × 0.6–1.2 cm. Spores smooth, nearly hyaline (transparent) under a microscope, ellipsoid; 5–7 × 4.0–5.5 μm. Pleurocystidia fusoid-ventricose; thickened and with 2–5 short, horn-like projections. Cheilocystidia similar to pleurocystidia, or more frequently smooth, thin-walled, and narrowly club-shaped.

Fruiting: Single or clustered; on decaying wood or sawdust piles. Widespread in U.S. and Canada; most abundant in North. Spring and fall.

Edibility: Edible. The radish-like flavor of raw specimens disappears upon cooking.

Similar species: (1) A larger species, Big Deer Mushroom (*Pluteus magnus,* not shown) is virtually indistinguishable on field characters alone; it consistently lacks the radish-like taste typical of Deer Mushroom (*P. cervinus*), but the taste is weak and therefore not reliable. (2) Washington Deer Mushroom (*P. washingtoniensis,* not shown) is more pinkish brown, with obscure scales on the disc (center of cap). Deer Mushroom's flesh-pink spore print, general shape, and habitat (on wood) may suggest (3) Silky Sheath (*Volvariella bombycina,* p. 252), but Silky Sheath has a *well-developed volva* that leaves a *broad, membranous cup sheathing* the *stalk base.* This emphasizes again the absolute necessity of collecting and observing the stalk base on any mushroom. Although both Silky Sheath and Deer Mushroom (*P. cervinus*) are edible, Silky Sheath may be confused with some of the poisonous Amanitas (see p. 215). Some pure white forms of Deer Mushroom resemble (4) Fluffy Roof (*Pluteus tomentosulus,* not shown), but the cap surface is *cottony* to *velvety* (not smooth to wrinkled) in *P. tomentosulus.* Deer Mushroom's radish-like taste (when raw) also helps to distinguish these 2 species, as does Fluffy Roof's preference for logs in *swampy areas,* but microscopic characters are most reliable. (5) See Sawdust Mushroom (*P. petasetus,* p. 252).

Remarks: Easy recognition, widespread occurrence, and abundant fruiting make this a favorite of many mushroom hunters. Deer Mushroom grows on various woody substrates and often has a long fruiting season. One of the most unusual specimens I have seen forced its way up between the vinyl floor tiles in the kitchen of a 6th floor apartment in a new high-rise building which had concrete floors! Feeling almost intimidated by this mysterious growth, the astonished tenant followed my suggestion to search for a woody substrate under the floor tiles, where he found a small pile of buried sawdust.

SIENNA ROOF *Pluteus chrysophaeus*   **Pl. 30**
Small, light to *dark brown cap*, on a *fragile, slender, white* or *grayish stalk*. *Cap:* Broadly rounded to conic at first, expanding to flat or nearly so, with a low, narrow hump; outline circular or irregularly lobed. Surface smooth, except somewhat wrinkled on disc in some specimens. *Hygrophanous — dark brown* at first, *fading* to yellowish brown or pinkish brown. Flesh white to pale watery brown below cuticle. *Odor and taste variable* (may be absent); sometimes has a strong odor or flavor of fresh grain or meal.* Gills close, free from stalk; white at first, but soon becoming *pinkish orange* to *pinkish brown* as spores mature. *Stalk:* Slender, cylindric; readily separating from cap. Solid at first, but sometimes hollow in age. Surface white above to brownish gray or yellowish brown at base; smooth but streaked with gray. **Technical notes:** Cap 1–4 cm across. Stalk 2.5–4.0 × 0.2–0.5 cm. Spores subglobose; 5–7 μm in diameter. Pleurocystidia fusoid-ventricose. Cheilocystidia clavate (club-shaped) to fusoid-ventricose. Gill trama convergent. Vesiculose cuticle cells 25–40 μm across; cells stain brown in KOH. Cystidioid elements lacking in cuticle.
Fruiting: *Scattered* to *grouped;* on *decayed wood of deciduous trees.* Michigan to New York and Texas. Summer.
Edibility: Unknown.
Similar species: Numerous small species of *Pluteus* (roof mushrooms) are difficult to distinguish without microscopic characters. For example, (1) *Pluteus seticeps* (not shown) is almost indistinguishable from Sienna Roof by field characters (although it lacks the "mealy" odor often present in Sienna Roof), but it has different cells in the cuticle. (2) Dwarf Roof (*P. nanus*, p. 252) is more reddish brown (see Pl. 30) and is also odorless. (3) Brown Roof (*P. lutescens*, p. 251) has a yellow stalk and young gills.
BROWNISH YELLOW ROOF   **Pl. 30**
Pluteus flavofuligineus
Medium-sized, *shiny yellow, velvety, thin caps* on *slender, twisted stalks.* Grows on *decaying wood.* *Cap:* Egg-shaped and brownish at first, later flat with a rounded to pointed hump. Predominantly yellow, but flushed with brown to olive or deep gray. Disc often wrinkled. Surface moist, often having scat-

---

* See p. 10 for cautions about using taste as an identifying characteristic.

tered, soft, mealy granules (visible under a lens). Odor and
taste not distinctive. Gills white at first, but eventually yellowish pink; free (unattached) and rounded next to stalk, edges
smooth or sometimes fringed. *Stalk: Slender,* cylindric or
slightly enlarged downward; solid. Surface *smooth,* but with a
spiral pattern of *streaks; variable in color,* but often *pinkish
to yellow. Spore print:* Yellowish pink. **Technical notes:** Cap
2.5–7.5 cm across. Stalk 4–8 cm $\times$ 4–6 mm. Spores smooth,
subglobose; 6–8 $\times$ 5.5–6.5 μm in diameter. Pleurocystidia and
cheilocystidia abundant; broadly fusoid-ventricose. Pilocysti-
dia fusoid; pointed, with yellow to brownish content in KOH.
Gill trama convergent.
Fruiting: Usually single; on well-decayed wood of deciduous
trees. Early summer and fall. Widespread across northern U.S.,
from Oregon to N.Y. and south to Tennessee.
Edibility: Unknown.
Similar species: Distinctive among yellow species of *Pluteus*
(roof mushrooms) in N. America by a combination of size,
color, and surface textures. Although not unique, the *apparently twisted stalk* is a good field character.

BROWN ROOF *Pluteus lutescens*   **Pl. 30**
Small, *fragile, brownish olive* to *yellowish brown cap* on a *yellow stalk. Gills yellow when young* (before spores mature).
Grows *singly* or *in small groups,* on *decaying wood of deciduous trees.* **Cap:** Broadly conic to convex when young, expanding to flat, sometimes lobed or irregular in outline. Surface
smooth to granulose, sometimes wrinkled on disc; hygrophanous (water-soaked). Flesh thin, soft; white to yellow, with a
watery layer just above gills. Odor and taste not distinctive.
Gills close, free from stalk; white to *yellow at first,* but becoming yellowish pink as spores mature. **Stalk:** Cylindric or nearly
so; yellow to orange at base, lighter above. Surface smooth,
tending to fibrillose. *Spore print:* Yellowish pink. **Technical
notes:** Cap 1.0–5.7 cm across. Stalk 2–7 cm $\times$ 3–7 mm. Spores
smooth, ovate (egg-shaped) to subglobose; 6–8 $\times$ 5.0–6.5 μm.
Pleurocystidia and cheilocystidia saccate (sac-shaped) to
broadly fusoid-ventricose, with a short neck. Gill trama convergent. Cuticle consists of saccate cells with brown pigment.
Fruiting: Solitary to grouped; on *decaying wood* of deciduous
trees. Common on aspens in the Rocky Mts. Spring to early
summer. Michigan to Washington, south to California.
Edibility: Unknown.
Similar species: Small specimens of Brown Roof (*P. lutescens*) may be mistaken for (1) Sienna Roof (*P. chrysophaeus,*
p. 250) if one overlooks the lack of odor and the different colors
of the stalk and gills—gills are *white* when young in Sienna
Roof and *yellow* before spores mature in Brown Roof (*P. lutescens*). (2) Dwarf Roof (*P. nanus,* below) has a more reddish
brown cap (see Pl. 30); it often grows on soil or needle beds.

DWARF ROOF *Pluteus nanus*   **Pl. 30**
Small, *fragile, dark reddish brown cap* on a *brittle yellow* stalk.
Gills yellow when young (before pink spores develop). No odor.
Spore print: Pink.
Fruiting: Solitary or scattered to grouped; on decaying wood
or soil by well-decayed wood. Widespread in U.S. from Rocky
Mts. eastward. Summer and fall.
Edibility: Unknown.
Similar species: See (1) Brown Roof (*P. lutescens,* above) and
(2) Sienna Roof (*P. chrysophaeus,* p. 250).

SAWDUST MUSHROOM *Pluteus petasetus*   **Pl. 30**
Medium-sized, white cap, streaked with brownish fibrils; dingy
yellowish, minutely scaly disc. Stalk similar in color and tex-
ture.
Edibility: Probably edible, as it has long been mistaken for
Deer Mushroom (*Pluteus cervinus,* p. 248).
Fruiting: Widespread and common on old sawdust piles.
Summer and fall.

 Sheath Mushrooms: Genus *Volvariella*

Medium to large, thin-fleshed, often fragile cap
with free gills (gills not attached to stalk). Stalk
slender, *ringless,* with a *cup-like volva at base.*
Volvariella Gills white when young, but becoming pink as
bombycina spores mature. Spore print pink to brownish.

SILKY SHEATH *Volvariella bombycina*   **Pl. 30**
Medium to large, *white, fibrillose, bell-shaped cap* on a *shiny
white stalk. Stalk* arises from a *broad, membranous sheath*
(volva). *Cap:* Round to egg-shaped at first, expanding to bell-
shaped or convex. Surface shiny, fibrillose, becoming somewhat
scaly in age; margin more or less fringed and not streaked or
ridged. Usually white, becoming dingy yellowish to grayish on
disc. Flesh soft, white, thin. Odor and taste not distinctive.*
Gills crowded, broad, free from stalk; white, but slowly becoming yellowish pink. *Stalk:* Solid, tapered upward, sometimes
from a bulbous base. Surface white, shiny, smooth; *sheathed at
base* by a *broad, cup-like volva. No ring* on stalk (compare
with Amanitas, Pls. 25–28). Volva *membranous,* thick; rim often lobed or torn. Outer surface of sheath white, with *indistinct, soft, yellowish* to *grayish patches. Spore print:* Yellowish pink. **Technical notes:** Cap 5–20 cm across. Stalk 6–20 ×
1–2 cm. Spores ovoid (egg-shaped) to elliptic; 6.5–10.5 ×
4.5–6.7 μm.
Fruiting: Solitary to clustered; *on wood*—logs and living
trunks of various deciduous trees, particularly beech and

---

* See p. 10 for cautions about using taste as an identifying characteristic.

maples, including box elder. Widespread in U.S. and Canada. Summer.

Edibility: Edible, but easily confused with some species of *Amanita* (see below and p. 215). See also Big Sheath Mushroom (below).

Similar species: A number of sheath mushrooms *(Volvariella)* grow *on soil.* Most are rarely encountered, but (1) Big Sheath Mushroom (*V. speciosa,* below) and (2) Streaked Sheath (*V. volvacea,* not shown) are sometimes common and, if habitat is ignored, may be mistaken for Silky Sheath *(V. bombycina).* The shiny or sticky cap surface (when moist) and typically longer, sometimes thicker stalk distinguish Big Sheath Mushroom. Although Silky Sheath has a tendency to develop yellowish or grayish colors (particularly on the disc) in age, this character is more evident and colors are often darker in Big Sheath *(V. speciosa),* although both species characteristically have white caps at first. Streaked Sheath *(V. volvacea)* is usually smaller and its dry, streaked cap surface is gray to grayish brown (not white) when first exposed by the ruptured universal veil (volva). It grows on soil or decaying vegetable matter. (3) Silky Sheath is sometimes confused with Amanitas (p. 215)—if spore color and substrate are ignored—but *no Amanitas grow on wood,* and sheath mushrooms *(Volvariella) never have a membranous ring* on the upper stalk. Amanitas produce *white* to yellowish (*not pinkish*) spore prints.

Remarks: A bright yellow form of *V. bombycina* (Silky Sheath) is found on magnolias in Florida.

BIG SHEATH MUSHROOM *Volvariella speciosa*   **Pl. 30**
Medium to large, *whitish, sticky cap* on a *slender stalk* rising from a *white, membranous sheath.* **Cap:** Egg-shaped to round at first, expanding to convex and finally flat, but more or less humped at center. Surface smooth, *sticky* when wet, sometimes with patches of volva tissue (veil remnants); white to grayish yellow. Margin not streaked or faintly so. Flesh thin except on disc (center); soft, white. Odor and taste unpleasant.* *Gills* crowded, broad, free from stalk, edges ragged; white at first, but *turning yellowish pink as spores mature.* **Stalk:** Solid; cylindric or enlarged at base. Surface smooth or with soft hairs; white to cream-colored. *No ring.* **Technical notes:** Cap 5–15 cm across. Stalk 9–20 × 0.5–2.0 cm. Spores ovoid (egg-shaped) to elliptic; 12–20 × 8.5–11.0 μm.

Fruiting: Solitary or grouped; on soil in gardens, fields, or woods, or on dung heaps, sometimes in greenhouses. Widely distributed and fruiting from late spring to summer; also during winter months in warm areas.

Edibility: Edible, but **be cautious** (see below).

Similar species: No poisonous species are known among the

---

* See p. 10 for cautions about using taste as an identifying characteristic.

sheath mushrooms *(Volvariella)*, but one should not ignore their similarities in field characters with Amanitas (deathcaps, p. 215). Many species of both genera have a well-developed volva, a cap that separates readily from stalk, and gills that are free from stalk and have pinkish tints at some time during development.

Field Mushrooms: Family Agaricaceae

Dark purplish brown to blackish brown spore print. Stalk typically stout. Cap colors range from white to some shade of brown or gray; surface texture smooth to fibrillose. Veil tissue usually leaves a ring but *no volva* on stalk. Gills free from stalk; gills and stalk readily separable from cap. These mushrooms grow on soil (often heavily fertilized) or on vegetable debris. Both edible and mildly poisonous species are present in this family, including *Agaricus bisporus,* the mushroom most commonly cultivated commercially in America.

Genus *Agaricus*

Small to large, fleshy gill fungi; mostly white to yellow or brown (rarely pinkish). Cap surface dry to moist but not slimy. Gills free from stalk; white to pink or gray when young, becoming dark purplish to blackish brown later, from maturing spores. Stalk has a membranous ring but *no volva* (compare with *Amanita,* p. 215).

Agaricus campestris

FLAT-BULB MUSHROOM *Agaricus abruptibulbus*   **Pl. 31**
Medium-sized, white, *yellow-staining* cap on a slender stalk that has a *wide, flat bulb* on base. *Stains yellow-orange* on wounding.
Fruiting: On soil under hardwoods. Eastern Canada and U.S. Summer and fall.
Edibility: Some report it as edible, but we urge **great caution** in eating any white, yellow-staining *Agaricus.* See Sylvan Mushroom (*A. sylvicola,* p. 261) and Yellow Stainer (*A. xanthodermus,* not shown—see discussion under Flat-top, *A. placomyces,* p. 258).

HORSE MUSHROOM *Agaricus arvensis*   **Pl. 31**
Medium to large, *white* cap and stalk. All parts *stain yellow when bruised. Odor of anise* usually present. Stalk has *membranous ring* but *no volva. Cap:* Nearly round at first, becoming convex and eventually flat, sometimes with a shallow, broad depression. Surface fibrillose (use a hand lens), with *little tendency* to form *minute scales.* Surface sometimes discolored, becoming yellowish gray on disc (center) at maturity. Flesh thick; white, except tinged with grayish pink above young

gills. Gills free from stalk, crowded; becoming grayish pink, then dark purple-brown. **Stalk:** Firm, cylindric or tapering upwards from a small bulb. Surface white, fibrillose. Ring broad, *membranous*, double; lower layer breaks into cottony patches. **Spore print:** Dark grayish reddish brown. **Technical notes:** Cap 8–20 cm across. Stalk 4.5–20 × 0.7–2.5 cm. Flesh turns bright lemon yellow in KOH when fresh. Spores ellipsoid; 6.5–8.0 × 4.5–5.5 μm.
Fruiting: Solitary to scattered; in open woods and grassy or shrubby places. Summer and fall. Widespread.
Edibility: Edible. Resembles the common cultivated mushroom. See **caution** below.
Similar species: Very commonly confused with several related species such as (1) Sylvan Mushroom (*A. sylvicola*, p. 261) and (2) Flat-bulb Mushroom (*A. abruptibulbus*, p. 254). Horse Mushroom *(A. arvensis)* prefers more open, grassy habitats; *A. sylvicola* and *A. abruptibulbus* are forest species. Both have smaller spores than *A. arvensis* (Horse Mushroom). (3) A much larger, more robust species of the western Rocky Mt. and Pacific states is Crocodile Mushroom (*A. crocodilinus*, p. 257). It can be easily recognized by its size and limited distribution. **Caution:** Anyone wishing to eat species in this group should be extremely careful, because the young "buttons" (unexpanded caps), which are most prized for food, are very frequently confused in the field with **deadly poisonous** species that are not related, such as (4) Green Gill (*Chlorophyllum molybdites*, p. 240, Pl. 29) and (5) several species of *Amanita*, such as Fool's Mushroom (*A. verna*, p. 238, Pl. 27). (6) Some species of *Agaricus* are also poisonous, such as Yellow Stainer (*Agaricus xanthodermus*, not shown), a species which is common and widespread in Europe but which thus far in N. America has been reported only in the Northwest.
Remarks: Confusion is rampant on identification of *Agaricus arvensis* (Horse Mushroom). Different mushrooms are called by this name in different areas both in Europe and in N. America, and the problem is not likely to be resolved soon. The anise odor is not always present in American specimens that are thought to be this species.

PRINCE *Agaricus augustus*   **Pl. 31**
Robust, brown, scaly cap on a *thick stalk*. Stalk *scaly below ring*. Surfaces of *all parts stain yellow* when handled or bruised. **Cap:** Convex at first, often flattened on disc, expanding slowly to a flat cap, sometimes with a broad, low hump. Surface dry, forming small, light grayish yellowish brown to light or moderate yellowish brown, fibrillose scales or patches at an early stage; background dingy pale yellowish. Disc remains brown and felted or cracked. Scales sometimes tend to recurve near the fringed margin of the cap. Flesh white, unchanging or becoming dull yellowish when bruised. Odor almond-like or absent. Gills close, free from stalk; *dingy white at*

first, but *soon pink* and *eventually dark brown.* **Stalk:** *Solid;* cylindrical to club-shaped. Surface *white, but stains yellow* and eventually brown when bruised; *sparsely* to *densely fibrillose-scaly below the ring,* may be smooth in age. Ring membranous, double, with patches of brownish fibrils underneath. **Spore print:** Dark grayish reddish brown. **Technical notes:** Cap 12–30 cm across. Stalk 8–20 × 0.7–3.5 cm. Spores ellipsoid; 8–11 × 5–6 μm.

Fruiting: Solitary to clustered; on soil in coniferous forests, grassy places, roadsides, etc. Summer and fall. Widespread in N. America and frequently collected in Rocky Mts. and on West Coast.

Edibility: Edible. Young caps are highly rated.

Similar species: *Agaricus subrufescens* (not shown), found in central and eastern U.S., can be distinguished by its smaller spore size.

MEADOW MUSHROOM *Agaricus campestris*   **Pl. 31**
Medium-sized, *white* to *brownish cap* on a *short stalk* with an *indistinct ring* and *no volva. Gills crowded; pale pink when young* (before spores develop), becoming *bright pink* before ring breaks (see below). **Cap:** Convex at first, expanding to flat: margin strongly incurved in young caps. Surface smooth at first or fibrillose (use a hand lens), soon developing small scales, which may be brownish gray. Surface typically dingy in age and when wet, often with gill color showing through cap; often breaks into irregular, coarse scales in dry weather. Flesh thick, firm; white, but slowly becoming flushed with pink to purplish brown. Odor and taste not distinctive when raw.* *Gills* free from stalk, *narrow; pale pink at first,* becoming *bright pink before ring breaks,* then *dark purple-brown* when spores mature. **Stalk:** Short; cylindric or tapered toward base. Surface white, fibrillose; eventually turns dingy reddish brown. *Ring thin, narrow, membranous* to *fibrillose, sometimes incomplete,* with *part remaining on cap edge.* **Spore print:** Dark grayish reddish brown. **Technical notes:** Cap 2.5–10 cm across. Stalk 2–6 × 0.5–1.5 cm). Spores ovoid (egg-shaped) to ellipsoid; 5.5–7.5 × 4.5 μm.

Fruiting: Solitary or grouped, often in "fairy rings"; on grassy soil in lawns, pastures, roadsides, or in barnyards or cultivated fields. Summer and fall. Widespread.

Edibility: Widely eaten and long prized for food. Flavor and texture much like cultivated mushroom of Europe and N. America. **Caution:** Recent research indicates the presence of hydrazines, which have a cumulative toxicity if taken in sufficient quantity and which are carcinogenic in smaller amounts. **Similar species:** White forms are easily confused with (1) other species of *Agaricus* which are not harmful except for a

---

* See p. 10 for cautions about using taste as an identifying characteristic.

few such as *A. xanthodermus* (Yellow Stainer) that *immediately stain yellow* when injured. The combination of bright pink, free (unattached) gills when young; the thin, more or less sparse ring tissue; and the stubby, tapered stalk with *no trace of volva* distinguishes Meadow Mushroom *(A. campestris)* from (2) deadly poisonous species of *Amanita* (deathcaps—see Pls. 26–27 and pp. 215–239) and (3) Green Gill (*Chlorophyllum molybdites*, p. 240, Pl. 29), which is also poisonous. In Green Gill the stalk is slender and the spores give the *gills* a distinctive *green* color.

YELLOW CAP *Agaricus comptuliformis*   **Pl. 31**
Small, fragile, pale greenish yellow cap with *darker, more orange scales. Slender, tapered stalk.* **Cap:** Flattened-convex, with an incurved margin, expanding to flat, sometimes with a broadly and shallowly depressed disc (center). Surface smooth at first, later fibrillose with scattered, fibrillose scales. *Vivid orange* in young buttons, *fading to pale greenish yellow* with maturity; all stages have *darker,* bright orange to yellow *scales.* Flesh moderately thick on disc, tapering to a thin margin; white, unchanging when cut. *Odor almond-like* or sometimes lacking; taste not distinctive.* Gills free from stalk, crowded; pink in unexpanded caps, eventually becoming dark brown from mature spores. **Stalk:** Slender, hollow; cylindric or expanded at base and tapered upward. Orange-yellow at first and remaining so at base, otherwise *fading* to white with a pinkish cast between orange to yellow scales as it expands. Stalk *scales* may form irregular *zones.* Ring membranous; upper surface white, usually streaked with gill marks, lower surface yellow with soft orange scales near margin. **Spore print:** Dark purplish brown. **Technical notes:** Cap 2.5–6.0 cm across. Stalk 4–10 mm × 3–6 cm. Spores thick-walled, subglobose to broadly ovoid; 4.0–5.5 × 3.5–4.5 μm. KOH (potash) turns all surfaces bright greenish yellow. $FeSO_4$ turns pink, then purplish, on cap surface.
Fruiting: Solitary to clustered; on soil. Summer and early autumn. Eastern U.S.
Edibility: Presumably edible, but **use caution,** as some people are poisoned by related species. **Not recommended.**
Similar species: The bright orange to yellow scales on cap and more or less in zones on stalk distinguish Yellow Cap from numerous other small species of *Agaricus.*

CROCODILE MUSHROOM *A. crocodilinus*   **Pl. 31**
Very large, white, thick-fleshed cap on a *short, stout stalk.* Cap surface often cracks in an angular pattern—especially in dry weather—forming *coarse,* wart-like *scales.* **Cap:** Broadly rounded—to hemispherical at first, becoming nearly flat at maturity. Surface fibrillose, *tending to split;* white flesh below is

---

* See p. 10 for cautions about using taste as an identifying characteristic.

exposed when surface cracks and forms scales. Scales become brownish in age as they dry. Gills free from stalk, crowded, narrow; pink at first, becoming dark purplish brown when spores mature. *Stalk:* White; fibrillose, with a high, membranous ring that sometimes leaves irregular patches on cap margin. *Spore print:* Dark purplish brown. **Technical notes:** Cap 10–35 cm across. Stalk 7–15 × 2–6 cm. Spores smooth, elliptic; 8–11 × 5.5–7.0 μm. No pleurocystidia; cheilocystidia 40–50 × 8–15 μm.

Fruiting: Solitary to scattered; in meadows, pastures, and other grassy areas. Western N. America. Fall.

Edibility: Edible and choice.

Similar species: Crocodile Mushroom may be the same species as (1) *Agaricus macrosporus* (not shown); both have very large spores for an *Agaricus.* (2) Parkway Mushroom (*A. bernardii,* not shown) is a mid-Atlantic species that is closely related to Sheathed Stalk (*A. rodmani*). Parkway Mushroom forms fairy rings along parkways and other grassy areas. It has a *double-edged ring* and flesh that *stains pink* when cut, fading to orange, then dingy brown. (3) Sheathed Stalk (*A. rodmani,* p. 259) is smaller and has a smooth cap surface (texture like that of kid leather).

BLOODY AGARIC *Agaricus haemorrhoidarius*   **Pl. 31**
Medium to large, brown, scaly cap; slender, white to brownish stalk. *Quickly stains red* on wounding. Compare with Forest Mushroom (*A. sylvaticus,* p. 260), which is larger and has a similar color reaction when cut or wounded.

Fruiting: Under deciduous trees. Central and eastern U.S. Summer and fall.

Edibility: Not recommended. The species in this group are not well known. Some cause **mild poisoning** (gastric upset).

GRAYSCALE *Agaricus meleagris*   **Pl. 32**
Large cap has *dark gray, fibrillose center and scales* on a whitish background. Stalk is thick, white. *Stains yellow,* then dark purplish brown, when cut or wounded. See **Similar species** discussion under Flat-top (*A. placomyces,* p. 258).

Fruiting: On forest soil. Summer and fall.

Edibility: Poisonous.

Remarks: Different species are called by this name in the East and West.

FLAT-TOP *Agaricus placomyces*   **Pl. 32**
Medium-sized, *thin cap* with *flattened, dark brown disc. Slender, bulbous stalk. Cap:* Bell-shaped at first, expanding to humped or flat; disc *flattened* at all stages. Blackish brown to grayish brown surface breaks into very small, dark scales over a dingy, whitish background; Flesh thin. *Odor unpleasant* (*creosote-like*) but *mild.* Gills free from stalk, close to crowded; pink at first, then dark brown. *Stalk:* Cylindrical or tapered slightly upwards, above a small, flattened bulb. Surface white; smooth below thin, broad, membranous ring. Ring breaks into

brownish, cottony patches on lower surface of stalk. *Stalk interior quickly stains vivid yellow at base* when exposed to air. *Spore print:* Dark grayish reddish brown. **Technical notes:** Cap 3–9 cm across. Stalk 5–8 × 0.6–2.0 cm. Spores broadly ellipsoid; 4.0–5.5 × 3.5–4.0 μm.

Fruiting: Solitary or scattered; on forest floor under hardwoods. Summer and fall. Midwest and eastward.

Edibility: Not recommended. Any mushroom with a creosote-like, carbolic, or "inky" odor should be avoided.

Similar species: Frequently confused with (1) Woollystalk (*A. subrutilescens*, p. 260) and (2) Grayscale (*A. meleagris*, above), both of which have similar patterns of scales on cap. Grayscale lacks the yellow stains when cut or bruised and Woollystalk has larger, redder brown scales and a fibrillose, sometimes zoned stalk. **Note:** The larger, more robust western species with a similarly shaped cap, often called "Flat-top Mushroom," is here also referred to as Grayscale, in reference to its grayer (often silvery gray) scales (see Pl. 32). It may be a different species from the fungus called by this name in eastern America. (3) Prince (*A. augustus*, p. 255) is also thicker, more robust, and has coarser, more yellowish brown scales, but its cap shape is similar to that of Grayscale and all parts slowly stain yellow. The yellow color develops more slowly in Prince *(A. augustus)* and is not confined to the stalk base. The 2 species are not closely related.

Remarks: Yellow-staining species of *Agaricus,* such as Flattop (*A. placomyces*) and **Yellow Stainer** (*A. xanthodermus,* not shown) characteristically have thin caps with a flattened disc, a disagreeable odor, and a *yellow wound reaction*—they turn yellow quickly when cut or scraped. The cap surface is usually smooth at first, but in most of these species it breaks into very small scales that form a more or less concentric pattern on the cap, sometimes with the disc remaining smooth. The very fast appearance of yellow to yellow-orange pigments on surfaces newly exposed to air by cutting or scraping contrasts with the slowly developing yellow colors of those related to *A. sylvicola* (Sylvan Mushroom) and *A. arvensis* (Horse Mushroom). In the Xanthodermus (Yellow Stainer) group, this color reaction, and likewise the disagreeable odor, may be restricted to the *interior* of the stalk at its *bulb.* These species also frequently have one or more coarse, white threads extending down into the soil from the stalk base. *A. xanthodermus* (Yellow Stainer) is a common species throughout continental Europe, but in N. America it is known at present only from the Northwest.

SHEATHED STALK *Agaricus rodmani*   **Pl. 31**
Squat, thick-fleshed, smooth, white cap on a *short stalk* with a *double-flanged ring.* **Cap:** Medium-sized, broadly convex or flattened with a strongly incurved margin at first, expanding to a flat cap, but usually with a margin that curves downward,

sometimes with a broad, low depression on disc (center). Surface appears smooth but is minutely fibrillose under a hand lens, sometimes with indistinct fibrillose scales or tending to form shallow cracks in age. Flesh thick, firm; white, except sometimes flushed with dull pink just above the gills. Odor and taste not distinctive. Gills free from stalk or attached by a tooth, narrow, abruptly rounded at end nearest stalk; white at first, but soon pink (light grayish reddish brown), then dark brown as spores mature. *Stalk:* Solid; tapering somewhat upwards from a rounded base at first, but in age usually having a pointed base. Ring a membranous sheath with 2 *flanges* that are not attached to the stalk. Base sheathed by remains of volva. Surface smooth; white, unchanging or slowly turning pinkish brown when handled. *Spore print:* Dark grayish reddish brown. **Technical notes:** Cap 5–12 cm across. Stalk 2.5–7.5 × 4.5–5.5 μm. Cheilocystidia saccate (sac-shaped).

Fruiting: Solitary or in groups; on soil in waste places, lawns, roadsides, trails, etc. Widespread. Spring to fall.

Edibility: Edible—one of the preferred species. Sometimes grown commercially as a substitute for *A. bisporus,* which it approaches in flavor, but *A. rodmani* (Sheathed Stalk) has a more "chewy" texture.

Similar species: The *double-flanged, sheathing ring* is distinctive among the squat, white, smooth-capped species of *Agaricus.* (1) Some specimens of the Parkway Mushroom (*A. bernardii,* not shown) may be mistaken for Sheathed Stalk (*A. rodmani*) if they are collected when young, especially in humid weather before the cap surface cracks. Both species have the firm, thick flesh, narrow gills, and double ring, but *A. bernardii* develops *coarse cracks* in the cap and *orange,* then stronger *pink tints* in the cut flesh before turning brown. (2) Meadow Mushroom (*A. campestris,* p. 256) has a more fibrillose cap surface and a stalk that is typically tapered. It *lacks the double-flanged ring.* There is no harm in confusing *A. rodmani* with *A. campestris* or *A. bernardii,* as all 3 are edible, but all white *Agaricus* species must be carefully distinguished from the **poisonous** Amanitas (p. 215, Pls. 26–27).

WOOLLYSTALK *Agaricus subrutilescens*   **Pl. 32**
Looks like Flat-top (*A. placomyces,* p. 258) with *reddish brown* scales on cap. No odor. No yellow stains. Stalk has *woolly fibrils* on surface.

Fruiting: Solitary to grouped, in forests. Northwestern U.S. Late summer and fall.

Edibility: Causes **mild poisoning** in some people.

FOREST MUSHROOM *Agaricus sylvaticus*   **Pl. 31**
Small to medium, *brown, scaly cap* on a *slender, white* to *brownish stalk. Stains red* when cut or wounded. *Cap:* Convex, sometimes flat or nearly so in age. Surface gray and fibrillose, with reddish brown to grayish reddish brown, flattened-down scales or streaked patches; surface often lighter toward

margin. Margin ragged. Flesh firm; white, but slowly staining red or reddish brown. *Odor not distinctive.* Gills crowded, rounded toward stalk but free (not attached); nearly white at first, then pale brownish pink and finally dark grayish reddish brown. **Stalk:** Slender, cylindrical or tapering upward from a small, rounded bulb; usually hollow with a single, narrow channel. Surface silky, whitish at first but becoming dingy brown as it ages or when handled. Flesh stains red when cut; ring membranous, thin, white, but soon brown. **Spore print:** Dull chocolate brown. **Technical notes:** Cap 2–8 cm across. Stalk 6–10 × 1–2 cm. Spores broadly ellipsoid; 5–6 × 3.0–3.5 μm. Cheilocystidia saccate (sac-shaped) to clavate (club-shaped).
Fruiting: Solitary to scattered or grouped; on soil throughout U.S. and Canada. Late summer to fall.
Edibility: Edible, but easily confused with some poisonous species (see below).
Similar species: (1) Bloody Agaric (*A. haemorrhoidarius,* p. 258) is larger and *stains immediately and intensely blood red* when cut or handled, but is otherwise nearly indistinguishable in the field from *A. sylvaticus* (Forest Mushroom). Both are edible. Two other similar species, (2) Flat-top (*A. placomyces,* p. 258) and (3) *A. hondensis* (not shown) are **poisonous,** at least to some people. These two are best distinguished by a characteristic *creosote-like or phenolic odor,* which is not always easy to detect. Flat-top (*A. placomyces*) also *stains yellow* in the stalk base when cut or broken open. *Agaricus hondensis* has less distinct scales and lighter colors, at least when young.

SYLVAN MUSHROOM *Agaricus sylvicola*   **Pl. 31**
Small to medium, *smooth, white cap; slowly stains yellow when bruised.* **Cap:** Hemispheric to convex at first, expanding to flat. Surface silky and fibrillose to obscurely scaly in age; sometimes tinged yellow on disc in age. Chocolate brown color of mature gills often shows through thin flesh. Flesh soft; white, unchanging or yellowing when cut or bruised. *Gills* free from stalk, crowded; *dingy white at first,* then *pink* and *finally dark brown* as spores mature. **Stalk:** White, but *stains yellow* when bruised and becomes pinkish brown in age. Cylindric, with a distinct bulb that is sometimes flattened at base. Interior usually hollow at maturity. Surface smooth to fibrillose or indistinctly scaly. Ring membranous, thick, with cottony patches on lower surface. **Spore print:** Dark grayish reddish brown. **Technical notes:** Cap 5–8 cm across. Stalk 8–15 × 1.0–2.5 cm (broader at base). Spores ellipsoid; 5.0–6.5 × 4.0–4.5 μm. Cheilocystidia abundant; club-shaped to fusoid-ventricose.
Fruiting: Solitary or clustered; on soil in both coniferous and hardwood forests. Widespread throughout N. America. Late spring to fall.
Edibility: Not recommended; some poisonings reported. Ap-

parently edible for some and not for others, but species in this group are not well defined.

Similar species: Easily confused with several other white species of *Agaricus.* Those with a *creosote-like odor* or which *stain yellow very quickly and intensely,* particularly in stalk base, such as (1) Yellow Stainer (*A. xanthodermus,* not shown), are definitely not to be eaten. Common edible species which might be mistaken easily for Sylvan Mushroom are (2) Horse Mushroom (*A. arvensis,* p. 254) and (3) Flat-bulb Mushroom (*A. abruptibulbus,* p. 254) (4) Crocodile Mushroom (*A. crocodilinus,* p. 257), (5) Meadow Mushroom (*A. campestris,* p. 256), and, in the Pacific Northwest, (6) Snowy Cap (*A. nivescens,* not shown). This last-named species is typically somewhat larger and more robust, with an almond-like odor and small, pointed scales on stalk (just above bulb). It does not stain yellow when cut or bruised.

Ringstalks, Scalecaps, and Smoothcaps: Family Strophariaceae

Spore print grayish brown to rusty brown or purplish brown. Stalk and cap not readily separable with a clean break. Gills adnate (broadly attached to stalk) to adnexed (notched at attachment with stalk). Cap smooth and sometimes sticky to fibrillose or scaly. Stalk with or without a ring or other veil remnants but not with membranous or cobwebby volva. Most species live on decaying wood but others grow on a great variety of substrates, such as soil, manure, and vegetable debris; some form a symbiotic relationship with plants (mycorrhizae). Microscopic characters of spores (smooth wall and distinct germ pore) and cap surface tissues (hymeniform or cellular) are sometimes needed to clearly distinguish Strophariaceae from related families. This group includes both edible and poisonous species, including hallucinogenic forms which are particularly dangerous.

Ringstalks: Genus *Stropharia*

S.
horne-
mannii

Medium to large cap on a *solid, ringed stalk.* Gills attached to stalk; brown to blackish. Spore print dark purplish brown. Spores thick-walled with a distinct germ pore, dark brown; walls fade to more yellowish brown in KOH.

VERDIGRIS MUSHROOM *Stropharia aeruginosa*   **Pl. 32**
Small to medium, *slimy, blue-green cap;* margin *often ragged. Stalk similar in color,* with a *whitish ring. **Cap:*** Rounded to

bell-shaped at first, later becoming flat but often retaining a low, rounded hump. Surface sticky or merely shiny as it dries. Color varies, but is some shade of blue or green, often flushed with yellow or yellowish brown, especially toward disc (center); color fades quickly as the mushroom dries, to yellow or light brown. Sparse, irregular, loose, white, scaly remnants (from ring) on margin are easily washed off by rain. Flesh soft; white or with a bluish tinge. Gills adnate (broadly attached), close; white or grayish at first, *becoming purplish brown as spores mature.* Odor radish-like. *Stalk:* Slender, cylindric or slightly enlarged at base. Surface white at apex, blue-greenish below; cottony to scaly. Ring white, breaking readily and leaving scattered scales on cap in young specimens but often disappearing completely. *Spore print:* Dark purplish brown. **Technical notes:** Cap 2.5–8.0 cm across. Stalk 3–7 × 0.4–1.0 cm. Spores ellipsoid; 6–8.5 × 4–5 µm. Chrysocystidia present. **Fruiting:** Solitary or in groups; on forest litter in Pacific Northwest and from Great Lakes east and south.
Edibility: Extremely variable in N. America and so **not recommended**; widely eaten in Europe.
Similar species: The shiny, blue-green cap and brown spores distinguish Verdigris Mushroom (*S. aeruginosa*) from Anise Funnelcap (*Clitocybe odora*, p. 144, Pl. 16), but when faded it is not easily distinguished from other brown-spored species.
Remarks: The blue and green colors, which are not common in mushrooms, make this a strikingly handsome fungus

FRINGED RINGSTALK *Stropharia ambigua*   **Pl. 32**
Medium to large, *pallid* to *yellow* or *brown-tinged, shiny* or *slimy cap,* with *ragged, white veil remnants hanging from margin. Gills attached* to apex of *long, slender stalk.* **Cap:** Obtuse to broadly convex at first, but soon becoming nearly flat, often with a low, rounded hump. Surface smooth, *shiny* when dry, but distinctly sticky to *slimy* when wet. Cottony veil remnants are easily washed off by rain or at maturity are evident only as a *sparse ring* or *patches* hanging on *thin, fibrillose cap margin.* Margin often *coated with spores.* Flesh white; thick, firm, tapered abruptly near margin. Odor not distinctive. Gills close, adnate (broadly attached), but often with a decurrent tooth extending down stalk. Gills white at first, but soon becoming more or less purplish gray, then dark purplish brown as spores mature. **Stalk:** Cylindrical or gradually tapering upward from a slightly expanded base. Upper stalk white, streaked above and when young; lower stalk fibrillose or with scattered patches of white, cottony veil. White, cord-like strands often extend from base. **Spore print:** Dark purplish brown. **Technical notes:** Cap 4–12 cm across. Stalk 7–15 × 1.0–1.5 cm. Spores smooth, ellipsoid; 11–14 × 6.0–7.5 µm. Spores stain dull yellow-brown in KOH. Pleurocystidia inconspicuous; embedded, with refractive content in KOH.

Fruiting: Solitary or in groups. Widespread in open, mixed conifer-hardwood forests in North and West. Spring and fall, but particularly abundant in Pacific Northwest in fall. Frequent along dirt roads, trails, or in other disturbed areas.

Edibility: Edible, but reportedly unattractive.

Similar species: The lighter colors, habitat, generally larger size, and ragged white veil distinguish it from (1) the poisonous Crown Toadstool (*S. coronilla,* below). Both are easily confused with (2) several species of *Agrocybe* (earthscales, p. 304) that have more grayish brown spore prints.

CROWN TOADSTOOL *Stropharia coronilla*   **Pl. 32**
Small to medium, *dingy light yellow, squatty mushrooms* with *adnate* (broadly attached) *gills*. Grows *in grassy places.* **Cap:** Convex, becoming flat or nearly so. *Surface smooth, greasy* to *somewhat sticky when moist.* Flesh thick, soft; white. Odor faint and slightly pungent or lacking; taste not distinctive (**poisonous**–do not try it).* Gills close, *adnate* or rounded next to stalk and sometimes notched in age; dingy whitish at first, but soon becoming grayish violet and finally deep purplish brown. **Stalk:** Short, cylindric. Surface white or nearly so; minutely cottony above, fibrillose below. Ring well developed and persistent, cottony-membranous; white, streaked on upper surface. **Spore print:** Dark purple-brown. **Technical notes:** Cap 2–5 cm across. Stalk 2–4 cm × 3–6 mm. Spores ellipsoid to obscurely angled, with a small apical pore; 7–9 × 4–5 μm. Pleurocystidia embedded, more or less clavate (club-shaped), with a sharply pointed tip and refractive content. Cheilocystidia similar.

Fruiting: Single, in clusters, or in rings; common on lawns and other grassy places throughout N. America, particularly in irrigated areas. Summer and fall.

Edibility: Poisonous.

Similar species: Species of *Agrocybe* that grow in grassy areas and have very similar field characters have lighter, more yellowish or grayish brown spore prints. (1) The cap of Cracked Earthscale (*Agrocybe dura,* p. 305, Pl. 38) is usually smaller, lighter in color and cracks more. (2) Roundtop Earthscale (*Agrocybe pediades,* p. 306) is consistently much smaller and more slender than Crown Toadstool (*S. coronilla*). (3) The closely related *Stropharia hardii* (not shown), which is common in some seasons in the South and East, is smaller and sometimes has brown spots. (4) Many other more or less nondescript "LBM's" (little brown mushrooms — some are **poisonous**) fade to a similar color and may be mistaken easily for this species, as well as many non-poisonous species. Obviously, it is foolish to experiment with any of these mushrooms for food, because of the difficulty in making a reliable identifica-

---

* See p. 10 for cautions about using taste as an identifying characteristic.

tion on the basis of field characters alone (see below).

Remarks: Species of several genera that resemble Crown Toadstool (*Stropharia coronilla*) in general characters are poorly known at present. Characters that are critical for identification — such as color, size, ring development, stickiness, and surface textures — often are inconsistent and vary greatly with changes in weather and habitat. Crown Toadstool (*S. coronilla*) was long regarded as being of questionable toxicity, but recent reports verify that it can cause **serious poisoning**, with some symptoms similar to those of muscimol-ibotenic acid poisoning (see p. 25).

LUXURIANT RINGSTALK *S. hornemanni* **Pl. 32**

Medium to large, *shiny, pale yellowish brown* to *dingy purplish* or *reddish brown cap*. *White ring* on stalk. Gills attached to *scaly white stalk*. **Cap:** Broadly conic to convex, with thin, inrolled margin at first; expanding to broadly convex, then flat, sometimes with a broad to narrow hump. Surface somewhat sticky when moist; brown but variable in color, often with soft, white wisps of veil tissue near the margin before cap expands. Flesh thick on disc (center), thin at margin; pale watery gray, becoming dingy yellowish in age. Odor not distinctive. Gills close, adnate (broadly attached) with a decurrent tooth extending down stalk in age; gills grayish white at first, becoming dull purplish brown as spores mature. **Stalk:** Cylindric; surface white and scaly below the *white* membranous *ring*, minutely fibrillose to smooth above. Interior soon hollow; flesh white to dingy yellow or brownish, with color sometimes showing through between white surface scales. **Spore print:** Dark purple-brown. **Technical notes:** Cap 5–14 cm across. Stalk 6–12 × 0.8–2.0 cm. Spores 10.5–13.5 × 5–7 μm. Cheilocystidia ventricose to fusoid, thin-walled. Some pleurocystidia are like cheilocystidia, but mucronate chrysocystidia are also present. **Fruiting:** Singly or clustered; on decaying conifer logs in coniferous forests in U.S. and Canada. Often found at high elevations. Late summer and fall.

Edibility: Unknown.

Similar species: The habitat, more or less robust form, and scaly white stalk make this a fairly distinctive species. The cap colors vary greatly and some of the more reddish variants could be confused with (1) the darker forms of Scaly Ringstalk (*S. squamosa*, p. 267) that have lost the characteristic scaly remnants of veil tissue from the cap surface. (2) Species of *Pholiota* (p. 270, Pl. 33) and *Agrocybe* (p. 304, Pl. 38) which might be confused with Luxuriant Ringstalk (*Stropharia hornemanni*) have *lighter-colored spore prints* that are more yellowish brown. Again, we emphasize the absolute necessity of obtaining a good fresh spore print on *white*, not colored, paper for accurate mushroom identification.

ROUGH-RING *Stropharia rugosoannulata* **Pl. 32**

Large, more or less *robust, purplish brown cap;* surface

streaked. White to *dingy yellowish stalk,* with a *thick, scaly ring.* **Cap:** Obtuse to broadly bell-shaped at first, finally rounded with a low hump and often upturned or split toward margin at maturity. Surface smooth at first but not sticky, becoming streaked and often developing radiating cracks or sometimes minute scales. Reddish to purplish brown at first, but fading quickly to light yellowish brown to grayish yellow, sometimes with olive tones. Flesh thick; firm. Odor not distinctive. Gills broad, close to crowded, adnate (broadly attached), nearly white, then bluish gray and finally dark grayish reddish brown. **Stalk:** Solid, tapering upward from a slightly enlarged base. Surface smooth to fibrillose or roughened, splitting in dry weather; white, but quickly turning dingy grayish and darkening somewhat on handling. *Interior firm, white* except yellowish just under surface. *Ring* set *high* on stalk, *membranous, thick, two-layered; lower layer separates* to form *hard, recurved, claw-like scales.* **Spore print:** Dark purplish brown. **Technical notes:** Cap 5–15 cm across. Stalk 10–15 × 1–2 cm. Spores 10–13 × 7–9 μm. Pleurocystidia have refractive content.

Fruiting: Solitary to clustered, often in distinct rings. Common on cultivated, heavily mulched soil, but also in woods; frequently abundant. Northern U.S. Spring.
Edibility: Edible and highly rated. Cultivated in Europe.
Similar species: The ring persists on the stalk of Rough-ring (*S. rugosoannulata*) and it is almost always possible to see the distinctive thick, tough, claw-like scales on its undersurface. Otherwise, the combination of size and colors of cap and stalk differentiate it readily from other Stropharias. Collectors who ignore the attached gills may look for it among the brown species of *Agaricus* (p. 254). Ordinarily the fibrillose, non-scaly stalk is a useful character in combination with the above characters, but the stalk has a strong tendency to split irregularly and recurve in unfavorable weather, sometimes forming very thick, irregular curls of tissue.

MANURE ROUNDHEAD *Stropharia semiglobata*   **Pl. 32**
Small, shiny yellow, hemispherical cap on a *very long, skinny stalk. Gills broadly attached.* Grows *on horse or cow dung.*
Cap: Broadly rounded at first and remaining so or expanding to nearly flat in age. Surface more or less sticky when moist, shiny as it dries; light yellow to yellowish pink, moderate orange-yellow or dark yellow. Flesh thick on disc, thin on margin; soft and watery, pale yellowish. Odor not distinctive. Gills subdistant, adnate (see inside front cover) very broad; grayish at first, later becoming dingy purplish brown with whitish edges. **Stalk:** Cylindric above a slightly bulbous base; very slender. Surface colored like cap or lighter; lower part sticky when moist. Ring poorly developed or lacking; sometimes evident as a fibrillose zone set high on stalk of young specimens. **Spore print:** Dark purple-brown. **Technical notes:** Cap 1–4

cm across. Stalk 5–8 cm $\times$ 3–5 mm. Spores ellipsoid, with a small apical germ pore; 15–20 $\times$ 7–10 μm. Spores dark purple-brown in H_2O, dull yellowish brown in KOH. Pleurocystidia present, but project only slightly, if at all, above basidia and contain refractive content in KOH. Cheilocystidia abundant; narrowly fusoid-ventricose, with narrow necks. Clamps present on hyphae.

Fruiting: Single to clustered; on dung of domestic animals. Common throughout the season in N. America.

Edibility: Reported as "edible" and as "inedible but harmless." **Not recommended** (see below).

Similar species: Other species of *Psilocybe, Stropharia,* and possibly *Panaeolus* growing on dung could be confused easily with Manure Roundhead (*S. semiglobata*) but cap shape, size and color and the noticeably "too long" stalk make this a distinctive species. Some *Panaeolus* species are **poisonous,** suggesting the inadvisability of experimenting with unknown dung-inhabiting fungi for food. Other than the obvious effects, the possible health hazards of the hallucinogenic Psilocybes is unknown, further suggesting the lack of wisdom in eating them or unknown mushrooms that grow on dung.

SCALY RINGSTALK   Pl. 32
Stropharia squamosa var. *squamosa*

Medium to large, *brown to orange* or *yellow, shiny caps;* surface sparsely ornamented with *soft, white scales.* Grows *in clumps on decayed logs or forest debris. Cap:* Conic to obtuse, with an incurved margin when young, becoming convex to flat, usually retaining a conic hump. Surface smooth, sticky when moist at first, with *soft, whitish scales* that are loose and easily washed off by rain. Flesh thin and watery; somewhat fragile; brownish, fading to pale yellowish gray. Odor faintly pungent. Gills subdistant, adnate (*broadly attached*), with a slight decurrent tooth extending down stalk; light bluish gray when young, becoming dark purplish gray as spores mature. *Stalk: Cylindric,* sometimes tapering slightly upward, white and fibrillose above ring, dingy brownish and covered with recurved scales below ring. *Lower portion* becomes *moderate* to *dark brown inside; brown shows between scales.* Ring set high on stalk, membranous. Upper surface nearly white and streaked before spores are shed; lower surface covered with brownish, fibrillose patches. *Spore print:* Dark purplish brown. **Technical notes:** Cap 3–8 cm across. Stalk 7–12 $\times$ 0.5–1.0 cm. Spores ellipsoid; 11–14 $\times$ 6–8 μm. Pleurocystidia lacking. Cheilocystidia filamentous, with acute apices.

Fruiting: Single to clustered; on soil or woody substrate. Northern U.S. and Canada.

Edibility: Some European authors report it as edible. There is always the question as to whether U.S. and European species are exactly the same. **Not recommended.**

Similar species: Most like (1) Luxuriant Ringstalk (*Stropha-*

ria hornemanni, p. 265), but easily distinguished on microscopic characters. Scaly Ringstalk (*S. squamosa*) typically has better developed scales on cap surface, more intense brown on lower stalk, and more orange color tones, lacking the purple tinges that are often conspicuous in Luxuriant Ringstalk (*S. hornemanni*). In rainy weather accurate identification of Scaly Ringstalk may be difficult due to loss of scales from cap surface as cuticular cells gelatinize and scales readily wash off. Without them, this variety of *S. squamosa* could be confused more easily with other Stropharias, such as (2) Crown Toadstool (*S. coronilla,* p. 264) and (3) faded specimens of Roughring (*S. rugosoannulata,* p. 265), which is more robust and has a scaly lower stalk. (3) Fringed Ringstalk (*S. ambigua,* p. 263) does not have a well-developed, membranous ring on the stalk. **Remarks:** A form of this species that is common in eastern U.S. is *more orange* (sometimes pumpkin orange) to brick red and is often *very slender*; it has *less conspicuous scales* on cap. This is variety *thrausta* (**Pumpkin Ringstalk**—see Pl. 32). Microscopically, it can be distinguished from variety *squamosa* by the eccentric (off-center) germ pore on its spores. It fruits on soil in hardwood forests in autumn.

Genus *Naematoloma*

Medium to large cap with gills that are attached to stalk apex. Stalk lacks a membranous ring but may have fibrillose fragments (veil remnants) from zone of fibrils fringing young cap. Spore print purple-brown.

ORANGE STUMP MUSHROOM   Pl. 33
Naematoloma capnoides
Medium-sized, *rounded, orange* to *yellow-brown cap;* surface *moist but not sticky. Slender, thin-ringed stalk.* Grows *in clusters on decaying conifer wood.* **Cap:** Convex, with an inrolled margin at first; eventually becoming flat, sometimes with a narrow, low, rounded hump. Surface smooth, or with scattered buff fibrils; moist but not sticky. Flesh thick; nearly white, unchanging when cut or bruised. Odor not distinctive. Gills close, rounded-adnate, but separating from stalk readily, moderately broad or narrower; white to grayish at first, but soon grayish or developing a purplish gray cast as spores mature, eventually becoming dark purplish brown. **Stalk:** Slender, cylindric or enlarged somewhat below; hollow in age. Surface nearly white at apex to pale, dull yellowish at base when young, darkening at base to rusty brown in age. Lower stalk has some stiff hairs; surface sparsely fibrillose up to the faint, incomplete, poorly developed ring left by the broken veil, indistinctly scurfy at apex. **Spore print:** Dark purple-brown.

Technical notes: Cap 2.5–6.0 cm across. Stalk 5–7 × 0.5–1.0 cm. Spores ellipsoid; 18–30 × 5–6 μm. Spores have smooth, thick walls and a small, flattened germ pore; walls turn purple-brown in water mounts, but dull yellowish brown in KOH. Pleurocystidia few to many, subclavate to obovate-mucronate. Cheilocystidia similar, or more commonly fusoid-ventricose.

Fruiting: Usually densely clustered on conifer wood. Widespread, but particularly common in western U.S. and Canada. Fall to winter.

Edibility: Edible and highly regarded by some, but easily confused with the noxious Sulphur Tuft (*Naematoloma fasciculare*, p. 269).

Similar species: Two species easily confused with Orange Stump Mushroom are (1) the edible Brickcap (*N. sublateritium*, p. 270) and (2) the inedible or poisonous Sulphur Tuft (*N. fasciculare*, below). Sulphur Tuft fruits at the same time as Orange Stump Mushroom and both are common on conifer wood. However, the more yellow to greenish colors, distinctly olive-tinted young gills, and often smaller size distinguish Sulphur Tuft. When fresh, the brick red to buff pink colors, larger size, and habitat on hardwood, particularly oak, distinguish Brickcap. The veil is typically better developed on Brickcap, covering the very young cap with a very thin, whitish, fibrillose layer and typically leaving pale yellowish to whitish marginal patches on older caps. There is little harm in confusing Brickcap and Orange Stump Mushroom, as both are edible when cooked. Sulphur Tuft, on the other hand, cannot be recommended for eating, as some people are poisoned by it.

SULPHUR TUFT *Naematoloma fasciculare*   **Pl. 33**
Small to medium, broadly bell-shaped to rounded, *greenish yellow* to *orange-yellow cap. Bitter taste* (do not try it).* *Gills broadly attached* to *slender, thin-ringed stalk.* Grows in clusters on *decaying logs* or *stumps.* **Cap:** Conic to bell-shaped at first, expanding to convex or flat, usually with a rounded hump. Surface orange-yellow on disc to greenish yellow outward, fading to greenish or olive-yellow, sometimes in age with brown disc and grayish yellow to dull olive limb; smooth or somewhat slippery when wet, sometimes minutely fibrillose toward margin or outermost layer breaking to form small, spot-like scales. Margin incurved at first, with an overlay of volval fragments. Flesh moderately thick, greenish yellow, eventually changing to dingy brown when cut. Odor not distinctive; taste typically *very bitter* (mild-tasting collections sometimes reported).* *Gills crowded, adnate (broadly attached)*, thin; pale yellow at first, becoming *greenish yellow* to *light green before spores mature.* **Stalk:** Slender, sometimes

---

* See p. 10 for cautions about using taste as an identifying characteristic.

narrowed toward base. Fleshy but hollow, round or compressed in cross-section. Flesh yellow at first, but soon yellow-orange to brown at base and lighter above. Surface fibrillose to smooth (hairless), often somewhat contorted. **Technical notes:** Cap 2–8 cm across. Stalk 5–12 × 0.3–1.0 cm. Spores ellipsoid; 6.5–8.0 × 3.5–4.0 μm. Pleurocystidia have yellow refractive content in KOH.

Fruiting: Scattered to densely clustered; on logs and stumps of coniferous and hardwood trees. Widely distributed. Spring and fall. Sometimes common during winter in mild climates. **Edibility:** Usually regarded as **poisonous,** or at least inedible. **Similar species:** Greenish tints on flesh and gills and sometimes on cap surface help to distinguish it from (1) the closely related edible Brickcap (*N. sublateritium,* below) and (2) Orange Stump Mushroom (*N. capnoides,* p. 268), but see discussion on p. 269. (3) A number of scalecaps (species of *Pholiota,* p. 270, Pl. 33) resemble Sulphur Tuft *(N. fasciculare);* the 2 genera intergrade. For example, mature specimens of *Pholiota astragalina* (not shown) have similar colors and it fruits on conifer logs in late summer and fall. Pholiotas typically have *more rusty brown spore prints,* however, and the greenish gill colors and lack of pink tones on young caps of Sulphur Tuft help to distinguish them. (4) *Naematoloma subviride* (not shown), which also has distinctly green gills, is smaller. It may be found in the Gulf Coast area and southeastern U.S.

BRICKCAP *Naematoloma sublateritium*   **Pl. 33**
Small to medium cap; *brick red on disc* (center), *yellowish pink near margin.* Cap *margin incurved* to *downturned. Thin, fibrillose veil leaves ring on stalk* or *patches on cap margin.* **Fruiting:** Clustered on hardwood logs or stumps. Common in hardwood forests throughout N. America. Late summer and fall.
Edibility: Edible.
Similar species: See (1) Orange Stump Mushroom (*N. capnoides,* p. 268) and (2) Sulphur Tuft (*N. fasciculare,* above).

Scalecaps: Genus *Pholiota*

Small to large cap with brown gills. Stalk has a membranous ring or fibrillose zones or scales. Yellowish brown spore print. Cuticle of cap filamentous. Spores have a distinct germ pore.

GOLDSKIN SCALECAP *Pholiota aurivella*   **Pl. 33**
Medium to large, *orange-yellow, rounded cap* with *scattered, reddish orange scales* embedded in surface (slime layer). Cap surface *sticky between scales. Scaly stalk.* Grows on *decaying wood. Cap:* Convex or broadly humped. Surface scales embedded in slime layer, sometimes disappearing in age. Flesh firm, yellow. Gills close, adnate (broadly attached) at first; yellowish

to reddish brown. **Stalk:** Central or eccentric (off center), cylindric, solid, firm. Surface cottony above poorly developed ring; fibrillose to *scaly* below. Scales dry, recurved, better developed toward base; yellowish to yellow-brown. **Technical notes:** Cap 4–15 cm across. Stalk 5–8 × 0.5–1.5 cm. Spores smooth, thick-walled, with distinct germ pore, elliptic; 7–10 × 4.5–6.0 μm. Pleurocystidia 30–45 × 4–7 μm, often branched near apex. Cheilocystidia slightly smaller, thick-walled.

Fruiting: Solitary to scattered or clumped; on trunks or logs of hardwoods. Widespread. Late summer to fall or early winter.

Edibility: Reported as edible, but **not recommended** (see below).

Similar species: Microscopic characters distinguish Goldskin Scalecap *(P. aurivella)* from a number of related species, including (1) Fat Pholiota *(P. adiposa,* not shown), which has gelatinous scales on stalk as well as cap. (2) *Pholiota squarrosa-adiposa* (not shown) has dry scales and forms large, dense clumps on alder and maple trees in the Northwest. Three fall species found on conifer wood in the same region are noteworthy: (3) *Pholiota abietis* (not shown) has dry scales and smaller spores; (4) *P. hiemalis* is a **poisonous** species found on logs of fir *(Abies).* Its stalk is typically flaring at the base and has gelatinous scales below. Its gills have yellow edges when young. (5) The brilliant yellow to orange-yellow Flame Scalecap *(P. flammans,* p. 272) is usually smaller, fruits earlier, and has dry, recurved scales on the stalk. The gills stain brown when injured.

CHARCOAL SCALECAP *Pholiota carbonaria*   **Pl. 33**
Small to medium, *brown, shiny cap. Reddish orange universal veil* leaves *scattered wisps on cap margin* and *thin zones* on *yellowish stalk.* Grows *on charcoal.* **Cap:** Convex to flat. Surface sticky; pale to moderate orange-yellow at first, soon darkening to moderate brown on disc, lighter toward margin. Flesh thick on disc, watery brown. Odor not distinctive. Gills close, adnate (broadly attached), narrow; whitish when young, becoming moderate yellowish brown at maturity. **Stalk:** Cylindric, solid or becoming hollow. Surface yellowish but darker at base; fibrillose beneath zones of moderate to dark reddish orange or strong brown, fibrillose universal veil. **Technical notes:** Cap 2–4 cm across. Stalk 3–6 × 0.4–0.6 cm. Spores smooth, thick-walled with narrow pore, broadly elliptic; 5.0–7.5 × 3.5–4.5 μm. Pleurocystidia and cheilocystidia abundant.

Fruiting: Scattered to densely clustered; on burned wood or charred soil; common in old fireplaces. From Rocky Mts. westward. Summer and fall.

Edibility: Unknown.

Similar species: Charcoal Scalecap *(P. carbonaria)* intergrades with (1) *Pholiota fulvozonata* (not shown), which has a dark cap and a less reddish universal veil. (2) *Pholiota highlandensis* (not shown) is more widespread. It has a pale yellowish universal veil and a more yellow-brown cap.

FLAME SCALECAP *Pholiota flammans*   **Pl. 33**
Small to medium, *bright orange-yellow, shaggy* cap with *bright yellow gills.* Thin, *shaggy,* like-colored stalk.
Fruiting: Grows on well-decayed conifer wood. Widespread in southern Canada and central to northern U.S. Summer and fall.
Edibility: Unknown.

TWO-TONED SCALECAP *Pholiota mutabilis*   **Pl. 33**
Clusters of medium-sized, *thin, brown, smooth caps. Caps fade* from *center outward. Brown gills. Stiff brown stalk. Cap:* Rounded or bell-shaped, sometimes expanding to flat with a low hump. Surface smooth, slightly sticky; moderate brown to strong yellowish brown when moist, fading to pale orange-yellow. Margin smooth, streaked and decorated with superficial universal veil fibrils when young. Flesh thin. Odor weak and more or less spicy. Gills close, thin, adnate (broadly attached) to decurrent (extending down stalk); pallid at first, becoming strong brown as spores mature. *Stalk:* Cylindric, sometimes tapered toward base; fibrous, becoming hollow. Surface smooth or streaked above ring; scaly below, with fibrillose, recurved scales. Pallid at first, becoming dark brown at base, lighter above. Ring variable, membranous and sometimes with scaly underside or sometimes merely a zone of fibrils. *Spore print:* Dull yellowish brown. **Technical notes:** Cap 2–6 cm across. Stalk 4–10 × 0.2–1.2 cm. Spores smooth, thick-walled with a well-developed, truncate pore; 5.5–7.5 × 3.5–7.0 μm. Pleurocystidia lacking. Cheilocystidia subcylindric to fusoid-ventricose.
Fruiting: In small to large clumps on decaying logs, stumps or occasionally buried wood. Widespread; common in Northwest. Fall.
Edibility: Edible, but **not recommended,** as it is frequently confused with Autumn Skullcap (*Galerina autumnalis,* p. 296). **Similar species:** Readily confused with (1) several species related to Spring Scalecap (*P. vernalis,* p. 274): *P. vernalis* and *P. veris* (Straw Scalecap, p. 273) have lighter, more yellow colors and smooth or less scaly stalks; they fruit in spring. (2) *Pholiota marginella* (not shown) also fruits in spring but lacks sticky surface and scaly stalk.

SHAGGY SCALECAP *Pholiota squarrosa*   **Pl. 33**
Medium to large, *yellowish brown cap;* surface *dry, coarsely scaly.* Grows *in clumps on decaying wood. Gills tinged with olive-green when young* (before spores mature). *Cap:* Obtuse to rounded, with a strongly incurved margin at first, expanding to nearly flat, with a low, broad hump. Surface scales dense, recurved; dingy yellow to orange-yellow or yellow-brown to

brownish orange in age. Margin often lacks scales. Flesh thick and flexible; yellowish. Odor variable—may be garlicky or onion-like, if present (may be absent). Gills close, narrow, adnate (broadly attached to stalk apex), sometimes with a decurrent line or tooth extending down stalk; yellowish at first, then greenish and brown as spores mature. *Stalk:* Firm, solid, cylindric. Surface of lower stalk (below ring) scaly like cap, dry. **Technical notes:** Cap 3–11 cm across. Stalk 4–10 × 0.4–1.2 cm. Spores elliptic to ovate, with a narrow, not truncate germ pore; 6.0–7.5 × 3.5–4.5 μm. Pleurocystidia have refractive content.

Fruiting: Small to large clumps; on decaying wood. Widespread; common in Rocky Mts. Summer and fall.

Edibility: Edible **with caution, but definitely not for everyone**—some people report mild poisoning.

Similar species: (1) Flame Scalecap (*P. flammans,* p. 272) is a dry, scaly species with *brilliant yellow* colors (see Pl. 33). (2) Sharpscales (*Pholiota squarrosoides,* below) has shaggy scales and colors like those of Shaggy Scalecap, but has a *gelatinous layer* under the scales and *lacks the greenish tones* on the gills.

SHARPSCALES *Pholiota squarrosoides*   **Pl. 33**
Colored like Shaggy Scalecap (*P. squarrosa,* above), except *lacking greenish tones* on gills; has gelatinous layer on cap under scales.

Fruiting: Common on wood in hardwood forests. Southern Canada and northern U.S. Autumn.

Edibility: Edible **with caution.** Do not confuse it with Shaggy Scalecap *(P. squarrosa).*

STRAW SCALECAP *Pholiota veris*   **Pl. 33**
Small to medium, *thin, light brown* to *yellowish cap;* surface smooth, hygrophanous (water-soaked). *Slender, ringed stalk.* Grows *in clusters* on *decaying wood.* **Cap:** Obtuse to rounded, with a narrow hump, becoming flat, sometimes with a depressed or perforated center or with a low central hump remaining. Surface shiny and *smooth,* streaked near margin; *hygrophanous,* fading first on disc. Flesh often tapers outward; fragile. Odor not distinctive. Gills close, adnate with a decurrent tooth to adnexed (see inside front cover); yellowish pink, becoming yellowish brown. *Stalk:* Cylindric; lighter than cap. Interior hollow or stuffed with cottony filaments. **Technical notes:** Cap 2–6 cm across. Stalk 4–8 × 0.4–1.2 cm. Spores smooth, truncate, elliptic; 5.5–7.5 × 3.5–8.0 μm. Pleurocystidia and cheilocystidia fusoid-ventricose with narrow necks; 35–65 × 3.5–9.0 μm.

Fruiting: Solitary or in small clusters; on hardwood logs and debris, including sawdust. North Carolina and Tennessee to Michigan and Ohio. Spring and early summer.

Edibility: Unknown, but **not recommended.**

Similar species: Very pale colors of faded specimens of Straw Scalecap (*P. veris*) and spring fruiting are distinctive among the Pholiotas. Spring Scalecap (*P. vernalis,* below) has crowded gills and a smooth stalk that is darker than cap and distinctly darker at base than above.

SPRING SCALECAP *Pholiota vernalis*   **Pl. 33**
Clusters of small to medium, *brown, shiny caps* with *narrow, crowded gills. Thin, brown stalk. Fruits in spring. Cap:* Conic or bell-shaped at first, expanding to flat, sometimes with low, narrow hump. Surface smooth, occasionally with sparse dull yellowish universal veil fibrils near margin; moderate yellow to strong yellowish brown, with translucent streaks near margin, fading to pale yellow when dry. Flesh thin, watery; pale orange-yellow. Odor and taste not distinctive.* Gills *crowded, narrow,* adnate (broadly attached); pale yellow to pale orange-yellow, becoming light yellow as spores mature. *Stalk:* Cylindric, flexible; interior hollow. Surface fibrillose, pale brownish at first; soon dark brown below, lighter above with a sheen of grayish surface fibrils. Ring poorly developed, fibrillose. **Technical notes:** Cap 1–4 cm across. Stalk 3–6 cm × 1.5–4.0 cm. Spores smooth with a narrow germ pore, elliptic; 5.5–7.0 × 3.0–4.5 μm. Pleurocystidia few or lacking. Cheilocystidia fusoid-ventricose, often with long, flexuous (zigzag) necks, 25–45 × 4–9 μm.
Fruiting: In small to large clumps; on decaying wood. Northern U.S. and Canada. Spring and early summer.
Edibility: Not recommended. Too easily confused with *Galerina autumnalis,* the deadly poisonous Autumn Skullcap (p. 296, Pl. 37), which fruits in both spring and fall.

Smoothcaps: Genus *Psilocybe*

Small to medium gill fungi. Thin, usually *brittle* or *fragile cap* on a *thin, ringless stalk.* Gills attached to apex of stalk. Spore print purplish brown. Spores thick-walled, with a distinct germ pore. Some species are hallucinogenic.

DUNG SMOOTHCAP *Psilocybe coprophila*   **Pl. 33**
Small, *dark reddish brown* to *yellowish, rounded, smooth cap. Slender, fibrillose, pallid* to *brownish stalk. Cap:* Convex at first, becoming flat, sometimes with a low, rounded hump; often with cottony patches along cap margin. Surface moist but not sticky when fresh; *hygrophanous* — dark brown colors *fade quickly* to a yellowish clay color. Flesh thin; brown, not staining when cut or bruised. Odor not distinctive. Gills broad, subdistant, adnate (broadly attached); pallid to brownish, becom-

* See p. 10 for cautions about using taste as an identifying characteristic.

ing dark violet-brown as spores mature. **Stalk:** Cylindric or nearly so; grayish yellow at first, then darkening to yellowish brown at base and lighter above. **Spore print:** Dark purplish brown. **Technical notes:** Cap 1–2 cm across. Stalk 2–5 × 0.1–0.3 cm. Spores 11–14 × 7–0 μm. Pleurocystidia and cheilocystidia fusoid-ventricose.

Fruiting: Singly or clustered; on manure. Widely distributed throughout the mushroom season. Common.

Edibility: Unknown, but too small to be of interest.

Similar species: (1) Easily confused with many other species that are distinguished mostly on microscopic characters. The combination of habitat (on dung), purple-brown spore print, lack of ring on stalk, and lack of blue or green stains on bruising help to distinguish Dung Smoothcap *(P. coprophila)*. (2) Another common species in the same habitat is Manure Roundhead *(Stropharia semiglobata*, p. 266). The more convex caps, which *remain rounded* instead of flattening; the more yellow, *sticky* cap surface; and the *thin but persistent ring* on *S. semiglobata* distinguish the 2 species in the field. (3) *Stropharia merdaria* (not shown) is more like Dung Smoothcap in shape and color, but like Manure Roundhead, it has a well-developed ring located high on its stalk.

BLUESTAIN SMOOTHCAP *Psilocybe cubensis*   **Pl. 33**
Small to medium, *rounded* to *nearly flat, thin, yellowish cap.* Cap *separates readily* from stalk. *Thin, ringed stalk stains blue at base when handled.* **Cap:** Hemispherical to broadly rounded at first, often with a low, rounded hump; expanding to flat or convex, sometimes with a hump remaining. Surface smooth to fibrillose or minutely scaly, sticky at first; yellowish white to light yellowish brown. Margin thin, often torn or split, usually with sparse, minute fragments of ring tissue (use hand lens). Gills adnexed (notched), close to subdistant (see inside front cover); pale dingy yellow at first, becoming purplish brown with light edges as spores mature. **Stalk:** Cylindric or tapering upward with a high ring. Surface colored like cap, with minute vertical streaks. Base readily *stains blue* when bruised and sometimes has cottony, blue-flushed filaments (mycelium) connecting to substrate. **Spore print:** Dark purplish brown. **Technical notes:** Cap 2.5–8.0 cm across. Stalk 3–7 × 0.7–1.5 cm. Spores smooth, thick-walled, with a narrow, non-truncate germ pore, elliptic; 12–17 × 8–10 μm. Pleurocystidia and cheilocystidia stain bluish in KOH.

Fruiting: Clustered on horse and cattle manure or manured soil. Southeastern U.S. and Caribbean Islands; also southward through Mexico.

Edibility: Not recommended. It is hallucinogenic and some people experience a variety of poisoning symptoms from its use. Children may develop high fevers and convulsions.

Remarks: The blue-staining Psilocybes are widely used for "recreational" purposes by the drug cult. Their possession is illegal. Species are very difficult to identify without a microscope.

Inky Caps, Crumblecaps, and Mottlegills: Family Coprinaceae

Typically fragile mushrooms, with spores which are black or nearly so and sometimes disseminated by dissolution of cap in an inky liquid, or with (in one species) a cap and gills that dry out and do not discharge spores. Gills free to adnate (broadly attached to stalk), sometimes with parallel sides (not tapered to edge) and very crowded. Mostly on dead organic matter such as animal manure, wood, or other plant debris. Both edible and poisonous species are included in this group.

Inky Caps: Genus *Coprinus*

Small to medium, very thin caps on slender stalks. Cap white to brown, with straight-sided, usually very crowded gills; both *cap and gills deliquesce* (*dissolve*) from edge inward, making an *inky mass*. Cap separates readily from stalk. Spore print black.

Coprinus comatus

INKY CAP *Coprinus atramentarius*   **Pl. 34**
Large, gray to *brownish cap* with *gray sheen; brownish tones, particularly toward apex* (pointed tip). *Dissolves* itself *in black, ink-like liquid at maturity.* **Cap:** Truncate-elliptic to broadly bell-shaped, typically with a lobed margin; sides often flattened or angled by pressure from other caps; flat or rounded, with an upturned, eroded margin when expanded. Surface sparsely covered with slender fibrils or minute scales, at least in center. Flesh very thin; gray at first, becoming pink, then *black* as it dissolves. Gills crowded; very wide, with parallel sides. **Stalk:** Cylindric or tapered upward; solid or with a narrow, hollow center. Surface white and smooth on upper stalk; gray and fibrillose below false ring. **Technical notes:** Cap 4–6 cm across. Stalk 8–15 × 0.8–1.2 cm. Spores 7–9 × 3.5–5.0 μm; slightly compressed.
Fruiting: Large clumps at bases of trees or stumps or rising from buried wood. Common and widespread. Spring and fall.
Edibility: Edible *when young* (before self-digestion begins), but **mildly poisonous** if consumed with or before or after alcoholic beverages.
Remarks: The large compact masses of shining gray caps pushing up through soil or grass are sometimes very attractive before liquefaction sets in. This inky cap (*Coprinus atramenta-*

rius) commonly grows in parks and residential areas, so it is one of the first mushrooms known to the amateur collector. The false ring below middle of stalk is caused by pressure from cap; it may also have very delicate, *dark fibrils* — remains of a rudimentary veil that may partially cover lower stalk.

GRAY SHAG *Coprinus cinereus*   **Pl. 34**
Small to medium, *gray cap* with *fibrillose to scaly or shaggy surface. Slender, gray stalk.* Grows on *dung.* **Cap:** Highly variable in size, but cylindrical to elliptic in button stage, expanding to bell-shaped or conic and eventually becoming flat and sometimes broadly funnel-shaped. Surface watery gray, hygrophanous; vertically streaked to cracked. Young specimens are completely covered with loose, fibrillose, whitish scales (remnants of universal veil), giving the mushroom a shaggy appearance as it matures. Margin even or lobed, appearing straight or slightly incurved at first but curling upward as cap expands. Flesh very thin; watery gray, then black as it deliquesces (digests itself). Odor and taste not distinctive. Gills crowded, free from stalk, very wide; watery gray at first, then black. **Stalk:** Cylindric and tapered upward, slender, fragile; hollow above and solid at the base. Surface shiny white under very delicate white scales. **Technical notes:** Cap 1.5–4.0 cm across. Stalk 5–10 × 0.4–1.0 cm. Spores 10–11 × 6–7 μm.

Fruiting: Single or in groups; common *on dung* heaps or heavily manured soil. Widespread. Spring to fall.

Edibility: McIlvaine (see p. 407) reports it to be excellent. Like all inky caps, it must be cooked at once.

Similar species: The gray caps with curved, whitish scales are key characters for Gray Shag *(C. cinereus).* The shaggy scales are remnants of the fibrillose universal veil which encloses the entire basidiocarp in the early button stage. *Coprinus sterquilinus* (not shown), another gray species of similar form that is also common on dung, can be distinguished by the *more powdery* veil remnants covering the young cap.

SHAGGY MANE *Coprinus comatus*   **Pl. 34**
Medium to large, *fibrillose to scaly, white cap; cylindric* with a *rounded tip before expansion.* Look for a *loose ring on stalk* in young specimens. **Cap:** Surface white to yellowish or light brown before breaking into scales. Scales curl upward and may become brownish at maturity, particularly in dry weather. Margin incurved and pressed against stalk at first, but curls upward as cap deliquesces (dissolves). Flesh very thin; white, then pink, purple, and finally black as it dissolves. No odor. Gills very crowded, free from stalk; white at first, then turning pink, purple, and finally black. **Stalk:** Cylindric or spindle-shaped, sometimes rooting; interior hollow. Surface white and fibrillose above ground level, with a *loose ring* just below the point at which cap margin touches stalk (see **Remarks**). **Technical notes:** Cap 2–6 cm across. Stalk 8–15 × 1.0–1.5 μm.

Spores smooth, with an apical pore, elliptic; 13–18 × 7–9 μm. **Fruiting:** Solitary, scattered, or in small clusters. Common throughout N. America in late summer to fall in the North and late fall to winter farther south.

Edibility: Edible. Some consider it one of the best. Be sure to use only young, fresh specimens.

Remarks: This is primarily a fungus of disturbed or open areas. In the Rocky Mts. it is common in spring or early summer. The loose ring on the stalk of these large, white, shaggy mushrooms is the volva remnant. It is one of the diagnostic characters of the species but *often falls away* at an early stage and is easily missed.

GLISTENING INKY CAP *Coprinus micaceus*   **Pl. 34**
Dense clumps of *very thin, yellow* to *light brownish caps;* surface hygrophanous. *Fragile, slender stalks.* **Cap:** Cylindric; margin often lobed, incurved at first, but curling outward as the cap deliquesces (dissolves). Surface smooth and shiny, usually with a *sparse coating of granules* which *glisten in bright light* under a hand lens. Brown on disc, lighter outwards, with translucent streaks extending toward margin in the button stage. Margin splits into radial folds as cap matures. Flesh *very thin,* fragile; dingy whitish to yellowish. Odor not distinctive. Gills crowded, adnate (broadly attached) at first, but separating from stalk as cap expands; very wide, with parallel sides. Gills whitish at first, but soon pinkish gray, then purplish and finally black as they deliquesce (dissolve). **Stalk:** Cylindric or sometimes enlarged slightly at base; hollow at maturity, brittle. Surface *white* and minutely fibrillose or faintly powdery. No ring. **Technical notes:** Cap 1.5–5.0 cm across. Stalk 4–8 × 0.3–0.5 cm. Spores elliptic; 8–11 × 5.0–6.5 μm. Pleurocystidia 40–70 × 20–40 μm.

Fruiting: In small to dense clumps; around hardwood stumps, tree roots, or buried wood in parks, lawns, or fields; also in forests. Common throughout temperate regions. Spring or early summer, and fall.

Edibility: Edible and said to have good flavor.

Remarks: The very large clumps of pale yellow to orange-yellow or light brown caps, often with a delicate granular coating, make this species easy to recognize. The granules are composed of smooth-walled, globose cells that are remnants of the universal veil. The granules are seen best on young buttons, but may not be present after the cap attains full size, especially since they are readily washed away by rain. In forests, where this inky cap is also common, the basidiocarps (fruiting bodies) are often solitary or in small clumps.

SNOWY INKY CAP *Coprinus niveus*   **Pl. 34**
Small to medium, *white, powdery cap* on a *thin, white stalk.* Grows *on dung.* **Cap:** Egg-shaped to bell-shaped; pure white prior to deliquescence. Surface powdery, with a *dense coating*

of granules (*veil tissue*); cuticle (cap surface) has vertical furrows beneath the granules, particularly toward the margin. Margin lobed, incurved at first but eventually curling upward as it dissolves and sometimes forming a tight roll. Flesh white to pale pinkish. Odor and taste not distinctive. Gills notched, crowded, very wide; white, then pink, and finally black as they dissolve. *Stalk:* Cylindric or narrowed above, *slender,* fragile. Hollow, *white.* **Technical notes:** Cap 1.5–4.0 cm across. Stalk 4–8 cm × 3–5 mm. Spores flattened; 12–17 × 8–12 μm.

Fruiting: Singly or in clusters; common on dung of large animals or on manure piles from spring to fall.

Edibility: Edible and said to have good flavor, but this inky cap is reduced to a very small substance with cooking.

Remarks: This handsome, pure white species varies greatly in size. It fruits singly or in small clusters. These characters, together with the habitat and the powdery veil remnants, make it easy to recognize. As in the Glistening Inky Cap (*C. micaceus,* above), the granules are made up of globose cells of the universal veil.

UMBRELLA INKY CAP *Coprinus plicatilis*   **Pl. 34**
Small, gray, very thin, fragile cap; surface wrinkled. Long, thin, fragile stalk. Gills attached to a collar around stalk. Grows on grassy soil. **Cap:** Long and oval to nearly cylindric with a rounded tip at first; spreading and becoming parasol-like to nearly flat, with a depressed center and downturned outer limb and margin. Margin eventually upturned or rolled up. Surface smooth at first, but soon wrinkled or pleated; light yellowish gray to brownish pink, darker on disc (center) after expansion. Flesh very thin and fragile. Odor and taste not distinctive. Gills distant (widely spaced) on expanded caps, attached to a sterile collar around stalk apex; dingy pale yellowish at first, then gray, finally black on edges as they deliquesce (dissolve). *Stalk:* Cylindric, sometimes with a bulbous base; often gracefully arched or curved. *Fragile* — extremely brittle. Surface smooth; white or translucent. No veil. *Spore print:* Black. **Technical notes:** Cap (expanded) 1–3 cm across. Stalk 4–7 cm × 1–2 mm. Spores thick-walled with a distinct germ pore, smooth, broadly elliptic; 7.5–10 × 10–12 μm.

Fruiting: Solitary to scattered; in grassy places, common on lawns. Widely distributed in N. America. Mid- to late summer or early autumn in hot weather.

Edibility: We know of no reports of poisoning but doubt that this inky cap will ever become attractive to mushroom gourmets due to its small size and the difficulty of finding enough to make it worthwhile.

Similar species: Numerous small species of *Coprinus* (inky caps) dissolve partially in dry weather, as *C. plicatilis* (Umbrella Inky Cap) does, but the combination of habitat, colors, and the attachment of the gills to a broad, sterile *collar* *around the stalk* make this a distinctive species. A similar genus, *Pseudocoprinus* (p. 285), has gills which *do not deliquesce* at all. (See Troop Crumblecap—*P. disseminatus,* p. 285, Pl. 35).

FELTSCALE INKY CAP *Coprinus quadrifidus*   **Pl. 34**
Medium-sized, *bell-shaped, gray cap* with *felt-like, patchy scales.* Grows *in clusters* on *hardwood logs. Cap:* Broadly elliptic to egg-shaped, with a rounded tip when young (in button stage), expanding to bell-shaped as spores begin to mature, eventually becoming flat with an upturned or recurved and ragged margin. Surface beneath scales yellowish white at first, darkening to medium or dark gray with maturity. Veil remnants on cap form ragged, soft, somewhat angular patches; patches are white at first, but soon become tinged with grayish yellow to brownish orange. Flesh thin. Odor unpleasant or absent. Gills narrowly notched, crowded, broad but thin; white at first, then purplish gray and finally black as they deliquesce (dissolve). *Stalk:* Cylindric or swollen, with a narrow, sharp rim at point of contact with cap margin in button stage; sometimes angular or flattened on one side in cross-section. Lower part white and cottony; attached to brownish, string-like strands at base. *Spore print:* Black. **Technical notes:** Cap 2–5 cm across. Stalk 4–12 cm × 5–8 mm. Spores thick-walled, smooth, elliptic; 7.5–10 × 4.0–5.5 μm.
Fruiting: Clustered; on hardwood logs and debris. Great Lakes area eastward. Spring to midsummer.
Edibility: Reports vary. Some report bad flavor, others claim gastric upset. No fatal poisonings known, but **not recommended.**
Similar species: Both (1) Gray Shag (*C. cinereus,* p. 277) and (2) Shaggy Mane (*C. comatus,* p. 277) have coarse, recurved, fibrillose scales, contrasting with the felt-like, patchy scales of Feltscale Inky Cap *(C. quadrifidus).* Those species have subtle color differences also, and their preferred substrates are different. (3) Inky Cap (*C. atramentarius,* p. 276) lacks a universal veil. (4) Numerous inky caps (species of *Coprinus*) have felty scales (remnants of universal veil), but *C. quadrifidus* is the most common large one that grows on decaying wood.

Genus *Montagnites*

DESERT INKY CAP *Montagnites arenarius*   **Pl. 34**
Medium to large, *whitish, dry cap* with *fragile, narrow, gill-like plates on underside. Slender, bulbous stalk.* Grows *on sandy soil or dunes. Cap:* Nearly round to oval in outline at first, soon becoming a flat, broadly depressed disc with coarse, irregular, black gill plates extending beyond cap edge and curving outward and downward. Surface smooth to scaly on persistent disc; gill plates wrinkled, *dry* and *fragile*—most often

quickly breaking and falling off so that frequently little remains below disc. **Stalk:** Cylindrical above a rounded or flat-topped bulb; fibrous to woody when dry. Surface fibrillose to scaly, sometimes with vertical ridges. Lower portion and bulb extend deeply into soil. **Technical notes:** Cap (including gills) 2.5–6.0 cm across. Stalk 5–20 × 0.3–1.0 cm. Spores very irregular, often misshapen and variable in size; 20–30 × 10–14 μm overall, but falling into 2 distinct size classes.
Fruiting: Solitary to scattered; on sandy soil in arid, desert shrub communities, sand dunes, roadsides or hillsides. Mexico to Texas and California, north to Oregon, southern Idaho, and Utah. Found throughout the frost-free season, following rains.
Similar species: Frequently confused with a sand-dune *Coprinus* (inky cap), to which it is closely related.

Crumblecaps: Genus *Psathyrella*

Small to medium, thin, fragile or brittle cap with gray to blackish gills. Slender, fragile stalk. Spore print black. Spores have a distinct germ pore. Cap may be hygrophanous, often streaked when fresh.

FRINGED CRUMBLECAP *Psathyrella candolleana*   **Pl. 35**
Medium-sized, *thin, yellowish cap;* surface *streaked, hygrophanous* (water-soaked). Margin of cap *thin, ragged* — decorated with *shreds of white veil. Whitish, fragile stalk.* **Cap:** Convex to bell-shaped at first, expanding to broadly conic or flat, with a low, rounded hump. Color changes gradually as it dries; moderate yellow to strong yellowish brown at first, darkening as spores mature, at least on the thin outer limb and margin; fading in age to whitish or remaining dingy yellowish on disc. Surface moist, smooth to slightly roughened, with translucent streaks at margin; young cap has scattered superficial fibrils or cottony wisps of whitish veil fragments. Flesh thin, fragile; color similar to that of cap surface but lighter. Odor not distinctive. Gills crowded, thin; dingy whitish at first, later tinged with grayish violet and finally dark grayish brown. **Stalk:** Cylindric or tapered slightly at base; hollow. Surface smooth or sometimes streaked at apex; lower part fibrillose or fibrillose-scaly. Veil remnants may form small, scattered, membranous scales on stalk or (rarely) a persistent ring. **Spore print:** Dark purplish brown. **Technical notes:** Cap 3–8 cm across. Stalk 6–10 × 0.5–1.0 cm. Spores smooth, thick-walled, with a hyaline (clear) germ pore; elliptic, sides flattened slightly or uneven in side view; 7–10 × 4–5 μm. No pleurocystidia. Cheilocystidia saccate (sac-shaped) to clavate (club-shaped), cylindric, or ventricose with blunt to rounded or knob-like tips; 32–46 × 9–15 μm.
Fruiting: In groups to large clumps; around old hardwood

stumps, or growing from buried wood, dead roots, and so on. Common throughout the range of hardwood forests, from Canada southward. Spring and early summer.

Edibility: Reported as edible, but **not recommended**—this mushroom could be confused with one of several "LBM's" (little brown mushrooms) with varying degrees of toxicity.

Similar species: Numerous species of *Psathyrella* (crumblecaps) and other dark-spored mushrooms can not be distinguished without careful evaluation of microscopic characters.

ARTIST CRUMBLECAP *Psathyrella delineata*   **Pl. 35**
Medium to large, *brown, thin, often wrinkled cap; more reddish brown on disc* (center). *Stalk whitish.* Grows on *decaying wood of deciduous trees. Cap:* Convex or slightly humped, expanding to nearly flat. Surface smooth to *wrinkled,* at first with thin, superficial, silky white fibrils forming a thicker layer outward and sometimes hanging from margin. Hygrophanous—moderate brown to grayish brown when moist, quickly fading to dingy yellowish. Flesh thick, fragile; colored like surface. Odor not distinctive. Gills close, adnate (broadly attached); colored like cap surface before spores mature. *Stalk:* Cylindric, hollow; whitish and not discoloring when cut or bruised. Surface white, fibrillose over lower part. *Spore print:* Blackish brown. **Technical notes:** Cap 3–10 cm across. Stalk 6–10 × 1.0–1.5 cm. Spores ovate (egg-shaped), flattened to indistinctly bean-shaped in side view; 7–9 × 4.5–5.5 μm; germ pore inconspicuous. Cystidia abundant; clavate-mucronate.

Fruiting: Scattered to grouped; on dead wood or other decaying vegetable debris in hardwood forests. More frequently reported in the East than the West. Spring to fall.

Edibility: Unknown.

HAYMAKER MUSHROOM *Psathyrella foenisecii*   **Pl. 35**
Small to medium, *bell-shaped, brown cap;* surface *smooth, hygrophanous* (fades unevenly as it dries). *Brown gills. Very fragile, spindly, whitish stalk.* Grows *in lawns. Cap:* Obtusely conic to convex, expanding to flat with a low, broad, rounded hump. *Hygrophanous* (water-soaked) at first, sometimes with a faintly streaked margin; grayish brown to light grayish yellowish brown when moist, fading quickly in a somewhat mottled pattern to light yellowish brown or lighter and then usually glistening. Surface smooth and moist at first, occasionally becoming slightly roughened on drying. Flesh very thin, fragile; watery brown, fading to pallid grayish yellow. Odor faint, not disagreeable; taste faintly acidic.* Gills adnate (broadly attached), with a very shallow, rounded notch at end near stalk apex, subdistant (see inside front cover), broad, tapering toward cap limb. Gills *brown* at first and darkening as spores mature, edges white; gills faces occasionally somewhat mottled

_____

* See p. 10 for cautions about using taste as an identifying characteristic.

as spores mature, eventually blackish brown. *Stalk:* Slender, cylindric or with a very small, hairy bulb at base; very fragile, hollow. Surface smooth to twisted and streaked, or with sparse, scattered superficial fibrils; colored like cap. *Spore print:* Deep grayish brown. **Technical notes:** Cap 1–3 cm across. Stalk 4–8 cm long or longer, 1.5–3.5 mm thick. Spores thick-walled, warty, ovate (egg-shaped) to broadly elliptic, with a truncate apical pore; 12–15 × 6.5–9.0 μm. No pleurocystidia. Cheilocystidia fusoid-ventricose with obtuse apices.

Fruiting: Scattered to grouped; common in grassy places such as lawns, pastures, and parks. Widely distributed from Canada southward. Spring to late summer.

Edibility: Reports vary. Although this is reportedly edible, we do **not recommend** it.

Remarks: This species and a very closely related one (*P. castaneifolia,* not shown) are intermediate between *Psathyrella* and *Panaeolus* (p. 286) and have been classified in both genera.

THIMBLECAP *Psathyrella gracilis*   **Pl. 35**
Small, fragile cap; brown to yellowish or gray—sometimes fading to *whitish* with a *pink tinge. Very thin, whitish stalk.* **Cap:** Broadly conic to bell-shaped, may expand to convex; sometimes scalloped at margin. Hygrophanous (water-soaked), with a translucent-streaked to grooved outer limb and margin; Moderate yellow to light yellowish brown or gray as spores mature when moist, fading quickly to dingy whitish with a yellow-tinged disc and often flushed with pink as it dries out. Surface smooth, polished, slippery. Flesh very thin and soon fragile; colored like surface. Odor and taste not distinctive. Gills adnate (broadly attached to stalk apex) or short-decurrent (extending slightly down stalk), close, broad; dingy whitish at first, becoming dark purplish brown as spores mature. **Stalk:** Cylindrical, hollow; very fragile. Surface whitish, smooth or slightly fibrillose, sometimes clothed with coarse hairs at base. **Spore print:** Dark grayish reddish brown. **Technical notes:** Cap 1–3 cm across. Stalk 5–10 cm × 1.5–3.0 mm. Spores smooth, with a distinct apical pore, elliptic; 11–15 × 6–8 μm. Pleurocystidia and cheilocystidia abundant; fusoid-ventricose, often with flexuous (zigzag) necks and acute apices. **Fruiting:** Scattered to grouped; on moist, sometimes grassy soil and vegetable debris or in boggy or swampy areas. Southern Canada and northern U.S. Late summer and fall.

Edibility: Unknown.

Similar species: Numerous species of *Psathyrella*—indistinguishable without a microscope. *Psathyrella atomata* (not shown) has a shorter stalk.

CLUSTER CRUMBLECAP *Psathyrella hydrophila*   **Pl. 35**
Small to medium, *rounded, brown cap;* surface *smooth, hygrophanous* (fades as it dries). *Young specimens* have *wisps of white, fibrillose veil* on *incurved margin.* **Cap:** Conic to convex,

expanding to nearly flat. Moderate brown to dark reddish brown when moist, sometimes with a streaked margin, *fading to dingy pale grayish yellow as it dries.* Surface moist and smooth or, on drying, sometimes shallowly wrinkled. *Margin incurved* at first; outer limb and margin covered with *fringe* of coarse, *whitish, fibrillose veil remnants* that are sometimes still evident on expanded caps. Flesh firm at first but soon fragile; watery brown, fading to pale grayish yellow. Odor and taste not distinctive. Gills adnate (broadly attached), close to crowded; pale reddish brown at first, sometimes with darker edges and occasionally beaded with watery droplets. **Stalk:** Cylindric, hollow. Surface white to grayish when young, may be brownish at base in age; smooth except at base, which is somewhat fibrillose from veil remnants. **Spore print:** Blackish brown. **Technical notes:** Cap 2–5 cm across. Stalk 3–8 cm × 3–6 mm. Spores elliptic; 4–6 × 3–4 μm; germ pore inconspicuous. Cheilocystidia clavate (club-shaped) to saccate (sac-shaped). Pleurocystidia broadly fusoid-ventricose, with long necks and rounded tips.

Fruiting: In groups or clumps; on decaying hardwood. Widely distributed. Late summer through fall.

Edibility: Unknown.

Similar species: Microscopic differences differentiate several species in mature state, but the *ring* or *fringe of veil remnants* on the *cap margin* distinguishes young specimens of this crumblecap *(P. hydrophila)* from others that grow on hardwood debris in the field. The veil remnants are not always present in older specimens, however.

ASPEN CRUMBLECAP *Psathyrella ulignicola*   **Pl. 35**
Medium to large, *gray, brittle, streaked cap;* cap *separates readily* from stalk. *Stalk thick, white, sometimes flushed with pink at base.* Grows *under aspen.* **Cap:** Broadly conic at first, expanding to nearly flat with a wavy, thin margin. Surface silky, fibrillose; gray, often tinged with brown, sometimes with scattered whitish veil fibrils, particularly near margin. Flesh thick on disc (center), tapering to very thin on outer limb; gray. Odor and taste not distinctive. Gills adnate (broadly attached), tapered to a narrow attachment at stalk, close, thin; pale grayish with white edges at first, becoming light to moderate brown as spores mature. **Stalk:** Cylindric and often twisted, firm but brittle; interior hollow. Surface fibrillose, usually with vertical streaks. **Spore print:** Blackish brown. **Technical notes:** Cap 5–10 cm across. Stalk 8–12 × 1.0–1.5 cm. Spores elliptic; smooth, thick-walled, with an inconspicuous germ pore. No pleurocystidia. Cheilocystidia variable. **Fruiting:** Solitary to grouped or clustered; on moist soil or well-decayed wood, often by the side of rotting logs or stumps of *aspen* or cottonwood. Common around beaver ponds in Rocky Mts. Spring and summer.

Edibility: Unknown.
Similar species: Microscopic characters are needed for positive identification of Psathyrellas, but the combination of large size, textured gray cap, and association with aspen or cottonwood trees in the western mountains distinguishes this species.
WEEPING WIDOW *Psathyrella velutina*   **Pl. 35**
Medium to large, *brown, thin, fragile cap;* surface *coarsely hairy. Deep brown,* somewhat *mottled gills. Slender, hairy stalk.* Grows on *soil and organic debris.* ***Cap:*** Broadly bell-shaped, at first with an incurved margin covered by a pale, fibrillose veil that forms a narrow superficial zone on outer limb or hangs as soft, cottony scales from margin; cap expands to broadly rounded, obtuse, or nearly flat. Surface *coarsely hairy* to indistinctly scaly; brownish orange to grayish yellow, lighter on margin. Flesh thick on disc (center), tapering to a thin outer limb and extending beyond gills; watery brown, fading to grayish yellow. Odor not distinctive. Gills close, adnate (broadly attached), with a narrow notch at stalk; gills separate readily from stalk. Gills dingy pale yellow at first, but soon *dark brown* from maturing spores; edges lighter, often beaded with droplets of moisture. ***Stalk:*** Cylindric; hollow. Surface fibrillose to scaly; lower part (below ring) colored like cap. Ring thin, fibrillose. ***Spore print:*** Blackish brown. **Technical notes:** Cap 5–12 cm across. Stalk 5–10 × 0.4–1.2 cm. Spores warty, thick-walled, elliptic, with a snout-like apex containing germ pore; 8–12 × 5.5–7.0 μm. Cheilocystidia filamentous. Pleurocystidia clavate (club-shaped) to narrowly fusoid-ventricose.
Fruiting: Scattered to grouped or in loose clumps; on bare soil, grassy places, compost heaps, sawdust piles, and so on. Widespread and common following rainy periods, with a long fruiting season.
Edibility: Reported as edible.
Similar species: Several large species of *Psathyrella* are distinguished mostly on microscopic characters. (1) *Psathyrella rugocephala* (not shown) has a smooth, wrinkled (in central part) cap. (2) *Psathyrella rigidipes* (not shown) is smaller, with brighter, more orange colors.

Genus *Pseudocoprinus*

Gills of mature mushrooms *do not deliquesce (dissolve)* into inky liquid. Compare with *Coprinus,* p. 276.

TROOP CRUMBLECAP   **Pl. 35**
Pseudocoprinus disseminatus
Small, *fragile, brownish* to *gray, pleated, umbrella-like caps* on *delicate, white stalks.* Grows *in troops* (large masses) *on soil* or *decaying wood.* ***Cap:*** Globose (spherical) at first, expanding to

hemispheric, rounded, or almost flat with a depressed center. Outer part folded (like an umbrella) and streaked. Surface somewhat granular (use hand lens); yellowish to brownish at center, whitish to gray outward. Flesh very thin. Gills adnate (broadly attached) to short-decurrent, subdistant (see inside front cover); white, but soon gray, then black as spores mature. *Gills do not dissolve.* **Stalk:** Hollow; *very fragile.* Surface smooth, with sparse, minute fibrils; white. **Spore print:** Black. **Technical notes:** Cap 0.5–1.5 cm across. Stalk 2–3 cm × 0.5–1.0 mm. Spores smooth, thick-walled, with a truncate germ pore, elliptic; 7–10 × 4–5 μm.
Fruiting: In *large, dense masses;* on *decaying wood and soil.* Common and widely distributed. Spring to fall.
Edibility: Too small to be of interest.
Similar species: Easily confused with (1) numerous very small inky caps (species of *Coprinus* — see p. 276), and with (2) crumblecaps (*Psathyrella* — previous group); in fact, *P. disseminatus* is sometimes placed in both of those genera. However, *P. disseminatus* and other species of *Pseudocoprinus* can be distinguished from true inky caps *(Coprinus)* by the *nondeliquescing gills,* and from crumblecaps *(Psathyrella)* by a combination of microscopic characters and the *folded* and *streaked cap.* (3) *Pseudocoprinus brunneus* (not shown) is more brownish and fruits in smaller clusters on grassy soil.

Mottlegills: Genus *Panaeolus*

Cap conic to bell-shaped or almost egg-shaped; thin, often fragile. Cap separates readily from stalk. Stalk very slender. *Gills mottled,* from uneven maturing of black spores. Cap has a cellular cuticle. It is unwise to eat any *Panaeolus.*

BELL MOTTLEGILL *Panaeolus campanulatus*   **Pl. 35**
Small to medium, *thin, gray cap* on a *brittle, skinny stalk. Gills* become *black* from maturing *spores.* Grows *on dung.* **Cap:** *Bell-shaped;* may have an incurved margin at first and a narrow, rounded knob at center. Margin thin and often fringed or irregularly toothed. Surface shiny and smooth; brownish gray to dingy pale yellow. Flesh very *thin,* fragile. Gills broad, subdistant (see inside front cover); dingy whitish at first, then *distinctly mottled as spores mature,* eventually *black* from spores. Gill edges may remain whitish. **Stalk:** Fragile, hollow, *very thin;* cylindric, with a slightly expanded base. Surface often streaked near apex, where gills are attached; colored like cap. **Spore print:** Black. **Technical notes:** Cap 2–5 cm across. Stalk 5–15 cm × 2–5 mm. Spores smooth, elliptic; 13–16 × 8–11 μm.
Fruiting: Solitary to clustered; *on horse or cow dung.* Widespread. Fruits after rainy spells; all seasons.

Edibility: Reports of poisoning suggest that it is unwise to eat any *Panaeolus.*

Similar species: Several species can be accurately distinguished only on microscopic characters. The poisonous and hallucinogenic *Panaeolus subbalteatus* (not shown) has more reddish brown colors and its stalk base *stains blue* when bruised.

STICKY MOTTLEGILL *Panaeolus semiovatus*   **Pl. 35**
Medium-sized, yellowish, sticky cap with *black gills. Separates readily from long, hollow stalk. Grows on dung.* **Cap:** More or less *bell-shaped;* rounded at top, incurved at thin, sterile margin. Surface smooth, sticky at times, otherwise shiny and smooth, sometimes with irregular, shallow, "pock-like" depressions; nearly white to dingy, pale orange-yellow. Flesh thin, fragile. Gills broad, adnexed with a narrow notch at stalk, subdistant (see inside front cover); pallid at first, but mottled as spores mature and eventually *black.* **Stalk:** Slender, cylindric with a gradually rounded, bulbous base; often rising from white strands or cottony filaments in substrate. Surface colored like cap; smooth, or streaked above a very thin, fibrillose-membranous ring that collapses early in stalk development. *Spore print:* Black. **Technical notes:** Cap 3–9 cm across. Stalk 8–15 × 0.5–1.5 cm. Spores smooth, thick-walled, with a distinct apical pore, elliptic; 15–20 × 8–11 μm. Chrysocystidia present on gill faces.

Fruiting: Solitary or in small clusters; common *on animal* (usually horse) *dung.* Widely distributed. Spring and summer.

Edibility: Not recommended. Some species of *Panaeolus* are poisonous.

Similar species: Almost indistinguishable from *Panaeolus solidipes* (not shown), which lacks a well-defined ring.

Webcaps, Flamecaps, Fiberheads, and Others: Family Cortinariaceae

One of the largest families of mushrooms, with more than 2000 species. Yellowish brown to rusty brown spore print. Cap and stalk firmly attached and not readily separating with a clean break; stalk lacking in some species. Veil often cobwebby. Members of this family have spores with no germ pore; spore surface may be wrinkled, warty, or spiny. Both edible and mildly to deadly poisonous species are included in this group.

Webcaps: Genus *Cortinarius*

Small to medium, occasionally large cap, with a *cobwebby veil* extending from stalk to margin of cap when young. Veil may leave a slight ring on stalk. Cap does not separate readily from stalk. Stalk varies from thin to stout. *Spore print brownish*—moderate reddish brown to yellowish brown or grayish yellowish brown. *Cortinarius* is one of the largest mushroom genera and is a very important part of the mushroom flora in our western coniferous forests. Unfortunately, very few species can be recognized with certainty in the field.

SMITH'S WEBCAP   **Pl. 36**
Cortinarius ahsii

Brown cap, often *flushed with yellow;* surface *hygrophanous. Brown gills. Stalk brownish,* sometimes *flushed with pink near top.* Veil remnants leave *bright greenish yellow ring* on stalk. **Fruiting:** On soil at high elevations, sometimes around snowbanks in coniferous forests. Rocky Mts. Spring to early summer.

 Edibility: Unknown, but **not recommended.**

CINNABAR BRACELET WEBCAP   **Pl. 36**
Cortinarius armillatus

Medium to large, *rounded* or *humped, reddish brown cap* on a *thick, bulbous stalk* with *cinnabar red bands. Cap:* Convex at first, soon bell-shaped, with an incurved margin. Surface moist, hairless to minutely fibrillose, sometimes with small, soft scales in age. Moderate to strong reddish brown or reddish orange. Flesh thick, soft; brownish pallid. Odor not distinctive. Gills broad, subdistant, adnate becoming adnexed (see inside front cover); light brown, becoming more reddish orange as spores mature. *Stalk:* Solid, thick, clavate (club-shaped). Surface dry, fibrillose; dull brownish, with reddish orange fibrils scattered over the surface—some form distinct *"bracelets."* Interior brownish. **Technical notes:** Cap 5–12 cm across. Stalk 7–15 × 1–2 cm above 3–4 cm diameter bulb. Spores thick-walled, without a germ pore, warty, broadly elliptic; 10–12 × 5.5–7.5 μm. Cheilocystidia more or less filamentous, scattered, 3–4 μm in diameter.

Fruiting: Solitary to clustered; on soil in mixed hardwood-conifer forests. Common in East and midwestern N. America, but uncommon from the Great Plains westward. Late summer and fall.

 Edibility: Edible, but **not recommended** (see below).

Similar species: Because the bright reddish orange rings and arcs of veil tissue on stalk and sometimes on cap margin stand out so prominently, this is often one of the first species of webcap mushrooms (genus *Cortinarius*) regularly recognized by novice mushroom hunters. It should be emphasized that a number of species in the genus have reddish orange veil remnants and at least one of them, Sorrel Webcap (*Cortinarius orellanus*) is **deadly poisonous.** Although, with experience, they can be separated (see under *C. orellanus,* p. 292) on field characters, the probability of making a mistake is high.

GREASED WEBCAP *Cortinarius collinitus*   **Pl. 36**
Medium-sized, *shiny yellow* to *brown, convex to humped cap. Stalk cylindric; white to violet,* with *zones of slime* on middle or lower part. *Cap:* Convex at first, then flat, sometimes with a persistent low, rounded *hump or knob* at center. Surface shiny when moist and not distinctly streaked or only faintly so on margin. Orange-yellow to brownish orange or yellowish brown, darkest on disc. Flesh thin, white, firm. Odor not distinctive. Gills subdistant, adnate to adnexed (see inside front cover), broad in swollen portion at middle. Gills pallid to grayish or bluish at first, becoming moderate brown in age. *Stalk:* Cylindric, often deeply buried in duff under conifers and hardwoods. White and fibrillose beneath thick, glutinous sheath of universal veil tissue. Universal veil colorless to tinged with violet; slime (veil) breaks into *zones* on mid- to lower stalk, often discoloring in age. **Technical notes:** Cap 3–10 (12) cm across. Stalk 5–13 × 0.5–1.5 cm. Spores thick-walled, surface wrinkled; elliptic to almond-shaped; 10–14 × 6–8 μm. Clamps present on hyphae.
Fruiting: Scattered to grouped; on forest duff under conifers and hardwoods, particularly in aspen forests. Mid to northern U.S. and Canada. Summer and fall.
Edibility: Reports vary, but apparently unattractive. **Not recommended.**
Similar species: It is easy to confuse the numerous species of *Cortinarius* (webcaps) that have cylindric, slimy stalks and brown, slimy caps. (1) *Cortinarius trivialis* (not shown) has a brownish stalk under the clear (non-violet) slime layer; the *slime* typically forms *more distinct rings or bands* on the lower stalk. This species is sometimes regarded as a variety of the Greased Webcap (*C. collinitus*). (2) *Cortinarius elatior* (not shown) has more grayish to olive-brown colors, a *distinctly ribbed* cap margin, and larger spores. Other American species with a brown, slimy cap and a violet-colored slime sheath on the stalk are (3) *Cortinarius cylindripes* (not shown) and (4) Splendid Webcap (*C. splendidus,* p. 294, Pl. 36). These 2 species can be distinguished from each other and from Greased Webcap (*C. collinitus*) by spore dimensions and other microscopic characters. Splendid Webcap also has a smoother stalk. Two similar species with a *white, non-zoned slime sheath* on the lower stalk are (5) *Cortinarius mucosus* (not shown), found in the Northwest, and (6) *C. mucigeneus* (not shown), found in the East.

BLUEGILL WEBCAP *Cortinarius delibutus*   **Pl. 36**
Medium-sized, *shiny yellow cap,* on a *sticky, yellow-banded club-shaped stalk. No odor. Cap:* Broadly convex to nearly flat or broadly humped. Surface smooth and shiny, *sticky.* Yellow to orange-yellow, sometimes flushed with greenish yellow near margin when young; may have a brownish tinge in age. Margin

thin and incurved at first. Flesh thick on disc, tapering gradually toward margin; white above to grayish yellow and bluish
lilac just above gills. Gills close, notched at stalk, with a decurrent tooth extending down stalk; bluish lilac when young, light
brown at maturity. *Stalk: Club-shaped; tinged with bluish lilac at apex, banded with yellow below* (from *sticky remnants of
universal veil*). **Technical notes:** Cap 4–8 cm across. Stalk 5–8
× 0.5–1.5 cm. Spores subglobose; 7–9 × 5–7 μm in diameter.
Fruiting: Scattered to grouped; under conifers and aspen.
Northern U.S. and Canada. Summer and fall.
Edibility: European authors report it as edible but not highly
esteemed. Obviously not worth the risk of confusing it with
other "LBM's."
Similar species: Frequently confused with the many yellow
species of *Cortinarius* (webcaps) and related groups or genera.
The sticky layers on cap and stalk (sometimes in bands or
zones on stalk) and bluish violet gills (when young) and stalk
apex are important for identification, particularly when stalk
shape is verified in young and old specimens. (1) Several species of *Cortinarius* in section *Myxacium* (such as *C. collinitus*
and *C. delibutus*) have sticky stalks of similar color that are
cylindric (equal in diameter) or tapered downward. (2) Other
species, in section *Bulbopodium,* have bulbous stalks with an
angular rim on the bulb in the button stage, but this character
is often lost as they mature. (See Bluefoot Webcap, p. 291.) (3)
Species in subsection *Inoloma* of section *Cortinarius* (such as
C. traganus — not shown) *lack the slime layer* from the universal veil but may be more or less tacky in moist weather.

GOLDBAND WEBCAP *Cortinarius gentilis*   **Pl. 36**
Medium-sized, *smooth, brown, rounded* to *flat* or *depressed,*
thin *cap* on a *cylindrical, brown stalk zoned with golden yellow
veil fibrils. Cap:* Conic to humped, becoming rounded or flat,
sometimes with an arching limb and margin. Surface smooth,
moist, hygrophanous (water-soaked) at first, but soon drying
out; strong brown to brownish orange when fresh, drying
lighter and more dull orange-yellow. Flesh thin, orange. Odor
not distinctive. *Gills subdistant,* adnate, *broad* (see inside front
cover); strong *brown, even in young caps. Stalk:* Cylindric,
sometimes tapered toward base. Surface fibrillose; brown, usually darkest at base. Universal veil usually forms a zone of
vivid yellow fibrils about midway on stalk. **Technical notes:**
Cap 2–5 cm across. Stalk 3–8 cm × 3–9 mm. Spores 7–9 × 6–7
μm.
Fruiting: Few to many; on moist (often mossy) soil. Common
in western coniferous forests; less common in the East. Summer and fall.
Edibility: Poisonous.
Similar species: Specimens having all important recognition
characters in perfect condition are recognized quite readily,

but these characters are quite short-lived in Goldband Webcap (*C. gentilis*), rendering it very easy to confuse with numerous other little brown mushrooms. The colors and hygrophanous (water-soaked) character of all parts fade quickly on drying in species such as this that have very thin flesh and widely spaced gills. Consequently, this is a very dangerous species.

BLUE-FOOT WEBCAP *Cortinarius glaucopus*   **Pl. 36**
Medium to large, *yellow* to *olive* or *brownish orange* cap on a *yellowish stalk flushed with blue-green at apex.* **Cap:** Convex at first, later flat or with a shallowly depressed disc. Surface smooth, sticky; color varies from greenish or grayish yellow to olive-brown, sometimes tinged with brownish orange, *often streaked* toward margin and outer limb. Flesh thick across disc and inner limb; nearly white or tinged with violet but soon dingy yellowish. Odor not distinctive. *Gills* close, adnate (broadly attached), thin, narrow at first; *tinged with violet before gill color is obscured by mature spores.* **Stalk:** Solid; cylindric above a more or less evanescent bulb with a distinct rim. Dingy *yellowish, tinged with blue-green,* especially *near apex;* at first often more or less streaked with veil remnants. Universal veil fibrils violet, soon coated by spores and colored strong brown. **Technical notes:** Cap 4–10 cm across. Stalk 4–8 × 1.5–3 cm. Spores broadly ellipsoid; 7–9 × 4.5–5.5 μm.
Fruiting: Grouped to clustered; on soil in coniferous woods. Northern U.S. and Canada. Common in the West but seldom reported east of Great Plains. Summer and fall.
Edibility: Apparently eaten by some people, but **not recommended** due to difficulty of accurate identification.
Similar species: Easily confused with (1) several other species of *Cortinarius* and possibly also with poisonous species of *Hebeloma* (p. 300). The colors, together with the *streaked pattern* on the cap surface, are important recognition characters for Blue-foot Webcap *(C. glaucopus).*
Remarks: Unfortunately, very few webcaps can be recognized with certainty in the field. The blue-green tints on young gills and both surface and interior of stalk in Blue-foot Webcap (*C. glaucopus*) are ephemeral and emphasize the necessity of recording such data in the field as soon as the mushroom is picked.

HELIOTROPE WEBCAP *Cortinarius heliotropicus*   **Pl. 36**
Small to medium, *slimy, heliotrope violet cap* and *stalk. Violet* to *brown gills. Grows on soil.* **Cap:** Convex to humped, expanding to flat; sometimes wavy on outer limb and margin. Surface *sticky when moist,* smooth; *light* to *dark purple,* usually *spotted, streaked,* or *splotched* with *orange-yellow.* Flesh tinged with violet at first, soon pallid; moderately thick on disc but thin over limb. Odor not distinctive. **Stalk:** Cylindric above a narrow, rounded bulb. Surface slimy; slime tinged with violet. Interior solid and tinged with violet above at first,

later becoming hollow. **Technical notes:** Cap 2–6 cm across. Stalk 4–8 × 0.5–1.2 cm. Spores 8–10 × 5.0–6.5 μm.

Fruiting: Single to grouped; on low ground under hardwoods. East of Great Plains. Summer and early fall.

Edibility: Unknown.

Similar species: Stature, coloration, and surface texture make this webcap a rather distinctive species. The *orange-yellow spots* are almost always present on some caps of a population. These help to distinguish Heliotrope Webcap (*C. heliotropicus*) from (1) the similarly colored and larger-spored *C. iodioides* (not shown), which has bitter-tasting slime, smaller spores, and fruits a little later in the same area. (2) The well-developed *violaceous slime layer* on *both cap and stalk* differentiate these webcaps from several species having sticky caps but *lacking slime* on stalks. Check young specimens.

Remarks: The pattern of coloration on the stalk of this species may be confusing, as the bulb is often whitest below the ground level, and the upper stalk, after the cap expands, is pallid to pale violet, soon tinged with orange-yellow or brown from the discharged spores that collect there.

HOARY WEBCAP *Cortinarius laniger*   **Pl. 36**
Medium to large, *moderate reddish brown, rounded cap* on a *robust, club-shaped stalk.* Grows *under conifers.* **Cap:** Rounded to bell-shaped; *subhygrophanous. Surface fibrillose;* moderate reddish brown, covered with *whitish fibrils,* giving it a *silvery or hoary cast* and sometimes a more or less spotted or streaked appearance when moist, drying to light brown. Margin whitish from veil remnants. Flesh light brown to nearly white. Odor not distinctive. Gills adnexed (notched); moderate reddish brown at first. **Stalk:** *Club-shaped* at first, with a bulbous base that is often not very evident at maturity. Solid, fleshy; *nearly white* over *reddish brown flesh* with *indistinct zones* or *patches* of *universal veil tissue* on lower part. **Technical notes:** Cap 4–10 cm across. Stalk 7–10 × 1–4 cm. Spores 8–10 × 5–6 μm.

Fruiting: Single to grouped; on soil under conifers. Northern U.S. and Canada; more common in the West. Late summer and fall.

Edibility: Unknown, but **not recommended.**

Remarks: Not easy to recognize because of the lack of distinctive field characters and considerable variability. The subhygrophanous character of cap and stalk is difficult to evaluate, and deceptive.

SORREL WEBCAP *Cortinarius orellanus*   **Pl. 36**
Medium-sized, *thin, reddish orange* to *brownish orange cap* on a *cylindrical, yellow stalk.* **Cap:** Bell-shaped, with a sharply inrolled margin at first, expanding to convex or flat, with a broad, low, rounded hump. Surface minutely fibrillose, tending to develop fine, depressed scales. Brownish orange to reddish

orange or dark grayish yellow. Margin thin, often flaring in age. Odor not distinctive. Gills subdistant, adnexed (notched), broad; brownish orange to dark orange-yellow. *Stalk:* Cylindrical, becoming hollow. Surface fibrillose; moderate yellow to moderate orange, with zones of reddish orange universal veil fibrils. Interior similar in color to surface but darker below. **Technical notes:** Cap 2–5 cm across. Stalk 3–6 × 0.4–0.7 cm. Spores 8–11 × 5.0–6.5 μm.

Fruiting: In groups; on beds of moss at high elevations in Rocky Mts. and Northwest. Summer and fall.

Edibility: Deadly poisonous.

Similar species: Many in *Cortinarius* and related genera. (1) Compare with Goldband Webcap (*C. gentilis,* p. 290). (2) A closely related European species, *C. speciosissimus* (not shown), which is likewise **deadly poisonous,** has a stalk colored more like the cap, with a zone of yellow universal veil remnants. It has not been recognized among the American species, but pothunters should watch for it and beware. Experimentation with any webcap in this group is both dangerous and foolish.

COPPER-RED WEBCAP *Cortinarius orichalceus*   **Pl. 36**
Large, firm, rounded or flat cap; reddish brown and yellow or greenish. Stalk has a *thick bulb* with a *distinct rim. Cap:* Convex at first, later almost flat, sometimes shallowly depressed. Surface smooth (hairless); old caps become cracked in dry weather. Reddish brown to deep orange on disc and light greenish yellow on outer limb and margin. Flesh thick; nearly white. Odor not distinctive. *Young gills greenish yellow. Stalk:* Solid, firm; *greenish yellow.* Distinctly bulbous; bulb *has a distinct rim.* **Technical notes:** Cap 5–10 cm across. Spores 10–12 × 5.5–7 μm. KOH (potash) on flesh turns green, then dark reddish brown.

Fruiting: In clumps, rings, or rows; under conifers. Western N. America. Late summer and fall.

Edibility: Unknown.

Similar species: (1) *Cortinarius rufoolivaceus* (not shown), which fruits in the same habitat and at the same time, has more violet and green colors and is dark grayish red overall when dried. (2) Many species resemble Copper-red Webcap *(C. orichalceus)* in size and stature, but the colors and particularly the potash reaction distinguish it.

Remarks: Most species of *Cortinarius* are mycorrhizal (have a symbiotic relationship with trees). We have seen the brightly colored caps of Copper-red Webcap appear in a straight line for as much as 6 meters (20 ft.) as if following a tree root.

REDGILL WEBCAP *Cortinarius semisanguineus*   **Pl. 36**
Medium to large, *orange-yellow* to *brown cap* — not hygrophanous. *Red gills. Yellow stalk. Single* to *clustered. Cap:* Obtuse to bell-shaped or convex, becoming flat, often with a rounded

knob. *Surface fibrillose,* tending to become *minutely hairy* or *scaly when dry;* light orange-yellow to light brown. Odor not distinctive. Gills close to crowded, adnate (broadly attached); moderate red to reddish brown. *Stalk:* Cylindric, sometimes tapered slightly at base; colored like cap or duller. Surface fibrillose, with remnants of poorly developed universal veil forming an indistinct ring near apex. **Technical notes:** Cap 3–9 cm across. Stalk 3–8 × 0.3–0.7 cm. Spores thick-walled, rough, elliptic; 6.0–8.5 × 3.5–5.0 μm. Some basidia have red content when revived in KOH (potash).

Fruiting: Single and scattered to clustered; on soil in forested areas. Widely distributed. Summer and fall.

Edibility: Unknown, but **not recommended,** as some of its close relatives are poisonous.

Similar species: The *blood-red gills* are found on several species of *Cortinarius.* A spore print must be obtained and young, fresh caps examined for the presence of a *"Cobwebby" universal veil* to verify the genus. Once this is determined, the combination of orange-yellow stalk, red gills, and non-hygrophanous orange-yellow cap sets Redgill Webcap *(Cortinarius semisanguineus)* apart. Both (1) *Cortinarius sanguineus* and (2) *Cortinarius californicus* (not shown) have red cap, gills, and stalk, but *C. californicus* has a *hygrophanous* (water-soaked) cap. (3) *Cortinarius phoenecius* (not shown) has a red cap and gills, but the stalk is orange-yellow as in Redgill Webcap.

SPLENDID WEBCAP *Cortinarus splendidus*   **Pl. 36**
Distinguished from Greased Webcap *(C. collinitus)* by microscopic characters and *less distinct zones or rings* formed by tissues of veil and outer stalk layers.

Fruiting: Great Lakes to Northeast.

Edibility: Unknown, but **not recommended.**

VIOLET WEBCAP *Cortinarus violaceus*   **Pl. 36**
Medium to large; *dark violet* to *dark purple overall, except for rusty brown spores. Grows on ground,* in *both coniferous* and *hardwood forests. Cap:* Convex to flat, with a low, rounded hump. Surface coarsely fibrillose, developing *small, soft,* more or less *erect scales.* Margin thin. Flesh thick over disc, tapering sharply to mid-limb, firm; light violet. Colors of surface and flesh do not change when cut or bruised. Gills subdistant, adnexed (notched), broad; moderate violet, flushed with warm brown as spores mature. *Stalk:* Firm, solid, or with a narrow hollow channel; cylindrical to club-shaped and tapering upwards from a rounded, often bent base. Interior colored like cap flesh at apex, lighter downwards. Violet fibrils of universal veil disappear at an early stage. **Technical notes:** Cap 5–12 cm across. Stalk 6–12 × 0.5–3.0 cm. Spores elliptic; 12–16 × 8–10 μm. Both pleurocystidia and cheilocystidia abundant, often with violet content that becomes purplish red in KOH (potash).

Fruiting: Solitary to scattered; on rich forest soil. Hardwood forests, from southern Canada to mid-South in U.S. Not uncommon in fall at times.

Edibility: Edible but unattractive. Probably best to avoid it.

Similar species: Frequently confused with any one of a great many species of *Cortinarius* which have some violaceous or purplish colors; few of these, however, have the more or less uniform, deep to almost blackish violet or purple colors peculiar to Violet Webcap *(C. violaceus)*. The main exception is (1) *Cortinarius hercynicus* (not shown), found in conifer forests of our western mountains. The two are very difficult to distinguish in the field, but the smaller, rounder spores of *C. hercynicus* distinguish them readily. (2) He-Goat (*Cortinarius traganus,* not shown) has a *much more copious veil* as well as lighter, pale violet colors that are soon flushed with or replaced by *yellowish to brown tones.* (3) Many violet-colored species of *Cortinarius* have *moist to sticky or slimy cap or stalk surfaces,* in contrast to the dry, fibrillose to minutely scaly surfaces of Violet Webcap.

Stumpfoots: Genus *Crepidotus*

There are more than 100 species of *Crepidotus* in N. America, most of which are indistinguishable on field characters. As a group they are quite distinctive, however; see below.

SOFT STUMPFOOT *Crepidotus mollis*   **Pl. 37**
Small to medium, *white* to *brownish, fan-shaped cap, laterally attached.* Grows *on hardwood debris.* **Cap:** Convex, becoming nearly flat; occasionally smooth and nearly white when young but *soon becoming fibrillose or scaly,* with small, soft, *orange-yellow to yellowish brown fibrils and scales.* Flesh soft, thin; white. Gills close, broad; pallid at first, but becoming dull brown as spores mature. **Stalk:** Rudimentary or lacking. No veil. **Spore print:** Moderate brown. **Technical notes:** Cap 1.5–5.0 cm across. Spores smooth, broadly elliptic; 7–10 × 4.5–6.5 μm. Cheilocystidia filamentous or swollen at base. Clamps lacking on hyphae.

Fruiting: Solitary or clustered; on decaying hardwood. Widespread in N. America. Spring to fall.

Edibility: Unknown.

Similar species: The combination of the *brown spore print, laterally attached cap,* and small to medium size makes stumpfoot mushrooms (*Crepidotus*) quite distinctive among genera growing on wood, if all 3 characters are considered. If a good spore print is not obtained, these fungi may be confused easily with (1) numerous small species of Tricholomataceae in several genera (see pp. 133–195) that have *white* to *dingy cream* or *pale violet spore prints.* (2) *Crepidotus applanatus* (not shown) has a cap that is smooth to downy, but not scaly, and more or less *fuzzy-edged gills* (use hand lens) with smaller spores. (3) *Crepidotus lanuginosus* (not shown) is a very small, white species found on decaying conifer logs, usually around melting snowbanks in our western mountains. (4) A very large (4–13 cm), white, southern species with a *sticky cap* and brown-staining gills is Giant Stumpfoot (*C. maximus,* not shown). (5) Spotted Stumpfoot (*C. maculans,* not shown), a small to medium species with a smooth, white cap that develops *small black spots* in age, fruits commonly on hardwood slash in the Great Lakes area. Some species of *Crepidotus* are more brightly colored: (6) Red Stumpfoot (*C. cinnabarinus,* not shown) is a northern species found from the Great Lakes eastward; and (7) Yellow Stumpfoot (*C. subnidulans,* not shown) is found from Missouri to the Chesapeake Bay and southward. Its more or less *salmon pink spore print, bright orange-yellow cap,* and very thin, *widely spaced gills* are most unusual in the genus *Crepidotus.*

Remarks: The amount and coloration of the surface fibrils varies greatly in Soft Stumpfoot *(C. mollis).* Some caps appear smooth and hairless except under a lens.

Skullcaps: Genus *Galerina*

AUTUMN SKULLCAP *Galerina autumnalis*   **Pl. 37**
Small to medium, *thin, brown, shallow, rounded* to *flat cap* and *thin, brown stalk. Scattered to clustered on wood.* **Cap:** Surface smooth, with a thin sticky layer. Strong brown to yellow-brown or brownish orange, fading quickly to dingy pale orange-yellow. Margin has translucent streaks. Flesh thin; brown. Odor not distinctive or faint and like that of cucumbers. Gills close, adnate (broadly attached) or subdecurrent (extending slightly down stalk); brownish, darkening in age. **Stalk:** Cylindric; brown, with whitish fibrils on surface and a *thin, fibrillose ring* high on stalk; surface darkens in age. *Interior dark brown at base, lighter* above. Ring sometimes not evident on mature specimens. **Technical notes:** Cap 2.5–6.0 cm across. Stalk 2–7 cm × 3–8 mm. Spores thick-walled, minutely roughened, lacking a germ pore; elliptic; 8–11 × 5.0–6.5 μm. Cheilocystidia fusiform (spindle-shaped) to fusoid-ventricose. Pleurocystidia similar; 40–65 × 9–12 μm.

Fruiting: Single to grouped or in large clusters; on decaying hardwood or conifer logs, stumps, and so on. Widespread. Typically fruits in autumn, but sometimes in spring and summer also.

Edibility: Deadly poisonous.

Similar species: (1) *Galerina venenata* (not shown), which has been shown to have the same toxins, grows on *grassy soil,* but is very similar in appearance. (2) Several other wood-rotting species of *Galerina* could be mistaken for Autumn Skull-

cap *(G. autumnalis)* and all may be poisonous. *Galerina margi-
nata* (not shown) *lacks a ring* on mature specimens. (3) Many
other "little brown mushrooms" in several genera are often
confused with these poisonous Galerinas and microscopic examination is often necessary to be sure of their identification.
The brown stalk interior, dark at base and lighter above, is a
good field mark for Autumn Skullcap *(G. autumnalis)*, but it is
also found in some brown, wood-rotting species of many other
genera, some of which are as closely related as *Gymnopilus*
(flamecaps—next group). Some species with a brown stalk interior are as distantly related as the Honey Mushroom *(Armillaria mellea)* in family Tricholomataceae (p. 136). *Spore print
color* will help to distinguish many of them, however. Honey
Mushroom, for example, has a *white* spore print.

Flamecaps: Genus *Gymnopilus*

Medium to large gill fungi. Cap firm; usually *yellow or orange.*
Cap does not separate readily from stalk. Flamecaps usually
grow on *decaying wood.* Spore print orange to grayish orange
or bright yellowish brown.

BLUE-GREEN FLAMECAP   Pl. 37
Gymnopilus punctifolius
Medium to large, *orange-brown, hygrophanous cap, gills,* and
stalk. All parts *flushed with blue-green.* Grows *on decaying
wood.* **Cap:** Convex to nearly flat, often with a low, rounded
hump. Surface smooth or minutely scaly toward center; may
be purplish pink to dull green at first, becoming *orange-brown,*
flushed with various tones of blue, green, or yellow, as it matures. Odor not distinctive. Gills greenish yellow when young,
becoming brown with a reddish orange cast as spores mature.
Stalk: Cylindric, but usually twisted, flattened, bent or contorted. Surface fibrillose; colored like cap, staining yellow to
dark yellow when cut or bruised. No ring. **Technical notes:**
Cap 2.5–10 cm across. Stalk 5–15 × 0.5–1.5 cm. Spores 4–6 ×
3.5–4.5 μm. Pleurocystidia and cheilocystidia similar; 20–40 ×
3–5 μm, capitate (enlarged at tip).
Fruiting: Solitary or in small clusters; on decaying conifer
wood. Rocky Mts. westward. Not uncommon, but typically
few found at one time. Fall.
Edibility: Suspect.
Remarks: The fresh brown color, with striking overtones of
green, blue, or yellow, makes this species quite easy for an experienced collector to recognize among the fall wood rotters, if
one has fresh specimens of different ages and a good spore
print.
FIR FLAMECAP   Pl. 37
Gymnopilus sapineus
Medium to large, *dry, orange-yellow cap and stalk.* Grows on

conifer wood, especially *slashings. Cap:* Convex to flat. Surface *strong orange-yellow* beneath a thin, brownish layer of fibrils or minute scales. Odor pungent. Gills close, broad; yellow at first. *Stalk:* Cylindric; surface fibrillose, dull orange yellowish. Ring fibrillose, yellow; often not evident on mature specimens. *Spore print:* Bright orange-brown. **Technical notes:** Cap 3–9 cm across. Stalk 3–8 × 0.4–1.0 cm. Spores elliptic; 7–10 × 4.0–5.5 μm. Cheilocystidia capitate or with rounded tips; 25–40 × 5–7 μm. Clamps present on hyphae. **Fruiting:** Single to clustered; on conifer logs, debris, or sawdust piles. Widely distributed in late summer and fall.

Edibility: Unknown, but **not recommended,** as others of this genus are **poisonous** (see below).

Similar species: Smaller size and the fairly rudimentary, often evanescent, fibrillose ring distinguish Fir Flamecap (*Gymnopilus sapineus*) from (1) Showy Flamecap or Big Laughing Mushroom (*G. spectabilis,* below), which is **poisonous.** (2) *Gymnopilus bellulus* (not shown), which is common on conifer stumps and logs in northern forests, is smaller than Fir Flamecap (*G. sapineus*), more reddish brown, and never forms a ring on the stalk. (3) Species of *Pholiota* (p. 270, Pl. 33) have a darker spore print.

SHOWY FLAMECAP *Gymnopilus spectabilis*   **Pl. 37**
(BIG LAUGHING MUSHROOM)
Medium to large, *orange-yellow cap* and *stalk; gills lighter. Stalk thick.* Grows in *large clumps on decaying wood. Cap:* Broadly convex, becoming flat, often with a broad, low, rounded hump. Surface fibrillose to fibrillose scaly, strong orange-yellow flushed with strong brown. Flesh thick, tapering very gradually to the thin margin; firm, pale yellow. Odor not distinctive; taste bitter (**poisonous**—do not try it).* Gills crowded, adnate (broadly attached) or subdecurrent, narrow; yellow, becoming orange-yellow and finally yellowish brown as spores mature. *Stalk:* Cylindric or narrowly club-shaped, tapering at base; solid, firm. Yellow above ring, orange-yellow flushed with brown below; streaked. Interior yellow at apex to brownish orange at base. Ring thin, sometimes lacking in old specimens. *Spore print:* Orange-brown. **Technical notes:** Cap 5–15 cm across. Stalk 5–15 × 0.8–2.5 cm. Spores 7.5–10.5 × 4.5–6.0 μm. FeSO₄ turns olive on cap and stalk. KOH (potash) turns reddish brown on flesh.

Fruiting: Usually clustered, on logs, stumps, buried wood, or roots of hardwood and coniferous trees, widespread. Throughout the season.

Edibility: Poisonous—sometimes hallucinogenic. Sometimes reported as non-poisonous, but we have seen people in Maryland made very ill by this flamecap *(Gymnopilus spectabilis).*

---

* See p. 10 for cautions about using taste as an identifying characteristic.

Similar species: (1) Do not mistake this poisonous *Gymnopilus* for one of the edible chanterelles (*Cantharellus,* p. 81, Pl. 7). (2) *Gymnopilus ventricosus* (not shown), found on wood of conifers in western N. America, has generally lighter colors, a more scaly cap surface, a stalk that is broader in lower part, and smaller spores (see **Remarks**). (3) *Gymnopilus validipes* (not shown) grows on stumps of hardwoods from the Great Lakes eastward. Like *G. spectabilis* (Showy Flamecap), it is poisonous. These 3 species of *Gymnopilus* look *very much alike* and **none of them should be eaten.** Similar colors, stature, and habitats cause frequent confusion between *G. spectabilis* and (4) Jack-O-Lantern (*Omphalotus illudens,* p. 178, Pl. 17), but their different spore print colors distinguish them readily: Jack-O-Lantern has a *white* to *yellowish* spore print (not orange-brown, as in *G. spectabilis*). (5) See also False Chanterelle (*Hygrophoropsis aurantiacus,* p. 154, Pl. 16).

Remarks: The present state of knowledge of species in the *G. spectabilis* complex indicates that although *G. spectabilis* causes serious poisoning, some closely related species apparently do not, at least for some people. Too little is known about *G. ventricosus* to recommend its use. We regard all species of *Gymnopilus* as dangerous and caution against their possible use for food or "recreation." Anyone tempted to take these mushrooms for their possible hallucinogenic effects should weigh carefully whether or not it is worth the high probability of serious and painful illness.

ORANGE FLAMECAP   Pl. 37
Gymnopilus terrestris

Medium-sized, *orange, hygrophanous cap, stalk, and gills. Single* or *in small clusters on soil in western conifer forests.* **Cap:** Broadly convex to flat, often lobed or irregular in outline. Surface smooth; uniformly orange or strong orange and orange-yellow on disc, grading outwards to strong brown, sometimes with an orange-yellow margin. Odor and taste not distinctive.* Gills close, adnate (broadly attached); dark orange-yellow at first, becoming darker and brighter as spores mature. **Stalk:** Cylindric, usually tapering upwards. Surface fibrillose; orange-yellow, staining brownish at base. No ring. **Spore print:** Yellowish brown. **Technical notes:** Cap 2.5–5.0 cm across. Stalk 3.5–6.0 × 0.7–1.5 cm. Spores ovoid (egg-shaped) to elliptic; 5.5–7.0 × 4.0–5.5 μm; dextrinoid (spores stain reddish brown in iodine).

Fruiting: *Singly* or in *small clusters; on soil in conifer forests.* Western U.S. and Canada. Late summer and fall.

Edibility: Suspect. Only the foolhardy experiment with little brown mushrooms, especially species of *Gymnopilus* or *Cortinarius.*

Similar species: The growth habit—on *soil,* not wood—is unusual for a flamecap *(Gymnopilus).* Microscopic characters also suggest a species of *Cortinarius* (webcap, pp. 287–295).

The orange colors in the range characteristic of *Gymnopilus*, the yellowish brown spore print color, and the complete lack of a veil are found in some webcaps (species of *Cortinarius*).

Poison Pie and Others: Genus *Hebeloma*

Small to large, usually sticky brown cap, firmly attached to stalk. Gills notched, often whitish. Stalk has remnants of fibrillose veil in some species, but is not ringed. Spore print dull yellowish brown.

POISON PIE *Hebeloma crustuliniforme*   **Pl. 37**
Medium to large, *rounded, cream-colored* to *brownish cap;* surface *smooth. Odor radish-like. Young gills* have *watery droplets on edges. Robust stalk.* **Cap:** Convex, with an inrolled margin at first, later broadly rounded to flat, often with a low, rounded hump. Surface has a thin sticky layer. Yellowish white on margin and outer limb, grading to grayish yellow on disc in young caps and light brown to light reddish brown over disc and inner limb at maturity. Flesh firm; white to brownish. *Odor of radishes.* Gills close, narrow, adnexed (notched); dingy yellowish white at first, becoming yellowish brown as spores mature. Gills beaded with minute droplets on edges when young. **Stalk:** Solid, abruptly bulbous; surface fibrillose to scurfy. Dingy yellowish white, sometimes darkening slightly at base. No veil. **Technical notes:** Cap 4–10 cm across. Stalk 4–9 × 0.7–2.0 cm. Spores thick-walled, minutely roughened (under highest magnification); elliptic. Cheilocystidia clavate (club-shaped) with rounded but not capitate tips; 50–85 × 7–9 μm. **Fruiting:** Single to grouped, sometimes in "fairy rings"; on soil under conifers or hardwoods. Widely distributed. Late summer and fall.
Edibility: Poisonous.
Similar species: (1) *Hebeloma sinapizans* (not shown) is also **poisonous.** It is darker, larger, and has a distinctly scaly stalk. (2) *Hebeloma sporadicum* (not shown) is similar, but lacks the radish-like odor and is also larger. It is found under spruce trees in the Great Lakes area.
DARK DISK *Hebeloma mesophaeum*   **Pl. 37**
Small to medium, *brown, shiny cap. Slender,* more or less *hairy, thin-ringed stalk. Radish-like odor.* **Cap:** Rounded, sometimes humped. Surface smooth, with a thin sticky layer. Moderate brown on disc when fresh, with a lighter outer limb and margin. Flesh firm; whitish, brown in stalk. *Odor radish-like.* Gills close, broad, adnate to adnexed (see inside front cover); dingy yellowish white to brownish, finally moderate brown with whitish; minutely hairy edges (use hand lens). **Stalk:** Cylindric, *slender.* Surface fibrillose-striate with a *thin, fibrillose ring.* Nearly white at apex, gradually becoming darker downward to brown at base (interior deep brown).

Technical notes: Cap 2–6 cm across. Stalk 3–9 × 0.3–0.7 cm. Spores minutely wrinkled, elliptic; 8–11 × 5–8 μm. Cheilocystidia 25–65 μm long; ventricose to subcylindric. Pleurocystidia lacking.

Fruiting: Grouped to scattered; on soil in coniferous forests, sometimes in bare or mossy places. Widespread in northern U.S. and Canada. Fall, occasionally in spring also.

Edibility: Reported as **poisonous.** Avoid all Hebelomas.

Similar species: The combination of a thin, non-membranous ring consisting of a zone of fibrils, as in the genus *Cortinarius* (webcaps), and a stalk, which is darker brown at base than above helps to distinguish Dark Disk from related species of *Heboloma. Heboloma gregarium* (not shown), for example, has a similar fibrillose ring, a dingy yellowish cap, and a more uniformly colored whitish stalk.

Fiberheads: Genus *Inocybe*

Small to medium gill fungi. Cap is *continuous* with slender stalk. Spore print dull yellowish brown. Spores smooth to angular or nodulose (under a microscope), with no germ pore.

CONIC FIBERHEAD *Inocybe fastigiata*   **Pl. 37**
Small to medium, *conic, brown caps;* surface *streaked* or *split. Twisted stalk. Cap:* Narrowly *conic* or bell-shaped, with an incurved margin at first, later becoming almost flat with an upturned margin and a narrow knob on disc. Surface fibrillose, with shallow cracks or *streaks* radiating from center. Yellowish brown. Margin lobed; typically split. Flesh thin; dingy white to yellowish. Odor of green corn or spermatic. Gills close, adnexed (notched); whitish, soon becoming olive to olive-brown. *Stalk:* Cylindric, sometimes tapered slightly upwards. Surface minutely fibrillose, twisted, streaked; dingy white to brownish. No ring. **Technical notes:** Cap 2–5 cm across. Stalk 4–8 × 0.3–1.0 cm. Spores smooth, elliptic; 9–15 × 5–7 μm. Cheilocystidia abundant; thin-walled, clavate (club-shaped).

Fruiting: Solitary to grouped; on bare, mossy, or grassy soil in open woods, pastures, or even on dunes. Widespread. Summer and fall.

Edibility: Poisonous.

Similar species: Many fiberheads (Inocybes) look like this and can not be distinguished in the field. Fortunately, they are fairly recognizable as Inocybes, as all are suspected of being poisonous.

EARTHBLADE FIBERHEAD *Inocybe geophylla*   **Pl. 37**
Small white, thin, fibrillose cap with a pointed knob. Slender white stalk. Cap: Conic to bell-shaped, soon broadly conic with a persistent, *pointed knob* and frequently a more or less lobed margin. Surface minutely radially fibrillose with a silky sheen; white or lilac at first, becoming dingy brownish in age.

Flesh thin except on disc. Odor variously described as earthy, nauseating, disagreeable, or spermatic. Gills close, adnate to notched, broad, becoming ventricose; colored like cap when young, becoming moderate yellowish brown as spores mature. *Stalk:* Cylindric. Color and surface texture like that of cap, with an indistinct zone of universal veil fibrils above. **Technical notes:** Cap 1.5–4.0 cm across. Stalk 2–6 × 0.2–0.4 cm. Spores smooth, thick-walled, elliptic, more or less inequilateral in profile; 7.5–10 × 4.5–6.0 μm. Pleurocystidia abundant.

Fruiting: Scattered to grouped; sometimes in small clumps on soil, in coniferous or hardwood forests, often in open or grassy places or under shrubs. Widespread. Summer and fall.

Edibility: Poisonous. Avoid all Inocybes.

Similar species: This is a very large genus with few species that can be reliably identified in the field. However, experienced collectors soon learn to recognize the genus, if not the species. This is important, as many Inocybes are poisonous.

Remarks: Several varieties of this species have been described. The white variety is less common than Lilac Earthblade (*I. geophylla* var. *lilacina*). Both the white and lilac forms flatten out in age, resembling a miniature Japanese umbrella. Both become brownish with age.

FLUFF FIBERHEAD *Inocybe lanuginosa*   **Pl. 37**
Small to medium, *dark brown cap;* surface *dry,* with *fluffy scales. Slender stalk. Grows on well-rotted wood. Cap:* Convex or hemispheric to bell-shaped at first, finally with a low, broad, rounded hump on disc. Surface dry; densely clothed with small, raised to erect, soft, fibrillose scales. Cap (cuticle) more or less uniformly dark brown; flesh lighter brown. Odor not distinctive. Gills subdistant, adnexed (notched); light yellowish brown at first, then strong brown when spores mature. *Stalk:* Cylindric; brownish, with a covering of soft, raised or recurved, dark brown scales. Universal veil brown, sparse, leaving no ring on stalk. **Technical notes:** Cap 1.5–4.0 cm across. Stalk 2.5–6.0 × 0.2–0.8 cm. Spores thick-walled, nodulose; 8–10 × 5–7 μm. Pleurocystidia thin-walled; 50–60 × 12–18 μm.

Fruiting: Solitary or in small clumps; on decaying logs, stump, or buried wood. Common but never abundant. Widespread in both coniferous and hardwood forests. Summer and fall.

Edibility: Poisonous.

Similar species: Several small, brown, scaly Inocybes can not be distinguished on field characters.

Genus *Rozites*

GYPSY NITECAP *Rozites caperata*   **Pl. 37**
Medium to large, *orange-yellow cap; hoarfrosted on disc, wrinkled near margin. Fleshy, whitish stalk with a persistent white*

ring. Spores brown. **Cap:** Rounded with an incurved, wrinkled margin, expanding to broadly bell-shaped or nearly flat with a low, rounded hump. Surface dry; smooth on disc and orange-yellow to yellow-brown (sometimes with gray-brown tones at first) beneath very minute whitish fibrils, lighter colors outward. Margin broadly grooved, wrinkled or scalloped. Flesh white, unchanging when cut or bruised, thick, firm. Odor and taste not distinctive. Gills close, broad, adnate, becoming adnexed; pale orange-yellow, then brownish orange as spores mature. Gill edges often remaining lighter, sometimes wrinkled (use hand lens). **Stalk:** Cylindric; sometimes expanded at base. Dingy white or pale brownish; sometimes showing an obscure zone from the universal veil. Ring about midway on stalk. **Technical notes:** Cap 5-10 cm across. Spores finely warty, elliptic in face view, inequilateral in profile; 11–14 × 7–9 μm. **Fruiting:** Scattered to grouped; on soil in both coniferous and hardwood forests, often abundant. Widespread in N. America. Summer and early fall.

Edibility: Edible and highly regarded.

Similar species: A distinctive species, if one pays attention to details, but it resembles a species of *Cortinarius* (webcap) with a membranous, not fibrillose ring. The veils are different, however. Gypsy Nitecap *(Rozites caperata)* has both a membranous partial veil, which leaves a well-developed ring about midway on the stalk, and a sparse, fibrillose universal veil, which frosts the cap surface and may leave a faint suggestion of a second ring near the base of the stalk. When both veils are present in *Cortinarius,* they are both fibrillose or cobwebby and do not leave a membranous ring.

Remarks: This mushroom is widely known in Europe as Gypsy Mushroom, but in Sweden it has the charming name of "Granny's Nitecap," perhaps from the broadly wrinkled or lobed cap margin and frequently projecting collar in the button stage.

Genus *Tubaria*

FLAKY SCALECAP *Tubaria furfuracea*   **Pl. 37**
Small to medium, *hygrophanous, smooth, brown,* more or less *fragile cap* with *wispy margin. Slender stalk. Grows on soil or decaying wood.* **Cap:** Slightly convex to flat. Surface moist; at first covered sparsely with wispy flecks of dull dingy yellowish veil remnants, often in a more or less concentric pattern, disappearing or evident only on the margin at maturity. Brownish orange to strong brown, fading to pale, dingy yellowish brown. Flesh thin, fragile; brownish. Odor and taste not distinctive. Gills broad, subdistant, broadly adnate, becoming subdecurrent (see inside front cover); colored like cap or darker at maturity, lighter when young. **Stalk:** Cylindric; hollow, fragile.

Surface smooth to minutely fibrillose, with scattered fibrillose flecks from universal veil; woolly white at base. *Spore print:* Light yellowish brown. **Technical notes:** Cap 1–4 cm across. Stalk 2–5 cm × 2–4 mm. Spores thin-walled, smooth, elliptic; 6.0–8.5 × 4–6 µm.

Fruiting: Scattered to grouped; on soil along side trails, road-sides, waste places or in forests, often on decaying twigs and chips. Widespread. Throughout the season.

Edibility: Probably harmless, but easy to confuse with *poisonous* Galerinas (see below).

Similar species: (1) Numerous other species of *Tubaria* are distinguished mostly on microscopic characters. The lighter spore print and smooth spores distinguish Flaky Scalecap from similar small, fragile species of (2) *Cortinarius* (p. 287) and (3) *Galerina* (p. 296).

Earthscales and Fairy Bonnets: Family Bolbitiaceae

Spore print grayish brown to bright rusty or yellowish brown. Often small and fragile (cap deliquesces in one genus). Microscopic characters of spores (smooth with apical pore) and cap cuticle (globose cells to hymeniform layer) often needed for definite identification of family. Both poisonous and edible species included.

Earthscales: Genus *Agrocybe*

Small to medium gill fungi. Cap white to yellow, brown, or olive, with a smooth surface. Stalk may be ringed or not. Mature gills and spore print dark yellowish brown. Spores have a thick, smooth, brown wall with a germ pore that is sometimes truncated (squared off).

MAPLE EARTHSCALE *Agrocybe acericola*   **Pl. 38**
Medium-sized, *hygrophanous, yellowish brown cap. Slender, white stalk. Grows on decaying hardwood logs. Cap:* Obtuse (bluntly convex) to *rounded* and humped, expanding to nearly flat in age. Surface smooth, moist; dark yellow-brown at first, later dark yellow while still hygrophanous. Margin incurved at first, opaque. Odor and taste not distinctive. Gills broad, adnate (broadly attached), sometimes with a decurrent tooth extending down stalk, close; dingy yellowish white at first, but grayish yellowish brown as spores mature. *Stalk:* Cylindric or slightly enlarged at base; hollow. Surface fibrillose; white at first, but becoming dark grayish yellowish brown at base and lighter above in age; apex remaining nearly white. Surface fibrillose-streaked; ring well developed, membranous, yellowish

white. *Spore print:* Dark grayish yellowish brown. **Technical notes:** Cap 3–9 cm across. Stalk 5–10 cm long. Spores ellipsoid, 8.0–0.5 × 5.0–6.5 μm; truncate. Pleurocystidia utriform to clavate-mucronate or with 2 or more apical projections. Cheilocystidia clavate (club-shaped).
Fruiting: Single to scattered; common on decaying hardwood logs and chips, especially maple. Widespread in N. America. Summer and fall.
Edibility: Not recommended.
Similar species: (1) Habitat (on soil) and lighter, non-hygrophanous colors distinguish *Agrocybe praecox* (not shown). Although their seasons overlap, *A. praecox* usually fruits earlier in the season. (2) Leather Earthscale (*A. erebia,* below) has more reddish brown colors, remaining dark until maturity. (3) *Agrocybe aegerita* (not shown) is usually on poplar or willow.

CRACKED EARTHSCALE *Agrocybe dura* **Pl. 38**
Small to medium, *yellowish, round to flat cap;* surface *cracks, showing white flesh. Firm, ringed stalk.* **Cap:** Broadly convex to nearly flat, sometimes with an obscure hump. Surface shiny, smooth and slightly sticky at first; soon develops shallow, often broad cracks, especially in dry weather. Nearly white to dingy pale yellowish. Flesh thick, soft. Odor not distinctive. Gills narrowly adnate, subdistant; whitish at first, but soon becoming dingy brown as spores mature. *Stalk:* Cylindric, usually tapering toward base, often stout, colored like cap; thin, cottony-fibrillose ring may leave an incomplete ring, wispy flecks on cap margin, or may disappear entirely on mature caps. *Spore print:* Dark grayish yellowish brown. **Technical notes:** Cap 3–12 cm across. Spores smooth, elliptic, with distinct germ pore; yellowish brown in KOH.
Fruiting: Scattered to grouped; in lawns, pastures, orchards, and grassy places in general. Widespread. Late spring and early summer.
Edibility: Edible. Be sure to get a spore print to distinguish it from deadly species of *Amanita* (p. 215).
Similar species: (1) *Agrocybe praecox* (not shown) has more brownish colors, smaller spores, and is found more commonly in wood-mulched plantings than in grassy places. (2) *Agaricus* species have free gills and darker, more purplish brown spore prints. (3) In the mid-Atlantic region and Southeast, *Stropharia hardii* (not shown), with a poorly developed ring, may be confused with Cracked Earthscale *(Agrocybe dura).*

LEATHER EARTHSCALE *Agrocybe erebia* **Pl. 38**
Medium to large, dark brown cap; surface *hygrophanous, wrinkled. Brown, ringed stalk.* **Cap:** Obtuse to rounded, becoming flat, often humped and with a broadly upturned margin in age. Surface smooth but typically radially wrinkled; sticky when young and moist. Dark brown to dark grayish brown, fading to yellowish or olive-brown. Flesh nearly white

at first, then brownish. Odor not distinctive. Gills subdistant, interveined, adnate to subdecurrent (see inside front cover); light grayish brown at first, becoming moderate brown. *Stalk:* Cylindric or tapering slightly. White and scurfy above, dull brown and fibrillose below the pallid, thin, membranous, persistent ring; darkest at base. *Spore print:* Moderate brown. **Technical notes:** Cap 3–9 cm across. Stalk 3.5–7.0 × 0.4–1.0 cm. Spores ellipsoid, with an elongated apex; 11–15 × 5.5–7.0 μm. Pleurocystidia fusoid-ventricose, with an obtuse apex; 40–75 × 9–15 μm. Cheilocystidia with a broad apex or fusoid-ventricose; 25–35 × 10–15 μm.

Fruiting: Single to grouped or clustered; on moist soil, in both hardwood and coniferous forests, often in luxuriant, fairly dark woods. Widespread in northern U.S. and Canada. Late summer and fall.

Edibility: Said to be edible but of inferior quality.

Similar species: Persistently darker colors (particularly brown stalk base) distinguish it from (1) Maple Earthscale (*A. acericola,* p. 304). Although both may have wrinkled cap surface, (2) Southern Earthscale (*A. aegerita*) has lighter, more reddish brown colors and is found only on wood — usually poplar.

ROUNDTOP EARTHSCALE *Agrocybe pediades*   **Pl. 38**
Small, rounded, dull brownish cap on a *very slender stalk.* Single or scattered *on grassy or disturbed soil.* **Cap:** Hemispheric to broadly rounded. Surface smooth; shiny and sticky when moist. Strong brown to strong yellowish brown at first, fading quickly to light yellowish brown or lighter. Flesh thick, whitish. Odor not distinctive. Gills close, adnate (broadly attached) but soon pulling free from stalk; pallid at first, becoming strong brown as spores mature. *Stalk:* Cylindric; fibrillose-furfuraceous. Yellowish white above, yellowish brown at base. Ring fibrillose, ephemeral. *Spore print:* Moderate brown. **Technical notes:** Cap 1.0–3.5 cm across. Stalk 2–5 cm × 1.5–3.0 mm. Spores thick-walled, with a distinct germ pore; elliptic, more or less compressed; truncate, 9–13 × 6.5–9.0 μm. Pleurocystidia and cheilocystidia fusoid-ventricose, with acute to subcapitate tips; 30–65 × 8–15 μm.

Fruiting: Solitary to grouped; on grassy areas, cultivated or disturbed soil, pasture land, etc. Common on bare or moss-covered soil in desert shrub zone. Widely distributed in N. America, throughout the growing season.

Edibility: Said to be edible, but **not recommended.** The risk of confusing it with a poisonous *Galerina, Hebeloma,* or *Inocybe* is too great, and the likelihood of finding enough for a meal too little to justify experimenting with one so small.

Similar species: Although common and widespread, the likelihood is great of confusing this with numerous other brown mushrooms of the same and other genera, as stated above. See (1) *Galerina* (p. 296), (2) *Hebeloma,* and (3) *Inocybe* (p. 301).

Remarks: In the complex of species around *A. pediades,* the name *Agrocybe semiorbicularis* is sometimes used for those with darker (brown) colors, slightly larger spores and sticky or tacky cap when moist. *A. pediades* then is restricted to those with lighter (more yellow) colors, smaller mean spore length, and non-viscid, sometimes broader cap. In this group of about 10 or more species are mostly small mushrooms, slender-stalked, and having fibrillose veil tissues which do not leave a conspicuous ring on the stalk. They are sometimes included in genus *Pholiota* (p. 270), but the microscopic structure of the cap cuticle separates them readily.

Genus *Bolbitius*

MANURE MUSHROOM   **Pl. 38**
Bolbitius vitellinus
Medium-sized, *thin, sticky, watery yellow cap* on a *thin, yellow stalk.* Grows *on manure* or *rich, moist soil.* **Cap:** Bell-shaped to conic, becoming broadly convex to flat, sometimes with depressed disc. Surface smooth, shiny; margin streaked or becoming grooved, sometimes somewhat warty. Flesh thin, soft; watery yellow. Gills close, ascending-adnate, thin, narrow; yellowish at first, tinged with rust as spores mature. ***Stalk:*** Cylindric; base often slightly expanded. Very fragile. Yellow, smooth beneath scattered soft hairs; base coated with whitish mycelium. ***Spore print:*** Moderate brown. **Technical notes:** Cap 2–6 cm across. Stalk 6–12 cm × 2–5 mm. Spores smooth, truncate with an apical pore, ellipsoid; 12–14 × 6–7 μm. Cheilocystidia saccate; 8–15 μm across. Cap cuticle consists of pyriform (pear-shaped) to saccate (sac-shaped) cells.
Fruiting: Single to clustered; on dung, in pastures, or bare soil. Widely distributed. Spring to fall.
Edibility: Unknown, but not likely to attract a following.
Similar species: May be mistaken for (1) a small, yellow inky cap *(Coprinus)* or (2) a roof mushroom *(Pluteus)*, but brown spore print and non-deliquescent gills readily distinguish it.

Genus *Conocybe*

Small to medium gill fungi. Cap usually conical to thimble-shaped, most often delicate or fragile. Stalk may have a ring. Spore print yellowish brown. Sterile cells on gill edge look bottle-shaped under a microscope. At least one species is deadly poisonous (see below).

WRINKLE RING *Conocybe arhenii*   **Pl. 38**
Small, fragile, brown cap on a slender, two-toned brown stalk with a cuff-like ring. **Cap:** Convex to bell-shaped or humped, eventually nearly flat, or flat with a depressed disc and sometimes an upturned outer limb and margin. Surface smooth, or

sometimes wrinkled or streaked; dark reddish brown to moderate brown on disc, lighter on limb with light brown to yellowish brown on margin. Flesh thin, brown. Odor not distinctive. Gills moderately close, narrowly notched, broad; yellowish brown. **Stalk:** Cylindric, sometimes slightly thickened toward base; hollow. Surface streaked and scurfy above, fibrillose-streaked below. Pale orange-yellow at apex, brown below to dark brown at base beneath surface scurf or fibrils. Ring about midway on stalk; felt-like and membranous or occasionally adhering to margin as minute scales. Upper surface streaked, and often coated with brown spore deposit. **Technical notes:** Cap 1–3 cm across. Stalk 2–6 cm × 1.5–3.0 mm. Spores ellipsoid, somewhat flattened on one side; 4–9 × 4–5 μm; thick-walled, with a narrow germ pore. Cheilocystidia densely packed, forming a sterile gill edge; narrowly fusoid-ventricose with obtuse apices to subcylindric, often flexuous (zigzag). Pleurocystidia lacking.

Fruiting: Solitary to grouped on soil; in open places or along trails or dirt roads in deciduous forests, parks, orchards, gardens, etc. Late summer and fall.

Edibility: Probably **poisonous.**

Similar species: (1) *Conocybe filaris* (not shown) — sometimes known as *Conocybe* or *Pholiota rugosa* — has a more distinctly wrinkled cap and cheilocystidia with narrower necks. Some species of the genus may be distinguished by habitat and time of fruiting, such as (2) *Conocybe stercoraria* and (3) *Conocybe fimicola* (not shown), which are found on animal dung in spring and early summer. (4) *Conocybe pinguis* and (5) *Conocybe intermedia* (not shown) grow on decaying hardwood logs and woody debris.

Remarks: Numerous species of *Conocybe* with ringed stalks are recognized with difficulty on field characters and are sometimes treated in a separate genus, *Pholiotina*. North American species of these charming, miniature mushrooms are not well known. Some are poisonous. This Conocybe and a number of other species have, until recently, been treated as a single species by American authors, under the name *Pholiota* (sometimes *Conocybe* or *Pholiotina*) *togularis*.

MILK BONNET *Conocybe lactea*   **Pl. 38**
Delicate whitish, conic to bell-shaped cap on a spindly stalk. Common in lawns on summer mornings. **Cap:** Slender and conic at first, expanding to narrowly bell-shaped. Surface smooth, white or tinged with pale yellow on disc. Flesh thin. Odor not distinctive. Gills close, very narrow; nearly white at first, becoming yellowish brown to brownish orange as spores mature. **Stalk:** Cylindric, with a slightly expanded base; hollow; very slender and fragile. Nearly white overall, or sometimes yellowish at base. Surface smooth beneath scattered, minute, soft white hairs. No ring. **Technical notes:** Cap 1.0–2.5 cm across. Stalk 4–9 cm × 1.5–3.0 mm. Spores thick-

walled, truncate; broadly elliptic; 11–15 × 7–9 μm. Cheilocystidia ninepin-shaped, with a rounded knob at tip. Cap cuticle
consists of compact, more or less pear-shaped cells.
Fruiting: Scattered to clustered on turf. Common on lawns,
pastures, parks, etc. Throughout northern N. America; less
common in the South. Summer.
Edibility: Unknown, but **not recommended,** as it could be
confused with a poisonous species of *Conocybe, Galerina,* or
Inocybe.
Similar species: The milky white, sometimes wrinkled
"dunce cap" on a spindly stalk and habitat help to distinguish
Milk Bonnet (*C. lactea*) from numerous other (1) Conocybes
and (2) Galerinas (p. 296). Unexpanded caps are commonly
confused with *Gastrocybe*—a Gastromycete relative of Manure Mushroom (*Bolbitius vitellinus,* p. 307) which often fruits
simultaneously in the same turf as Milk Bonnet. *Gastrocybe*
caps never expand, they are darker watery brown than Milk
Bonnet, and the whole mushroom is translucent.
Remarks: Like many others, this charming little mushroom
has a marvelous timing mechanism. From the northern Rocky
Mts. to the mid-Atlantic Coast we have observed this as a
warm-season mushroom characteristic of the midsummer flora.
Even so, it seemingly shuns the oppressive heat of midday and
afternoons. Its delicate white caps dot the green sward in the
cool dewy hours of early morning, then wilt and wither into
the grass, usually before noon.
RUSTY HOOD *Conocybe tenera*   **Pl. 38**
Delicate reddish brown, bell-shaped cap on a *like-colored,
fragile, ringless stalk.* **Cap:** Narrowly conic at first, becoming
broadly bell-shaped, often with a flaring margin or an upturned margin and limb. Surface smooth, hygrophanous—
orange-yellow when young, becoming brownish orange, fading
to yellowish pink. Flesh thin, brown. Odor not distinctive. Gills
subdistant, ascending-adnate, narrowly attached (see inside
front cover); yellowish at first, but becoming brown as spores
mature. **Stalk:** Cylindric and more or less enlarged at base;
hollow, fragile. Color of cap or lighter; surface streaked. No
ring. **Technical notes:** Cap 1.0–3.5 cm across. Stalk 4–8 cm ×
1.5–3.0 mm. Spores 7–10 × 5.5–7 μm; thick-walled, with a distinct germ pore. Pleurocystidia lacking. Cheilocystidia scattered, capitate (enlarged at tip). Cap cuticle consists of pear-
shaped cells.
Fruiting: Scattered to clustered; in grassy places such as
lawns and pastures. Widespread. Spring and summer.
Edibility: Unknown.
Similar species: Faded specimens may be mistaken for (1)
Milk Bonnet (*Conocybe lactea,* above), which grows in the
same habitat. Numerous small species of *Conocybe* and (2)
Galerina (p. 296) look so much alike that they can be distinguished only on microscopic characters. They have the same

stature as (3) species of *Mycena* (fairy helmets, p. 170), but Conocybes and Galerinas have brown spores, whereas Mycenas give white spore prints.

Pinkgills: Family Entolomataceae

Spore color and spore shape distinguish this family. Spores are some shade of pink and when seen under a microscope are angular to longitudinally streaked or grooved. Cap and stalk not readily separable; typically absent. Gills attached to stalk or free from it. Both edible and poisonous species included.

Pinkgills: Genus *Entoloma*

Small to medium (rarely large) gill fungi with *pink spores.* Caps of various shapes, firmly attached to stalks. Stalk slender to stout, ringless. Spores angular. This group includes some poisonous species.

ABORTED PINKGILL *Entoloma abortivum*   **Pl. 38**
Medium to *large, light brownish gray cap* with *grayish* to *pink gills. Pale stalk.* Often has *soft, whitish, irregular masses of tissue* ("aborted" form—see below) *nearby.* ***Cap:*** Broadly conic or rounded at first, expanding to convex or flat, often retaining a low, rounded hump and incurved margin. Surface smooth to fibrillose or becoming minutely scaly; sometimes indistinctly zoned and fading to grayish brown in age. Flesh soft, white, fragile. Odor and taste not distinctive.* Gills close, shallowly and narrowly notched at first, decurrent (extending down stalk) in age; grayish at first, but becoming pink as spores mature. ***Stalk:*** Cylindric or thicker downward, sometimes off-center; solid. Surface white to light gray; minutely fibrillose to scurfy, cottony white at base. No veil. ***Spore print:*** Pink. *"Aborted" form:* Sessile or with a *rudimentary* or *short stalk. Irregularly rounded* to *flattened; soft. Surface white; wrinkled* to *roughened* or *veined. Interior pale watery pink, marbled* or *veined. Solitary* or *in masses,* sometimes *fused.* **Technical notes:** Cap 4–10 cm across. Stalk 3–10 × 0.5–1.0 cm. Spores angular-elliptic. No cystidia.
Fruiting: Scattered or clumped; on soil, often around well-decayed logs. Widely distributed, common. Late summer and fall.
Edibility: Edible **with caution** but **not recommended.** Non-aborted forms are easily confused with poisonous species of *Entoloma* (see below).
Similar species: The aborted form is distinctive. It forms

---

* See p. 10 for cautions about using taste as an identifying characteristic.

when the *Entoloma* is parasitized by the common wood rotter *Armillaria mellea* (Honey Mushroom, p. 136). When aborted and non-aborted forms are found together, the species may be quite readily recognized. Non-aborted forms found by themselves are easily confused with other species of *Entoloma,* some of which are **poisonous,** such as *Entoloma lividum* (Gray Pinkgill), which is slightly more robust, often larger, has yellowish gills when young, and differs on microscopic characters.

GRAY PINKGILL *Entoloma lividum*   **Pl. 38**
Medium to large, *grayish cap* on a *thick white stalk. Mature gills pink; spore print pink.* Grows in oak woods. *Cap:* Convex to broadly humped at first, may be nearly flat or wavy in age, sometimes with a downturned margin. Surface smooth, slightly slippery when wet; not hygrophanous (water-soaked). Pale gray to brownish gray or pale grayish brown, brownish tones becoming more dominant as it ages. Flesh thick near stalk, firm; white. Odor faint and somewhat mealy. Gills adnate (broadly attached) to broadly and shallowly notched at stalk apex, close; pale grayish yellow when young, later becoming pink from maturing spores. *Stalk:* Cylindric; solid. Surface smooth or wavy, somewhat scurfy above and silky below. White; does not discolor from handling. **Technical notes:** Cap 5–15 cm across. Stalk 7–15 × 1.0–2.5 cm. Spores angular, subglobose; 7–10 μm. No cystidia.
Fruiting: Scattered or grouped; on soil in oak woods. Widespread east of Great Plains. Fall.
Edibility: Poisonous.
Similar species: Easily mistaken for a *Tricholoma* (p. 185) or possibly a *Clitocybe* (p. 138), especially when young — before spores have matured. A spore print is essential!

UNICORN PINKGILL *Entoloma murraii*   **Pl. 38**
Looks like a bright yellow version of Salmon Pinkgill (*Entoloma salmoneum,* below).
Fruiting: Uncommon but occasionally abundant on soil in hardwood and mixed forests. Great Lakes region eastward to mid-South. Summer and fall.
Edibility: Unknown, but see under Salmon Pinkgill.

SALMON PINKGILL *Entoloma salmoneum*   **Pl. 38**
Small to medium, *orange, conic cap with a nipple-like tip. Fragile, skinny, orange stalk. Cap:* Broadly conic to bell-shaped, with a *pointed tip.* Surface smooth, moist; margin translucent-streaked at first. *Salmon orange* when fresh, fading quickly as it dries. Flesh very thin on limb and margin. Odor not distinctive. Gills close to subdistant, broad, narrowly attached (see inside front cover); colored like cap. *Stalk:* Cylindric. Surface smooth, *colored like cap,* with soft white mycelium at base. *Spore print:* Pink. **Technical notes:** Cap 1–4 cm across. Stalk 4–8 cm × 1–3 mm. Spores angular, almost square in section; 9–12 μm across. No cystidia.
Fruiting: Scattered; on moist, often mossy soil or very well-

decayed wood in mixed woods or bogs, sometimes under rhodo-
dendrons. East of the Great Plains. Late summer and fall.

Edibility: We know of no reports, but definitely do not encourage experimenting with species of *Entoloma.*

Similar species: (1) Unicorn Pinkgill (*E. murraii,* above) is
bright yellow; otherwise the two are very similar. (2) The
bright colors suggest a waxycap (species of *Hygrophorus,* p.
202, Pls. 22–24). Spore print color separates them readily.

STRAIGHT-STALK PINKGILL *Entoloma strictior*   **Pl. 38**
Medium-sized, *dark brown* to *grayish brown, conic cap* on
a grayish stalk. Pink gills when mature. Fruits in early spring.
Cap: Conic to broadly conic or bell-shaped at first, often almost as wide as high, sometimes almost flat with a narrow,
pointed hump at maturity. Surface smooth, hygrophanous, often with translucent streaks at maturity. Flesh thin, brittle.
Odor and taste not distinctive.* Gills adnate, broad, subdistant, (see inside front cover); dingy white at first, becoming
pink as spores mature. *Stalk:* Very slender, cylindric or with a
slightly swollen base; fragile. Surface longitudinally or spirally
streaked or twisted; nearly white or tinged with cap color,
white and cottony at base. *Spore print:* Pink. **Technical
notes:** Cap 2.5–6.0 cm across. Stalk 6–12 × 0.3–1.0 cm. Spores
angular-elliptic; 6-sided, 9–12 × 6–8 µm. No cystidia.

Fruiting: Solitary to scattered; on moist ground or well-
decayed wood; frequent in bogs. East of Great Plains. Spring
to fall.

Edibility: Said to be **poisonous.**

Similar species: (1) Easily mistaken for a species of *Melanoleuca* (Cavalier, p. 169, Pl. 18), especially when young or before
spore print is obtained. (2) Numerous other species of *Entoloma* are reliably distinguished only with a microscope.

Brimcaps: Family Paxillaceae

A small family with a close relationship to the boletes (Boletaceae, p. 100) by the microscopic spore characteristics (dark
color, long and narrow, no germ pore) and slime layer above
gills, which allows them to be easily separated from cap flesh;
also gills frequently intervened. Spore print pale to dark yellowish or pinkish brown. Contains both edible and poisonous
species.

Brimcaps: Genus *Paxillus*

Cap thick-fleshed, with a gill layer that is easily peeled off
underside of cap. Cap firmly attached at center or at one side

---

* See p. 10 for cautions about using taste as an identifying characteristic.

to stalk, which is tough and solid. Gills narrow, close, decurrent (extending down stalk); often stain brownish when bruised. Spore print yellowish brown.

VELVET-FOOT BRIMCAP *Paxillus atrotomentosus*   **Pl. 38**
Large, brown, velvety cap; laterally attached by a *short, robust, velvety stalk* to *decaying conifer wood.* ***Cap:*** A shallow, rounded knob at first, expanding to more or less fan-shaped. Thick, dry surface; unpolished to velvety, sometimes with a matted layer of hairs. Dark orange-yellow to moderate brown or darker; sometimes blackish. Margin thin, hairy; long remaining inrolled. Flesh firm, thick; whitish. Gills close, narrow, long-decurrent (extending down stalk), forked to more or less poroid on decurrent portion; strong yellow, sometimes darkening when bruised. ***Stalk:*** Eccentric (off center) to nearly lateral, sometimes slightly narrowed upwards; solid, firm. Surface *densely velvety;* dark brown to brownish black, colored like gills at apex. ***Spore print:*** Moderate to strong yellowish brown. **Technical notes:** Cap 5–15 cm across. Stalk 3–12 × 1.0–2.5 cm. Spores smooth, dextrinoid, ovoid; 5–7 × 3–4 μm.
Fruiting: Single or in groups or clumps; on decaying conifer logs, stumps, roots or partially buried wood. Widely distributed. Summer and fall.
Edibility: Unknown, but hardly tempting.
Similar species: The close, decurrent, yellow gills and dark brown, stout, velvety cap and stalk make this a distinctive species. Although highly variable, it is easily recognized by beginners. The cap of *Paxillus panuoides* (not shown) is smaller, thinner, lighter colored, and is laterally attached *directly* to the woody substrate, lacking a stalk.

NAKED BRIMCAP   **Pl. 38**
Paxillus involutus
Medium to large, *brown cap;* surface *dry, fibrillose.* Margin *strongly inrolled. Crowded, decurrent gills* extend down *firm stalk. Grows on ground.* ***Cap:*** Slightly convex at first, soon becoming flat with a shallow, central depression. Margin hairy, sometimes more or less ribbed; persistently *inrolled.* Surface *matted with fibrils,* sometimes tending to tear irregularly on the limb, in a more or less radial pattern. Light brown to strong brown; may be indistinctly zoned. Flesh yellowish, firm; thick on disc and inner limb. Gills *crowded,* forked, broad, *decurrent* (extending down stalk); gills *separate readily* from *flesh of cap.* Gills *dingy yellow,* sometimes flushed with olive, staining brown when bruised. ***Stalk:*** *Central* or *slightly off-center,* sometimes enlarged downwards; solid. Surface smooth (hairless), brown. **Technical notes:** Cap 5–15 cm across. Stalk 4–10 × 1.5–2.0 cm. Spores smooth, elliptic; 7–9 × 4–6 μm. Pleurocystidia 50–70 × 9–12 μm.
Fruiting: Solitary to grouped; on ground in woods. Widely distributed. Early summer to fall.

Edibility: Not recommended. Reports vary, but when raw or poorly cooked it is definitely **poisonous** to some people. **Remarks:** The combination of colors, shape and easily removable gills make Naked Brimcap (*P. involutus*) easy to recognize. The brown spore print color and lack of latex distinguish it readily from species with similar overall appearance in several genera which give white to pale spore prints.

Genus *Phylloporus*

Some authors place this genus in family Boletaceae.

GOLDGILLS *Phylloporus rhodoxanthus*   **Pl. 38**
Medium to large, *rounded, red, velvety cap. Bright yellow gills extend down yellow* to *reddish stalk.* **Cap:** Broadly convex to flat; often with an indistinct, low, narrow hump at first, and a shallowly depressed disc in age. Surface dry, velvety; bright red to reddish brown, often cracking to expose firm yellow flesh. Odor and taste not distinctive. Gills subdistant, thick, decurrent (extending down stalk); yellow. **Stalk:** Cylindric, sometimes tapered gradually toward base. Surface yellow, flushed with red in an irregular pattern. **Spore print:** Moderate brown. **Technical notes:** Cap 3–8 cm across. Stalk 4–10 × 0.5–1.5 cm. Spores smooth, cylindric; 11–14 × 0.5–1.5 or 11–14 × 3.5–5.0 μm.
Fruiting: Solitary to scattered or grouped; on soil in both hardwood and conifer forests. Widely distributed. Summer and fall.
Edibility: Edible.

Slimecaps and Woollycaps: Family Gomphidiaceae

Spore print dark gray to blackish. Cap and stalk not readily separable. Gills thick, decurrent, and typically spaced widely apart. Spores seen under a microscope are long and thin, like those of boletes (Boletaceae, p. 100). Veils may be present or absent. Cap and stalk not readily separable. These fungi grow on soil and all species appear to be mycorrhizal. No poisonous species known from this family.

Slimecaps: Genus *Chroogomphus*

Small to large, fleshy fungi with thick, decurrent gills. Gills some shade of yellow to orange, at least when young (before spores mature); spores black. Some tissues *stain violet* in iodine. No known poisonous species.

BROWN SLIMECAP *Chroogomphus rutilus*   **Pl. 39**
Medium to large, *rounded to flat, reddish brown, sticky cap.*
Gills extend down dingy, firm stalk. **Cap:** Broadly convex, expanding to flat, with a narrow, low, pointed knob. Strong
brown to reddish brown; may darken to blackish red. Margin
thin; incurved at first. Flesh firm; dull orange-yellow to yellowish pink. Odor not distinctive. Gills subdistant, broad, decurrent (extending down stalk); dull orange-yellow to light yellowish brown, becoming more olive-brown as spores mature.
Stalk: Solid; cylindric or tapering downwards. Surface dry to
moist, with a thin band of fibrils (universal veil remnants) midway on stalk. Orange-yellow flushed with reddish tones. Interior light yellowish at base. **Spore print:** Dark gray. **Technical notes:** Cap 3–12 cm across. Stalk 4–16 × 1.5–3.-2.5 cm.
Spores smooth, cylindric; 14–22 × 4.5–7 µm. Pleurocystidia
long-cylindric, projecting, thin-walled. Tissues of cap amyloid.
Fruiting: Solitary or scattered; on soil under conifers, especially pines. Widespread in northern U.S. and Canada. Summer and fall.
Edibility: Edible.
Similar species: (1) *Chroogomphus ochraceous* (not shown)
and (2) Orange Woollycap (*Chroogomphus tomentosus*, below)
have an orange cap and stalk. *C. tomentosus* has a *dry,* fibrillose cap and is found only west of the Great Plains. *Chroogomphus ochraceous* has a sticky layer on cap surface, as in Brown
Slimecap (*C. rutilus*), but is more consistently *orange. Chroogomphus vinicolor* (not shown) has a narrower cap, which is
more bell-shaped when young (before it expands), with a very
thin slime layer on cap in a range of colors similar to those of
Brown Slimecap (*C. rutilus*). Microscopic characters distinguish the 2 species readily, as *C. vinicolor* has thick-walled,
clavate (club-shaped) to narrowly spindle-shaped cystidia, contrasted with the *thin-walled, more cylindric* cystidia in *C. rutilus* (see **Technical notes** above).
ORANGE WOOLLYCAP *Chroogomphus tomentosus*   **Pl. 39**
Small to medium, *dry, orange cap. Widely spaced gills extend
down orange stalk. Western N. America.* **Cap:** Rounded to
broadly conic with a blunt apex, or flat and sometimes shallowly depressed on disc (center). Surface fibrillose; tacky when
moist, dull and downy in dry weather. Orange to brownish
orange. Flesh firm; light orange. Gills distant (widely spaced),
thick, long-decurrent (extending down stalk); yellowish orange,
flushed with blackish spores at maturity. **Stalk:** Cylindric, tapered toward base; firm. Surface smooth with scattered fibrils;
colored like cap. No ring. **Spore print:** Blackish. **Technical
notes:** Cap 2–6 cm across. Stalk 4–17 × 1–1.5 cm. Spores
smooth, cylindric; 15–25 × 6–9 µm. Pleurocystidia thick-
walled.
Fruiting: Single to grouped; on soil under western conifers,

especially Douglas fir and hemlock. *Rocky Mts. westward,* at
low to medium elevations (below 1500 meters). Late summer
and fall.
Edibility: Edible.
Similar species: *Chroogomphus leptocystis* (not shown) has
more brownish colors, typically with grayish tones, at least on
margin, and thin-walled cystidia. It grows in the same habitat
and fruits at the same time as Orange Woollycap.

Slimecaps: Genus *Gomphidius*

Small to large, fleshy fungi with thick, *decurrent* gills. Cap
flesh and gills white at first (before spores mature); *spores
black.* Stalk usually lemon yellow at base. Tissues do *not* stain
blue or violet in iodine (see *Chroogomphus,* above).

SLIMECAP *Gomphidius glutinosus*   **Pl. 39**
Medium to large, *slimy, gray* to *brown, rounded cap; stains
black* when cut or bruised. *White* to *smoky gills extend down
white* to *yellow stalk.* **Cap:** Broadly convex to flat; margin
sometimes upturned in age. Surface smooth, shiny, with a *gelatinous or slimy outer layer* when wet. Color highly variable —
light grayish brown to reddish brown, reddish gray, or grayish
purple, often stained or spotted with black. Flesh thick, soft;
whitish except pink just under cap cuticle. Gills subdistant to
close, arched, broadly decurrent (extending down stalk).
Stalk: Solid; cylindric or tapered downwards. White at apex,
yellow at base. Veil two-layered, sheathing stalk; outer layer
slimy, inner layer white and fibrillose, leaving a slight ring
which is soon colored by blackish spores. Interior colored like
surface. **Technical notes:** Cap 2–10 cm across. Stalk 4–10 ×
0.7–2.0 cm. Spores smooth, cylindric; 15–20 × 4–7 μm.
Fruiting: Scattered to grouped, or often clustered; on soil under conifers. Frequent under spruce. Widespread in N. America, often abundant in the Northwest.
Edibility: Edible, but not popular — slimy texture (see **Remarks**).
Similar species: Several color varieties of *G. glutinosus* have
been described. (1) *Gomphidius largus* (not shown) is a much
larger species that also differs on microscopic characters. (2)
Gomphidius subroseus (not shown) is smaller, with a bright
pink to red cap.
Remarks: All of the American species of *Gomphidius* (and the
closely related *Chroogomphus*) are edible. The blackish spore
prints, long-decurrent gills on rounded to flat caps, and somewhat waxy gills render them comparatively easy to recognize,
at least as members of the family Gomphidiaceae. None are
especially popular edibles, however, possibly because of the
slimy texture. Some people recommend peeling off the outer
layer before cooking. This will not eliminate all of the slime in

certain species such as *G. glutinosus,* as some of the inner tissues also gelatinize.

Brittlegills and Milkcaps: Family Russulaceae

Spore print white to yellow. Cap and stalk mostly not readily separable. Gills variously attached to stalk, but not free. Cap often has brittle texture and many exude transparent to white or colored, *milk-like latex.* Veils lacking. Microscope characteristics of flesh (clusters of globose cells) and spores (no germ pore; variously ornamented, but ornamentations black in iodine solution) help to distinguish the 2 genera (*Russula* and *Lactarius*) of this large family. Both (mildly) poisonous and edible species included.

Brittlegills (Russulas): Genus *Russula*

Russula brevipes

Medium to large, mostly thick-fleshed cap has brittle consistency—crumbly like cheese. Thick, fragile to tough, usually hollow to stuffed stalk. Spore print white to orange-yellow. Strong spiny to netted ornamentation on spores stains black in iodine; flesh heteromerous.

WHITISH BRITTLEGILL *Russula albidula*   **Pl. 39**
Size varies—small to medium or occasionally large, *white, fragile cap* on a *thick, white stalk. Taste peppery.** *Mature gills pale yellowish. Cap:* Broadly rounded to flat, with a low, broadly and shallowly depressed disc (center) and faintly streaked margin. Surface *sticky* when wet. Flesh white; fragile. Odor not distinctive. Gills close, adnate (broadly attached); white at first; but becoming pale yellow as spores mature; sometimes forked. *Stalk:* Cylindric or slightly expanded at base; *white, fragile.* **Spore print:** Pale yellow. **Technical notes:** Cap 2–8 cm across. Stalk 2.5–7.0 × 1.0–2.3 cm. Spores subglobose; 8–11 × 6.5–8.5 μm.
Fruiting: Solitary to grouped; in pine woods and hardwoods. Eastern U.S. Summer and fall.
Edibility: Unknown.
Similar species: Easily confused with (1) white species of *Hygrophorus* (waxycaps, p. 202, Pls. 23–24) and *Tricholoma* (p. 185, Pl. 21). The combination of cream-colored spore print and brittle consistency identify Whitish Brittlegill as a *Russula.* (2) *Russula albella* (not shown) is similar but lacks the sticky surface and is slightly larger. (3) *Russula albida* (not shown) is larger.

---

* **See p. 10 for cautions about using taste as an identifying characteristic.**

STUBBY BRITTLEGILL *Russula brevipes*   **Pl. 39**
Large, dry, white, broadly funnel-shaped cap. Stalk stubby; centrally attached. Gills faintly flushed with green. ***Cap:*** Convex at first, with a broad, low depression and inrolled outer limb and margin; expanding to broadly and shallowly *funnel-shaped;* margin downturned to flaring at maturity. Surface dry and unpolished; white, staining dingy yellow to brown. Flesh firm; white. Gills close, decurrent (extending down stalk), sometimes forked or with veins between gills; white, with a faint blue-green tinge on gills and upper stalk. Odor not distinctive. ***Stalk:*** Short, thick, firm, cylindric; interior solid or hollow in age. Surface dry and unpolished; white, with brownish stains when bruised. ***Spore print:*** Pale yellowish. **Technical notes:** Cap 6–20 cm across. Stalk 2.5–8.0 × 2–5 cm. Spores amyloid on warts and ridges, short-elliptic; 8–11 × 6.5–8.5 μm. **Fruiting:** Solitary to grouped; under conifers or in mixed conifer-hardwood forests. Widespread. Summer and fall. **Edibility:** Edible.
Similar species: A number of large, white species of *Russula* and *Lactarius* are very hard to distinguish on field characters alone. Careful attention should be given to gill color and staining, spacing, forking, and presence or absence of latex.
Remarks: This species has long been called *Russula delica,* a European species with more widely spaced gills which apparently does not occur in N. America.

COMPACT BRITTLEGILL *Russula compacta*   **Pl. 39**
Medium to large, *stout, whitish caps;* surface *dry, unpolished. All parts stain orange-brown.* ***Cap:*** Convex, with a broad, shallowly depressed disc, becoming nearly flat, with a broad, shallow depression over disc and most of limb. Surface shiny and sticky when wet, soon *dry and dull;* not streaked but sometimes shallowly cracked, especially on disc. Yellowish white to pale orange-yellow, soon developing yellowish brown to brownish orange colors in age or when injured. Flesh thick, hard and brittle at first, but spongy in age; initial color and color changes same as for cap surface. Odor absent or fishy. *Gills close,* moderately broad, adnate (broadly attached to stalk apex), often forked near stalk and sometimes outward. Short gills abundant; mostly coming halfway or closer to stalk, interveined. Gills are colored like cap. ***Stalk:*** Cylindric and flared at apex, sometimes enlarged at base. Colored like cap. Solid and hard when young, in age central part becomes spongy or chambered (see inside front cover). ***Spore print:*** White. **Technical notes:** Cap 4–12 cm across. Stalk 3–8 × 1.0–3.5 cm. Spores warty, broadly ovate (egg-shaped) to subglobose; 7.5–10.0 × 6.5–8.5 μm. Warts convex to bluntly convex, mostly connected to form an incomplete network.
Fruiting: Solitary to grouped; in deciduous and mixed coniferous-deciduous forests. Midwest to East Coast and south to Texas.

Edibility: Edible.
Similar species: (1) *Russula crassotunicata* (not shown) is often smaller than *R. compacta.* It has white to yellow colors that stain brown, a rubbery cuticle, and a puffball-like odor. It commonly fruits under conifers in Pacific Northwest. (2) Numerous large, whitish dry species of *Russula* stain *gray to black,* sometimes first showing pink or red tints or occasionally brown, but then becoming *more grayish* than *R. compacta.* (3) The large, dry milkcaps (*Lactarius,* p. 326) are easily distinguished by the *latex* they exude when cut.
Remarks: Compact Brittlegill (*R. compacta*) is a distinctive and easily recognizable species.

DENSE BRITTLEGILL *Russula densifolia*   **Pl. 39**
Large, white to *dingy brown cap* on a *thick stalk.* Cap *convex to depressed;* surface *dry to sticky. All parts stain red,* then *black,* when injured. *Cap:* Rounded with a broadly depressed disc and an incurved, sometimes streaked or grooved margin at first, expanding to flat or broad and shallowly funnel-shaped at maturity. Flesh firm; dingy whitish, but *quickly staining red,* then *black,* in fresh specimens. Odor not distinctive. Gills *close, narrow,* adnate (broadly attached); yellowish at first, darkening in age. *Stalk:* Short, cylindric; dull white. *Spore print:* White. **Technical notes:** Cap 5–20 cm across. Stalk 2–7 × 1–4 cm. Spores thick-walled with amyloid ridges, short-elliptic; 7–10 × 6–8 μm.
Fruiting: Solitary to grouped; in both hardwood and coniferous forests. Widespread in N. America. Summer and fall.
Edibility: Not recommended — as reports vary from "poisonous" to "edible," there is apt to be little satisfaction in being the one to prove that the first of these is correct!
Similar species: (1) *Russula nigricans* (not shown) has thicker, more widely spaced gills and smaller spores, a thinner cuticle (cap surface), and is said to have a "fruity" odor. It is apparently not uncommon in the Northwest, but elsewhere in N. America *R. densifolia* seems to be confused frequently with other white species that stain darker when cut or bruised. In the East, a species with these characters and larger spores is (2) *Russula dissimulans* (not shown). When cut, the flesh of both *R. nigricans* and *R. dissimulans* stains reddish orange, then grayish red, and finally black. (3) Pepper-and-salt Brittlegill (*R. albonigra,* not shown) and (4) *R. adusta* (not shown) both stain *directly gray or black* when bruised or wounded. There is no intermediate pink or red coloration. *Russula adusta* is less common but perhaps easier to recognize by its *gills,* which are *very thick, widely spaced,* and often interveined.
Remarks: Color changes in response to bruising, handling, or injury as described above may occur also, very slowly, in response to harsh environmental conditions, such as very dry air or possibly intense sunlight, or simply in response to aging.

Thus, one finds undisturbed specimens of Dense Brittlegill *(R. densifolia)* of almost any age which are partially or wholly dingy brown, gray, or almost black. Pink or red colors which characterize *R. nigricans* and *R. densifolia* may be hard to demonstrate under these conditions, especially on old fruiting bodies. Cut the cap or stalk, or scrape these surfaces deeply with a tool or fingernail. If the underlying tissues are already brown or gray, the pink or red colors may develop very slowly and weakly or not at all.

SICKENER *Russula emetica*   **Pl. 40**
Medium to large, *fragile, shiny red cap* with *white gills* on *thick, white stalk. Taste sharply peppery* (**poisonous** — do not try it). *Cap:* Slightly convex to flat, often with a shallowly depressed disc; margin warty-streaked. Surface sticky; bright red to pink, sometimes with patches of yellow. Flesh soft; white, except pink just under cuticle. Gills close, broad, adnate (broadly attached to stalk apex). *Stalk:* Cylindric, hollow in age or stuffed with filaments; very fragile. Surface smooth, white. *Spore print: White.* **Technical notes:** Cap 4–10 cm across. Stalk 4–10 × 1.0–2.5 cm. Spores amyloid, broadly elliptic; wall thick, warty to spiny with low connecting ridges.

Fruiting: Scattered to grouped; on soil, well-decayed wood, or moss beds, including sphagnum bogs. Widespread. Summer and fall.

Edibility: Poisonous. As the species name indicates it is well known to act as an emetic, and thus is not likely to be fatal. **Similar species:** There are many red species of *Russula* and most have probably been misidentified as Sickener (*R. emetica*). Some can not be distinguished without a microscope; they may have a colored spore print, although it may be pale. Fragile Brittlegill (*R. fragilis*, p. 321) is smaller; it usually has some purple to greenish or yellow colors and lacks the pink flesh just under the cuticle. It, too, is poisonous. **Remarks:** We advise against eating any fragile red *Russula*. Some claim that *R. emetica* is harmless, but reports of it having been eaten with impunity may involve misidentification, particularly when a species is so frequently confused as this one.

GOLDEN BRITTLEGILL *Russula flavipes*   **Pl. 40**
Medium-sized, *yellow* to *orange, dry, rounded* to *flat cap* on a *short, firm, yellow stalk. Cap:* Convex at first, expanding to flat with a shallowly depressed disc. Surface smooth; scurfy to velvety, especially on margin. Brilliant yellow to orange-yellow or orange on disc, sometimes fading to nearly white on margin. Flesh white. Odor not distinctive. Gills close, adnate (broadly attached), white at first, becoming dingy yellowish in age. *Stalk:* Cylindric or flaring upwards; solid at first, but later becoming spongy and sometimes hollow. Colored like cap, usually darkest at base. *Spore print:* Yellowish. **Technical**

notes: Cap 3.5–7.5 cm across. Stalk 3–7 × 0.8–1.5 cm. Spores warty, subglobose; 7–8 × 6–7 μm.

Fruiting: Solitary or scattered; on soil, sometimes in grassy places, deciduous woods. Eastern U.S. south to Alabama. July and August.

Edibility: Unknown.

Remarks: The combination of small to medium size, bright colors and dry, unpolished surfaces, and habitat (in eastern hardwood forests) make this a distinctive species that is easily recognized on field characters. In the Chesapeake Bay area it is encountered very frequently but never in great abundance.

FRAGILE BRITTLEGILL *Russula fragilis*   **Pl. 40**
Small to medium, *thin, fragile, multicolored cap* on a *brittle white stalk. Pale yellowish gills* and *spore print.* **Cap:** Convex with an incurved margin and sometimes with a distinct but small, central hump at first, expanding to flat with a shallow, broadly depressed disc. Margin and outer disc streaked and sometimes warty. Surface sticky when wet. *Color variable—*dark grayish purple, dark to moderate red, dark pink to strong yellowish pink, often flushed with areas of grayish olive or pale grayish yellow. *Cuticle peels off readily.* Flesh thin, soft and brittle; white, or sometimes colored like surface just below cuticle. Odor not distinctive or "apple-like" to unpleasant. Gills close to subdistant, occasionally forked near stalk, broadly adnate (attached) to adnexed (notched) or almost free from stalk apex; yellowish white, sometimes becoming more yellowish in age. **Stalk:** Cylindrical; solid or stuffed with cottony filaments. Surface white; dry to moist, smooth or with vertical wrinkles. **Spore print:** Yellowish white. **Technical notes:** Cap 2–6 cm across. Stalk 2.5–6.0 × 0.5–1.5 cm. Spores subglobose to ovoid (egg-shaped), with scattered, amyloid warts and thin, more or less reticulate ridges.

Fruiting: Solitary to scattered; on soil or well-rotted wood in coniferous, mixed, or hardwood forests. Widely distributed in N. America. Summer and fall.

Edibility: Poisonous.

Similar species: Red Russulas are both frequent and common throughout N. America. They are very frequently misidentified, thus none should be eaten. Fragile Brittlegill (*R. fragilis*) is one of the more distinctive species among them because of its great variability, especially in color. Typically it will have several variants of the colors listed above in patches or zones that blend subtly from one to another. It is a most attractive small species.

STINKING BRITTLEGILL *Russula fragrantissima*   **Pl. 39**
Large, yellow to *brown, sticky cap* with a *strong offensive odor* and *brown-staining, yellowish, brittle gills. Firm, yellowish stalk.* **Cap:** Nearly round to egg-shaped at first, expanding to flat with a shallowly depressed disc or at times funnel-shaped;

split or lobed on margin. Surface shiny, sticky; often radially streaked on limb, margin distinctly warty-streaked. Flesh thick, hard, brittle; yellowish white to brownish, stained moderate brown around larval channels but unchanging when cut. Odor fetid to aromatic or almond-like; taste acrid, nauseating to some.* Gills close to subdistant, occasionally forked and interveined, adnexed (notched) to adnate (broadly attached); short gills mostly reaching at least halfway to stalk. Gill edges are often beaded with transparent liquid. *Stalk:* Cylindrical or tapering. Surface dry, dull; smooth, or minutely scurfy at apex when young, later smooth or with faint, indistinct, lengthwise ridges. Yellowish white at first, but soon staining brown, or in age becoming light to moderate brown at base; sometimes brown almost overall. Interior solid and hard throughout; central part is later stuffed with softer tissue than cortex and eventually becomes hollow, with rough, brown-staining inner walls. *Spore print:* Pale orange-yellow. **Technical notes:** Cap 7-20 cm across. Stalk 7-15 $\times$ 1.5-6.0 cm. Spores subglobose to ovate (egg-shaped) or broadly elliptic; 6.5-9.5 $\times$ 6.8 μm. Cell wall (surface) ornamented with conic to cylindric warts or isolated to connected, more or less reticulate ridges up to 1 μm high.

Fruiting: Solitary to grouped; on soil, in both coniferous and hardwood forests. Widespread. Late summer and fall.

Edibility: Not recommended.

Similar species: (1) *Russula laurocerasi* (not shown), which fruits under similar conditions, has a more slender stalk, a more yellow cap, retains a cleaner aspect, has a stronger, more fragrant (less fetid) odor, and has larger spores with higher ornamentation. The 2 species intergrade and are very frequently confused. Both are confused with (2) *R. subfoetans* (not shown), which is smaller, has a more fetid odor, and smaller spores. (3) Red streaks on stalk and red gill edges, along with habitat (on sandy soil), distinguish Sand Brittlegill (*R. ventricosipes,* p. 324).

Remarks: This is the species commonly incorrectly identified in the U.S. as *Russula foetans,* a European species of similar appearance but with flesh which turns yellow when cut.

SCALLOP BRITTLEGILL *Russula pectinatoides*   **Pl. 39**
Medium to large, *thin, fragile, dingy light brownish cap,* with *radiating streaks* and *grooves;* surface *sticky. Fragile stalk.* *Cap:* Convex with a depressed disc, becoming flat, often with a flaring limb and margin, sometimes split radially; outer limb warty and streaked, with broad, shallow channels between rows of warts. Surface shiny and smooth at first, at least on disc; network of cracks develops with age and drying. Grayish

---

* See p. 10 for cautions about using taste as an identifying characteristic.

brown, fading to pale orange-yellow, moderate yellow, or light yellowish brown overall, or with a dark disc. Cuticle thin and readily separable from flesh below. Flesh thin, fragile; yellowish white, except brownish just under cuticle. Odor faint and disagreeable. Gills subdistant, often forked near stalk, interveined, adnate (broadly attached) or less often notched. Short gills few and of various lengths. Gills yellowish white, becoming pale yellow, sometimes stained yellowish brown. *Stalk:* Cylindric or flaring slightly at apex. Surface dry, dull and smooth (hairless), but with minute, soft scales at apex. Yellowish white, variously stained brown to orange or gray, sometimes flushed with yellowish gray at base or overall. Interior stuffed with cottony filaments or hollow; sometimes chambered. *Spore print:* Pale orange-yellow. **Technical notes:** Cap 3–8 cm across. Stalk 1.5–7.0 × 0.5–2.0 cm. Spores warty, broadly elliptic to ovate (egg-shaped); 5.5–8.5 × 4.5–6.5 μm. Warts conic to cylindric or bluntly conic.

Fruiting: Solitary to grouped; in deciduous or mixed deciduous-coniferous forests and pine plantations. Midwest and eastern N. America. Early summer to early autumn.

Edibility: Unknown, but **not recommended.**

Similar species: (1) *Russula amoenolens* and (2) *R. cerolens* (not shown) have darker, more somber colors with more yellow (less orange) tones, stronger odor and taste, and a lighter-colored spore print. The thicker, more firm flesh, brown and yellow colors with a stronger red element, and stronger, distinctive odors distinguish species of the *R. foetans* complex, such as Stinking Brittlegill (*R. fragrantissima*, p. 321).

Remarks: The species in this group have all been called *Russula pectinata*, a European species of similar appearance. The Latin name refers to the distinct ribs that radiate outward on the outer cap surface, roughly reminiscent of the shell of a sea scallop.

VARIEGATED BRITTLEGILL *Russula variata*   **Pl. 40**
Large, multicolored or *predominantly green* to *pink, purplish,* or *gray cap. Gills repeatedly forked.* **Cap:** Convex, with an incurved margin at first; later becoming flat with a depressed disc or broadly funnel-shaped. Margin sometimes wavy and split. Surface sticky or dry and dull, smooth, sometimes streaked in age. Color highly variable over a great range of dull, often grayed tones, from purple to green, often with several colors on a single cap or with nearby caps of mostly solid but strikingly different colors. Cuticle readily separable from flesh below; thin, more or less elastic. Flesh firm and brittle, thick; white, unchanging when cut or bruised. Odor mild or disagreeable. Gills narrow, close, adnate (broadly attached); *repeatedly forked* to form short gills. Gills white to yellowish, sometimes spotted or splotched with brown. **Stalk:** Solid to stuffed with filaments or hollow; cylindric. Surface white or

spotted with yellow or brown. ***Spore print:*** White. **Technical notes:** Cap 5–14 cm across. Stalk 3–8 × 1.5–3.0 cm. Spores warty, ovate (egg-shaped) to subglobose; 7–10 × 5.5–8.0 μm. Warts mostly isolated; short, cylindric to conic.

Fruiting: Solitary to grouped; on soil under hardwoods (common under oak and aspen), but also under pine or in mixed pine-hardwood forests. Great Lakes eastward; Canada south to Florida. Summer.

Edibility: Edible.

Similar species: Green forms may be mistaken for (1) *Russula aeruginea* (not shown) but the forking of gills on Variegated Brittlegill *(R. variata)* is a good distinguishing character. *Russula aeruginea* and (2) Green Brittlegill (*R. virescens,* p. 325) both have a cream to yellow spore print; Variegated Brittlegill *(R. variata)* gives a white spore print.

SAND BRITTLEGILL *Russula ventricosipes*   **Pl. 39**
Medium to large, *yellow* to *brown, firm, rounded* to *flat cap* with a *depressed center* and *sticky surface. Short, hard stalk.* Grows *in sandy soil.* **Cap:** Convex with a depressed disc and incurved margin at first, expanding to flat or broadly funnel-shaped with a warty-streaked margin. Surface shiny and smooth, with sand adhering to it; pale yellowish pink to pale yellow, reddish orange, or yellowish brown. Flesh thick, brittle; yellowish white, becoming pale yellow to light yellowish brown when cut or in age. Odor not distinctive. Gills moderately broad, brittle, close, often forked near stalk; adnate (broadly attached to stalk) or adnexed (notched). Short gills mostly extend nearly to stalk. Gills yellowish white to yellow, later becoming orange-yellow with reddish edges. **Stalk:** Tapered at base or both at base and apex; hard and solid at first, later stuffed with filaments, sometimes becoming hollow or chambered. Slowly stains yellow to brownish when cut. Surface dry, dull, with faint lengthwise ridges. Yellowish white, *streaked or splotched with red or reddish brown.* ***Spore print:*** Pale orange-yellow. **Technical notes:** Cap 4–13 cm across. Stalk 2–10 × 1.5–5.0 cm. Spores elliptic; 7–10 × 4.5–6.0 μm. Surface appears almost smooth but is sparsely ornamented with low warts or short, unconnected ridges.

Fruiting: Solitary to grouped; in sandy soil, often associated with pines. Midwest to Southeast. Late summer and fall.

Edibility: Unknown.

Similar species: (1) *Russula lilaceps* (not shown) has purplish colors on stalk, smaller spores, and lacks red streaks on upper stalk (connecting to gill edges). Reddish colors and lack of distinctive odor also distinguish Sand Brittlegill *(R. ventricosipes)* from (2) Stinking Brittlegill *(R. fragrantissima)* and related species.

Remarks: Caps of Sand Brittlegill often do not fully expand and remain partially buried in the sand. They are found on forested dunes near the Great Lakes and Atlantic seashore. In Maryland this Russula is common under pines in clearings around golf courses. The Latin name *ventricosipes* refers to the shape of the more or less stubby stalk, which tapers both toward the apex and the base.

GREEN BRITTLEGILL *Russula virescens*   **Pl. 40**
Medium to large *cap* with a *green, dull surface* that *breaks into crust-like patches.* Does *not stain* (change color) when handled. *Cap:* Thick; convex with a slightly depressed disc and incurved margin, becoming flat to concave, not streaked at first but becoming warty-streaked in age for about 1 cm inward from margin; surface slightly sticky when moist, soon dry, dull and patchy, at least near margin. Cuticle thin, readily separable from flesh halfway or more inward from margin. Flesh firm and brittle, later becoming spongy but brittle; white to faintly yellowish when cut. Odor very weak. *Stalk:* Solid to stuffed with filaments. Surface dry, dull; smooth, or with faint lengthwise ribs; yellowish white, sometimes becoming pale grayish yellow where bruised or brownish in soft interior tissue when cut. *Spore print:* Yellowish white. **Technical notes:** Cap 5–15 cm across. Stalk 4–8 × 1.5–3.5 cm. Spores warty, broadly elliptic to subglobose; 6–9 × 5–7 μm. Warts broadly to bluntly convex; surface sometimes has short ridges.
Fruiting: Solitary to grouped; common on soil, in deciduous or mixed coniferous-deciduous woods. East of Great Plains. Summer.
Edibility: Edible; sometimes highly regarded, if one can eliminate the particles of soil or sand.
Similar species: The surface of *Russula crustosa* (not shown) breaks into the same patchy pattern, but colors are usually more yellowish, reddish, or grayish brown. Faded caps of Green Brittlegill *(R. virescens)* assume similar colors, but *R. crustosa* produces a darker yellow spore print.

SHELLFISH BRITTLEGILL *Russula xerampelina*   **Pl. 40**
Medium to large, *hard-fleshed cap; color varies* (often *dark red* or *purple*). Mature plants have a *fishy odor* (may develop slowly). All parts *slowly stain dingy yellow-brown* when cut or bruised. *Cap:* Convex, becoming flat, with a broad, shallow depression. Surface sticky when moist, but soon dry; smooth — not streaked or warty. Color most often *dark red,* but may be dark purple, pink, green, or brown, often with traces of yellow. Flesh white; firm. Odor variable — may be absent at first, but present in mature or old specimens and variously described as similar to that of *fish, crab, herring, rotten shrimp, or shellfish.* Gills broad, close to subdistant, adnate (see inside front cover); yellowish white. *Stalk:* Solid at first, later spongy. Surface white or flushed with pink; dry, smooth to wrinkled. *Spore print:* Yellowish. **Technical notes:** Cap 4–15 cm across. Stalk 4–10 × 1.5–3.5 cm. Flesh *turns green* in FeSO$_4$. Spores broadly

elliptic to ovoid (egg-shaped); 8–11 × 6.5–8.5 μm. Warts mostly connected.

Fruiting: Solitary to grouped; on soil in coniferous or various mixed coniferous-deciduous forests. Widely distributed. Common in late summer and fall.

Edibility: Edible and good. Some people report a nut-like flavor for young buttons; others report that it imparts a shellfish-like or crab-like flavor to all dishes in which it is an ingredient.

Remarks: The "*Xerampelina* complex"—a group of closely related species—is readily recognized by a combination of 3 characters: (1) the *shrimp-like* or *fishy odor,* (2) the *brown staining* of *all parts* when cut or bruised, and (3) the *green staining reaction* of flesh *to iron salts* such as iron alum. The last-named character is the most reliable, as the odor and brown-staining reactions are often weak and slow to develop.

Milkcaps: Genus *Lactarius*

Lactarius deliciosus

Cap small to large; firm but sometimes fragile. Cap is continuous with stalk. All parts exude latex when cut or broken; latex clear to white or colored. Spore print white to orange-yellow.

KINDRED MILKCAP *Lactarius affinis*   **Pl. 42**
Medium to large, *slimy, dull yellow* or *brownish cap. Latex white—unchanging or drying as green spots.* Stalk and cap colored alike. **Cap:** Convex with an incurved margin at first, later nearly flat with a broad, shallowly depressed disc, margin often lobed. Surface smooth; dingy pale orange-yellow, becoming light brown, not zoned. Flesh firm; white at first, later flushed with brown. Odor not distinctive. Latex *white; unchanging,* or *sometimes leaving green spots on gills or flesh* when it dries (variety *viridolacteus*). Gills close, broad, adnate (broadly attached) to subdecurrent; yellowish. **Stalk:** Cylindric, becoming hollow; often brownish at base. **Spore print:** White to yellowish. **Technical notes:** Cap 5–15 cm across. Stalk 4–12 × 1–3 cm. Spores reticulate with isolated warts, elliptic; 8.0–9.5 × 6.5–8.0 μm.

Fruiting: Scattered to grouped; on soil in mixed conifer-hardwood forests and pastures. Southern Canada to mid-South; common in Great Lakes area. Late summer and fall.

Edibility: Unknown.

Similar species: (1) *Lactarius pallidus* (not shown), common in Europe but rare in America, *lacks* peppery taste. (2) Old or faded specimens of Ordinary Milkcap (*L. trivialis,* p. 338) are easily mistaken for Kindred Milkcap *(L. affinis),* but *L. trivialis* can be distinguished readily when young and in good condition by its *violet-gray* colors, often in concentric zones on cap. It is not uncommon in western N. America but is rarely found in the East. (3) *Lactarius pseudoaffinis* (not shown) has smaller spores. It is found in North Carolina and Tennessee.

WATERDROP MILKCAP *Lactarius aquifluus*   **Pl. 40**
Medium to large, *brown cap; sometimes indistinctly spotted or zoned. Latex transparent, watery. Odor of brown sugar.* **Cap:** Nearly flat, expanding to broadly and shallowly depressed at first, with an incurved margin and usually with a small, pointed knob on disc. Surface smooth at first, becoming somewhat fibrillose or developing shallow cracks as it matures. Light to moderate reddish brown or grayish reddish orange. Flesh thick on disc but tapering sharply on limb to a thin outer limb and margin; colored like surface or paler. Gills close, sometimes forked near stalk; narrow at first, later broad; pinkish white at first, developing brownish tones with maturity, but *not staining* when bruised. **Stalk:** Cylindric. Surface colored like cap or paler; dry, smooth. Interior stuffed with filaments to hollow. **Spore print:** Pale yellowish. **Technical notes:** Cap 4–15 cm across. Stalk 4–8 × 1–2 cm. Spores reticulate, broadly elliptic; 7–9 × 6.0–7.5 µm.

Fruiting: Solitary to grouped; in forested areas east of Great Plains, especially in bogs and other low, wet places. Late summer and fall.

Edibility: Not recommended—see below.

Similar species: The combination of non-slimy or non-sticky cap surface, non-staining tissues, and unique odor distinguish Waterdrop Milkcap from half a dozen or more N. American milkcaps which may have colorless, watery, or whey-like latex. Waterdrop Milkcap *(L. aquifluus)* is very close to the European species *L. helvus,* and is sometimes considered to be the same species. However, *L. helvus* (not shown) has whitish latex. A series of related species or varieties varying in these and microscopic characters are very hard to distinguish. *Lactarius helvus* is known to be **poisonous** to some people, although a powder ground from dried specimens is sometimes used as a condiment. In view of the confusing taxonomy of this group, we recommend that none of the milkcaps with clear latex be eaten.

DARK-SPOTTED MILKCAP *Lactarius atroviridis*   **Pl. 40**
Large, dingy green cap and stalk; often spotted. Latex white; slowly stains gills greenish when cut. **Cap:** Convex when young, with a strongly incurved margin, later becoming nearly flat with a broad, shallow depression over disc and inner limb. Surface tacky at first, soon becoming dry and somewhat rough. Light to dark green, with irregular dark spots in a concentric pattern. Flesh thick, firm. Odor not distinctive. Latex white; slowly turns greenish when exposed to air. Gills close, narrow; yellowish white to pinkish white, spotted with greenish or brownish in age, adnate to short-decurrent, short gills often numerous. **Stalk:** Cylindric. Surface dry; colored like cap, with dark spots. **Spore print:** Pale yellowish. **Technical notes:**

Cap 5–15 cm across. Stalk 2–8 × 1–3 cm. Spores elliptic; 7–9 × 5.5–6.5 μm. Surface reticulate with free (unconnected) warts.

Fruiting: Scattered or in small clumps; on soil, in coniferous and deciduous forests. Great Lakes eastward and south to Tennessee. Summer and fall.

Edibility: Not recommended.

Similar species: (1) *Lactarius olivaceoumbrinus* (not shown) is larger and is found in pine forests of Pacific Northwest. Its colors tend more to brown and its spores are broader. (2) *Lactarius sordidus* (not shown), growing in the same area as Dark-spotted Milkcap (*L. atroviridis*), is *more brown than green* and often has dark spots *on stalk* but not on cap.

GRAY MILKCAP *Lactarius caespitosus*   **Pl. 42**
Medium to large, *firm, gray to grayish brown* cap and stalk. Surface *slightly sticky. Latex white, unchanging* when exposed to air. *Cap:* Convex, with an incurved margin, becoming flat or shallowly depressed. Flesh thick, brittle; white and unchanging or very slowly staining yellowish when cut. Odor not distinctive. Gills close, adnate (broadly attached) to short-decurrent (extending slightly down stalk); white to pale yellowish pink. *Stalk:* Cylindric, firm but soon hollow. Surface smooth, *sticky* at first; brownish gray. *Spore print:* Pale yellowish. **Technical notes:** Cap 4–10 cm across. Stalk 3–6 × 1–3 cm. Spores broadly ellipsoid; 9–12 × 7–9 μm. Surface reticulate with free ribs and warts.

Fruiting: Solitary to grouped or clumped; on soil in spruce-fir forests. Northern Rocky Mts. to Pacific Northwest. Summer and early fall.

Edibility: Unknown. Not recommended.

Similar species: Kauffman's Milkcap (*L. kaufmanii,* not shown) has a darker cap.

GOLD-DROP MILKCAP *Lactarius chrysorrheus*   **Pl. 42**
Medium-sized, *yellowish, convex* to *flat, shiny cap. Abundant white latex changes quickly* to *bright yellow* when exposed to air. *Cap:* Convex at first, with a strongly inrolled margin and shallowly depressed disc, becoming flat to shallowly funnel-shaped. Surface smooth, moist to slightly sticky; pale orange-yellow, with darker, watery spots in concentric zones. Flesh whitish, soon yellow when cut. Gills pale yellowish; close, adnate (broadly attached) to short-decurrent. *Stalk:* Cylindric; becomes hollow in age. Surface smooth, colored like cap. *Spore print:* Pale yellow. **Technical notes:** Cap 3–8 cm across. Stalk 3–5 × 1.0–1.5 cm. Spores broadly ellipsoid; 8.0–9.5 × 7.0–7.5 μm. Surface reticulate, with scattered warts and short ridges. Cap cuticle a thin ixocutis, hyaline (transparent).

Fruiting: Solitary or in clusters or rings; on soil in hardwood and mixed hardwood-conifer forests. S. Canada to Mexico.

Edibility: Not recommended.

Similar species: (1) In *L. vinaceorufescens* (not shown) *all parts turn slowly reddish brown,* eventually brownish red when injured or in age. It is more common in the Northeast, particularly in low, mixed conifer-hardwood forests, whereas Gold-drop Milkcap seems to prefer well-drained soil under oak. (2) *Lactarius colorascens* (not shown) stains *red* (not yellow) on cap but not on gills.

WRINKLED MILKCAP *Lactarius corrugis*   **Pl. 40**
Medium to large, *dry, brown cap,* with *concentric wrinkles. Abundant white latex* seeps from gills when cut; gills and flesh *stain brown. Cap:* Convex with a flat or depressed disc and incurved margin, becoming nearly flat. Surface minutely velvety; variously but distinctly wrinkled, at least on margin and outer limb. Brownish orange to dark reddish brown, sometimes darker at center than outward. Flesh firm; white, *staining brown* when cut. Odor and taste not distinctive. Gills close, adnate (broadly attached) to subdecurrent; dingy yellowish, sometimes with clear drops of liquid on edges. *Stalk:* Cylindric; solid, firm. Surface dry, velvety; colored like cap or lighter. *Spore print:* White. **Technical notes:** Cap 5–11 cm across. Stalk 5–10 × 1.5–2.5 cm. Spores globose; 9–12 μm. Surface reticulate, with occasional isolated narrow bands and fine lines.
Fruiting: Solitary to scattered; on soil in hardwood and mixed conifer-hardwood forests. Eastern and midwestern N. America, but most common in southeastern U.S. Midsummer to fall.
Edibility: Edible; some rate it choice.
Similar species: Frequently confused with (1) wrinkled forms of Tawny Milkcap (*Lactarius volemus,* p. 340), which has lighter and *more yellowish* (tawny) colors, a *less wrinkled* or smooth cap, a *strong odor* (fishy when dry), and smaller spores. (2) Orange Milkcap (*L. hygrophoroides,* p. 331, Pl. 41) has brighter colors, does *not* stain brown, and has *distant* (widely spaced) *gills.*

COTTONROLL MILKCAP *Lactarius deceptivus*   **Pl. 41**
Large, *dull white, dry cap;* flesh *stains brownish* when cut or bruised. *Young cap* has a *large cottony roll* on *incurved margin.* Latex white, unchanging when exposed to air. *Cap:* Convex with a depressed disc, becoming funnel-shaped and cracking with age, forming angular patches on surface. May become light yellowish brown overall. Flesh firm, thick; white. Odor mild at first, later strong and pungent. *Gills white* to *pale yellowish; subdistant,* adnate (broadly attached) to decurrent (extending down stalk). *Stalk:* Cylindric, short, solid, hard; white, staining brownish. *Spore print:* White to faintly yellowish. **Technical notes:** Cap 8–20 cm across. Stalk 4–8 × 2–4 cm. Spores minutely warty, broadly elliptic; 9–12 × 7.5–9.0 μm.

Fruiting: Solitary to grouped; under oak, hemlock, and in mixed conifer-hardwood forests. Southern Canada to southern U.S.; east of Great Plains.

Edibility: Not recommended. Although it is sometimes regarded as edible (but not very palatable), this species is frequently misidentified.

Similar species: (1) *Lactarius tomentoso-marginatus* (not shown) has a hairy margin which may be mistaken for the cotton roll of *L. deceptivus* (Cottonroll Milkcap) in any except very young caps. The subdistant gill spacing of Cottonroll Milkcap (*L. deceptivus*) is very important in distinguishing this from a number of "look-alikes." (2) Fleecy Milkcap (*L. vellereus*, p. 339) has *more widely spaced gills* and (3) Pepper Milkcap (*L. piperatus*, p. 333) has *very narrow, crowded gills*. (4) *Lactarius caeruleitinctus,* known only from Florida, has close gills and a blue-tinged stalk which darkens after harvesting — not to be confused with the narrow, blue-green zone found rarely on the stalk apex of otherwise typical Cottonroll Milkcaps (*L. deceptivus*) reported from New England and Michigan. These remind one of certain large, white Russulas, such as Stubby Brittlegill (*R. brevipes,* p. 318). Indeed, this species varies in so many characters as to be truly deceptive.

SAFFRON MILKCAP *Lactarius deliciosus*   **Pl. 42**
A medium to large milkcap. *Orange overall; stains green* from *handling or bruising. Cap zoned. Latex orange at first;* turns *green* when exposed to air. *Cap:* Convex to flat, with a shallow central depression; margin incurved at first, often flaring in age. Surface slimy to sticky, soon becoming dry. Colors highly variable; *zoned,* from concentric orange to orange-yellow spots, streaks, and pock marks. Flesh firm and fragile, variable in thickness; orange to reddish orange near surface when first cut, often slowly becoming more red to brownish red and finally *green* (from latex). Odor not distinctive. Gills pale orange-yellow to light orange; close, sometimes interveined, adnate (broadly attached), sometimes with a decurrent line extending down stalk. *Stalk:* Cylindric; firm but often hollow in age. Surface smooth or "pock-marked" in some specimens; base sometimes stains reddish when first cut. *Spore print:* Yellowish. **Technical notes:** Cap 5–15 cm across. Stalk 3–7 × 1.0–2.5 cm. Spores ellipsoid; 7–11 × 6–8 μm. Surface warty, with an incomplete reticulum (network).

Fruiting: Solitary to grouped; under conifers. Alaska to Mexico and east across the conifer zones. Summer and fall.

Edibility: Edible, but don't be deceived by the species name, *(deliciosus),* as quality varies in different subspecies. When cooked with trout, flavors of both are improved.

Similar species: Easily confused with numerous other species having latex that is some shade of orange or red-orange. (1) Orange-ring Milkcap (*L. thyinos,* p. 337) has a *more sticky* stalk surface, similar orange colors of cap and latex, but *does* *not stain green* as it gradually changes to grayish red. It is reported from southern Canada south to New England and Michigan. (2) Peck's Milkcap (*L. peckii*, p. 333), known from New England southward, has a similar zoned pattern of darker and more reddish orange colors on the cap but has *white latex.* In Peck's Milkcap the latex and wounded flesh do not become reddish when exposed to air, but dried latex in southern varieties is *blue-green.* Faded or aged specimens of some varieties of Saffron Milkcap *(L. deliciosus)* could be confused with (3) *L. rubrilacteus*, (4) *L. salmoneus*, and (5) *L. barrowsii* (not shown), all of which have *more latex;* and even with (6) the dingy *white to yellowish Lactarius pseudodeliciosus* (not shown), which has orange, green-staining latex. (7) *Lactarius chelidonium* (not shown) has dingy yellowish to "muddy" orange latex.

Remarks: The above description is broad enough to encompass all of the varieties of Saffron Milkcap *(L. deliciosus)*, including variety *deterrimus,* which is sometimes regarded as a separate species. These varieties and this series of "look-alikes" emphasize the necessity of having specimens of mushrooms of all ages in good condition in order to make identifications as accurately as possible on field characters.

SMOKY MILKCAP *Lactarius fumosus*   **Pl. 40**
Similar to Sooty Milkcap *(L. lignyotus*, p. 332), but lighter and more grayish.
Fruiting: Scattered or grouped on forest soil, east of Great Plains. Summer and fall.
Edibility: Unknown.

ORANGE MILKCAP *Lactarius hygrophoroides*   **Pl. 41**
Medium sized, *orange* to *reddish orange cap. White, unstaining latex.* Gills widely spaced. **Spore print:** White.
Fruiting: On soil in hardwood forests. Great Lakes to Maine and Florida. Summer and early fall.
Edibility: Edible.

INDIGO MILKCAP *Lactarius indigo*   **Pl. 41**
Medium to large; *indigo blue overall,* including the *abundant latex. Sticky cap surface* has a *silvery sheen.* **Cap:** Firm; convex, with a depressed disc and inrolled margin at first, becoming shallowly funnel-shaped. Surface smooth; pale to light or purplish blue when fresh and moist, fading quickly to grayish or silvery. Cap *slowly* turns *greenish* from *bruising, handling,* or *aging.* Flesh whitish at first, but quickly stains blue, then green when cut. Gills often are darker blue than cap or stalk, dusted with yellowish powder from mature spores in age; close, broad, adnate (broadly attached) to decurrent (extending down stalk). **Stalk:** Cylindric; hard, hollow. Surface sticky, sometimes spotted. **Spore print:** Pale yellowish. **Technical notes:** Cap 5–15 cm across. Stalk 2–7 × 1.0–2.5 cm. Spores reticulate, broadly ellipsoid; 7–9 × 5.5–7.5 μm.
Fruiting: Solitary to grouped; on forest soil. Canada to Mex-

ico, Midwest to East Coast; common in the Southeast. Summer and fall.

Edibility: Edible.

Remarks: The *blue latex* makes this one of the easiest milkcaps to recognize. Be sure to check fresh, healthy specimens that have not dried out.

SOOTY MILKCAP *Lactarius lignyotus*   **Pl. 40**
Small to medium, *thin, blackish brown cap;* surface *dull, velvety. Slender stalk. Latex white; slowly stains cut surfaces pink. Gills close. Cap:* Convex with a narrow, pointed knob and incurved margin at first, expanding to nearly flat with a shallow depression; sometimes wrinkled around a low central knob. Surface often ribbed and sometimes lobed in age near margin; occasionally more or less mottled with lighter spots but remaining dark brown. Gills white at first, becoming yellowish in age (from mature spores), sometimes with dark edges; adnate (broadly attached) to decurrent (extending down stalk). *Stalk:* Cylindric; colored like cap except lighter (sometimes white) at base. Surface ribbed at apex; base stains reddish to violet when cut. *Spore print:* Yellow. **Technical notes:** Cap 2–7 cm across. Stalk 5–10 × 0.4–1.0 cm. Spores globose; 9.0–10.5 µm in diameter. Surface reticulate, with high ridges.

Fruiting: Solitary to scattered; on wet, usually mossy soil in coniferous forests and bogs. Common on peat moss. Southern Canada to mid-South; east of Great Plains. Summer and fall.
Edibility: Unattractive as food, but apparently not poisonous.
Similar species: A number of species that look like Sooty Milkcap (*Lactarius lignyotus*) can be distinguished by a combination of field and microscopic characters. Among them, (1) *L. gerardii* (not shown) has a *white* spore print, more widely spaced gills, *usually* lacks pink or violet stains, and is common *under hardwoods* as well as conifers. (2) *Lactarius fallax* (not shown) has *more crowded gills,* sometimes with dark brown edges. It is found under conifers in the Northwest from Alaska to California. (3) Smoky Milkcap (*L. fumosus,* p. 331) is similar in appearance but has a lighter (smoky brown) cap surface.

SLIMY MILKCAP *Lactarius mucidus*   **Pl. 40**
Medium to large, *shiny, brown* to *gray cap;* surface *slimy* to *sticky. Latex white, drying* as *green* to *olive spots. Cap:* Rounded, with a depressed disc (sometimes with a low knob). Surface smooth, not zoned. Grayish brown to dark gray on disc, pale pinkish buff to light gray on margin. Flesh firm; white to pale brownish pink, unchanging when cut or bruised. Odor not distinctive. Gills close, adnate (broadly attached); white, later yellowish. *Stalk:* Cylindric; solid or becoming hollow with age. Surface smooth, sticky; colored like cap but lighter. *Spore print:* White or pale yellowish. **Technical notes:** Cap 3–10 cm across. Stalk 3–7 × 0.7–2.0 cm. Spores

ellipsoid; reticulum complete or with open ends and some free ridges.

Fruiting: Solitary to scattered; on soil in moist coniferous woods, sometimes on peat moss. Widespread in N. America, Canada to mid-South. Summer and early fall.

Edibility: Said to be non-poisonous, but unpalatable.

Similar species: (1) Kauffman's Milkcap (*L. kauffmanii,* not shown), common in the Pacific Northwest, is larger and has a darker, more uniformly colored cap. (2) Another western species, *Lactarius pseudomucidus* (not shown), is known from Alaska to California and eastward to Idaho. It has darker, more grayish colors than Slimy Milkcap *(L. mucidus),* an *extremely* slimy stalk, and latex which does *not* produce greenish or bluish spots on drying.

PECK'S MILKCAP *Lactarius peckii*   **Pl. 42**
Medium to large, *reddish orange overall; cap zoned* with *darker spots* and *streaks. Latex white, unchanging* when exposed to air. *Cap:* Convex with a depressed disc, margin streaked at first and remaining long incurved, later shallowly funnel-shaped. Surface dry, minutely velvety at first but soon smooth. Gills close, narrow, decurrent (extending down stalk); darkening and becoming more red to grayish red at maturity. *Stalk:* Cylindric; interior soon stuffed with filaments and finally hollow. Surface colored like cap or lighter, sometimes spotted with reddish brown or discolored from handling. *Spore print:* White. **Technical notes:** Cap 5–15 cm across. Stalk 2–6 × 1.0–2.5 cm. Spores globose; 6.0–7.5 μm in diameter. Surface has a partial to complete reticulum (network).

Fruiting: Scattered or in groups or small clumps; in open, often grassy places in deciduous forests. Eastern and southern U.S.; New England southward.

Edibility: Reported as not poisonous, but said to be unpalatable. **Not recommended.**

Similar species: The reddish orange, zoned caps may be confused with (1) Saffron Milkcap *(L. deliciosus)* — see comparison above. Old and faded specimens of (2) *L. allardii* (not shown) and Peck's Milkcap *(L. peckii)* could be confused, but in *L. allardii* caps are more pink, not zoned; the latex dries greenish; and the short, thick stalk gives it a more squatty appearance. *Lactarius allardii* is a white mushroom which becomes grayish pink in age; *L. peckii* is reddish orange, fading somewhat in age.

PEPPER MILKCAP *Lactarius piperatus*   **Pl. 41**
Medium to large, *dry, white cap* with *thin, narrow, very crowded gills. White latex. Cap:* Convex to flat or depressed on disc. Surface smooth or wrinkled in age or where damaged, becoming spotted or smudged with dingy yellow-brown. Gills white at first, then pale yellowish; often forked one or more times. *Stalk:* Cylindric; firm, solid. Surface white, dry. *Spore*

print: White. **Technical notes:** Cap 5–15 cm across. Stalk 2–8 × 1.0–2.5 cm. Spores short-ellipsoid; 5–7 × 5.0–5.5 μm. Surface ornamented with fine lines and isolated warts.

Fruiting: Scattered to grouped; on soil in deciduous woods. Eastern N. America. Summer.

Edibility: Not recommended. Poisoning has been reported from this species in N. America.

Similar species: Variety *glaucescens* of Pepper Milkcap *(L. piperatus)* has pale cream latex which dries greenish. Several closely related species with crowded gills have white latex that slowly turns yellow or stains cut surfaces yellow on drying. (1) *Lactarius neuhoffii* (not shown) is found in eastern and midwestern U.S. (2) *Lactarius angustifolius* is known only from Texas. Some of the large, white, dry *Russula* species resemble Pepper Milkcap, but, of course, they *lack the white latex.*

Remarks: The *narrow, very crowded gills* are an important recognition character for *L. piperatus* (Pepper Milkcap).

SHAGGY BEAR *Lactarius representaneus* **Pl. 41**
Large, *sticky, yellow cap;* surface *scaly,* with a *hairy margin. Spotted stalk. White* or *cream-colored latex quickly stains cut surfaces purple. Grows under conifers. Cap:* Convex with a depressed disc to flat or shallowly funnel-shaped. Surface hairy, particularly toward margin, which is shaggy from stiff hairs; sometimes faintly zoned. Flesh thick, firm, brittle; white, but quickly staining grayish reddish purple when cut (from latex). Odor variable. Gills close; pale yellowish, *staining purplish* when injured. *Stalk:* Cylindric or expanded downwards; hard. Surface sticky to dry; usually spotted, yellowish. *Spore print:* Yellowish. **Technical notes:** Cap 6–15 cm across. Stalk 5–10 × 1–4 cm. Spores elliptic, with warts and ridges on surface; 9–11 × 6.5–8.0 μm.

Fruiting: Scattered to clustered; on soil under spruce. Western U.S. and Canada. Late summer and fall. Common in Rocky Mts.

Edibility: Poisonous.

Similar species: *Lactarius speciosus* (not shown) is usually smaller, has a distinctly zoned cap, duller and paler colors, and grows under hardwoods in southeastern U.S. If the color changes of latex or wound reaction are not noted or are ignored, this species could be confused easily with Spotstalk (*L. scrobiculatus,* p. 335), and related species.

RED–JUICE MILKCAP *Lactarius rubrilacteus* **Pl. 42**
Medium to large, orange, concentrically ringed cap. Latex scanty, dard red to orange-red. All parts slowly stain blue-green on injury.

Fruiting: Scattered to grouped on soil in pine forests. Rocky Mts. and westward. Summer and fall.

Edibility: Edible.

RED-HOT MILKCAP *Lactarius rufus* **Pl. 42**
Medium to large, *reddish brown cap* and *stalk;* surface *moist*

to dry. Gills lighter brown. Latex white. **Cap:** Convex to flat or broadly depressed and often with a narrow, pointed central knob. Surface smooth at first, but later minutely fibrillose or cracked, and more or less indistinctly spotted or streaked, dry to moist or tacky. Moderate reddish brown; fading in age. Flesh dingy pale yellowish pink. Odor not distinctive. Latex often thin, scanty. Gills close, whitish at first, but soon becoming yellowish pink or darker in age. **Stalk:** Cylindric, colored like cap or lighter at apex, often whitish at base. Surface smooth, dry; flesh firm but interior usually hollow at maturity. **Spore print:** White to yellowish. **Technical notes:** Cap 4–12 cm across. Stalk 5–10 × 0.8–1.6 cm. Spores ellipsoid; surface reticulate, with an open net and isolated warts.

Fruiting: Scattered to grouped or clumped; on light soil or moss beds under conifers in northern forests. Summer and early fall. Sometimes fruits in great abundance in Rocky Mts. We have counted over 300 caps in a square meter.

Edibility: Not recommended. Although some forms of this complex species in Europe are eaten after parboiling, the American material may be different.

Similar species: Commonly misidentified as *Lactarius alpinus,* a smaller, more yellow-orange species (not shown).

Remarks: This is a highly variable species, not too well understood. The form shown here is common in our Rocky Mts. In the field it looks like specimens we have seen in Norway and Sweden.

SPOTSTALK   Pl. 41
Lactarius scrobiculatus

Medium to large, *straw yellow cap; young* specimens have a *sticky surface* and *hairy margin. Latex white,* but *changes quickly to yellow* when exposed to air (when gills are cut). *Stalk spotted.* **Cap:** Convex at first, with a strongly incurved margin; soon shallowly depressed. Surface hairy; spotted or streaked, sometimes zoned and more or less scaly toward margin. Pale yellow to brownish, sometimes faintly tinged with olive. Flesh firm, somewhat brittle; white. Odor faint or lacking, sometimes fruity. Gills close, often forked near stalk, adnate (broadly attached), white or yellowish. **Stalk:** Cylindric, firm, stuffed to hollow. Surface dry, white to yellowish, appearing pitted from dark yellow spots. **Spore print:** Yellowish. **Technical notes:** Cap 4–14 cm across. Stalk 3–10 × 1–3 cm. Spores warty and ridged but not reticulate, elliptic; 7–9 × 5.5–7.0 μm.

Fruiting: Solitary to grouped; in coniferous forests. Nova Scotia to British Columbia and Alaska to California and Colorado. **Edibility: Poisonous.** Avoid all species of *Lactarius* with white latex which stains yellow.

Similar species: (1) *Lactarius payettensis* and (2) *L. alnicola* (not shown) are common western species of similar appearance. *Lactarius alnicola* has a cottony, not bearded, margin on young, unfolding caps, contrasted with that of Spotstalk (*L. scrobiculatus*). Marginal hairs on cap of *L. payettensis* become grayish and the white latex does not *itself* become yellow but stains cut tissues yellowish to brown. (3) *Lactarius gossypinus* (not shown) has a distinct *pinkish cast* to gills. (4) Latex of Shaggy Bear (*L. representaneus*, p. 334) is white at first, but soon *stains purplish.* (5) Numerous other white to yellowish, hairy species, some dry and others sticky, resemble Spotstalk (*L. scrobiculatus*) in some features, but *lack the spotted stalk.*

MARYLAND MILKCAP *Lactarius subplinthogalus*   **Pl. 41**
Medium-sized, *dry, pale orange-yellow cap; gills and stalk slightly darker.* Latex *stains cut surfaces strong yellowish pink. Gills very widely spaced. Cap:* Flat, with a narrow, shallow depression on disc; margin usually lobed, minutely scalloped, or pleated. Surface smooth, unpolished; sometimes wrinkled and tinged with gray in age. Flesh soft, nearly white at first, but staining yellowish pink when cut. Odor not distinctive. Gills distant (widely spaced), broad, adnate (broadly attached) to decurrent (extending down stalk). *Stalk:* Cylindric or tapered at base; surface smooth, dry. *Spore print:* Pale orange-yellow. **Technical notes:** Cap 3–7 cm across. Stalk 3–6 × 0.7–1.5 cm. Spores subglobose; 7–9 μm in diameter. Surface has spines and ridges but is not reticulate.
Fruiting: Scattered to grouped; on soil in hardwood and mixed conifer-hardwood forests. Central Atlantic and southeastern U.S.; not uncommon in Chesapeake Bay region. Summer to early fall.
Edibility: Unknown.
Similar species: The very widely spaced gills, stature, and fruiting time suggest (1) Orange Milkcap (*L. hygrophoroides,* p. 331), a species of the hardwood forests throughout N. America from the Great Plains eastward. Orange Milkcap has brighter and usually more intense orange to reddish orange colors; white, unstaining latex (or staining brownish in some specimens); and a white spore print. The "washed-out" colors of Maryland Milkcap, together with its pale-colored spore print and the yellowish pink staining distinguish it readily from Orange Milkcap. (2) Light or faded forms of *Lactarius fumosus* (Smoky Milkcap, p. 331, Pl. 40) may resemble Maryland Milkcap, but the drab colors and close gill spacing of *L. fumosus* distinguish the two species readily.

RED–WINE MILKCAP *Lactarius subpurpureus*   **Pl. 41**
A medium to large milkcap. *Purplish* to *yellowish pink overall,* with *darker spots* or *zones. Purplish red latex slowly stains light green. Cap:* Convex with a depressed disc, expanding to flat or shallowly funnel-shaped. Surface smooth, developing a silvery sheen as it loses moisture, becoming more yellowish in age or as it dries out; sometimes streaked and retaining purplish color longest near margin. Odor not distinctive. Latex

sometimes scanty. Gills subdistant, adnate (broadly attached) to decurrent (extending down stalk); flushed with green when injured. **Stalk:** Cylindric, smooth, stuffed to hollow. **Spore print:** Pale yellowish. **Technical notes:** Cap 3–10 cm across. Stalk 3–8 × 0.7–1.5 cm. Spores reticulate, ellipsoid; 8–11 × 6.5–8.0 μm.

Fruiting: Solitary to grouped; on soil in mixed forests and coniferous woods, often under hemlock. Eastern Canada and U.S. south to Florida.

Edibility: Edible.

Similar species: Colors distinguish it readily from all other milkcaps growing in the same area except *L. paradoxus* (not shown), which has purplish red latex also. Faded specimens of the two are frequently confused, but young fresh specimens of *L. paradoxus* have *blue* and often *more brownish* colors that are lacking in *L. subpurpureus* (Red-wine Milkcap).

ORANGE-RING MILKCAP *Lactarius thyinos*   **Pl. 42**
Medium to large, *orange, slimy* to *sticky, cap* and *stalk. Cap zoned. Latex orange;* does *not stain* flesh and gills *green* when exposed to air. **Cap:** Convex at first, becoming depressed on disc and later broadly funnel-shaped, often with a flaring outer limb and margin. Surface smooth, sticky to slimy at first, with alternating zones of strong to moderate orange and moderate orange-yellow, fading to grayish. Flesh thin. Odor faintly fragrant. Gills subdistant (see inside front cover); orange, very slowly staining grayish red when injured. **Stalk:** Cylindric or tapered upwards; hollow, fragile. Surface smooth; orange, sometimes with a whitish sheen in age; staining grayish red when cut, but *no green stains. Spore print:* Pale yellow. **Technical notes:** Cap 3–9 cm across. Stalk 4–8 × 1–2 cm. Spores broadly elliptic; 9–12 × 7.5–9.0 μm. Surface reticulate, with some isolated warts and ribs. Cap and stalk with a thin ixocutis (cuticle).

Fruiting: Scattered to grouped; in cedar woods, swamps, and bogs. Great Lakes area eastward to Vermont and Nova Scotia.

Edibility: Edible.

Similar species: Orange-ring Milkcap looks like (1) Saffron Milkcap (*L. deliciosus,* p. 330) and (2) *L. rubrilacteus* (p. 334), but both of those species *stain green when cut or bruised.* Peck's Milkcap (*L. peckii,* p. 333) has *white latex.*

POWDERPUFF MILKCAP *Lactarius torminosus*   **Pl. 41**
Mostly large; *pink overall. Cap hairy,* especially *on margin. Latex white, unchanging* when exposed to air. **Cap:** Convex to flat, with a depressed disc and strongly incurved margin, expanding to shallowly funnel-shaped. Surface sticky on center at first, often more or less zoned and fading to white, at least on margin. Flesh firm to flaccid (limp); white or pinkish, not changing when cut. Gills close, narrow, yellowish pink, some forking near stalk, short-decurrent. **Stalk:** Smooth, dry; occa-

sionally spotted, colored like cap. Interior stuffed with filaments to hollow. **Spore print:** White to pale yellowish. **Technical notes:** Cap 4–12 cm across. Stalk 3–7 × 0.6–1.5 cm. Spores reticulate with some isolated warts, elliptic; 7.5–9.0 × 6.0–7.5 μm.

Fruiting: Scattered to grouped; on soil, usually associated with birch trees. Alaska to California, Missouri, and Nova Scotia. Late summer and fall.

Edibility: The European form of this species is eaten and even harvested commercially for market in Finland. It is consistently reported as **poisonous** in America. We advise against experimenting with it, as there appear to be differences between European and American specimens.

Similar species: Variants of Powderpuff Milkcap *(L. torminosus)* and (1) *Lactarius pubescens* (not shown) are almost indistinguishable without a microscope. Both fruit under birch trees in the same area. (2) *Lactarius villosus,* also similar, is white, becoming tinged with orange; it has smaller spores. It is reported from Nebraska and California.

Remarks: The name Shaggy Milkcap, used in a number of European English language books, refers to the thick, hairy coat on the cap. This and the pink colors when fresh are important field characters.

ORDINARY MILKCAP *Lactarius trivialis*   **Pl. 42**
Large, sticky, gray cap and *stalk,* suffused with *violet;* both *fade to brownish. Latex white. Grows under conifers* in *western N. America.* **Cap:** Convex with an incurved, downy margin at first, soon nearly flat with shallowly depressed disc; margin often upturned. Surface smooth; indistinctly zoned or lacking zones. Reddish gray, fading quickly to light brown or lighter. Flesh thick, firm; whitish. Odor not distinctive; taste faint, slowly peppery.* Gills pallid to light yellowish pink. Latex white, drying olive-brown. **Stalk:** Cylindric; hollow, more or less fragile. Surface slimy at first but soon dry. **Spore print:** Pale yellow. **Technical notes:** Cap 5–15 cm across. Stalk 5–10 × 1.0–2.5 cm. Spores broadly ellipsoid; 7.5–9.5 × 6.0–7.5 μm. Surface reticulate, with some isolated warts and bars.

Fruiting: Solitary to scattered; on soil in conifer forests. Alaska to Washington and Utah; seldom found in the East. Fruits in fall.

Edibility: Not recommended. In Europe this milkcap (*L. trivialis*) is eaten only after boiling. It is sold on the market in Finland. In America this species is hard to recognize.

Similar species: Faded specimens are easily confused with (1) Kindred Milkcap (*L. affinis,* p. 326) and (2) Slimy Milkcap (*L. mucidus,* p. 332) in our western conifer forests. (3) *Lactarius*

---

* See p. 10 for cautions about using taste as an identifying characteristic.

argillaceifolius (not shown) is a species of hardwood forests that has been widely misidentified as Ordinary Milkcap *(L. trivalis)*. The brown-staining gills, early summer fruiting, hardwood forest habitat, and microscopic characters distinguish *L. argillaceifolius*.

DAMP MILKCAP *Lactarius uvidus*   **Pl. 42**
Medium to large, *gray* to *brown cap,* flushed with *purple;* surface *sticky. Latex white* to *yellowish; slowly stains* cut surfaces *purplish,* then *brown. Cap:* Convex, sometimes with a small knob, becoming nearly flat with a broad, shallow, central depression. Surface smooth, slimy to sticky; may be zoned or not (see **Remarks**), sometimes spotted with grayish purple to grayish red or grayish to light yellowish brown. Odor not distinctive. Gills close, adnate (broadly attached); white, becoming yellowish to pale brownish pink. *Stalk:* Cylindric or enlarged downwards. Surface may be somewhat slimy or dry; often yellowish around base. *Spore print:* Pale yellowish. **Technical notes:** Cap 3–10 cm across. Stalk 3–7 × 1.0–1.5 cm. Spores elliptic; 8–11 × 6.5–7.5 µm. Surface incompletely reticulate, with isolated warts and ribs. KOH (potash) on cuticle turns green.
Fruiting: Scattered to grouped; on ground under mixed birch, aspen, and pine or coniferous forests throughout N. America. Summer and fall.
Edibility: Poisonous.
Similar species: (1) *Lactarius maculatus* (not shown) and (2) *L. subpalustris* (not shown) have whey-like latex. *L. maculatus* has a distinctly spotted or zoned cap surface and a peppery taste. Both are found in eastern hardwood forests.
Remarks: The above description is written broadly enough to encompass both the eastern variety of *L. uvidus* and the darker-colored, more distinctly zoned western varieties of the species illustrated on Pl. 42.

FLEECY MILKCAP *Lactarius vellereus*   **Pl. 41**
Large, hard, white cap; surface dry, *minutely velvety at first.* Cap *convex, depressed at center. Gills* usually *widely spaced.* Cut surfaces *stain yellowish* to *light brown. Latex white. Cap:* Broadly and shallowly funnel-shaped or nearly flat, with a dry, unpolished surface. Sometimes lobed at maturity and sometimes becoming brownish all over in age. Flesh white, thick. Gills subdistant to distant, sometimes forked or interveined, adnate to decurrent; may be flushed with green. *Stalk:* Thick, cylindric; sometimes eccentric (off center). Interior may be solid or stuffed. *Spore print:* White or yellowish. **Technical notes:** Cap 5–25 cm across. Stalk 2–5 × 1.5–4.0 cm. Spores minutely warty, subglobose; 7.5–9.5 × 6.5–8.5 µm.
Fruiting: Grouped to scattered; on ground in hardwood and mixed hardwood-conifer forests. Midwest and eastern U.S. and southern Canada.

Edibility: Not recommended.
Similar species: *Lactarius subvellereus* (not shown), which
has smaller spores, is apparently more common than Fleecy
Milkcap *(L. vellereus).* The two are very commonly confused.
TAWNY MILKCAP *Lactarius volemus*   **Pl. 40**
Similar to Wrinkled Milkcap *(L. corrugis,* p. 329), but cap
more yellowish (tawny); rarely wrinkled.
Fruiting: Common and often abundant on ground in hard-
wood forests easts fo Great Plains. Summer.
Edibility: Edible.

PART III

Puffballs and Relatives
GASTROMYCETES

7

GASTROMYCETES
Puffballs, Stinkhorns, and Others

Basidiomycete mushrooms which produce spores enclosed inside a spore case and which have no means of forcefully discharging their spores are classified as Gastromycetes. Many common edible fungi are Gastromycetes. A few species are poisonous; some (such as the stinkhorns, Pl. 43, p. 344) are unappealing as food because of their odor or texture.

Earthstars and puffballs are among the most common Gastromycetes. They produce spores inside a persistent spore case, which may be smooth or distinctively ornamented on the surface. Some puffballs (such as species of *Lycoperdon,* p. 354) have spore cases that eventually open by means of a distinct pore or "mouth." Some Gastromycetes are stalked (see *Tulostoma,* p. 364). Many puffballs are edible when young and white inside, but be sure to cut them in half lengthwise to make sure there are no signs of a developing cap and gills. Young puffballs are occasionally confused with early stages ("buttons") of poisonous Amanitas (see Pls. 26 and 27).

False truffles (see *Truncocolumella,* p. 349) are Gastromycetes that grow under ground; many are a favored food of rodents and larger animals, such as deer. The presence of these fungi may be evident to mushroom hunters by humps or cracks in the soil.

Family Calostomataceae

Lattice Puffballs: Genus *Calostoma*

Small to medium, stalked puffballs with a *lattice-like stalk* that is gelatinous at first. Spore powder whitish.

LATTICE PUFFBALL *Calostoma lutescens*   **Pl. 43**
Medium to large, *net-like gelatinous stalk* and *round, red-mouthed spore sac. Spores white.* **Spore case** three-layered: outer layer thin, gelatinous; middle layer breaks into irregular, hard, red scales that fall away with gelatinous outer layer. Inner spore sac persistent, tough but papery; yellowish, with red

"teeth" along slit-like opening. **Stalk:** Orange-yellow when fresh, drying hard and tough. Base more or less roots in soil and incorporates soil and debris. **Technical notes:** Spore case 1–2 cm across. Stalk 3–6 × 1–2 cm. Spores globose, with pitted walls; 6–8 μm in diameter.

Fruiting: Scattered to clustered; on soil in hardwood forests. Southeastern U.S. and Mexico.

Edibility: Unknown, but obviously less attractive to the palate than the eye.

Similar species: (1) *Calostoma cinnabarina* (below) has a red inner spore case, thicker and more gelatinous outer layers, and a shorter stalk. (2) *Calostoma ravenelii* (not shown) has yellowish inner spore case as in *C. lutescens,* but lacks conspicuous gelatinous tissues on spore case and stalk.

ASPIC PUFFBALL *Calostoma cinnabarina*   **Pl. 43**
Red spore case has an *orange, gelatinous outer layer. Stalk net-like.*

Fruiting: On soil in hardwood forests, often along trails and roadsides. Southeastern U.S. Late summer and fall.

Edibility: Unknown.

Similar species: See Lattice Puffball (above).

Stinkhorns: Family Clathraceae

Genus *Anthurus*

LIZARD CLAW *Anthurus gardneri*   **Pl. 43**
Large, white, sponge-like stalk. Orange and *brown head splits vertically. Unpleasant odor.* **Cap:** Consists of 4–6 angular, clawlike arms; more or less ribbed with white or yellowish pink to reddish orange colors outward, inner surfaces colored dark olive-brown from slimy, fetid spore mass. Arms separate and spread outward at maturity. **Stalk:** Cylindrical or enlarged upwards or in midportion; hollow. Stalk rises from a white, cup-like, membranous volva with a slimy inner layer. **Technical notes:** Head 2.5–5.0 × 1.0–1.5 cm. Stalk 7–10 × 1.0–1.5 cm. Spores elliptic; 3–4 × 1–2 μm.

Fruiting: Solitary to clustered; on soil in grassy places, gardens, and greenhouses. Widespread in N. America; southern Canada to California in the West, Massachusetts to Ohio and southward in the East. Late summer.

Edibility: Unknown.

Similar species: *Lysurus mokusin* (below) has broad, shallow, lengthwise (vertical) ribs and depressions on stalk and head, giving the stalk an *angular* outline in cross-section, contrasted with the round stalk of Lizard Claw *(A. gardneri)* seen in cross-section. *Lysurus mokusin* has spore slime in depressions on *outer* surface of arms, whereas spore slime of *A. gardneri* coats *inner* and *side* surfaces of arms.

RIBBED LIZARD CLAW *Lysurus mokusin* **Pl. 43**
Large, pink to *reddish orange, hollow, deeply grooved stalk* rises from a *whitish, membranous cup. Outer* surface of arms coated with *slimy brown spore mass.* Stalk *angular* in cross-section.
Fruiting: Reported from Chesapeake Bay area southward. Common in California. May to October. Also fruits in greenhouses.
Edibility: Unknown.
Similar species: See Lizard Claw (*Anthurus gardneri,* above).

Stinkhorns: Genus *Clathrus*

COLUMN STINKHORN **Pl. 43**
Clathrus columnatus
Medium-sized, *pink, spongy receptacle* consisting of *2–5 thick columns united at apex. Odor unpleasant.* Columns narrowed at base, wider above, curved, more or less angular; rising from membranous, white volva. Columns deep reddish orange above to yellowish pink below. Spore mass slimy, dark olive-brown, coating inner surface of upper part of columns. **Technical notes:** Receptacle up to 8 cm high. Spores 3.5–5.0 × 2.0–2.5 μm.
Fruiting: Scattered to grouped; on sandy soil, sometimes in lawns, especially on coastal plains. Carolinas south to Florida and Gulf Coast, also Mexico and Hawaii. Late fall and winter.
Edibility: Unknown. Other species of *Clathrus* are said to be **poisonous.**
Similar species: (1) Lattice Stinkhorn (*Clathrus ruber,* below) has a larger, more globular, net-like receptacle. It has been reported in the same area as Column Stinkhorn (*C. columnatus*) and north to Virginia, also in California. The columnar arms of Column Stinkhorn are free of each other at their bases within the volval cup, thus somewhat reminiscent of (2) an upside-down Stinky Squid (*Pseudocolus fusiformis,* below). Differing habitats emphasize their differences, as Column Stinkhorn is found on sandy soil, whereas Stinky Squid shows a preference for rotting logs and chip-mulched soil.
LATTICE STINKHORN *Clathrus ruber* **Pl. 43**
Medium-sized, reddish, round, lattice-like, hollow ball from white, cuplike volva membrane. Spore mass on inside of lattice.
Fruiting: Southeastern U.S. and California.
Edibility: Unknown.
Similar species: See Column Stinkhorn (*Clathrus columnatus,* above).

Genus *Pseudocolus*

STINKY SQUID *Pseudocolus fusiformis* **Pl. 43**
Small to medium, *soft, pink, spongy columns united at base;*

tips free or fused but usually touching. Odor unpleasant. **Head:** Consists of 3–4 slender arms that arch outward and then come together at pointed apex. Individual arms more or less angular and tapering upwards, with greenish spore slime on inner surfaces toward the apex. Arms reddish orange to yellowish pink at tip, lighter downwards to nearly white at slender, rounded to bulbous stalk. Volva white, membranous above; brownish at base, with numerous threadlike strands radiating out into substrate. **Technical notes:** Receptacle 4–9 × 1.5–2.5 cm overall; arms 2–5 mm in diameter × 2.5–6.5 cm long. Spores smooth, hyaline (clear), elliptic; 3.5–5.0 × 1–2 μm. **Fruiting:** Solitary to grouped or clustered; on decaying logs or chip-mulched soil. Eastern U.S., from Massachusetts to Georgia. **Edibility: Not recommended.**
Similar species: Column Stinkhorn (*Clathrus columnatus,* above) has thicker columns that are separate at base and united in a flattened "roof" above. Species of Lizard Claw (*Anthurus gardneri,* p. 343) have a long stalk and more brownish spore slime.

Stinkhorns: Genus *Simblum*

CHAMBERED STINKHORN   Pl. 43
Simblum sphaerocephalum

Medium-sized, *round, red, lattice-like head* on a *spongy, hollow stalk. Slimy, greenish spore mass* on inner surfaces of *lattice* has a *strong, repulsive odor.* **Cap:** Subglobose, hollow; ribs of lattice strong yellowish pink. Spore mass dark olive-brown. **Stalk:** Colored like lattice ribs above; lighter below, sheathed at base by membranous, white, cup-like volva. **Technical notes:** Cap 1.5–2.5 cm across. Stalk 6–8 × 0.5–1.5 cm; wall 1–4 mm thick. Spores smooth, elliptic; 3.5–4.5 × 1.5–2.0 μm.
Fruiting: Solitary or scattered; on soil in pastures, lawns, orchards, and other grassy places. New York southward and west to Nebraska, Kansas, and New Mexico. **Edibility:** Unknown, but **not recommended.**
Similar species: *Simblum texensis* (not shown) is yellow and has larger spores.
Remarks: *Simblum sphaerocephalum* (Chambered Stinkhorn) is occasionally found in a "twin" form having fused heads on 2 gracefully arched stalks arising from a single volva.

Family Hysterangiaceae

Genus *Phallogaster*

SAC STINKHORN *Phallogaster saccatus*   **Pl. 43**
Medium-sized, *white head* and *stalk, flushed* with *pink or lilac.*

Stinky odor develops *slowly. Greenish spore slime inside.*
Fruit body: An irregularly pear- to egg-shaped head, tapering downward to a short, pointed stalk, attached to substrate by pink, cord-like strands. Surface smooth at first, then pitted, eventually developing a more or less star-shaped opening to expose olive-tinged gleba. Interior *chambered* in head, solid in stalk. **Technical notes:** Fruiting body 2.5–5 × 1–3 cm. Spores smooth, long-elliptic; 4–5 × 1–2 μm.
Fruiting: Solitary or clustered; on well-decayed wood. Central and eastern N. America. Spring to midsummer.
Edibility: Unknown.
Similar species: Not likely to be confused with anything except an immature stinkhorn, from which it is readily distinguished by the *chambered gleba* seen in longitudinal section.

Family Phallaceae

Genus *Dictyophora*

NET STINKHORN *Dictyophora duplicata*   **Pl. 43**
Large, white, spongy stalk with a *net-like skirt* originating under *thin, slime-covered cap.* Odor weak to strong, repulsive.
Cap: Bell-shaped, most often with an apical hole that is continuous with the hollow stalk. White, except upper surface is covered with olive-tinged spore slime, having a network of low, thin ridges under spore layer. *Stalk:* Cylindric and tapered upwards, often curved; rising from membranous white to pinkish volval cup with slimy inner layer. **Technical notes:** Cap 4–5 × 3.5–4 cm. Stalk 12–17 × 2–4 cm. Spores smooth, hyaline (transparent), elliptic; 3.5–4.5 × 1–2 μm.
Fruiting: Solitary or grouped; on soil in hardwood and mixed conifer-hardwood forests. Southeastern Canada west to Great Lakes and south to Mexico.
Edibility: Young "eggs" are said to be non-poisonous.
Similar species: (1) Common Stinkhorn (*Phallus impudicus*) and (2) Eastern Stinkhorn (*Phallus ravenelii*, p. 348) both look like Net Stinkhorn minus the beautiful netted skirt. The skirt may be slow to develop and not observed in young specimens or may be shed or broken off in older specimens.

Stinkhorns: Genus *Mutinus*

DOG STINKHORN *Mutinus caninus*   **Pl. 43**
Long, slender, more or less *pointed stalk. No cap.* Stalk rises from an *elongate, membranous volva* with a *gelatinous inner layer.* Upper part of *stalk coated with fetid spore slime.* **Stalk:** Cylindric with a blunt apex; hollow, spongy. Reddish orange under olive-brown spore slime, gradually lighter below. Volva *membranous,* white to yellowish. **Technical notes:** Stalk 6–12

$\times$ 1.0–1.5 cm. Spores hyaline, smooth, cylindric, 3.5–5.0 $\times$ 1.5–2.0 μm.

Fruiting: Solitary to grouped; on soil and leaf litter in hardwood forests. Widespread in N. America, but more common in East and Midwest. Summer and fall.

Edibility: Inedible.

Similar species: Spore slime directly coating stalk with no head distinguishes Dog Stinkhorns *(Mutinus)* from all others. *Mutinus elegans* (not shown) has a larger stalk with a longer, more narrowly tapered, and more rosy pink upper portion.

Stinkhorns: Genus *Phallus*

EASTERN STINKHORN Pl. 43
Phallus ravenelii
Large, white, spongy stalk with a *thin cap* and more or less *granular, dark grayish olive, strongly fetid spore mass.* **Cap:** Narrowly bell-shaped, with apex open to hollow stalk. Surface granular and white under slimy, olive-tinged spore mass. Odor repulsive to nauseating. **Stalk:** Cylindric, tapering upwards from a tough, membranous, cup-like volva, which is smooth (hairless) and wrinkled on outside and white to pinkish or lilac-tinged inside. Volva has thick, colorless, gelatinous inner layer. **Technical notes:** Cap 3–5 $\times$ 2.5–4.0 cm. Stalk 10–15 $\times$ 1–2 μm.

Fruiting: Solitary to clustered; on soil, often on decaying woody debris or sawdust. Hardwood forests in eastern to midwestern N. America. Late summer and fall.

Edibility: Young "eggs" are said to be non-poisonous, but definitely **not recommended.**

Similar species: (1) Upper surface of cap of Common Stinkhorn *(Phallus impudicus)* has a network of ridges under the spore slime, as in (2) Net Stinkhorn (*Dictyophora duplicata,* p. 347). Common Stinkhorn is found from the Great Lakes west and southward, whereas Net Stinkhorn and Eastern Stinkhorn are found in midwestern and eastern N. America. Both species of *Phallus* may have a short skirt projecting below the cap, but it is never as well developed or conspicuous as in *Dictyophora,* and is usually lacking. (3) *Itajahya galericulata* (not shown), found in Arizona and New Mexico, has a nearly globose cap in several overlapping layers, with spore slime sandwiched between the layers.

Remarks: When they first emerge from the membranous volva and when the spore slime is lost in age, stinkhorns often have no odor. This may lead to occasional deception, due to careless statements in mycological literature suggesting that one always encounters the smell before sighting a stinkhorn, or that they can be "tracked down" by smell. In our western states at least, such pursuit will lead most often to a spot inhabited by well-disguised insects having the same fetid odor.

False Truffles: Family Rhizopogonaceae

Genus *Truncocolumella*

CITRINE FALSE TRUFFLE **Pl. 43**
Truncocolumella citrina
Small to medium, *greenish yellow, irregularly rounded* or
lobed. Matures underground. Fruiting bodies pear- to egg-
shaped; often wrinkled, lobed, or vertically flattened, with a
short, thick, rudimentary, pointed stalk. Surface dry; nearly
white at first (before exposure to light), then light to brilliant
greenish yellow, becoming grayish olive in age. Gleba olive-
gray to brownish gray; firm. Stalk branches in lower gleba to
form several strands radiating outward to surface (see lengthwise section). **Technical notes:** Fruiting body 1.5–5.0 ×
2.0–3.5 cm. Spores elliptic, thin-walled, smooth, 6.5–10.0 ×
3.5–4.5 µm.
Fruiting: Single to clumped; often pushing up a hump of soil.
Western conifer forests containing Douglas fir. Summer and
fall.
Edibility: Unknown.
Similar species: The many species of false truffles in western
N. America are distinguished mostly on microscopic characters. However, the combination of citrine outer surface and
radiating branches from stalk tip in Citrine False Truffle (*T.
citrina*) is quite distinctive.

Family Astrogastraceae

Genus *Gastroboletus*

BOLETE FALSE TRUFFLE **Pl. 43**
Gastroboletus turbinatus
Small to medium, *thick, dry, red* to *brown cap* with *red* to
yellow tubes. Stubby stalk. Flesh stains blue. **Cap:** Convex;
surface felty, dark brown to red flushed with orange. Flesh
thick; yellow to pinkish, *staining blue* when cut or bruised.
Tubes crowded, curved or twisted, with red to orange or yellow
mouths; tubes *stain blue* when cut or injured. **Stalk:** Short,
cylindric but often flattened and tapering at base. Yellow to
orange or red, more or less marbled; injured places *stain blue,
then red*. Does not give a spore print. **Technical notes:** Cap
2–6 cm across. Stalk 1–3 × 0.7–2.0 cm. Spores smooth, elliptic;
14–18 × 6.5–9.5 µm.
Fruiting: Scattered, on soil under conifers, Pacific Northwest
to Rocky Mts. Summer and fall.

Edibility: Unknown, but definitely **not recommended.**
Similar species: Relationship with boletes is obvious, and this may be thought to be an aborted bolete. The curved tubes and failure to make a spore print distinguish the genus *Gastroboletus,* which has about 10 species in western N. America. Like other false truffles, they often mature completely under the forest duff, making only a hump or crack in the surface above them.

Family Hymenogastraccae

Genus *Thaxtergaster*

SLIMY POUCH *Thaxtergaster pinguis*   **Pl. 43**
Small to medium, *slimy, yellow, rounded cap; does not open completely* and *does not give a spore print.* **Cap:** Globose at first, usually wrinkled or lobed and often flattened at maturity and breaking away from stalk; yellow to olive-brown, sometimes streaked or splotched with orange-yellow to yellow-brown. Surface slimy to sticky. Interior consists of thick, solid continuation of stalk to top of cap, surrounded by irregularly chambered, *yellow-brown gleba.* **Stalk:** Cylindric, sometimes enlarged downwards; surface sticky, often tinged with violet. *Does not make a spore print.* **Technical notes:** Cap 1–5 cm across. Stalk 1–4 × 1–2 cm thick. Spore walls brown, warty; spores elliptic; 14–17 × 8–10 μm.
Fruiting: Solitary to clustered; on soil in coniferous forests west of Great Plains. Early summer to fall.
Edibility: Unknown.
Similar species: Looks like a species of *Cortinarius* (webcap, p. 287, Pl. 36) in which the cap failed to open and expand completely.

Puffballs: Family Lycoperdaceae

Fruiting bodies single or grouped, mostly forming spore case above ground. Spore case globose to rounded or pear-shaped; not stalked but sometimes with a sterile base; surface at maturity sometimes has a distinctive pattern of scales. Interior forms a spore powder at maturity, sometimes with a conspicuous thread-like capillitium. Spores are discharged passively through one or more distinct pores or by breaking or disintegration of the spore case.

Mostly edible when young and white inside. **Caution:** Before eating puffballs, be sure to section young spore cases longitudinally to be sure that they are white throughout, solid to spongy-firm in texture, and do not form a structure which could be the cap and gills of a gill mushroom. Remember, deadly poisonous white Amanitas may look like puffballs from the outside!

True Puffballs: Genus *Bovista*

PUFFBALL *Bovista pila*   **Pl. 45**
Medium-sized, *round, brown, spore case with a paper-thin wall; opens by an irregular apical pore or tear; on surface of ground*. Round spore case sometimes grooved or ribbed around central basal attachment. Surface at first white, sometimes staining pinkish when handled. Thin, dull outer covering cracks, then flakes off at maturity, leaving shiny, brown, persistent wall originally attached to soil by a single, thin strand which breaks at point of attachment, allowing dry spore cases to be blown over soil by wind. Gleba purplish brown; no sterile base. **Technical notes:** Globose to (occasionally) ellipsoid spore case; 3–8 cm across. Capillitium much branched from main axis, 10–12 μm in diameter, tips pointed; spores smooth, pedicel short or lacking; globose; 3.5–4.5 μm in diameter.
Fruiting: Solitary to grouped; on soil in pastures, along roadsides, and in open places in woods or around stables. Common and widely distributed. Late summer and fall.
Edibility: Edible.
Similar species: (1) The smaller Plum Puffball (*Bovista plumbea,* not shown) has a bluish gray to more purplish brown spore case with a slightly thicker and more persistent outer wall. It is attached to soil by a clump of fibers, contrasted with the single cord of *B. pila*. Microscopically, the larger, oval (5–7 × 4.5–6.0 μm) spores and thicker capillitium of *B. plumbea* separate them readily. (2) Another small species, *Bovista minor* (not shown) is found occasionally in the Great Lakes region and southward. It has olivaceous gleba and small, oval, minutely warted spores. (3) Some species of *Lycoperdon* (e.g., *L. echinatum, L. marginatum, L. pulcherrimum*) have deciduous scales and other small species such as *L. pusillum* (Mini Puffball) may have indistinct but persistent surface scales. These remain attached to soil at maturity. (4) The flattened inner spore cases of *Disciseda,* Sandcase Puffball, may become separated from the outer sandcase, then resembling *Bovista,* but they are never globose.
Remarks: Species of *Bovista* represent the true puffballs. There are few species but they are not uncommon. Characteristically, they are produced on the surface of the soil, becoming readily detached at maturity, although *B. minor* originates under ground. The persistent, colored inner spore case separates readily from the thinner, more or less ephemeral outer spore case. It often lasts over the winter and is frequently seen blown about by the wind.

Giant Puffballs: Genus *Calvatia*

Medium to large puffballs. Spore case lacks a definite apical mouth or pore. Spore mass (gleba) is not separated from sterile base by a papery membrane. Glebal threads lack distinct main axis.

VASE PUFFBALL *Calvatia cyathiformis*   **Pl. 44**
Large, globose to *pear-shaped, white* to *brownish spore case* with *violaceous gleba at maturity.* Surface of spore case smooth at first, but often cracking and sometimes forming flat scales over rounded upper part as it matures; usually smooth but wrinkled or grooved over narrowed sterile base. Wall of upper spore case eventually disintegrates to expose gleba. Sterile base persists long after spores are dispersed. Gleba white at first, then yellow to yellow-brown and eventually violaceous. **Technical notes:** Spore case 8–20 × 5–15 cm. Capillitium sparingly branched, septate, approx. 5 μm in diameter; walls thick, pitted. Spores spiny, globose; 4.0–7.5 μm in diameter. **Fruiting:** Solitary, grouped, or in fairy rings; in pastures, lawns, parks, golf courses, or grassy fields. Widely distributed from Great Plains eastward. Midsummer to late fall.
Edibility: Edible.
Similar species: The purplish color of mature, dry gleba distinguishes this from most other Calvatias, although *C. leiospora* and *C. sigillata* are found in grasslands of the Great Plains. A smaller variety or form in which the sterile base is inconspicuous or lacking is sometimes regarded as a separate species, *C. fragilis.* This is widespread and often common in grasslands of the Great Plains and in the Rocky Mts., where it grows among sagebrush and other desert shrubs.

SMOKY PUFFBALL *Calvatia fumosa*   **Pl. 44**
Medium-sized, *gray, thick-walled spore case* has *smooth* to *slightly undulate* or *very shallowly cracked surface.* Grows in *western mountains.* Round spore case may be smooth and white at first but soon becomes light to medium gray, developing very shallow depressions, bumps, or cracks with maturity. May have a strong, very unpleasant odor. Thick, persistent wall breaks irregularly to release spores. Mature gleba dark brown, powdery. Often attached to soil by persistent string-like strand. **Technical notes:** Spore case 3–8 cm across. Capillitium sparsely branched, blunt-tipped, 2.5–15.0 μm in diameter, with slit-like pits in thick walls. Spores warty, globose; 5.0–7.5 μm in diameter.
Fruiting: Solitary to grouped or small clusters; on soil in spruce-fir forests; Rocky Mts. and westward. Summer to fall.
Edibility: Unknown.
Similar species: (1) *Calvatia subcretacea* (not shown) is

white with gray-tipped, low warts, cones, or bumps. It is wide-spread in western mountains. (2) *Calvatia hesperia* (not shown) has a smooth, gray spore case which breaks up at maturity to release spores. It is known only from southern California. Both species have smooth spores. (3) *Calvatia pachyderma* (not shown) is usually larger. The thin outer wall of spore case separates from the thick inner wall in irregular patches. Smooth to finely warted spores are round to elliptic.

GIANT PUFFBALL   **Pl. 44**
Calvatia gigantea
One of the largest puffballs. White, round spore case with thin, smooth outer layer flaking away at maturity. Giant spore case remains globose or somewhat flattened at maturity, with a single root-like attachment. Surface white, becoming dingy to brownish. Texture like that of kid leather but eventually cracking into shallow flakes, especially when dry; inner layer gradually breaks, exposing yellow to olive-brown gleba. Sterile base rudimentary or lacking. **Technical notes:** Peridium 20–50 cm across. Spores smooth to spiny, globose; 3.5–5.5 µm in diameter. Capillitium septate; walls thick with round pits, narrowed at tips; 2–9 µm in diameter.
Fruiting: Solitary or scattered; in meadows or other open places. Common in eastern N. America. Late summer and fall.
Edibility: Good.
Similar species: (1) Western Giant Puffball *(Calvatia booniana,* not shown), which may be as large or larger, has a more flattened shape overall and coarse, rounded knobs or bumps. It has smooth spores and grows in arid areas of Rocky Mts. and Northwest. (2) *Calvatia cretacea,* (3) *C. lepidophora,* and (4) *C. polygonia* are all smaller (10–20 cm in diameter) and have distinctly warty spores. *C. cretacea* is found in arctic and alpine areas. *C. lepidophora* and *C. polygonia* are found in prairie regions.

SCULPTURED PUFFBALL *Calvatia sculpta*   **Pl. 44**
Medium to large, *pear- to top-shaped spore case* with *large warts united at tips.* Grows *at high elevations in western mountains.* Very large, longitudinally or horizontally streaked warts are distinctive. They become split at base, but remain attached at tips and shed when fully mature. Gleba yellow to olive-brown, powdery at maturity. **Technical notes:** Peridium 5–10 cm across. Spores minutely warty, globose; 3–6 µm in diameter. Capillitium septate, branches narrowed toward tips; 3–8 µm in diameter.
Fruiting: Solitary to scattered; in conifer duff at high elevations in western mountains. Summer and fall.
Edibility: Unknown.
Similar species: (1) *Calvatia subcretacea* (not shown) has a thicker, tough peridial wall. (2) *Calbovista subsculpta* (not shown) is much larger and has a felt-textured outer wall which

breaks into flat or pyramidal patches and completely disintegrates at maturity.

Genus *Disciseda*

SANDCASE PUFFBALL *Disciseda candida*   **Pl. 45**
Small, flattened, acorn-like spore case; opens by a single pore.
Grows *on exposed soil.* Distinctly two-layered spore case forms
below surface of soil. Outer layer is intertwined with soil particles, forming a "sand case" with no apparent attachment to
soil. When mature part of sand case breaks off, it exposes a
gray to brownish, membranous inner spore case with an irregular to short-tubular pore. Gleba olive-brown to purplish brown.
Technical notes: Mature spore case 1.5–3.0 cm. across. Spores
smooth, globose; 3–6 μm. Capillitium rarely branched.
Fruiting: Widespread in waste areas or open soil in grass- or
pasturelands, prairie or shrub communities; often in sandy soil.
Matures after summer rains but persistent spore cases may be
found at any time of year.
Edibility: Not a likely candidate.
Similar species: (1) *Disciseda subterranea* and (2) *D. muelleri* (not shown) are reportedly found rarely in Midwest and
East. Both have smaller spore cases and larger spores.

Puffballs: Genus *Lycoperdon*

Small to medium, usually stalkless puffballs. Spore
case *two-layered;* opens by an *apical pore,* exposing yellow-green to violaceous spore powder and
filaments. Outer wall of spore case forms *spines,*
Lycoperdon warts, or felty scales; may have a sterile base.

SPINY PUFFBALL *Lycoperdon echinatum*   **Pl. 46**
Small to medium, *rounded spore case, narrowed below* to a
stubby sterile base. Often attached to soil by *string-like*
strands. Long spines leave *reticulated pattern* on surface *when*
shed. Spore case (including spines) yellowish white at first,
darkening to brown or blackish at maturity; spines often with
convergent tips readily shed to show net-like pattern of minute, scurfy particles; sterile base not well developed, has very
small chambers; *gleba dark purplish brown* at maturity. **Technical notes:** Spore case 2–5 cm across. Spores indistinctly
warted, globose to subglobose, often with long pedicels, 4–6 μm
in diameter.
Fruiting: Often abundant on soil in hardwood forests. Eastern
U.S. and Canada. Fall.
Edibility: Edible.
Similar species: Beautiful Puffball (*L. pulcherrimum,* p. 356)
has long spines which leave a *smooth surface* when they fall

off. It is less common than *L. echinatum,* and less abundant.
NAKED PUFFBALL *Lycoperdon marginatum*   **Pl. 46**
Small to medium *spore case. Outer wall* covered with *thick, long spines* that are shed in *small sheets* or *scales,* exposing *brown, scurfy* to *pitted inner spore case.* Flattened, globose spore case is narrowed below to a persistent, short, thick sterile base with small chambers. Pure white at first, but soon becoming pinkish to clay-colored and deep brown in age. Spines thick or more slender with tips united, at maturity falling away in sheets except over sterile base. Gleba olive, becoming grayish to purplish brown at maturity. **Technical notes:** Spore case 1–5 cm in diameter. Capillitium seldom branched, with attenuated tips; 3–6 μm in diameter; thick-walled, brownish. Spores smooth or nearly so, globose; 3.5–4.5 μm in diameter.
Fruiting: Common on sandy soil. Widespread. Summer and fall.
Edibility: Presumably edible when young.
Similar species: Immature specimens are confused with (1) the smaller *Lycoperdon curtisii* (not shown), which lacks the netted pattern on inner spore case characteristic of *L. marginatum* (Naked Puffball). (2) Beautiful Puffball (*L. pulcherrimum,* p. 356) is also easily confused with *L. marginatum* and has a purple-brown spore mass at maturity, but it also *lacks the netted pattern* on inner spore case after scales are shed.
SMOOTH PUFFBALL *Lycoperdon molle*   **Pl. 46**
Small to medium, *usually pear-shaped, brown spore case* with *small spines* or *granules on surface. Spore mass dark brown.* Spore case typically taller than wide. Sterile base well developed, with large chambers; often nearly as wide as fertile portion of spore case but sometimes narrowed to a distinct stalk. Inner spore case opens by a wide, irregular pore. **Technical notes:** Spore case 1–4 cm across × 1–6 cm high. Capillitium approx. 6 μm in diameter; wall thick, pitted. Spores globose or nearly so; 3.5–5.0 μm in diameter.
Fruiting: Common but rarely abundant; grows on soil and humus, in both hardwood and coniferous forests. Widely distributed. Late summer and fall.
Edibility: Presumably edible.
Similar species: Mycologists often include *L. molle* in a broad concept of (1) *Lycoperdon umbrinum* (not shown); if so, it can also be confused with (2) *L. muscorum* and with (3) *L. foetidum* (not shown), which has darker, brown- to black-tipped spines. *L. molle* has a smaller average spore size. (4) *Lycoperdon flavotinctum* (not shown) has yellow-tinged spore case at maturity.
GEM PUFFBALL *Lycoperdon perlatum*   **Pl. 46**
Small to medium, *pear-* or *top-shaped, white* to *grayish spore case* with *deciduous, cone-shaped scales* and *olive-brown gleba.* Fruits *on the ground.* Large, white (later brown-tipped)

scales, usually separated from smaller surrounding ones by a narrow bare space and leaving a fairly distinctive pattern when large scales drop first. Sterile base with large chambers forms a thick, often persistent stalk. **Technical notes:** 3–7 × 2–6 cm. Spores 3.5–4.5 μm; minutely spiny, no pedicel. Capillitial threads thick-walled with occasional pits, flexuous, tapered toward apex; 3–7 μm thick.

Fruiting: Solitary to densely clustered; on soil or humus in forests, along roads or trails, or in open areas. Common throughout N. America. Summer to fall.

Edibility: Edible and good by all accounts, but be sure interior is white and undifferentiated.

BEAUTIFUL PUFFBALL *Lycoperdon pulcherrimum* **Pl. 46**
Similar to Naked Puffball (*L. marginatum,* p. 355), but *lacks* network of minute scurfy scales on inner spore case when outer scaly case is first shed.

Fruiting: Solitary to dense clusters, on sandy soil in open hardwood, forests; often in clearings for fire lanes or in pastures.

Edibility: Presumably edible.

Similar species: See Naked Puffball (*L. marginatum,* above).

MINI PUFFBALL *Lycoperdon pusillum* **Pl. 46**
Small, globose spore case, attached to soil by *one or a few string-like strands. Lacks sterile base. Outer wall smooth* or nearly so; *apical pore large,* with a *lobed margin.* Surface of spore case white at first, then grayish brown and finally dark brown. Surface minutely flocculose (cottony) at first, with fibrils flattening down "like drying suds" and separating into very small patches, giving a somewhat netted appearance (use hand lens); or surface may be covered with delicate powder or very soft warts, finally falling away. Inner spore case smooth to obscurely spotted. Gleba yellow to olive-brown or dark yellowish brown. **Technical notes:** Spore case 1–2 cm across. Capillitium thick-walled except at tapered tips, pitted in thickest portion, somewhat wavy; 2.5–6.0 μm in diameter. Spores minutely ornamented, globose; 3.5–4.5 μm in diameter.

Fruiting: Solitary to clustered; on bare soil, pastures, roadsides, etc. Widespread and common. Spring to fall.

Edibility: Presumably edible.

Similar species: Readily distinguished in the field from most other species of this size by the olive-tinged gleba, lack of a sterile base, and peculiar surface covering. *Lycoperdon oblongisporum* (not shown) is a rare species with ellipsoid spores.

PEAR PUFFBALL *Lycoperdon pyriforme* **Pl. 46**
Clusters of medium-sized, globose to pear-shaped, fairly smooth, *white* to *brownish spore cases,* attached by *conspicuous, string-like strands* to *decaying woody substrate.* Spore case smooth and white at first, gradually becoming brown. Surface becomes roughened, then cracked, forming small, firmly attached scales or spines which may eventually fall off;

apical pore irregular, often slit-like. Sterile base well developed, with small chambers. Gleba white, then olivaceous to olive-brown, eventually with a grayish cast. **Technical notes:** Spore case 1.5–3.5 cm across × 2–3 cm high. Capillitium sparingly branched; thick-walled and brownish except at thin, tapered tips; somewhat wavy; 3–6 μm in diameter. Spores smooth, globose; 2.5–3.5 μm in diameter.

Fruiting: Scattered or in large, sheet-like clusters; usually on or beside decaying logs, stumps, sawdust, or other woody debris. Widely distributed. Fruits in fall, but spore cases persist throughout the year and old ones from a previous season's fruiting are often collected.

Edibility: Highly rated by some people. **Caution:** *Only young, pure white specimens should be eaten.*

Remarks: Great clusters of comparatively smooth, pear-shaped spore cases on decaying wood with conspicuous white strands at base readily identify this choice puffball in the field.

Puffballs: Genus *Vascellum*

PASTURE PUFFBALL *Vascellum depressum*   **Pl. 45**
Medium-sized, *top-shaped puffball* with *olive-brown gleba* and a *broad, chambered, sterile base* that is separated from the *gleba* by a *papery membrane.* White to pale brownish outer surface of a spore case is granular to soft-spiny at first. Inner wall metallic brownish, shiny. Both inner and outer walls open irregularly to form broad lobes which break off at top but remain attached at lower part, leaving a broad, persistent bowl-like base. Chambers in sterile base large. **Technical notes:** Spore case 2–5 cm across — a little taller than wide. Sparingly branched, septate, non-pitted capillitial threads 3.5–6.5 μm in diameter, breaking into small segments.

Fruiting: Common in grassy places (pastures, lawns, golf courses, parks, etc.) in Northwest and widely distributed over N. America. Fruits in fall.

Edibility: Edible.

Family Mycenastraceae

Giant Puffballs: Genus *Calbovista*

SCULPTURED GIANT PUFFBALL   **Pl. 45**
Calbovista subsculpta
Medium to large, *rounded, white* to *brownish spore case. Outer wall breaks into thick, angular patches* that separate from the *very thin, shiny inner spore case.* The fragile inner spore case fractures very early as the dark brown gleba dries out, leaving the spore mass exposed in cracks between scales. Scales py-

ramidal to flat-topped, thick, angular; grayish to brownish. Lower third (or quarter) of spore case is a firm, whitish sterile base. **Technical notes:** Spore case 8–25 cm across; usually *wider than tall.* Capillitial threads have short, thorn-like branches. Spores nearly smooth, globose; 3–5 μm in diameter. **Fruiting:** Solitary to grouped; on bare soil or open places in high mountains. Rocky Mts. to West Coast. Spring to late summer or fall.

Edibility: Excellent when interior is white and firm.

Genus *Mycenastrum*

GIANT PASTURE PUFFBALL   Pl. 45
Mycenastrum corium
Medium to large, flattened spore case; two-layered. *Comparatively thin, felty outer wall breaks into patches* or is *shed. Thick, tough, persistent inner wall breaks into irregular lobes.* Tough, white, inner spore case eventually becomes pale dingy brownish and breaks into broad, somewhat star-like, sometimes recurved lobes. Mature gleba dark brown, powdery. No sterile base or stalk. **Technical notes:** Spore case 5–20 cm across. Capillitium thick-walled, branched, spiny. Spores warty, brown, globose; 8–12 μm in diameter.
Fruiting: Solitary to grouped; on bare soil in pastures, barnyards, feedlots. Widespread in N. America, often common in Rocky Mts. Summer and fall.

Edibility: Edible.

Family Astreaceae

Earthstars: Genus *Astreus*

WATER-MEASURE EARTHSTAR   Pl. 47
Astreus hygrometricus
Small to medium, *flattened, stalkless spore case* sits on *6 or more rays* which *expand* or *recurve when wet* and *fold inward when dry.* Spore case two-layered; outer layer splits at maturity, forming hard, sometimes branched rays that soon become *cracked on inner surface.* Inner layer persists as a thin, grayish to brownish spore case with a surface that is felted or netted with fibrous lines; opens by an irregular, often torn or slit-like mouth. Spore case develops under soil surface and base is connected to soil by black, thread-like strands. **Technical notes:** 1–5 cm wide, including expanded rays. Spores tuberculate, globose; 7–11 μm in diameter. Capillitium very thick-walled, aseptate, branched; smooth or encrusted.
Fruiting: Scattered to grouped on soil; often in open, fairly sandy soil, seaside dunes, or waste places. Worldwide in distri-

bution and common. Matures in late summer and fall in temperate climates.

Similar species: (1) Bracken Earthstar (*A. pteridis,* not shown) is larger, having expanded spore cases that are 7–15 cm across. It is found in the Pacific Northwest. These 2 species are universally confused with (2) some earthstars of the genus *Geastrum* that also have a stalkless inner spore case. At maturity *Astreus* earthstars are almost indistinguishable in the field from *Geastrum* earthstars, but their spore mass (gleba) develops differently.

Family Geastraceae

Earthstars: Genus *Geastrum*

Geastrum rufescens

Small to medium, dry, gray to brownish puffball; stalkless. Tough outer wall of spore case splits into *starlike pattern of recurved rays* (see Pl. 47). Round inner spore case opens by an apical pore or tubular mouth.

FRINGED EARTHSTAR *Geastrum fimbriatum*   **Pl. 47**
Small, globose smooth-walled spore case lacking stalk recessed in bowl of 5–8 recurved rays has indistinct, fibrillose mouth. Spore case originates under soil surface with soil particles adhering to dingy, thin, cottony, outer layer which peels off, leaving a smooth, pale grayish brown surface. Inner spore case light to dark yellowish brown with a raised, conical, *fibrillose mouth area* that is *not* sharply delimited from remainder of spore case and not grooved or markedly streaked. Gleba dark grayish brown. **Technical notes:** Spore case up to 3 cm across, with expanded rays. Capillitium unbranched; thick-walled, encrusted; 4–7 μm in diameter. Spores minutely asperulate, globose; 2.5–4.0 μm in diameter.
Fruiting: Grouped to clustered around stumps in hardwood forests; often abundant if not common. Widespread in eastern N. America. Fall.
Similar species: Specimens with cracked upper surface of rays near base of inner spore case will be mistaken for (1) Bowl Earthstar (*G. saccatum,* p. 361). Fringed Earthstar (*G. fimbriatum*) is somewhat smaller, has a less distinct mouth zone, and lacks any suggestion of the *pinkish colors* that are often seen on (3) Reddish Earthstar (*G. rufescens,* p. 360).
FLOWER EARTHSTAR *Geastrum floriforme*   **Pl. 47**
Small, round spore case with small, indistinct apical pore has ring of tough, pointed lobes of outer wall that are bent inward when dry and expanded outward when moist. Subterranean until mature; outer spore case at first covered with soil and

debris, becoming smooth, pale brownish; gleba brown at maturity. **Technical notes:** Spore case 2.0–2.5 cm across, with rays expanded. Thick-walled capillitial threads approx. 10 μm in diameter. Spores warty, globose; 2.5–3.5 μm in diameter.

Fruiting: Solitary to scattered; on soil. Widespread in N. America, from Canada to Florida and westward. Common in Rocky Mts. and the West.

Similar species: Small size and indistinct mouth distinguish Flower Earthstar (*G. floriforme*) from other earthstars with hygroscopic rays, such as (1) Water-measure Earthstar (*Astreus hygrometricus,* Pl. 47), (2) *Geastrum campestre,* and (3) *Geastrum umbilicatum* (not shown).

GROOVED EARTHSTAR *Geastrum pectinatum*   **Pl. 47**
Small spore case with a *pointed, grooved mouth* and *grooved lower portion,* just above attachment to stalk. *Outer rays remain recurved when fully mature.* Mouth area of brownish spore case long, conical; *streaked or grooved,* but otherwise not clearly delimited from spore sac. Spore sac separated from outer spore case by a short but *distinct stalk.* Outer surface of rays (outer spore case) somewhat felty, incorporating particles of soil debris. Mature gleba dark brown. **Technical notes:** Spore case 1–2 cm across. Capillitium unbranched or sparingly branched; 4–7 μm in diameter. Spores coarsely warty, globose; 4.5–6.0 μm in diameter.

Fruiting: Uncommon. Eastern N. America.

Remarks: The relatively long-stalked spore case with a long, streaked or grooved mouth and the ribbed surface of lower part of inner spore case, plus the debris incorporated in the felty outermost layer, are good and distinctive field characters of this uncommon species.

REDDISH EARTHSTAR   **Pl. 47**
Geastrum rufescens
Small to medium, round, apically pointed, dull brownish spore case. When fresh, spore case often shows *pinkish tints after soil debris is removed. Mouth area fibrillose; opening not distinct.* Spore case originates under soil surface and at first is subglobose or more flattened, often with a low, obscure beak and with sparse, cottony fibrils adhering to soil particles. Mature spore case on short stalk above 5–9 extended, pointed, occasionally split rays. *Mouth* of spore case *not sharply defined* but somewhat elevated; fibrous or torn around edge. Surface elsewhere dull to unpolished or granular-velvety. Gleba dark brown. **Technical notes:** Spore case 1–5 (8) cm across. Capillitium unbranched; 3–6 μm in diameter, with thick, smooth, encrusted walls. Spores minutely warty, globose or nearly so; 3.0–4.5 μm in diameter.

Fruiting: Usually clustered in light soil around decaying hardwood stumps. Sometimes common in eastern N. America. Late summer and fall.

Similar species: In (1) *Geastrum limbatum* (not shown), an earthstar found occasionally in southern U.S., an outer layer of the spore case separates, leaving it clean and free of soil debris and the mouth area is more clearly delimited. (2) Bowl Earthstar (*G. saccatum,* below) has a more sharply delimited mouth area and an outer spore case with less soil debris. The inner spore case is not stalked and is often surrounded by a rim of tissue split from the inner layer of the outer spore case.

BOWL EARTHSTAR *Geastrum saccatum*   **Pl. 47**
Small to medium, *nearly round, light grayish brown, stalkless spore case* with a *distinct, conical, fibrillose mouth.* Spore case is *recessed* in a *bowl of recurved rays. Often grows under junipers.* Outer surface of spore case has little adhering soil or debris and is minutely velvety to spongy-felted; pale yellowish gray to grayish brown. Inner surface lighter, smooth. Inner spore case smooth; light brownish, with a paler mouth area set off from remaining spore case by a distinct ring and sometimes a shallow groove. Gleba dark brown. **Technical notes:** Spore case 2–5 cm across, including recurved rays. Capillitium very thick-walled, heavily encrusted; 4–8 μm in diameter. Spores warty, globose; 3.5–4.5 μm.
Fruiting: Grouped around decaying stumps in hardwood forests or under junipers. Widely distributed in eastern N. America. Late summer.
Similar species: The light-colored, distinct mouth distinguishes Bowl Earthstar (*G. saccatum*) from (1) Fringed Earthstar (*G. fimbriatum,* p. 358) and (2) the short-stalked Reddish Earthstar (*G. rubescens,* p. 359).

COLLARED EARTHSTAR *Geastrum triplex*   **Pl. 47**
Medium to large, *nearly round spore case,* with *wide, pointed, recurved rays.* Spore case has a *prominent "beak"* (mouth area) but *no stalk. Cracked upper surface* of rays forms a *saucer-like base* for *persistent inner spore case.* Rays of outer spore case thick and fleshy at first, usually 4–6 in number; rays become expanded to arched or recurved at maturity. Outer surface nearly free of soil and debris, with a distinct scar at base from attachment. Inner spore case grayish brown to yellowish brown, becoming lighter with age. Surface smooth; mouth area a *pointed,* radially fibrillose but not grooved *beak* with a ragged opening. **Technical notes:** Spore case 1–5 cm across (unexpanded), up to 8 cm with rays expanded. Capillitium very thick-walled, slightly encrusted; 3–6 μm in diameter. Spores warty, globose; 3.5–4.5 μm in diameter.
Fruiting: Grouped to scattered on rich soil in hardwood forests. Widely distributed. Late summer and fall.
Remarks: Large size, well-defined, beaked mouth, and stalkless spore case make this a fairly distinctive species, particularly those specimens which have a *saucer-like collar* at base of inner spore case.

Family Sclerodermataceae

Earthballs: Genus *Scleroderma*

Medium to large, thick-walled spore case opens by an irregular tear, exposing powdery spore mass (gleba) at maturity. Young gleba white at first, becoming marbled as spores mature.

EARTHBALL *Scleroderma citrinum*   **Pl. 48**
Medium to large, *nearly round, yellowish* to *brownish spore case* has *angular scales*. Each scale *usually* has a *smaller central wart*. Round, somewhat flattened spore case may be attached to soil or forest debris by a very short stalk and coarse, white strands. Distinctly yellowish, with cut edge turning pink when young, darkening to yellowish brown as it matures. Opens by irregular tears at apex but not with recurved lobes. Gleba white at first, then pebbled violet-gray, becoming blackish brown as spores mature. **Technical notes:** Peridium 3–9 cm across. Spores verrucose-reticulate, globose; 8–11 μm in diameter.
Fruiting: Solitary or in small clusters; on soil or well-rotted logs. Coniferous and hardwood forested areas; widely distributed. Summer and fall.
Edibility: Poisonous to some people. Experimenting with Sclerodermas should be avoided, as some species are much more toxic than this one and the likelihood of confusion is too great to warrant the risk.
Remarks: The combination of marbled flesh (when neither very young nor fully mature) and the dingy yellowish, scaly-cracked outer skin is fairly distinctive. This is the only earthball or puffball which is parasitized by a bolete (see *Boletus parasiticus*, Pl. 11, p. 107).

SMOOTH EARTHBALL *Scleroderma flavidum*   **Pl. 48**
Small to medium, *comparatively thin-walled, brownish spore case; smooth* or *may split* to form *shallow, angular scales*. Spore case *opens by recurved scales*. Young, white spore case is globose to flattened with thick folds above a short, stalk-like base. It forms under surface of sandy soil, becoming dingy pale yellowish, then pale yellowish brown. Surface sometimes cracks or splits, forming shallow, irregular scales; top *splits at maturity* into broad, usually blunt *scales* that *bend backward,* exposing dark grayish to yellowish brown, powdery spore mass (gleba). **Technical notes:** Peridium 2–5 cm in diameter. Spores thick-walled, with stout spines up to 1.5 μm long; globose; 8–13 μm in diameter.
Fruiting: Solitary to grouped; on (often sandy) bare soil, lawns, parks, old fields, ditchbanks, etc. Common in late summer and fall.

Edibility: Do not eat Sclerodermas.
Similar species: Star Earthball (*S. polyrhizum,* below) is similar but larger.

STAR EARTHBALL *Scleroderma polyrhizum*   **Pl. 47**
Large, whitish, thick-walled spore case with *roughened surface* splits into *wide, star-like rays. Forms under ground.* Spore case flattened to round or irregular in shape; sometimes lobed. No stalk. More than half of case often remains below soil surface, attached by white, string-like or flattened strands. Wall thick, hard and tough. Surface white at first, then yellowish or light brownish; cottony to rough or shallow-scaly with adhering soil. At maturity spore case splits irregularly into a varying number of recurved lobes, exposing dark brown, powdery spore mass. **Technical notes:** Peridium 4–14 cm in diameter. Spores brown, globose; spines project into deciduous hyaline sheath from complete or incomplete reticulum; 6–10 μm in diameter.
Fruiting: Solitary to clustered; on hard clay or sandy soil under hardwoods, in lawns, or on bare soil. East of Rocky Mts., most common in Southeast. Late summer and fall.
Edibility: Not recommended.
Similar species: Both this Scleroderma and *S. flavidum* (Smooth Earthball, above) open by splitting into broad, recurved scales. *S. flavidum* has a smaller spore case with a smoother outer surface.

Stalked Puffballs: Family Tulostomataceae

Genus *Battarraea*

FLATCAP STALKED PUFFBALL   **Pl. 48**
Battarraea stevensii
Medium to large, *flattened* to *round spore case* on a *thick, coarse-scaled, woody stalk. Opens by a marginal tear.* Grows *on desert soil.* Papery to tough spore case opening all around margin leaves wall of 2 bowl-shaped halves; upper half falls away, leaving powdery spore mass on lower (everted) half. Stalk somewhat *woody;* surface brownish with long, *ragged,* sometimes overlapping *scales.* Base sheathed in two-layered, cup-like volva. **Technical notes:** Peridium 3–6 cm across, 2–3 cm thick. Stalk 10–25 × 0.5–1.5 cm. Spores brownish, punctate, globose; 6–7 μm in diameter. Capillitium hyaline, thin-walled, or with annular to spiral thickenings.
Fruiting: Solitary or scattered; on soil in regions of West and Southwest. Fruits following rains, but stalk and empty spore case persists.
Similar species: *Battarraea phalloides* (not shown) is larger and emits a very strong, unpleasant odor as it matures. The peculiar, flattened spore case with a circumscissile opening and

persistent, well-developed volval cup distinguish this genus from other large desert puffballs.

Stalked Puffballs: Genus *Tulostoma*

STALKED PUFFBALL *Tulostoma brumale*   **Pl. 48**
Small, nearly round, smooth, papery spore case on a thin, woody, somewhat *bulbous stalk has a distinct tubular opening.* Grows *on sandy soil.* Globose or somewhat flattened, light grayish yellowish brown spore case has non-granular, smooth wall not with persistent sand particles or acorn-like base. *Stalk:* Hollow, colored like spore case; smooth or with sparse, small, rough scales; cylindrical with small, inconspicuous bulb at base. **Technical notes:** Spore case 1–2 cm across. Stalk 1–5 × 0.2–0.4 cm. Spores minutely verrucose, globose, some pedicellate; 3–5 μm in diameter. Hyaline capillitium 4–7 μm in diameter.
Fruiting: Solitary to grouped; on sandy soil, often in waste places. Widely distributed in N. America.
Similar species: (1) *Tulostoma striatum* and (2) *Tulostoma simulans* (not shown) both have a tubular mouth, as in *T. brumale,* but the former 2 species also have a spore case with *acorn-like* basal remains of *outer peridium* or have a *more roughened* to *sandy wall* on spore case, compared with the smooth spore case of *T. brumale.* (3) Other species with a smooth spore case *lack* the tubular mouth.

Family Podaxaceae

Stalked Puffballs: Genus *Podaxis*

Medium to large, ellipsoid, dry, scaly, fragile spore case on a long, slender, somewhat woody, scaly stalk. Bottom of spore case separates from stalk, releasing brown to black spore powder. Grows in desert areas.

GIANT STALKED PUFFBALL *Podaxis longii*   **Pl. 48**
Large, white oval spore case with a thick but fragile wall. Thick, scaly stalk. Spore case contains *dark reddish brown spore powder.* Young spore case pure white and shiny at first, but may be discolored by soil or maturing spores; surface has adherent, round to angular, sometimes recurved scales. Wall fairly persistent but separates from stalk at its base as spores mature. *Stalk:* persistent; woody in outer part, with a narrow

hollow or stuffed interior. Stalk is nearly cylindric or enlarged to distinctly bulbous at base, sometimes with a short, tapered, "rooting" tip. Surface lustrous to shiny, longitudinally grooved or ribbed and shaggy or with angular scales; scales adherent but often recurved. Gleba *dark reddish brown*. **Technical notes:** Spore case 7–16 × 5–8 cm. Stalk 8–25 × 1–4 cm. Spores thick-walled, with a broad germ pore and no evident apiculus, subglobose; 6–9 × 5–8 μm.

Fruiting: Solitary to scattered; fruits following rainy periods, on sandy soil along roadsides or under mesquite or giant cacti. Known from southern Arizona to southeastern California and Argentina.

Edibility: Unknown, but the species which is known as *P. pistillaris* (Khumbi) is widely eaten in India and the Near East.

Remarks: This is the species of *Podaxis* most easily identified in the field by its consistently large, robust form with a thick, often bulbous and ribbed stalk, and lustrous white color.

KHUMBI *Podaxis pistillaris*   **Pl. 48**

Medium to large, white to brownish, oval spore case with a papery-thin wall. Slender, bulbous stalk. Spore case contains *powdery, dark brown spores.* Spore case originates underground, often has adherent soil particles when fully expanded. Case is two-layered; outer layer breaks up, forming irregular, flattened to shaggy scales which may drop off as inner wall matures and weathers. Both wall layers are white at first and usually become dingy pale brownish to moderate brown. Wall soon becomes loose from stalk at bottom and splits longitudinally; it eventually is shed completely. Stalk persistent; somewhat woody, with a hollow or stuffed interior; bulbous or cylindric and tapering downwards from ground level. Surface smooth to longitudinally ridged, twisted, or shaggy-scaly; interior wall reddish brown. **Technical notes:** Spore case 2–10 × 1.5–4.0 cm. Stalk 4–10 × 1–3 cm. Spores ellipsoid; 10–17 × 9–12 μm.

Fruiting: Solitary to scattered or rarely clumped. Fruits following seasonal rains; on desert soils, along roadsides, or in sandy areas. California to southern Idaho south to Mexico and east to Texas.

Edibility: Edible when young — widely eaten in northern India, where it was first described.

Similar species: Several species, including (1) *Podaxis argentinus* and (2) *Podaxis farlowii* (not shown) are distinguishable only on microscopic characters. (3) *Podaxis microporus* has a distinctly orange-brown to rusty brown spore mass at maturity. (4) Giant Stalked Puffball (*Podaxis longii,* above), known only from southern Arizona and adjacent California, can sometimes be distinguished in the field by its *thicker, scaly stalk.*

Remarks: This is one of 2 kinds of stalked puffball popularly known as Khumbi in India, where they are the most popular edible commercial mushrooms on the market. *Phellorinia inquinans,* also known as Khumbi, has a spore case that is not penetrated by the stalk; the case opens by an irregular apical rupture. *Phellorinia* has light reddish brown spores.

Family Pisolithaceae

Genus *Pisolithus*

PEA ROCK *Pisolithus tinctorius*   **Pl. 48**
Large, top-shaped to *club-shaped, brown spore case. Thinwalled spore case* contains *pea-sized nodules* of *powdery spore mass,* separated by *fragile filaments. Grows on soil.* Spore case flattened to nearly round, and rarely nearly stalkless; more often it has a distinct, irregular, thick stalk that is intergrown with soil particles. Interior white at first, but becoming oliveyellow, then purplish brown to blackish brown and somewhat watery before it dries out as brown spore mass develops. Wall of spore case *very fragile.* Base fibrous, persistent; attached to soil by numerous, persistent, cord-like strands. **Technical notes:** Spore case 5–20 × 4–10 cm. Spores warty with a hyaline envelope, globose; 7–12 μm in diameter. Capillitium hyaline, clamped.
Fruiting: Solitary to grouped; on soil in fields, along roadsides, and in pasturelands. Widespread, but most common in Southeast and Northwest. Summer and fall.
Similar species: The very thin, fragile spore case and peashaped, nodular "spore balls" readily distinguish mature plants from the closely related Sclerodermas (p. 362).

Family Nidulariaceae

Genus *Crucibulum*

BIRD'S NEST *Crucibulum levis*   **Pl. 48**
Small, brownish, thin-walled, dry cups with *whitish spore cases, each attached* to *inner cup surface* by a *tiny, coiled cord.* Grows on *vegetable debris.* Stalkless cups almost cylindrical or tapered downward from expanded, sometimes flattened lip. Cups are covered at first by a thin membrane which ruptures at a very early stage. Outer surface velvety to unpolished, grayish yellow to brownish orange; inner surface and mouth smooth. Spore cases (peridioles) thin, disk-shaped; white. **Technical notes:** Cup diameter and height about equal, 5–10 mm. Peridioles 1–2 mm across. Spores 7–10 × 4–6 μm.
Fruiting: Grouped to clustered; on decaying wood or other

vegetable debris. Late summer and fall. Common throughout
N. America.
Edibility: Inedible.
Similar species: In general appearance this *Crucibulum* resembles the slightly smaller *Nidula* (p. 368) or *Nidularia* (not
shown), both of which have *gel-filled* young cups and *lack* the
cord on peridioles.

Genus *Cyathus*

SPLASH-CUP BIRD'S NEST *Cyathus stercoreus*   **Pl. 48**
Small, goblet-shaped cups with a *smooth inner wall.* Cup contains *brown, flattened spore cases* that are attached to wall by
a *thin, coiled cord.* Grows *on soil* and *manure.* Each cup is
shaped like a goblet or a slender cup, often with a recurved
margin, and occasionally with a short, thick stalk, sometimes
seated on a velvety, rusty brown pad. Immature cups are covered with a thin, whitish membrane (epiphragm) which disappears early with maturity. Outer surface brownish orange to
grayish brown or dingy yellowish brown; woolly at first but
hairs eventually wear off, leaving smooth surface. Inner surface
smooth, not streaked or grooved; grayish brown to blackish.
Flattened spore cases dark grayish brown; usually attached by
a *slender, fragile cord* but cord is often not evident on some
spore cases. **Technical notes:** Cups 5–15 × 4–8 mm. Peridioles 1.5–2.5 mm in diameter. Spores thick-walled, nearly hyaline, subglobose to ovoid; 22–35 × 18–30 μm.
Fruiting: Scattered or in large, dense clusters (which look like
wasp's nests), on *soil, dung, manured soil,* sawdust, etc. Common and widespread throughout N. America.
Edibility: Inedible.
Similar species: Streaked Bird's Nest (*C. striatus,* below) has
streaks or *grooves* on the inner wall of its cups that distinguish
it from *C. stercoreus.*
STREAKED BIRD'S NEST *Cyathus striatus*   **Pl. 48**
Small, brownish, goblet-shaped cups, with *streaks* and *grooves*
on *inside wall.* Cup contains *dark spore cases,* attached by a
coiled cord. Splashcups vary from slender goblets to narrow
cups, often with a recurved or flaring margin at maturity; sessile or with a very short stalk, sometimes seated on a brown,
tufted pad. Top of cup covered by a thin, whitish membrane
(epiphragm) which splits at an early stage, exposing gleba. Inner surface of cup smooth between grooves and streaks; outer
surface streaked, at least near margin, beneath coarse, shaggy
hairs; brownish orange to dark brown. Dark grayish to grayish
brown spore cases (peridioles) are confined to lower part of
cup. Each case is flattened and attached by a *strong, elastic
cord.* **Technical notes:** Cups 8–12 × 6–8 mm. Peridioles
(spore cases) 1–2 mm in diameter. Spores hyaline, thick-walled,
elliptic; 15–22 × 8–12 μm.

Fruiting: Scattered to grouped; on dead wood and other vegetable debris. Common and widely distributed throughout N. America.
Edibility: Inedible.
Similar species: Streaks and grooves on inner wall of splash-cup of *C. striatus* (Streaked Bird's Nest) distinguish it from Splash-cup Bird's Nest (*C. stercoreus,* above).

Genus *Nidula*

GEL BIRD'S NEST *Nidula candida*   **Pl. 48**
Small, brownish, nearly straight-sided cups. Each cup contains *tiny, flattened, brown spore cases* that are *embedded in* a *gelatinous matrix when fresh.* Grows *on decaying wood* or *soil.* Short, cylindric fruiting body (peridium) lacks a stalk and has *nearly vertical sides* that taper somewhat at base and flare at apex. Top of cup is covered at first with a membrane (epiphragm). Exterior of cup pale dull orange-yellow, beneath soft, light brownish scales; gray to light grayish brown when weathered. Cup interior smooth. Numerous smooth, brown spore cases (disc-shaped peridioles) are *embedded in a transparent gel or mucilage* inside the cup when fresh; later glued together by dried mucilage or free, *with no attachment to inner wall.*
Technical notes: Cups 5–20 × 3–8 mm. Peridioles (spore cases) 1–3 mm wide. Spores colorless, elliptic; 6–10 × 4–8 μm.
Fruiting: Grouped to clustered; on decaying wood, other debris, or soil. Common in Northwest. May be seen throughout the season as old (usually empty) cups persist.
Edibility: Inedible.
Similar species: The much smaller *Nidularia* (not shown) *lacks* the membranous epiphragm. It is rarely found in N. America. These are the only 2 "bird's nest" fungi which have cups that are *filled with a gel* before they mature and *lack* cord-like attachment of flattened peridioles (spore cases).

Palate Pointers: Recipes

Glossary

Selected References

Index

WARNING: These recipes should be used only by those who are expert at mushroom identification. Do not eat any wild mushroom without first obtaining an expert opinion on identification of the mushroom. This book is intended to be a field guide to mushrooms, and as such, it focuses on identification, not on mushroom toxicology. For details on that subject, we refer you to one of the excellent treatises now available (see p. 407).

It is also important to remember that edibility often depends as much on the person as on the mushroom (see p. 24). Even when properly cooked, some mushrooms that can be eaten safely by many people can nonetheless trigger a toxic reaction in a sensitive individual.

Finally, keep in mind that proper collection, preparing, and cooking techniques are as essential as identifying the mushroom species accurately: some cases of suspected mushroom poisoning are simple food poisoning.

Palate Pointers:
Going Wild with Mushrooms in the Kitchen

by Anne Dow

Milkcaps? Black Trumpets? Sulphur Shelf? These are mushrooms? Hen-of-the-Woods, Oysters, Ruffles—*these* are mushrooms? Among the common species the beginning pothunter first learns to recognize, these creatively named wild mushrooms are distinctive and delectable. Fresh mushrooms from field and forest have the perfection of peas in May and tomatoes in August. With the help of several good field guides that are now available, even a newcomer can learn to recognize several common edible species safely. For beginners, though, it's wise to remember that the guidance of experienced collectors provides the best possible introduction to mushrooming. Many states have clubs that offer field trips and other activities for amateurs, including lectures, often by a professional mycologist. For the address of the club nearest you, write: North American Mycological Association, 4245 Redinger Road, Portsmouth, Ohio, 45662.

Along with hints on preserving your finds, the following recipes will show you ways to exploit not only the particular tastes and textures of wild mushrooms, but also their spectacular colors and forms. No edible species that a beginner is likely to confuse with poisonous species have been included in these recipes. Similarly, no species that is edible for some people but which must be parboiled and have the water thrown out has been used. Some species of edible wild mushrooms are know to produce digestive upsets when eaten raw, so in general they should all be cooked. In addition, some individuals may be allergic to certain wild mushrooms, as to any other food. It is always a good idea not to overindulge, particularly with a new species. The logo of the Minnesota Mycological Society reads: "There are old mushroom hunters, there are bold mushroom hunters—but there are no old, bold mushroom hunters!" The place for boldness is in the kitchen, *after* identification.

There are documented cases of foragers returning home with 2000 morels and bushels of chanterelles. Instances of foragers returning home with very scant finds need no documentation, and since your luck is bound to vary so much, I have not attempted to specify the amount of mushrooms to be used in each recipe, unless more is definitely not better (see recipe, p. 383). All the recipes that follow will serve four generously, or can be stretched to feed six. I hope you will consider these recipes a starting point on the enticing path of mushroom cookery, letting the magnificent attributes of the mushrooms themselves guide your imagination.

Tips on Preparing and Preserving

Chances are you have gone to considerable lengths to collect your wild mushrooms. They are worth the extra care of preparing and cooking them carefully, using only the best and freshest ingredients.

Unpacking the Basket. Be as fussy about your mushrooms as you are about fish. If you couldn't resist woody, yellowed or mushy specimens in the woods, resist them now! Some cases of alleged "mushroom poisoning" have turned out to be ordinary food poisoning, caused by the spoilage of otherwise edible mushrooms. With freshness as with identification, "if in doubt, throw it out." Cutting mushrooms down the middle will reveal any damage done by insect larvae. Their small holes usually start in the stalk and proceed upwards and outward. If the colony has not advanced too far, you can cut it out. Or dropping whole mushrooms into cold salted water will quickly discover unwanted occupants.

To Wash or Not to Wash? Once the dirty or woody base has been cut off, then what? Gilled mushrooms and the softer pored fungi, such as the boletes in genus *Leccinum,* absorb water like a sponge. Unless the caps are very young and firm, these mushrooms will retain their texture best if brushed with a mushroom brush or wiped with a damp paper towel. Firm species, such as Ruffles *(Sparassis),* can stand up to washing, and generally are most effectively cleaned by a spray of cold water from the faucet. Fortunately, the species with structures that trap sand and soil—such as the morels with their pits, and the chanterelles with their crevices—tend to be firm, while the softer mushrooms are often found in relatively pristine condition. Much of the flavor and fragrance of wild mushrooms are in the "skin" of the cap; only those with sticky outsides, such as slipperycaps *(Suillus),* should be peeled.

When the Basket is Empty. What if you've looked in your yard, your neighbor's yard, and in field and wood, without finding a single choice edible? It's been known to happen. In this emergency you can use dried Cepes *(Boletus edulis)* saved from an earlier, more serendipitous foray, or fresh Shiitake *(Lentinus edodes)*, which can be bought or grown from your own logs. If bought in a gourmet specialty shop or ordered by mail, dried Cepes are expensive, but they are so richly flavored that half an ounce can transform a meal for four. To properly reconstitute them, two hours in cold or tepid water is ideal. You can get by with half an hour in warm water, but the texture may be rather leathery. The process can be hurried by weighting the mushrooms down so they can't float, but not by using hot water. Since a lot of flavor leaches into the soaking liquid, use dried Cepes only when you can use the liquid in the same recipe, as with soups and stews.

When the Basket Overflows. What if you find too much? How do you set some aside for another day? I generally find that gentle sautéing or quick steaming followed by freezing produces the most satisfactory results. Taste and texture are preserved as well as possible, and the most options for future use are kept open.

Canning, Pickling, and Drying. I prefer not to can wild mushrooms, since the long boiling tends to level the gustatory peaks wild mushrooms offer. I also avoid pickling, which substitutes the taste of vinegar and spices for subtle wild mushroom flavors. Fresh specimens of many species can be dried with reasonable success, but I find that their distinctive taste, as well as texture, is usually lost. Even with Shiitake, drying does not concentrate the flavor so much as subtly sour it. The one exception is the boletes (species of *Boletus, Leccinum,* and *Suillus*). Anyone who has tasted a soup made with dried Cepes *(Boletus edulis)* knows that it has retained a *lot* of flavor.

Marinating. Putting sliced fresh mushrooms into a boiling marinade of olive oil and lemon, with just a hint of herb or spice, is a very satisfactory way to handle small quantities. Otherwise, it consumes too much time and olive oil! Cooled and refrigerated, marinated mushrooms will keep for a week or longer, and are especially good in salads. Mushrooms can also be frozen in the marinade for up to a year; frozen mushrooms that were previously sautéed or steamed can be used on the spur of the moment by thawing them quickly in hot marinade.

Sautéing and Freezing. When you have a reasonably small amount of mushrooms, sautéing is the best way to preserve taste and texture. Slice the mushrooms, and sauté in butter or olive oil *very gently* for only a minute or two. When the mushrooms are still decidedly underdone, remove them from the heat, cool, and place them in plastic pint containers to freeze. That way you can pop them into hot marinade later if you decide you want mushroom salad, and they will still be reasonably firm. You can always cook them *more*.

Steaming and Freezing. What if you are overwhelmed by dozens of huge King Boletes *(Boletus edulis)*? Very occasionally, it does happen. When the mind boggles at the prospect of hours spent slicing and sautéing, steaming is the answer. Always steam rather than boil, since much less flavor leaches out.

Trim off the base of the stems, then cut off the stems just below the caps. Halve the stems and scoop out the little insect colony that often starts there. Check to make sure it has advanced no further. Halve the caps and steam them with the stems for 3–4 minutes, depending on their size. Cool, then package the steamed mushrooms in plastic containers before freezing.

What if you want the trumpet shape of whole golden chanterelles *(Cantharellus)* or black trumpets *(Craterellus)* to glorify a dish? Again, steaming is the answer. The shape of these mushrooms is open, so no slicing is necessary for them to steam thoroughly in 3 minutes, or 2 minutes, in the case of very thin *Craterellus*. Drain on paper towels and freeze with special care, like fresh raspberries, by setting the mushrooms in a single layer on a pie pan. When frozen, transfer to rigid plastic freezer containers.

Cooking Times. All times given in the recipes that follow are for altitudes near sea level; at higher altitudes, lengthen them accordingly.

Other Cookbooks to Consult. Several mycological clubs have published wild mushroom cookbooks, which are available to non-members—when in print! I can personally recommend the following cookbooks.

Rocky Mountain Mushroom Cookbook, © Colorado Mycological Society, 1981, 3024 South Winona Court, Denver, Colorado 80236.

Kitchen Magic with Mushrooms, © Mycological Society of San Francisco, Inc., 1963, P.O. Box 11321, San Francisco, California 94101.

Wild Mushroom Recipes, © Puget Sound Mycological Society, 1969, 2559 N.E. 96th Street, Seattle, Washington 98115.

Manna From the Wild Mushroom, by Louise Priest (former President of the Mycological Society of Washington, D.C.) and Dave Fisher, © Louise Priest, 1981, M.A.W., 3654 North Mitchner, Indianapolis, Indiana 46226

Clear Soup with Black Trumpets
(*Craterellus cornucopioides*, p. 85)
(*Craterellus fallax*, p. 85)

Fresh Black Trumpet or Horn of Plenty mushrooms
  (Craterellus)**
Approximately 2 quarts clear chicken stock, fresh or
  canned
2 tablespoons sake (Japanese rice wine)
Salt and freshly ground green peppercorns
A few fresh spinach leaves or sprigs of watercress
Optional: 2 or 3 small shrimp per person, shelled and
  deveined, or 1 whole softshell Louisiana red crayfish
  per person

** Substitutes: wild Brown Ear Fungus (*Auricularia auricula,* p. 64);
fresh kit-grown or dried Chinese Wood Ears, also known as Black Fungus *(Auricularia polytricha);* or fresh Shiitake *(Lentinus edodes)*

Bring chicken stock to a boil. Add sake, and salt and pepper to
taste. If available, add shrimp or crayfish and simmer over low
heat until red. Stir in mushrooms and simmer for 1 minute
before putting spinach or watercress into the pot, then turn off
the heat and cover the pot. Before serving, wait 1 minute to
allow thorough wilting.

Clear Soup with Black Trumpets can be made into Black
and White Soup by the addition of bits of Ruffles (*Sparassis
crispa,* p. 76), either fresh or marinated. See recipe for Mushroom Marinade on p. 397. Create a more formal, quite stunning
soup with cut-outs from the white Bearded Hedgehog (*Hericium erinaceus,* p. 91), made with a cookie or truffle cutter. See
recipe for Poor Man's "White Truffle" Cut-Outs on p. 398.

Note: Before using any white mushrooms, be very sure you can properly identify the deadly white Amanitas (see pp. 215–239).

Bolete Chestnut Vichyssoise
(edible *Boletus,* p. 103)

This recipe works very well for all edible species in the family
Boletaceae (p. 100). As Vincent Marteka explains in his beginners' guide *Mushrooms Wild and Edible,* avoid boletes that
have red pores, stain blue, or taste bitter. The slightly slippery
texture evident in specimens of *Suillus* (slipperycaps, p. 113)
even when raw, and also in some cooked boletes (*Boletus,*
p. 103, and *Leccinum,* p. 111) complements the potato beautifully, producing a distinctive smoothness. When cold, the soup
is a delicious vichyssoise, but it is equally heavenly when hot.
Let the weather be your guide!

> Fresh or dried boletes *(Boletus)***
> 2 pounds whole potatoes, preferably waxy new potatoes
> 1 quart chicken stock, fresh or canned
> 1 pound chestnuts (or ½ half pound dried chestnuts,
>   soaked overnight)
> 2 leeks
> 3 tablespoons fresh butter
> Salt and freshly ground green peppercorns to taste
> 1 cup heavy cream

** Substitutes: fresh *Suillus* (slipperycaps, p. 113) or *Leccinum* (scaberstalks, p. 111)

If dried mushrooms are used, soak them 1–2 hours in tepid
water. Save the water and use it in place of a like amount of
the chicken stock.

Bring a large pot of water to boil and add the potatoes.
When the water boils again, turn the heat down low and cover
the pot. Simmer 20–30 minutes, until fork-tender. Put cooked
potatoes in a large bowl of cold water to cool. When cool, peel
and slice the potatoes, and purée them in a blender with half
the chicken stock. Set this mixture aside.

Cut a cross on the flat side of each chestnut with a sharp
knife. Put chestnuts into a small pot of boiling water, and simmer for 5 minutes. When the drained chestnuts have cooled,
peel off the shells and brown inner skins.

Cut leeks in half lengthwise, rinse off grit, and slice, including the tender green part. Slice the dried or fresh mushrooms.
Melt butter in a frying pan and add leeks and mushrooms.
Stir, cover, and sauté over low heat until the vegetables are
soft, but not brown. Add half of the chicken stock (or a combination of chicken stock and the water used to soak dried mush-

rooms), the peeled chestnuts, and salt and pepper to taste. Simmer over low heat for 15 minutes, then cool the mixture by placing the pot in a bowl of cold water. Once it has cooled, purée in a blender and combine with the potato purée. Add salt and pepper to taste, stir in cream and refrigerate until well chilled.

Pink and White Bolete Salad Meinhard Moser
(*Boletus edulis,* p. 104)

As mild and delicious as peaches and cream, this delicate dream of a salad was news to me when Meinhard Moser served it to our research crew at Jackson Hole. He says it is very common in Switzerland's Tessene province. The white bolete slices look so much like potatoes that every bite is a surprise.

> Firm young King Bolete mushrooms—fresh, not dried*
> 3 tablespoons extra virgin olive oil
> 3 eggs
> 2 tomatoes
> 1 small onion
> 3 slices of ham
> Salt and freshly ground white pepper to taste
> 3 tablespoons wine vinegar

Slice the mushrooms ⅛ inch thick. (If they are mature, first peel the tube layer off the underside.) Sauté in the olive oil over low heat just until they become a bit transparent but are still *al dente*. Transfer to a bowl and cool briefly in the freezer.

Hard-boil, peel, and slice the eggs. Scald the tomatoes briefly and peel. Dice tomatoes, onion, and ham. Combine with mushrooms and salt and pepper to taste. Add the vinegar and stir lightly.

* Dried Cepes when reconstituted in water have excellent flavor but poor texture—tough and leathery. Succulent texture is the essence of this dish.

King Bolete Brie Quiche
(*Boletus edulis,* p. 104)

This recipe is a variation of Julee Rosso's and Sheila Lukins's "Brie Soufflé" from *The Silver Palate Cookbook.* They call it "a most luxurious brunch dish," and suggest serving it with champagne and fresh fruit. I feel this version, made with the king of boletes, can reign alone over a brunch table.

Fresh or dried King Bolete mushrooms (Cepes)**
3 tablespoons butter
½ pound ripe Brie (easiest to peel and mince if frozen)
Half a loaf of crusty French bread, grated into crumbs
3 eggs
¾ teaspoon salt
Dash of Tabasco
1 cup milk (if using dried mushrooms, replace milk with ½ cup heavy cream and ½ cup soaking liquid)
Fast & Trusty, Light & Crusty, French Bread Quiche Shell (see recipe below)

** Substitutes: Any edible species of *Boletus, Leccinum,* or *Suillus* (pp. 103–118), fresh or dried; or fresh Shiitake mushrooms *(Lentinus edodes)*

To make the quiche shell:

My family was not treated to many quiches until I discovered that the pastry shell could be replaced by buttered crumbs grated from half a loaf of crusty French bread. Since I make French bread a dozen loaves at a time, and usually manage to freeze ten, I always have this on hand in the way I never did pâte brisée. But a crusty bakery loaf will freeze, thaw, and grate just as well as homemade, as long as you avoid the limp supermarket brands. This recipe can also be used in Chicken Breast Quiche with Morels (p. 384), or any time you're not in the mood to make pastry.

Fast & Trusty, Light & Crusty
French Bread Quiche Shell

> ½ loaf crusty French bread
> 3 tablespoons sweet butter

Finely grate bread into a bowl. Melt butter, dribble it over the bread crumbs, and mix thoroughly. Press the mixture against the bottom and sides of a 10-inch porcelain quiche dish or pie pan. Voilà!

To make the quiche:

Soak the dried sliced mushrooms for 1–2 hours in tepid water. If quantity is small, chop slices after soaking.

Preheat oven to 325°. If the mushrooms are fresh, slice them ¼ inch thick. Melt butter in a frying pan and sauté over low heat for about 3 minutes, until golden. Set aside. Slice the rind off the Brie with a sharp knife, then mince the peeled Brie. Sprinkle half of the cheese in an even layer over the prepared quiche shell, and add half of the mushrooms. Top with bread crumbs, and repeat Brie and mushroom layers.

Whisk together eggs, salt, Tabasco, and milk. Pour this mixture into the quiche dish and bake for 25–30 minutes, until golden and bubbling.

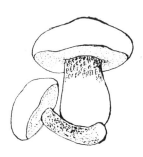

Hedgehog Needle "Noodles"
(*Hericium erinaceus*, p. 91)

One October, my family was returning by car to Maryland from a "persimmoning" expedition to Virginia when we saw a huge hedgehog mushroom *(Hericium)* about twenty feet up one of the trees lining the road. Luckily we had our long-handled fruit picker in the car! The mushroom was too big to fit in one of the large grocery bags that are standard equipment in our car, so we cradled it on top of the bag. When we got home and cut it open, it was plain that the inside—crumbly and slightly yellowed instead of smooth, firm, and white—was past eating. But the white and supple needles (spines) were still in prime condition. Carefully, I cut them all off at the base, going over the giant globe in strips. A quick boil, a bit of butter and dill, and presto, fungal pasta!

If your *Hericium* is smaller and younger than this one was, the needles will be shorter and less like noodles. But they'll taste just as good, and the inside is more likely to be fresh and firm. If it is, you could try the Poor Man's "White Truffle" Cut-outs on p. 398.

Needles cut off at the base from a large hedgehog mushroom *(Hericium)*
Approximately 2 quarts chicken stock or water for boiling
Salt and freshly ground green peppercorns to taste
A few drops of olive oil
2 tablespoons sweet butter
Minced fresh dill, or dried dill leaves

Bring chicken stock or water to the boil. (Chicken stock will add flavor to the mushrooms, and vice versa. Stock used in this way can be frozen and will make a delicious soup base for recipes like Black and White Clear Soup on p. 375).Throw a pinch of salt and a few drops of olive oil into the water, as you would with pasta, and add the needles (spines). Turn down the heat and simmer for 2 minutes. Strain, reserving liquid for another use if desired, and put the "noodles" into a serving dish. Top with butter, dill, and a bit more salt and freshly ground pepper to taste.

Milkcap Manna

(*Lactarius corrugis*, p. 329)
(*Lactarius volemus*, p. 340)
(*Lactarius deliciosus*, p. 330)

The velvety, deep chocolate brown caps of *Lactarius volemus* (Tawny Milkcap) are so beautiful that it's almost a shame to cook them, since this completely alters their appearance. But one is encouraged to get on with it, not only because of the treat to come, but because it's fun to watch the pure white milk bead up as the mushrooms are sliced. In *Lactarius deliciosus* (Saffron Milkcap) the milk is orange!

Fresh milkcap mushrooms (edible *Lactarius* species)
2 ounces prosciutto
A few sprigs of parsley
1 cup whole wheat flour
Salt and freshly ground green peppercorns to taste
4 tablespoons sweet butter

Mince prosciutto and parsley, and set aside. Slice mushrooms ¼ inch thick. Put the flour, salt, and pepper in a small paper bag and shake to mix. Pop mushrooms into the bag (in successive batches if you have a lot) and shake several times to coat them thoroughly. The milk exuded by the mushrooms will make the flour stick.

Melt butter in a frying pan and sauté the floured mushrooms for about 5 minutes, turning once. When the mushrooms are a deep gold, sprinkle with minced prosciutto and parsley, and toss gently in pan before transferring them to a warm serving dish.

Pine Cluster Against White Sky
(*Morchella* species, pp. 37–41)

The Morel is one of the easiest wild mushrooms to identify and
it satisfies that primal pothunting urge, after a winter of being
cooped up, to go out in the woods and *find* something. Bill
Roody, founder of the wild plants bimonthly *Coltsfoot,* can't
remain inside when he "hears the mycelium rumbling." The
taste of a morel is wonderful, wild and woodsy, but very mild
and delicate. It needs a bland background such as chicken
breasts and the simplest of sauces, in order not to be overpow-
ered. Capitalizing on the morel's resemblance to a pine cone,
this dish woos the eye as much as the stomach. Fresh chives
make a realistic cluster of "pine needles" to lay the "cones"
against, and the thick white sauce on top of the chicken breast
complements colors and flavors perfectly. If collecting has been
poor, a successful dinner for two can be made with only one
morel, sliced in half. The "pine cones" are most realistic, however, when the caps are left whole. If you can spare a pair per
serving, or a cluster of three, you'll have an artful composition
that evokes the simplicity of a Japanese painting.

To make the sauce:

    4 tablespoons sweet butter
    4 tablespoons flour
    1/8 tablespoon freshly grated nutmeg
    Salt and freshly ground green peppercorns to taste
    1 cup milk or light cream

In a medium-sized frying pan melt the butter over very low
heat. Remove the pan from the heat and add the flour, stirring
the roux on and off heat for 5 minutes to thoroughly cook the
flour with no trace of scorching. Turn off the heat and add
the nutmeg and salt and pepper to taste and the cup of milk or
light cream, all at once. Turn the burner back on low heat and
stir until it simmers. Cover to keep warm and set aside.

To make the chicken:

    2–12 choice small, fresh morels *(Morchella),* left whole
    4 tablespoons sweet butter
    4 boneless fillets of chicken breasts
    Fresh whole chives

Caution: Do not drink alcohol before, during, or after the same
meal at which you eat inky caps (*Coprinus*) or morels (*Morchella*).

Cut off morel stems so that the whole caps look like pine cones. Reserve the stems for stuffing the fillets. Extra morels, or a few broken ones, can also be saved for this purpose. In a frying pan large enough for the chicken breasts, melt 2 tablespoons of butter and sauté the morel caps very gently, turning as little as possible, until they have wilted a bit. With a slotted spoon or rubber spatula carefully remove the caps to a plate and reserve.

Mince the leftover mushroom pieces and put them in the frying pan after melting an additional tablespoon of butter. Sauté until thoroughly wilted, but not brown. Using a sharp knife, make a lateral pocket in the middle of each chicken fillet, and put a portion of the sautéed mushroom pieces inside. Add the last tablespoon of butter to the frying pan, and sauté the chicken fillets over very low heat for 3 or 4 minutes per side. The fillets should be barely white. Transfer to dinner plates.

Spoon a bit of sauce over each fillet. Take 5 chives cut at slightly uneven lengths and lay them in a fan along the top of each fillet, pinching them together at one end and pressing down lightly. One by one, set the morel caps into the base of chive clusters, putting a tiny bit of sauce over the aperture where the stems were cut off.

If your morels are too big to fit on a chicken breast, the Chicken Breast Quiche (see next page) will provide a smooth, white expanse of "sky" that will accommodate "pine clusters" made of outsize morels such as *Morchella crassipes* (Thick-footed Morel, p. 39). Cut the stems off 2–3 large, choice morels, leaving the caps whole. Make the quiche (next recipe) using the stems. Sauté the caps in melted butter very gently over low heat until they wilt slightly. Decorate the Chicken Breast Quiche with them.

   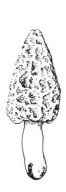

Frittered Ruffles

(*Sparassis crispa*, p. 76)

Have you ever dipped a lacy elder blossom in batter, deep-fried it, and feasted on the world's lightest doughnut? The thin ruffles of these mushrooms (which are sometimes nicknamed "cauliflowers," but which look more like a head of looseleaf lettuce) are almost as delicate and airy as elder blossoms, and are much tastier!

    1 "head" of Ruffles *(Sparassis)*
    1 cup whole wheat flour
    ½ teaspoon salt
    ⅔ cup milk
    2 eggs
    Oil for deep frying

Soak the whole mushroom in cold salted water for 15 minutes to evict possible insect larvae that may be lurking in the many hiding places. Steam for 10 minutes. Cool, and cut off the flattened branches just at their base, keeping each branch whole.

Measure flour, salt, and milk into a bowl, stirring well. Separate the eggs and add the yolks to the batter. In another bowl, beat the whites until stiff, then gently fold them into the batter.

Heat oil to 375°. Holding a mushroom branch at its base, dip it into the batter, then drop it into the hot oil. When golden brown, use a slotted spoon to lift it out, and drain on paper towels. Repeat with each branch.

Chicken Breast Quiche with Morels

(*Morchella* species, pp. 37–41)

    Stems from 3 large morels, and any extra morels available
    Recipe for Fast & Trusty, Light & Crusty, French Bread Quiche Shell (p. 379)
    8 ounces whole-milk mozzarella cheese
    8 tablespoons sweet butter
    4 boneless chicken breast fillets

Caution: Do not drink alcohol before, during, or after the same meal at which you eat inky caps (*Coprinus*) or morels (*Morchella*).

3 shallots
2 tablespoons dry sherry
3 egg yolks
1 cup heavy or light cream
¼ cup milk
Salt and freshly ground green peppercorns to taste
⅛ teaspoon freshly grated nutmeg
Optional: 3 ounces prosciutto, thinly sliced

Prepare quiche shell and preheat the oven to 300°, a low setting that will give a much smoother texture to the custard than the higher settings commonly used. Grate the mozzarella, and spread ⅓ of it over the quiche shell. If prosciutto is to be used, tear the slices into bite-size pieces and lay on top of the cheese.

Melt 2 tablespoons of butter in a medium-sized frying pan and sauté the chicken breasts over low heat, covered, for roughly 4 minutes on each side. When the fillets are barely cooked, put them on a plate to cool.

Mince the shallots and morel stems, plus any extra morels. Melt 3 tablespoons of butter in a small frying pan, add the mushrooms and shallots, and sauté over low heat for 5 minutes. Add the sherry and stir. Spoon this evenly into the quiche shell.

Cut the cooled chicken into bite-size pieces and spread them over the mushroom and shallot layer. Beat together egg yolks, cream, milk, salt, pepper, and nutmeg. Pour this mixture into the quiche dish. Bake for 30–40 minutes until the quiche has set. Cover the top of the quiche with the remaining grated cheese, and run the dish under a red-hot broiler for about 30 seconds. The cheese should just barely melt to provide a smooth, white topping. Decorate with the large sautéed morels.

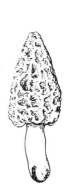  

Golden Duck with Apricots and Chanterelles

(*Cantharellus cibarius*, p. 81)
(*Cantharellus lateritius*, p. 83)

Chanterelles usually have to be dug up from a semi-buried position in the soil, and the dirt trapped in their many nooks and crannies betrays this fact. A strong jet of cold water is the quickest and most effective way to clean them. Fortunately, unlike gilled mushrooms or softer, pored mushrooms, chanterelles can stand up to washing. They also keep well. I once spent an hour cleaning part of my first haul with a half-inch watercolor brush I had borrowed from Vera McKnight. I didn't get very far before I gave up and put the rest in the fridge. When I got back to them four days later, they were still in good condition.

These golden trumpets smell and taste of apricots, and their extra spiciness complements the sweetness of the actual fruit in the recipe.

Fresh chanterelles, left whole
1 duckling (5–6 pounds)
1 6-ounce package dried apricots, or ½ pound fresh apricots
2 tablespoons to 1 cup Madeira, to taste (if dried apricots are used, choose a Sercel Madeira rather than a Rainwater Madeira)
2 tablespoons sugar
2 tablespoons white vinegar
2 cups duck stock from giblets, or chicken stock
Zest of 1 lemon
2 tablespoons arrowroot or flour
2 tablespoons lemon juice

To prepare the roast and mushrooms:

Preheat oven to 300°. Roast the duckling until a leg can be moved up and down easily. While it cooks, soak dried apricots in Madeira. Wash the chanterelles and steam for 3 minutes, then cool on paper towels.

To make the sauce:

Make a glaze of the sugar and the white vinegar. Caramelize the liquid, but don't scorch it. Add ½ cup of the stock, stir and simmer, then add the remaining 1½ cups. Mix in the lemon zest, arrowroot or flour, and 2 tablespoons of Madeira.

Put the roast duckling on a large platter. Separate the fat from the pan juices, and add the juices to the sauce. Deglaze roasting pan with more Madeira, and add to the sauce. If you used dried apricots, add the Madeira "marinade" to the sauce now. Dip the chanterelles into the sauce and set aside.

Peel and slice the apricots, adding them to the sauce along with the lemon juice. Heat the sauce and pour half of it over the duckling. Arrange the chanterelles on and around the duckling. Serve the rest of the sauce separately.

Chanterelle Schnapps Meinhard Moser (*Cantharellus cibarius,* p. 81)

Amber in color, ambrosial in taste, the original Austrian recipe for this intriguing drink calls for schnapps made from rye. Vodka, also colorless and unsweetened, is a very satisfactory substitute, according to Dr. Moser. The spiked chanterelles are a welcome bonus that makes an unusual, attractive, and tasty cocktail snack.

    1 pint fresh golden chanterelle mushrooms**
    1 fifth vodka or unflavored schnapps

** Substitute: Dried chanterelles (½ cup), usually unsatisfactory for culinary purposes, work well in this recipe.

Wash the fresh mushrooms under cold running water and drain on paper towels. Dehydrate them at 105° in a dehydrator, in the sun, or over a light bulb, until completely dry, as wet chanterelles will make the vodka cloudy. Crumble the dried mushrooms into a large, wide-mouthed jar. Add the vodka, reserving the empty bottle. Soak off the label and replace it with one of your own.

After 2 days, strain the golden liquid back into the bottle. The spiked chanterelles can be served as appetizers.

Hen-of-the-Woods Turkey
(*Grifolia frondosus,* p. 128)

"To the imaginative eye, a clump of this fungus looks like a setting hen that has just fluffed its feathers after being disturbed on the nest . . . ," writes Vincent Marteka in *Mushrooms Wild and Edible.* "The fluffed feathers are actually smoky gray to brown mushroom caps that grow at the tips of short white stems. The caps grow so close together that the short stems aren't visible to an observer standing over a mushroom clump."

This evocative paragraph suggested to me a splendid, easy way to serve leftover turkey the day after Thanksgiving in a dish that suggests a live turkey with its arcs of feathers. It takes foresight, since this mushroom's season is late September through October. Fortunately, as Mr. Marteka adds, "a typical Hen of the Woods provides more than enough mushrooms for one meal." The extra mushrooms can be frozen after parboiling or steaming for ten minutes, then slicing and patting the pieces dry before freezing them in separate bags. For this recipe, though, be sure to break off the "feathers" at the base of their short stems, rather than slicing them.

    1 fresh or frozen Hen-of-the-Woods
    3 tablespoons sweet butter
    Boned, left-over turkey, at room temperature, cut into
      bite-size pieces
    Leftover gravy

If the mushroom is fresh, steam it for 10 minutes, then break off the "feathers" at the base of their short stems and discard the hard central core. Allow a frozen mushroom to thaw slightly first. Melt the butter in a frying pan and sauté the "feathers" for 5 minutes over low heat, being careful not to break up the pieces. Remove from the burner and cool in the pan.

Mound the boned, diced turkey in an oval shape on a platter and arrange the mushroom "feathers" over the surface, wedging the stems lightly in between the turkey pieces to create a ruffled look. Heat the gravy and carefully pour it around the feathers to fill in the cracks between turkey pieces.

Sulphur Shelf Saffron Pilaf
(*Laetiporus sulphureus,* p. 128)

The brilliant bands of orange and yellow on the Sulphur Shelf mushroom tempt one to prepare a dish that explores that end of the color spectrum. So much do the coral-colored strips resemble shrimp that there is a further temptation to make an all-vegetable *trompe l'oeil.* This dish joyfully gives in to both impulses. Remember, though, that only the tenderest part of this huge mushroom is worth eating. Unless you have very young specimens in prime condition, only a thin strip along the outer growing edge of each "petal" should be used in cooking. Be firm when your knife encounters firmness: leave it on the tree!

> Tender outer edges of Sulphur Shelf mushroom, cut in 2 inch × ½ inch strips
> 3 tablespoons sweet butter
> Salt and freshly ground green peppercorns to taste
> Approximately 1 quart chicken stock
> 1–2 yellow and/or red sweet peppers, cut into diamonds
> 2 tablespoons dry vermouth or white wine
> ⅛ teaspoon saffron
> 1 teaspoon olive oil
> ⅓ cup uncooked rice per person

Melt the butter in a frying pan, add mushroom strips and salt and pepper to taste. Cover, and sauté over low heat for 5 minutes. Add 1 cup chicken stock and simmer slowly for 25 minutes.

While this is cooking, warm the vermouth or white wine in a small metal container, add the saffron, and let it sit for 2 minutes. The alcohol will draw the saffron flavor out and make the most of it—a great help at $2000 the pound! Bring the remaining chicken stock to a boil, and add a pinch of salt and a few drops of olive oil along with the uncooked rice. Stir, and add the vermouth and saffron, then cover and cook over low heat for 20 minutes. Add the yellow or red peppers to the mushrooms and simmer for another 5 minutes. Put the rice into a deep serving dish and pour the mushrooms and peppers over it, mixing so that the yellow rice shows.

Persimmon Pork and Beans with Blewits
(*Clitocybe nuda,* p. 143)

This blue, green, and orange dish is pork and beans with a difference! If you live in the eastern United States, you can pick a delicious harvest of wild persimmon in October and November after the leaves have fallen. Persimmons need plenty of sun to ripen properly (contrary to the old wives' tale, a hard frost has nothing to do with it), so don't look for them in the woods. You can often see them along the road—look for a tree with bare branches decorated by hundreds of small, apricot-colored globes. Persimmons are a contrary fruit: if they are still smooth, their taste will not be. If the skin looks puckered, make a taste test on the spot. If the fruit is still astringent when picked, no amount of "ripening" on a sunny windowsill will make it less so, nor will sugar or honey disguise the disaster. Come back in a week or two, and—if you can find a good tree at the right time—what a treat you'll have in store.

Fresh Blewit mushrooms**
1 cup seedless pulp of American persimmon, fresh or frozen
1½ pounds pork loin
4 tablespoons sweet butter
1½ pounds fresh Romano green beans (or 2 9-ounce packages of frozen Italian cut green beans)
3 tablespoons apple jelly

** Substitutes: Fresh or dried boletes (edible *Boletus* species, p. 104, fresh *Suillus* species, p. 113, or *Leccinum* species, p. 111) or fresh Shiitake mushrooms (*Lentinus edodes,* p. 135).

Persimmons and Blewits usually fruit at the same time. If you have persimmons and Blewits in hand and Romano beans in the garden (before a hard frost has struck), you have luck on your side. If not, frozen Italian cut green beans from the supermarket will do fine.

Remove the stem ends and the seeds from the persimmons, until you have 1 cup of seedless pulp on hand. This is admittedly a chore by hand, but easy if you have an electric sieve. Frozen persimmon pulp can also be used.

Slice the pork ½ inch thick and cut diagonally into bite-size pieces. Melt 2 tablespoons of butter in a small frying pan and sauté the pork over low heat just until pink color is gone, then set aside. Slice the mushrooms. Melt 2 more tablespoons of butter in the frying pan and sauté them over low heat for 2 minutes. Set aside.

Top and tail the beans, cut them diagonally into bite-size pieces and steam until just tender, but still a deep forest green.

Reheat the pork. Add apple jelly and persimmon pulp and stir. Combine this mixture with the beans and mushrooms.

Blue Blewit Salad
(*Clitocybe nuda,* p. 143)

This salad is as breathtaking as a salad with April violets, especially if the Blewits are very young. At that age they are a bright blue (they fade to buff with age) and are small enough to be marinated and served whole, instead of in slices. And while violets are beautiful and quite harmless, Blewits are far more tasty.

> Very young Blewit mushrooms**, left whole
> 1½ cups Mushroom Marinade (see recipe on p. 397
> Tender leaf lettuce
> *Optional:* other tender greens

** Substitutes are the "White Truffle" Cut-Outs (see recipe on p. 398), made with *Hericium erinaceus* (Bearded Hedgehog, p. 91), or fresh Shiitake *(Lentinus edodes)*

Prepare the mushroom marinade. Bring it to a boil before adding whole Blewits. Turn off heat, cover, and wait for only one minute to prevent fading. Remove the mushrooms with a slotted spoon and cool on a plate.

Cool the marinade by putting the pan in a larger pot of cold water. Trim, wash, and dry the greens, then put them into a large salad bowl. Dress with a bit of the cooled marinade and toss. Sprinkle the mushrooms on top, turning them right side up to show off their blue color.

Fillet of Sole with Shaggy Manes
(*Coprinus comatus,* p. 277)

These distinctive denizens of roadsides, vacant city lots, and disturbed ground are also called Inky Caps and Lawyer's Wigs. The names are properly descriptive because these mushrooms dissolve into a black ink and, according to Jane Grigson, author of *The Mushroom Feast,* are "only to be eaten when decidedly white and clean, like a new barrister's wig in an English court."

If you don't plan to serve Shaggy Manes as a post-foray snack, how do you stop these beauties from turning into an inky mess? A. Paul Jensen microwaves them briefly, a method he finds superior to blanching or submerging them in water, either of which causes sogginess. He uses a glass dish and watches them until they start to break down and give up a considerable amount of water. After microwaving, the mushrooms can be refrigerated or frozen until needed.

The recipe below preserves as much as possible of the Shaggy Mane's succulent texture.

Shaggy Mane mushrooms
4 fillets of sole
1 tablespoon lemon juice
1 bay leaf
2 shallots, peeled and diced
½ cup water
Freshly ground green peppercorns
3 tablespoons sweet butter
2 tablespoons flour
¼ cup heavy cream

Preheat oven to 350°. Lay the sole fillets in a buttered baking dish. Add lemon juice, bay leaf, shallots, and water. Grind pepper over the fish and dot with 1 tablespoon of butter. Bake about 25 minutes, until done. Cover to keep warm.

Melt 2 tablespoons of butter in a saucepan and add 2 tablespoons of flour, stirring a few minutes over low heat until the raw flour taste is gone. Add the juice from the baking pan, and

Caution: Do not drink alcohol before, during, or after the same meal at which you eat inky caps (*Coprinus*) or morels (*Morchella*).

cook for another few minutes, stirring until the sauce has thickened. Mix in cream and remove from the heat.

Steam fresh Shaggy Manes for 2 or 3 minutes. If mushrooms have been previously blanched or microwaved, just reheat them briefly. Arrange the sole fillets on a serving dish, top each with one or more Shaggy Manes, and pour the sauce over all.

Fish with Lemon Twist
(*Suillus americanus,* p. 113)

"None so poorly shod as the shoemaker's wife," and none so poorly equipped as the angler caught with fish but no lemon! The day may yet be saved if your luck extends to finding *Suillus americanus* (American Slipperycap), for this mushroom has a distinctive lemony tang. And if you have a bit of butter or oil, salt, pepper, and a dried herb, you're home safe.

> Fresh slipperycap mushrooms *(Suillus)*
> Freshly caught fish
> 3 tablespoons butter or oil
> Salt and pepper to taste
> A few pinches of any dried herb

Clean the fish. Peel off the slimy skin from the mushroom caps. (The tube layer may be left on.) Cut off and discard tough stems. Heat the butter or oil in a frying pan. Add the fish, mushrooms, salt, pepper, and herb. Sauté until the fish is cooked.

Real Oyster Gumbo with Slipperycaps
(edible *Suillus* species, pp. 113-118)

Slipperycaps are aptly named where texture is concerned, and in concert with the similar quality of okra and oysters, they will produce a splendid dish for devotees who can't have too much of a good thing. If you have access to Louisiana red crayfish, particularly softshells, their satiny texture is a marvelous addition. One whole bright red crayfish floating half-submerged in the dusky green of each soup bowl makes a truly spectacular dish. If you don't have any slipperycaps, but you do have oyster mushrooms *(Pleurotus),* you can use this recipe to make Double Oyster Gumbo!

> Fresh slipperycap mushrooms *(Suillus)***
> 1 tablespoon of uncooked white rice per person
> 3 tablespoons extra virgin olive oil
> Salt and freshly ground black pepper to taste
> 8 tender fresh young okra pods, or a package of frozen okra
> 2 scallions
> 1 tomato
> 6 tablespoons sweet butter
> 1/3 cup flour
> 1 quart hot water
> 2 bay leaves
> 1-2 cloves garlic
> 1 pint shucked oysters
> Small bowl of filé powder to be passed around at the table
> *Optional:* Louisiana red crayfish, 1 per person if softshell, 2-4 if hardshell

** Substitutes: Dried Cepes (*Boletus edulis,* p. 104), or oyster mushrooms (*Pleurotus ostreatus,* p. 181, or *Pleurotus porrigens*).

If dried Cepes are to be used, soak them for 1-2 hours in tepid water.

Measure the rice, heat a little over double the amount of water to boiling, adding a few drops of olive oil and a pinch of salt. Cook rice over very low heat for 25 minutes. Turn off the heat and set aside.

Slice the okra 1/4 inch thick. Mince the garlic, white parts of the scallion, and the tomato. Put in a bowl and reserve.

Make a five-minute golden Creole roux—heresy! In Louisiana, where there is more time, this takes 45 minutes. Use any large, heavy pot that is not cast iron. Melt 3 tablespoons of butter with 3 tablespoons of olive oil over medium heat, then add the flour. Cook for 5 minutes, stirring constantly with a rubber spatula, until the roux is the color of peanut butter. Be careful not to scorch it.

Slowly pour 1 quart of hot water into the pot, and stir to thin the roux. Bring this to a boil and add the reserved okra, garlic, scallion, and tomato, bay leaves, and salt and pepper to taste. When it boils again, turn the heat to low, cover the pot, and simmer for 8 minutes.

Hardshell crayfish should be added to the pot at this point. Remove them with a slotted spoon as soon as they have turned bright red, and put them on a plate to cool. Once they are cool, remove the tails, and the yellow "fat" in the heads, if desired, and set aside.

Slice the fresh slipperycaps, and sauté gently in 3 tablespoons of melted butter for 5 minutes. If using dried Cepes instead, drain and sauté them, and add the soaking water to the gumbo.

Softshell crayfish should go into the gumbo pot at this point. Then add the mushrooms and the oysters with their liquid, and simmer about 3 minutes, *only* until the oysters barely begin to plump up.

Put a little rice in each soup bowl and ladle the gumbo over it. If you are serving crayfish, add them to the bowls. Filé, a tasty thickener made of powdered sassafras leaves, should be brought to the table in a separate dish, since it becomes stringy if added before cooking is completed. To appease the Louisiana contingent for having rushed the roux, pass the filé around. It should be sprinkled on the gumbo like salt.

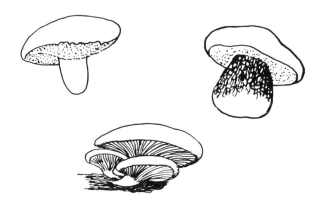

Coquilles St. Jacques Margaret Lewis

(Pleurotus ostreatus, p. 181)
(Pleurotus porrigens, p. 182)

Margaret Lewis finds that oyster mushrooms *(Pleurotus)* are a great extender in expensive seafood dishes, since the flavor of just one large scallop will permeate six or more mushrooms. A ratio of twelve oyster mushrooms to three scallops per person makes a delicious entree, or smaller portions can be used for a light hors d'oeuvre. "I have known mycologists to sprinkle meat tenderizer on tough *Pleurotus,* so as to use everything," says Lewis. "It works!"

6 or more fresh oyster mushroom *(Pleurotus)* caps per
    shell, cut to scallop size if necessary
Scallop shells
A few sprigs of fresh parsley
1 lemon
2 shallots and/or 2 garlic cloves
3 tablespoons sweet butter
1 large scallop per shell
$\frac{1}{4}$ teaspoon powdered mustard
Garlic salt to taste
2 tablespoons vermouth
$\frac{2}{3}$ cup bread crumbs
1 tablespoon flour
$\frac{1}{3}$ cup milk
Salt and freshly ground green pepper to taste
Dash of paprika

Butter the scallop shells, chop the parsley, and cut the lemon into narrow wedges. Mince the shallots and/or garlic, and sauté with mushroom caps in a tablespoon of butter. Place 1 or more scallops in the center of each shell, then surround with 6 or more oyster mushroom caps. Dribble the shallots evenly over the filled shells and sprinkle very lightly with mustard powder, garlic salt, and the vermouth.

Preheat oven to 350°. Melt a tablespoon of butter in a frying pan and brown the bread crumbs. Set aside.

In another frying pan, add a tablespoon of flour to a tablespoon of melted butter. Stir for a few minutes over low heat, until the raw taste of the flour is gone. Slowly whisk in $\frac{1}{3}$ cup of milk and salt and pepper to taste. The "cream" sauce should be thin, so cook it for only another minute or two.

Top each of the filled scallop shells with a tablespoon or so of the sauce to prevent drying out, and bake until the scallops are firm (about 15 minutes). Cover with the buttered bread crumbs and chopped parsley, adding a pinch of paprika. Serve the shells with a narrow wedge of lemon.

Mushroom Marinade

This basic recipe makes a third of a cup of marinade that can be used with any edible mushroom. Adding one or more of the optional ingredients will give this a different taste each time you try it.

⅔ cup extra virgin olive oil
⅓ cup lime or lemon juice or red or white vinegar
⅓ cup water
Salt and freshly ground green peppercorns to taste
2 tablespoons minced shallots or scallions, white part only
1 bay leaf
1 sprig parsley
Optional: a fresh sprig or ¼ teaspoon dried tarragon, oregano, thyme, or basil
½ teaspoon freshly cracked cumin or coriander seeds, or ½ teaspoon ground cumin or coriander
The thin outer peel of a lemon or lime

Combine all ingredients in a saucepan, including salt and pepper to taste, and bring the liquid to a boil. Turn the heat down very low, cover the pan, and barely simmer for 10 minutes. Strain into another saucepan, discarding the herbs. The marinade is now ready to be brought back to a boil and poured over cleaned mushrooms, as in the following recipe. When cooling mushrooms in the marinade, don't refrigerate right away or the oil will congeal before the mushrooms have a chance to soak up the flavor.

Poor Man's "White Truffle" Cut-Outs in Marinade

(*Hericium erinaceus,* p. 91)

You can make a foray into fancy gourmet shops and buy Italian White Truffles at the current price of $50 per ounce. Or you can wait for this most expensive of mushrooms to be grown commercially, as is currently being attempted with the Black Perigord Truffle. Or you can go for a drive or walk along a tree-lined city street, and lift up your eyes unto the branches in search of the hedgehog mushroom (Bearded Hedgehog), an amazing white mass covered with spines up to three inches long and often weighing many pounds. Adults and children alike find this pure white, easily sliced fungus willing material for cookie or truffle cutters.

> A fresh young, firm, white hedgehog mushroom *(Hericium)***, or portion thereof
> Juice of 1 lemon, or 2 for a large mushroom
> 1½ cups of Mushroom Marinade (see recipe, p. 397)
> Cookie or truffle cutters, or a sharp knife

** Substitutes: Very firm young puffballs (*Calvatia,* p. 352; *Calbovista,* p. 357; or *Lycoperdon,* p. 354). Be firm about demanding firmness! Old puffballs leave a particularly sour taste in the mouth.

Slice mushroom thinly. Brush slices with lemon juice to retain whiteness, and cut into clubs, hearts, spades, diamonds, or whatever shapes take your fancy. If your mushroom is a large specimen, let the kids have a field day with their cookie cutters. Using a slotted spoon, dip the cut-outs into lemon juice, or brush them again. Bring the marinade to a boil and add the mushroom cut-outs. Immediately remove from heat and allow to cool at room temperature for 1 hour. Pour through strainer, reserving the marinade for salad dressing.

The cut-outs can be used in the "Black and White Soup" (p. 375). They also taste excellent on sliced fresh tomatoes, topped with some marinade, and they make an elegant decoration for whole roast chicken and for pâté slices. If brushed with a little dissolved gelatin or beef consommé that contains gelatin, the cut-outs will stick properly and have an attractive shine.

Glossary

The terms below are defined as they apply specifically to mushrooms. Anatomical features which are illustrated in this book are indicated with a cross-reference following the definition: **(F)** = inside front cover; **(Fig.)** = text figure. Figures are scattered throughout the text.

Acidulous: Mildly caustic, biting, or acidic; tart.
Adnate: Refers to gills that are broadly attached to the stalk. **(F)**
Adnexed: Refers to gills that are narrowly attached to the stalk. **(F)**
Agglutinate: To join together as with glue; refers to clumps of fibrils or scales.
Allantoid: Slightly curved with rounded ends; shaped like a curved sausage.
Amyloid: Staining blue-black or grayish violet in iodine solution (Melzer's reagent).
Angular: Having angles or sharp corners, as opposed to having a circular shape.
Annulus: A ring of tissue around the upper portion of the stalk, formed when the partial veil breaks away from the cap margin. **(F)**
Apex (pl., apices):   The highest point of something; the tip or top.
Apothecium: A cup-shaped ascocarp (except for certain Ascomycetes such as morels, in which the spore-bearing layers may be convoluted so as to look like a brain). **(Fig. 10, p. 17)**
Apiculate: Refers to spores that have a short projection on one end that was attached to a sterigma.
Appressed: Closely flattened down against surface; refers to scales or fibrils (hairs) on surface of cap or stalk.
Arcuate: Arc-like; refers to gill attachment.
Areolate: Divided into smaller areas by cracks; refers to surface of cap or stalk.
Ascocarp: A fungus fruiting body bearing spores in microscopic, sac-shaped cells.
Aseptate: Lacking cross walls or partitions; compare with **septate.**

Asperulate: Slightly roughened with fine projections or points.

Ascus (pl., asci): A spore-bearing cell that produces spores internally following nuclear fusion and reduction division; a spore sac found in the group of fungi called Ascomycetes (see **Fig. 9, p. 16,** and **Fig. 10, p. 17**).

Basidium: A spore-bearing cell that produces spores externally following nuclear fusion and reduction division; found in the group of fungi called Basidiomycetes (see **Fig. 9, p. 16** and **Fig. 15, p. 20**).

Broom cell: A sterile cell with an apex divided into many small, fingerlike branches so as to appear broomlike.

Biguttulate: Having 2 oil-like drops inside (see **Fig. 27, p. 53**).

Bilateral: Having gill tramal hyphae that form a divergent pattern towards the gill tip.

Capitate: Having an enlarged, rounded tip resembling a well-formed head.

Caulocystidium: A cystidium (sterile cell) found on the stalk of a mushroom fruiting body. See **cystidium.**

Central: Refers to a type of attachment of the mushroom cap and stalk in which the stalk is attached to the center of the cap.

Cheilocystidium: A cystidium (sterile cell) on the gill edge. See **cystidium.**

Clamp connection: A microscopic, elbow-like or semicircular hyphal branch that connects adjacent cells of Basidiomycetes (see **Fig. 15, p. 20**).

Clamps: Short for clamp connections; elbow-like connections between cells (see above).

Clavate: Widened at one end; club-shaped. **(F)**

Cleistothecium: A spherically shaped Ascomycete fruiting body with no opening for spore discharge (see **Fig. 10, p. 17**).

Close: Refers to gill spacing in which the gills are closer together than in the spacing described as **distant** or **subdistant** but farther apart than **crowded. (F)**

Coprophilous: Dung-inhabiting; refers to fungi that grow on manure.

Crenate: Scalloped or with uniform rounded lobes; refers to margin of cap. **(F)**

Chrysocystidium: A smooth, thin-walled **cystidium** (sterile cell) having cell contents that stain brightly in certain dyes, or yellow in a strong base such as KOH (caustic potash); when dried they show a coagulated or amorphous content.

Cuticle: The uppermost tissue layer of the cap or stalk of a Basidiomycete mushroom fruiting body (see **Fig. 8, p. 9**).

Cyanophilous: Readily absorbing blue stains, such as cotton blue dye.

Cystidium: A sterile hyphal end-cell that has a distinctive shape, size, or content.

Decurrent: Extending down the stalk; refers to attachment of gills or tubes to stalk. **(F)**

Deliquescent: Becoming liquid at maturity as a result of self-digestion; refers to flesh of inky caps (*Coprinus,* p. 276).

Depressed: Refers to a mushroom cap in which the central part is lower than the outer part.

Dextrinoid: Staining yellowish brown or reddish brown in iodine solution (Melzer's reagent).

Distant: Refers to gill spacing in which the gills are very widely spaced. **(F)**

Disc: The central part of the cap over the stalk (see **Fig. 8, p. 9**).

Duff: The partially decayed plant material on the forest floor.

Eccentric: Off center; refers to attachment of cap on stalk.

Elliptic: Having the shape of a flattened circle. Refers to the shape of a mushroom spore. **(F)**

Epiphragm: A membrane over the peridioles in the young fruiting body of bird's nest fungi (see Pl. 48 and **peridiole**).

Eguttulate: Not containing one or more oily globules.

Evanescent: Fleeting; likely to vanish; having a short existence.

Excipular trichomes: Sterile hairs protruding from the outer surface of an apothecium.

Fibrillose: Having threadlike or hairlike filaments; refers to surface of cap or stalk. **(F)**

Flexuous: Bent alternately in opposite directions; zigzag or wavy.

Floccose: Cottony.

Friable: Readily breaking into small pieces. **(F)**

Fruiting body: The reproductive (spore-producing) structure of a fungus.

Fusiform: Spindle-shaped; tapering at both ends.

Fusoid-ventricose: Swelling out at the middle (or one side), with both ends somewhat tapered.

Glabrous: Smooth; having no hairs or pubescence.

Glandular dots: Darkly colored, pinhead-sized dots found on the stalks of some agarics and boletes (see **Fig. 31, p. 101**).

Gleba: The spore-bearing tissue of a Gastromycete fungus, such as a puffball.

Gleocystidium: A cystidium (sterile cell) with oily, resinous, or granular contents. See **cystidium.**

Globose: Having a spherical shape. See also **subglobose.** Refers mostly to the shape of the cap or spores of a mushroom or of an entire fruiting body.

Glutinous: Slimy.

Guttate: Having a spotted appearance, as if from drops of liquid.

Guttulate: Containing one or more oily globules (see **Fig. 27, p. 53**).

Guttule: A small, drop-like particle.

Hilum: The mark or scar on the basidiospore indicating the point of attachment of the basidiospore to the sterigma.

Hyaline: Transparent or translucent; glassy.

Hydrazine: A colorless, volatile, corrosive, liquid used in jet and rocket fuels. Poisonous chemical compounds produced by certain mushrooms have been found to be the same (see p. 48).

Hygrophanous: Having a water-soaked appearance when wet and changing color (usually fading gradually) as drying progresses.

Hymenium: The layer of spore-bearing cells and associated structures found on a mushroom fruit body. Examples: The layer of cells found on gill and tooth surfaces of agarics and hydnums) or on tube walls of boletes (see **Fig. 8, p. 9**).

Hypha (pl., **hyphae):** One of the threadlike filaments of a mycelium (see **Fig. 15, p. 20**); the cells may or may not be connected by **clamps** (see above).

Ibotenic acid: An isoxazole derivative that is toxic in very minute quantities (see p. **25**).

Inamyloid: Not amyloid; refers to tissue that does not turn blue-black or grayish violet in iodine solution (Melzer's reagent).

Inoperculate: Opening by an irregular split to discharge the spores; see also **operculate** and **suboperculate.**

Intervenose: Interveined; having veins on the surface and at times crossing from gill to gill.

Ixocutis: A sticky, outermost layer of horizontally flattened hyphae on the surface of a cap.

KOH: Potassium hydroxide; used in a weak (2–3%) solution.

Latex: A clear, milky, or colored liquid that exudes from cut or broken surfaces or wounds of mushrooms such as milkcaps (*Lactarius,* p. 326).

Lateral attachment: Having a stalk attached to the side of the cap.

Limb: The part of the cap between the central **disc** and the edge, or **margin** (see **Fig. 4, p. 7**).

Lubricous: Slippery, oily, or greasy.

Margin: The edge or border or a mushroom cap or cup (see **Fig. 4, p. 7**).

Marginate: Gills having edges colored differently from faces; or a bulb that has a raised edge or rim. **(F)**

Micron (abbrev., **μm**): One one-millionth of a meter.

Mucronate: Ending in a short, sharp point.

Muscimol: An isoxazole derivative that is toxic in very minute amounts (see p. 25).

Mycelium: A mass of threadlike, microscopic filaments (**hyphae**) comprising the fungus body. **(F)**

Mycorrhiza (pl., **mycorrhizae):** A symbiotic association between the roots of a plant and the hyphae of a fungus; a relationship beneficial to both partners.

Obovate: Egg-shaped, with the narrow end attached to the stalk.

Operculate: Opening by an apical lid to discharge the spores; as in the ascus of a morel (see **Fig. 9, p. 16**).

Ovate: Egg-shaped. **(F)**

Partial veil: A layer of tissue that covers the gills or pores of mushroom fruiting body during the initial stages of development. Remnants of the partial veil may later form a ring around the stalk, as in *Amanita* (p. 215), or a cobweb-like covering over the gills, as in the webcaps (*Cortinarius,* p. 287). **(F)** (See also **Fig. 3, p. 6,** and **Fig. 12, p. 19.**)

Peridiole: A detachable spore case (usually lentil-shaped) that is a part of the gleba of fruiting bodies of bird's nest fungi. (Nidulariaceae, p. 366)

Peridium: The outer wall of a perithecium or of some puffball-like fruiting bodies. Also applied to the entire fruiting body of a puffball.

Perithecium (pl., **perithecia**): A flask-shaped Ascomycete fruiting body (see **Fig. 10, p. 17**).

Phenol: A caustic, poisonous compound derived from benzene; also called carbolic acid (see p. 261).

Pileus: The cap of the mushroom fruiting body.

Pleurocystidium: A cystidium (sterile cell) found on the side (or face) of a gill or pore. See also **cystidium**.

Pruinose: Scurfy; having a white, powdery covering.

Pyriform: Pear-shaped.

Receptacle: (1) The part of an apothecium of a cup fungus not including the stalk. (2) A structure supporting the spore-bearing layers of a stinkhorn.

Recurved: Bent downwards or backwards; refers to scales on many types of fungi **(F)** or rays of earthstars (see *Geastrum,* Pl. 47).

Reticulate: Net-like.

Saccate: Bag- or sac-like. Refers to a cystidium or to the cup-like volva remnant at the stalk base. **(F)**

Sclerotium: A hardened mass of hyphae resistant to unfavorable conditions.

Septate: Divided by partitions, as in some **spores** or **hyphae.**

Sphaerocysts: Large globose or round cells.

Spore: A microscopic reproductive cell of a mushroom, capable of reproducing the organism whence it came. **(F)**

Squamose: Having scales.

Squamulose: Having minute scales.

Stalk: The part of the mushroom fruiting body that elevates the spore-producing layer above the ground (see **Fig. 3, p. 6; Fig. 4, p. 7;** and **Fig. 12, p. 19**).

Sterigma (pl., **sterigmata**): A small pointed branch off a hypha bearing a spore (see **Fig. 15, p. 20**).

Storied: Alternating layers of fungus tissue and hollow spaces (as in some stalk interiors). **(F)**

Striate: Marked with lines, grooves, or ridges.

Strigose: Rough with stiff, closely appressed hairs or bristles.

Subdistant: Intermediate (in spacing) between **close** and **distant;** refers to spacing of gills. **(F)**

Subglobose: Almost spherical; rounded or almost round in optical section.

Suboperculate: Intermediate between truly **operculate** and **inoperculate;** refers to the ascus opening for discharging spores.

Suprahilar depression: The round, smooth area on a spore just above the **hilum.**

Teliospore: A rust or smut spore from which the basidium is produced.

Trama: The flesh of a gill between 2 hymenial (spore-producing) layers (see **Fig. 6, p. 8**); also used for the fleshy portion of a mushroom cap above the gills of an agaric or the tube layer of a bolete or polypore.

Trichodermium: The outermost layer on the surface of a cap, composed of hair-like hyphal tips perpendicularly oriented to the cap surface.

Truncate: Ending abruptly, as though the end were cut off; refers to end of spore, top of cap, etc. **(F)**

Tuberculate: Having small wart-like or knob-like projections.

Universal veil: A layer of tissue that covers the entire mushroom (fruiting body) during the initial stages of development. Remnants of the universal veil sometimes form scales or patches on the cap, or a cup-like **volva** at the base of the stalk. **(F)** (See also **Fig. 3, p. 6,** and **Fig. 12, p. 19.**)

Ventricose: Broad at the middle and tapered toward the ends.

Verrucose: Having small, wart-like or knob-like projections, as in spores of *Cortinarius* (webcaps, p. 287).

Viscid: Sticky or tacky when moist.

Volva: The cup-like remains of universal veil tissue around the base of the mushroom stalk. **(F)** (See also **Fig. 3, p. 6.**)

Zoned: Arranged in layers, rings, bands, or alternating patches; can refer to different-colored layers of flesh (see Sweet Spine, Pl. 8) as well as the cap or stalk surface (see Saffron Milkcap, Pl. 42).

Selected References

Most of the literature consulted in preparation of this Field Guide consists of technical papers and books not cited here because of the nature of this book and space limitations. Listed below are a few references, some of which have been cited in the text, pertaining to two subjects of special interest to mushroom enthusiasts: mushroom poisoning and mycophagy. See also the cookbooks listed on p. 372 of the recipe section.

Ammirati, J. F., Traquair, J. A., and P. A. Horgen. 1985. *Poisonous Mushrooms of the Northern United States and Canada.* University of Minnesota Press. Minneapolis, Minn.

Kelly, K. L., and Judd, D. B. 1976. *Color—Universal Language and Dictionary of Names.* Nat. Bur. Stand. (U.S.) Spec. Publ. 440, Washington, D.C.

Lincoff, G., and Mitchel, D. H. 1977. *Toxic and Hallucinogenic Mushroom Poisoning.* Van Nostrand Reinhold Co., New York.

McIlvaine, C., and Macadam. 1973. *One Thousand American Fungi.* Dover Publ. Inc., N.Y.

McKenney, M., and Stuntz, D. 1971. *The Savory Wild Mushroom.* University of Washington Press. Seattle, Wash.

Peck, C. Annual Report New York State Museum 32:44, 1875.

Rumack, B. H., and Salzman. 1978. *Mushroom Poisoning: Diagnosis and Treatment.* CRC Press Inc., West Palm Beach, Fla.

Smith, A. H. 1975. *A Field Guide to Western Mushrooms.* The University of Michigan Press. Ann Arbor, Mich.

———, Smith, H. V., and Weber, N. 1979. *How to Know the Gilled Mushrooms.* Wm. C. Brown Co., Dubuque, Iowa.

———, and Weber, N. S. 1980. *The Mushroom Hunter's Field Guide.* The University of Michigan Press. Ann Arbor, Mich.

Index

The scientific and recommended common names of all mushroom discussed in this *Field Guide* are listed in the index below. Some commonly used alternate or obsolete names are listed, followed by an equals sign (=) and the current name used in this book. References to plates on which species are illustrated are given in **boldface** type after the common and latinized species names. Species for which no plate reference is given do not have a separate species description in the text accounts; the page reference indicates the **Similar species** entries where they are mentioned.